KALLIS' 2017 REDESIGNED
SAT® PATTERN
STRATEGY 2nd Edition

KALLIS' Redesigned SAT Pattern Strategy

KALLIS EDU, INC.
7490 Opportunity Road, Suite 203
San Diego, CA 92111
info@kallisedu.com
www.kallisedu.com

ISBN-13: 978-1546724773
ISBN-10: 154672477X

Our **Redesigned SAT Pattern Strategy** gives students the tools to approach each SAT topic with confidence and provides a variety of practice exercises to help students master test-taking skills. Each chapter is divided into numerous **Question Topics** that break down each concept tested on the official exam, giving students a simple, systematic approach to even the most difficult concepts. Practice includes **Quick Practices** and **Practice Activities** for focusing on particular question types as well as six full-length **Practice Tests**.

KALLIS

KALLIS'

SAT

PATTERN

STRATEGY

Table of **Contents**

Getting Started

Introducing the Redesigned SAT

What is the SAT?

The SAT has been the go-to standardized test for assessing a student's college readiness for nearly a century. When the test was first administered in 1926, it was called the "Scholastic Aptitude Test," but over the years it has come to be called just the "SAT."

One reason the SAT intimidates students and parents alike is that it is so "big." For one, it is "big" in terms of sheer length: the SAT takes three hours to complete unless you decide to write the optional essay, in which case it clocks in at around four hours. The SAT is also "big" in terms of its perceived impact on a student's academic future. According to many students, your SAT score dictates which colleges you can hope to get in to, which scholarships you can apply for, and whether your parents will keep or disown you. Okay, maybe not so much the last part, but the fact remains—the SAT gets treated as a big deal.

But size alone is not what makes the SAT so intimidating—the SAT intimidates because it seems so unknowable. To appreciate the SAT's air of mystery, look no further than its name. To most students and parents, the abbreviation "SAT" does not stand for anything—it simply is. For many, "SAT" is a title without meaning, and the contents of the SAT remain equally unknowable. That the writers of the SAT have now redesigned it may only add to the anxiety that students feel.

This study guide will remove the mystery from the SAT. After all, just by reading this introduction you probably learned that "SAT" once stood for "Scholastic Aptitude Test." You will likely find that the redesigned SAT focuses on fundamental skills that you have already been working on in school for years. As you continue reading this study guide, you will find that the SAT is far from unknowable. Reviewing the approaches and practicing the strategies outlined in this study guide will transform the SAT from "the test" to "just another test."

Introducing the Second Edition

Welcome to the second edition of KALLIS' *SAT Pattern Strategy*. We released the first edition back in 2015, not long after the College Board announced the changes to the SAT and released the first few practice tests. Since then, the overall content and difficulty of the new SATs have changed little by little, and this second edition is designed to reflect these changes.

Naturally, the most dramatic revisions in this edition are to the six Practice Tests. We have replaced several reading passages, swapping the old and obscure topics for more contemporary and relevant ones. A number of writing and langauge tests have been updated, too, and now test a wider variety of grammatical and stylistic concepts. And finally, we have reduced the overall difficulty level of each math test and balanced our tested topics to match those tested on the new SAT. You will also find that the six Practice Tests' answers and explanations now list what concept(s) are tested in each question, allowing students to identify their strengths and weaknesses and modify their study plans accordingly.

While the SAT itself may be intimidating, preparing for it does not have to be. These pages demonstrate that the SAT tests a limited set of concepts in fairly predictable ways. Once you understand *what* the SAT tests and *how* it tests these concepts, it becomes evident that the test's bark is much bigger than its bite.

Out with the Old, in with the New

Starting in 2016, the College Board™ is introducing the Redesigned SAT. Thus, any student who graduates in 2017 or later takes the Redesigned SAT. This section briefly outlines the differences between the old SAT and the Redesigned SAT.

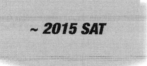

	~ 2015 SAT	2016 Redesigned SAT
Testing Time	• **3 hours and 45 minutes**	• **3 hours** (plus 50 minutes for the **optional** Essay Test)

Test Breakdown	• **Critical Reading Test**
	(scored on a 200 – 800 point scale)
	
	• **Writing Test (with Essay)**
	(scored on a 200 – 800 point scale)
	
	• **Math Test**
	(scored on a 200 – 800 point scale)
		• **Evidence-Based Reading and Writing**
		   - Reading Test
		   - Writing Test
		(scored on a 200 – 800 point scale)
		• **Math Test**
		(scored on a 200 – 800 point scale)
		• **Essay Test**
		(separate reading, writing, and analysis scores ranging from 2–8 points)

Score Breakdown	• Score Range: **600 – 2400**	• Score Range: **400 – 1600** (plus separate reading, writing, and analysis scores for the **optional** Essay Test)

How do I register for the SAT?

The SAT is offered year-round in the United States and internationally. The vast majority of students take the SAT during their junior and senior years of high school. The majority of students take the SAT more than once, and most students receive a better score the second time they take it.

Most students register for the SAT online. To do so, just go to College Board's "Register" page on its website, select a convenient test date and location, print your "Admission Ticket," and take it with you on the day of the test.

However, you must register for the SAT by mail if you:

- choose to pay for the test using a check or money order.
- are less than 13 years old.
- are unable to submit a digital photo during the online registration process.
- need to register for Sunday testing because of a religious observance.
- take the test in Nigeria, Ghana, or Cameroon.
- are requesting that a testing center be opened nearer to your home.

The Student Registration Guide for the SAT includes an SAT registration form and a return envelope. See your school's counselor for a registration guide and any additional information necessary for SAT mail registration.

If you are unable to pay the fee for the SAT, there are many resources available that may allow you to take the test at no cost, as well as provide assistance throughout the college application process. More information is available on the College Board's website.

An Overview of the SAT

The Redesigned SAT consists of a Reading Test, a Writing and Language Test, a Math Test, and an optional Essay Test. Below you will find an outline of the number of questions and time allotted for each test section of the SAT.

Test Name	Test Components	Number of Questions	Time Allotted (minutes)
Reading Test	• Four reading passages • One pair of reading passages • One to two visual components (such as graphs, tables, or diagrams)	52	65
Writing and Language Test	• Four reading passages containing grammatical and stylistic errors • One to two visual components (such as graphs, tables, or diagrams)	44	35

Math Test	• **No-Calculator portion**
	  - Multiple-choice section
	  - Student-produced response section
		20	25

	• **Calculator portion**
	  - Multiple-choice section
	  - Student-produced response section
		38	55

Essay Test (Optional)	• One reading passage with a corresponding writing prompt	1	50

Scoring the SAT

Scoring at a Glance

The Redesigned SAT employs a multi-level scoring system. The score report will contain an overall score, individual sub-scores for each of the three sections (Reading, Writing, and Math), a breakdown of your performance in each of the test's subtopics, and a score for the optional Essay Test.

The overall, or composite, score ranges from 400 – 1600. Thus, 400 points are awarded just for showing up and taking the test, and 1600 points are awarded for answering every question on the test correctly.

The composite score is broken into two sub-scores: a 200 – 800 point Reading and Writing Test score and a 200 – 800 point Math Test score. Each of these sub-scores are broken down further. The Reading Test score, Writing and Language Test score, and Math Test score will be reported individually and on a 10 – 40 point scale. Additionally, the Redesigned SAT score report will show test takers' skills in a number of Reading, Writing and Language, and Math Test subtopics.

Optional student essays will be reviewed by two graders, each of whom will assign an essay a reading score, a writing score, and an analysis score ranging from 1 to 4 points. The graders' scores will then be added together, meaning each essay will receive three scores, with each score ranging from 2 to 8 points. These Essay scores are not calculated into a student's composite score, but they provide academic institues with a comprehensive overview of a student's writing abilites.

There is no penalty for wrong answers on the Redesigned SAT. Only correct answers will contribute toward a test taker's score; incorrect and unmarked answers will not negatively affect a test taker's score. This means that you should never leave a question blank, even if it means that you have to guess.

Scoring Flowchart

COMPOSITE SCORE
(400 - 1600)

Area Score Reading and Writing Test (200 - 800)	Area Score Math Test (200-800)

Test Score Reading Test (10 - 40)	Test Score Writing and Language Test (10 - 40)	Test Score Math Test (10 - 40)

Preparing for the SAT

Each student will develop different strategies and approaches when preparing for the SAT. The tips below can help you focus your studies, but ultimately, you must determine what study methods work best for you.

 Create a study schedule so you have at least two study sessions devoted to the SAT per week.

 Review the chapters of this book and complete the quizzes at the ends of the chapters.

 Take the practice tests in a quiet place under timed conditions.

 Focus on areas that you have difficulty with by reviewing the relevant sections in this book.

The practice sections in this book have been aligned to the rubrics published by the College Board. Therefore, if you see it here, you are likely to see something like it on the actual test. Use the indexes of your text books to reference difficult concepts. Ask your teachers when you need extra help. Be proactive.

Do not study yourself into exhaustion. Take time to sleep, eat healthy food, exercise, and socialize with family and friends. A refreshed, happy brain will be much more nimble. After all, the SAT is just another test.

Mastering
The Reading Test

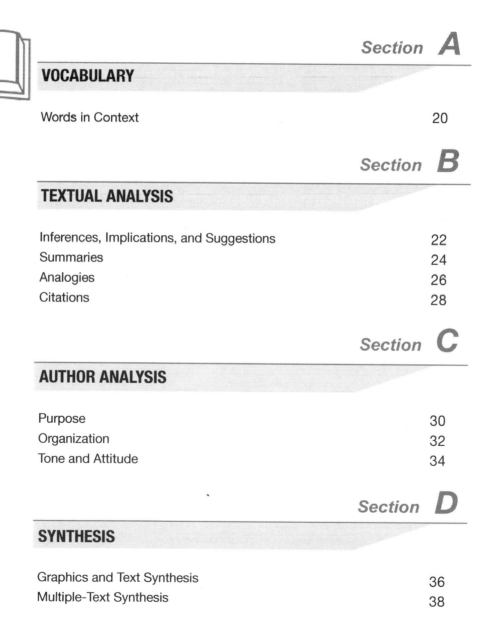

Reading Test Basics

A. Breaking Down the Reading Passages

The SAT Reading Test consists of four reading passages and one pair of passages. Each passage (or passage pair) is accompanied by ten to eleven multiple-choice questions. Two of the four reading passages will include supplementary materials, such as charts, diagrams, or tables, that contain information relevant to the passage's topic.

The SAT Reading Section will always contain the following:

• One literature passage
• One or two history/social science passages
• One or two science passages
• One passage pair (history, social science, or science)

B. Understanding the Reading Questions

Each multiple-choice question will have four answer choices with one correct answer. You will not be penalized for incorrect answers.

Certain types of questions will appear in nearly every set of questions. Generally, a question set will include two words-in-context questions and two citation questions. Additionally, passage pairs as well as passages containing a chart, diagram, or table will always include several synthesis questions. By mastering the three types of questions just mentioned, you will be prepared for nearly half of the questions on the Reading Test.

C. Reading with Purpose

Although it does not require physical exertion or even movement, reading is an active task. When you read academic material—especially when being timed, as is the case with the SAT—you should set certain reading "goals" for yourself. Doing so will immerse you in what you are reading. At the very least, it will keep your mind from wandering. Such goals may already be second nature to you. As you read, try to answer the following questions:

• What is/are the main topic(s) of the passage(s)?
• How is/are the passage(s) structured?
• How does the author feel about the topic he or she is discussing?
  (Is he/she excited? Impartial? Critical? Supportive?)

If the answers to these basic questions are not clear to you by the time you finish, it may be a good idea to read the questions and then quickly reexamine parts of the passage before answering.

Reading Test Quick Reference Chart

Question Type	Description	Specific Topics (SAT)	Common Question Formats
Vocabulary (approximately 15 – 20% of questions)	Use the context of a sentence, paragraph, or passage to determine the meaning of a word.	Words in Context	• As used in line xx, "_____" most nearly means…
Textual Analysis (approximately 50% of questions)	Make a reasonable, supportable deduction based on information presented in the text. In other words, summarize what the author says or tries to say.	Inferences, Implications, and Suggestions	• The author suggests that… • The author indicates that…. • It can most reasonably be inferred that… • The author most strongly implies which of the following about…
		Summaries	• The author's main point about _____ is… • The author uses _____ and _____ as examples of…
		Analogies	• Which situation is most similar to the one described in lines xx – xx?
		Citations	• Which choice provides the best evidence to the previous question?
Author Analysis (approximately 20% of questions)	Explain why or how the author does something.	Purpose	• The main purpose of the passage is to… • The discussion of _____ in lines xx – xx primarily serves to…
		Organization	• Which choice best describes the structure of the paragraph/passage?
		Attitude and Tone	• The passage is written from the perspective of someone who is… • The author's attitude is primarily characterized by… • What main effect does _____ have on the tone of the passage?
Synthesis (approximately 15% of questions)	Explain a relationship between two passages or between a passage and its supplementary material.	Graphics and Test Synthesis	• Which information best summarizes the information presented in the graph? • According to the graph, which statement is true about _____? • What information presented in paragraph xx is represented by the graph? • Which statement about _____ is best supported by the graph?
		Multiple-Text Synthesis	• How would the author of Passage 1 most likely respond to the claim (lines xx – xx) made in Passage 2? • Which choice best states the relationship between the two passages?

Section A: Vocabulary

001 Question Topic

→ **WORDS IN CONTEXT**

APPROACH

Being able to discern the meaning of a word through context is an important skill. In fact, up to 20 percent of SAT Reading Test questions ask you to do just that. The words used for "Words in Context" questions may be relatively common; in these cases, the difficulty lies in determining the word's nuanced meaning in the sentence. Use the context of the phrase, sentence, or paragraph in which the word appears to determine its meaning.

Example

Although the envelope containing the classified documents appeared unopened, the government agent feared that the documents had been doctored.

As used in the sentence above, "doctored" most nearly means

(A) adulterated.

(B) treated.

(C) repaired.

(D) altered.

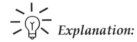 *Explanation:*

"Doctored" is a relatively common word that, when used as a verb, has multiple meanings. Because all the answer choices provide an accurate definition of "doctored," we must use the context of the sentence to decide which synonym is best suited to the sentence. The process of "doctoring" is something done to the documents, and a process the agent fears. From this, we can infer that choice (D), "altered," is the best choice because a government agent would fear that important ("classified") documents had been altered.

Question Formats

Although question formats vary from test to test, the most common format for a words-in-context questions is

• As used in line xx, "_____" most nearly means...

Focus Questions

What kinds of words does the author choose to use in the passage?
What are the nuances of meaning in the passage?

This passage is adapted from **Arvind Suresh** (Editor) & **Sharman Apt Russell** (Author), "**Nature's Notebook: Through the Eyes of a Citizen Scientist**," *Scistarter Blog,* published in 2015.

line   Here in the Chihuahuan Desert of southwestern New Mexico, I am intimate now with three trees in my backyard: a box elder, a desert willow, and a honey mesquite. I know when these plants become luminous with the green of new leaves, when they flower, when their flowers turn to fruit, and when their fruit falls. I also have a warm relationship with a male
5 four-winged saltbush, having rubbed his yellow pollen sensuously between my fingers, and with a female four-winged saltbush, admiring her extravagant and seasonal cloak of papery seeds. Perhaps my greatest new friend, however, is a soaptree yucca, whose single stalk grows up quickly and prominently in late spring, its buds producing a mass of scented creamy-white flowers—like a six-foot-high candle glowing in the dusk.
10   This spring is my third year with my selected plants. Phenology is too dull a word for what is happening here. For how I must search along a stem for the smallest of leaves, peer into the heart of a bud, and rub my fingers against a catkin. This is one-to-one, a real conversation, me and this catkin, me and this honey mesquite.

1) As used in line 1, "intimate" most nearly means
(A) confidential.
(B) private.
(C) familiar.
(D) devoted.

2) As used in line 4, "warm" most nearly means
(A) friendly.
(B) charitable.
(C) tepid.
(D) snug.

3) As used in line 8, "prominently" most nearly means
(A) proudly.
(B) importantly.
(C) obtrusively.
(D) noticeably.

4) As used in line 10, "dull" most nearly means
(A) blunt.
(B) unimaginative.
(C) somber.
(D) faint.

Section B: Textual Analysis

Questions in this category ask you to make reasonable, supportable deductions based on the information presented in the passage. In other words, you must summarize or analyze what the author says or implies.

002 Question Topic

INFERENCES, IMPLICATIONS, AND SUGGESTIONS

APPROACH

The Reading Test will often ask you to make an inference, identify an implication, or determine what an author is suggesting in a passage. When you encounter a question that asks you to do any of these, you must choose an answer that is not explicitly stated. In other words, you must interpret meaning. At the same time, the correct answer will be entirely supported by the text. If an answer choice contains a detail or idea that seems logical and yet overreaches the implications in the passage, rule it out.

Example

Andrew and Alice have been close friends for years. But lately, whenever Andrew has tried to talk to Alice, she pointedly ignores him.

What can reasonably be inferred based on the sentences above?
(A) Andrew lied to Alice.   (B) Andrew said something to offend Alice.
(C) Alice is upset with Andrew.   (D) Alice has found a new friend.

 Explanation:

In this case, we do not have enough evidence to assume that "Andrew lied to Alice," or even that he "said something to offend" her. After all, he could have offended her with his actions and not his words. Ultimately, we do not know why Alice is ignoring him. Moreover, there are no hints that "Alice has found a new friend." Thus, the safest and most supportable choice is (C) because it includes an inference that is much harder to disprove than the other choices.

Question Formats

Although question formats vary, the most common formats for inference, implication, and suggestion questions are

- The author suggests/indicates that…
- It can most reasonably be inferred that…
- The author most strongly implies which of the following about _____?
- Which choice best reflects the narrator's view of _____?

Focus Questions

Does a direct explanation of the text's meaning seem to be missing?

Does the author provide hints and clues that might lead to a conclusion?

Does the author use words such as "may," "might," and "probably?"

The following is adapted from **V.S. Vernon Jones**, *Aesop's Fables*, originally published in 1912.

A thirsty Crow found a Pitcher with some water in it, but so little was there that, try as she might, she could not reach it with her beak, and it seemed as though she would die of thirst within sight of the remedy. At last she hit upon a clever plan. She began dropping pebbles into the Pitcher, and with each pebble the water rose a little higher until at last it reached the brim, and the knowing bird was enabled to quench her thirst.

1) The fable suggests which of the following?

(A) Necessity inspires ingenuity.

(B) Patience is often rewarded.

(C) It is better to be hungry than thirsty.

(D) Intelligence is preferable to wealth.

A dispute arose between the North Wind and the Sun, each claiming that he was stronger than the other. At last they agreed to try their powers upon a traveler, to see which could soonest strip him of his cloak. The North Wind had the first try; and, gathering up all his force for the attack, he came whirling furiously down upon the man, and caught up his cloak as though he would wrest it from him by one single effort: but the harder he blew, the more closely the man wrapped it round himself. Then came the turn of the Sun. At first he beamed gently upon the traveler, who soon unclasped his cloak and walked on with it hanging loosely about his shoulders: then he shone forth in his full strength, and the man, before he had gone many steps, was glad to throw his cloak right off and complete his journey more lightly clad.

2) What is implied by the Sun's victory over the North Wind?

(A) Most people would rather be too hot than too cold.

(B) Excessive pride always results in failure.

(C) Persuasion is a stronger motivator than force.

(D) Nature seeks to make man as uncomfortable as possible.

There were two Cocks in the same farmyard, and they fought to decide who should be master. When the fight was over, the beaten one went and hid himself in a dark corner; while the victor flew up on to the roof of the stables and crowed lustily. But an Eagle espied him from high up in the sky, and swooped down and carried him off. Forthwith the other Cock came out of his corner and ruled the roost without a rival.

3) Which of the following morals is suggested by the fable?

(A) Few animals will challenge an eagle.

(B) Pride comes before a fall.

(C) Time makes losers of us all.

(D) Fighting leads to chaos and disorder.

003 Question Topic

→ **SUMMARIES**

APPROACH

When recalling something you have read, you probably do not remember it word-for-word. You most likely remember the main idea and a few details or examples. What you are doing in your mind is summarizing. Often, the best strategy for answering summary questions is to reread the relevant part(s) of the passage, paying close attention to the author's main points and corresponding details.

Example

Kayla and Brittany nervously paced up and down the street, glancing at the unremarkable house each time they passed it. Finally, they each took a deep breath and went to ring the doorbell.

Which choice best summarizes the passage?
(A) Two friends spent a long time staring at a house.
(B) Kayla and Brittany eventually found the courage to approach the house.
(C) Two friends cannot find the house that they are trying to locate.
(D) Kayla and Brittany fear whoever lives in the "unremarkable house."

Explanation:

When answering summary questions, avoid choices that include implications or inferences. Choices (A) and (C) are incorrect because they identify Kayla and Brittany as friends, which is neither mentioned nor suggested in the example sentences. Moreover, they "glance" rather than "stare" at the house, and the example does not indicate that they are lost. (D) is incorrect because, although the example states that Kayla and Brittany are nervous, there is no indication that they fear the resident of the house they approach. (B) accurately summarizes Kayla and Brittany's transformation from nervousness to confidence by saying they "eventually found the courage to approach the house," leaving out non-essential detail and description.

Question Formats

Although question formats vary from test to test, the most common formats for summary questions are

- The author's main point about _____ is...
- The author uses _____ and _____ as examples of...
- Which choice best summarizes the passage?
- The central claim in the passage is that...
- The central problem that the author describes in the passage is...
- In the passage, the author contends that...
- The passage identifies which of the following as _____?

Focus Questions

What is the main topic of the passage?

What details contribute to the main topic of the passage?

This passage is adapted from **Steve Silberman**, "**Music to Write By: 10 Top Authors Share Their Secrets for Summoning the Muse**," *Neurotribes*, published in 2012.

line

Writing is a hell of a way to make a living. It only seems easy to those who haven't tried it. I've somehow managed to survive that way for the past 20 years or so—for richer and for poorer—and still don't know how my favorite authors, journalists, and bloggers manage to pull it off with such verve and panache. Sometimes, being a writer feels like

5   getting paid to pull a rabbit out of a hat over and over again—but each time it has to be a new breed of rabbit, "miraculously" emerging from a different style of hat.

Days under the spotlight that I reach into the fraying dark with sweaty fingers, and feel warm fur, are good days. Other days, it's nothing but hat in there; but I say "*Voilà!*" with a practiced flourish anyway and hope the audience doesn't notice that the alleged rabbit is

10   just a tattered old stuffed thing, a patchwork made to twitch by sleight-of-hand

But writers have their secrets and rituals for courting the fickle favor of the Muse. For some, it's sitting in a certain chair at the right time of day—or getting out of familiar surroundings to type busily away in a café filled with people that might someday be readers. For others, it's a brisk walk in the open air. Or it's potions; woe to the poet who

15   finally decides to undertake her epic sestina sequence only to discover that her cupboard is bare of aged Sumatra.

1) The author's main point about pulling "a rabbit out of a hat over and over again" (line 5) is that
   (A) most professional writers believe in miracles.
   (B) most people who enjoy writing also enjoy magic.
   (C) professional writers must consistently produce unpredictable and varied work.
   (D) some people feel that writers mainly trick and deceive their readers.

2) The author uses "sitting in a certain chair…" (line 12) and "getting out of familiar surroundings…" (line 12) as examples of
   (A) superstitious traditions that the author rejects.
   (B) practices that help writers produce high-quality work.
   (C) actions that help the author focus on his writing.
   (D) pieces of advice given to the author by his friends.

004 Question Topic

→ **ANALOGIES**

APPROACH

Analogy questions require you to relate a situation from the passage to a situation described in the answer choices. Analogy questions require you to understand the implications of a relationship or situation in the passage, and then to recognize which choice contains similar implications, even though the situation itself may seem completely different.

Example

The piano teacher's parrot would sit nearby during lessons and frequently say, "Bravo!"

Which of the following situations is most like the one in the sentence?
(A) Dogs who know each other engage in greeting rituals with their tails wagging.
(B) Mastering the piano requires learning how to count beats in a measure.
(C) The students voted on the best name for the new classroom goldfish.
(D) The kindergarten teacher always ink-stamped smiley faces on homework.

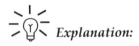

Explanation:

All the choices have something to do with learning or pets, but only (D) serves as an accurate analogy of the sentence. The parrot in the sentence voices approval regardless of piano students' performance, and similarly, the teacher in (D) ink-stamps encouraging symbols on homework papers regardless of the quality of the work.

Question Formats

Although question formats vary from test to test, the most common formats for an analogy question are

- Which situation is the most similar to the one described in lines xx-xx?
- The author uses the figurative phrase "_____" mainly to emphasize what he/she sees as _____.

Focus Questions

What are the main ideas and relationships in the passage?
What images does the passage create?

This passage is adapted from **Jane Austen**, *Persuasion*, originally published in 1818.

line   Captain Frederick Wentworth who being made commander in consequence of the action off St. Domingo, and not immediately employed, had come into Somersetshire, in the summer of 1806; and having no parent living, found a home for half a year at Monkford. He was, at that time, a remarkably fine young man, with a great deal of intelligence, spirit, and brilliancy;

5   and Anne an extremely pretty girl, with gentleness, modesty, taste, and feeling. Half the sum of attraction, on either side, might have been enough, for he had nothing to do, and she had hardly anybody to love; but the encounter of such lavish recommendations could not fail. They were gradually acquainted, and when acquainted, rapidly and deeply in love. It would be difficult to say which had seen highest perfection in the other, or which had been the

10   happiest: she, in receiving his declarations and proposals, or he in having them accepted.

A short period of exquisite felicity followed, and but a short one. Troubles soon arose. [Anne's father] Sir Walter, on being applied to, without actually withholding his consent, or saying it should never be, gave it all the negative of great astonishment, great coldness, great silence, and a professed resolution of doing nothing for his daughter. He thought it a

15   very degrading alliance; and [Anne's late mother's friend] Lady Russell, though with more tempered and pardonable pride, received it as a most unfortunate one.

Anne Elliot, with all her claims of birth, beauty, and mind, to throw herself away at nineteen; involve herself at nineteen in an engagement with a young man, who had nothing but himself to recommend him, and no hopes of attaining affluence, but in the chances of a

20   most uncertain profession, and no connexions to secure even his farther rise in the profession, would be, indeed, a throwing away, which she grieved to think of!

1) Which situation is most similar to the one described in lines 11 – 16?
   (A) A university research proposal is not approved.
   (B) A swimming pool is too cold to swim in.
   (C) A pair of shoes no longer fits.
   (D) An "ugly duckling" turns out to be a beautiful swan.

2) Which situation is most similar to the one described in lines 17 – 21?
   (A) Deciding to quit your job so you can travel around the world.
   (B) Ending a relationship because the other person lacks commitment.
   (C) Attending a community college when your parents want you to attend a private university.
   (D) Avoiding your parents because you think they are upset with you.

005 Question Topic

→ **CITATIONS**

APPROACH

Citation questions test your ability to recognize evidence for conclusions you draw from text. These questions will ask you to select a quote that supports (or, as the SAT says, "provides the best evidence for") the answer to the preceding question. Double check any relevant information in the passage before answering a citation question. When answering, choose the sentence or phrase that has the most substantial and direct relationship to the previous question.

Example

Paul heard the teacher call his name, and he knew it was time. His heart pounding in his chest, Paul reviewed what he would say as he approached the front of the class.

Which choice best provides evidence for the idea that Paul is feeling nervous?
(A) "Paul heard the teacher call his name…"
(B) "…he knew it was time."
(C) "His heart pounding in his chest…"
(D) "Paul reviewed what he would say…"

Explanation:

Although the example above is formatted differently than most SAT citation questions, the gist of the question is the same. Here, we might ask ourselves, "What makes me think that Paul is feeling nervous?" One of the most common signs of nervousness is an increased heart rate. "His heart [is] pounding in his chest" provides direct evidence for Paul's nervousness, making (C) the correct answer.

Question Formats

Although question formats vary from test to test, the most common formats for summary questions are

- Which choice provides the best evidence for the answer to the previous question?
- Which choice best supports the author's claim that _____?
- A student claims that _____. Which of the following statements from the passage best supports/contradicts the student's claim?
- Which statement from the passage best supports the information presented in the graph/table/diagram?

Focus Questions

How is the author trying to convince me?
Which part of the passage proves that?

This passage is adapted from **Kate Chopin**, *The Awakening and Selected Short Stories*, originally published in **1899**.

> *line*   "One of these days," Edna said, "I'm going to pull myself together for a while and think—try to determine what character of a woman I am; for, candidly, I don't know. By all the codes which I am acquainted with, I am a devilishly wicked specimen of the sex. But some way I can't convince myself that I am. I must think about it."
>
> 5   "Don't. What's the use? Why should you bother thinking about it when I can tell you what manner of woman you are?" Arobin's fingers strayed occasionally down to her warm, smooth cheeks and firm chin, which was growing a little full and double.
>
> "Oh, yes! You will tell me that I am adorable; everything that is captivating. Spare yourself the effort."
>
> 10   "No; I shan't tell you anything of the sort, though I shouldn't be lying if I did."
>
> "Do you know Mademoiselle Reisz?" she asked irrelevantly.
>
> "The pianist? I know her by sight. I've heard her play."
>
> "She says queer things sometimes in a bantering way that you don't notice at the time and you find yourself thinking about afterward."
>
> 15   "For instance?"
>
> "Well, for instance, when I left her to-day, she put her arms around me and felt my shoulder blades, to see if my wings were strong, she said. 'The bird that would soar above the level plain of tradition and prejudice must have strong wings. It is a sad spectacle to see the weaklings bruised, exhausted, fluttering back to earth.'"
>
> 20   "Whither would you soar?"
>
> "I'm not thinking of any extraordinary flights. I only half comprehend her."

1) In the context of the passage, Edna's attitude is best described as
   (A) fearful.
   (B) pensive.
   (C) distraught.
   (D) witty.

2) Which choice provides the best evidence for the answer to the previous question?
   (A) Line 1 ("'I'm going to…and think'")
   (B) Line 8 – 9 ("'You will…the effort'")
   (C) Line 13 ("'She says…at the time'")
   (D) Line 21 ("'I'm not thinking…comprehend her'")

Section C: Author Analysis

Generally, when speaking with someone face-to-face, you subconsciously perceive the person's goals. You make inferences about the person's overall intention based on social cues as well as the context and content of the conversation. Author analysis questions require you to employ many of the same skills. The cues that you absorb as you read will help you select the choice that best articulates the author's intentions.

006 Question Topic

→ **PURPOSE**

APPROACH

When inferring an author's purpose in using a particular word, sentence, idea, or structure, it helps to consider the overall intent of the passage. Ultimately, context is everything when answering purpose questions, so quickly take a second look at the section in question before answering.

Example

Isabella was apparently unaware that not everyone loved science fiction; as she explained the minutiae of interstellar travel to her friend Logan, he could not keep from yawning.

The author mentions yawning primarily to
(A) emphasize Logan's boredom.
(B) imply that Logan is sleepy.
(C) provide evidence that Logan is impolite.
(D) criticize Logan's viewpoint on science fiction.

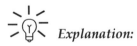 *Explanation:*

The word "yawning" occurs in a sentence that is mainly about Isabella's lack of social awareness. Choice (A) is the only possible answer. The context indicates that the author inserts an instance of yawning to show how much Isabella is boring Logan, not to comment on Logan's character or personality.

Question Formats

Although question formats vary from test to test, the most common formats for purpose questions are

- The main purpose of the (sentence, paragraph, passage, etc.) is to…
- The discussion of _____ in lines xx – xx primarily serves to…
- The (first, second, third, etc.) paragraph is primarily concerned with establishing a contrast between…

PURPOSE

Focus Questions

Why did the author write the passage?
How do details contribute to the main topic of the passage?

This passage is adapted from **Caren Cooper, "Coop's Scoop: Speak for the Trees on next #CitSciChat,"** *CitizenSci,* published in **2015.**

line　　In the mid-1800s, when J. Sterling Morton moved to the Nebraska Territory, he soon was homesick for trees. Maybe he missed the sound of leaves rustling in the breeze. Or maybe the pine-fresh scent. In 1872, as secretary for the Territory, Morton established Arbor Day, and 1 million trees were planted on that first Arbor Day in the Nebraska Territory.

5　　Most fundamentally, trees provide fresh air. Not only do they take in carbon dioxide and release oxygen, they reduce pollutants in the air, improving overall air quality. The benefits include the shade of full-grown trees, which can lower heating bills. Trees are also habitat (food and shelter) for wildlife, they provide privacy, and places for tire swings and tree houses. Being outside is revitalizing, and being in a landscape with trees and greenery helps people cope with
10　chronic stress.

　　Because trees provide so many benefits to people, tree-planting events continue, particularly for city trees. Cities have programs for residents to help with the care and stewardship of city trees, as with the million tree initiative in New York City. In Philadelphia, residents map planting sites and newly planted trees in PhillyTreeMap in order to visualize and
15　keep track of the positive impacts of the city's trees.

　　Many species of trees face blights of insect pests and diseases. Citizen science efforts monitor tree health. For example, in OakMapper, participants in California can report suspected cases of Sudden Oak Death, which is caused by a pathogen. Seventh and eighth graders in Ohio discovered the emerald ash borer parasitoid in woods adjacent to their school. As millions of
20　ash trees across Europe are killed by a fungus, citizen scientists participate in a Facebook game, Fraxinus, to help align DNA sequences to assess variability in different strains of the pathogen. The results can help researchers understand the genetic code behind the disease.

1) The main purpose of the passage is to
    (A) explain how J. Sterling Morgan ushered in a new age of environmentalism.
    (B) describe the ways in which trees and humans benefit one another.
    (C) weigh the benefits imparted by trees against the high cost of planting them.
    (D) encourage young people to plant trees in their neighborhoods.

2) The discussion of "citizen science efforts" to monitor tree health in paragraph 4 (lines 16 – 22) primarily serves to
    (A) illustrate that conservation efforts are international and available to non-scientists.
    (B) imply that America takes environmentalism more seriously than Europe does.
    (C) explain how tree-planting efforts have caused the spread of parasites and diseases.
    (D) warn readers of the imminent extinction of numerous species of trees.

007 Question Topic

ORGANIZATION

APPROACH

Organization questions ask you how the author structures and presents information in a passage. An organization question may ask you how one piece of information relates to another piece of information, or how that piece of information contributes to the passage's main idea(s). You may be asked to identify the rhetorical strategies that the author uses and recognize how they are arranged. As examples, an author might describe a cause and effect relationship, present events in chronological order, or contrast two sides of an issue.

Example

The forest was very dense. The first night of the camp, they left their flashlights and cell phones on and used up the batteries. The second night, rain soaked all the firewood that they had brought. So on the third night they were sitting in the dark when they thought they heard footsteps.

The last sentence in the passage serves mainly to
(A) introduce a character.
(B) describe a consequence.
(C) summarize events.
(D) provide explanations.

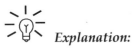

Explanation:

The last sentence hints that something might be about to happen. Yet the sentence simply does not introduce any characters. Likewise, the passage as a whole lists reasons why the campers ended up sitting in the dark, which could divert attention to words like "explanations." However, we are being asked about the function of the last sentence, not the passage as a whole. One clue that the answer is (B) is that it begins with "so," which indicates consequence. To paraphrase the last sentence, "As a consequence of the reasons just listed, the campers were sitting in the dark..."

Question Formats

Although question formats vary from one test to another, the most common formats for organization questions are

- Which choice best describes the structure of the paragraph/passage?
- What function does the paragraph serve in the passage as a whole?
- The paragraph is primarily concerned with establishing a contrast between...
- During the course of passage, the narrator's focus shifts from…

Focus Questions

This passage is adapted from **Henry Lee**, *Sea Monsters Unmasked*, originally published in 1883.

line Here let me say—and I wish it to be distinctly understood—that I do not deny the possibility of the existence of a great sea serpent, or other great creatures at present unknown to science, and that I have no inclination to explain away that which others have seen, because I myself have not witnessed it. "Seeing is believing," it is said, and it is not agreeable to
5 have to tell a person that, in common parlance, he "must not trust his own eyes." It seems presumptuous even to hint that one may know better what was seen than the person who saw it. And yet I am obliged to say, reluctantly and courteously, but most firmly and assuredly, that these perfectly credible eye-witnesses did not correctly interpret that which they witnessed. In these cases, it is not the eye which deceives, nor the tongue which is untruthful, but the
10 imagination which is led astray by the association of the thing seen with an erroneous idea. I venture to say this, not with any insolent assumption of superior acumen, but because we now possess a key to the mystery which Archdeacon Deinbolt and his neighbours had not access to, and which has only within the last few years been placed in our hands. The movements and aspect of their sea monster are those of an animal with which we are now well acquainted, but
15 of the existence of which the narrators of these occasional visitations were unaware; namely, the great calamary, the same which gave rise to the stories of the Kraken, and which has probably been a denizen of the Scandinavian seas and fjords from time immemorial.

1) Which choice best describes the structure of the passage?
   (A) A polite disclaimer is followed by a firm assertion.
   (B) A general description is followed by a specific instance.
   (C) A historical event is described and then given a broader context.
   (D) A problem is presented and then a solution is suggested.

2) The passage is primarily concerned with establishing a contrast between
   (A) Archdeacon Deinbolt and the author.
   (B) presumption and courtesy.
   (C) the great calamary and the Kraken.
   (D) past and present knowledge.

008 Question Topic

TONE AND ATTITUDE

APPROACH

When you call a friend, you can usually determine how your friend is feeling right away. You listen to what your friend says and how he or she says it. It is not so different when you are asked to identify tone and attitude in a text. A quick look back at the first few lines of the text, as well as the segment in question, will help you absorb clues such as word choice, sentence structure, and content.

Example

Horses evolved to live in herds, constantly close enough to swish flies off each other with their tails. Today's horses still *hate* to be alone. But for one reason or another, they cannot always be with other horses. And while the occasional barn cat or chicken might become a friend, many horses have been known to deeply cherish goat companions. Goats are social and see eye-to-eye with horses on the topic of solitude: they oppose it.

The author's attitude toward horses and goats can best be described as

(A) practical.   (B) sentimental.
(C) affectionate.   (D) ambivalent.

Explanation:

The author is explaining sociability from the horses' point of view. The diction is not overly tender or sweet, and thus could not be described as "sentimental." Rather, the author describes negative emotions of both horses and goats ("hate to be alone") in a bemused way, while also noting that many horses "deeply cherish" their goat friends. Overall the author expresses understanding of the two species, so "affectionate" is a fitting description, and choice (C) is correct.

Question Formats

Although question formats vary, the most common formats for tone and attitude questions are

- The author's attitude toward _____ is best described as...
- What main effect does _____ have on the tone of the passage?
- How do the words "___" and "___" in paragraph xx help establish the tone of the paragraph?
- The author uses the word "___" throughout the passage mainly to...
- Over the course of the passage, the narrator's attitude shifts from...
- The passage is written from the perspective of someone who is...

Focus Questions

If the author were reading this out loud to me, how would he or she sound?

This passage is adapted from **H.P. Lovecraft**, "**The Shunned House**," originally published in *Weird Tales*, October **1937**.

line   What I heard in my youth about the shunned house was merely that people died there
in alarmingly great numbers. That, I was told, was why the original owners had moved out
some twenty years after building the place. It was plainly unhealthy, perhaps because of
the dampness and fungous growths in the cellar, the general sickish smell, the drafts of the
5   hallways, or the quality of the well and pump water. These things were bad enough, and
these were all that gained belief among the persons whom I knew. Only the notebooks of
my antiquarian uncle, Doctor Elihu Whipple, revealed to me at length the darker, vaguer
surmises which formed an undercurrent of folklore among old-time servants and humble
folk; surmises which never travelled far, and which were largely forgotten when Providence
10   grew to be a metropolis with a shifting modern population.
       The general fact is that the house was never regarded by the solid part of the community
as in any real sense "haunted." There were no widespread tales of rattling chains, cold
currents of air, extinguished lights, or faces at the window. Extremists sometimes said the
house was "unlucky," but that is as far as even they went. What was really beyond dispute is
15   that a frightful proportion of persons died there; or more accurately, had died there, since after
some peculiar happenings over sixty years ago the building had become deserted through the
sheer impossibility of renting it. These persons were not all cut off suddenly by any one cause;
rather did it seem that their vitality was insidiously sapped, so that each one died the sooner
from whatever tendency to weakness he may have naturally had. And those who did not die
20   displayed in varying degree a type of anemia or consumption, and sometimes a decline of the
mental faculties, which spoke ill for the salubriousness of the building. Neighboring houses, it
must be added, seemed entirely free from the noxious quality.

1) The author's attitude toward "the shunned house" can most accurately be characterized as one of
   (A) justifiable fear.
   (B) open hostility.
   (C) scholarly fascination.
   (D) unhealthy obsession.

2) The passage is written from the perspective of someone who
   (A) is considering purchasing a particular house.
   (B) has taken an academic interest in a mysterious subject.
   (C) lets his superstitious tendencies guide his research.
   (D) is determined to disprove a controversial theory regarding a house.

3) What effect does the phrase in lines 6 – 8 ("Only the notebooks…humble folk") have on the tone of
   the passage?
   (A) It adds an element of superstition regarding the reputation of the house.
   (B) It interjects an element of nostalgia to a passage otherwise concerned with the present.
   (C) It attempts to add humor to an otherwise somber account.
   (D) It reveals the author's fear of "the shunned house."

Section D: Synthesis

Synthesis questions require you to understand the relationship between two passages, or between a passage and a graphical representation of data, such as a table, chart, or graph.

009 Question Topic

→ **GRAPHICS AND TEXT SYNTHESIS**

APPROACH

You have studied graphs, tables, and charts in math; on the Reading Test, graphics questions require you to apply your knowledge. Take a careful look at the title and at the "x" and "y" axes of the graphic to insure that you have a firm grasp of what is (and what is not) represented. The graphic information might support or contradict the text, or it might not apply to the text at all.

Example

Hey mom
Homecoming game is over! We lost, as usual :/
Can you pick me up from the high school?
I NEED food like now : {

What information in the text message is suggested by the graph?
 (A) Many teens text while driving.
 (B) Many teens do not know how to drive.
 (C) Many teens cannot afford to buy cars.
 (D) Many teens do not have driver's licenses.

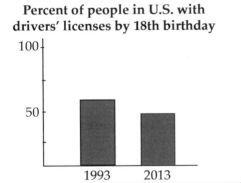

Percent of people in U.S. with drivers' licenses by 18th birthday

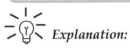

Explanation:

The graph presents information only about driver's licenses, ruling out all choices except (D). The writer of the text message asks to be picked up from "the high school," so we can assume that the writer is a teen and is not in a situation to drive independently. The graph indicates simply that such a situation is fairly common for teens.

Question Formats

Although question formats vary from test to test, some common formats for graphics and text synthesis questions are

- Which claim about _____ is supported by the graph?
- What information presented in paragraph xx is represented by the graph?
- It can be reasonably inferred from the passage and the graph that _____.
- Which choice best summarizes the information presented in the graph?
- According to the graph, which statement is true about _____?

Focus Questions

Why has the graphic been paired with the passage?
What information do the works share?

Passage 1 is adapted from John Bound, Michael Lovenheim, et al, "Understanding the Decrease in College Completion Rates and the Increased Time to Baccalaureate Degree," published in 2007.

The graph is from the U.S. Dept. of Education, **National Center for Education Statistics "The Condition of Education,"** published in 2013.

line   Enrollment is relatively elastic among public universities outside of the most selective few. Here, we expect increased demand to lead to increased enrollment and consequent reductions in resources per student.

    That aggregate increases in time to degree are not tied directly to changes in characteristics
5   of students suggests that the underlying rate at which students complete college studies may be impeded by limited availability of courses and institutional resources more generally at public colleges...The evidence that we have put together points strongly towards declines in the resources, both monetary and non-monetary, available to students at public colleges and universities playing a central role in explaining the decrease in completion rates and the
10 increased time it is taking college students within the U.S. to obtain BA degrees.

Percentage of students seeking a bachelor's degree at 4-year degree-granting institutions who completed a bachelor's degree within 6 years, 2006

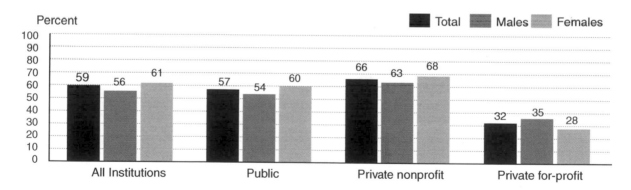

1) Which claim about graduation rates is supported by the graph?
   (A) A greater total number of people graduate from public colleges than private nonprofit ones.
   (B) About two-thirds of students who start at private nonprofit institutions tend to graduate within six years.
   (C) A majority of people who start college do not have a bachelor's degree at the end of six years.
   (D) It is easier to graduate from private nonprofit colleges than private for-profit ones.

2) From the passage and the graph, it can be reasonably inferred that
   (A) the only way to graduate within a reasonable amount of time is to attend private colleges.
   (B) a public college or university has to waste a lot of money educating students who drop out.
   (C) public institutions need more money to make it easier for students to graduate in a timely manner.
   (D) smaller enrollment means that private nonprofit institutions can provide a better education.

010 Question Topic

→ **MULTIPLE-TEXT SYNTHESIS**

APPROACH

When you see a movie and it reminds you of another movie, you are recognizing similarities between them. When you compare which is better, you are recognizing differences between them. When you wonder, "What would so-and-so do in a situation like this?" you are extrapolating based on what you know about so-and-so. All of this thinking constitutes synthesis, and you can use the same skills to answer questions about the paired texts on the Reading Test.

Example

(The following sources and passages are fictitious.) Ingredients List 1 is from the label of Soup Playground's "Condensed Tomato Soup"; Ingredients List 2 is from Jackson Yee, *Simplest Soups*.

Ingredients List 1: Tomato puree (water, tomato paste), high fructose corn syrup, wheat flour, water, salt, potassium chloride, flavoring, citric acid, sea salt, ascorbic acid, monopotassium phosphate.

Ingredients List 2: 2 cups vegetable broth, 1 cup chopped onion, 1 cup chopped celery, 1 tablespoon fresh basil, 1 tablespoon tomato paste, 2 pounds fresh tomatoes (cut into wedges), ½ teaspoon salt, dash of pepper. Combine ingredients, simmer for 30 minutes. Serve hot, topped with spoonfuls of plain yogurt.

How would the author of List 2 most likely respond to the recipe in List 1?
(A) With curiosity, because it does not include preparation instructions
(B) With admiration, because its ingredients are low in calories
(C) With nostalgia, because he ate Soup Playground soups as a child
(D) With criticism, because it does not include an allergy warning

Explanation:

Essentially, you are being asked to infer how one author would react to another's work. The best way to do so is to find the differences and similarities between the two works. One of the most noticeable differences between the two lists above is that List 2 includes preparation instructions whereas List 1 does not. Thus, (A) is the clearest, most supportable inference that can be made from the choices provided.

Question Formats

Although question formats vary, some common formats for multiple-text synthesis questions are

- How would the author of Passage 1 most likely respond to the claim about _____ made in Passage 2?
- Which choice best states the relationship between the two passages?
- Is the principle described in Passage 1 consistent with the situation described in Passage 2?
- One difference between the _____ in Passage 1 and the _____ in Passage 2 is...
- On which of the following would the authors of both passages most likely agree?

Focus Questions

Passage 1 is adapted from **John Locke**, *Essay Concerning Human Understanding*, originally published in **1689**. Passage 2 is adapted from **William Henry Pyle**, *The Science of Human Nature*, originally published in **1917**.

Passage 1

line   Let us then suppose the mind to be, as we say, white paper, void of all characters, without any ideas:—How comes it to be furnished? Whence comes it by that vast store which the busy and boundless fancy of man has painted on it with an almost endless variety? Whence has it all the materials of reason and knowledge? To this I answer, in one word, from experience. In

5   that all our knowledge is founded; and from that it ultimately derives itself. Our observation employed either, about external sensible objects, or about the internal operations of our minds perceived and reflected on by ourselves, is that which supplies our understandings with all the materials of thinking. These two are the fountains of knowledge, from whence all the ideas we have, or can naturally have, do spring.

Passage 2

10   Observation of children shows that they are selfish, envious, and quarrelsome. They will fight and steal until they are taught not to do such things. How can we understand this? There is no way of understanding such actions until we come to see that the children and men of to-day are such as they are because of their ancestors. It has been only a few generations, relatively speaking, since our ancestors were naked savages, killing their enemies and eating

15   their enemies' bodies. The civilized life of our ancestors covers a period of only a few hundred years. The pre-civilized life of our ancestors goes back probably thousands and thousands of years. In the relatively short period of civilization, our real, original nature has been little changed, perhaps none at all. The modern man is, at heart, the same old man of the woods.

1) How would Locke respond to Pyle's claim that children's temperaments are shaped by humanity's "original nature"?
   (A) Children are only savage if they learn to be so through experience.
   (B) Experience teaches children to reject their innate savage nature.
   (C) Children's lack of logic and reasoning drive them to selfishness.
   (D) Children only reveal their "original nature" when striving for material goods.

2) Which choice best states the relationship between the two passages?
   (A) Passage 2 defends a controversial theory presented in Passage 1.
   (B) Passage 2 questions the line of reasoning that Passage 1 uses to reach a conclusion.
   (C) Passage 2 refutes the process describing the role of learning outlined in Passage 1.
   (D) Passage 2 expands upon the philosophical stance presented in Passage 1.

ANSWERS

&

Explanations

Question Topics

1-10

Answers & Explanations...
Mastering the Reading Test

1) ➡ C

Although all choices provide accurate definitions of "intimate," only (C) works in the context of the sentence. After the author claims that she is "intimate" with her plants, she describes some of their physical characteristics, so we can infer that she is familiar with the qualities of plants in her backyard.

2) ➡ A

The author clarifies that her "warm" relationship with plants involves familiarity and admiration. These qualities also characterize many friendships, so we can presume she has a friendly relationship with the plants.

3) ➡ D

The author gives hints at the soaptree yucca's noticeability. She describes its flower stalk as a "six-foot-high candle glowing in the dusk." Because we can safely assume that a human-sized, glowing candle is *noticeable*, (D) is the correct choice.

4) ➡ B

Each of the choices represents a correct meaning of "dull." In the the context of the sentence, the author uses "dull" to describe the word "phenology," which is the study of seasonal changes in plants and animals. The author says that watching the plants in her backyard leaf out, produce seeds , and so on, cannot be described by a word as dull as phenology. The best choice is (B), "unimaginative," because the author implies that "phenology" does not begin to encompass her experience with plants.

1) ➡ A

When making an inference, one must ensure that an entire choice is supportable based on the information presented in the text before selecting that choice. For instance, (C) mentions the Crow's thirst, which is an element of the fable, but it also mentions hunger, which is not. Because we can eliminate one part of the choice, we must eliminate the entire choice. (B) and (D) are too general to serve the purpose. Only choice (A) is fully supportable based on the text; the Crow needs water (necessity) and so comes up with a clever solution to get water (ingenuity).

2) ➡ C

This question requires you to recognize that the forces of nature (the North Wind and the Sun) represent concepts (force and persuasion, respectively). (C) is correct because the North Wind unsuccessfully uses force to rip the traveler's cloak away, whereas the sun uses persuasion (heat) to convince the traveler to remove his cloak of his own volition.

3) ➡ B

The fable suggests that the victorious Cock is ultimately the loser because he was carried off by an Eagle, whereas the beaten Cock keeps his life. The victorious one is carried off because his excessive pride impels him to brag about his victory, drawing the Eagle's attention.

Question Topic 003: Summaries

1) ➡ C

The main idea of the passage is that writing for a living is very difficult. Thus, when the author mentions the magic trick of pulling a rabbit from a hat, he is linking this imagery to his main point: writers must consistently produce new ideas, which "only seems easy to those who haven't tried it."

2) ➡ B

In Greek mythology, Muses are goddesses who are the sources of creativity. Paragraph 3 mainly points out that authors "court the...Muse"; that is, they purposefully engage in rituals that will inspire them. New ideas are necessary for "high-quality work." Therefore, (B) provides the best summary of the examples.

Question Topic 004: Analogies

1) ➡ A

Lines 11–16 describe a situation in which Anne Elliot wants approval from her fater regarding her engagement to be married, but that approval is withheld. The only choice that describes a situation in which approval is being withheld is (A), wherein a university will not approve a researcher proposal.

2) ➡ C

Lines 17–21 characterizes Anne Elliot's decision to marry as a poor one because she and her family will not advance socially or monetarily from the marriage. In other words, Anne is not living up to social expectations. The only choice that describes a similar situation in which someone fails to live up to the expectations laid out for him or her is (C), as a private university is generally thought to be more prestigious than a community college.

Question Topic 005: Citations

1) ➡ B

To be pensive is to be thoughtful. We can determine that Edna is primarily thoughtful in the passage because she seems to be pondering her own character and that of Mademoiselle Reisz. This contemplative tone persists throughout the passage, with no indications that she is feeling fearful, distraught, or witty.

2) ➡ A

The correct choice is (A) because line 1 is the first mention Edna makes about thinking; it is the most appropriate textual evidence to support calling her attitude "pensive."

Question Topic 006: Purpose

1) ➡ B

The passage begins with the origins of Arbor Day, a holiday that celebrates environmentalism through the planting of trees. The following paragraphs discuss how "trees provide so many benefits to people," and how these benefits encourage "tree-planting efforts," which is especially important in cities. Thus, the majority of the passage discusses the mutually beneficial relationship between trees and humans, making (B) the correct choice.

2) ➡ A

Choice (A) is correct because the final paragraph mentions efforts by "seventh and eighth graders in Ohio" and "citizen scientists" in Europe to improve trees' health by identifying pathogens. Thus, the efforts described are international (they take place in America and Europe) and available to non-scientists (they are performed by students and Facebook users).

1) ➡️ A

The first half of the passage serves as a disclaimer; this is best evidenced in lines 1 – 3 ("I do not deny the possibility of the existence of a great sea serpent..."). But the author then turns to his purpose: "And yet I am obliged to say...most firmly and assuredly," where he explains "sea monster" sightings.

2) ➡️ D

The author introduces the primary contrast of the passage when he writes, "we now possess a key to the mystery which Archdeacon Deinbolt...had not access to." The author then proceeds to explain the "key to the mystery" (recent knowledge), making (D) the most appropriate choice.

Question Topic 008: Tone and Attitude

1) ➡️ C

The author's diction indicates a scholarly, level-headed approach when discussing the house. He entertains the possibility that the house's danger arises from the fact that it is "plainly unhealthy" while also mentioning the "darker, vaguer surmises" of others. He discusses facts and describes "what was really beyond dispute." Moreover, we can presume that the author is fascinated by the house because of how much research he conducts into the house's history.

2) ➡️ B

The author's academic interest can be surmised based on how many sources he consulted concerning the house's history. He mentions claims about the house from when he was young, the research conducted by his uncle, and opinions from members of the community. Moreover, because no one knows why so many people have died in the aforementioned house, we can safely say the author is investigating a mysterious subject.

3) ➡️ A

With the exceptions of lines 6 – 8, the author does not mention any instances of people attributing the house's danger to superstitious or folkloric causes. Thus, the addition of lines 6 – 8 primarily serves to introduce an element of superstition into the author's investigation of the house.

Question Topic 009: Graphics and Text Synthesis

1) ➡️ B

The correct choice must be completely supported by the graph. Since two-thirds of 100 is close to 66, the information in (B) is accurate based on the graph. Other choices incorrectly interpret the information. (A) includes information on the total number of people graduating, which cannot be supported because the graph displays percentages of students, not total number of students. (C) is factually incorrect because the "Total" for "All Institutions" is 59 percent, so the majority of college students *do* earn bachelor's degrees within 6 years. (D) is incorrect because we cannot determine how easy a type of school is based on graduation rates.

2) ➡️ C

The passage claims that a lack of resources "both monetary and non-monetary" at public universities play "a central role in explaining the decrease in completion rates." This information is supported by the graph, which demonstrates that public institutions have lower graduation rates than private nonprofit universities.

Question Topic 010: Multiple-Text Synthesis

1) ➡️ A

Locke proposes that people are born with minds like "white paper," and that all knowledge and characteristics come from experience. Thus, it follows that Locke would maintain that a savage child learned to be so through his or her experiences, making (A) the correct choice.

2) ➡️ C

The author of passage 1 claims that humans are completely shaped by experience, whereas the author of passage 2 maintains that humans are driven by an "original nature" that is savage unless taught to be civilized. Therefore, the author of passage 2 presents a different hypothesis on the same topic, refuting the author of passage 1.

CHAPTER 2

Mastering
The Writing and Language Test

1

STRUCTURING SENTENCES

2

CORRECTING GRAMMAR MISTAKES

3

IMPROVING STYLE AND STRUCTURE

Writing and Language Test Basics

A. About the Passages

The SAT Writing and Language Test consists of four reading passages. Each passage is accompanied by eleven multiple-choice questions. One or two of the reading passages will include supplementary materials, such as tables, charts, or graphs, that display information relevant to the passage's topic.

The SAT Writing and Language Test will always contain the following:

- A career-related passage
- A science passage
- A history/social science passage
- A literature/humanities passage

The passages will be in a variety of different modes. Some will be descriptions of an event, some will explain concepts, and some will present arguments.

B. About the Questions

Each multiple-choice question will have four answer choices, and each question will have only one correct answer. As with other sections of the SAT, you will not be penalized for incorrect answers.

Certain types of questions will appear in nearly every set of questions. Generally, a question set will include at least one vocabulary question, and each passage with an associated table, chart, or graph will contain about two questions regarding the relationship between the passage and the visual. The overall breakdown of questions on the Writing and Language Test is as follows:

- Approximately 55 percent of questions relate to the structure, style, or precision of the passage. These questions do not necessarily ask you to fix grammatical errors; rather, they require you to improve the *quality* and *clarity* of the passage as a whole.

- Approximately 45 percent of questions relate to locating and fixing grammatical errors within the passage. Thus, a strong understanding of English grammar and the ability to spot grammatical mistakes are crucial to mastering the Writing and Language Test.

C. Test-Taking Strategies

As a whole, the Writing and Language Test covers a wide range of grammatical and stylistic concepts, but each question will only test one or two concepts. Thus, one of your first priorities when answering Writing and Language Test questions should be determining which *specific* concept or concepts a question is testing. Doing so will allow you to proceed quickl and confidently.

- **Use the underlined text to determine what is being tested.**
  If the underlined text is an entire sentence, the corresponding question will likely be testing your knowledge of sentence structures or your organizational abilities. If the underlined text is a single word or a phrase, it could be testing vocabulary.

- **Use the answer choices to determine what is being tested.**
  Before selecting an answer, look carefully at all of your choices. Determine what part or parts of the answers change from choice to choice. For example, if one answer choice contains a comma, and another a semicolon, you can be fairly certain the question is testing punctuation. Or, if one answer choice replaces "it" with "they," you can be fairly certain that the question is testing your knowledge of pronouns.

- **Use the information around the underlined portion.**
  Use the passage as a whole and the sentences just before and after underlined portions to double-check your answers. Ensure that the choice you have selected fits the context of the passage and the paragraph.

Writing & Language Test PATTERN Approach

Going into any test with a strategy in mind will reduce test anxiety and boost confidence. You can actively develop a strategy using the following pattern approach to fine-tune your effectiveness.

PATTERN Approach

Start with the Question

Determine exactly what the question is asking you to do. Doing so will prevent you from becoming distracted as you look back in the passage for relevant information.

Determine what specific concept or concepts a question is testing. Doing so will allow you to apply an appropriate rule or strategy to each question, taking the guesswork out of answering the question.

Narrow Your Search
Specific Concepts

Ex: If a question wants you to determine the tense of a verb, look at other verbs in the sentence or paragraph for guidance.

Look back at the passage and search for any information or grammatical structures near the underlined portion that might help you.

Review the Passage
Underlined Portion

Quickly eliminate answers that you are confident contain incorrect or inaccurate information. Select the correct answer from the remaining choices.

Use the Process of Elimination

Structuring Sentences

SENTENCE STRUCTURE

1 Subjects and predicates are like actors and actions in a film. Subjects generally perform an action; predicates tell the reader what subjects do or what they are like.

Subject	Predicate
The "who" or the "what" that is either doing something or is being described	A description of what the subject does or what the subject is like

I believe a leaf of grass is no less than the journey-work of the stars. –Walt Whitman

Subject (I) + Predicate (believe a leaf of grass is no less than the journey-work of the stars.)

"I" is the subject because it is doing something. The rest of the sentence is the predicate because it describes what the subject is doing: believing.

Suspicion always haunts the guilty mind. –William Shakespeare

Subject (Suspicion) + predicate (always haunts the guilty mind.)

"Suspicion" is the subject, because it is doing something. The rest of the sentence is the predicate because it describes what suspicion does: always haunting.

2 Subjects and Predicates can become difficult to sort out when the writer adds clauses, prepositional phrases, adverbs, and so on.

Change in all things is sweet. –Aristotle

Subject (Change in all things) + Predicate (is sweet.)

In this case, the subject includes a prepositional phrase ("in all things") but is still a single concept. The predicate describes what the subject of the sentence is like. In this case, the subject—"change"—"is sweet."

My aim is to put down on paper what I see and what I feel in the best and simplest way.
–Ernest Hemingway

Subject (My aim) + Predicate (is to put down on paper what I see and what I feel in the best and simplest way.)

Although Hemingway uses "I see" and "I feel" in the predicate, the subject is "My aim." The rest of the sentence is the predicate and describes "My aim."

Section A: Clauses

Most spoken communication does not consist of simple subject-predicate expressions. Rather, it spans the spectrum from long and complicated to short and elliptical. Yet spoken communication is effective because we supplement our words with natural pauses, facial expressions, and gestures. With our voices, we indicate meaning through tone, volume, and emphasis.

Written language, however, must rely on diction, sentence structure, and punctuation to communicate meaning. Understanding the basic components of sentences—including **clauses**—can help you identify and correct confusion and errors.

INDEPENDENT AND DEPENDENT CLAUSES

▶ A **clause** is a group of words containing a subject and a verb. An independent clause can stand on its own as a sentence while a dependent clause cannot. Structurally, the only difference between the two types of clauses is that a dependent clause begins with a subordinate conjunction while an independent clause does not.

▶ **Subordinate conjunctions** show that one event is a result of another, or that one event depends on another event. Some of the most common subordinate conjunctions are (al)though, because, if, since, that, when, whether, and while. Let's look at how adding a subordinating conjunction to a clause changes its structure and meaning.

INDEPENDENT CLAUSE		SUBORDINATE CONJUNCTION		DEPENDENT CLAUSE
John is very tired		because		because John is very tired
the dog plays with its owner	+	while	=	while the dog plays with its owner
swimming is great exercise		although		although swimming is great exercise
the car is expensive		if		if the car is expensive

Notice how the examples in the Independent Clause column could be complete sentences given proper capitalization and punctuation. The examples in the Dependent Clause column are all fragments that do not express a complete thought.

011 Question Topic

→ **FRAGMENTS AND RUN-ONS**

DESCRIPTION

You have probably been hearing about "checking for complete sentences" since elementary school. As you know, a complete sentence includes a subject and a predicate. Incomplete sentences are called "fragments," and sentences that ignore necessary punctuation are called "run-ons." Sentence fragments need finishing, and run-on sentences need punctuation.

Example

I have always loved playing **1** <u>soccer I do not play</u> on a team.

    (A) NO CHANGE   (C) soccer when possible, not

    (B) soccer, not   (D) soccer, but I do not

 Explanation:

The correct choice is (D) because it is the only choice that provides a natural pause between thoughts, a clear relationship between ideas, and a complete thought.

Sentence Fragments

▶ Some sentences are fragments because they lack a subject and/or a verb.

    Fragment sentence: Right in front of me.

    Complete sentence: *A ball rolled* right in front of me.

▶ Other fragments have all the components of a complete sentence, but they begin with a subordinate conjunction, making them incomplete thoughts that require an independent clause to be complete.

    Fragment sentence: Even though I kicked the ball gently.

    Complete sentence: Even though I kicked the ball gently, *it bounced down the street.*

Run-on Sentences

▶ Many run-on sentences result from mispunctuation and unnecessary wordiness. When possible, rephrase run-ons to reduce wordiness and ensure that punctuation clarifies rather than confuses.

    Run-on sentence: A child came barreling toward me the child was panting as he said "Hey!"

    Complete Sentence: A child came barreling toward me, *panting as he said, "Hey!"*

012 Question Topic

COMPLEX SENTENCES

DESCRIPTION

Sentences containing an independent clause as well as a dependent clause are called **complex sentences**. When a sentence contains an independent clause and a dependent clause, the order in which the clauses are presented determines whether a comma must come between them.

Complex Sentence Structures

> **Dependent Clause + Comma (,) + Independent Clause + Period (.)**

> **Independent Clause + Dependent Clause + Period (.)**

Example

Morgan and Andy always enjoy 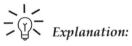 traveling...once they are actually on the road.

(A) NO CHANGE	(C) traveling; once
(B) traveling once	(D) traveling. Once

Explanation:

Choice (B) is correct because the example sentence above consists of an independent clause followed by a dependent clause, so no punctuation is needed between clauses.

▶ A dependent clause that precedes an independent clause is set apart by a comma.

> ***Before you speak,*** take a deep breath.
>
> ***Wherever they looked,*** they saw lion footprints.
>
> ***As soon as the diamond ring hit the water,*** he regretted throwing it.

▶ A dependent clause that comes after an independent clause does not need to be set apart by a comma.

> Take a deep breath ***before you speak***.
>
> They saw lion footprints ***wherever they looked***.
>
> He regretted throwing the diamond ring ***as soon as it hit the water***.

▶ However, in long, convoluted sentences containing the structure outlined above, add a comma between independent and dependent clauses if doing so improves the clarity of the sentence.

> Freed from all obligations, Darla and Connie decided to take a long road trip to an undecided location, ***even though they hardly had enough money for a full tank of gas.***

013 Question Topic

→ **COMBINING SENTENCES**

DESCRIPTION

While there are many ways to combine two sentences, the simplest method is often to replace the period that separates the two sentences with a semicolon or a comma plus a coordinating conjunction.

Two Sentences: I love exploring nature. My sister prefers the city life.

Combined Sentences: I love exploring nature, **but** my sister prefers the city life.

I love exploring nature; my sister prefers the city life.

Example

We had never seen a waterfall in this **1** canyon, my sister did not believe that one existed.

(A) NO CHANGE

(C) canyon; my sister

(B) canyon so my sister

(D) canyon; although my sister

 Explanation:

The correct choice is (C) because a semicolon accurately joins two independent clauses. Choice (D) is incorrect because the semicolon is followed by a dependent clause.

▶ A semicolon is traditionally used to combine sentences when the ideas in the two sentences have a relationship that does not need to be explained with a conjunction:

We stepped into the creek; small fish swam around our feet.

The rocks were slippery; we picked our way carefully.

▶ A comma plus a coordinating conjunction is traditionally used to combine sentences to clarify the relationship between the ideas in the two sentences:

We waded upstream, *for* the creek provided the clearest path. Sunlight filtered through the trees, *and* birds sang.

💬 **TEACHER'S TIP**

If you are having trouble memorizing the coordinating conjunctions, use the acronym FANBOYS:

For And Nor But Or Yet So

014 Question Topic

COMPOUND VERBS

DESCRIPTION

In some sentences, one subject will perform multiple actions. These sentences are said to have **compound verbs**. How these sentences are punctuated depends on whether the subject is mentioned more than once in the sentence.

Example

We scrambled over and around **1** boulders and we reached a bend in the creek.

(A) NO CHANGE

(C) boulders, we

(B) boulders; and then we

(D) boulders and

 Explanation:

Choice (D) is correct; the subject of the sentence, "we," does not need to be repeated between actions ("scrambled" and "reached"). If it is not repeated, no punctuation is necessary between verbs.

▶ If the subject is repeated between verbs, which have been italicized in the examples below, then the sentence contains two independent clauses and must be punctuated with a semicolon or a comma and a coordinating conjunction. It can also be split into two sentences.

Compound Sentence: We *spotted* the waterfall; we *decided* it was not within walking distance.

Compound Sentence: We *spotted* the waterfall, but we *decided* it was not within walking distance.

Two Sentences: We *spotted* the waterfall. We *decided* it was not within walking distance.

▶ The examples above can also be written **without repeating the subject.** This produces a shorter, more concise sentence:

Compound Verbs: We *spotted* the waterfall but *decided* it was not within walking distance.

CLAUSES

Read the passage and answer the corresponding questions.

PASSAGE

Shackleton's Journey

In January of 1915, a British ship crossed the South Atlantic Ocean to Antarctica. It contained a crew of 27 men led by Ernest Shackleton. After becoming stuck when the seawater **froze solid they gave up** on their goal of reaching land and crossing the polar continent on foot.

The crew lived in the ship, going out on the ice to hunt seals and penguins. They waited for the ice to melt enough so that their ship could float. It was hugely disappointing when, after nine months, the wooden ship began to crack under the pressure of the ice. By November, the ship had sunk. The men camped on ice floes until April, hoping to drift to an island. When their ice floe **2 cracked in half, they** had no choice but to get into three small wooden lifeboats. They were at sea for a **3 week before they managed** to reach the tiny Elephant Island, which was uninhabited, barren, and snow-covered.

Leaving most of the men camped under two overturned lifeboats, Shackleton and five other men got back in the third lifeboat and headed out again. **4 After becoming caught** in a hurricane. After 16 harrowing days, they managed to land on an island where they knew there was a whaling station on the other side. Three of them hiked through snow without sleeping for 36 hours to reach the whaling **5 station and when they** reached it, they sent help back for the men on the other side of the island. Almost immediately, Shackleton made rescue attempts for the rest of the men as well. He borrowed ships to reach the men on Elephant Island three **6 times. He had to turn back** because of icy waters. During his fourth attempt, on August 30, 1916, Shackleton reached the men and rescued them. Amazingly, the entire crew survived the ordeal.

1

(A) NO CHANGE
(B) froze solid, they gave up

2

(A) NO CHANGE
(B) cracked in half they

3

(A) NO CHANGE
(B) week, before they managed

4

(A) NO CHANGE
(B) They were caught

5

(A) NO CHANGE
(B) station. When they

6

(A) NO CHANGE
(B) times but had to turn back

Section B: Phrases

As discussed in the previous section, a clause is a group of words containing a subject and a verb. A **phrase** is a group of words that conveys an idea but does not contain a subject and a verb. Thus, on their own, phrases cannot be complete sentences.

Let's look at how some of the most common types of phrases fit into sentences.

015 Question Topic

→ **PREPOSITIONAL PHRASES**

DESCRIPTION

Prepositional phrases begin with prepositions and end with their objects. In the sentence, "Brian offered carrots to the horse," the prepositional phrase is "to the horse." A **preposition** helps clarify the relationship between a subject and a verb in a sentence. For example, prepositions such as *over, beneath, under, behind, outside, in, on, between,* and *through* indicate **spatial** relationships. Prepositions such as *from, before, since,* and *after* indicate **temporal** relationships. And prepositions such as *by, for, with, from,* and *to* mainly describe **logical** relationships. Selecting the most precise preposition clarifies meaning.

Example

Jade boarded a ship **1** of Shanghai.

    (A) NO CHANGE   (C) to Shanghai.

    (B) into Shanghai.   (D) through Shanghai.

Explanation:

The correct choice is (C), because it indicates the direction (a spatial relationship) in which the ship is going.

▶ Longer prepositional phrases that introduce a sentence must be followed by a comma. The following sentence includes three prepositional phrases, but only the introductory phrase needs a comma to avoid confusion.

    After conquering the English Channel, the ocean swim team made plans **for a relay swim** that involved swimming **across the Santa Barbara Channel**.

▶ Some authors choose not to punctuate **introductory** prepositional phrases when they are short, as in the following sentence.

    In a day an orca may swim 100 miles or more.

► In most cases, do not use punctuation between a verb and any prepositional phrase that modifies it.

Incorrect: Many historians estimate that over 20,000 Puritans emigrated ***to the United States, between 1630 and 1640.***

Correct: Many historians estimate that over 20,000 Puritans emigrated ***to the United States between 1630 and 1640.***

The propositional phrase "between 1630 and 1640" modifies "emigrated" by describing when the emigration occured. Thus, no comma should separate the verb from the phrase.

► Do not use use any punctuation between a preposition and its object (the noun that completes the phrase):

Incorrect: The forest was ablaze, and the air was thick ***with: hot smoke and ash***.

Correct: The forest was ablaze, and the air was thick ***with hot smoke and ash***

The nouns "smoke" and "ash" are the objects of the preposition "with," so no punctuation should separate these nouns from the preposition.

016 Question Topic

DESCRIPTION

An **appositive** is a noun or noun phrase that identifies or describes another noun that appears immediately before or after it. Appositive phrases need to be separated from the rest of a sentence with commas, parentheses, or em dashes. Additionally, as explained in this topic, appositives differ in subtle but important ways from titles.

Example

A documentary  filmmaker Madison Pace decided to try making a fictional film.

(A) NO CHANGE

(B) filmmaker,

(C) filmmaker:

(D) filmmaker such as

Explanation:

The phrase "a documentary filmmaker" describes Madison Pace, and it begins with the article "a." Thus, it is an appositive phrase. It must be separated from the rest of the sentence with a comma, so the correct choice is (B).

Punctuating Appositives

▶ Each of the examples below uses appropriate punctuation to separate the appositive phrase from the rest of the sentence.

> I would like you to meet my friend, ***the finest musician around***.
> The teacher (***the only person not sleeping by the end of the lecture***) looked up in surprise.
> He held out a flower—***a sweet pea***—as she walked toward him.

Titles vs. Appositives

▶ You must be able to differentiate between a **title** and an **appositive**. If a title appears before the noun it labels with no articles ("a," "an," and "the"), the title should not be separated from the noun by any punctuation.

> **Title:** The music of ***iconic jazz musician*** Louis Armstrong remains popular even today.

> **Appositive:** The music of Louis Armstrong, ***an iconic jazz musician***, remains popular even today.

> *In the first example, "iconic jazz musician" acts as Louis Armstrong's title. Thus, it is not separated from the rest of the sentence by any punctuation. In the second example, the same informationis an appositive that comes after the noun it describes, so the information must be set apart from the rest of the sentence with commas.*

▶ Remember, the difference between a title and an appositive is as small as an article ("a," "an," and "the").

> **Title:** ***Famous explorer*** Marco Polo introduced aspects of Mongolian and Chinese culture to Europe.

> **Appositive:** ***A famous explorer,*** Marco Polo introduced aspects of Mongolian and Chinese culture to Europe.

017 Question Topic

→ PARTICIPIAL PHRASES

DESCRIPTION

Participial phrases begin with participles, which look like verbs but act as modifiers. Participial phrases can compress information and help create concise sentences. They usually serve to describe the subject of the sentence, but in some cases they describe other nouns.

Example

1 While believing it could win someday, the team continued to enter tournaments.

(A) NO CHANGE

(C) While believing in winning

(B) Believed to win

(D) Believing it could win

 Explanation:

The correct choice is (D) because "Believing it could win someday" describes "the team," the subject of the sentence.

Forming Participial Phrases

▶ **Present participles** end in "-ing." They indicate that a condition or action relates to the subject.

> ***Sweeping down the canyon of skyscrapers**, **the wind*** turned my umbrella inside-out.
> *The participle "sweeping" describes an action taken by the wind, which is the subject.*

▶ **Past participles** often end in "-ed" or "-en." They indicate that the subject is the recipient of a condition or action.

> **Isaiah** finally arrived home, ***soaked to the bone***.
> *The participle "soaked" describes the subject, "Isaiah," who has been soaked by something, most likely rain.*

Punctuating Participial Phrases

▶ In most cases, participial phrases should be separated from the rest of a sentence by commas, especially when they serve as an introductory phrase:

> ***Determined to tackle the problem first thing in the morning***, the detectives went home.

▶ If a comma causes confusion about which noun the phrase is modifying, eliminate the comma:

> **Confusing**: The waves slid gently toward the children, ***wriggling their feet in the sand***.

> **Clear**: The waves slid gently toward the children ***wriggling their feet in the sand***.

> *A comma before the participial phrase "wriggling their feet" creates confusion because the phrase seems to apply to the waves. The author clearly wants to indicate that the children are wriggling their feet, not the waves, which is more clearly implied by removing the comma.*

018 Question Topic

→ **DANGLING MODIFIERS**

DESCRIPTION

Whether it be a single word or an entire phrase, a modifier provides description. *Where* a modifier is placed in a sentence determines *what* it modifies. A "dangling modifier" comes at the beginning of a sentence but ends up with nothing to modify; the intended subject of the sentence is missing.

Example

With no warning, **1** the couch became a launching pad to the bookcase.

(A) NO CHANGE

(B) the couch was used as a launching pad

(C) the kitten launched from the couch

(D) the couch launched the kitten

 Explanation:

The phrase "With no warning" is left dangling. It cannot refer to the couch, as couches cannot give warnings. The correct choice is (C), which correctly makes the kitten the sentence's subject.

▶ When a description comes at the beginning of a sentence, make sure the thing being described is the subject of that sentence.

Incorrect: Daringly, experiments near the edge of the volcano began.

> *Experiments cannot be daring. The sentence must explain who daringly began the experiments.*

Correct: Daringly, ***graduate students*** began experiments near the edge of the volcano.

Incorrect: Turning the corner, the imposing bank building came into view.

> *Bank buildings cannot turn corners. The subject must explain who was "Turning the corner."*

Correct: Turning the corner, ***the bank robber*** saw the imposing bank building.

PHRASES

Read the passage and answer the corresponding questions.

PASSAGE

The Romance of the Three Kingdoms

The classic Chinese historical novel, *The Romance of the Three Kingdoms*, includes the tale of a particularly wily character who outsmarts powerful men. In the tale, **1 Zhou Yu, a military general, is searching** for a pretext to get rid of his rival, the clever Zhuge Liang. So, he asks Zhuge Liang to pledge to produce 100,000 arrows within 10 days or give his life. To General Zhou Yu's **2 surprise Zhuge Liang** replies, "Oh, I only need three days for that."

To ensure Zhuge Liang's failure, Zhou Yu orders that no one should provide Zhuge Liang with any arrow-making supplies. **3 Appeared unconcerned, Zhuge Liang** arranges to have 20 boats on the nearby river covered in bunches of straw, but he does nothing else. On the third night, fog sets in. Zhuge Liang and some soldiers row the straw-covered boats upstream to the camps of the **4 enemy—the** forces of Cao Cao. Just before daylight, Zhuge Liang orders the soldiers to begin pounding war drums and shouting. The enemy mistakenly thinks it is a surprise attack, and enemy archers shoot across the dark, misty river. Their arrows **5 stick, in the straw.** Zhuge Liang then directs the boats to turn around, and arrows stick in the other sides. Speeding away as daylight breaks, **6 arrows bristle** by the thousands. The men aboard chant, "Thanks for the arrows, Cao Cao!" In this way, Zhuge Liang sidesteps the internal plot against him and also depletes the enemy's resources.

1

(A) NO CHANGE
(B) Zhou Yu, a military general is searching

2

(A) NO CHANGE
(B) surprise, Zhuge Liang

3

(A) NO CHANGE
(B) Appearing unconcerned, Zhuge Liang

4

(A) NO CHANGE
(B) enemy the

5

(A) NO CHANGE
(B) stick in the straw

6

(A) NO CHANGE
(B) the boats bristle with arrows

Section C: Verb Tense

While you may have little need to know the specific terms for verb tenses and aspects (past, present, future, perfect, progressive, conditional, and so on), you should have a clear idea of when and how to use them. On the Writing and Language Test, expect several questions about verb tense and aspect. Common sense will guide you in answering many such questions, but let us review a few general rules for tricky situations.

019 Question Topic

CONSISTENT TENSES

DESCRIPTION

Writing with **consistent tenses** means making sure that the verbs clearly indicate *when* something occurs or takes place. Often, sentences must use the same tense throughout in order to make sense.

Past: Yesterday I *sat* on the beach and *watched* people surf.
Present Progressive: Right now I *am sitting* on the beach and *watching* people surf.
Future: Tomorrow I *will sit* on the beach and *watch* people surf.

> *In sentences with compound verbs (as in the examples above), auxiliary verbs such as "am" and "will" do not need to be repeated.*

Example

Ryan and Kayla sat next to each other in almost every class. He was left-handed and she was right-handed, a difference which, no doubt, **1** has resulted in many bumped elbows.

(A) NO CHANGE

(C) has been resulting

(B) resulted

(D) would result

 Explanation:

The correct choice is (B) because "resulted" is consistent with "was." Both are in the simple past tense, which makes sense in this sentence.

Processes and Routines

▶ Processes (often scientific facts), routines, and universal truths are generally written using the simple present tense.

> **Process**: Humpback whales *migrate* up to 25,000 kilometers each year to breed and find food.
>
> **Process**: The Earth *completes* one orbit around the Sun every 365 days.
>
> **Routine**: On most days, Jacob *wakes* up at 8:00 am and *eats* cereal for breakfast.
>
> **Universal Truth**: The only constant in life *is* change.

Literary Present

▶ Descriptions of art and summaries of plot in literature are usually expressed using the simple present tense. Analysis of art and literature and what an author is expressing are described using the simple present tense, as well.

> In the play, Aristophanes essentially ***voices*** his opposition to the war between Athens and Sparta.

▶ When writing about an author who is writing history, the literary present is only used when discussing the author:

> The author ***claims*** that the ancient Greeks ***loved*** comedy.
>
> *The author's claims are in the literary present, but saying that ancient Greeks "love" comedy is paradoxical.*

Interrupted actions

▶ One case in which verbs do not appear to be consistent is when an ongoing activity is interrupted.

> I **was sitting** on the beach and **watching** the waves when I ***heard*** a shout.
>
> *The past-progressive tense ("was sitting" and "watching") is interrupted by an event ("heard").*

QUICK PRACTICE **VERB TENSE**

Read the passage and answer the corresponding questions.

PASSAGE

SERVICE ANIMALS

When I was in high school, I decided to become a trainer for service animals. My high school counselor called it a meaningful career because service animals, mainly dogs, **1** **helped** people with disabilities live more independently. I decided to major in Animal Behavior in college.

For a class assignment, I visited a dog-training center. The trainers patiently **2** **coax** the dogs to use their noses and mouths to undertake many tasks. For example, a trainer pointed to a Post-it on a door. She put her finger on it and prompted the curious dog to investigate the Post-it with its nose, at which point she gave the dog a treat. Gradually, the dog learned to touch the Post-it with its nose in order to get a treat, and then the trainer opened the door a bit. The dog began to get treats if it touched the Post-it with a little push of the nose. The trainer said that eventually the dog **3** **would** learn to push the door shut without a Post-it.

During my career, I will be excited if service-animal organizations **4** **will put** more resources into training capuchin monkeys as service animals. I have read that the little primates **5** **are** very helpful to people who are housebound because of weakness or paralysis. Monkeys are intelligent and have opposable thumbs, so they can do many tasks around the house based on verbal prompts and laser pointers. For example, they can unscrew lids or caps, turn pages of magazines, and operate televisions and DVD players. They may be able to check that their owners' limbs **6** **are supported**. As with dogs, capuchin monkeys also provide good company and affection.

1
(A) NO CHANGE
(B) help

2
(A) NO CHANGE
(B) coaxed

3
(A) NO CHANGE
(B) will

4
(A) NO CHANGE
(B) put

5
(A) NO CHANGE
(B) were

6
(A) NO CHANGE
(B) would be supported

Section D: Mood and Voice

Language must be flexible enough to express many varieties of meaning. When evaluating text, check to make sure that the text's mood and voice fit the writer's purpose.

020 Question Topic

→ **MOOD**

DESCRIPTION

Every sentence possesses a quality called **mood**, which refers to a writer's intentions. In addition to conveying intent, a sentence's mood affects its word order and verb form.

Example

Joelle said that if she **1** is president for a day, she would give more government funding to NASA.

(A) NO CHANGE   (C) was being

(B) was   (D) were

 Explanation:

The correct choice is (D) because it correctly conjugates the verb "to be" to show that the sentence's mood is subjunctive (the sentence describes a condition not likely to come true).

INDICATIVE MOOD	IMPERATIVE MOOD	SUBJUNCTIVE MOOD
Provides facts or opinions	Gives a command	Expresses doubts, wishes, demands
Asks questions	Makes a request	Refers to the non-factual
Ex: I think I see an owl.	*Ex: Look at that owl!*	*Ex: I wish that the owl were visible.*

In English, subjunctive patterns are only discernible in a few specific situations.

▶ In statements with "if," first- and third-person singular nouns use the subjunctive form of "to be" (were) when the statement is doubtful or not factual:

     If that chihuahua *were* a big dog, she would be scary.

▶ Phrases about requirements or preferences ending in "that" are in the subjunctive. The verb that follows must be in the "base form," which means it is the simplest form, with no special ending. For example, the base form of the verb "to speak" is "speak."

- The subjunctive difference is only noticeable when the subject is in the third-person singular because there is no "-s" or "-es" verb ending:

    [It is important, etc. that + [*third-person singular noun*] + [**base form of verb**].
        Everyone **stays** together. → It is preferable that *everyone* **stay** together.
        Her son **goes** to a tutoring center. → Antonia insisted that *her son* **go** to a tutoring center.

021 Question Topic

→ **VOICE**

DESCRIPTION

Every sentence has **voice**, either active or passive. A sentence's voice primarily communicates the relationship between the subject, verb, and object (if any) of the sentence. Writers indicate voice by word order

Example

1 The college has been attended by thousands of students.

(A) NO CHANGE

(B) Thousands of students have attended the college.

(C) Thousands of students were being attended to by the college.

(D) The college always has thousands of students in attendance.

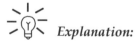 *Explanation:*

As written, the statement is in the passive voice, which is usually not as desirable as the active voice. Of the choices, only (B) conveys the same information, so it is the best change.

▶ In English, the subject of a sentence usually comes before the action. That way, the listener or reader knows who performed the action. This structure is called the **active voice**.

Emily baked cookies.
This sentence is active because the subject (Emily) is the one performing the action (baking).

▶ The **passive voice** either places the subject after the action or leaves the subject out. Often, using the passive voice makes a sentence unclear, unnecessarily wordy, or both. The following examples demonstrates how to improve some common passive voice sentence structures by making the sentences active:

> **Passive**: The cookies **were eaten** by Emily's brothers.
>
> *Often, when a sentence claims that something was done by someone, the sentence can be easily restructured into the more concise active voice.*
>
> **Active**: Emily's brothers **ate** the cookies.

> **Passive**: The asteroid **was drawn** closer by the star's strong gravitational pull.
>
> **Active**: The star's strong gravitational pull **drew** the asteroid closer.

▶ There are cases in which the passive voice is appropriate and sometimes even preferable to the active voice, some of which include:

- When the subject is inanimate.

  > The massive shipwreck *was discovered* in 1963.
  >
  > *The shipwreck itself, not the person who discovered it, is the focus of the sentence. The use of the passive voice draws attention to the shipwreck, making it appropriate for this sentence.*

- When the subject is unknown.

  > Stonehenge *was constructed* approximately 5,000 years ago.
  >
  > *Because archaeologists are not sure who created Stonehenge, the passive voice is appropriate here.*

- When you want to emphasize the recipient of an action.

  > Modern calculus *was developed* in part by Isaac Newton nearly 400 years ago. Since then, it has provided the basis for countless scientific and mathematical discoveries.
  >
  > *The two sentences focus on the impact of calculus. Thus, it is appropriate to make calculus the focus of the first sentence by placing it before Isaac Newton, who would be the subject of the sentence if it were in the active voice.*

- When you want to emphasize the subject.

  > Some problems *cannot be solved* by computers
  >
  > *The sentence emphasizes the subject of the sentence, computers, by withholding it until the end of the sentence*

MOOD AND VOICE

Read the passage and answer the corresponding questions.

PASSAGE

Power from the Wind: Kinetic Energy

It is possible to understand how wind provides **electricity, first focus** on kinetic energy. Anything that is in motion possesses kinetic energy. Planets moving through space have kinetic energy, as do the tiniest particles. The bigger and heavier a thing is, the more kinetic energy **2 it has and the more it can transfer**. A bowling ball falling into a swimming pool will create a bigger splash than a ping-pong ball because the bowling ball has more kinetic energy to transfer to the water.

Windmills have captured kinetic energy for centuries. Wind consists of moving air molecules that transfer kinetic energy to other air molecules. In order for modern windmills to create electricity, it is crucial that the air **3 contains** enough kinetic energy to push against a windmill's blades. The blades then rotate, causing the center shaft to rotate; that sets in motion rotating parts that **4 are used to turn** a magnet within a pocket of copper coils.

The magnet's turning electromagnetic poles push or pull on electrons in the atoms of the nearby copper coils. Electrons are forced from their atoms, but they **5 would be instantly attracted by** new atoms. The receiving atoms then have an excess of electrons, and they lose other electrons, which then attach to other copper atoms, and so on. The chain-reaction moving along the copper wire **6 is called** an electric charge.

1

(A) NO CHANGE
(B) electricity, if one first focuses

2

(A) NO CHANGE
(B) will be contained and transferred by it

3

(A) NO CHANGE
(B) contain

4

(A) NO CHANGE
(B) turn

5

(A) NO CHANGE
(B) instantly attract

6

(A) NO CHANGE
(B) calls

Section E: Comparing and Listing

In English, there are multiple ways to make **comparisons.** This section will review some comparative structures and common comparison errors. Additionally, we will focus on **parallel structure.** We will practice ensuring that two or more terms, phrases, or clauses use a parallel word pattern to avoid confusion.

022 Question Topic

→ **DEGREES OF COMPARISON**

DESCRIPTION

Degrees of comparison can take one of two forms: the **comparative degree** or the **superlative degree.**

Example

In wind chimes, the longest hollow tubes produce **1** lower, fuller tones.

(A) NO CHANGE

(B) lowest, most full

(C) more lower, fuller

(D) the lowest, fullest

 *Explanation:*

As written, the sentence leaves the reader wondering "lower and fuller than what?" The "longest" tubes produce the "lowest, fullest" sounds of all. (D) is the answer because it correctly maintains the superlative degree.

Degrees of Comparison

The Comparative Degree

When ONE noun or noun phrase is being compared to ONE other noun or noun phrase, use the comparative degree.

The bassoon is **harder** to learn than the clarinet.

Hip-hop is often **more exciting** than country music.

The Superlative Degree

When ONE noun or noun phrase is being compared to TWO OR MORE other nouns or noun phrases, use the superlative degree.

The **largest** brass instrument is the tuba.

The **most lucrative** music genre is rock.

023 Question Topic

→ **LOGICAL COMPARISONS**

DESCRIPTION

The word "than" indicates that two nouns or noun phrases are being compared. It is logical to compare a person to a person, an object to an object, a concept to a concept, and so on. Yet even a single misplaced word can create an **illogical** comparison. The mistake commonly occurs when there is a possessive form on one side of the comparison.

Example

Robotic bees' tolerance of pesticides is higher than 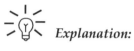 organic bees, but robotic bees do not make honey.

(A) NO CHANGE

(C) that of organic bees

(B) organics' tolerance

(D) those of organic bees

Explanation:

Choice (C) is correct because it compares levels of tolerance. As written, the sentence illogically compares tolerance (a concept) to organic bees (living creatures).

Illogical: The *population* of New York City is larger than Alaska, Idaho, Montana, North and South Dakota, Wyoming, and Nebraska combined.

> *The sentence above is attempting to compare the* population *of a city to the* combined population *of several states, but instead it illogically compares a population to several states.*

Logical: The *population* of New York City is larger than the **combined population** of Alaska, Idaho, Montana, North and South Dakota, Wyoming, and Nebraska.

▶ Many of the trickiest comparisons (and the ones that are most commonly tested on the SAT) use the pronouns "that" or "those" to replace the second use of the term being compared. "That" replaces singular nouns, and "those" replaces plural nouns:

Illogical: The company's *hiring process* for accountants is significantly less rigorous than *those* for managers.

> *Because "hiring process" is singular, it must be replaced by "that" in the second half of the comparison.*

Logical: The company's *hiring process* for accountants is significantly less rigorous than *that* for managers.

024 Question Topic

→ PARALLEL STRUCTURE

DESCRIPTION

Two or more terms, phrases, or clauses have **parallel structure** if they use a consistent word pattern to show that two or more ideas are equally important. Parallel structures are often combined using a coordinating conjunction, such as "and" or "but."

A shopping list that says, "milk, eggs, and avacodos" is clearer and more concise than one that says, "milk, eggs, and check for ripe avocados." Similarly, in any writing, lists are clearer if items are grammatically consistent.

Example

Corey bought headphones, a microphone, and **1** he bought a guitar. He was ready to become a musician.

(A) NO CHANGE

(C) a guitar.

(B) additionally a guitar.

(D) that guitar.

Explanation:

The correct choice is (C) because "a guitar" is parallel in structure to the previously listed items, "headphones" and "a microphone."

► When nouns and participial phrases are joined in lists, the result can be awkward:

   Incorrect: Becoming a professional musician requires **dedication** and **being naturally talented**.
   Correct: Becoming a professional musician requires *dedication* and *natural talent*.

► Similarly, one should avoid listing nouns and verbs together:

   Incorrect: Jamie learned to play **keyboards, drums**, and sometimes **practiced guitar**.
   Correct: Jamie learned to play *keyboards, drums,* and *guitar.*
   Correct: Jamie learned to play *keyboards* and *drums,* and sometimes *he practiced guitar.*

► Another common error is to list gerunds together with infinitives:

   Incorrect: As a professional musician, Jamie likes **practicing, performing**, and **to travel**.
   Correct: As a professional musician, Jamie likes *practicing, performing*, and *traveling*.
   Correct: As a professional musician, Jamie likes **to** *practice, perform*, and *travel*.

COMPARING AND LISTING

Read the passage and answer the corresponding questions.

PASSAGE

Music on the Mind

The final few minutes of Igor Stravinsky's *The Firebird* are one huge crescendo, which comes to a climax with a resounding "boom" from the timpani. That moment, more than **1** **any moment in** any other song, gives me chills. Indeed, most people know of at least one song that sends shivers down their spines. And these shivers are only the tip of the iceberg.

Medical researchers say that music provokes a host of physiological reactions. Culturally familiar music has more of an impact than **2** **people thinking that something** sounds strange. Individual subjects in studies have similar reactions to favorite musical pieces: increased heart rates, dilated pupils, and **3** **high levels** of dopamine. Dopamine is a substance in the brain associated with feelings of pleasure. One study even found that **4** **the most** dopamine is released shortly *before* the chill-inducing moment than during. It appears that humans take pleasure in both anticipating and experiencing certain points in music.

Although researchers know how music affects the body, they still do not know why it does so. As is so often the case in neurological research, different theories exist. When it comes to the physical and neurological responses to music that are familiar to an individual—such as *The Firebird's* boom on me—there may be a complex interplay in the brain between expectations, **5** **adaptations**, and pleasure when expected outcomes occur. In human evolution, individuals who could detect certain patterns among sounds in the environment may have been more likely to sense what would happen next. When sound patterns affected their emotions, they might have been able to react more quickly (as in the ability to run away from a predator). If humans enjoyed listening to crickets, owls, wind, waves, and so on, they would be more likely to do it. In short, the enjoyment of music might be a lucky side-effect of natural selection.

Although other theories exist, they have proven **6** **more** harder to support because they rely on factors that are difficult to test and quantify, such as individuals' personalities or social dynamics.

1
(A) NO CHANGE
(B) Delete the underlined portion

2
(A) NO CHANGE
(B) music that

3
(A) NO CHANGE
(B) increased levels

4
(A) NO CHANGE
(B) more

5
(A) NO CHANGE
(B) adapting

6
(A) NO CHANGE
(B) Delete the underlined portion

Section F: In-Sentence Punctuation

Understanding sentence structures requires some familiarity with the types of punctuation used to connect or separate ideas in a sentence. In this section, we will look at some of the fundamental rules for comma, semicolon, colon, em-dash, and parentheses usage.

025 Question Topic

→ **COMMAS**

DESCRIPTION

Most types of punctuation serve one or maybe two functions. Take the period, for example: it indicates that a sentence has ended or that a word has been abbreviated. The comma, however, is the overachiever of the punctuation world. Depending on how and where it is used in a sentence, a comma will serve one of many functions.

Example

Meilani wanted to become a molecular biologist. **1** Still, she loved philosophy.

(A) NO CHANGE   (C) Still she,

(B) Still she   (D) She, still,

 Explanation:

The underlined section is correct as written, because transition words such as "still" are usually separated from the rest of the sentence with a comma to represent a natural pause. The correct choice is (A). In this sentence, "still" is being used to mean "nevertheless."

1. SEPARATING DEPENDENT AND INDEPENDENT CLAUSES

▶ A comma separates a dependent clause from an independent clause *if the dependent clause comes first.*

> While waiting for the bus, I found a dollar on the ground.
>   *(dependent clause)*   *(independent clause)*

▶ Generally, no comma separates a dependent clause from an independent clause *if the independent clause comes first.*

> I found a dollar on the ground while waiting for the bus.
>   *(independent clause)*   *(dependent clause)*

▶ Use a comma followed by a coordinating conjunction to separate two independent clauses.

> The bus pulled up to the bus stop ten minutes late, *so* I knew that I would be late for work.
>   *(independent clause)*   *(independent clause)*

2. SEPARATING ITEMS IN A SERIES

▶ When listing more than two of anything (nouns, verbs, phrases, etc.), separate each element using a comma.

> Every morning Daniel *wakes up, eats breakfast, drinks coffee, and brushes his teeth* before driving to work. At work, Daniel's responsibilities include *responding to emails, interacting with customers, and training new employees.*

3. SEPARATING LENGTHY INTRODUCTORY ELEMENTS FROM THE REST OF THE SENTENCE

▶ Long introductory phrases generally need to be separated from the rest of a sentence with commas. Short introductory phrases (usually of four words or less) do not necessarily need to be set off by commas, but when in doubt, it is often best to include a comma.

> *Lifting the flat gray rock,* Jordan discovered a world teeming with insect life.
>
> *On top of the antique bookshelf,* the cat stretched lazily.

4. SEPARATING TRANSITION WORDS FROM THE REST OF THE SENTENCE

▶ Transition words, such as **however, therefore,** and **moreover,** clarify the relationship between two or more sentences. Transition words must be separated from the rest of a sentence with a comma.

> The giant squid has fascinated and terrified people for centuries. *However,* researchers know very little about the elusive deep-sea denizen.
>
> The tumultuous sea rocked the ship violently for days. *Consequently,* most of the crew became seasick.

5. SEPARATING NONESSENTIAL INFORMATION FROM THE REST OF THE SENTENCE

▶ If a phrase or clause could be removed from a sentence without changing the sentence's meaning, the information should be bookended by commas. Commonly, nonessential elements appear as appositives and relative clauses.

> The book, *an old leather-bound tome,* sat neglected on the top shelf of the bookcase.
> Jessica, *who visited the library at least once a week,* decided to check out the old tome sitting high on the bookshelf.

6. SEPARATING QUOTES FROM THE REST OF A SENTENCE

▶ A comma should come immediately before a quotation. If the quote is a statement and if the sentence continues after the quote, put a comma at the end of the quote, before the quotation marks.

> Mark said to Kerry, *"Let me help you carry that,"* after seeing Kerry struggle to haul the box down the hallway.
>
> After much deliberation, Ashley set her pen to the page and wrote, *"Nothing causes student writers more trouble than the comma."*

026 Question Topic

→ **SEMICOLONS**

DESCRIPTION

A semicolon can connect two complete sentences. Generally, a semicolon is used instead of a period if the two sentences are closely related and the relationship between them requires no explanation.

Example

The surf forecast is calling for mostly sunny skies and a swell of two to three **1** feet. Light offshore winds early in the morning will turn into moderate west winds by the afternoon.

Which choice most effectively combines the two sentences at the underlined portion?

(A) feet, and thus light

(B) feet; light

(C) feet and; light

(D) feet; but, light

 Explanation:

Choice (B) is correct because a semicolon is sufficient; the relationship between the sentences is obvious and does not need explanation by "thus," "and," or "but."

▶ If the relationship between two independent clauses is not self-evident, it is usually preferable to combine the two ideas with a comma followed by a coordinating conjunction (for, and, nor, but, or, yet, so) to clarify the exact nature of the relationship:

Unclear: The surfer swam to the surface unharmed; the force of the wave had cracked his board.

Clear: The surfer swam to the surface unharmed, **but** the force of the wave had cracked his board.

Both of the sentences above are grammatically correct, but the second version of the sentence is preferable because, without the conjunction "but," the relationship between the surfer being unharmed and his board being cracked is unclear. With the inclusion of "but," it is clear that the relationship is one of contrast.

027 Question Topic

→ **COLONS**

DESCRIPTION

On the SAT Writing and Language Test, **colons** most commonly function to introduce explanations or examples. In other words, colons separate statements from elaborations.

Example

In the 2000 film *Castaway*, the protagonist survives four years of complete isolation by using a unique survival **1** strategy; talking to a volleyball.

(A) NO CHANGE

(B) strategy: talks

(C) strategy by which: he talks

(D) strategy: he talks

 Explanation:

The correct choice is (D) because a colon indicates that what follows will explain what the author means by "unique survival strategy."

▶ The main rule to remember is than an **independent clause** must precede a colon. However, elaborations after colons can consist of a single noun, a phrase or list, or an entire clause.

> **Single-Word Elaboration**: Fictional archaeologist Indiana Jones faces many dangers during his travels, but he only fears **one**: *snakes.*

> **Phrase/List Elaboration**: A good friend must possess **three qualities**: *compassion, generosity, and a sense of humor.*

> **Clause Elaboration**: In recent years, biologists have come to recognize the intelligence of many bird species. **Take crows, for example**: *scientists have only recently discovered that these remarkable birds can recognize human faces, solve complex puzzles, and maintain complex social groups.*

028 Question Topic

EM DASHES AND PARENTHESES

DESCRIPTION

Em dashes (—) and **parentheses** [( )] both separate nonessential information from the rest of a sentence. As we learned earlier in the section, commas can perform the same role, so the punctuation used to separate nonessential information is a matter of stylistic preference.

Example

Evelyn longed to be reunited with her **1** son who—by the way was a war veteran—and searched for him in homeless shelters.

(A) NO CHANGE

(B) son—a war veteran—and

(C) son the war veteran—and

(D) (war-veteran son) and

 Explanation:

Choice (B) correctly separates out the information about Evelyn's son being a war veteran. Although the information adds to the reader's understanding, it is nonessential because the sentence would make sense without it.

▶ Like pairs of commas, pairs of em dashes or parentheses set apart nonessential clauses (clauses that, when omitted, do not change the meaning of the sentence). For the sake of the SAT, the most important rule of em dash and parentheses usage is to be **consistent**: you cannot mix-and-match commas, em dashes, and parentheses when separating nonessential information from the rest of a sentence.

Incorrect: On weekends, the group took hot meals—*usually spicy stews,* to the migrant camp.

Correct: On weekends, the group took hot meals—*usually spicy stews*—to the migrant camp.

Incorrect: The stranger was clean-shaven and wore clean—*(if slightly shabby)*—clothes.

Correct: The stranger was clean-shaven and wore clean *(if slightly shabby)* clothes.

▶ A single em dashe can take the place of a colon, comma, or a pair of parentheses at the end of a sentence if the writer wishes to emphasize the information.

We now have powerful means for finding old friends—*social media.*

IN-SENTENCE PUNCTUATION

Read the passage and answer the corresponding questions.

PASSAGE

Jeju Island

South Korea's Jeju Island was formed by volcanic activity. Much like the **1 Hawaiian Islands, Jeju** contains evidence of its fiery beginning in rocky **2 features, that** are stunning. In the center of the island stands the tallest mountain in South Korea—Halla Mountain. It was once a volcanic **3 inferno; today,** the mountain's topmost peaks form a rim around a lake.

When molten rock was cascading out of the sea to form **4 Jeju Island in** some areas the lava on top of the flow **5 cooled—forming insulation—that** kept hot lava beneath at high temperatures. The sub-surface lava continued its downward path wherever there was an opening. **6 Subsequently, the** lava dispersed to lower elevations as though it were emptying out of giant garden hoses. It left behind a network of caves known as "lava tubes."

Another intriguing rock formation created by the volcanic activity is Seongsan Peak on the island's east edge. From a bird's-eye view, the peak looks like an elevator button that has been **7 pushed in. Perfectly** round, with a bowl-like center.

1

(A) NO CHANGE
(B) Hawaiian Islands Jeju

2

(A) NO CHANGE
(B) features that

3

(A) NO CHANGE
(B) inferno, today,

4

(A) NO CHANGE
(B) Jeju Island, in

5

(A) NO CHANGE
(B) cooled, forming insulation that

6

(A) NO CHANGE
(B) Subsequently the

7

(A) NO CHANGE
(B) pushed in: perfectly

Correcting Grammar Mistakes

PARTS OF SPEECH

Each word used in a sentence fills a particular role. Understanding what some of these roles are will help you as you review common errors in grammar.

Subject	Verb	Object
Expresses the "who" or the "what" that is either doing something or is being described.	Expresses action or describes the subject's state of being.	Receives the action of the verb.

The empty vessel makes the loudest sound. – William Shakespeare

Subject (The empty vessel) + *verb* (makes) + *object* (the loudest sound).

NOUN: a person, place, thing, or idea

My _mind_ is not a _bed_ to be made and re-made. —James Agate

VERB: an action or state of being. Helper (auxiliary) verbs include *be, do, have, can, must, may, might, should, could,* and *will.*

You _can't hold_ a man down without staying down with him. —Booker T. Washington

ADJECTIVE: describes a noun or noun phrase

A _good_ book is the _purest_ essence of the _human_ soul. —Thomas Carlyle

ADVERB: describes a verb or an adjective

A _good_ book is the _purest_ essence of the _human_ soul. —Thomas Carlyle

PRONOUN: takes the place of a noun (a person, place, or thing); pronouns include *I, you, he, she, it, we, they, me,* and *mine.*

Very few of _us_ are what _we_ seem. – Agatha Christie

PREPOSITION: shows the relation of a noun or pronoun to something; prepositions include *in, to, at, for, by, with, under, behind, above, around, over, from,* and *through.*

Let me listen _to_ me and not _to_ them. – Gertrude Stein

CONJUNCTION: joins words or groups of words together; conjunctions include *and, but, or, because, although, if,* and *unless.*

We may encounter many defeats, _but_ we must not be defeated. – Maya Angelou

Section G: Subject-Verb Agreement

Even experienced writers sometimes lose sight of the subject of a sentence and use the wrong verb form. This section reviews irregular verb forms and focuses on a few of the tricky instances of subject-verb agreement.

029 Question Topic

→ **PRESENT-TENSE VERBS**

DESCRIPTION

Verbs **conjugate**, or change form, based on the person and number of the noun(s) to which they refer. If the action is in the simple present tense (if it describes a habit, routine, or condition) then the third-person form of regular verbs adds an "-s" or "-es" to the base verb ("give" becomes "gives," "do" becomes "does," etc.). But some verbs are **irregular**—they do not conjugate according to the normal pattern.

Irregular Verb Forms

	Singular	Plural
1st **Person**	I have; *I am.*	we have; we are.
2nd **Person**	you have; you are.	you all have; you all are.
3rd **Person**	*it has; it is.*	they have; they are.

Example

Under normal conditions the flight to the United States **1** take two hours, but it has been delayed today.

(A) NO CHANGE   (C) is taking

(B) takes   (D) took

Explanation:

Choice (B) is correct because it provides a verb that corresponds with the third-person singular subject "flight." The verb should be in the present tense because it is describing a routine action.

▶ Sentences that begin with "There is" or "There are" must match the subject of the sentence in number:

> **Incorrect: There is tables** loaded down with tasty dishes over there; please help yourself.
>
> **Correct:** *There are tables* loaded down with tasty dishes over there; please help yourself.

▶ Abstract nouns (such as "humor" or "condition") and uncountable nouns (such as "air") are usually singular.

> **Incorrect: The state** of the students' academic and athletic achievements at the schools in the cities within the region **are** improving, but rural districts are lagging.
>
> **Correct:** *The state* of the students' academic and athletic achievements at the schools in the cities within the region *is* improving, but rural districts are lagging.

→ VERBS SPLIT FROM SUBJECTS

DESCRIPTION

Sometimes writers pack in a great deal of information between the subject of a sentence and the actual verb. In order to evaluate the correct form of the verb, mentally eliminate "extras" and pare the sentence down to the minimum information that still forms a complete thought.

Example

The mountain, which thrusts its spiky peaks into the sky like frozen flames, often **1** <u>awe</u> travelers into complete silence.

(A) NO CHANGE

(C) are awing

(B) have awed

(D) awes

Explanation:

Eliminating the long phrase beginning with "which," the adverb "often," and the prepositional phrase "into complete silence" simplifies the example to "The mountain awes travelers." Thus, the subject of the sentence is "The mountain," which takes the present-tense singular third-person verb "awes," making (D) correct.

▶ Plural nouns in the midst of a sentence do not necessarily take plural verb forms if they are not the subject:

> Every afternoon, my sister, toting textbooks, snacks, pillows, and ear phones, claims the couch in the living room.

> ~~Every afternoon,~~ my sister, ~~toting textbooks, snacks, pillows, and ear phones~~, claims the couch ~~in the living room~~.

> ***My sister*** *claims* the couch.

▶ Singular nouns in the midst of a sentence do not necessarily take plural forms of the verb, either:

> Most spies, given their job description, training, and knowledge of current technology, know a bit about tracking cell phones.

> Most spies~~, given their job description, training, and knowledge of current technology,~~ know a bit about tracking cell phones.

> ***Most spies*** *know* a bit about tracking cell phones.

031 Question Topic

GROUPS AND PARTS OF GROUPS

DESCRIPTION

Nouns that represent groups are known as "**collective nouns.**" They are words such as "team," "staff," and "load." Collective-noun subjects take a singular verb. This can be confusing when the collective noun is followed by a prepositional phrase beginning with "of."

Example

The sign on the door read: "Our staff of dedicated nurses and doctors **1** are here to serve the public."

(A) NO CHANGE   (C) be

(B) is   (D) being

Explanation:

The subject of the sentence is "The staff," a third-person singular noun that corresponds to "is." The words "nurses and doctors" describe "staff," but they are not the main subject of the sentence. Thus, choice (B) is correct.

▶ **Individual parts** of groups, described by phrases such as "a member of," "one piece of," and "a collection of," are singular nouns.

> **Incorrect:** **The collection** of first-edition books **sit** on the bookshelf.
>
> **Correct:** *The collection* of first-edition books *sits* on the bookshelf.

• The noun phrase "The number of _____" is singular whereas the phrase "a number of _____" is plural:

> *The number of wolves* in the national park *is* increasing steadily.
>
> *A number of park rangers are* investigating the cause of this recent wolf resurgence.
>
> *Notice that the subject "the number of wolves" takes a singular verb ("is"), whereas the subject "a number of park rangers" takes a plural verb ("are").*

▶ Nouns that begin with "each," "either," "neither," or "none" express one part of the pair or group. Thus, they require a singular verb.

> **Incorrect:** **Each** of the musicians **want** to lead the band; **each have** the necessary charisma.
>
> **Correct:** *Each* of the musicians *wants* to lead the band; *each has* the necessary charisma.
>
> **Incorrect:** **Neither** the groom nor the bride **envision** a formal wedding reception.
>
> **Correct:** *Neither* the groom nor the bride *envisions* a formal wedding reception.

032 Question Topic

→ **PARTICIPLES, GERUNDS, AND INFINITIVES**

DESCRIPTION

Sometimes "action words" do *not* serve as verbs in a sentence. **Participles**, **gerunds**, and **infinitives** allow us to talk *about* actions and their effects. Depending on the context in which they are used, participles, gerunds, and infinitives serve as nouns, adjectives, or adverbs. Therefore, they cannot serve as a sentence's main verb and do not change according to subject-verb agreement.

Example

One of my favorite movies, *Ben Hur*, **1** taking place in ancient Rome.

(A) NO CHANGE

(C) taken

(B) takes

(D) to take

 Explanation:

*Because a participle, gerund, or infinitive cannot serve as the main action of a sentence, choices (A), (C), and (D) are incorrect. Choice (B) is correct because it contains a present-tense verb that agrees with the singular subject of the sentence, "**One** of my favorite movies."*

▶ A participle acts as a modifier (an adjective or adverb), so it provides description. Present participles are formed by adding "-ing" to the end of a verb's base form (i.e., "running," "jumping," and "being"). Past participles are often formed by adding "-en" or "-ed" to a verb's simple past-tense form, which sometimes undergoes a minor spelling change as well (i.e., "forgotten," "spoken," and "written").

- Often, past participles are used to describe a person's feelings:
  Andrew was **bored** by the abstract, black-and-white film.

- Present participles usually describe the person, thing, or circumstance that provoked the feeling:
  The abstract, black-and-white film was **boring**.

▶ A gerund acts as a singular noun that describes an activity. Gerunds are formed by adding "-ing" to a verb base form, so distinguishing present participles from gerunds requires using the context of the sentence. Remeber that gerunds act as nouns:

  Jules and Lina loved **watching** abstract films.
  Andrew avoided **going** to films with them.

▶ An **infinitive verb**, or just an "infinitive," acts as a noun, adjective, or adverb. Infinitives are formed by adding the word "to" before a verb's base form. Thus, "to fly," "to dive," and "to be" are infinitive verbs.

  Infinitive as a noun: Diana tries **to walk** for at least an hour every day.
  Infinitive as a adjective: Andrea is looking for an exciting book **to read**.
  Infinitive as an adverb: Eric is going to the store **to return** a recent purchase.

033 Question Topic

→ **AUXILIARY VERBS**

DESCRIPTION

Frequently, writers and speakers of English express nuances about time (tense) through auxiliary, or helping, verbs. For example, consider the difference in the statements "I eat" and "I will be eating," or "You were brave" and "You could have been brave." Auxiliary verbs include forms of the words *be, do,* and *have*, as well as the modal verbs *can, could, must, might, would, will,* and *shall*.

Example

Arturo isn't here yet. He **1** had been walking slowly due to his knee injury.

(A) NO CHANGE

(C) is walking

(B) have walked

(D) walk

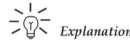 *Explanation:*

Logically, "is walking" explains what the singular subject "Arturo" is doing in the present, which matches the phrase "isn't here yet" in the present tense, so the correct choice is (C).

Auxiliary Verbs and Tense

▶ Although participles can take past or present forms, they cannot be used to determine a sentence's tense. If applicable, use the auxiliary verb instead.

- Casey *has* traveled to Burma four times.

  Because "has" is a present-tense form of the verb "have," the sentence is in the present perfect—a variation of the present tense. The present perfect shows that something happened in the past but has consequences that affect the present. The past participle "traveled" indicates that Casey's visits to Burma occurred in the past, but it does not determine the tense of the sentence.

- Arturo *was* walking when he *tripped* on a crack in the sidewalk.

  Although the sentence includes the present participle "walking," the verbs "was" and "tripped" indicate that the sentence takes place in the past.

Auxiliary Verbs and Subject-Verb Agreement

▶ The auxiliary verbs "be," "do," and "have" must agree in number with the subject.

> Most **students** *have* finished the test, but **Zoe** *has* not finished yet.
> While **you** *were* studying yesterday, **I** *was* too.
> **Noah and I** *have* wanted to go skiing for a long time; **he** *has* never been before.

SUBJECT-VERB AGREEMENT

Read the passage and answer the corresponding questions.

PASSAGE

Land of Sagas

Iceland is a land of superlatives. The small island sits at the top of the world, undergoes constant volcanic activity, and **1 commands** some of the most breathtaking vistas on Earth. It also happens to have more writers, per capita, than anywhere else on Earth; one in ten Icelanders **2 are published authors.**

Since the earliest Viking settlers set foot on the island over 1,000 years ago, Iceland has been a land of stories, or "sagas," as Icelanders call them. Then as well as now, a large repertoire of stories **3 help** communities get through long, harsh winters, such as those in Iceland, and dramatic landscapes are likely to inspire dramatic plots. The island reportedly inspired aspects of J.R.R. Tolkien's setting for the seminal *Lord of the Rings* trilogy. More recently, it has provided the backdrop for filmed fantasy epics such as television's *Game of Thrones* series.

Undoubtedly, Iceland's natural beauty and history of storytelling **4 contributes** to the nation's incredible literary output. However, a more practical factor may drive Iceland's publishing phenomenon. The Icelandic government, in a bid to support Icelandic culture both through the writing of literature and the translation of literature, **5 provides some funding** for writers. This state support is significant enough to keep some authors on salary. Ultimately, finding inspiration to write about your nation's natural beauty and rich culture **6 is** wonderful, but being paid by your government to give voice to your inspiration is both wonderful and practical.

1

(A) NO CHANGE
(B) command

2

(A) NO CHANGE
(B) is a published author

3

(A) NO CHANGE
(B) helps

4

(A) NO CHANGE
(B) contribute

5

(A) NO CHANGE
(B) provide some funding

6

(A) NO CHANGE
(B) are

Section H: Pronouns

Pronouns are tricky parts of speech. A **pronoun** replaces a noun, noun phrase, or another pronoun. Despite this simple description, English speakers commonly make mistakes with pronouns when they speak and write.

► While there are many types of pronoun, this section focuses primarily on **personal pronouns**, which are used to refer to first-person, second-person, and third-person noun and noun phrases.

► A pronoun's **case** shows how the word functions in a sentence. It can be in the subjective case, the objective case, or the possessive case.

- A pronoun will be in the **subjective case** when it functions as the **subject** of a sentence.
- A pronoun will be in the **objective case** when it functions as the **object** of a sentence.
- A pronoun will be in the **possessive case** when it is being used to show **ownership**.

The table below shows the different cases of personal pronouns.

Person	Subjective Case	Objective Case	Possessive Case
First-Person Singular	I	me	my/mine
First-Person Plural	we	us	our(s)
Second-Person Singular/Plural	you	you	your(s)
Third-Person Singular	he, she, it	him, her, it	his, her(s), its
Third-Person Plural	they	them	their(s)

► "Uncountable nouns" are nouns that are always singular quantities: "energy," "water," "money," etc. It would sound strange to say "We spent all of our monies." Uncountable nouns take the pronoun "**it**."

► "Countable nouns" are nouns that can appear as two or more: "people," "bananas," "dollars," etc. It would sound strange to say "How many dollar do you have?" Countable nouns can be singular or plural, as can any pronouns that refer to them.

- Some modifiers and pronouns that express inexact quantities apply to only "uncountable" or to "countable" nouns, not both.

Uncountable Modifiers/Pronouns (Singular)	Countable Modifiers/Pronouns (Plural)
(a) little	several
less	(a) few, fewer
much	many

The coffee **is** ready. Would you like *a little*? Is that too *much*? Would you prefer *less*?
The cookies **are** ready. Would you like *a few*? Is that too *many*? Would you prefer *fewer*?

→ **INDEFINITE PRONOUNS**

DESCRIPTION

Indefinite pronouns refer to an unspecified person, place, or thing. The indefinite pronouns in the box are always singular, and pronouns that replace them must be singular as well.

Common Indefinite Pronouns

Everyone	Anyone	Someone	No one
Everything	Anything	Something	Nothing
Everybody	Anybody	Somebody	Nobody

Example

Everybody is entitled to **1** his or her opinion.

(A) NO CHANGE   (C) one's

(B) their   (D) whose

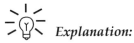 *Explanation:*

Because "everybody" is singular, it must be replaced by a singular pronoun. Choice (A) is correct because "his" and "her" are both singular. Although "one's" is singular, the pronoun "one" does not take a specific referent, making (C) incorrect.

▶ Since indefinite pronouns do not indicate gender, plural pronouns seem to fit with them naturally, as plural pronouns are gender-neutral in English. However, such a construction is still not acceptable in most published or academic writing, and when answering questions on the Writing and Language Test, you must be ready to correct such mistakes:

    Incorrect: **Someone** is knocking at the door; please find out what **they** want.

    Correct: *Someone* is knocking at the door; please find out what *he* or *she* wants.

    Incorrect: **No one** seems to think that the rules apply to **them**.

    Correct: *No one* seems to think that the rules apply to *him* or *her*.

▶ "Each" also indicates that a noun is singular, and must be replaced by a singular pronoun. Another possibility is to change the noun to a plural one.

    Incorrect: **Each child** got a permission form, which **they** promptly lost.

    Correct: *Each child* got a permission form, which *he* or *she* promptly lost.
    Correct: *All of the children* got permission forms, which *they* promptly lost.

035 Question Topic

PRONOUNS WITH COLLECTIVE NOUN REFERENTS

DESCRIPTION

Collective nouns describe groups, such as "the Lopez family" or "the volleyball team." Because collective nouns are often singular nouns that refer to multiple individuals, deciding whether they should correspond with singular or plural pronouns may appear difficult but can easily be mastered.

Example

The Federal Bureau of Investigation, better known as the FBI, receives **1** their funding from the U.S. government.

(A) NO CHANGE   (C) this

(B) its   (D) it's

Explanation:

The pronoun at the underlined portion refers to the singular subject of the sentence, "The Federal Bureau of Investigation," so choice (B), the singular personal pronoun "its," is correct.

▶ On the other hand, when you see a phrase that follows the pattern *(noun) of (noun)*—as in "each of the businessmen" or "all of the employees"—remember that the antecedent will always be the **first** word:

  The board of directors asked for a review of *its* financial records.

   The phrase "of directors" simply describes "The board," which is the true antecedent of "its."

  The herd of elephants traversed *its* territory.

▶ The proper name of a business or organization, even if it is a plural, takes a singular pronoun:

  Plants & Things donated one of *its* most beautiful orchids to the school auction.

  Friends of the Symphony held *its* annual dinner outdoors this year.

036 Question Topic

→ **PRONOUNS AS OBJECTS**

DESCRIPTION

Objective pronouns include the words "me," "you," "him," "her," "it," "us," and "them." The object of a sentence or clause receives the action.

Example

The project was an extraordinary learning experience for **1** my group and myself.

(A) NO CHANGE

(C) my group and me.

(B) my group and I.

(D) I and my group.

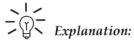 *Explanation:*

Choice (C) is correct because the speaker and the group are objects of the preposition "for," so the pronoun for the speaker must be "me." If we were to take out "my group and," it would be clear that the phrase should be "for me," not "for I."

Pronouns as Objects of Prepositions

▶ When a pronoun is the object of a preposition, make sure that it is in the **objective case,** even if it is separated by another noun. The most common mistake here is using "I" where one should use "me," or using "we" instead of "us."

Incorrect: She sent a letter *to* my sister and *I*.
Correct: She sent a letter *to* my sister and *me*.

Incorrect: *For we* beginning surfers, the waves were just right.
Correct: *For us* beginning surfers, the waves were just right.

Incorrect: After handing in his exam, Kessler leaned over to his classmate and whispered, "*Between you and I*, I think I just failed that test."

Correct: After handing in his exam, Kessler leaned over to his classmate and whispered, "*Between you and me*, I think I just failed that test."

037 Question Topic

AMBIGUOUS PRONOUNS

DESCRIPTION

Ambiguous pronoun errors occur when a writer uses a pronoun that can refer to more than one noun.

Example

Kaitlyn picked up her friend Brooke from class, and they went to **1** her house to load up the skis.

(A) NO CHANGE

(C) one's

(B) the

(D) Brooke's

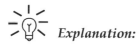 *Explanation:*

The correct choice is (D) because it clarifies whether "her house" is the home of Kaitlyn or of Brooke.

▶ Most ambiguous pronouns are fixed by repeating the target noun instead of using a pronoun.

- **Ambiguous:** The assignment was to read **the book**, write **an essay** about it, and give **it** to the teacher.

    As is, the sentence is unclear as to whether the assignment is to give "the book" or the "essay" to the teacher.

- **Revised:** The assignment was to read *the book*, write *an essay* about it, and give *the essay* to the teacher.

- **Ambiguous:** Curtis passed Anthony the basketball, and *he* sprinted down the court.

    As is, the sentence is unclear as to whether Curtis or Anthony "sprinted down the court."

- **Revised:** Curtis passed Anthony the basketball, and *Anthony* sprinted down the court.

038 Question Topic

→ **WHO AND WHOM**

DESCRIPTION

The pronoun "who" and its objective form "whom" can serve many purposes in a sentence, making the mastery of them tricky for many students.

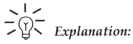

Example

The student asked his academic advisor, "To **1** who should I give my letter of recommendation?"

(A) NO CHANGE

(C) who is the person that I

(B) whom should I

(D) whom is the person that I

Explanation:

The correct choice is (B); the pronoun at the underlined portion is the object of the preposition "To," so the pronoun must be in the objective case, making "whom" correct. Choices (C) and (D) are incorrect because they are unnecessarily wordy.

▶ "Who" and "whom" can form questions, making them interrogatives.

> **Who** loves you? **Whom** do you love?

▶ They also introduce **relative clauses**, which give further information about a person or persons.

> My friend, **who** always gets As, has been helping me prepare for an upcoming midterm.

▶ They are also used to define or identify a person or persons. A common mistake is to use "that" to refer to a person or persons:

> **Incorrect**: The head coach is the person **that** is wearing sunglasses.
> **Correct**: The head coach is the person *who* is wearing sunglasses.

▶ Some experts claim that the pronoun "whom" is disappearing from the English language. In most published or academic writing, however, the word "whom" is still expected where appropriate. The pronoun "whom" acts as the object of an action or a preposition.

> **Incorrect**: **Who** did you call when you won the award?
> **Correct**: *Whom* did you call when you won the award?

> **Incorrect**: It is not clear yet **who** the director is going to hire.
> **Correct**: It is not clear yet *whom* the director is going to hire.

PRONOUNS

Read the passage and answer the corresponding questions.

PASSAGE

Business Management

In the business world, management styles are always changing. However, two of the most enduring management styles are "Management by Objectives" (MBO) and "Total Quality Management" (TQM).

MBO was first popularized by German-American professor and business consultant Peter Drucker. In **1** his 1954 book, *The Practice of Management*, Drucker describes MBO as the process of an organization's employees and managers agreeing on objectives so that **2** it is working toward the same goals. This style is symbolically represented by the now ubiquitous "statement of purpose" often posted on the websites of companies or other entities. A typical employee may experience MBO without realizing it when a manager gives **3** them written objectives and evaluations. Before MBO, these practices were uncommon in employee management.

TQM focuses on improving the quality of products and services through continuous modifications in response to employee and customer feedback. It is unclear to **4** whom the credit for TQM methods should go, but they were first used on a large scale in Japanese industry. The U.S. Navy may have begun to incorporate the methods during the 1960s in its air systems production. TQM first became popular in the manufacturing sector but spread to other areas, including retail sales, hotels, educational institutions, airlines, and even government. Nearly everyone participates in TQM at some point when **5** they answer a "customer feedback survey" or some other response form.

One characteristic that distinguishes TQM from MBO is flexibility: although companies using TQM have goals, **6** they are constantly changing based on feedback from consumers and employees.

1
(A) NO CHANGE
(B) their

2
(A) NO CHANGE
(B) they are

3
(A) NO CHANGE
(B) him or her

4
(A) NO CHANGE
(B) who

5
(A) NO CHANGE
(B) he or she answers

6
(A) NO CHANGE
(B) the goals

Section I: Commonly Confused Words

In the English language, it is not uncommon for words with very different meanings to sound similar or the same. When speaking, the differences rarely matter. But in writing, using the correct word is crucial for expressing thoughts accurately.

039 Question Topic

→ HOMOPHONES

DESCRIPTION

Some commonly confused words are **homophones**—words that sound the same but are spelled differently and have different meanings.

Example

No matter what **1** <u>your</u> doing, you will do it better if you are in a good mood.

(A) NO CHANGE   (C) you're

(B) yours is   (D) you were

Explanation:

The sentence as written confuses the possessive pronoun "your" with "you're," the contraction of "you are." Thus, choice (C) contains the correct contraction.

▶ The homophones "they're," "there," "their" also cause trouble for many students.

THEY'RE	THERE	THEIR
"**They're**" is the contracted form of "they are." In other words, they + are = **they're**. *They're* going to the barbecue at the park.	"**There**" can be a place, a demonstrative pronoun that answers "where?" The barbecue is over *there*, next to the swimming pool. OR, "**there**" can be a strange pronoun that does not actually replace a noun; it is sometimes called an "existential pronoun" because it declares that something exists. *There* is a large crowd gathering.	"**Their**" is a possessive adjective like "his" or "our." I believe that they are bringing *their* swimming suits.

► An apostrophe can make a big difference. The homophones "its" and "it's" have completely different meanings.

IT'S	ITS
"It's" is the contracted, or shortened, form of "it is" and "it has." In other words, it + is/has = **it's**. *It's* time to transplant the flower. *It's* been too long since I have gone fishing.	"Its" is a possessive pronoun like "his," "her," "ours," or "their." The flower is outgrowing *its* container.

040 Question Topic

→ **PHONETIC SIMILARITY**

DESCRIPTION

Commonly confused words are not always exact homophones; they may have **phonetic similarity**, meaning they sound similar even though they have different meanings or play different roles in communication.

Example

The doctor walked **1** through a snowstorm to get to the hospital and perform the emergency surgery.

(A) NO CHANGE

(B) threw

(C) thru

(D) though

 *Explanation:*

The correct choice is (A); "through" means passing into and out of, as the doctor did by walking into the storm and out of it at the hospital.

► "**Affects**" is a verb whereas "**effect**" is a noun.

   Rain often *affects* traffic.

   The *effect* of rain is usually more traffic jams.

► "**Than**" is used when forming comparisons. "**Then**" is used when forming conditional statements; "**then**" also means "at that time" or "in that case."

   There are more bananas *than* you can imagine in that truck.

   If you want a banana, *then* just follow that truck.

   Then you will have all the bananas that you want.

► Example sentences of other commonly confused words with phonetic similarity include:

   Incorrect: He likes every vegetable **accept** onions.
   Correct: He likes every vegetable *except* onions.

   Incorrect: We **past** the school on the way to the park.
   Correct: We *passed* the school on the way to the park.

Additional Commonly Confused Words

NOTE The following definitions/synonyms only summarize the most common uses for each word.

Commonly Confused Words	Part(s) of Speech	Definition/Synonyms
accept	verb	receive, gain; accept something as true, believe
except	preposition	not including, besides
adverse	adjective	harmful, unlucky, unfavorable
averse	adjective	having a strong feeling of opposition
bare	verb, adjective	(verb) uncover, expose; (adjective) simple, unclothed
bear	verb, noun	(verb) transport, support; tolerate; (noun) a type of large mammal
capital	noun	money; a city or town with political and economic importance
capitol	noun	a building that houses the legislative branch of a government
complement	verb, noun	(verb) improve something by adding a part or component; (noun) an addition that completes something
compliment	verb, noun	(verb) praise someone or something; (noun) an expression of mild praise
lose	verb	have something taken away, misplace
loose	adjective	unsecured, detached
passed	verb (past tense)	leave behind, progress, travel
past	adjective, noun, adverb	(adjective) no longer existing; (noun) the time before the present moment, former times; (adverb) pass from one side to another
principal	adjective, noun	(adjective) main, primary; (noun) a person of authority, director
principle	noun	a concept that serves as the foundation of a behavior or system
to	preposition	indicating a particular direction, identifying something that is affected
too	adverb	extremely, excessively; additionally, also
two	number	2
whose	determiner/pronoun	showing that something belongs to or is associated with a person
who's	contraction	a shortened form of "who is" or "who has"

COMMONLY CONFUSED WORDS

Read the passage and answer the corresponding questions.

PASSAGE

Apocalypse Soon

Doomsday prophecies have become almost commonplace. In the **1** **passed** two decades alone, Americans have harbored apocalyptic fears based on the new millennium and the Mayan calendar. Religious cult leaders are infamous for heralding the end of civilization, the end of mankind, the end of Earth, the end of the end itself!

Although most modern doomsday prophecies are built on shaky foundations, we must **2** **accept** that **3** **their** remains a chance that environmental factors will conspire to spell out the end of life as we know it. Scientists refer **4** **too** these ecological disasters as extinction events—periods in which a large portion of life on Earth suddenly dies. There have been at least five such events in the past 600 million years, and each one has had a huge **5** **affect** on Earth's biodiversity.

The most recent extinction event is called the Cretaceous-Paleogene (K-Pg) extinction event, but most people know it as "the one that killed the dinosaurs." The K-Pg extinction event occurred approximately 66 million years ago, when a large meteor collided with present-day Mexico. The meteor impact triggered ecological catastrophes that killed an estimated 75 percent of all life on Earth. In fact, most if not all extinction events were caused by **6** **adverse** environmental changes that contributed to or coincided with widespread ecological catastrophes such as volcanic eruptions or runaway greenhouse effects.

Today, human activities such as overhunting and the exploitation of natural resources contribute to the extinction of an estimated 30,000 species per year. Many researchers claim that we are in the midst of another extinction event, one for which the blame falls squarely on humanity's shoulders. As humans continue to look at supernatural prophecies or social paranoia for signs of the apocalypse, the majority of life on Earth must look no further **7** **then** humanity to see **8** **its** impending demise.

1
(A) NO CHANGE
(B) past

2
(A) NO CHANGE
(B) except

3
(A) NO CHANGE
(B) they're
(C) there

4
(A) NO CHANGE
(B) to
(C) two

5
(A) NO CHANGE
(B) effect

6
(A) NO CHANGE
(B) averse

7
(A) NO CHANGE
(B) than

8
(A) NO CHANGE
(B) it's

Section J: Additional Topics

English grammar is filled with tricky little rules that do not make much difference in casual conversation but make a difference in the coherence of written expression. This section illuminates two types of idiomatic word groups that must be memorized.

041 Question Topic

CORRELATIVE CONJUNCTIONS

DESCRIPTION

All conjunctions show how ideas are "con-joined," or how they relate to each other. Correlative conjunctions come in pairs. For example, "neither/nor" is a correlative conjunction: "neither" always pairs with "nor." The purpose of correlative conjunctions is to connect two equal units of grammar.

Example

Many adolescents do not get enough sleep, often due to either social media **1** nor homework.

(A) NO CHANGE

(B) with homework.

(C) or homework.

(D) and homework.

 Explanation:

The word "either" in the sentence is one part of a correlative conjunction: it must be paired with "or." Thus, (C) is the correct choice.

▶ The chart below lists of some of the most frequently used correlative conjunctions, along with examples that demonstrate proper use.

Correlative Conjunction	Example Sentence
either…or	The waiter said, "You may choose **either** soup **or** salad."
neither…nor	Jane was not hungry, so she ordered **neither** soup **nor** salad.
both…and	Alex, being very hungry, asked, "Can I have **both** soup **and** salad?"
between…and	The waiter responded, "You must choose **between** soup **and** salad."
not only…but also	Alex was **not only** hungry, **but** he was **also** very talkative.
as…as	Alex retorted, "But I want **as** much food **as** possible."
whether…or	Jane said to Alex, "I don't know **whether** you are hungry **or** rude."

042 Question Topic

→ **PHRASAL VERBS**

DESCRIPTION

A **phrasal verb** consists of either a **verb + preposition** or a **verb + adverb** combination. These phrases have meanings that differ from the meanings of the individual words from which they are formed. For example, the phrasal verb "ran into" does not convey the same meaning as the verb "ran."

Example

Because he was so tired, Jonas could not **1** focus toward the conversation with his manager.

(A) NO CHANGE

(C) focus to

(B) focus on

(D) focus with

 Explanation:

The preposition that pairs with "focus" is "on." Therefore, (B) is correct.

▶ On the Writing and Language Test, you may be asked to pair a preposition with a verb to form an appropriate phrasal verb based on the context of the sentence. Consequently, it is crucial to know the specific prepositions used in phrasal verbs as well as the phrasal verb's meaning.

> **Incorrect:** The psychology student was able to **point against** many flaws in Jung's dream theory.
>
> **Correct:** The psychology student was able to *point out* many flaws in Jung's dream theory.

> **Incorrect:** The make-up promised to **block against** UVB rays.
>
> **Correct:** The make-up promised to *block out* UVB rays.

▶ The chart below lists some frequently used phrasal verbs, along with their meanings and examples that demonstrate proper use.

Phrasal Verb	Meaning	Example Sentence
get by	manage, survive	Although they did not have much money, the young couple managed to **get by.**
focus on	pay attention to	The professor became angry when she realized her students were not **focused on** the lecture.
go through	undergo a difficult experience	Recently, the country has **gone through** much political turmoil.
	search	Jacob had to **go through** his entire dresser to find his favorite sweater.
add up	make sense	As the detective interviewed the suspect, he realized that her story did not **add up.**

Read the passage and answer the corresponding questions.

Sleep Paralysis

Sleep paralysis is a physical and psychological condition that occurs in some individuals during REM sleep. Under normal circumstances, the body is paralyzed during REM sleep to **1 prevent it from** mimicking the actions taken in a dream. However, when sleep paralysis occurs, a person's brain awakens during REM sleep. This leaves a person fully aware of his or her surroundings but unable to move.

Because sleep paralysis renders sufferers helpless and disoriented, it is often a very traumatic experience. Sleep paralysis can render a person **2 both immobile or** mute for up to several minutes at a time. Likewise, it can **3 result from** auditory, tactile, and visual hallucinations that manifest themselves in horrifying ways. Many cultures have unique names for this condition, most of which **4 center on** the disturbing nature of sleep paralysis. For instance, the Japanese call sleep paralysis *kanashibari*, which translates to "bound in metal." Likewise, the Kurdish people call sleep paralysis *mottaka*, which means "suffocating ghost." According to Mexican culture, sleep paralysis is caused by a deceased person's spirit preventing the sleeper's movement, referred to as *se me subio el muerto*, meaning "the dead person is on me."

5 Whether sleep paralysis is a result of neurological and environmental factors is still up for debate. Some psychiatrists believe that sleep paralysis is caused by the misfiring of neurons in the pons area of the brain. Other possible causes of sleep paralysis include irregular sleep schedules, increased levels of stress, and the use of artificial sleep aids. Ironically, some drugs used to induce sleep and relaxation are also used to treat sleep paralysis. The benzodiazepine Clonazepam has been used to treat sleep paralysis, as has the antidepressant drug fluoxetine, commonly referred to as Prozac. Ultimately, because **6 neither a definite cause or a reliable cure** has been discovered, sleep paralysis remains as perplexing as it is terrifying.

1

(A) NO CHANGE
(B) prevent it to

2

(A) NO CHANGE
(B) both immobile and

3

(A) NO CHANGE
(B) result in

4

(A) NO CHANGE
(B) center toward

5

(A) NO CHANGE
(B) Whether sleep paralysis is a result of neurological or

6

(A) NO CHANGE
(B) neither a definite cause nor a reliable cure

Improving Style and Structure

Section K: Development and Organization

The Writing and Language Test measures not only your knowledge of the technical aspects of writing, but also your ability to comprehend and evaluate content. Many of these questions require you to gain the "big picture," meaning the logical progression of ideas in the passage. You may be asked whether the writer should add information or delete details. You may be asked to select changes for clarity or coherence. Questions may also require evaluating how information presented in a graph or diagram relates to the passage.

Faces and Feelings

Title provides a general focus point.

Introductory sentence makes initial claim.

Researchers say that a person's facial expression affects the person's own mood, and also the moods of others. So if a woman smiles, the muscles in her face affect her brain in such a way that she actually feels happier. If another person sees her smiling face, that person's brain is also affected and *he* feels happier. Frowns have the opposite effect.

Explanations set up information that follows.

Transition phrase and sentence acknowledge counterpoint and set up the information that follows.

Of course, most people do not walk around either smiling or frowning. Most faces we see have in-between expressions, and we have to interpret the emotions behind them. Studies have found that people can be trained to perceive ambiguous facial expressions more positively.

Logical deduction

New claim sets up the information that follows.

Evidence supports the claim.

For example, in one study, aggressive, at-risk teenagers were shown 15 photos at a time of the same face in a range of expressions from smiling to frowning. The teens had to determine if the expression was happy or angry. For some of the expressions in the mid-range, if a teen identified the expression as angry, the computer responded with a message that the answer was incorrect; the expression was happy. After a week of training, the teens apparently perceived the people around them differently; they became significantly less aggressive.

Ultimately, It seems that people are strongly affected not only by what they see in other people's faces, but also by what they *think* they see.

Conclusion connects and reflects upon the passage's main ideas.

043 Question Topic

→ **PASSAGE AND PARAGRAPH DEVELOPMENT**

DESCRIPTION

Some Writing and Language questions may ask whether information in the passage includes too many details, or conversely, not enough support/explanation. You may also be asked to evaluate an introductory or concluding statement. Make sure that you have a clear idea of the passage's and paragraph's main ideas; the title of the passage is a crucial clue.

Example

A Popular "Spider"

Chlorophytum comosum is a grass-like, clumping perennial plant. It sends out wiry, arching stalks with flowers that then develop into plantlets. **1** In its natural setting, its stalks droop until the plantlets reach the soil and send out roots of their own. In homes, however, Chlorophytum comosum is usually displayed as a hanging plant, which allows its slender leaves to swing below the plant. **2** The species is native to southern Africa.

1　The writer is considering deleting the underlined portion of the sentence. Should it be kept or deleted?
(A) Kept, because it provides an important clarification.
(B) Kept, because it maintains the stylistic pattern established previously.
(C) Deleted, because it provides an unnecessary detail.
(D) Deleted, because it undermines the previous sentence.

2　Which sentence provides the best conclusion for the passage?
(A) NO CHANGE
(B) Consequently, one of its common names is "Spider plant," referring to the spider-like appearance of the plantlets.
(C) The plantlets' resemblance to a spider has earned it the nickname "Spider plant," but I don't call it that because I hate spiders.
(D) Many people regard it as one of the easiest houseplants to grow.

Explanation:

▶ **1** *The correct choice is (A); the phrase helps clarify the description of the plant's natural characteristics.*

▶ **2** *The correct choice is (B) because the sentence about the common name is more appropriate to conclude the paragraph. (B) improves the focus by further developing the previous sentence's description of the plant's display in homes.*

044 Question Topic

PASSAGE ORGANIZATION

DESCRIPTION

Communicating effectively requires coherence. In other words, facts and ideas should be presented logically and should be appropriately connected and complete.

Example

Teacher for a Day

[1] Substitute teachers must find the classroom, find the light switch, and find several pages of written instructions from the teacher. [2] They must comprehend the purpose of piles of instructional materials and supplies, and they must log on to an unfamiliar computer to find the attendance site. [3] The slightest problem, such as where the teacher keeps extra pencils, means that the substitute must pause instruction; whereupon students can hardly be expected to refrain from loud conversations. [4] Within short order, they meet and manage large groups of students whom they do not know, follow routines that they do not know, and provide instruction for learning activities that they may never have seen before.

To make the paragraph more logical, sentence 4 should go
- (A) before sentence 1.
- (B) before sentence 2.
- (C) before sentence 3.
- (D) where it is now.

 Explanation:

The correct choice is (C) because it is more coherent to mention meeting students before mentioning problems with instruction.

▶ SAT Writing and Language Test passages may include bracketed numbers such as "[1]" before several sentences in a paragraph, or for each paragraph. One of the questions will then ask you to decide whether to move a particular sentence (such as "sentence 1") to a different place in the paragraph. Or, you may be asked where to place a new sentence.

▶ When answering coherence questions, you must consider the logical flow of facts and ideas. Within paragraphs, you can also confirm your selection by looking for clues in diction, such as pronouns in a sentence that must have particular antecedents. If you are asked to rearrange complete paragraphs, you can re-check the topic sentences of each paragraph.

045 Question Topic

→ **TRANSITIONS**

DESCRIPTION

Whereas conjunctions clarify the relationship between ideas *within a sentence*, transition words clarify the relationship between the ideas presented in *different sentences*. SAT Writing and Language Tests often include questions requiring you to select an appropriate connecting word or phrase. You will have to look carefully at the sentences or clauses to consider how to indicate the progression of thought accurately.

Example

Peyton and Aveline admitted to leaving out a few ingredients. **1** <u>Nonetheless,</u> their cake was arguably edible.

(A) NO CHANGE

(B) In fact,

(C) Similarly,

(D) For instance,

Explanation:

Choice (A) is correct because "nonetheless" reinforces the assertion that the cake was "edible" in spite of ingredients being left out.

▶ Following are some categories of functions for transition words and phrases:

Add and strengthen	also, additionally, furthermore, in fact, moreover, what is more
Describe an effect	as a result, consequently, hence, therefore, thus
Describe order	next, subsequently, thereafter
Show factors in common	likewise, similarly
Contrast	however, in comparison, in contrast, on the other hand
Reinforce an assertion	all the same, even so, nevertheless, nonetheless, despite, still
Introduce specifics	for example, for instance, in this case, specifically
Suggest	alternatively, if not, instead, otherwise, then again
Prepare to conclude	thus, finally, in short, hence, therefore

▶ Transitions that **contrast** or **introduce specifics** may be placed in commas *after* a subject that you want to emphasize:

His family went to the mountains frequently. Mine, ***however,*** always went to the beach.

Some bird species are incredibly efficient flyers. The albatross, ***for example,*** can glide hundreds of miles without once flapping its wings.

DEVELOPMENT AND ORGANIZATION

Read the passage and answer the corresponding questions.

PASSAGE

Swimming Giants

1 **Living in weight-supporting water allows some aquatic animal species to become huge.** Even behemoths are able to stay afloat and mobile. The most obvious example is the blue whale, the largest animal on Earth. The blue whale is about as long as three school buses, and usually weighs around 200 tons. It usually ambles along at about 5 miles per hour (mph). However, if it is in a hurry, it can swim much faster, up to 20 mph. The giant Pacific octopus can grow to as long as 20 feet end to end and weigh 50 pounds—big enough to wrap around a small car. Yet it can dart after prey at jet-like speed.

2 **On the other hand**, water's buoying properties allow some species to thrive even though they appear quite slow and ungainly. **3** **For example, tree sloths, penguins, and elephants are all expert swimmers.** The heaviest bony fish, the Mola mola (or ocean sunfish) can weigh up to 2,200 pounds. **4** The Mola mola can therefore be an awkward giant in an aquarium tank. In the open ocean, however, it is perfectly shaped to glide down to deep, cold waters to eat, and then gracefully swim up to the surface to expose one of its large, flat sides to the sun.

1

Which choice most effectively establishes the main topic of the passage?

(A) NO CHANGE
(B) Animals that live in water have the advantage of speedy mobility.

2

Select the answer that best transitions between the first and second paragraphs.

(A) NO CHANGE
(B) As a result,

3

The writer is considering deleting the underlined sentence. Should the sentence be kept or deleted?

(A) Kept, because it supports the topic sentence by listing animals that are ungainly on land.
(B) Deleted, because it lists land animals, distracting from an emphasis on marine life.

4

The writer wants to add a sentence here. Which choice would best support the writer's main point about the Mola mola?

(A) Its body is tall (10 feet) but narrow, so that it looks like a swimming pancake.
(B) It periodically swims into kelp beds, where smaller fish clean parasites from its skin.

Section L: Concision, Style, and Syntax

In writing, "style" refers to the manner in which content is conveyed to fulfill the writer's purpose. Questions involving style can refer to diction, tone, and consistency. In the past, people often preferred elaborate and decorative styles of writing, but today's texts tend to be more direct. In general, academic writing should be concise, formal, and clear.

046 Question Topic

→ **IMPROVING CONCISENESS**

DESCRIPTION

Concision, or **conciseness**, means presenting an idea clearly and simply. The correct answers on Writing and Language Test questions will not necessarily be the fanciest-sounding or most elaborate ones. Rather, correct answers often convey information in as few words as possible.

Example

The scenes sculpted on the Parthenon in ancient Athens were designed **1** <u>in such a way as</u> to inspire awe.

(A) NO CHANGE

(C) as

(B) so as

(D) DELETE the underlined portion

 Explanation:

The correct choice is (D) because the underlined portion adds no information to the sentence, making it unnecessary and deletable.

► The Writing and Language test will likely include several questions pertaining to wordy or redundant information and will test your ability to pare down such information.

  Wordy: Serving as entertainment for audiences both young and old, Greek myths are also recognized for their abilities to reveal facets of Greek cultural values and practices.

  The sentence may sound academic, but it lacks clarity because of unnecessary wordiness.

  Concise: Greek mythology is not only entertaining, but it also reveals many details about ancient Greek culture.

047 Question Topic

→ **ELIMINATING REDUNDANCIES**

DESCRIPTION

When writers repeat themselves, they are being "redundant." When you choose an answer, be careful to **distinguish between redundancy and support.** While it is redundant to say "The ancient structure was incredibly old," saying, "The ancient structure is more than 2,000 years old" is not redundant because the phrase "more than 2,000 years old" adds new information.

Example

Offerings left in ancient graves tell us what **1** the community valued and what people believed was worth having.

    (A) NO CHANGE   (C) people considered

    (B) the community valued as   (D) was

 *Explanation:*

  Choice (C) is correct because it maintains the same meaning as the underlined portion without the repetition of ideas.

▶ Redundancies are especially common in descriptions. When you notice a long description, make sure none of the terms that comprise the description repeat or overlap with each other.

    Redundant: The archaeologist looked for subtle clues that were barely noticeable as he combed through the foundations of the ancient structure, which was incredibly old.

        Which phrases are redundant?
        subtle = barely noticeable
        ancient = incredibly old

    Concise: The archaeologist looked for subtle clues as he combed through the foundations of the ancient structure.

048 Question Topic

→ **IMPROVING DICTION**

DESCRIPTION

Diction refers to the overall characteristics of the words the writer uses. When evaluating answer choices for Writing and Language questions, take note of how effectively the words serve the author's purpose.

Example

The soldier's torch cut through the darkness, providing a **1** buffer around which his comrades could rally.

(A) NO CHANGE   (C) beacon

(B) sign   (D) message

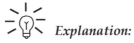 *Explanation:*

The correct choice is (C). A "beacon" is a source of light that serves as a signal to others, which fits best with the context of the example above. Because a "sign" is usually a written indication or a gesture, (B) does not work as well in the context of the sentence.

▶ The most appropriate word choice in each case depends largely on the context. In most cases answer choices that include informal, non-standard diction will *not* be the correct answers.

   Less formal: The aquarium's simulated flash flood displays **scary** force.

   More formal: The aquarium's simulated flash flood displays *frightening* force.

▶ In most cases, the best answer to a diction question will be the one that is specific and that most precisely conveys the author's meaning.

   Less specific: Passengers hurriedly **got** their bags from the overhead bins.

   More specific: Passengers hurriedly *retrieved* their bags from the overhead bins.

   Less specific: Astronauts at the international space station have an important **job**.

   More specific: Astronauts at the international space station have an important *mission*.

049 Question Topic

IMPROVING CONSISTENCY

DESCRIPTION

Good writing often includes rhythms and patterns. For that reason, the Writing and Language Test may ask you to choose an answer that will **maintain a pattern** already established in the text.

Example

It is possible that high heels were invented for a purely practical reason. Ninth-century pottery images show Persian horseback riders wearing high heels, probably to grip the stirrups **1** and so their feet did not slip.

Which choice most closely matches the stylistic pattern established earlier in the sentence?

(A) which meant that their feet did not slip.

(B) whenever their feet started to slip.

(C) and keep their feet from slipping.

(D) preventing any foot slippage.

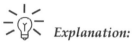 *Explanation:*

In the sentence with the underlined portion, the author speculates that the purpose of the high heels was "to grip the stirrups." Choice (C) is the answer because it follows the same grammatical pattern of an infinitive plus an object: "(to) keep their feet."

▶ At the paragraph level, using consistent sentence patterns often makes information easier for readers to absorb. Matching an establised pattern requires rereading the previous sentences and noting their structure and tone.

> The ancient Egyptian festival of Opet was a multi-day public holiday. The Nile River flooded every summer, covering agricultural fields with nutrients for the soil. Next year's crops would flourish. The flooding was life-giving. It was a symbol of rebirth. It was a sign that the gods were pleased. The floods meant that there was a lot of water for a beautiful floating parade.

> *The underlined portion does not match the pattern or tone that precedes it. An improved version is:*

> The ancient Egyptian festival of Opet was a multi-day public holiday. The Nile River flooded every summer, covering agricultural fields with nutrients for the soil. Next year's crops would flourish. The flooding was life-giving. It was a symbol of rebirth. It was a sign that the gods were pleased. It even provided the means for beautiful floating processions.

CONCISION, STYLE, AND SYNTAX

Read the passage and answer the corresponding questions.

PASSAGE

"Lost" Watermelon Variety

Farmers in the American South have a long history of growing watermelon, a vine fruit that consists mostly of water. **1 Nearly every single Southerner of every income level and ethnic background has** found watermelon to be refreshing during the region's hot summers. Consequently, watermelon **2 appears frequently** in regional dishes.

A recent interest in authentic Southern dishes has led to a return of some "lost" varieties of watermelon. One of these is the Bradford melon. The Bradford was a longtime favorite among Southern cooks. Not only was its interior red and sweet, but its soft rind made delicious pickles. **3 Once commercial farming developed and began using trains and trucks to transport crops to market**, however, the Bradford melon was no longer commercially viable. Its rind was simply too soft for stacking.

The Bradford melon's history stems from the American Revolutionary war in the 1770s. The story begins with British forces **4 capturing some American soldiers and placing them** on a prisoner-of-war ship bound for the West Indies. At one point, the ship's captain ordered that the prisoners be given some slices of watermelon. One of the imprisoned soldiers **5 loved the fruit so much that he saved every seed from his slice.** After the war, that soldier went home to his farm in Georgia, where he planted the seeds. Eventually he developed a successful crop.

Many years later, a farmer named Bradford managed to cross the former soldier's variety with another one, creating the famous Bradford melon. **6 Fortunately, even after it was no longer grown as a commercial crop, members of the Bradford family decided that they liked the Bradford melon so much that they preserved small fields of the melon variety for their own enjoyment.** Today, they have revived the crop. They sell the melons to specialty producers of Southern syrups and pickles.

1

(A) NO CHANGE
(B) Southerners of every background income have

2

(A) NO CHANGE
(B) shows up here and there

3

(A) NO CHANGE
(B) With the advent of the modern transportation industry,

4

(A) NO CHANGE
(B) placing some captive American soldiers

5

(A) NO CHANGE
(B) was enchanted; he pocketed the seeds from his slice.

6

(A) NO CHANGE
(B) After the melon's commercial demise around the beginning of the 20th century, the Bradford family preserved it in their own gardens for generations.

ANSWERS
&
Explanations
QUESTION TOPICS
11-49

Answers & Explanations...
Mastering the Writing and Language Test

1) ➡ B

The sentence containing the underlined portion consists of a dependent clause ("After...solid") followed by an independent clause ("they...foot"). Generally, when a dependent clause comes before an independent clause, a comma separates the two clauses, making (B) the correct choice.

2) ➡ A

The sentence containing the underlined portion consists of a dependent clause ("When...half") followed by an independent clause ("they... lifeboats"). Generally, when a dependent clause comes before an independent clause, a comma separates the two clauses, making (A) the correct choice.

3) ➡ A

The underlined portion includes the prepositional phrase beginning "before they managed." It describes *when* something is happening. Thus, it does not need separating from the rest of the sentence, making choice (A) correct.

4) ➡ B

The underlined portion is part of a dependent clause. ("After" is a subordinate conjunction, signaling that a dependent clause follows.) Dependent clauses cannot stand alone as sentences; they need to be connected to an independent clause. Thus, as written, the sentence is a fragment. "They were caught in a hurricane" is an independent clause, so (B) forms a complete sentence.

5) ➡ B

Choice (A) creates a run-on sentence by connecting two complete sentences with only a conjunction

("and" in this case). Two sentences can be connected using a semicolong or a comma and a conjunction. Because (B) uses a period to separate the sentences, it is the better choice.

6) ➡ B

As written, the underlined section creates confusion because it is not clear that Shackleton had to turn back each of the the three times. The phrase at (B) more clearly connects the ideas by using the transition word "but" and by making the second half a dependent clause.

1) ➡ A

The phrase "a military general" is an appositive that adds information about Zhou Yu. The appositive must be separated from the rest of the sentence using commas, em dashes, or parentheses. Because (A) places commas at the beginning and end of the appositive, it is the correct choice.

2) ➡ B

"To General Zhou Yu's surprise" begins with the preposition "to," so it is a prepositional phrase. When a lengthy prepositional phrase appears at the beginning of a sentence, a comma should always end the phrase. Thus, (B) is the correct answer.

3) ➡ B

The past participle "appeared" is incorrect here because the action is occurring at the same time as the main verb, "arranges." (B) is correct because the participle "appearing" creates a parallel time frame.

4) ➡ A

The phrase "the forces of Cao Cao" is an

appositive that describes "the enemy." End-of-sentence appositives must be separated from the rest of a sentence using either a comma, an em dash, or a pair of parentheses. (A) correctly uses an em dash to separate the appositive from the rest of the sentence.

5) ➡ B

Generally, short prepositional phrases, such as "in the straw," do not need to be separated from the rest of the sentence with a comma, making (B) the correct choice.

6) ➡ B

The participial phrase "speeding away as daylight breaks" describes a noun that is not included. As written, the dangling modifier indicates that the arrows sped away, rather than the boats. (B) clarifies the sentence by restoring the subject.

Question Topics 019: Verb Tense

1) ➡ B

Because service animals still help people with disabilities today, the verb "to help" should be in the present tense. Although the counselor said it in the past, the usage falls into the category of being a universal truth.

2) ➡ B

The verb tense in the sentence should be consistent with the verb tense in the surrounding sentences. (B) correctly changes "coax" to the past tense.

3) ➡ A

The trainer said "the dog would learn..." in the past, so it is appropriate to use "would" instead of the future-tense "will."

4) ➡ B

In sentences that include conditions that start with "if" or "when," there are fixed pairing of tense. A present-tense condition, ie., "if service-animal organization put more resources..." pairs with a

future-tense statement such as " I will be excited."

5) ➡ A

Although the speaker is mentioning a fact that he or she "has read," it falls in the category of a universal truth. Also, it makes sense to describe the monkeys' qualities in the present tense to match the descriptions in the following sentences.

6) ➡ A

The sentence immediately after the underlined portion says that monkeys "provide good company." The verb "provide" is in the present tense. Thus, we can safely assume that the underlined portion should be in the present tense, making (A) the correct choice.

Question Topics 020 – 021: Mood & Voice

1) ➡ B

As written, the sentence inappropriately switches from the indicative mood to the imperative mood at the underlined portion. Choice (B) is correct because it changes the sentence into a conditional statement, which is clearer and more consistent.

2) ➡ A

The underlined portion correctly uses the active voice; the structure conveys the information about a bigger and heavier thing's capabilities directly and concisely. There is no reason to use the more convoluted passive voice, as in choice (B).

3) ➡ B

Many subjunctive sentences, including the one containing the underlined portion, describe requirements. When a subjunctive statement contains a third-person singular, present-tense verb, make sure the verb does not have an "s" at the end, as it would for an indicative sentence. (B) is the correct choice because the verb "contain" must express the subjunctive mood.

4) ➡ B

Choice (A) is incorrect because it unnecessarily uses the passive voice ("are used") to express an action that can be stated using the active voice. (A) causes the reader to wonder whether the rotating parts turn the magnet, or whether they only help the magnet turn. (B) is preferable because it uses the active voice to clarify that rotating parts turn a magnet.

5) ➡ B

Because the sentence containing the underlined portion is expressing a process that occurs in reality, the indicative is more appropriate than the subjunctive, making (B) correct.

6) ➡ A

The underlined portion correctly uses the passive voice, "is called." In this case, the reader understands that the subject is "people" or "the public," "everyone," etc.

> ### Question Topics 022 – 024:
> ### Comparing & Listing

1) ➡ A

The sentence containing the underlined portion compares a moment in the *Firebird Suite* to moments in other songs. The underlined portion is crucial to this comparison because without it, "that moment" would be compared to "any other song," forming an illogical comparison. Thus, the correct choice is (A).

2) ➡ B

As written, the sentence at 2 compares music to "people thinking something," which does not make sense. Choice (B) corrects the problem, with familiar music being compared to unfamiliar music.

3) ➡ B

The underlined words are part of a list, and should be consistent grammatically with other parts of the list. In this case, the list consists of past participles: "*increased* heart rate, *dilated* pupils…" As a result, (B) is a better match.

4) ➡ B

The sentence containing the underlined portion is comparing two things: the amount of dopamine released before a "chill-inducing moment" of music and the amount of dopamine released after that same moment. When comparing two things, use the modifier "more"; when comparing more than two things, use the modifier "most." (B) is correct because this comparison involves only two things, making "more" the appropriate modifier.

5) ➡ A

The underlined portion is part of a list composed of the simple nouns "expectation" and "pleasure." Thus, the noun "adaptation" is a good fit, while the gerund "adapting" would be out of place.

6) ➡ B

When forming the comparative degree, add the "-er" ending to a one-syllable quality and the word "more" before a two-syllable quality. However, adding both the "-er" ending and "more" is redundant, so the underlined portion must be deleted to maintain conciseness.

> ### Question Topics 025 – 028:
> ### In-Sentence Punctuation

1) ➡ A

The introductory phrase "Much like the Hawaiian Islands" is lengthy enough to need a comma to separate it from the rest of the sentence. Thus the sentence should not be changed.

2) ➡ B

The phrase "that are stunning" modifies "rocky features." Modifiers that begin with "that" are rarely preceded by a comma, making (B) the correct choice.

3) ➡ A

The semi-colon correctly joins two related independent clauses in the same sentence.

4) ➡ B

The dependent clause "When molten rock was cascading out of the sea to form Jeju Island" comes before a prepositional phrase ("in some areas") that is part of the independent clause about the lava. Therefore, a comma must follow the dependent clause.

5) ➡ B

The information "forming insulation" is essential to the sentence; without it, the reader would not know what kept the lava hot. Therefore, it should not be set off from the rest of the sentence with em dashes. (B) appropriately adds a comma to separate the independent clause from the participial phrase "forming insulation that…"

6) ➡ A

"Subsequently" is a transition word, so it needs a comma to separate it from the rest of the sentence.

7) ➡ B

A colon is correct in this case because the phrase "perfectly round…" explains the preceding description of the peak looking like an elevator button. Thus, the colon introduces an elaboration. (A) would create a sentence fragment with no subject or verb in the second sentence.

Question Topics 029 – 033: Subject-Verb Agreement

1) ➡ A

The noun to which the verb "commands" refers is the subject of the sentence, "the small island." Because the noun "island" is singular, the third-person singular verb "commands" is the appropriate form of the verb, making (A) the correct choice.

2) ➡ B

The subject of a sentence is never located in a prepositional phrase. Thus, "Icelanders" is NOT the subject of the sentence because it is part of the prepositional phrase "in ten Icelanders." The subject of the sentence, and the noun to which the verb "is" refers, is "one." "Is" agrees in number with "one," as both are singular, so (B) is the correct choice.

3) ➡ B

The subject in this clause is the collective noun, "a repertoire of stories." Since there is only one repertoire, the verb must be in the third-person singular, as in "helps."

4) ➡ B

The full subject of the sentence, and the noun phase to which the verb "contribute" refers, is "Iceland's natural beauty and history." This noun phrase is plural, as it mentions both "natural beauty" and "history." Thus, the correct verb form is "contribute" because it corresponds to a plural subject.

5) ➡ A

The sentence's essential meaning is that the *Icelandic government provides*. Since "government" is singular, it is correct that the verb "provides" should also be singular in form.

6) ➡ A

The verb "is" refers to "finding inspiration" ("finding inspiration…is wonderful"). Because all gerunds (words that look like verbs but act like nouns—"finding" in this case) are singular, "is" is the correct form of the verb, and (A) is the correct choice.

Question Topics 034 – 038: Pronouns

1) ➡ A

The description of Peter Drucker includes both "professor" and "business consultant." In spite of the two titles, Drucker is singular, so the pronoun "his" is appropriate.

2) ➤ B

The underlined words occur in a phrase that begins "an organization's *managers and employees* agreeing..." Since the agreeing is being done by more than one, the pronoun must be plural.

3) ➤ B

The subject of the sentence is "a typical employee." Since the subject is singular, a manager can only give a written evaluation to "him" or "her," not to "them."

4) ➤ A

If we turn the indirect question about credit into a hypothetical answer, we would say "The credit for the methods should go **to him** (or "her" or "them"). Remember the rule of thumb that "whom" and "him" sound alike and play a similar role: as the object of a preposition (such as "to") or of an action.

5) ➤ B

"Everyone" is an indefinite pronoun. It does not refer to a definite person, but it does refer to an abstract "individual." Since "everyone" is singular, the pronoun referring to it must be singular as well.

6) ➤ B

In the sentence as written, it is unclear whether "they" refers to "TQM and MBO," "companies," or "goals." Choice (B) clears up any confusion by restating "the goals."

Question Topics 039 – 040: Commonly Confused Words

1) ➤ B

The correct choice is (B) because "past" refers to durations of time that have ended, and the underlined portion is referring to the two decades before the present (the past).

2) ➤ A

"To accept" something is to admit or to agree to take something, and "to except" something is to omit it or leave it out of a list or group. When we plug in these definitions at the underlined portion, it becomes clear that (A) is the correct choice, as it makes sense to say, "we must admit...that environmental factors will conspire..."

3) ➤ C

The correct choice is the existential pronoun "there," as the underlined portion emphasizes that "a chance" exists.

4) ➤ B

The preposition "to" often follows the verb "refer," making (B) the correct choice.

5) ➤ B

"Huge" is an adjective that describes the word at the underlined portion. Adjectives generally modify nouns, and "affect" is a verb, so (A) must be incorrect. (B) is correct because "effect" is a noun, so it is logical that "huge" modifies "effect."

6) ➤ A

"Averse" means having feelings of dislike or opposition. From this, we can conclude that (B) is incorrect because the underlined portion describes "environmental changes," and environmental changes cannot have feelings, making (B) illogical in the context of the sentence. "Adverse" means harmful, which makes sense in the sentence, as harmful environmental changes can lead to the extinction of animal species.

7) ➤ B

Although it may not be immediately evident, the sentence containing the underlined portion includes a comparison, which is evidenced in the use of the comparative word "further" (the comparative form of "far"). Because "than" is used when forming a comparison, (B) is the correct choice.

8) ➤ A

The underlined portion refers to "life on Earth,"

which is showing possession over its "impending demise." "Its" is the possessive form of "it," making (A) the correct choice. "It's" is the contracted form of "it is," which does not work in the context of the sentence.

Question Topics 041 – 042: Additional Topics

1) ➡ A

The verb "prevent" is often followed by the preposition "from," making (A) the correct choice. As is evidenced by the underlined portion, a noun or pronoun usually comes between "prevent" and "from."

2) ➡ B

When it introduces two alternatives, the adverb "both" always pairs with the conjunction "and," making (B) the correct choice. "Or" is used in the correlative conjunction "either…or" to indicate that only one of two choices can be selected.

3) ➡ B

"To result in" is to cause or produce; "to result from" is to be caused by. Based on the context of the sentence, sleep paralysis can cause/produce hallucinations. Thus, (B) is correct choice.

4) ➡ A

The verb "center" often pairs with the preposition "on," making (A) the correct choice.

5) ➡ B

"Whether" is a conjunction that expresses a choice between two options. The conjunction "and" indicates that all of two or more options can be chosen, whereas the conjunction "or" indicates that only one option may be selected. Thus, (B) is correct because both "whether" and "or" suggest that only one of two options can be selected.

6) ➡ B

The word "neither" always pairs with "nor," making (B) the correct choice.

Question Topics 043 – 045: Development and Organization

1) ➡ A

The second sentence of the passage says, "Even behemoths are able to stay afloat." That sentence enhances the idea from (A) that huge species can thrive in water. Furthermore, the rest of the passage discusses huge aquatic animals, including slow ones.

2) ➡ A

The paragraphs have opposite focuses (fast vs. slow giant aquatic creatures), and the transition "on the other hand" indicates that opposing information will follow. Thus, (A) is the correct choice.

3) ➡ B

The topic sentence of the passage suggests that aquatic animals are the focus of the passage. Because tree sloths and elephants do not live in water, we can conclude that the underlined sentence distracts from the topic's focus. Furthermore, penguins do not fit the passage's focus on "huge" marine animals, specfically blue whales, the giant Pacific octopus, and the Mola mola.

4) ➡ A

The author focuses on the Mola mola's size, characterizing it as an "awkward giant." Because (A) lists the dimensions of a Mola mola while also describing its "ungainly" shape, it is the correct choice. (B) adds information about the Mola mola that is irrelevant to the main topic of the passage.

1) ➡ B

Choice (B) is concise. It expresses "income level and ethnic background" as "background," for example, which improves the passage's focus on watermelon itself. Also, (B) corrects unnecessary emphasis: "nearly every single Southerner" becomes simply "Southerners."

2) ➡ A

The tone of the passage is formal, whereas the tone of the phrase "shows up here and there" is informal. Thus, "appears frequently" is consistent in tone and should remain unchanged.

3) ➡ B

As written, the phrase is wordy and awkward; it references "commercial farming" without explanation, and its syntax makes it sound as if farming began using trucks, which is muddled. In contrast, (B) is concise and clear.

4) ➡ B

Choice (B) conveys the same information as (A), but (B) is much more concise.

5) ➡ B

Both of the choices are grammatically correct, but (B) incorporates more precise and interesting diction.

6) ➡ B

As written, the use of the word "fortunately" is jarring in an otherwise neutral passage. Secondly, the sentence at (B) conveys the information more clearly.

Mastering
The Essay Test

Essay Test Basics

In the Redesigned SAT, the Essay Test is optional. Some colleges and universities do not require SAT Essay scores as part of the application process, but many do. That's why it is a great idea to tackle the Essay Test: it may give you more choices later. The good news is that the Redesigned SAT Essay has a standard prompt which includes very specific directions. Completing the following activities will help you practice, so when you face the Redesigned SAT essay prompt, you will know exactly what to do.

NOTE

All SAT Essay Tests follow the same procedure: within 50 minutes, you must read a passage and write an analysis of it.

1   First, you will be presented with the following instructions:

As you read the passage below, consider how the author uses:
- evidence, such as facts or examples, to support claims.
- reasoning to develop ideas and to connect claims and evidence.
- stylistic or persuasive elements, such as word choice or appeals to emotion, to add power to the ideas expressed.

2   After reading the instructions, you will be presented with a 650- to 750-word passage that argues a certain point. As you read the passage, take notes based on the considerations listed above. After the passage, a variation of the following prompt will appear:

Write an essay in which you explain how the author builds an argument to persuade his/her audience about the author's claim. In your essay, analyze how the author uses one or more of the features listed above (or features of your own choice) to strengthen the logic and persuasiveness of his/her argument. Be sure that your analysis focuses on the most relevant features of the passage.
Your essay should not explain whether you agree with the author's claims, but rather explain how the author builds an argument to persuade his/her audience.

Essay Test Skills

The SAT Essay Test is scored based on the following criteria: **Reading, Analysis,** and **Writing**.

You are evaluated on your understanding of the passage, on the basis of:

▶ including accurate descriptions of overarching and central ideas, major details, and the relationships between ideas and details.

▶ accurately using quotes and/or paraphrases.

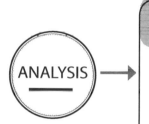

You are scored based on how well you explain the author's use of reasoning and stylistic elements in a passage. You can demonstrate analytical abilities by:

▶ showing that you understand what you are being asked to do by writing an analysis.

▶ commenting on several elements that the author uses to build the argument.

▶ supporting your points with references to the text.

▶ quoting and referencing the most relevant portions of the passage.

You are scored based on how clearly and concisely you present an analysis. You can demonstrate your writing abilities by:

▶ making and supporting a central claim regarding the passage.

▶ using varied sentence structures and a diverse vocabulary.

▶ connecting ideas in such a way that all information is relevant to the prompt.

▶ writing a well-organized essay that shows a logical progression.

▶ demonstrating proper grammar and use of punctuation.

NOTE

Essays are scored by two graders, each of whom assigns a score of 1 to 4 points (1 being the lowest) to each of the categories listed above. Thus, each category receives a score of 2 to 8 points.

Approaching the Passage

Use the standard directions below for guidance when taking notes:

> As you read the passage below, consider how the author uses:
> - evidence, such as facts or examples, to support claims.
> - reasoning to develop ideas and to connect claims and evidence.
> - stylistic or persuasive elements, such as word choice or appeals to emotion, to add power to the ideas expressed.

Your primary goal when reading the passage is to **comprehend the issue** that the author is discussing and the author's position on it.

You must also notice how the author builds his or her argument (evidence), how the author explains his or her views (reasoning), and how the author addresses readers' senses and emotions (style). You may have to read the passage more than once to absorb these elements. As you read and review the passage, quickly take notes regarding the author's main strategies.

Making an Argument: Author Strategies

1. SUPPORTING EVIDENCE:

- *Citation of facts or statistics*
- *Citation of a source of authority*
- *Examples*

2. REASONING AND LOGIC:

- *What the writer thinks, based on the evidence (arguments, claims, connections, and conclusions)*
- *Demonstrations by contrast, analogy, metaphor, and comparison*

3. STYLISTIC OR PERSUASIVE STRATEGIES:

- *Word choices that appeal to emotions*
- *Sentence or paragraph structures used for a particular effect (juxtaposition, repetition, short sentences, and questions)*
- *Descriptive wording, comparisons, and imagery*
- *Reminiscences, warnings, calls to action, reassurances, irony, and humor*

Practice Activity 1: Recognizing Rhetorical Devices

Each of the following short texts employs at least one rhetorical device. In the spaces that follow each short text, identify one or more functions it serves. Write:

"E" for supportive Evidence
AND/OR
"R" for Reasoning and logic
AND/OR
"S" for Stylistic or persuasive strategies

1. People generally tend to comply with expectations and follow rules; therefore, the authors of this study hypothesized that most grocery shoppers would change their shopping patterns if they had partitioned shopping carts.

    Function of text: _____

2. Scarlet macaws—those raucous and bustling rulers of the rainforest's upper canopy—are facing extinction as their habitat shrinks.

    Function of text: _____

3. The company's data revealed that its employees produced 10 percent more work during the workday if they joined large groups to eat lunch.

    Function of text: _____

4. Consider that Ludwig van Beethoven composed his most sublime and innovative music after he became deaf. It is nothing short of stunning that he was able to use a kind of "inner ear" to express visceral emotions with music.

    Function of text: _____

5. A study led by geneticists at Oxford University used DNA sequences from living people to confirm historical accounts of events that led to the genetic mixing of populations, such as conquests and trade routes.

    Function of text: _____

6. When typical DNA sequences of two populations match, it can be assumed that they have shared ancestry. It also makes sense that the longer the matching sequence is, the more recently the populations intermingled, because the matching is less diluted.

    Function of text: _____

7. Roman coins found at the archaeological site indicate that the ancient village was part of a far-reaching network of trade routes.

    Function of text: _____

8. The Mexican region of Oaxaca (prounounced "wa-ha-ka") has a reputation for quality folk art based on the hand-loomed wool rugs that have been produced in Oaxacan villages since the Zapotec empire (500 BCE to 900 CE).

    Function of text: _____

9. Critics of mixed-gender schools say that rather than helping students overcome shyness, the schools make students feel painfully self-conscious.

    Function of text: _____

10. If you had a thermos of hot chocolate and you tried to drink it through a straw in the thermos's cap, the straw would concentrate the liquid's heat and would probably burn your tongue and the roof of your mouth. Similarly, geothermal energy is captured by drilling narrow vents deep into the ground to reach water heated by the Earth's inner core of magma. The water is drawn up as steam, which can power turbines.

    Function of text: _____

* You can find sample answers with explanations at the end of this chapter.

Annotating the Passage

Below you will find a short text accompanied by sample notes. The student went back after writing the notes and underlined the most relevant points. Next, the writer can use the notes to outline an analytical essay.

The following passage is adapted from Peter Janiszewski, Ph.D., "30% of people with a 'healthy' BMI are actually obese," 2015 Obesity Panacea (PLoS BLOGS)

Passage

Although I've discussed this issue a number of times over the years, every now and then a new study comes out that provides further evidence of the limitations of **body mass index** (BMI) as a measure of health, or even adiposity (level of fat in the body).

Recall that BMI is the most common metric used to assess body weight status, and to identify the presence of overweight and obese individuals. While it is great when used in epidemiological studies across thousands of people, it's a pretty lousy measure on an individual basis. So why does it keep being used? It is relatively easy and inexpensive to measure height and weight – hence, the measure persists in clinical practice.

In this cross-sectional study the authors assessed the BMI, body fat percentage, and cardiometabolic risk factors of 6,123 (924 lean, 1,637 overweight and 3,562 obese, classified according to BMI) Caucasian subjects (69% females) between the ages of 18 and 80 years.

What did they find?

First, 29% of subjects classified as normal weight and 80% of individuals classified as overweight according to BMI had a body fat percentage within the obese range. Thus, on an individual basis BMI tends to consistently underestimate a person's adiposity. This data implies that there are many individuals who don't weigh that much on an absolute scale, but a large proportion of their weight is composed of fat tissue. These are people who may look thin, but tend to be soft, with little muscle tone. In a clinical setting, these folks may easily be overlooked by their physician due to their "normal weight."

Sample Notes

> Topic is new study: BMI limited as measure of health

> BMI based on height, weight; easy/inexpensive way to identify overweight/obesity (counterpoint)
Author: BMI is "lousy" measure for individual health (stylistic; word choice)

> New study uses body fat % and cardiometabolic risk factors;
Author begins to support his case with factual evidence

> Study findings: some BMI normal weight and most overweight have body fat % in "obese" range
▶ Data support argument that BMI "lousy" measure for individuals
▶ Supporting example: someone who looks thin but has little muscle

Conversely, approximately 5% of individuals classified as overweight and 0.2% of those classified as obese by BMI actually had low levels of fat mass. These individuals would be the bodybuilders of the bunch – high absolute body weight that is composed mostly of muscle mass. This is often the line of argument used to illustrate how ineffective BMI is at measuring adiposity. And yet, as I've criticized before, the misclassification in this direction appears to occur only rarely. This simply suggests there are simply few body builders around. More importantly, any physician should be able to conclude that the patient in front of them with a BMI of 31 kg/m^2 is not actually obese when their biceps are bigger than their waist.

Finally, when compared to individuals who were actually lean (both on BMI and body fat), those with a high levels of adiposity, regardless of their BMI (normal weight, overweight or obese BMI) had poorer cardiometabolic profiles, including elevated blood pressure, blood glucose and lipid levels, as well as markers of systemic inflammation.

So how can a physician determine whether a patient with a normal or overweight BMI is actually obese? Measuring waist circumference certainly seems to help. This one measure can help distinguish those with a low versus high adiposity despite similar BMIs.

Even better, physicians could start paying less attention to weight or adiposity altogether, and evaluate more relevant markers of a patient's health, including metabolic factors, psychological status, mobility, etc.

Study data show converse also true, BMI mistaking muscle mass for obesity.

Author: dismisses supportive data because cases occur so rarely
Reasoning: not likely doctors will misclassify muscular individuals

Evidence: Subjects with high levels of body fat also had high blood pressure, etc.
Implication: doctors may be missing signs (supports "lousy individual care" argument)

Alternative simple measure proposed: measure waist

Reasoning: if weight and body fat not meaningful, doctors should focus on "more relevant markers" of health

Outlining and Writing Your Essay

Outlining your essay allows you to organize and connect information mentioned in your notes before you start writing. Without an outline, an essay may become disorganized, wordy, and redundant. By the end of your outlining process, you should know how you will respond to each aspect of the prompt.

▸ Prompt ◂

Write an essay in which you explain how Peter Janiszewski builds an argument to persuade his audience that BMI is not an accurate measurement of an individual's health. Your essay should not explain whether you agree with Janiszewski's claims, but rather explain how Janiszewski builds an argument to persuade his audience.

▶ WE CAN BREAK THIS LARGE PROMPT INTO THREE CENTRAL QUESTIONS:

THREE CENTRAL QUESTIONS

1 **What is the author's attitude toward using BMI to measure an individual's health?**

Confirm that you understand the central argument made by the author and jot it down. Be very careful to identify this argument correctly, as the author may use counterexamples to prove his points which, if misread, would lead you to think that the author is saying the opposite of what he is saying.

2 **What evidence and stylistic techniques does the author use to support his attitude?**

Look at your notes and **identify** the broader techniques used by the author. Begin to plan the structure of your essay based on these broader points.

3 **How does this evidence support his attitude?**

Always **relate** the evidence or stylistic element to the specific point being made. Explain why the strategy in question helps (or does not help) the author build a persuasive argument. For example, you may discuss why particular imagery used by the author is useful, how descriptive diction helps the author prove his or her point, or how the author's use of data persuades the reader.

By answering each of the above questions in an essay, you will have identified the passage's **main topic, evidence, reasoning,** and **stylistic elements.** In other words, you will know what you want to say in your essay.

Once you know what you will say in your essay, quickly determine how you will say it:

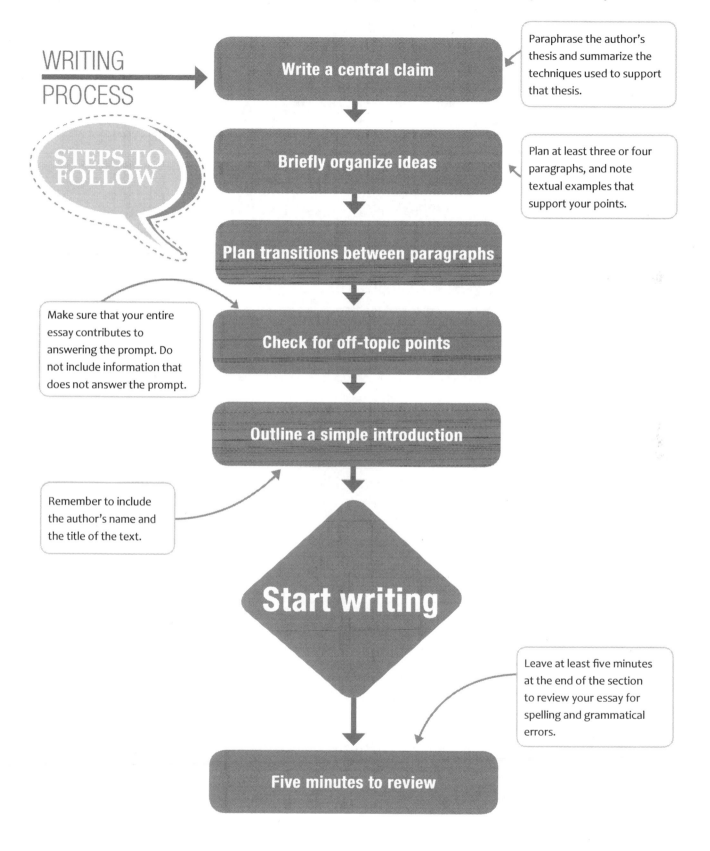

WRITING PROCESS

STEPS TO FOLLOW

Write a central claim

Paraphrase the author's thesis and summarize the techniques used to support that thesis.

Briefly organize ideas

Plan at least three or four paragraphs, and note textual examples that support your points.

Plan transitions between paragraphs

Make sure that your entire essay contributes to answering the prompt. Do not include information that does not answer the prompt.

Check for off-topic points

Outline a simple introduction

Remember to include the author's name and the title of the text.

Start writing

Leave at least five minutes at the end of the section to review your essay for spelling and grammatical errors.

Five minutes to review

How to Practice

The Essay Section will always be based on a source text and accompanied by the standard prompt. As a result, practicing is very easy:

Source materials are abundant. You can find persuasive texts in columns and editorials in newspapers, magazines, and media websites. You are virtually surrounded by people who are trying to persuade you of something. All persuaders use **reasoning**, **evidence**, and **stylistic elements** to make an argument.

Once you have a source article, **practice** notating it.

Practice writing essays. Start without a time limit, and then try timing yourself for 50 minutes.

In the weeks leading up to the test, you should aim to write two practice essays a week. The more you practice, the better your essays will be. And the more awareness you have of current issues, the easier it will be for you to quickly grasp the issue presented.

CHAPTER 3

> **NOTES**
>
> An essay's introduction provides the framework for everything that follows. It sets the tone of an essay while providing the reader with crucial background information. Possibly because so much is expected of introductions, many students find writing them difficult. On the SAT Essay Test, however, composing a thorough introduction is as simple as making a precise claim about the passage you are analyzing. If possible, include the author's name, the passage's title, any relevant context (such as the year published), the author's overall argument, and the author's primary strategies.

TO START YOUR ESSAY WITH CLEAR, PRECISE IDEAS:

▶ include the title of the article and the name of the author, if available.

▶ make a claim about the author's primary strategies.

▶ state the author's overall argument.

DIRECTIONS

The authors and titles excerpted below are imaginary, purely for practicing. Complete the claims about the excerpts with your own ideas. The first one is done for you.

EXCERPT 1   From "The Irony of Bronze," by Hilda Door.

> The year is 300 BCE; stormy seas toss a small ship crossing the Mediterranean Sea. After a valiant struggle, the ship's crew—along with its heavy cargo—is sunk. The families of the crew members wait and wait for them to come home, and finally mourn their loved ones.
>
> Some 2,300 years later, however, an exquisite bronze statue carried by the ship is found in the mud. The statue is dug up; mud is cleaned from its face and hair; it is displayed in the world's finest museums, where children can look into its eyes and connect with people of an ancient era. The irony is that sinking into the sea saved the statue from destruction; most other bronze statues of the period were later melted down to make tools or weapons.

> **Claim:** *In her article "The Irony of Bronze," Hilda Door uses imagery to emphasize a painful fact: sometimes human tragedy preserves ancient art.*

EXCERPT 2 From "Weighing Group Projects," by Tyler Chun.

Daniel and Grace have opposite viewpoints. Daniel loves group project assignments because he is very social. He likes breaking down the project so that each person can choose what to do, and he does not mind hounding his peers if he thinks that they are slacking. But Grace hates group projects because she gets bored and frustrated by how long it takes to coordinate jobs.

Claim: *In his article "Weighing Group Projects," Tyler Chun uses reasoning to* _____

_____

_____

_____

EXCERPT 3 From "Underwater Photographer," by Steven Sealberg.

Most people think that professional underwater photographers are lucky to get to swim about, shooting scenes of breathtaking marine life. But their art is also a business. Meeting deadlines can require a great deal of knowledge and creativity, mainly because underwater visibility is unpredictable. Rough seas cause reduced visibility for several reasons. One is that the rough surface reflects more sunlight, so that less light penetrates underwater. Another is that wave surges can stir up the silt and sand on the sea bottom, so that the water becomes murky.

Claim: *In his article "Underwater Photographer," Steven* _____

_____

_____

_____

_____

From "Public Libraries," by Magnolia Wordsmith.

I've heard it said that libraries are on their way out. Some claim that the Internet renders libraries obsolete; after all, why spend time sifting through shelf after dusty shelf when virtually any text is just a Google search or Wikipedia article away? I myself have fallen victim to the convenience of online research—my writing consistently references more hyperlinks than it does brick-and-mortar publishers.

Yet convenience does not necessarily lend itself to learning. Online research is simple, and it puts the learner in a passive position: type a few words, click "Search," and all your questions are answered. But learning is neither simple nor passive. Learning should be challenging, riddled with false starts and dead ends. Learning should be active and tactile. Too often, I've turned to the Internet for research and found exactly what I was looking for after a few minutes of searching. The process is quick and easy. However, that which comes easy is rarely that which stays with us.

More vivid than any memory of online research are my memories of conducting research in my alma mater's labyrinthine library. Memories of diving into the stacks intent on finding one book but ending up with five. Memories of thumbing through entire books looking for just two or three excerpts to strengthen my argument. Memories of frustration when those two or three excerpts didn't exist, and of triumph when I would find four instead of three.

Learning is a journey, not a destination. Online research allows us to teleport from destination to destination, forgoing the memories that come from the journeys. Libraries allow us to walk to our destinations; sure, it takes longer, but it makes the trip memorable.

Claim: _____

_____

_____

_____

_____

_____

_____

_____

_____

* You can find sample answers with explanations at the end of this chapter.

Practice Activity 3 — Insightful Analysis

NOTES

SAT Essay Test responses must focus on the "art and craft of writing." You must demonstrate that you can identify and analyze the methods an author uses to persuade readers. In other words, once you have determined what an author says, you must explain how he or she says it. One way to analyze an author's work is to discuss what makes their writing unique. Do they ask questions? Do they use humor to prove their point? The more thorough your analysis, the higher your score will be. Ultimately, SAT Essay Test evaluators are looking for insightful student responses. "Insight" means "seeing into," implying a deep and profound understanding.

TO DEMONSTRATE INSIGHTFUL ANALYSIS IN YOUR ESSAY RESPONSE:

▶ Name a strategy the author uses.
▶ Explain what point the strategy is supporting.
▶ Elaborate on how and why it works (or does not work).

It may help to remember the analytical task in this format:

The strategy of (x) supports the author's idea that (y) because...

One way to elaborate on your point is to consider how persuasive the passage would be if the author did not use the strategy:

If the author did not use the strategy of (x), then....

Read the brief excerpts and fill in the blanks below with analytical ideas of your own. The first one is done for you.

 EXCERPT 1   From *Not That it Matters*, by A.A. Milne, originally published in 1920.

Golf is so popular simply because it is the best game in the world at which to be bad…At golf it is the bad player who gets the most strokes. However good his opponent, the bad player has the right to play out each hole to the end; he will get more than his share of the game. He need have no fears that his new driver will not be employed. He will have as many swings with it as the scratch man; more, if he misses the ball altogether upon one or two tees. If he buys a new niblick [a golf club] he is certain to get fun out of it on the very first day.

1. Persuasive strategy: *Reasoning.*

2. Idea that it supports: *Golf is more fun if you are bad at it.*

3. How and why it is supportive:

The author's logical process gives readers a new way to look at golf, and an alternative way of thinking about what makes a sport fun. He points out that in golf, "however good the opponent, the bad player has the right to play out each hole to the end." Rather than being embarrassed by his poor skills, Milne chooses to point out that even as a beginner with new golf clubs, he can have fun "on the very first day."

Milne's reasoning reminds readers of typical childhood goals in any game--to get to one's own turn. Milne reasons that "our turn" is long in golf when we are less proficient. It is a humorous point, because it is unexpected and reminds us that golf is just a game. More importantly, he models un-self-conscious enjoyment.

If Milne did not use reasoning, and just stated that golf is popular because it is fun even for beginners or bad players, readers would not be persuaded; it would seem a strange idea.

EXCERPT 2 From *My Man Jeeves*, by P.G. Wodehouse, originally published in 1919.

> Do you know Marvis Bay? …It isn't what you'd call a fiercely exciting spot, but it has its good points. You spend the day there bathing and sitting on the sands, and in the evening you stroll out on the shore with the gnats. At nine o'clock you rub ointment on the wounds and go to bed.

1. Persuasive strategy: *Sarcastic humor.*

2. Idea that it supports: *Marvis Bay is boring.*

3. How and why it is supportive:

Wodehouse says that Marvis Bay "has its good points," but the "good points" sound uncomfortable (gnat bites) and boring ("sitting on the sands," and going to bed at 9 p.m.) The sarcastic humor persuades the reader because _____

_____

_____

_____

_____

If the author did not use sarcastic humor, and just said "Marvis Bay is boring," _____

_____

_____

_____

_____

From *Jean François Millet* by Estelle M. Hurll, originally published in 1900. The following is a collection of comments on Jean François Millet's drawing "Woman Feeding Hens."

Once more let us recall [John] Ruskin's teaching in regard to enclosed spaces. The artist is unhappy if shut in by impenetrable barriers. There must always be, [he] says, some way of escape, it matters not by how narrow a path, so that the imagination may have its liberty.

This is the principle which our painter has applied in his picture ["Woman Feeding Hens"]. [He] wisely gives us a glimpse of the sky above, and shows us the shady vista of the garden walk leading to the great world beyond.

1. Persuasive strategy: *Referring to an expert authority, "Ruskin."*

2. Idea that it supports: *Artists such as Jean François Millet add openings and pathways to invite imagination about the larger setting.*

3. How and why it is supportive:

The author's strategy of referring to "Ruskin," who is clearly considered an expert authority on art, _____

_____

_____

_____

_____

If the author did not refer to an expert, the reader might think _____

_____

_____

_____

_____

_____

_____

EXCERPT 4 From *Oh, Well, You Know How Women Are!* by Irvin S. Cobb, originally published in 1919.

[Women are said to be single-minded.] But that which is ordinarily a fault may, on occasion of extraordinary stress, become the most transcendent and the most admirable of virtues. I think of this last war [World War I] and of the share our women and the women of other lands have played in it. No one caviled nor complained at the one-ideaness of womankind while the world was in a welter of woe and slaughter. Of all that they had, worth having, our women gave and gave and gave and gave. They gave their sons and their brothers, their husbands and their fathers, to their country; they gave of their time and of their energies and of their talent; they gave of their wonderful mercy and their wonderful patience, and their yet more wonderful courage; they gave of the work of their hands and the salt of their souls and the very blood of their hearts.

1. Persuasive strategy: *Repetition.*

2. Idea that it supports: *Women's single-mindedness can be* _____

_____

_____

3. How and why it is supportive:

   The author's repetition of the word "gave" _____

_____

_____

_____

_____

_____

   If the author did not use repetition, _____

_____

_____

_____

_____

EXCERPT 5

From *"Animal Claws"* by Kallis Edu staff, 2015.

Many mammals, including cats, dogs, and bears, have claws that are strong and long, useful for climbing, digging, and catching prey. But the most important use for claws in many cases is to assist animals with simply walking and running. The principle is the same as that for treads on the soles of athletic shoes: traction. When a cheetah can dig its claws into the ground, it can push off with more power and thus, more speed. When a polar bear has to walk across slippery ice, the traction from its claws can prevent slipping.

1. Persuasive strategy: *Providing examples.*

2. Idea that it supports: _____

_____

_____

_____

3. How and why it is supportive: _____

_____

_____

_____

_____

_____

_____

_____

_____

_____

_____

_____

From *"Arizona Universities"* by Kallis Edu staff, 2015.

Many people are familiar with the University of Arizona (UA), located in Tucson, Arizona, partly due to its high-ranking athletic teams, the Wildcats.

But in terms of enrollment, UA is dwarfed by two universities located in Phoenix, Arizona. One of these, Arizona State University (ASU), is the largest public (government-supported) university in the nation, with more than 83,000 students spread over its six campuses and online. The University of Phoenix, a private for-profit institution, has 112 campuses worldwide, and many online programs. It has the largest enrollment of any university in the United States, with about 227,000 students in 2015.

1. Persuasive strategy: _____

2. Idea that it supports: _____

_____

_____

_____

3. How and why it is supportive: _____

_____

_____

_____

_____

_____

_____

_____

_____

_____

_____

* You can find sample answers with explanations at the end of this chapter.

CHAPTER 3

Using Quotations Skillfully

> **NOTES**
>
> Your primary task on the SAT Essay Test is to analyze an author's work. Quoting an author allows you to show the reader exactly what part of the text you intend to analyze while simultaneously demonstrating your own understanding of the text. Moreover, referring to the text frequently helps your response stay focused. When summarizing information from a passage, paraphrasing (using your own words) is often preferable to direct quotations, yet quoting is often effective when you want to highlight a unique stylistic element used by the author.

1. TO USE QUOTATIONS SKILLFULLY:

To complete the writing task, you must be able to:
- ▶ Choose parts of the text that have the most to do with your point.
- ▶ Integrate them smoothly into sentences of your own.

2. WRITERS INTEGRATE QUOTATIONS IN MANY WAYS, BUT HERE ARE THREE BASIC METHODS:

- ▶ following a complete thought and a colon
- ▶ following a comma
- ▶ following "says that" or its equivalent

Three basic methods		Example
1) **(Complete thought):**	→	*In "The Star-Spangled Banner," Francis Scott Keys begins with a rhetorical question: "Oh, say can you see, by the dawn's early light...?"*
2) **The author says,**	→	*The flag's stars and stripes, Keys says, "were so gallantly streaming."*
3) **The author says that**	→	*Keys says that "the rockets' red glare, the bombs bursting in air" provided light to see the flag.*

Read the brief excerpt and fill in the blanks below with quotations. The first one is partially done for you.

 EXCERPT 1 From "The Star-Spangled Banner," by Francis Scott Keys, 1814.

> Oh, say can you see by the dawn's early light
> What so proudly we hailed at the twilight's last gleaming?
> Whose broad stripes and bright stars through the perilous fight,
> O'er the ramparts we watched, were so gallantly streaming?
> And the rocket's red glare, the bombs bursting in air,
> Gave proof through the night that our flag was still there.
> Oh, say does that star-spangled banner yet wave
> O'er the land of the free and the home of the brave?

Three basic methods		Example
1) **(Complete thought):**	→	*Keys finishes the verse with a second question: "Oh, say does that star-spangled banner yet wave...?"*
2) **The author says,**	→	*The light from explosions, Keys says, "Gave ____* _____ _____ _____ _____ _____ _____ _____ _____ ."*
3) **The author says that**	→	*Keys says that the United States of America is "the land* _____ _____ _____ _____ _____ _____ ."*

CHAPTER 3

From "Take Me Out to the Ballgame," lyrics by Jack Norworth, 1908.

Take me out to the ball game,
Take me out with the crowd.
Buy me some peanuts and cracker jack,
I don't care if I never get back,
Let me root, root, root for the home team,
If they don't win it's a shame.
For it's one, two, three strikes, you're out,
At the old ball game.

Three basic methods	Example
1) **(Complete thought):** →	*The speaker in the song seems to want to be swept up in something big and exciting: "Take_____* _____ _____ _____."
2) **The author says,** →	*The speaker cheerfully imitates an umpire and says, "For_____* _____ _____ _____."
3) **The author says that** →	*Showing lighthearted competitive spirit, the speaker says that "If_____* _____ _____ _____."

From *"Auld Lang Syne,"* lyrics by Robert Burns, 1788.

> Should old acquaintance be forgot,
> and never brought to mind?
> Should old acquaintance be forgot,
> and auld lang syne [times gone by]?
> CHORUS:
> For auld lang syne, my dear,
> for auld lang syne,
> we'll take a cup of kindness yet,
> for auld lang syne.
> And surely you'll buy your pint cup!
> and surely I'll buy mine!
> And we'll take a cup o' kindness yet,
> for auld lang syne.

Three basic methods		Example
		In Robert Burns' "Auld Lang Syne," the speaker
1) **(Complete thought):**	→	_____ _____ _____ _____."
2) **The author says,**	→	*The speaker in the song* _____ _____ _____ _____ _____."
3) **The author says that**	→	_____ _____ _____ _____ _____."

* You can find sample answers with explanations at the end of this chapter.

MODEL
ANSWERS
PRACTICE ACTIVITIES

1-4

In every case, answers will vary. Model answers are merely examples of possible answers.

Model Answers...
Mastering the Essay Test

1. ■■▶ R

The author describes a prediction about typical human behavior based upon a generalization. The author thus describes a reasoning process: if x is true, then y must be true.

2. ■■▶ S, E

In the middle of a factual statement about scarlet macaws facing extinction, the author interjects an emotionally appealing description of the birds. The stylistic strategy serves to heighten readers' concern about the birds by highlighting their lively and humorous qualities.

3. ■■▶ E

The sentence summarizes research data, which can serve as evidence in a text.

4. ■■▶ S

Choosing words such as "sublime," "stunning," and "visceral" adds a stylistic layer to an otherwise purely factual sentence. The author's purpose is to persuade the reader to share his or her attitude toward Beethoven's compositions.

5. ■■▶ E, R

The text introduces a research study and its general results. Thus, the text provides an introductory sentence that alludes to evidence in the form of facts (DNA findings). It also makes use of reasoning when it indicates the types of claims that will be based on the facts (connections to events in history).

6. ■■▶ R

The text primarily describes a reasoning process: in cases where populations' DNA sequences match, it is reasonable to assume that populations have shared ancestry. The more they match, it is reasonable to conclude that they have mingled more recently.

7. ■■▶ E, R

The text describes solid evidence in the form of ancient Roman coins found at the site of an archaeological dig. It also contains reasoning and interpretation: the coins must mean that there was a trade network that reached from the site to ancient Rome.

8. ■■▶ E

The author packs the sentence full of evidence in the form of facts, including the region, how to pronounce the name of the region, the reputation of the region, the product that provides its renown, and its ancient history.

9. ■■▶ S, R

Claims are by definition forms of reasoning, based on some type of deduction or interpretation. The sentence functions as reasoning in that it describes a claim made by "critics of mixed-gender schools." The sentence also includes stylistic devices. Phrases such as "overcome shyness" and "painfully self-conscious" serve to provoke readers' interest and empathy.

10. ■■▶ R, E

The text includes many facts about heat, straws, and geothermal energy. It uses reasoning in the form of analogy to explain the facts: if you have experienced x, or can imagine experiencing x, you can understand y, because it has similarities.

Practice Activity 2

EXCERPT 2 Sample Answer

Claim: In the article "Weighing Group Projects," Tyler Chun uses reasoning to explain the pros and cons of group projects.

EXCERPT 3 Sample Answer

Claim: In his article "Underwater Photographer," Steven Sealberg uses an explanatory style to spell out the challenges of professional underwater photography.

EXCERPT 4 Sample Answer

Claim: In "Public Libraries," Magnolia Wordsmith makes use of rhetorical questions, personal anecdotes, and metaphor to strengthen her argument that libraries still serve an important function despite the growing popularity of online research.

Practice Activity 3

EXCERPT 2 Sample Answer

3. it is a compliment to the reader; it makes the reader feel that the author trusts him or her to "get" the joke. It places the reader with the author, sharing a viewpoint. If the author did not use sarcastic humor, and just said "Marvis Bay is boring," the reader might feel alienated, because it would sound like a complaint. The author would seem to be negative and overly critical. Instead, readers probably find themselves laughing with the author and assuming that he is correct about the bay.

EXCERPT 3 Sample Answer

3. helps the reader feel that the perspective is trustworthy. If the author did not refer to an expert, the idea might seem to be just something that the author herself thinks.

EXCERPT 4 Sample Answer

2. a virtue during times of chaos and crisis.

3. emphasizes the massive outpouring of support by women during the war. If the author did not repeat the word over and over, the reader would not have the same emotional response. The repetition makes the author sounds very serious as he attempts to overturn a conventional view of women during his era. The repetition seems like the beating of a fist on a table, which shows strong feeling and is very persuasive.

EXCERPT 5 Sample Answer

2. Animal claws help with simply walking and running by providing traction.

3. The examples help the reader visualize the effect of the animals' claws. Without the examples of the cheetah and the polar bear, the reader might not pay as much attention to the author's claim, and might not really agree that claws are necessary for providing traction. Once the reader can visualize the examples, the reader is much more likely to remember and accept the notion.

EXCERPT 6 Sample Answer

1. Use of data as evidence

2. In the U.S., ASU and University of Phoenix are the largest institutions of their categories.

3. The author's use of enrollment figures and number of campuses for each institution is persuasive because the numbers are huge. The numbers surprise the reader, who might have trouble imagining so many students in one university. If the author had not included the data as evidence, the reader might think that ASU and the University of Phoenix were only slightly larger than other campuses, and would not have been convinced. The numbers, however, are inarguable evidence.

EXCERPT 1 Sample Answer

2. proof through the night that our flag was still there.

3. of the free and the home of the brave.

EXCERPT 2 Sample Answer

1. me out to the ballgame, take me out with the crowd."

2. "For it's one, two, three strikes you're out."

3. they don't win it's a shame."

EXCERPT 3 Sample Answer

1. asks a rhetorical question: "Should old acquaintance be forgot?"

2. apparently does not want to forget old times, and says, "We'll take a cup of kindness yet."

3. The speaker indicates trust when he says that "surely you'll buy your pint cup."

MASTERING
SAT MATHEMATICS

Math Test Basics

A. Breaking Down the Math Test

The Math portion of the SAT consists of two tests:

- **One No-Calculator Math Test, 25 minutes**
  20 questions total: 15 multiple-choice questions, 5 student-produced response questions.

- **One Calculator Math Test, 55 minutes**
  38 questions total: 30 multiple-choice questions, 8 student-produced response questions including a pair of related questions (numbers 37 and 38) that are worth two points each.

Each correctly answered question is worth one point, with the exception of the pair at the end of the Calculator Test, which are worth two points per correctly answered question. Unanswered and incorrectly answered questions are worth zero points.

> **Note**
> There is no scoring penalty for wrong answers—this means you should always guess even if you are unsure of the answer to a question.

B. Introducing the Questions You Will See

The questions on the Math Tests can be classified according to four categories that correspond to the chapters of this book:

- **Mastering SAT Algebra:**
  Modeling and solving single equations and systems of equations; linear functions and their graphs

- **Mastering Advanced Topics in Math:**
  Polynomials and their graphs; factoring

- **Mastering SAT Geometry:**
  Geometry and trigonometry; complex numbers

- **Mastering SAT Data Analysis:**
  Graph and table analysis; probability and statistics

FLUENCY

ARITHMETIC

Fluency with arithmetic operations (addition, subtraction, multiplication, and division) is tested explicitly in the No-Calculator Test, but it is also essential in mastering the Calculator Test, as excessive use of your calculator will slow you down and can lead to errors.

ALGEBRAIC

Fluency with algebraic operations means identifying structures in algebraic expressions and using these structures to manipulate, factor, and solve expressions.

TRENDS AND RELATIONSHIPS

UNDERSTAND

The Math Test expects you to predict how manipulating one variable will affect related variables. The test evaluates your understanding of statistical measures (e.g. mean and median) by asking you how changes in data affect these measures. These questions can be conceptual, or they may ask you to calculate actual values.

DEMONSTRATE

You are expected to demonstrate an understanding of trends and relationships by identifying and describing graphical representations such as scatterplots and two-way tables.

GRAPHS

TYPES

Graphs are important across all four categories. The types of graphs you will encounter range from simple linear functions to polynomials with multiple roots to geometric figures in the coordinate plane.

ANALYSIS

You are expected to create, sketch, and transform graphs from their functions, as well as determine equations from graphs.

CHAPTER 4

Mastering
SAT Algebra

Fundamental Concepts and Techniques

NUMBER PROPERTIES

Real number : any number that can be located on a number line, including positive numbers, negative numbers, fractions, decimals, and square roots.

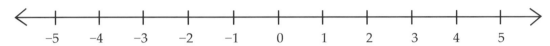

Integer : a whole number, including positive whole numbers, negative whole numbers, and zero.

| Negative: −4, −9, −12... | Zero: 0 | Positive: 1, 2, 3, 4..... |

Consecutive integers : whole numbers that follow each other in numerical order. Thus, the sequence 1, 2, 3, 4 consists of four consecutive positive integers, and the sequence 2, 4, 6, 8 consists of four consecutive even integers.

050 Question Topic

→ NUMERICAL CALCULATIONS

▶   Questions that require purely numerical calculations, including questions that involve plugging in numerical values for variables, can be effectively solved by adhering to the order of operations (see Teacher's Tip).

Example

What is the value of $7-5+\dfrac{6(4-2)^2}{2}$?

 Solution :

First, calculate anything inside parentheses: $(4 - 2) = 2$

Second, calculate any value that has an exponent: $(2)^2 = 4$

Multiply: $6(4) = 24$

Divide: $\dfrac{24}{2} = 12$

Add and subtract: $7 - 5 + 12 = 14$

The correct answer is 14.

💬 TEACHER'S TIP

Solve equations and inequalities in the following way:
1. Calculate values contained in parentheses, ( ).
2. Calculate values involving exponents.
3. Calculate values being multiplied or divided.
4. Calculate values being added or subtracted.

▶ **Equation :** a mathematical statement in which two expressions are equal to one another and set on either side of an equal sign:

$$10 + 5 = 7 + 8$$

(*expression*)   (*expression*)

(*equation*)

▶ **Variable :** a symbol (often a lower–case or upper-case letter) that represents one or more numbers. For instance, in the equation $a + b = c + 5$, a, b, and c are variables.

When an equation includes a variable, the numerical value of that variable which makes the equation true (makes the two sides equal to each other) is called the **solution** to the equation. An equation may have more than one solution, or it may have no solutions.

▶ **Properties of Equality :**

- Addition Property of Equality: For all real numbers a, b, and c, if $a = b$, then $a + c = b + c$.
- Subtraction Property of Equality: For all real numbers a, b, and c, if $a = b$, then $a - c = b - c$.
- Multiplication Property of Equality: For all real numbers a, b, and c, if $a = b$, then $a \cdot c = b \cdot c$.
- Division Property of Equality: For all real numbers a, b, and c, if $a = b$, then $\dfrac{a}{c} = \dfrac{b}{c}$.
- Distribution Property of Equality: For all real numbers a, b, and c, $a(b + c) = ab + ac$.

051 Question Topic

ALGEBRA PROBLEMS IN ONE VARIABLE

▶ Always begin by examining the question for structures and expressions that consist of more than just a single variable or number that will help manipulate the equations. Most questions will contain such a structure, and difficult questions may require you to recognize a question's structure to answer the question at all.

▶ Use the properties of equality to isolate the variable on one side of the equation.

▶ Confirm the solution by plugging the value back into the original equation.

Example

If $4x + 5 = 8$, then $8x + 9$ equals

(A) 8   (C) 12

(B) 10   (D) 15

 TEACHER'S TIP

Always assess an equation's structure before attempting to solve it.

 **Solution :**

Recognize that $8x$ has twice the value of $4x$. Multiply the first equation by 2:

$2 \cdot [4x + 5] = [8] \cdot 2 \longrightarrow 8x + 10 = 16$

Subtract 1 from both sides of the equation:

$8x + 10 - 1 = 16 - 1 \longrightarrow 8x + 9 = 15$.

The correct choice is (D).

INEQUALITIES

An **inequality** shows that two mathematical expressions are NOT equal to one another. Inequalities are used to show that one quantity is greater than (>), less than (<), greater than or equal to (≥), less than or equal to (≤), or not equal (≠) to another quantity. Below are simple inequality statements with their meanings:

▶ $10 > 8$ means "ten is greater than eight."

▶ $15 < 20$ means "fifteen is less than twenty."

▶ $10 + x \geq 9$ means "any quantity that is ten greater than x is greater than or equal to nine."

▶ $6 - y \leq 4$ means "any quantity that is y less than six is less than or equal to four."

▶ $0 \neq 1$ means "zero is not equal to one."

Properties of Inequality

▶ Transitive Property of Order: For all real numbers a, b, and c, if $a < b$ and $b < c$, then $a < c$.

▶ Addition Property of Order: For all real numbers a, b, and c, if $a < b$, then $a + c < b + c$.

▶ Multiplication Property of Order: For all real numbers a, b, and c:

  (A) If $a < b$ and $c > 0$, then $ac < bc$.

  (B) If $a < b$ and $c < 0$, then $ac > bc$.

052 Question Topic

→ **SOLVING INEQUALITIES**

▶ Solving inequalities is much like solving equations, but with one very important exception: *when solving inequalities, reverse the direction of the inequality sign whenever you multiply or divide the inequality by a negative number.*

▶ Use the properties of inequality to isolate the variable on one side of the inequality.

Example

If $3p - 9 < 6$ and $2q + 2 < -6$, and if p and q are integers, then the largest value of $p + q$ is

(A) –2

(B) –1

(C) 0

(D) 1

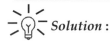 **Solution :**

To find a possible sum for p and q, first solve the inequalities above for p and q respectively.

Solving for p :   Solving for q :

$3p - 9 < 6$ $2q + 2 < -6$

$3p < 15$ $2q < -8$

$p < 5$ $q < -4$

Now add the largest values for p and q. Since $p < 5$, the largest whole-number value for p is 4, and since $q < -4$, the largest whole-number value for q is –5:

$4 + (-5) = -1$

The correct choice is (B).

 TEACHER'S TIP

When solving inequalities, reverse the direction of the inequality sign whenever you multiply or divide the inequality by a negative number.

CHAPTER 4

053 Question Topic

ALGEBRAIC WORD PROBLEMS

When you encounter an algebraic word problem, convert the sentences into algebraic expressions by converting words that indicate relations and operations into symbols. Examples include:

▶ "is" means "="
▶ "more than," "the sum of," and "increased by" mean "+"
▶ "less than" and "the difference" mean "−"
▶ "the product of" means "×"

Example

If $19 + x$ is 6 more than 11, what is the value of $3x$?

(A) −6   (C) 5
(B) −3   (D) 10

 **Solution :**

First convert the problem into a mathematical equation. The word "is" means "is equal to," and "more than" means "plus." The problem becomes the equation:

$19 + x = 6 + 11$

Before we find the value of $3x$, we must solve the equation for x:

$19 + x = 6 + 11$
$x = 17 - 19$
$x = -2$

If $x = -2$, then $3x = 3 \cdot -2 = -6$

The correct choice is (A).

 TEACHER'S TIP

> Convert a word problem into a mathematical equation before attempting to solve it.

SYSTEMS OF EQUATIONS

A system of equations is a set of two or more equations with the same variables. There are two methods for solving systems of equations, which are outlined in the Question Topics below.

As with single variable equations, whenever you see a question involving a system of equations, begin by looking for structures that will help you solve the question. Recognizing these structures will always save you time, and occasionally will be necessary to complete the question.

Systems With No Solutions or Infinite Solutions

Some systems will have either no solutions or infinite solutions. Before trying to solve a system of equations, examine it to see if either of the following cases is applicable:

▶ A system of equations has no solution when two equations contradict each other. For example, the system of equations that consists of the equations $x + y = 1$ and $x + y = 2$ has no solution.

▶ A system of equations consisting of two equations has infinite solutions if it can be demonstrated that the two equations are equivalent to each other. For example, the system of equations that consists of $2x = 8y$ and $4x = 16y$ has an infinite number of solutions.

054 Question Topic

THE ADDITION-OR-SUBTRACTION METHOD

The Addition-or-Subtraction Method requires you to recognize relationships of structure between equations. Apply the following steps when using the Addition-or-Subtraction Method:

1. Determine whether one equation can be transformed through division or multiplication so that either or both coefficients of the variable(s) match(es) the coefficient(s) in the other equation.
2. Multiply or divide one equation so that it matches the other equation as described above.
3. Add or subtract one equation from the other to eliminate one variable.
4. Solve the resulting equation for a single variable.
5. If necessary, substitute the value of the variable into one of the original equations to find the value of the other variable.

> **Example**
>
> If $2x = y + 7$ and $5x = 2y + 15$, what is the value of x?

 Solution :

To find the value of x, we must eliminate y. Multiply the first equation by 2, and then subtract this equation from the second equation to get the answer:

$$5x = 2y + 15 \quad \rightarrow \quad 5x = 2y + 15$$
$$2(2x) = 2(y + 7) \quad \rightarrow \quad -)\ 4x = 2y + 14$$
$$\overline{\hspace{3cm} x = 1}$$

 TEACHER'S TIP

For systems of equations, always begin by looking for structures that will help solve the question.

055 Question Topic

The Substitution Method is very useful when there is no easily discernible relationship between two equations, or when you are presented with equations that only have one variable in common. Apply the following steps when using the Substitution Method:

1. Solve one equation for one of the variables.
2. Substitute the solution from step 1 into the other equation and solve for the other variable.
3. Substitute this value in the equation used in step 1 and solve.

Example

If $\dfrac{x}{y} = \dfrac{7}{3}$ and $\dfrac{y}{z} = \dfrac{4}{5}$, then $\dfrac{x}{z} = ?$

(A) $\dfrac{12}{35}$

(C) $\dfrac{12}{7}$

(B) $\dfrac{5}{7}$

(D) $\dfrac{28}{15}$

Solution :

Since both equations have the y variable, solve both equations for y:

$$y = \frac{3}{7}x \text{, and } y = \frac{4}{5}z$$

According to the Substitution Method:

$$\frac{3}{7}x = \frac{4}{5}z$$

Convert the equation above into the form $\dfrac{x}{z}$:

$$x = \frac{28}{15}z \rightarrow \frac{x}{z} = \frac{28}{15}$$

The correct choice is (D).

056 Question Topic

When working with an equation or inequality with more than one variable, it will often be necessary to solve for one variable. Certain questions will ask you to do only this. To solve for a given variable, transform the equation or inequality so that the variable is isolated on one side of the equation. This variable is then said to be expressed in terms of the other variable(s).

Example

If $6y(3 - 4x) = z$ and $x = -\dfrac{3}{2}$, what is y in terms of z?

(A) $-\dfrac{z}{18}$

(C) $16z$

(B) $-\dfrac{z}{12}$

(D) $\dfrac{z}{54}$

 **Solution:**

Our goal is to isolate y on one side of the equation. First plug in the value for x, then simplify the equation:

$$6y\left[3 - 4\left(-\frac{3}{2}\right)\right] = z$$

$$6y\left(3 + \frac{12}{2}\right) = z$$

$$6y(3 + 6) = z$$

$$6y(9) = z$$

$$54y = z$$

$$y = \frac{z}{54}$$

The correct choice is (D).

> **TEACHER'S TIP**
>
> Always check that minus signs are distributed correctly.

CHAPTER 4

THE SLOPE AND MIDPOINT OF A STRAIGHT LINE

▶ The slope of a non-vertical line that contains point A (x_1, y_1) and B (x_2, y_2) is given by the formula:

$$\text{Slope } (m) = \frac{\text{Rise}}{\text{Run}} = \frac{\text{Change in } y}{\text{Change in } x} = \frac{y_2 - y_1}{x_2 - x_1}$$

▶ Horizontal lines have a slope of zero.

▶ Vertical lines have an undefined slope.

▶ Word problems will often describe slope as "rate of change," or they ask how quickly or slowly a quantity changes given two data points. In these cases, use the slope formula above to get the answer.

▶ The midpoint between two points (x_1, y_1) and (x_2, y_2) is the point $\left[\dfrac{x_1 + x_2}{2}, \dfrac{y_1 + y_2}{2}\right]$

057 Question Topic

PARALLEL AND PERPENDICULAR LINES

▶ If the line l_1 has slope m_1 and line l_2 has slope m_2, then l_1 is parallel to l_2 if and only if $m_1 = m_2$

▶ If the line l_1 has slope m_1 and line l_2 has slope m_2, then l_1 is perpendicular to l_2 if and only if $m_1 \cdot m_2 = -1$.

Example

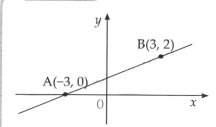

If the point C (not shown), with coordinates $(a, 41)$, lies on the line AB in the figure above, what is the value of a?

Solution :

To solve for a, we must find the slope of AB, which is equal to the slope of BC, as points A, B, and C lie on the same line:

$$\text{Slope } AB = \frac{2 - 0}{3 - (-3)} = \frac{2}{6} = \frac{1}{3}$$

$$\text{Slope } BC = \frac{41 - 2}{a - 3} = \frac{1}{3}$$

$$\frac{39}{a - 3} = \frac{1}{3}$$

$$a - 3 = 117$$

$$a = 120$$

TEACHER'S TIP

The phrase "rate of change" means "slope."

LINEAR FUNCTIONS

▶ The graph of a linear function is always a straight line.

▶ When lines intersect, the point of intersection is the common solution to the equations of the two lines.

▶ A line that rises as it moves from left to right has a positive slope. A line that falls as it moves from left to right has a negative slope.

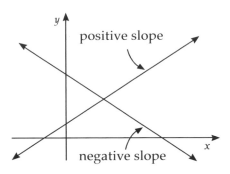

058 Question Topic

➤ THE EQUATION OF A LINE

▶ There are several ways to write the equation of a linear function. Each form highlights certain features of the graph:

- **Point-Slope Form:** $y - y_1 = m(x - x_1)$, or $\dfrac{y - y_1}{x - x_1} = m$. A line in this form has slope m and includes the point (x_1, y_1).

- **Slope-Intercept Form:** $y = mx + b$. A line in this form has slope m and y-intercept b (which is the point $(0, b)$).

- **Standard Form:** $Ax + By = C$. Most SAT math questions will present the equation of a line in this form

- **Intercept Form:** $\dfrac{x}{a} + \dfrac{y}{b} = 1$. A line in this form has x-intercept a and y-intercept b.

Example

What is the equation of a line with y-intercept -3 that is parallel to the line with equation $2x + 5y = 8$?

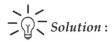 Solution :

Rewrite the equation $2x + 5y = 8$ in slope-intercept form to determine slope:

$$y = -\frac{2}{5}x + \frac{8}{5}$$

Because the lines are parallel, the slope of both lines is $-\frac{2}{5}$.

The slope–intercept form of the line is $y = mx + b \rightarrow y = -\frac{2}{5}x - 3$.

 TEACHER'S TIP

Each form of the equation of a line highlights certain features of the graph.

▶ In any pair of nonzero opposites, such as –8 and 8, one number is negative and the other is positive. The positive number of any pair of nonzero opposites is called the absolute value of each number in the pair. An absolute value is indicated by straight vertical brackets. For example, $|-8| = 8$, and $|8| = 8$.

▶ The absolute value of a number, x, can also be defined as the distance between zero and x on the number line, which always produces a positive value.

▶ The graph of the function $y = |x|$ consists of two parts:
- For $x < 0$, the graph of $f(x) = |x|$ is the line $y = -x$
- For $x \geq 0$, the graph of $f(x) = |x|$ is the line $y = x$

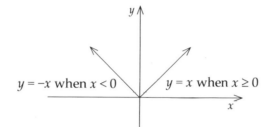

$y = -x$ when $x < 0$ $y = x$ when $x \geq 0$

059 Question Topic

ABSOLUTE VALUE PROBLEMS

▶ The absolute value of zero is zero: $|0| = 0$.
▶ If $|x| = a$, then $x = a$ or $x = -a$.
▶ If $|x| < a$, then $-a < x < a$.
▶ If $|x| > a$, then $x > a$ or $x < -a$.

Example

If x and y are consecutive negative odd integers whose sum is –120, and $x > y$, what is the value of $|y - x|$?

 **Solution:**

Since x and y are consecutive negative odd integers with a sum of 120 and $x > y$, we can write the following equations:
$x = y + 2$
$x + y = -120$
Using substitution, we can write:
$(y + 2) + y = -120 \rightarrow 2y + 2 = -120$.
Subtracting 2 from both sides gives us $2y = -122$.

Divide both sides by 2 to get $y = -61$.

Therefore, $x = -59$.

The value of $|y - x|$ is $|-61 - (-59)| = |-2| = 2$.

TEACHER'S TIP

When solving absolute value problems, start by removing the absolute value sign and solving for the nonzero opposites of the value separately.

QUADRANTS ON THE COORDINATE PLANE

Questions on the SAT Math Test may test your understanding of the four quadrants of a coordinate plane. These quadrants may also be referenced in any question that includes the coordinate plane, including certain questions in trigonometry:

Quadrant I: x and y are positive

Quadrant II: x is negative, y is positive

Quadrant III: x and y are negative

Quadrant IV: x is positive, y is negative

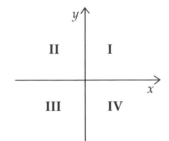

060 *Question Topic*

GRAPHING INEQUALITIES

▶ Inequalities are graphed as regions. First, graph the inequality as if it were an equation. This line separates the points on the plane that satisfy the inequality from those that do not.

▶ If the inequality is > or <, then the points on the boundary line itself do not satisfy the inequality and the line is drawn as broken. If the inequality is ≥ or ≤, the points on the line are included in the region and the boundary is represented as a solid line.

▶ The boundary line divides the plane into two regions. When a linear inequality is expressed in slope-intercept form, and the inequality is < or ≤, then the region is below the line. If the inequality is > or ≥, the region is above the line.

Example

$$2y + x < 1$$
$$y + 3x \geq 5$$

If the system of inequalities above is graphed on a coordinate plane, the solution to the system will fall into which of the following sets of quadrants?

(A) I, II, and IV

(B) III and IV

(C) III only

(D) IV only

 *Solution :*

Change the first inequality to slope-intercept form:

$2y + x < 1$

$2y < -x + 1$

$y < -\dfrac{x}{2} + \dfrac{1}{2}$

The boundary of the region represented by this is inequality is the line $y = -\dfrac{x}{2} + \dfrac{1}{2}$. As the inequality is "less than," the line is broken and the region is below the line.

Now graph the second inequality:

$y + 3x \geq 5$

$y \geq -3x + 5$

The boundary of the region represented by the second inequality is the line $y = -3x + 5$. As the inequality is "greater than or equal to," the line is solid and the region is above the line.

  TEACHER'S TIP

When a linear inequality is expressed in slope-intercept form, and the inequality is < or ≤, then the region is below the line. If the inequality is > or ≥, the region is above the line.

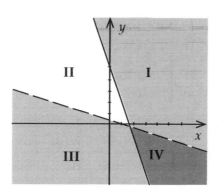

All of the points that satisfy the system are in Quadrant IV. The correct choice is (D).

Word Problems

WORD
PROBLEM

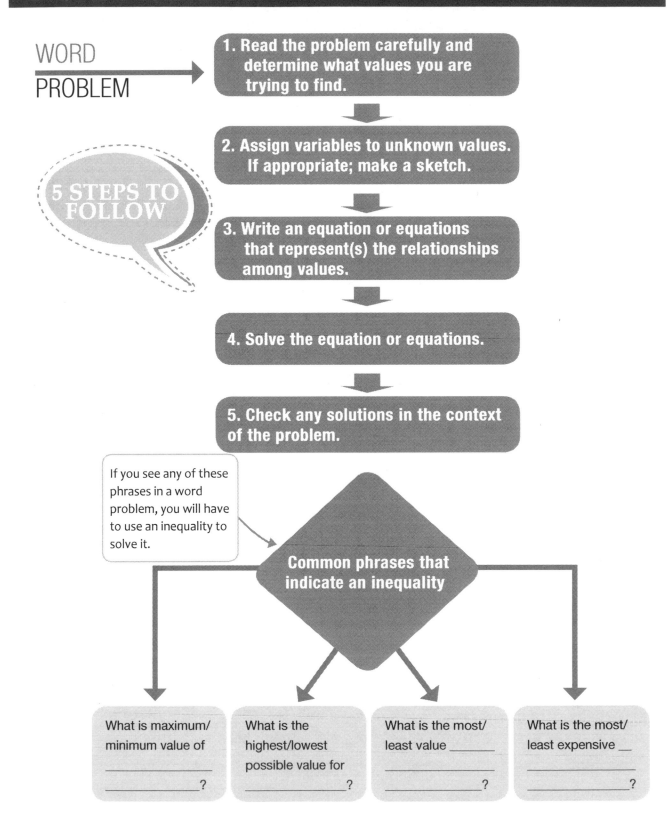

5 STEPS TO FOLLOW

1. Read the problem carefully and determine what values you are trying to find.

2. Assign variables to unknown values. If appropriate; make a sketch.

3. Write an equation or equations that represent(s) the relationships among values.

4. Solve the equation or equations.

5. Check any solutions in the context of the problem.

If you see any of these phrases in a word problem, you will have to use an inequality to solve it.

Common phrases that indicate an inequality

What is maximum/ minimum value of _____ ?

What is the highest/lowest possible value for _____ ?

What is the most/ least value _____ _____ ?

What is the most/ least expensive __ _____ ?

CHAPTER 4

061 Question Topic

Example

The length of a rectangular field is 10 meters greater than three times its width. A roll of fencing that is 180 meters long and 1 meter high will enclose the field with no fencing left over. What are the dimensions, in feet, of the field?

Solution :

1. As you read the problem, determine what you are trying to find. In this problem we are looking for the dimensions (the length and width) of the field.

2. Refer to the length of the field as l and the width of the field as w. Sketch the figure described in the problem:

3. Create equations from the information in the word problem. Using the sentence, "The length of a rectangular field is 10 meters greater than three times its width," we can create the equation:

$$l = 10 + 3w$$

Additionally, the problem tells us, "A roll of fencing that is 180 meters long… will enclose the field with no fencing left over." Thus, the 180–foot roll of fencing will encircle the *perimeter* (P) of the field. The general equation for calculating perimeter is

$$P = 2l + 2w$$

4. Before solving, we need to reduce the number of variables in our equation for perimeter. This can be accomplished through substitution: Since $P = 180$ and $l = 10 + 3w$, we can rewrite the equation for the perimeter of the field as $180 = 2(10 + 3w) + 2w$ and solve for w :

$$180 = 2(10 + 3w) + 2w$$
$$180 = 20 + 6w + 2w$$
$$160 = 8w$$
$$20 = w$$

Knowing the width allows us to find the length. Since $l = 10 + 3w$ and $w = 20$, $l = 10 + 3(20)$, so $l = 70$. Thus, the dimensions of the field in feet are $w = 20$ and $l = 70$.

5. Plugging the solutions into one of the original equations allows us to check our answer.

$$180 = 2(70) + 2(20)$$

062 Question Topic

WORD PROBLEMS IN STATISTICS

Example

The average grade, x, of a class of 30 students was below the passing grade 70. If 10 of the students had raised their test scores by 15 points each, the average for the class would have been passing or above. Which of the following describes all possible values of x?

(A) $67 \le x < 70$ (C) $65 \le x < 70$

(B) $67 < x < 70$ (D) $65 < x < 70$

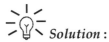 *Solution :*

1. After reading the problem, determine what you are trying to find. The problem asks for the range of average test scores in the class.

2. The problem tells us that the average test score in the class is represented by the variable x. Instead of sketching a diagram, we must determine what formulas the question is asking us to use. Here, we must be able to calculate average (arithmetic mean), which uses the formula:

$$Arithmetic\ mean = \frac{sum\ of\ all\ values\,(test\ scores)}{total\ number\ of\ values\,(test\ scores)}$$

3. Now we must create the equations and/or inequalities that will allow us to find the value(s) of x. The sentence, "The average grade, x, of a class of 30 students was below the passing grade 70" can be summarized by the inequality $x < 70$. The sentence, "If 10 of the students had raised their test scores by 15 points each, the average for the class would have been passing or above" can be expressed using the equation:

$$x + 5 = \frac{30x + (15 \times 10)}{30}$$

The expression $x + 5$ represents the average score after 10 students raised their scores by 15 points each. Ten students each scoring 15 points above their original scores results in an increase in the sum of all scores of 150 points; distributed equally to all students, this results in an average score increase of 5 points. $30x$ represents the number of students (30) times the original average test score. The expression 15×10 represents the 10 students who raised their scores by 15 points each.

4. Now we can solve the problem. We know that the average test score would be equal to or above 70 if 10 students had scored 15 points higher. Therefore, $x + 5 \ge 70$.

   By solving for x, we determine that $x \ge 65$. Since we know that the original average was less than 70, we combine the two inequalities to get the correct answer: $65 \le x < 70$

5. Plugging in any possible value of x into the equation created in step 3 confirms this solution.

063 *Question Topic*

WORD PROBLEMS WITH INEQUALITIES

> **Example**
>
> David can spend no more than $160 on pants and shirts for school. He buys 4 pairs of pants at $24 each. If k represents the dollar amount he can spend on shirts, which of the following inequalities could be used to determine the possible values for k?
>
> (A) $4 \times 24 - k \leq 160$ (C) $4 \times 24 + k \leq 160$
>
> (B) $4 \times 24 - k \geq 160$ (D) $4 \times 24 + k \geq 160$

Solution :

1. After reading the problem, determine what you are trying to find. The problem asks for an inequality that expresses amount of money David can spend on shirts after he buys 4 pairs of pants at $24 each.

2. The problem tells us that the dollar amount David can spend on shirts is represented by k. Before creating an inequlity, sketch the information provided in the word problem:

$$(\boxed{} \times 4) + \boxed{}_{\text{(k)}} \leq 160$$

3/4. Because the answer to this question does not require us to solve an equation or inequality, the "solution step" can be combined with the "creating an equation/inequality step."
Convert the information presented in the problem into an inequality. Start with the sentence, "David can spend no more than $160 on pants and shirts for school." The phrase, "no more than $160" means that his total spending on pants and shirts must be "less than or equal to $160." Then incorporate the infomation in the sentence, "He buys 4 pairs of pants at $24 each." This sentence tells us that he spent 4×24 dollars on pants. The final sentence gives us the rest of the information we need to create an inequality: "If k represents the dollar amount he can spend on shirts, which of the following inequalities could be used to determine the possible values for k?" If k is the amount of money he can spend on shirts and he has already spent 4×24 dollars on pants, we can state:

$$4 \times 24 + k \leq 160$$

Thus, the correct choice is (C).

5. For this problem, checking an answer simply means ensuring that all relevant information in the problem is accounted for in the inequality above.

064 Question Topic

WORD PROBLEMS WITH MULTIPLE VARIABLES

Example

There are eight fewer students on the Debate Club than on the Math Team, and there are only half as many students on the Ecology Force as on the Debate Club. How many students are on the Debate Club if there is a total of 68 students, and if each student can only participate in one activity?

(A) 12

(C) 32

(B) 24

(D) 36

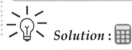 Solution :

1. After reading the problem, determine what you are trying to find. The problem asks for the number of students on the Debate Club.

2. Assign variables to the different clubs: d = Debate Club, m = Math Team, e = Ecology Force.

3. Using the information in the sentence, "There are eight fewer students in the Debate Club than on the Math Team, and there are only half as many students on the Ecology Force as on the Debate Club," we can create the equations:

$$d = m - 8$$
$$e = \left(\frac{1}{2}d\right)$$

As there are a total of 68 students, we can write:

$$68 = d + m + e$$

Next, we must reduce the number of variables we have to deal with. The question wants us to find the number of students in the Debate Club, so substitute d for m and e. Doing so gives us the equation:

$$68 = d + (d + 8) + \left(\frac{1}{2}d\right)$$

4. Now solve for d:

$$68 = 2\frac{1}{2}d + 8$$
$$60 = 2\frac{1}{2}d$$
$$d = 24$$

Thus, the correct choice is (B).

5. Check your solution by using the number of students on the Debate Team to find the number of students in the other clubs; ensure that the total number of students in all clubs equals 68.

CHAPTER 4

065 Question Topic

WORD PROBLEMS WITH RATIONAL EXPRESSIONS

Example

Peter owes his friend p dollars. Last month he paid $\frac{1}{4}$ of the amount owed. This month he paid his friend $\frac{1}{5}$ of the remaining amount plus $15.00. In terms of p, how much money does he still owe?

(A) $\dfrac{p-15}{20}$

(C) $\dfrac{4p-15}{5}$

(B) $\dfrac{3}{4}p-15$

(D) $\dfrac{3}{5}p-15$

Solution:

1. After reading the problem, determine what you are trying to find. The problem asks for the amount of money Peter owes his friend.

2. The problem tells us that the variable p is the total amount owed.

3. Before we determine how much Peter still owes, we must calculate how much he has already repaid. Last month he paid $\frac{1}{4}p$, so the remaining amount owed is

$$p-\frac{1}{4}p=\frac{3}{4}p$$

This month, he paid one fifth of this amount, which is $\left(\frac{1}{5}\right)\left(\frac{3}{4}\right)p$, plus an additional fifteen dollars. Thus, the amount paid this month is

$$\left(\frac{1}{5}\right)\left(\frac{3}{4}\right)p+15=\frac{3}{20}p+15$$

4. The amount he owes is

$$\frac{3}{4}p-\left(\frac{3}{20}p+15\right)=\frac{15}{20}p-\frac{3}{20}p-15=\frac{3}{5}p-15$$

Therefore, the correct choice is (D).

5. Once you have found the solution, double check your work by quickly reviewing each step to ensure that no steps were skipped and that there are no calculation errors.

Quick Practice

1. If $x + 3 = 12$, what is the value of $(x + 7)^2$?

   (A) 144

   (B) 169

   (C) 196

   (D) 256

2. If the function ∇ is defined as $x \nabla y = x^2 + y^2 + xy$ for all integers x and y, what is the value of $-3 \nabla -5$?

   (A) 29

   (B) 38

   (C) 49

   (D) 54

3. If $y = 2x - 3$ and $23y - 15y = 30$, what is the value of x?

   (A) $\frac{3}{2}$

   (B) 2

   (C) $\frac{5}{2}$

   (D) $\frac{27}{8}$

4. If $6(p + q) + 5 = 29$, what is the value of $p + q$?

   (A) 3

   (B) 4

   (C) 5

   (D) 6

5. A sequence begins with the number a_0 and subsequent numbers are determined by taking the previous number, tripling it, and adding six to the product. What is the smallest starting number a_0 in a sequence whose fifth term is greater than 10,000?

   (A) 120

   (B) 121

   (C) 362

   (D) 368

6. Dorothy receives a paycheck every two weeks for $750. Every month, she must pay $800 in rent and $450 in bills. She has also committed to putting 15% of her monthly income into a savings account. What is the most she can allocate to other expenses each month?

   (A) $0

   (B) $25

   (C) $100

   (D) $250

7. If p, q, and r are positive integers, and $pq = 25$ and $qr = 24$, which of the following must be true?

   (A) $p > r > q$

   (B) $q > r > p$

   (C) $q > p > r$

   (D) $r > p > q$

8. If p is $\frac{3}{4}$ of q and q is $\frac{4}{7}$ of r, what is the value of $\frac{p}{r}$?

   (A) $\frac{3}{5}$

   (B) $\frac{3}{7}$

   (C) $\frac{4}{7}$

   (D) $\frac{8}{9}$

9. If $x = y^2$ for any positive integer y, and $z = x^3 + x^2$, what is z in terms of y?

   (A) $y^3 + y^2$

   (B) y^2

   (C) $y^2 + y$

   (D) $y^6 + y^4$

10. If $y = 3x + 2$ and $x > 5$, which of the following represents all possible values of y?

(A) $y < 15$

(B) $y > 15$

(C) $y < 17$

(D) $y > 17$

11. At a bottling company, machine A fills a bottle with spring water and machine B accepts the bottle only if the number of fluid ounces is between $7\frac{9}{10}$ and $8\frac{1}{10}$. If machine B accepts a bottle containing x fluid ounces, which of the following describes all possible values of x?

(A) $|x - 8| = \frac{1}{10}$

(B) $|x + 8| = \frac{1}{10}$

(C) $|x - 8| < \frac{1}{10}$

(D) $|x + 8| < \frac{1}{10}$

12.

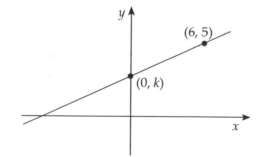

In the figure above, the slope of the line is $\frac{1}{2}$. What is the value of k?

(A) $\frac{1}{2}$

(B) $\frac{3}{2}$

(C) 2

(D) 3

13.

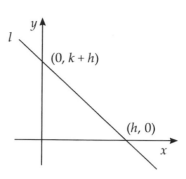

In the figure above, if the slope of line l is k, what is h in terms of k?

(A) $\dfrac{k}{1+k}$

(B) $\dfrac{-k}{1+k}$

(C) $\dfrac{k}{1-k}$

(D) $1+k$

14. What is the y-intercept of the line that passes through the points $(4, -2)$ and $(1, 3)$?

(A) $-\dfrac{8}{5}$

(B) 1

(C) $\dfrac{14}{3}$

(D) 8

15. On the coordinate plane, the line $\overline{AB}$ passes through the origin. If $\overline{AB} \perp \overline{CD}$ and they intersect at $(10, 6)$, where does $\overline{CD}$ cross the x-axis?

(A) $(0, 12)$

(B) $(0, 22\frac{2}{3})$

(C) $(13\frac{3}{5}, 0)$

(D) $(20, 0)$

16.

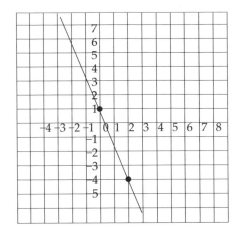

Which of the following equations is graphed in the figure above?

(A) $y = -\dfrac{5}{2}x + 1$

(B) $y = \dfrac{5}{2}x + 1$

(C) $y = -\dfrac{5}{2}x - 1$

(D) $y = \dfrac{5}{2}x - 1$

17. At a computer store, Peter bought USB drives at eight dollars each and David bought USB drives at thirteen dollars each. If they bought a combined eight USB drives and spent $89 between them, how many USBs did David buy?

(A) 2

(B) 3

(C) 4

(D) 5

18. A politician proposes a flat-rate tax scheme that would use the same rate for every taxpayer regardless of income. He presents this scheme in the form of an equation, $T = 200 - 0.25x$, where T is the total taxes collected and x is a taxpayer's annual income. What is the significance of the value 200 in this equation?

(A) The taxes assigned to a person who has an income of zero

(B) The number of taxable days in the year

(C) The administrative costs of processing a single payer's taxes

(D) The amount of tax collected per $1,000 of income

19. If $12f + 5g = 15$ and $8f + 15g = 17$, what is the value of $f + g$?

(A) $\dfrac{2}{3}$

(B) $\dfrac{3}{2}$

(C) $\dfrac{5}{2}$

(D) $\dfrac{8}{5}$

20. James has $x + 23$ apples, Scott has $x + 25$ apples, and John has $x + 12$ apples. All of their apples are put into three empty boxes with exactly y apples in each box. What is the value of y in terms of x?

(A) $x + 20$

(B) $3x + 20$

(C) $3x + 60$

(D) $3x + 10$

CHAPTER 4

MASTERING SAT ALGEBRA

ANSWERS

&

EXPLANATIONS

1-20

Answers & Explanations...
Mastering SAT Algebra

1.	Ⓓ	6.	Ⓑ	11.	Ⓒ	16.	Ⓐ
2.	Ⓒ	7.	Ⓐ	12.	Ⓒ	17.	Ⓓ
3.	Ⓓ	8.	Ⓑ	13.	Ⓑ	18.	Ⓐ
4.	Ⓑ	9.	Ⓓ	14.	Ⓒ	19.	Ⓓ
5.	Ⓑ	10.	Ⓓ	15.	Ⓒ	20.	Ⓐ

1) ➤ D

$x + 3 = 12$

$x + 3 + 4 = 12 + 4$, so $x = 9$

$x + 7 = 16$

$(x + 7)^2 = 256$

2) ➤ C

$x \nabla y = x^2 + y^2 + xy$

$-3 \nabla -5 = (-3)^2 + (-5)^2 + (-3)(-5)$

$= 9 + 25 + 15 = 49$

3) ➤ D

$23y - 15y = 30 \rightarrow 8y = 30 \rightarrow y = \frac{15}{4}$

Substitute this result into the first equation:

$y = 2x - 3$

$\frac{15}{4} = 2x - 3 \rightarrow 2x = \frac{27}{4} \rightarrow x = \frac{27}{8}$

4) ➤ B

$6(p + q) + 5 = 29$

$6(p + q) = 24$

$p + q = 4$

5) ➤ B

The sequence begins with the number a_0, so the fifth term of the sequence is a_4:

$a_1 = 3a_0 + 6$

$a_2 = 3(3a_0 + 6) + 6 = 9a_0 + 24$

$a_3 = 3(9a_0 + 24) + 6 = 27a_0 + 78$

$a_4 = 3(27a_0 + 78) + 6 = 81a_0 + 240$

The fifth term must be greater than 10,000:

$81a_0 + 240 > 10,000$

$81a_0 > 9,760$

$a_0 > 120.5$

As a_0 is an integer, the smallest starting value is 121.

6) ➤ B

Monthly income $= \dfrac{\$750}{2\,weeks} \times \dfrac{4\,weeks}{1\,month} = \$1,500$

Expenses = Rent + Bills = $800 + $450 = $1,250

Savings = (0.15)(1500) = $225

Remaining income = $1,500 - (800 + 450 + 225)$

$= \$25$

7) ➡ A

$$q = \frac{25}{p} = \frac{24}{r}$$

As the numbers 24 and 25 have no factors in common, and all three numbers are integers, we can infer that $p = 25$, $r = 24$, and $q = 1$. Therefore, $p > r > q$ must be true.

8) ➡ B

$$p = \frac{3}{4}q \rightarrow q = \frac{4p}{3}$$

Also, $q = \frac{4r}{7}$

We can write: $\frac{4p}{3} = \frac{4r}{7} \rightarrow \frac{p}{r} = \frac{3}{7}$

9) ➡ D

$$x = y^2$$
$$z = x^3 + x^2$$

Substitute y for x in the second equation:

$$z = (y^2)^3 + (y^2)^2$$
$$z = y^6 + y^4$$

10) ➡ D

$$y = 3x + 2$$
$$x > 5$$

Therefore,

$$y > 3(5) + 2 \rightarrow y > 17$$

11) ➡ C

$$7.9 < x < 8.1$$

Subtract 8 from the inequality:

$$-0.1 < x - 8 < 0.1$$

This implies that: $x - 8 > -0.1$ for $x < 8$ and $x - 8 < 0.1$ for $x > 8$.

These two inequalities can be combined into an expression using an absolute value:

$$|x - 8| < 0.1$$

12) ➡ C

The value of k is the y-intercept, which is equivalent to the value of b in the slope intercept form of a line. The slope, m, is given in the question as $\frac{1}{2}$. Using the point specified on the graph:

$$y = mx + b \rightarrow 5 = \frac{1}{2}(6) + b \rightarrow b = 2$$

13) ➡ B

The slope of l is k, and the y-intercept of l is $k + h$. The equation of the line is:

$$y = kx + (k + h)$$

Plug in the point $(h, 0)$:

$$0 = kh + k + h$$

$$kh + h = -k$$

$$h(k + 1) = -k$$

$$h = \frac{-k}{1 + k}$$

14) ➡ C

Determine the slope of the line:

$$m = \frac{3 - (-2)}{1 - 4} = \frac{5}{-3}$$

Solve for b:

$$y = -\frac{5}{3}x + b$$

$$3 = -\frac{5}{3}(1) + b$$

$$b = \frac{14}{3}$$

15) C

Only choices (C) and (D) are points on the x-axis. $\overline{AB}$ passes through the points $(0, 0)$ and $(10, 6)$. The slope of $\overline{AB}$ is:

$$m_{AB} = \frac{6}{10} = \frac{3}{5}$$

The slope of $\overline{CD}$ is the negative reciprocal of the slope of $\overline{AB}$:

$$m_{CD} = -\frac{5}{3}$$

Since we know $\overline{CD}$ passes through $(10, 6)$, we can determine the equation for the line and then its x-intercept:

$$6 = -\frac{5}{3}(10) + b \;\rightarrow\; b = \frac{68}{3}$$

$$y = -\frac{5}{3}x + \frac{68}{3}$$

As we are looking for the x-intercept, we subsititute zero for y:

$$0 = -\frac{5}{3}x + \frac{68}{3}$$

$$5x = 68$$

$$x = 13\frac{3}{5}$$

16) A

The line passes through the point $(0, 1)$ so the y-intercept is 1. Eliminate (C) and (D). From the graph, we see that the slope of the line is negative. We can eliminate (B). The correct choice is (A).

17) D

x = number of \$8 USBs

y = number of \$13 USBs

$x + y = 8$

$8x + 13y = 89$

Solve for y:

$8(8 - y) + 13y = 89$

$64 - 8y + 13y = 89$

$5y = 25$

$y = 5$

18) A

The variable x represents a taxpayer's annual income. When $x = 0$, $T = 200$. Choices (B) and (C) are incorrect because there is no mention of administrative costs or taxable days in the question. Choice (D) is incorrect because the equation gives the amount of taxes collected in terms of a taxpayer's total income, not per \$1,000 of income.

19) D

$12f + 5g = 15$

$8f + 15g = 17$

Multiply the first equation by a factor of 3 :

$36f + 15g = 45$

Subtract the second equation in the system from the equation above:

$$\begin{array}{r} 36f + 15g = 45 \\ -\quad 8f + 15g = 17 \\ \hline 28f = 28 \end{array}$$

$28f = 28 \;\rightarrow\; f = 1$

Solve for g:

$$12(1) + 5g = 15 \rightarrow 5g = 3 \rightarrow g = \frac{3}{5}$$

Finally, $f + g = \dfrac{8}{5}$

20) A

Total number of apples $= (x + 23) + (x + 25) + (x + 12)$

$$= 3x + 60$$

The number of apples in each box, y, is:

$$y = \frac{3x + 60}{3} = x + 20$$

CHAPTER 5

Mastering
Advanced Topics In Math

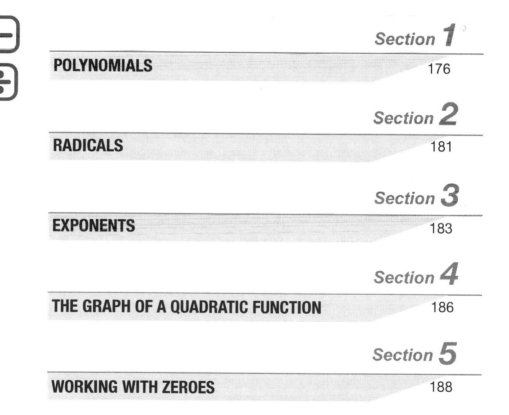

Fundamental Concepts and Techniques

POLYNOMIALS

You will encounter the following terms on the SAT:

▶ Monomial: a polynomial with one term; for example, $5x$ or $6b^2$

▶ Binomial: a polynomial with two terms; for example, $3x + 2y$ or $2x^2 + y^2$

▶ Trinomial: a polynomial with three terms; for example, $2x + 3y + 5z$ or $x^2y + 3y + z^2$

▶ Polynomial: a monomial or any combination of two or more monomials. Each of the six terms above, and any combination that can be formed from them, are referred to as polynomials.

066 Question Topic

ADDITION AND SUBTRACTION OF POLYNOMIALS

Terms must consist of the same variables raised to the same powers in order to add or subtract them. For example: $ax^n + bx^m + cx^n + dx^m = (a + c)x^n + (b + d)x^m$

Example

Simplify the expression $(9n^2 + 5n) + (n^2 - 6n + 12)$.

 **Solution :**

The expression can be rearranged to:

$(9n^2 + n^2) + [5n + (-6n)] + 12$

$10n^2 - n + 12$

TEACHER'S TIP

Polynomial operations, like numerical calculations, are subject to the order of operations.

067 Question Topic

MULTIPLICATION OF POLYNOMIALS

▶ When multiplying terms of the same variable, add the exponents.
▶ When raising a term to a power, multiply exponents.
▶ When multiplying a polynomial by a polynomial, multiply each term in one polynomial by each term in the other, and add similar terms.

Example

Simplify the expression $(y + 2)(y^3 - 5y^2 + 2)$.

 **Solution:**

$(y + 2)(y^3 - 5y^2 + 2)$
$= y(y^3 - 5y^2 + 2) + 2(y^3 - 5y^2 + 2)$
$= y^4 - 5y^3 + 2y + 2y^3 - 10y^2 + 4$
$= y^4 - 5y^3 + 2y^3 - 10y^2 + 2y + 4$
$= y^4 - 3y^3 - 10y^2 + 2y + 4$

 TEACHER'S TIP

Keep careful track of minus signs.

068 Question Topic

DIVISION OF POLYNOMIALS

▶ When dividing monomials, subtract exponents.
▶ When dividing a polynomial by a monomial, distribute the monomial across the terms of the polynomial.

Example

What is the quotient of $\dfrac{6p^3 - 3p^2 - 4p + 15}{6p}$?

 **Solution:**

$$\frac{6p^3 - 3p^2 - 4p + 15}{6p} = \frac{6p^3}{6p} - \frac{3p^2}{6p} - \frac{4p}{6p} + \frac{15}{6p} = p^2 - \frac{1}{2}p - \frac{2}{3} + \frac{5}{2p}$$

 TEACHER'S TIP

When subtracting polynomials, subtract coefficients. When dividing polynomials, subtract exponents.

069 Question Topic

When dividing a polynomial by a polynomial:

▶ Set up the division, adding zero coefficients so that every power is included.

$$\frac{DIVIDEND}{DIVISOR} = QUOTIENT \qquad DIVISOR\overline{)DIVIDEND}^{QUOTIENT}$$

▶ The quotient is the expression that is multiplied by the divisor to give the next term of the dividend.

▶ The product of the quotient and the divisor **is subtracted** from the next two terms of the dividend.

▶ Remember that your remainder is a quotient of the divisor.

Example

If the expression $\dfrac{x^3 + 8x + 10}{x+2}$ is rewritten in the equivalent form $A - \dfrac{B}{x+2}$, and B is an integer, what is the value of B?

Solution :

First set up the operation:

$$x+2\overline{)x^3 + 0x^2 + 8x + 10}$$

Note the zero coefficient that has been added to the term x^2 so that all powers of x are included. Next, determine the first term of the quotient:

$$
\begin{array}{r}
x^2 \\
x+2\overline{)x^3 + 0x^2 + 8x + 10} \\
\underline{x^3 + 2x^2} \\
-2x^2
\end{array}
$$

Complete the operation:

$$
\begin{array}{r}
x^2 - 2x + 12 \\
x+2\overline{)x^3 + 0x^2 + 8x + 10} \\
\underline{x^3 + 2x^2} \\
-2x^2 + 8x \\
\underline{-2x^2 - 4x} \\
12x + 10 \\
\underline{12x + 24} \\
-14
\end{array}
$$

TEACHER'S TIP

Add zero coefficients if necessary so that every power is included.

The quotient is $x^2 - 2x + 12 - \dfrac{14}{x+2}$. If this is written in the form $A - \dfrac{B}{x+2}$, $B = 14$.

CHAPTER 5

070 Question Topic

→ **FACTORING POLYNOMIALS**

When factoring a polynomial, always look first for a Greatest Common Factor (GCF). The GCF is the variable with the highest power that is common to all terms in a polynomial. If there is a GCF, factor it first. For example, the GCF of the polynomial $x^4 + x^3 - x^2$ is x^2. The factored form is $x^2(x^2 + x - 1)$.

Example

Factor the polynomial $6x^4 - 15x^3 + 3x^2$.

 **Solution :**

Identify the Greatest Common Factor.
The GCF is $3x^2$. The factored form is:
$6x^4 - 15x^3 + 3x^2 = 3x^2(2x^2 - 5x + 1)$

TEACHER'S TIP

When factoring a polynomial, always look for a GCF first.

071 Question Topic

→ **FACTORING QUADRATICS 1**

▶ A quadratic trinomial of the form $ax^2 + bx + c$ for which $a = 1$ can be factored in the following way: If $x^2 + bx + c = x^2 + (p + q)x + pq$, where $b = p + q$ and $c = pq$, then the factored form is $(x + p)(x + q)$.

▶ Try using the schema below (or some similar diagram) to factor quadratics. Begin by writing the product pq (coefficient c) in the top segment and the sum $p + q$ (coefficient b) in the bottom segment. Then determine the values of p and q by observation:

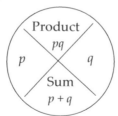

TEACHER'S TIP

Example

Factor the quadratic trinomial $x^2 - 5x + 6$.

 **Solution :**

$x^2 - 5x + 6 = x^2 + [(-2) + (-3)]x + (-2)(-3)$
The factored form is $(x - 2)(x - 3)$.

Using the diagram above for the example would give:

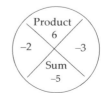

072 Question Topic

→ **FACTORING QUADRATICS 2**

A quadratic trinomial of the form $ax^2 + bx + c$ for which $a \neq 1$ can be factored in the following way:

If $ax^2 + bx + c = pqx^2 + (ps + qr)x + rs$, where $a = pq$, $b = ps + qr$, and $c = rs$, then the factored form is $(px + r)(qx + s)$.

Example

Factor the quadratic trinomial $5x^2 + x - 4$.

 **Solution :**

$5x^2 + x - 4 = (5)(1)x^2 + [(5)(1) + (1)(-4)]x + (-4)(1)$

The factored form is $(5x - 4)(x + 1)$.

 TEACHER'S TIP

Quadratics can be solved by factoring or using the quadratic equation:

$$x = \frac{-b \pm \sqrt{b^2 - 4ac}}{2a}$$

073 Question Topic

→ **SPECIAL PRODUCTS**

▶ A polynomial of the form $a^2 - b^2$ is called a *difference of squares* and can be factored as:
$a^2 - b^2 = (a - b)(a + b)$.

▶ The square of a binomial can be expanded as follows:
- Binomial sum squared: $(a + b)^2 = a^2 + 2ab + b^2$
- Binomial difference squared: $(a - b)^2 = a^2 - 2ab + b^2$

▶ The cube of a binomial can be expanded as follows:
- Binomial sum cubed: $(a + b)^3 = a^3 + 3a^2b + 3ab^2 + b^3$
- Binomial difference cubed: $(a - b)^3 = a^3 - 3a^2b + 3ab^2 - b^3$

Example

If $(p + q)^2 = 82$ and $pq = 12$, what is the value of $p^2 + q^2$?

(A) 8   (C) 43
(B) 36   (D) 58

 TEACHER'S TIP

The difference of squares is the most important special product to remember.

 **Solution :**

Use the expansion of a binomial squared to expand the first equation: $(p + q)^2 = p^2 + 2pq + q^2 = 82$

We can then substitute $pq = 12$ into the equation above and solve: $p^2 + q^2 + 2(12) = 82$

$p^2 + q^2 = 82 - 24 = 58$

The correct choice is (D).

▶ A number, b, is called the square root of a positive real number, a, if the equation $b^2 = a$ is true. It follows that the equation $b = \pm\sqrt{a}$ is also true.

▶ The symbol $\sqrt{\ }$ is called a radical and, as above, is used to indicate a square root. A number or expression under a radical is referred to as a radicand.

▶ For any real number a, $\sqrt{a^2} = |a|$

▶ A square root is also denoted by an exponent of value $\frac{1}{2}$, that is, $a^{\frac{1}{2}} = \sqrt{a}$

   • Product Property of Square Roots: For any numbers a and b, where $a \geq 0$ and $b \geq 0$, $\sqrt{ab} = \sqrt{a} \cdot \sqrt{b}$

   • Quotient Property of Square Roots: For any numbers a and b, where $a \geq 0$ and $b > 0$, $\sqrt{\dfrac{a}{b}} = \dfrac{\sqrt{a}}{\sqrt{b}}$

074 Question Topic

EQUATIONS WITH RADICALS

▶ When you encounter an equation that contains a variable as a radicand, begin by rewriting the equation so that the radical containing the variable is isolated on one side of the equation.

▶ Next, square both sides of the equation to remove the radical.

▶ The resultant equation is not necessarily equivalent to the original equation. All solutions must be checked against the original equation to ensure that they are not extraneous. In general terms, an extraneous solution is a solution that works with a transformed or simplified equation but that does not work with the original equation. In the case of radicals, an extraneous solution will sometimes be a solution that results in a negative radicand, or otherwise not satisfy the equation.

Example

Solve $\sqrt{5x - 4} - x = -2$.

Solution:

$\sqrt{5x-4} - x = -2 \rightarrow \sqrt{5x-4} = x - 2 \rightarrow (\sqrt{5x-4})^2 = (x-2)^2$
$5x - 4 = x^2 - 4x + 4 \rightarrow 0 = x^2 - 9x + 8 \rightarrow 0 = (x-8)(x-1)$

Therefore, $x = 1$ and $x = 8$.

Next, we must test for extraneous solutions. First, check the solution $x = 8$ by plugging into the original equation:

$\sqrt{5(8)-4} - 8 = -2 \rightarrow \sqrt{36} - 8 = -2 \rightarrow 6 - 8 = -2$

Yes, $x = 8$ is a solution to the equation.

Next, we test the second solution, $x = 1$:

$\sqrt{5(1)-4} - 1 = -2 \rightarrow \sqrt{1} - 1 = -2 \rightarrow 1 - 1 \neq -2$

No, $x = 1$ is not a solution to the equation. It is extraneous.

💬 **TEACHER'S TIP**

All solutions must be checked against the original equation to ensure that they are not extraneous.

075 Question Topic

→ **SIMPLIFYING RATIONAL EXPRESSIONS**

► A rational expression, or algebraic function, is a quotient of two polynomials. The following are examples of rational expressions: $\frac{2x+1}{x^2}$, $\frac{2x^2+3x-5}{x^2+4}$, $\frac{ab^2}{a^2+a}$

► You cannot divide by zero. Solutions that make the denominator equal to zero are examples of extraneous solutions.

Example

Simplify $\frac{2x^2+x-3}{2-x-x^2}$.

 **Solution:**

TEACHER'S TIP

A solution is considered extraneous if it contains a zero in the denominator, or if it contains a variable that results in a zero in the denominator.

$$\frac{2x^2+x-3}{2-x-x^2} \rightarrow \frac{2x^2+x-3}{-x^2-x+2} \rightarrow \frac{2x^2+x-3}{-(x^2+x-2)} \rightarrow \frac{(x-1)(2x+3)}{-(x-1)(x+2)} \rightarrow -\frac{2x+3}{x+2}$$

The final form $-\frac{2x+3}{x+2}$, is the original expression in simplified form. We must, however, check all rational expressions for extraneous solutions. According to the original equation, the variable x cannot take the values 1 and −2 because these values make the denominator of the equation equal to zero. We write the final form as: $-\frac{2x+3}{x+2}$, for $x \neq 1, -2$.

076 Question Topic

→ **CONJUGATES AND RATIONALIZING THE DENOMINATOR**

► If we have a fraction with a radical in the denominator, we are required to manipulate the expression so that the radical in the denominator is removed. This is called simplifying the expression or rationalizing the denominator.

► If the denominator is a monomial, multiply the entire expression by the radical in the denominator over itself.

► If the denominator is a binomial, use the conjugate of the denominator over itself to rationalize the denominator. Conjugates are defined as follows: if b and d are both nonnegative, then the binomials $a\sqrt{b}+c\sqrt{d}$ and $a\sqrt{b}-c\sqrt{d}$ are called conjugates of one another. If, a, b, c and d are integers, the product of conjugates follows the difference of squares and their product will be an integer.

Example

Simplify the expression $\frac{3}{5-2\sqrt{7}}$

 *Solution :*

$$\frac{3}{5-2\sqrt{7}} = \frac{3}{\left(5-2\sqrt{7}\right)} \times \frac{\left(5+2\sqrt{7}\right)}{\left(5+2\sqrt{7}\right)} = \frac{3\left(5+2\sqrt{7}\right)}{\left(5\right)^2 - \left(2\sqrt{7}\right)^2}$$

$$= \frac{15+6\sqrt{7}}{25-28}$$

$$= \frac{15+6\sqrt{7}}{-3}$$

$$= -5-2\sqrt{7}$$

 TEACHER'S TIP

The binomials $a\sqrt{b}+c\sqrt{d}$ and $a\sqrt{b}-c\sqrt{d}$ are called conjugates of one another. Their product is a difference of squares.

EXPONENTS

▶ **Fractional Exponents:** Fractional exponents are equivalent to roots. A fractional exponent of $\frac{1}{2}$ is equivalent to a square root; a fractional exponent of $\frac{1}{3}$ is equivalent to a cube root; and so on. In mathematical notation, we can write, $x^{\frac{1}{2}} = \sqrt{x}$, and $x^{\frac{1}{3}} = \sqrt[3]{x}$

▶ **Negative Exponents:** Negative exponents are equivalent to the reciprocal of the base (the variable or number raised to some power) raised to the absolute value of the exponent. For example, $x^{-2} = \frac{1}{x^2}$

▶ **Zero Exponents:** Any base raised to the power zero equals 1. That is, $x^0 = 1$

▶ **Exponential Equations:** An exponential equation is an equation that contains a term with a variable in the exponent. For example, $a^x = b$ is an exponential equation, where a and b are any two real numbers.

077 Question Topic

→ **TRANSFORMATIONS**

The operations of exponents are summarized below. Assume all bases and denominators are nonzero.

• $(a^m) \cdot (a^n) = a^{m+n}$ → $(2^3) \cdot (2^4) = 2^7 = 128$	• $\dfrac{a^m}{a^n} = a^{m-n}$ → $\dfrac{3^6}{3^3} = 3^3 = 27$
• $(a^m)^n = a^{m \cdot n}$ → $(6^2)^3 = 6^6$	• $\left(\dfrac{a}{b}\right)^n = \dfrac{a^n}{b^n}$ → $\left(\dfrac{2}{x}\right)^3 = \dfrac{2^3}{x^3} = \dfrac{8}{x^3}$
• $\left(\dfrac{a}{b}\right)^{-n} = \dfrac{a^{-n}}{b^{-n}} = \dfrac{b^n}{a^n}$ → $\left(\dfrac{2}{x}\right)^{-3} = \dfrac{2^{-3}}{x^{-3}} = \dfrac{x^3}{2^3} = \dfrac{x^3}{8}$	• $\left(\dfrac{a}{b}\right)^0 = \dfrac{a^0}{b^0} = 1$ → $\dfrac{x^0}{2^0} = 1$
• $(ab)^n = a^n \cdot b^n$ → $(2x)^3 = 2^3 \cdot x^3 = 8x^3$	• $a^{\frac{m}{n}} = \sqrt[n]{a^m}$ → $(2x)^{\frac{2}{3}} = \sqrt[3]{(2x)^2}$

Example

Simplify the expression $\left(\dfrac{2p^2q^{-3}}{3r^{-4}s}\right)^{-2}$.

 **Solution :**

$$\left(\frac{2p^2q^{-3}}{3r^{-4}s}\right)^{-2} = \frac{\left(2p^2q^{-3}\right)^{-2}}{\left(3r^{-4}s\right)^{-2}} = \frac{2^{-2}p^{-4}q^{6}}{3^{-2}r^{8}s^{-2}} = \frac{\dfrac{1}{4}\cdot\dfrac{1}{p^4}\cdot q^6}{\dfrac{1}{9}\cdot r^8 \cdot \dfrac{1}{s^2}} = \frac{9q^6s^2}{4p^4r^8}$$

💬 **TEACHER'S TIP**

Fractional exponents are equivalent to roots. Negative exponents indicate the reciprocal.

FUNCTIONS AND THEIR GRAPHS

► A **function** is a set of ordered pairs with a consistent relation between the two values of each pair.
► The equation $y = f(x)$ represents the graph of a function.
► The domain of $y = f(x)$ is the set of *x-coordinates* on the graph of the function.
► The range of $y = f(x)$ is the set of *y-coordinates* on the graph of the function.
► The zeros of $y = f(x)$ are equivalent to the *x-intercepts* of the graph.

078 Question Topic

→ TRANSFORMATIONS

A **transformation** of a function is its conversion to another function by the introduction of a constant. The result is called a translation. The most common transformations and translations are summarized below:

When the function $f(x)$ is changed to:	The graph is changed:	When the function $f(x)$ is changed to:	The graph is changed:
$y = f(x + a),\ a > 0$	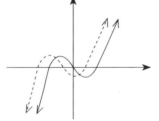	$y = c[f(x)],\ c > 1$	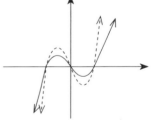
The graph shifts to the left a units. Minimum and maximum values stay the same. Zeros are changed.		The graph is stretched vertically. Minimum and maximum values are changed. Zeros stay the same.	
$y = f(x - a),\ a > 0$	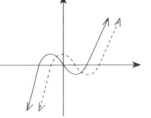	$y = c[f(x)],\ 0 < c < 1$	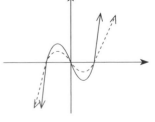
The graph shifts to the right a units. Minimum and maximum values stay the same. Zeros are changed.		The graph is shrunk vertically. Minimum and maximum values are changed. Zeros stay the same.	

CHAPTER 5

When the function $f(x)$ is changed to:	The graph is changed:	When the function $f(x)$ is changed to:	The graph is changed:
$y = f(x) + a,\ a > 0$ 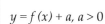	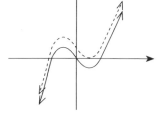	$y = f(cx),\ c > 1$	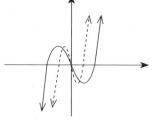
The graph shifts upwards *a* units. Minimum values, maximum values, and zeros are changed.		The graph is shrunk horizontally. Minimum and maximum values are the same. Zeros are changed.	
$y = f(x) - a,\ a > 0$	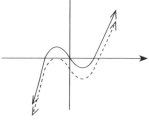	$y = f(cx),\ 0 < c < 1$ 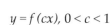	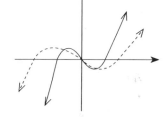
The graph shifts downward *a* units. Minimum values, maximum values, and zeros are changed.		The graph is stretched horizontally. Minimum and maximum values are the same. Zeros are changed.	
$y = -f(x)$	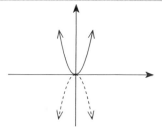	$y = f(-x)$	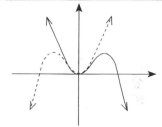
The graph is reflected across the *x*-axis.		The graph is reflected across the *y*-axis.	

Example

The graph of function $f(x)$ is translated 3 units to the left, 4 units upwards, and stretched vertically by a factor of 2, to produce a new function. If $f(x) = x^2 - 12x + 9$, what is the new function?

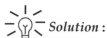 **Solution :**

Approach this question by considering the translation step-by-step:

- Translation 3 units to the left produces the new function f':

$$f'(x) = f(x + 3) = (x + 3)^2 - 12(x + 3) + 9$$
$$= x^2 + 6x + 9 - 12x - 36 + 9 = x^2 - 6x - 18$$

- Translation 4 units upwards produces the new function f'':

$$f''(x) = f'(x) + 4 = x^2 - 6x - 18 + 4 = x^2 - 6x - 14$$

- A vertical stretch by factor of two produces the function f''':

$$f'''(x) = 2 \cdot f''(x) = 2(x^2 - 6x - 14)$$
$$f'''(x) = 2x^2 - 12x - 28$$

The new function is $f'''(x) = 2x^2 - 12x - 28$.

 TEACHER'S TIP

Approach translation questions step-by-step.

The graph of a quadratic function is a parabola. The characteristics of this graph can be determined from either the standard form or the vertex form of the equation:

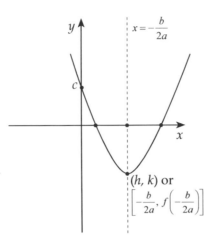

▶ For the standard form, $y = ax^2 + bx + c$

- The vertex is $\left[-\dfrac{b}{2a}, f\left(-\dfrac{b}{2a}\right)\right]$

- The axis of symmetry is $x = -\dfrac{b}{2a}$

- The y-intercept is $(0, c)$

- The x-intercepts are $\left(\dfrac{-b - \sqrt{b^2 - 4ac}}{2a}, 0\right)$ and $\left(\dfrac{-b + \sqrt{b^2 - 4ac}}{2a}, 0\right)$

▶ For the vertex form, $y = a(x - h)^2 + k$:

- The vertex is (h, k)

079 Question Topic

TRANSFORMATIONS ON QUADRATIC FUNCTIONS

▶ If the quadratic $y = x^2$ is transformed to $y = (x + h)^2$, the parabola is translated to the left h units. If the same quadratic is transformed to $y = (x - h)^2$, the parabola is translated to the right h units.

▶ If the quadratic $y = x^2$ is transformed to $y = x^2 + k$, the parabola is translated vertically k units.

▶ If the quadratic $y = x^2$ is transformed to $y = ax^2$, the parabola is scaled vertically by a factor of a units.

Example

The path of a basketball can be modeled by the equation

$y = -4x^2 + 16x + 6$, where x represents time and y represents the height of the basketball. Which of the following is the maximum height reached by the ball?

      (A) 18   (C) 22

      (B) 20   (D) 24

Solution :

First, change the standard form of the quadratic to the vertex form by completing the square:

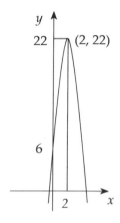

TEACHER'S TIP

The vertex form is best for translations of quadratic functions.

$y = -4x^2 + 16x + 6$
$ = -4(x^2 - 4x) + 6$
$ = -4(x^2 - 4x + 4 - 4) + 6$
$ = -4(x - 2)^2 + 16 + 6$
$ = -4(x - 2)^2 + 22$

From the vertex form, we can determine that the vertex of the parabola is (2, 22). When $a < 0$ for a quadratic equation written in the form $a(x - h)^2 + k$, the graph of the parabola opens downward. Since $a = -4$, the parabola is inverted, as we would expect since the function models the path of a ball in the air. The maximum height of the basketball is 22 meters. The correct choice is (C).

WORKING WITH ZEROES

▶ A zero for a polynomial, also called a solution to that polynomial, is a value such that when it is plugged into the polynomial, the value of the polynomial is zero.
▶ Zeros are related to factors of polynomials as follows: if a is a zero of a polynomial, then $(x - a)$ is a factor of the polynomial.
▶ Zeros represent the values at which the graph of the polynomial crosses the x-axis; that is, the zeros are the x-values at which $y = 0$.

080 Question Topic

→ **WORD PROBLEMS WITH QUADRATICS**

When working on a word problem involving a quadratic, follow these steps:
1. Read the question carefully.
2. Determine what the question is asking you to find, and note information that is given. If possible, make a sketch.
3. Assign a variable and write an equation that represents the relationships between the numbers that are given in the question.
4. Solve the equation.
5. Check solutions in the context of the problem.

Example

A landscaper designed a rectangular grass plot with a length three meters less than four times its width. If the plot has an area of 175 square meters, what is the width of the plot?

Solution :

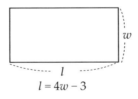

$l = 4w - 3$

If x is the width of the plot, then the length of the plot is $4x - 3$. Since the area is 175 square meters, we can write the relationships as: $x(4x - 3) = 175$

Expand the parentheses: $4x^2 - 3x - 175 = 0$

Use the quadratic formula: $x = \dfrac{-b \pm \sqrt{b^2 - 4ac}}{2a}$

$x = \dfrac{-(-3) \pm \sqrt{(-3)^2 - 4(4)(-175)}}{2(4)} = \dfrac{3 \pm \sqrt{9 + 2800}}{8}$

$= \dfrac{3 \pm \sqrt{2809}}{8} = \dfrac{3 \pm 53}{8}$

$x = \dfrac{56}{8} = 7$ and $x = \dfrac{50}{8} = -6.25$

> ### TEACHER'S TIP
>
> Zeros represent the values at which the graph of the polynomial crosses the x-axis because they are x-values for which $y = 0$.

Check solutions in the context of the problem. Since the width of a field cannot be a negative value, the solution
$x = -6.25$ is not relevant. The width of the field is 7 meters.

081 *Question Topic*

An exponential function is a function of the form $f(x) = b^x$ in which the input variable x occurs as an exponent. A function of the form $f(x) = a \cdot b^x$ is also considered an exponential function.

Two common examples of exponential functions are exponential growth (interest, population, etc.), and exponential decay (finances, half-life, and chemistry). When working with an exponential function , the function is exponentially growing if $a > 0$ and $b > 1$. The function above is exponentially decaying if $a > 0$ and $1 > b > 0$.

Example

A space probe measures the radioactivity of a meteorite at M units. If the meteorite has a radiation half-life of 2 days, how can we describe its radioactivity in terms of d, days after the initial measurement?

(A) $f(d) = M(4)^{2d}$

(B) $f(d) = M\left(\dfrac{1}{2}\right)^{\frac{d}{2}}$

(C) $f(d) = d\left(\dfrac{1}{2}\right)^{\frac{1}{M}}$

(D) $f(d) = M\left(\dfrac{1}{4}\right)^{d}$

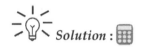 *Solution :*

M is the starting radioactivity, which is represented by "a" in the exponential function $f(x) = a(b)^x$ listed in the table on the previous page. Every two days, $\dfrac{1}{2}$ of M is left, so our "b" is $\dfrac{1}{2}$, and the manipulation of a such that $1 > b > 0$ means we know our half-life equation describes decay.

Our x variable is $\dfrac{d}{2}$ because the units are halved every $2(d)$ days, giving us the function $f(d) = M\left(\dfrac{1}{2}\right)^{\frac{d}{2}}$ and making (B) the correct choice.

Quick Practice

1. If $y = x^2 + x$ for any positive integer x, and if $z = y^2 + y$, what is z in terms of x?

   (A) $x^4 + x^2 + x$

   (B) $x^4 + x^3 + x^2 + x$

   (C) $x^4 + x$

   (D) $x^4 + 2x^3 + 2x^2 + x$

2. The side of one square is three centimeters longer than the side of a second square, and the area of the second square is 51 square centimeters less than the area of the first square. What is the length of the second square?

   (A) 3 centimeters

   (B) 5 centimeters

   (C) 6 centimeters

   (D) 7 centimeters

3. Which of the following is equivalent to the expression $\dfrac{x^2 - 16}{x^3 + x^2 - 20x}$?

   (A) $\dfrac{4}{x+5}$

   (B) $\dfrac{x+4}{4}$

   (C) $\dfrac{x+4}{x+5}$

   (D) $\dfrac{x+4}{x^2 + 5x}$

4. Which of the following is equivalent to the expression $x^2 - zx + xy - zy$?

   (A) $(x - y)(x + z)$

   (B) $(x - z)(x + y)$

   (C) $x(x + z - y) - zy$

   (D) $x^2 + x(z - y) - zy$

5. Which of the following is a simplified form of $\dfrac{5x + 10}{15(x+2)^2}$?

   (A) $\dfrac{x}{(x+2)^2}$

   (B) $\dfrac{3}{x+2}$

   (C) $\dfrac{1}{3(x+2)}$

   (D) $\dfrac{x+10}{3(x+2)^2}$

6. If $ax^2 - bx = ay^2 + by$, what is the value of $\dfrac{a}{b}$?

   (A) $\dfrac{1}{x - y}$

   (B) $\dfrac{1}{x + y}$

   (C) $\dfrac{x - y}{x + y}$

   (D) $\dfrac{x + y}{x - y}$

7. If $\dfrac{a^2 - 4}{(a-2)^2} = b$ and $a \neq 2$, what is the value of a in terms of b?

   (A) $\dfrac{2 + b}{2 - b}$

   (B) $\dfrac{4}{b - 1}$

   (C) $\dfrac{b + 2}{b - 2}$

   (D) $\dfrac{2b + 2}{b - 1}$

Chapter 5

8. If $\dfrac{x^2 + A + 1}{x + y} = x - y + \dfrac{1}{x + y}$, what is A in terms of x and y?

(A) xy

(B) $-y^2$

(C) x^2

(D) y^2

9. If $\sqrt{\dfrac{9^{x+3}}{27^x}} = 81$, what is the value of x?

(A) -2

(B) -1

(C) 0

(D) 1

10. Which of the following is equivalent to the expression $y^{\frac{1}{2}}\left(y^{\frac{1}{2}} + y^{-\frac{1}{2}}\right)$?

(A) $y + 1$

(B) y

(C) 1

(D) 0

11. An urban planner is calculating the cost of building maintenance in a proposed housing structure. The cost of maintenance can be approximated by dividing the number of residents by the number of units, and multiplying that number by $44. The following function is used to determine the cost of maintenance:

$$C = \dfrac{(475)(44)(1.12)^x}{(200)}$$

Where C is the cost of maintenance and x is the number of years from the present (year 0). What is the significance of the value 475 in the function?

(A) The number of units in the building

(B) The number of residents currently in the building

(C) The number of resident in the building after year one

(D) The cost of maintenance per resident

12. A chemist has 80 pints of 20 percent salt solution. How many pounds of pure salt must be added to produce a solution that is 30 percent salt?

(A) 4.6

(B) 8

(C) 11.4

(D) 16

13. Which of the following is equivalent to the expression $\dfrac{6 + 2\sqrt{2}}{\sqrt{2} - \sqrt{3}}$?

(A) $-4 - 6\sqrt{2} - 6\sqrt{3} - 2\sqrt{6}$

(B) $4 + 6\sqrt{2} + 6\sqrt{3} + 2\sqrt{6}$

(C) $-4 + 6\sqrt{2} - 6\sqrt{3} + 2\sqrt{6}$

(D) $4 - 6\sqrt{2} + 6\sqrt{3} - 2\sqrt{6}$

Quick Practice

14. Which of the following is true of the equation
$x + 1 = \sqrt{x+1}$?

(A) It has no roots.

(B) It has only one root.

(C) The roots are zero and −1.

(D) The roots are zero and 2.

15.

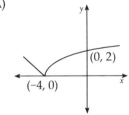

The figure above is the graph of function f. Which of the following could be the graph of $y = f(2x)$?

(A)
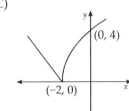
(−4, 0)   (0, 2)

(B)
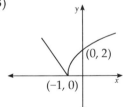
(−1, 0)   (0, 2)

(C)
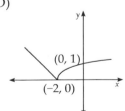
(−2, 0)   (0, 4)

(D)
(−2, 0)   (0, 1)

16. A certain function g has the property that $g(x + y) = g(x) + g(y)$ for all values of x and y. Which of the following statements must be true when $p = q$?

I. $g(p + q) = 2g(p)$

II. $g(p + q) = [g(p)]^2$

III. $g(q) + g(q) = g(2p)$

(A) None.

(B) I only.

(C) I and III only.

(D) II and III only.

17.

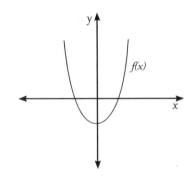

The figure above is the graph of the function $f(x) = px^2 - 2$, where p is a constant. If $g(x) = \dfrac{p}{2}x^2 - 2$, which of the following describes the graph of $g(x)$ in the relation to the graph of $f(x)$?

(A) It will be narrower and opens upward.

(B) It will be wider and opens downward.

(C) It will be wider and opens upward.

(D) It will be narrower and opens downward.

CHAPTER 5

18. The functions f, g, and h are defined as $f(x) = -2x^2$, $g(x) = 4x$, and $h(x) = f(x) - g(x)$. For $x > 5$, which of the following describes the value of h as x increases in value?

(A) h increases only.

(B) h decreases only.

(C) h stays the same.

(D) h decreases then increases.

19.

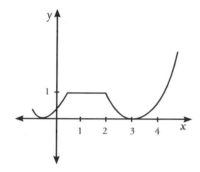

The figure above is the graph of $y = f(x)$. Which of the following could be the graph of

$$y = \frac{1}{2} f(x)?$$

(A)

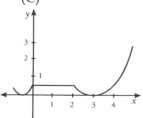

(B)

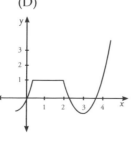

(C)

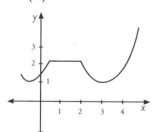

(D)

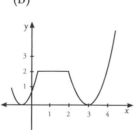

20.

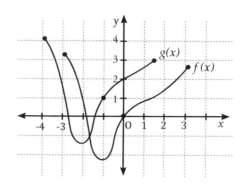

The graphs of functions f and g in the interval $-4 \le x \le 3$ are shown above. Which of the following is the function g in terms of f?

(A) $g(x) = f(x + 1)$

(B) $g(x) = f(x) + 1$

(C) $g(x) = f(x + 1) + 1$

(D) $g(x) = f(x - 1)$

ANSWERS

&

EXPLANATIONS

1-20

Answers & Explanations...
Mastering Advanced Topics

1.	Ⓓ	6.	Ⓐ	11.	Ⓑ	16.	Ⓒ
2.	Ⓓ	7.	Ⓓ	12.	Ⓒ	17.	Ⓒ
3.	Ⓓ	8.	Ⓑ	13.	Ⓐ	18.	Ⓑ
4.	Ⓑ	9.	Ⓐ	14.	Ⓒ	19.	Ⓒ
5.	Ⓒ	10.	Ⓐ	15.	Ⓑ	20.	Ⓒ

1) ▶ D

$y = x^2 + x$

$z = y^2 + y$

Substitute the first equation into the second:

$z = (x^2 + x)^2 + (x^2 + x)$

$= (x^4 + 2x^3 + x^2) + (x^2 + x)$

$= x^4 + 2x^3 + 2x^2 + x$

2) ▶ D

Let x be the length of the second square. We can write the following equation relating the areas of the two squares, and solve for x:

$(x + 3)^2 - x^2 = 51$

$(x^2 + 6x + 9) - x^2 = 51$

$6x + 9 = 51$

$6x = 42$

$x = 7$

3) ▶ D

$\dfrac{x^2 - 16}{x^3 + x^2 - 20x} = \dfrac{(x-4)(x+4)}{x(x^2 + x - 20)} = \dfrac{(x-4)(x+4)}{x(x-4)(x+5)}$

$= \dfrac{(x+4)}{x(x+5)} = \dfrac{x+4}{x^2 + 5x}$

4) ▶ B

Choice (B) can be written as:

$(x - z)(x + y) = x^2 + xy - zx - zy$

5) ▶ C

$\dfrac{5x + 10}{15(x+2)^2} = \dfrac{5(x+2)}{15(x+2)^2} = \dfrac{1}{3(x+2)}$

6) ▶ A

$ax^2 - bx = ay^2 + by$

$ax^2 - ay^2 = by + bx$

$a(x^2 - y^2) = b(x + y)$

$\dfrac{a}{b} = \dfrac{x+y}{(x^2 - y^2)} = \dfrac{x+y}{(x-y)(x+y)} = \dfrac{1}{x-y}$

7) ▶ D

$\dfrac{a^2 - 4}{(a-2)^2} = b \rightarrow \dfrac{(a-2)(a+2)}{(a-2)^2} = b \rightarrow \dfrac{(a+2)}{(a-2)} = b$

$a + 2 = b(a - 2)$

$a + 2 = ba - 2b$

$a - ba = -2b - 2$

$a(1 - b) = -2b - 2$

$a = \dfrac{2b + 2}{b - 1}$

8) ➡ B

$$\frac{x^2 + A + 1}{x + y} = x - y + \frac{1}{x + y}$$

$$\frac{x^2 + A + 1 - 1}{x + y} = x - y$$

$$x^2 + A = (x + y)(x - y)$$

$$x^2 + A = (x^2 - y^2)$$

$$A = -y^2$$

9) ➡ A

$$\sqrt{\frac{9^{x+3}}{27^x}} = 81 \rightarrow \sqrt{\frac{(3^2)^{x+3}}{(3^3)^x}} = 3^4 \rightarrow \frac{3^{x+3}}{3^{\frac{3x}{2}}} = 3^4$$

$$3^{(x+3) - \frac{3x}{2}} = 3^4$$

$$x + 3 - \frac{3x}{2} = 4 \rightarrow \frac{2x}{2} - \frac{3x}{2} = 4 - 3$$

$$-\frac{x}{2} = 1$$

$$x = -2$$

10) ➡ A

$$y^{\frac{1}{2}}\left(y^{\frac{1}{2}} + y^{-\frac{1}{2}}\right) = y^{\frac{1}{2} + \frac{1}{2}} + y^{\frac{1}{2} - \frac{1}{2}} = y^1 + y^0 = y + 1$$

11) ➡ B

The denominator of the function is the number of units (200). The numerator must include the number of residents. As x represents the number of years after year 0, 1.12 must be the growth rate and 475 the number of residents in year 0.

12) ➡ C

The amount of salt in the solution is:

$$(0.2)(80) = 16 lb$$

To increase the concentration of salt to 30%, add x lb. of salt, but note that this increases the mass of the sample to $80 + x$ lb:

$$0.3 = \frac{16 + x}{80 + x}$$

$$24 + 0.3x = 16 + x$$

$$x = 11.4$$

13. ➡ A

$$\frac{6 + 2\sqrt{2}}{\sqrt{2} - \sqrt{3}} = \left(\frac{6 + 2\sqrt{2}}{\sqrt{2} - \sqrt{3}}\right)\left(\frac{\sqrt{2} + \sqrt{3}}{\sqrt{2} + \sqrt{3}}\right)$$

$$= \frac{\left(6 + 2\sqrt{2}\right)\left(\sqrt{2} + \sqrt{3}\right)}{2 - 3}$$

$$= \frac{6\sqrt{2} + 6\sqrt{3} + 2(2) + 2\sqrt{6}}{-1}$$

$$= -4 - 6\sqrt{2} - 6\sqrt{3} - 2\sqrt{6}$$

14. ➡ C

First, square both sides to eliminate the radical:

$$(x + 1)^2 = \left(\sqrt{x + 1}\right)^2 \rightarrow x^2 + 2x + 1 = x + 1$$

Then, solve the equation for x:

$$x^2 + 2x + 1 - 1 - x = 0$$
$$x^2 + x = 0$$
$$x(x + 1) = 0$$
$$x = 0, \ x = -1$$

Both solutions work when plugged into the original equation, so it has two solutions 0 and -1.

15) ⟹ B

When $x = 0$, $x = 2x = 0$ and $f(x) = f(2x)$. Thus, we can infer that the y-intercept of $f(x)$ is the same as the y-intercept of $f(2x)$ and is the point $(0, 2)$; on this basis we can eliminate (C) and (D). From the graph, we can also see that $f(-2) = 0$. Therefore, the value $y = f(2x) = 0$ when $x = -1$, and (B) is correct.

The function h is the product of two expressions, $-2x$ and $x + 2$. Consider them separately. For $x > 5$, $-2x$ is negative in value and decreases as x increases. Over the same range, $x + 2$ is positive in value and increases as x increases. Their *product* must decrease in value as x increases, so (B) is the correct choice.

16) ⟹ C

Begin by evaluating Roman numeral I. When $p = q$, it is also true that $g(p) = g(q)$. If we substitue p for x and q for y in the form of the function given in the question, $g(x + y) = g(x) + g(y)$, we get the function $g(p + q) = g(p) + g(q)$. Since $g(p) = g(q)$, we can substitute $g(p)$ for $g(q)$, which means that $g(p + q) = g(p) + g(p) = 2g(p)$. Roman numeral I must be true. We can eliminate choices (A) and (D) because they do not include Roman numeral I. To choose between (B) and (C), we need only to evaluate Roman numeral III. Because $p = q$, it is also true that $2p = 2q$ and $g(2p) = g(2q)$. Also, $g(2q) = g(q + q) = g(q) + g(q)$ according to the property of the function. Therefore, $g(q) + g(q) = g(2p)$, and III is true. The correct choice is (C).

19) ⟹ C

The graph of $y = \dfrac{1}{2} f(x)$ will have values of y that are one-half those of $y = f(x)$ for all values of x.

From the graph of $y = f(x)$, we see that when $0.5 < x < 2$, $f(x) = 1$. This means that for the graph of $y = \dfrac{1}{2} f(x)$, the value of y when $0.5 < x < 2$ is $\dfrac{1}{2}(1) = \dfrac{1}{2}$. This corresponds to choice (C).

20) ⟹ C

The graph of $g(x)$ is the graph of $f(x)$ translated vertically 1 unit and horizontally 1 unit to the left. This transforms the function in the following ways:

Vertical translation: $g(x) = f(x) + 1$
Horizontal translation: $g(x) = f(x + 1) + 1$

17) ⟹ C

From the graph, we know that $p > 0$ because the parabola opens upwards. The value of $\dfrac{p}{2}$ will also be positive and the graph of $g(x)$ will open upwards. Also, $p > \dfrac{p}{2}$ for $p > 0$, so for all values of x except $x = 0$, $f(x) > g(x)$. This implies that the graph of $g(x)$ will be wider (or flatter) than the graph of $f(x)$.

18) ⟹ B

$h(x) = f(x) - g(x)$
$h(x) = -2x^2 - 4x$
$h(x) = -2x(x + 2)$

CHAPTER 6

Mastering
SAT Geometry

Fundamental Concepts and Techniques

082 Question Topic

→ **VOLUME OF SOLIDS**

Prisms and Cylinders

▶ A prism is a type of general cylinder. Both prisms and cylinders are named for the shape of their bases. For example, a cylinder with a circle as the base is called a circular cylinder, and a prism with a hexagon as the base is called an hexagonal prism.

Formula for a Cylinder

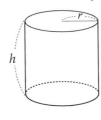

$Volume = \pi r^2 h$

Formula for a Prism

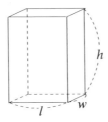

$Volume = lwh$

Note: If a pyramid and a rectangular prism have equal height and base measurements, the volume of the pyramid is $\frac{1}{3}$ the volume of the rectangular prism.

Pyramids and Cones

▶ A cone is a solid in which lines that begin on the perimeter of the base meet at a single point called the vertex.

▶ A pyramid is a cone that has a polygon as its base. Both cones and pyramids are named by the shape of their base (a triangular pyramid, a circular cone, etc.).

Formula for a Cone

$Volume = \frac{1}{3}\pi r^2 h$

Formula for a Pyramid

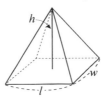

$Volume = \frac{1}{3}lwh$

Note: If a cone and a cylinder have equal height and base measurements, the volume of the cone is $\frac{1}{3}$ the volume of the cylinder.

Spheres

▶ A sphere is a surface that represents the set of all points a fixed distance from a single point. The fixed distance is the radius, r, and the point is the center of the circle.

▶ A hemisphere is one-half of a sphere.

Formula for a Sphere

$Volume = \left(\frac{4}{3}\right)\pi r^3$

Formula for a Hemisphere

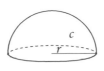

$Volume = \left(\frac{2}{3}\right)\pi r^3$

Example

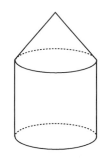

A cylinder is attached to a cone as shown and the entire object has a height of 1 meter. If the radius of both the cylinder and the cone is 10 centimeters, and the volume of the entire solid is 8000π cubic centimeters, what is the height of the cylinder?

(A) 30 centimeters

(B) 50 centimeters

(C) 70 centimeters

(D) 100 centimeters

Solution :

Let x be the height of the cylinder in centimeters, and y be the height of the cone affixed to the cylinder in centimeters. The total volume of the solid is the sum of the volumes of the cylinder and the cone:

$$V = \pi r^2 x + \frac{1}{3}\pi r^2 y$$

This expression can be rearranged to: $x + \frac{1}{3}y = \frac{V}{\pi r^2}$

The combined height of the solid is 1 meter, or 100 centimeters. As we are calculating in centimeters, we can write the following equation: $x + y = 100 \rightarrow y = 100 - x$

Substitute for y in the equation for total volume, and solve for x:

$$x + \frac{1}{3}(100 - x) = \frac{V}{\pi r^2} \rightarrow x = \frac{3}{2}\left(\frac{V}{\pi r^2} - \frac{100}{3}\right) \rightarrow x = \frac{3}{2}\left(\frac{8000\pi}{\pi(10)^2} - \frac{100}{3}\right) \rightarrow x = \frac{3}{2}\left(80 - \frac{100}{3}\right)$$

$$\rightarrow x = \frac{240}{2} - \frac{300}{6} = 120 - 50 = 70$$

The height of the cylinder is 70 centimeters. The correct choice is (C).

083 Question Topic

VOLUME AND AREA

Relationships Between Two Solids

▶ If the ratio of sides or heights between two similar solids is $a : b$, then the ratio of their surface areas is $a^2 : b^2$ and the ratio of their volumes is $a^3 : b^3$. If we assign the solids a scale factor k such that the ratio $a : b = k$, then the ratio of their surface areas is equal to k^2 and the ratio of their volumes is equal to k^3.

Transforming a Single Solid

▶ If a solid is re-scaled in three dimensions, then the volume of the rescaled solid will be the products of the scale factors. For example, if a rectangular prism has its length, width, and height doubled, the final volume will be eight times $(2 \times 2 \times 2)$ the volume of the original solid.

Example

If a sphere has a surface area of $3x$ cm^2, and another sphere has a surface area of x cm^2, what is the ratio of the volume of the first sphere to the volume of the second sphere?

(A) $\dfrac{1}{3}$

(C) 3

(B) $\sqrt{3}$

(D) $3\sqrt{3}$

Solution :

The two objects referred to in the question are both spheres, so their shapes are similar. Because their shapes are similar, we can calculate a scale factor from their areas: if the ratio of surface areas between solids is $a^2 : b^2$, the scale factor k is equivalent to $a : b$, and the ratio of their volumes is k^3:

$$\frac{a^2}{b^2} = \frac{3x}{x} \rightarrow k = \frac{a}{b} = \sqrt{\frac{3x}{x}} = \sqrt{3} \rightarrow k^3 = 3\sqrt{3}$$

The correct choice is (D).

 TEACHER'S TIP

For two similar objects with scale factor k, the ratio of their areas is k^2, and the ratio of their volumes is k^3.

TRIANGLES

Naming and Definitions

▶ A triangle is typically named using three upper-case letters, each of which is used to label one of the triangle's three vertices..

▶ Sometimes, angles will be named with a single letter, such as $\angle A$, and other times they will be named using the three letters that represent the sides that form the angle (such as $\angle BAC$).

▶ There are two ways of naming the sides of a triangle. The first way is to use the letters that represent the bounds of the line, such as $\overline{AB}$. The second way is to use a single letter that corresponds to the angle that faces the side. The side is typically named using a lower case letter in italics (such as the letter a).

▶ An *obtuse triangle* is a triangle in which one angle is an obtuse angle. An obtuse angle is an angle that is greater than ninety degrees. An obtuse triangle must have one obtuse angle and two acute angles.

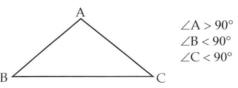

$\angle A > 90°$
$\angle B < 90°$
$\angle C < 90°$

▶ An *acute triangle* is a triangle in which all angles are acute angles. An acute angle is an angle that is less than ninety degrees.

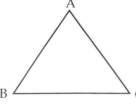

$\angle A < 90°$
$\angle B < 90°$
$\angle C < 90°$

► A *right triangle* is a triangle which contains a 90 degree angle. The sides of right angles are named according to their positions with respect to the right angle (as with the hypotenuse) or according to which of the other angles is being discussed (as with adjacent and opposite sides):

- The side opposite the right angle is called the hypotenuse. It is always the longest side of a right triangle. In the triangle below the hypotenuse is the side $\overline{BC}$.

- The remaining sides are named in relation to the angle being discussed. The side that meets the hypotenuse at the angle being discussed is called the adjacent side, and the side that does not meet the hypotenuse at the angle is called the opposite side.

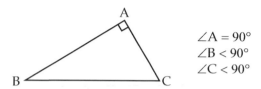

$\angle A = 90°$
$\angle B < 90°$
$\angle C < 90°$

► An *isosceles triangle* is a triangle with two equal angles.

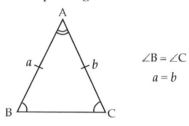

$\angle B = \angle C$
$a = b$

► An *equilateral triangle* is a triangle in which all three angles are 60°. The three sides of an equilateral triangle are the same length.

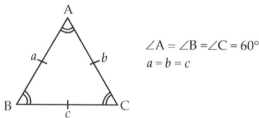

$\angle A = \angle B = \angle C = 60°$
$a = b = c$

► An *exterior angle* is the angle that is formed when a side of a triangle is extended. The exterior angle is the supplement of the angle adjacent to it, which is in the triangle. As the angle measure of a triangle is 180 degrees, the exterior angle will be equal to the sum of the other two (non-adjacent) angles of the triangle, which is also the supplement of the previously mentioned adjacent angle.

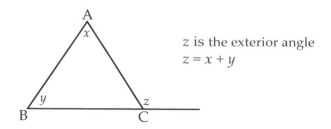

z is the exterior angle
$z = x + y$

084 *Question Topic*

→ **THE PYTHAGOREAN THEOREM AND SPECIAL RIGHT TRIANGLES**

▶ The Pythagorean Theorem gives the relationship between the lengths of the sides of a right triangle. It states that the sum of the square of the two non-hypotenuse sides of a right triangle is equal to the square of the hypotenuse. This theorem is given in the Reference Section at the start of each SAT Math Test:

The Pythagorean Theorem: $a^2 + b^2 = c^2$

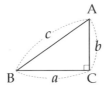

▶ The distance formula is used to calculate the distance between two points (x_1, y_1) and (x_2, y_2), and is a special case of the Pythagorean theorem:

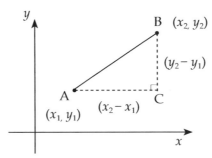

- Any two points (marked A and B in the figure to the right) can be used to form a right triangle.
- The distance between A and B is the length of the hypotenuse of the triangle with sides of length $(x_2 - x_1)$ and $(y_2 - y_1)$:

$$d^2 = (x_2 - x_1)^2 + (y_2 - y_1)^2$$
$$d = \sqrt{(x_2 - x_1)^2 + (y_2 - y_1)^2}$$

The equation above is referred to as the distance formula.

▶ There are four right triangles that appear regularly on the SAT. The first two are the 3–4–5 right triangle and the 5–12–13 right triangle. The numbers 3–4–5 and 5–12–13 refer to ratios between the sides of the right triangles, and not necessarily the actual lengths of the sides. The other two common right triangles are the 30–60–90 triangle and the 45–45–90 trianngles, where the numbers correspond to the number of degrees in each of the triangle's three angles. The sides of a 30–60–90 triangle always equal x, $x\sqrt{3}$, and $2x$, where x is the length of the shortest side. The sides of a 45–45–90 triangle always equal x, x, and $x\sqrt{2}$, where x is the length of both legs.

Example

In the figure above, $\angle BAC$ and $\angle ABD$ are right angles, and AC = 9, BC = 15, and DB = 5. What is the length of AD ?

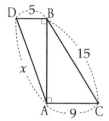

(A) 17

(B) $\sqrt{74}$

(C) $5\sqrt{2}$

(D) 13

TEACHER'S TIP

Use the Pythagorean Theorem $(a^2 + b^2 = c^2)$ to find the missing side length of a right triangle.

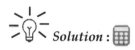 **Solution :**

In $\triangle ABC$, $15^2 = 9^2 + (AB)^2 \rightarrow (AB)^2 = 225 - 81 = 144 \rightarrow AB = 12$

We can see that the non-hypotenuse sides of $\triangle ABD$ are 5 and 12 units long. This means that $\triangle ABD$ is a 5-12-13 right triangle, and $\overline{AD} = 13$. The correct choice is (D).

Congruence between triangles means that the angles and sides of the triangles are exactly the same. There are four ways to establish congruence between two or more triangles :

▶ **SAS :** If two triangles have two pairs of sides of equal length and the angles between the sides are equal, the triangles are congruent.

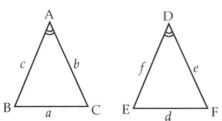

If $c = f$, $b = e$, and $\angle A = \angle D$, then
$\triangle ABC \equiv \triangle DEF$

▶ **SSS :** If two triangles have three pairs of sides of equal length, then the triangles are congruent.

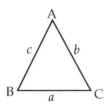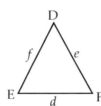

If $a = d$, $b = e$, and $c = f$, then
$\triangle ABC \equiv \triangle DEF$

▶ **ASA :** If two triangles have two pairs of equal angles and the sides between the angles are the same length, then the triangles are congruent.

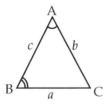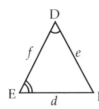

If $\angle A = \angle D$, $\angle B = \angle E$, and $c = f$, then
$\triangle ABC \equiv \triangle DEF$

▶ **AAS:** If two triangles have two pairs of angles of equal size and one pair of sides of equal length, the triangles are congruent.

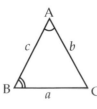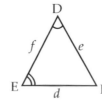

If $\angle A = \angle D$, $\angle B = \angle E$, and $a = d$, then
$\triangle ABC \equiv \triangle DEF$

NOTE : AAA and SSA are not sufficient to prove congruence between triangles.

Similarity between two triangles indicates that corresponding angles are equal and corresponding sides are proportional. There are three ways to establish similarity between triangles:

▶ **AA :** It is sufficient to demonstrate similarity between two triangles if they have two pairs of angles that are the same size.

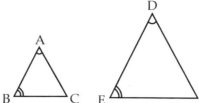

If $\angle A = \angle D$, and $\angle B = \angle E$, then
$\triangle ABC \sim \triangle DEF$
(the two triangles are similar)

▶ **SAS :** Two triangles are similar if they have one pair of angles that are equal and if the sides that are adjacent to that angle on the two triangles are proportional.

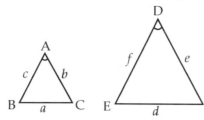

If $\angle A = \angle D$, and $\dfrac{c}{f} = \dfrac{b}{e}$, then

$\triangle ABC \sim \triangle DEF$

▶ **SSS :** Two triangles are similar if three pairs of corresponding sides on the triangles are proportional.

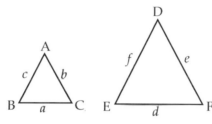

If $\dfrac{a}{d} = \dfrac{b}{e} = \dfrac{c}{f}$, then $\triangle ABC \sim \triangle DEF$

Example

In the figure below, AC = 12, DC = 18, and DB = 15. What is the length of line segment AF?

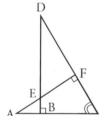

(A) 8   (C) 10

(B) 9   (D) 11

💬 **TEACHER'S TIP**

Similarity between two triangles indicates that corresponding angles are equal and corresponding sides are proportional.

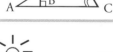 **Solution :**

Since $\angle B = \angle F = 90°$ and $\angle C$ is an angle in both triangles, $\triangle AFC$ is similar to $\triangle DBC$ according to AA criteria. This means that corresponding sides are proportional, and we can write:

$$\frac{DB}{AF} = \frac{DC}{AC} = \frac{CB}{CF}$$

If AC = 12, DC = 18, and DB = 15, then $\dfrac{15}{AF} = \dfrac{18}{12} \rightarrow AF = \dfrac{12 \cdot 15}{18} = 10$ The correct choice is (C).

▶ **Angle Bisector Theorem:** An angle bisector of a triangle splits the opposite side into segments that have the same ratio of lengths as the sides adjacent to the angle.

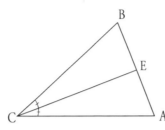

If ∠BCE = ∠ACE, then

$$\frac{CB}{CA} = \frac{BE}{EA}$$

▶ **Triangle Side-Splitter Theorem:** Lines parallel to the side of a triangle and inside the triangle divide the other two sides into proportional segments.

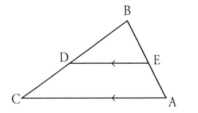

$$\frac{CD}{DB} = \frac{AE}{EB}$$

▶ The altitude of a right triangle drawn from the right angle creates three similar triangles. This is due to the fact that each of the two resultant smaller triangles shares a common acute angle with the largest triangle.

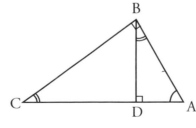

$$\triangle ABC \sim \triangle ADB \sim \triangle BDC$$

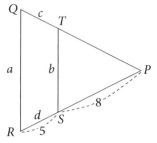

Note: Figure not drawn to scale

Jim wants to measure the area of two plots of land bounded by four roads. Road a and Road b are parallel to each other, and Road c and Road d are transversals to the other two roads and meet each other at point P. Road b divides Road d into two parts of lengths 5 miles and 8 miles, as marked in the diagram. If the area of both plots together is 65 square miles, what is the area, in square miles, of the plot bounded by the points P, S, and T?

(A) 9.6   (C) 24.6

(B) 13.0   (D) 25.0

 **Solution :**

Road b is parallel to Road a, so it creates two pairs of equivalent interior angles : $\angle PST$ and $\angle PRQ$, and $\angle PTS$ and $\angle PQR$. As the angle at P is common to $\triangle PTS$ and $\triangle PQR$, the two triangles are similar by the AA criteria. The areas of the two triangles are proportional according to the scale factor of the two triangles, k, squared. (See page 207 for more on this.) The scale factor for the two triangles is the ratio between the lengths of corresponding sides:

$$k = \frac{PS}{PR} = \frac{8}{13}$$

The ratio between the areas of the triangles is the scale factor squared:

$$k^2 = \left(\frac{8}{13}\right)^2 = \frac{64}{169}$$

Set this ratio equal to the areas of the triangles. According to the question, the area of $\triangle PRQ$ is 65 square miles. Solve for the area of the triangle $\triangle PST$:

$$\frac{64}{169} = \frac{\triangle PST}{\triangle PRQ} \rightarrow \frac{64}{169} = \frac{\triangle PST}{65}$$

$$\frac{(64)(65)}{169} = \triangle PST$$

$$\triangle PST = 24.6$$

The correct choice is (C).

> **TEACHER'S TIP**
>
> Look for similar triangles when solving complicated geometry questions.

A **circle** is the curved line formed by all points which are equidistant from a single point in two dimensions.

▶ **Radius**: A line segment that runs from the center point to a point on the circle.
▶ **Diameter**: A line segment that joins two points on the circle and passes through the center point. The diameter is twice the radius.
▶ **Chord**: A line segment that joins two points on the circle.

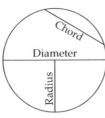

Diameter = 2 × Radius

Area and Circumference

▶ The circumference of a circle (C) is equal to π multiplied by the diameter (*d*) of the circle: $C = \pi d = 2\pi r$
Both this formula and the formula for the area of a circle are given in the Reference Section at the beginning of each SAT Math Test.
▶ The area of a circle (A) is π multiplied by the square of the radius: $A = \pi r^2$.

Chords

▶ The perpendicular bisector of a chord passes through the center of the circle.

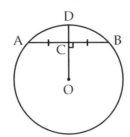

If $\overline{AC} = \overline{CB}$ and $\overline{OD} \perp \overline{AB}$, then OD passes through the center of the circle.

▶ Congruent chords have congruent arcs; congruent arcs have congruent chords.

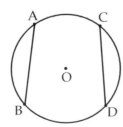

If $\overline{AB} = \overline{CD}$ (that is, their lengths are equal), then $\overparen{AB} = \overparen{CD}$.

▶ Arcs between parallel chords are congruent.

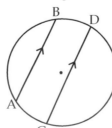

If $\overline{AB} \mathbin{/\!/} \overline{CD}$, then $\overparen{AC} = \overparen{BD}$.

087 Question Topic

→ TANGENTS TO A CIRCLE

▶ A **tangent** to a circle is a straight line which touches the circle at only one point.

▶ A tangent to a circle forms a right angle with the circle's radius at the point of contact with the tangent.

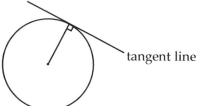

tangent line

▶ Two separate tangents will meet at a point equidistant from their points of contact with the circle.

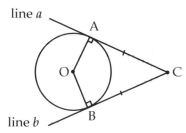

If line a and line b are tangent to the circle O, then $\overline{AC} = \overline{BC}$.

Example

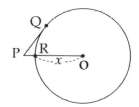

In the figure above, $\overline{QP}$ is tangent to circle O at point Q. If $\overline{PQ} = 15$ and $\overline{PR} = 5$, what is the radius of circle O?

(A) 12   (C) 18
(B) 15   (D) 20

 **Solution :**

As $\overline{PQ}$ is tangent to the circle O, $\angle OQP = 90°$ and $\triangle OQP$ is a right triangle. According to Pythagorean theorem:

$$\overline{OP}^2 = \overline{OQ}^2 + \overline{QP}^2$$

Taking x as length of the radius, we can write :

$$(x + 5)^2 = x^2 + 15^2$$
$$x^2 + 10x + 25 = x^2 + 225$$
$$10x = 200 \rightarrow x = 20$$

The correct choice is (D).

💬 TEACHER'S TIP

Many students find that sketching a diagram helps them solve geometry problems. For example, a helpful sketch for the question on this page might look like this:

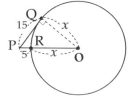

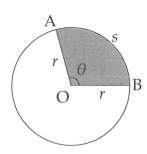

► An **arc,** *s*, is a continuous segment of a circle's circumference.

► If line segments are drawn from the endpoints of an arc to the center of the circle, the bounded region is called a **sector**. The line segments are radii.

► The angle formed by the two radii of a sector is called the **central angle**. The measure of this angle in unit radians is equal to the number of radius units (that is, some factor of the length of the radius) in the corresponding arc. This relationship is expressed in the formula $\theta = \dfrac{s}{r}$, where θ is the measure of the central angle, *s* is the arc length, and *r* is the radius.

► If we use the equation above and take the arc length as the circumference of an entire circle, the result is the radian measure of a circle:

$$\theta = \frac{s}{r} = \frac{2\pi r}{r} = 2\pi$$

This result implies that a radian measure of π is equivalent to the radian measure of a semi-circle. As the degree measure of a circle is $360°$, the following conversion factors can be used to convert radians into degrees and vice versa:

$$1 \text{ radian} = \frac{180}{\pi} \text{ degrees} \qquad\qquad 1 \text{ degree} = \frac{\pi}{180} \text{ radians}$$

► The formula $\theta = \dfrac{s}{r}$ can also be used to find the arc length or area of a sector in the following circumstances:

- To determine the arc length of a sector, *s*, given the radius, *r*, and the measure of the central angle, θ, in radians: $s = \theta r$

- To determine the arc length of a sector, *s*, given the radius, *r*, and the measure of the central angle, θ, in degrees: $s = \dfrac{\theta}{180} \cdot \pi r$

- To determine the area of a sector, A, given the radius, *r*, the arc length of the sector, *s*, and the measure of the central angle, θ, in radians: $A = \dfrac{1}{2} rs$

- To determine the area of a sector, A, given the radius, *r*, and the measure of the central angle, θ, in degrees: $A = \dfrac{\theta}{360} \cdot \pi r^2$

CHAPTER 6

Example

A sector of a circle has an arc length of six centimeters and an area of 75 square centimeters. What is the radius of the circle?

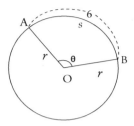

What is the measure of the central angle?

 **Solution :**

- Area $= \dfrac{1}{2}rs \rightarrow 75 = \dfrac{1}{2}r(6)$

    $6r = 150,\ r = 25$

    The radius of the circle is 25 centimeters.

- To find the measure of the central angle, we use the formula

    $s = \theta r$:

    $6 = 25\theta \rightarrow \theta = \dfrac{6}{25} = 0.24$

    The measure of the central angle is 0.24 radians, or approximately 14 degrees.

TEACHER'S TIP

To convert degrees to radians, multiply by the conversion factor $\dfrac{\pi}{180°}$.

▶ **Thales' theorem:** If $\overline{AB}$ is the diameter of a circle on which A, B, and C are inscribed, then ΔABC is a right triangle.

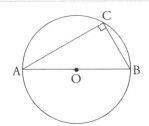

▶ **Inscribed angle theorem:** The measure of the central angle is twice the measure of any inscribed angle that intercepts the same arc.

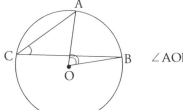

$\angle AOB = 2 \angle ACB$

▶ Angles inscribed in the same arc are congruent

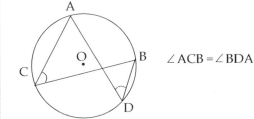

$\angle ACB = \angle BDA$

089 *Question Topic*

EQUATION OF A CIRCLE

▶ A circle can be defined in a coordinate plane as the set of all points that are equidistant from a given point in the plane.

▶ The standard form of the equation for a circle can be derived as follows:

- (x, y) are the coordinates of a point on the circle below. The center is the point (h, k), and r is the radius.
- The distance formula gives us the distance between any two points in the plane (x_1, y_1) and (x_2, y_2):

$$\sqrt{(x_2 - x_1)^2 + (y_2 - y_1)^2} = d \; c$$

- The distance formula is applied to the points on the circle with respect to the center:

$$\sqrt{(x - h)^2 + (y - k)^2} = r$$

- Squaring both sides, we have the standard form for the equation of a circle:

$$(x - h)^2 + (y - k)^2 = r^2$$

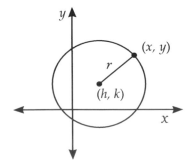

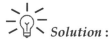
Find the coordinates of the points at which the line $y = 2x - 2$ and the circle $x^2 + y^2 = 25$ intersect.

Solution:

A line and a circle can intersect once (if the line is tangent to the circle), twice (if the line passes through the circle), or not at all. Begin by solving the two equations simultaneously:

$y = 2x - 2$

$x^2 + y^2 = 25$

Substitute the first equation into the second equation:

$x^2 + (2x - 2)^2 = 25 \rightarrow x^2 + (4x^2 - 8x + 4) = 25$

$5x^2 - 8x - 21 = 0 \rightarrow (5x + 7)(x - 3) = 0$

$x = -\dfrac{7}{5}$ and $x = 3$

There are two points of intersection.

Substitute the x-values into the first equation to find the points of intersection:

For $x = -\dfrac{7}{5}$,

$y = 2\left(-\dfrac{7}{5}\right) - 2 = -\dfrac{24}{5}$

For $x = 3$,

$y = 2(3) - 2 = 4$

The points of intersection are $\left(-\dfrac{7}{5}, -\dfrac{24}{5}\right)$ and $(3, 4)$.

TEACHER'S TIP

The standard form for the equation of a circle:
$$(x - h)^2 + (y - k)^2 = r^2$$

Trigonometric Ratios

The trigonometric ratios are the ratios between the lengths of the sides in a right triangle. Similarity proves that the ratios associated with any given angle are constant for any right triangle with the same angle measures (the lengths of the sides are proportional so their ratios are constant).

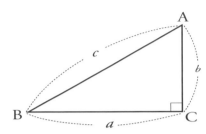

Trigonometric Ratio	Abbreviation	Definition
Sine of $\angle A$	sin A	$\dfrac{leg\ opposite \angle A}{hypotenuse} = \dfrac{a}{c}$
Cosine of $\angle A$	cos A	$\dfrac{leg\ adjacent \angle A}{hypotenuse} = \dfrac{b}{c}$
Tangent of $\angle A$	tan A	$\dfrac{leg\ opposite \angle A}{leg\ adjacent \angle A} = \dfrac{a}{b}$

090 Question Topic

SINE AND COSINE OF COMPLEMENTARY ANGLES

The sine and cosine of complementary angles in a right triangle are equal. This relationship appears consistently on the SAT, and is represented by the formulas:

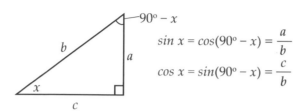

$$\sin x = \cos(90° - x) = \frac{a}{b}$$

$$\cos x = \sin(90° - x) = \frac{c}{b}$$

We can also express this relationship by saying that the sine of one non-right angle in a right triangle is equal to the cosine of the other non-right angle in the right triangle:

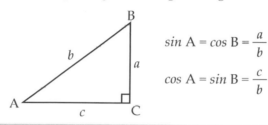

$$\sin A = \cos B = \frac{a}{b}$$

$$\cos A = \sin B = \frac{c}{b}$$

Example

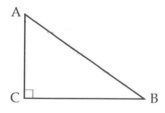

In the triangle above, the sine of angle A is $\frac{4}{5}$. Which of the following is the value of the cosine of angle B?

(A) $\frac{3}{5}$

(B) $\frac{6}{10}$

(C) $\frac{4}{5}$

(D) $\frac{10}{8}$

TEACHER'S TIP

Here's an easy way to recall trigonometric ratios:

o = side opposite angle θ
h = hypotenuse
a = side adjacent to angle θ

$$\sin \theta = \frac{o}{h} \rightarrow \text{SOH}$$

$$\cos \theta = \frac{a}{h} \rightarrow \text{CAH}$$

$$\tan \theta = \frac{o}{a} \rightarrow \text{TOA}$$

Solution:

Triangle ABC is a right triangle, and angles A and B are non-right angles in the right triangle. According to the formula $\sin A = \cos B$, the cosine of angle B is equal to the sine of angle A, $\frac{4}{5}$. The correct choice is (C).

ANGLES OF ELEVATION AND DEPRESSION

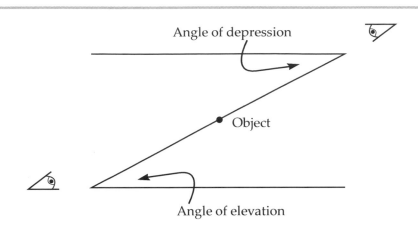

Angle of depression

Object

Angle of elevation

► The angles of elevation and depression to an object can be used to find the distance to the object.

► The tangent, cosine, or sine of the angle of elevation or depression can be used to relate the height, distance to, or direct-line distance from an the object, respectively, keeping in mind that

$$\tan \theta = \frac{\text{opposite angle}}{\text{adjacent angle}}$$

Example

John wants to measure the height of a tree. He walks exactly 100 feet from the base of the tree and measures the angle from the ground to the top of the tree as 33 degrees. How tall is the tree?

Solution :

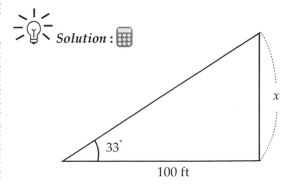

33°

100 ft

x = height of the tree

$$\tan 33° = \frac{x}{100} \rightarrow x = 100 \tan 33° = 64.94$$

The height of the tree is 64.94 feet.

 TEACHER'S TIP

Sketch the situation described to determine what you need to do to solve the question.

▶ The imaginary unit i is defined as having the following properties:

$$i = \sqrt{-1}, \ i^2 = -1, \text{ and } i^4 = 1$$

▶ The square root of any negative number can be defined as follows:

$$\text{For } a > 0, \ \sqrt{-a} = \sqrt{-1} \cdot \sqrt{a} = i\sqrt{a}$$

▶ Any number of the form $a + bi$—where a and b are real numbers, $b \neq 0$, and i is the imaginary unit—is called a *complex number*.

▶ In $a + bi$, a is called the real part and bi the imaginary part of the complex number.

092 Question Topic

→ SIMPLIFYING EXPRESSIONS WITH COMPLEX NUMBERS

When a complex number is in the denominator of a fraction, it must be rationalized in the same way as a radical in the denominator. This is accomplished by multiplying the complex number by its conjugate. The conjugate of the complex number $a + bi$ is the complex number $a - bi$. When conjugates are multiplied, they give as product the difference of two squares:

$$(a + bi)(a - bi) = a^2 - b^2(i^2) = a^2 + b^2$$

Example

Simplify the expression $\dfrac{5 - 2i}{4 + 3i}$.

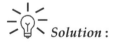 **Solution:**

Rationalize the denominator by multiplying out the imaginary part of the complex number.

$$\frac{5 - 2i}{4 + 3i} = \left(\frac{5 - 2i}{4 + 3i}\right)\left(\frac{4 - 3i}{4 - 3i}\right)$$

$$= \frac{20 - 15i - 8i + 6i^2}{16 - 9i^2}$$

$$= \frac{20 - 23i - 6}{16 + 9}$$

$$= \frac{14 - 23i}{25}$$

 **TEACHER'S TIP**

The imaginary unit i is defined as $i^2 = -1$.

Quick Practice

1.

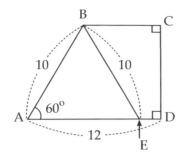

What is the area of the trapezoid BCDE?

(A) $16\sqrt{3}$

(B) $\frac{45}{2}\sqrt{3}$

(C) $8+4\sqrt{3}$

(D) $4+12\sqrt{3}$

3.

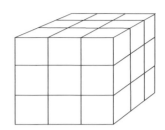

In the figure above, the cube is divided into twenty-seven smaller cubes of equal volume. If twelve of these smaller cubes have a combined volume of 36 cubic units, what is the volume in cubic units of the entire cube?

(A) 54

(B) 81

(C) 108

(D) 135

2.

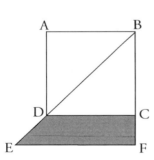

In the figure above, ∆*BEF* is an isosceles right triangle and ABCD is a square as shown. If AB = 1 and EB = 2, what is the area of the shaded region CDEF?

(A) $\frac{1}{2}$

(B) $\frac{\sqrt{2}}{2}$

(C) 1

(D) $\sqrt{2}$

4. A rectangular fish tank has a base four feet wide and nine feet long. While the tank is halfway filled with water, a heavy cube with an edge of three feet is placed in the tank. By how many inches will the water in the tank rise when the cube is completely submerged?

(A) 2

(B) 4

(C) 6

(D) 9

5.

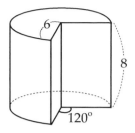

Note: Figure not drawn to scale

What is the volume of the solid in the figure above?

(A) 84π

(B) 96π

(C) 144π

(D) 192π

7.

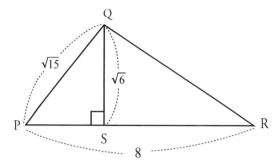

In △PQR above, what is the length of the side $\overline{QR}$?

(A) $\sqrt{29}$

(B) $\sqrt{31}$

(C) $\sqrt{37}$

(D) 7

6.

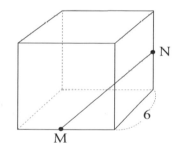

The figure above is a cube with edges of length 6 units. Points M and N are the midpoints of two edges of the cube. Line segment $\overline{MN}$ connects point M to point N. What is the length of $\overline{MN}$?

(A) 8

(B) $3\sqrt{6}$

(C) $2\sqrt{6}$

(D) $6\sqrt{2}$

8.

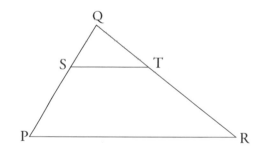

Note: Figure not drawn to scale

In the figure above, $SQ = 4$, $SP = 8$, $QR = 15$, and $\overline{ST}$ is parallel to $\overline{PR}$. What is the length of $\overline{TR}$?

(A) 8

(B) 9

(C) 10

(D) 12

Quick Practice

9.

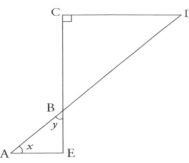

Note: Figure not drawn to scale

In the figure above, $\overline{AE}$ and $\overline{CD}$ are each perpendicular to $\overline{CE}$. If $x = y$, $\overline{AB} = 8$, and the length of $\overline{BD} = 16$, what is the length of $\overline{CE}$?

(A) $3\sqrt{2}$

(B) $6\sqrt{2}$

(C) $8\sqrt{2}$

(D) $12\sqrt{2}$

10.

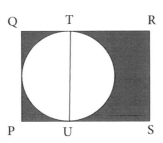

In the figure above, PQRS is a rectangle, and $\overline{TU}$ is the diameter of the circle. If the length of $\overline{RS}$ is six centimeters and the length of $\overline{PS}$ is eight centimeters, what is the area of the shaded area in square centimeters?

(A) $48 - 6\pi$

(B) $48 - 8\pi$

(C) $24 - 6\pi$

(D) $48 - 9\pi$

11. If $\cos\dfrac{\pi}{3} = x - 1$, then what is the value of x?

(A) $\dfrac{1}{2}$

(B) $\dfrac{3}{2}$

(C) $\dfrac{\pi}{3} + 1$

(D) x has two values

12.

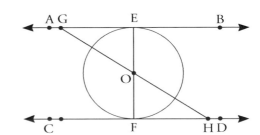

In the figure above, $\overleftrightarrow{AB} \parallel \overleftrightarrow{CD}$ and both lines are tangent to the circle O. The diameter of circle O is equal to the length of segment $\overline{OH}$ If the diameter of the circle O is 24, what is the measure of $\angle BGH$?

(A) $30°$

(B) $45°$

(C) $60°$

(D) $75°$

13.

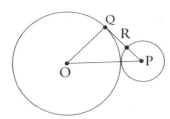

Note: Figure not drawn to scale

In the figure above, the circle with center O has radius 8 units and the circle with center P has radius 2 units. The circles are tangent to each other. Segment $\overline{PQ}$ is tangent to the larger circle and intersects the smaller circle at R. What is the length of segment $\overline{QR}$?

(A) $\sqrt{12}$

(B) $\sqrt{14} - 2$

(C) $\sqrt{18}$

(D) 4

14. A bird sits on top of a lamppost. The angle of depression from the bird to the feet of an observer is 35°. The distance from the bird to the observer is 25 meters. How tall is the lamppost?

(A) 14.34 meters

(B) 20.48 meters

(C) 17.5 meters

(D) 10.7 meters

15. Which of the following is equivalent to the term

$$\frac{2+i\sqrt{5}}{3-i\sqrt{5}}?$$

(A) $\frac{1}{14} + \frac{\sqrt{5}}{14}i$

(B) $\frac{1}{14} - \frac{5\sqrt{5}}{14}i$

(C) $\frac{1}{14} - \frac{\sqrt{5}}{14}i$

(D) $\frac{1}{14} + \frac{5\sqrt{5}}{14}i$

16.

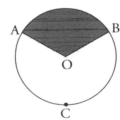

The radius of the circle shown is 9 units. If the area of the shaded sector is 9π square units, what is the length of $\overset{\frown}{ACB}$?

(A) 3π

(B) 15π

(C) 16π

(D) 18π

Quick Practice

17. What is the degree measure of an angle of 60 radians?

    (A) $\dfrac{\pi}{6°}$

    (B) $\dfrac{60°}{\pi}$

    (C) $\dfrac{10800°}{\pi}$

    (D) $\dfrac{1080°}{\pi}$

18. $$(2a + b) + (3 - 5a)i = 1 + 8i$$

    If a and b are integers such that the equation above is true, what is their sum?

    (A) –3
    (B) –2
    (C) –1
    (D) 2

19. What are the coordinates of the center of the circle represented by the following equation?

    $$x^2 - 2x + y^2 - 6y = 9$$

    (A) (−1, −3)

    (B) (1, 3)

    (C) (−3, −1)

    (D) (3, 1)

20. What are the coordinates at which the line $3y + x = 6$ and the circle $x^2 + y^2 = 10$ intersect?

    (A) $\left(\dfrac{9}{5}, \dfrac{13}{5}\right)$, $(3,1)$

    (B) $\left(-\dfrac{9}{5}, \dfrac{13}{5}\right)$, $(3,1)$

    (C) $\left(-\dfrac{9}{5}, \dfrac{13}{5}\right)$, $(-3,-1)$

    (D) $\left(\dfrac{9}{5}, -\dfrac{13}{5}\right)$, $(-3,-1)$

ANSWERS

&

EXPLANATIONS

1-20

Answers & Explanations...
Mastering SAT Geometry

1.	Ⓑ	6.	Ⓑ	11.	Ⓑ	16.	Ⓒ
2.	Ⓐ	7.	Ⓑ	12.	Ⓐ	17.	Ⓒ
3.	Ⓑ	8.	Ⓒ	13.	Ⓓ	18.	Ⓓ
4.	Ⓓ	9.	Ⓓ	14.	Ⓐ	19.	Ⓑ
5.	Ⓓ	10.	Ⓓ	15.	Ⓓ	20.	Ⓑ

1) ➡ **B**

The base angles $\angle BAE = \angle BEA = 60°$, which means that $\angle AB = 60°$, $\triangle ABE$ is an equilateral triangle, and $BA = BE = AE = 10$. Therefore:

$$ED = AD - AE = 12 - 10 = 2$$

Because $\triangle ABE$ is an isosceles (and equilateral) triangle, the altitude from the peak angle to the base bisects the base into two segments of 5 units each. As $BC \parallel AD$, we can infer that:

$$BC = 5 + ED = 5 + 2 = 7$$

BC and ED are the two bases of the trapezoid BCDE. Calculate the altitude of the trapezoid using the Pythagorean theorem:

$$\text{Altitude}^2 + 5^2 = 10^2 \longrightarrow \text{Altitude} = \sqrt{75} = 5\sqrt{3}$$

The area of the trapezoid is:

$$\text{Area}_{BCDE} = \left(\frac{BC + ED}{2}\right)(\text{Altitude})$$

$$\left(\frac{7 + 2}{2}\right)\left(5\sqrt{3}\right) = \frac{45}{2}\sqrt{3}$$

2) ➡ **A**

$\triangle BEF$ is a 45–45–90 right triangle, with a side to hypotenuse ratio of $1 : \sqrt{2}$. The length of the sides is:

$$BF = EF = \frac{2}{\sqrt{2}} = \sqrt{2}$$

and the area of $\triangle BEF$ is:

$$\text{Area}_{\triangle BEF} = \frac{1}{2}(\sqrt{2})(\sqrt{2}) = 1$$

The area of the square ABCD is 1. The area of the triangle $\triangle BCD$ is half the area of the square:

$$\text{Area}_{\triangle BCD} = \frac{1}{2}$$

The area of the shaded region is:

$$\text{Area}_{CDEF} = \text{Area}_{\triangle BEF} - \text{Area}_{\triangle BCD} = 1 - \frac{1}{2} = \frac{1}{2}$$

3) ➡ **B**

Let x be the volume of the entire cube:

$$\frac{12\,cubes}{36\,unit^3} = \frac{27\,cubes}{x}$$

$$x = \frac{27}{12} \cdot 36\,unit^3 = 81\,unit^3$$

4) ➡ **D**

The volume of the cube is equal to the amount of water displaced by the cube. This amount of water will have the dimensions 4 feet × 9 feet × d. The volume of the cube is:

Volume = 3 feet × 3 feet × 3 feet = 27 feet^3

The water rises by d:

4 feet × 9 feet × d feet = 27 feet^3

$d = \dfrac{27}{36}$ feet $= \dfrac{3}{4}$ feet = 9 inches

5) D

The general formula for the volume of a right solid is:

Volume = Base area × Height

The base of this solid is a circle with one third removed (the central angle of the segment removed is 120°). The volume of the solid is:

Volume $= \left(\dfrac{2}{3}\pi r^2\right)\cdot h = \left(\dfrac{2}{3}\pi(6)^2\right)\cdot 8 = 192\pi$

6) B

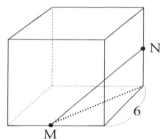

$\overline{MN}$ is the hypotenuse of a triangle which has one side half the edge of the cube and another side the distance from the vertex below N to the point M. This latter side is itself the hypotenuse of a triangle with one side which is the full length of the edge of the cube and another side one-half the edge of the cube. Calculate the square of this latter side, which we will label b^2:

$b^2 = 3^2 + 6^2 = 45$

Calculate the length of $\overline{MN}$:

$\overline{MN}^2 = b^2 + 3^2 = 45 + 9 = 54$

$\overline{MN} = \sqrt{54} = \sqrt{9\cdot 6} = 3\sqrt{6}$

7) B

First calculate the length of $\overline{PS}$ using the Pythagorean theorem:

$(PS)^2 = (QS)^2 + (PS)^2$

$15 = 6 + \overline{PS}^2$

$9 = \overline{PS}^2$

$\overline{PS} = 3$

Calculate the length of $\overline{RS}$:

$\overline{RS} = \overline{PR} - \overline{PS} = 8 - 3 = 5$

Finally, calculate the length of $\overline{QR}$ using the Pythagorean theorem:

$\overline{QR}^2 = \overline{QS}^2 + \overline{RS}^2$

$QR^2 = 5^2 + \left(\sqrt{6}\right)^2$

$QR^2 = 31$

$\overline{QR} = \sqrt{31}$

8) C

According the Triangle Side–splitter Theorem, lines parallel to the side of a triangle and within the triangle divide the other sides of the triangle into proportional segments. We can write the following ratios in order to solve for $\overline{TR}$:

$\dfrac{\overline{SP}}{\overline{QP}} = \dfrac{\overline{TR}}{\overline{QR}} \rightarrow \dfrac{8}{12} = \dfrac{TR}{15}$

$\overline{TR} = \dfrac{2}{3}(15) = 10$

9) D

$x = y = 45°$

$\angle CBD = 45°$ (vertical angles are identical)

$\angle BDC = 45°$ (sum of interior angles of a triangle)

Therefore, $\triangle ABE$ is similar to $\triangle DBC$ and both are 45–45–90 right triangles. For a 45–45–90 right triangle, the ratio of the side to the hypotenuse is:

$\text{Side} = \dfrac{\text{Hypotenuse}}{\sqrt{2}}$

The length of $\overline{CE}$ can be written as:

$\overline{CE} = \overline{CB} + \overline{BE}$

$\overline{CE} = \dfrac{16}{\sqrt{2}} + \dfrac{8}{\sqrt{2}} = \dfrac{24}{\sqrt{2}}$

Rationalize the denominator:

$\overline{CE} = \dfrac{24}{\sqrt{2}}\cdot\dfrac{\sqrt{2}}{\sqrt{2}} = \dfrac{24\sqrt{2}}{2} = 12\sqrt{2}$

10) ➡ D

The diameter of the circle is 6 centimeters. The radius is 3 centimeters, and the area of the circle is:

$$\text{AREA}_{circle} = \pi r^2 = \pi(3)^2 = 9\pi$$

The area of the shaded region is the difference between the areas of the rectangle and the circle:

$$\text{AREA}_{Shaded} = \text{AREA}_{PQRS} - \text{AREA}_{circle}$$
$$= (6 \times 8) - 9\pi$$
$$= 48 - 9\pi$$

11) ➡ B

$$\cos\frac{\pi}{3} = \cos 60^\circ = \frac{1}{2}$$

$$\frac{1}{2} = x - 1$$

$$x = \frac{3}{2}$$

The correct choice is (B).

12) ➡ A

A tangent line to a circle is perpendicular to the radius of the circle at the point of contact, so $\angle OFH$ is a right angle. The diameter of the circle is the line segment $\overline{OH}$, so the radius $\overline{OF} = \frac{1}{2} \cdot \overline{OH}$. This implies the ratio:

$$\sin \angle OHF = \frac{\overline{OF}}{\overline{OH}} = \frac{1}{2}, \text{ and } \angle OHF = 30^\circ$$

$\angle OHF$ and $\angle BGH$ are alternate interior angles between parallel lines, so $\angle OHF = \angle BGH = 30^\circ$

13) ➡ D

The line $\overline{PQ}$ is tangent to the circle O, so $\angle OQP = 90^\circ$ and ΔOQP is a right triangle. The length of $\overline{OP}$ is the sum of the radii of the two circles:

$$\overline{OP} = 8 + 2 = 10$$

Using the Pythagorean theorem, solve for $\overline{QP}$:

$$\overline{OP}^2 = \overline{OQ}^2 + \overline{QP}^2$$
$$10^2 = 8^2 + \overline{QP}^2$$
$$36 = \overline{QP}^2$$
$$6 = \overline{QP}$$

The length of $\overline{QR}$ is: $\overline{QR} = \overline{QP} - \overline{RP} = 6 - 2 = 4$

14) ➡ A

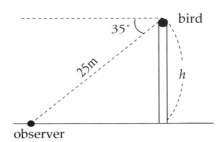

(Diagram not to scale)

The angle of depression from the bird to the observer is equal to the angle of elevation from the observer to the bird because the two are interior alternate angles between parallel lines. The ratio of the height of the post to the distance from bird to observer is the sine of the angle of elevation:

$$\sin 35^\circ = \frac{h}{25}$$
$$h = 25 \sin 35^\circ$$
$$= 14.34 \text{ meters}$$

15) ➡ D

$$\frac{2+i\sqrt{5}}{3-i\sqrt{5}} \cdot \frac{3+i\sqrt{5}}{3+i\sqrt{5}}$$

$$= \frac{6 + 2\sqrt{5} \cdot i + 3\sqrt{5} \cdot i + 5i^2}{9 - 5i^2}$$

$$= \frac{6 + 5\sqrt{5} \cdot i + 5(-1)}{9 - 5(-1)}$$

$$= \frac{1 + 5\sqrt{5} \cdot i}{14}$$

$$= \frac{1}{14} + \frac{5\sqrt{5}}{14}i$$

16) ➡ C

The area and arc length of a segment are both proportional to the central angle. This allows us to write the proportion:

$$\frac{Area\ of\ \overset{\frown}{ACB}}{Area\ of\ circle} = \frac{Length\ of\ \overset{\frown}{ACB}}{Circumference\ of\ circle}$$

To find the area of the segment of $\overset{\frown}{ACB}$:

$$Area\ of\ \overset{\frown}{ACB} = Area\ of\ circle - Area\ of\ \overset{\frown}{AB}$$

$$= \pi(9)^2 - 9\pi = 81\pi - 9\pi = 72\pi$$

As the circumference of the circle is 18π, we can write the proportion above as:

$$\frac{72\pi}{81\pi} = \frac{\overset{\frown}{ACB}}{18\pi}$$

$$\overset{\frown}{ACB} = \frac{8}{9} \cdot 18\pi$$

$$= 16\pi$$

17) ➡ C

$$60\ radians \cdot \frac{360°}{2\pi\ radians} = \frac{10800°}{\pi}$$

18) ➡ D

$$(2a + b) + (3 - 5a)i = 1 + 8i$$

Therefore,
$$2a + b = 1\ \text{and}\ 3 - 5a = 8$$

Solve the second equation:

$$-5a = 8 - 3 \rightarrow -5a = 5 \rightarrow a = -1$$

Solve for b:
$$2(-1) + b = 1 \rightarrow b = 3$$

Calculate their sum: $a + b = -1 + 3 = 2$

19) ➡ B
$$x^2 - 2x + y^2 - 6y = 9$$
$$x^2 - 2x + 1 + y^2 - 6y + 9 = 9 + 1 + 9$$
$$(x - 1)^2 + (y - 3)^2 = 19$$

The center of the circle has coordinates (1 , 3)

20) ➡ B

To find points of intersection, solve the system of equations:

$$3y + x = 6 \rightarrow x = 6 - 3y$$
$$x^2 + y^2 = 10$$

Substitute the first equation into the second:
$$(6 - 3y)^2 + y^2 = 10$$

$$36 - 36y + 9y^2 + y^2 = 10$$

$$10y^2 - 36y + 26 = 0$$

$$(2y - 2)(5y - 13) = 0$$

There are two solutions:
$$2y - 2 = 0 \rightarrow y = 1$$

And,
$$5y - 13 = 0 \rightarrow y = \frac{13}{5}$$

Solve for x–coordinates:
For $y = 1$,
$$3(1) + x = 6 \rightarrow x = 3$$

For $y = \frac{13}{5}$:

$$3\left(\frac{13}{5}\right) + x = 6$$

$$\frac{39}{5} + x = 6$$

$$x = -\frac{9}{5}$$

The two points of intersection are:

$$\left(-\frac{9}{5}, \frac{13}{5}\right)\ \text{and}\ (3, 1).$$

Mastering
Data Analysis

Fundamental Concepts and Techniques

CATEGORICAL DATA

Categorical data is data that can take on one of a fixed number of values or falls into a category. Examples of categorical data are polling results (how many people would vote for each of a group of political candidates), demographic information (groups by location, ethnicity, age, etc.), and quantitative measurements that are organized by range (such as boys in a grade-school class organized by weight ranges). This final example shows that quantitative data can be organized in two ways, either by plotting individual data points (each boy's weight is represented on a graph) or by category (the number of boys that are between 0 – 50 lbs., 51 – 60 lbs., 61 – 70 lbs., etc.). Only the latter of these is referred to as categorical data.

Bar Graphs

▶ Bar graphs are used to represent categorical data only. A category is represented by a vertical or horizontal bar. One axis will have categories on it, and the other will indicate the number of individuals that are in each category.

▶ Below is an example of a vertical bar graph (on the left) with adjacent bars for each state representing different years:

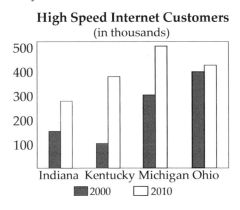

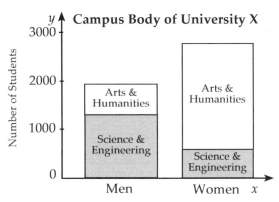

▶ A segmented bar graph (above right) groups multiple categories in a single bar. In this way, a segmented bar graph divides larger category groupings further into subcategories.

▶ Above (on the right) is an example of a segmented bar graph that groups a campus body by gender and each gender by area of study.

Pie Graphs

▶ Pie graphs are a way of representing categorical data by proportion. The proportions may be explicitly marked by way of percentages, and they will always be visible in the structure of the chart.

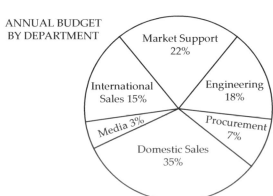

093 Question Topic

→ **BAR GRAPHS AND PIE GRAPHS**

▶ When working with a bar graph, pay close attention to the axes: be clear on the categories and on the scale of the units provided. For example, on the bar graph of the Internet users on the previous page, data for two years are provided for each state, and a legend is provided below the horizontal axis. Be clear on which bar represents which year—the dark bars represent the year 2000 and the lighter bars represent the year 2010. On the horizontal axis, the number of users is presented in thousands, so that the number "200," for example, that is on the vertical axis marks the level at which the number of internet users is 200,000.

▶ When working with a pie graph, look for the total number of elements (people, dollars, units) that is being divided up in the graph. As a pie graph displays proportions, the number of elements assigned to each category must be calculated according to the following formula:

Number of Elements in a Group = (Total Number of Elements) × (Proportion of Elements in a Group)

Example

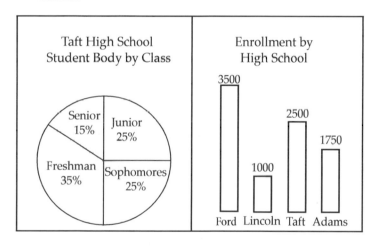

According to the graphs, how many more freshmen are enrolled than sophomores at Taft High School?

(A) 125   (C) 375

(B) 250   (D) 500

 *Solution* :

To determine how many freshmen and sophomores are at Taft High School, first establish how many students are at Taft. This information is obtainable from the bar graph, which gives total student enrollments by high school. The third column from the left is labeled "Taft" and represents enrollment at Taft High School. It shows that enrollment at Taft is 2,500 students.

To calculate the number of freshmen and sophomores at Taft, consider the pie chart, which shows the proportion of students that belong to each class. The proportion of students that are freshmen and sophomores at Taft are 35% and 25% respectively. We can now calculate the numbers of each:

Number of freshmen at Taft = (0.35)(2500) = 875
Number of sophomores at Taft = (0.25)(2500) = 625

There are 250 more freshmen than sophomores at Taft. Choice (B) is correct.

TWO-WAY TABLES

▶ Two-way tables present numerical values grouped into two types of intersecting categories, which are listed in the top row and leftmost column of the table.

▶ The two–way table below contains the number of undergraduate students enrolled in four California universities, organized by gender and school:

	UC Los Angeles	UC Berkeley	UC San Diego	UC Santa Cruz	Total
Female	15,849	13,495	11,535	8,384	49,263
Male	12,825	12,456	12,270	7,311	44,862
Total	28,674	25,951	23,805	15,695	94,125

▶ Review the table above and note the categories: The categorical variables are gender (male or female) and university (UC Los Angeles, UC Berkeley, UC San Diego, and UC Santa Cruz). This is seen more clearly when the numbers are removed (below):

	UC Los Angeles	UC Berkeley	UC San Diego	UC Santa Cruz
Female				
Male				

▶ Now review the table below. Note that the totals for each category are not included. The numerical values in the table below are called **joint frequencies**. They are the number of members that correspond simultaneously to two categorical variables:

	UC Los Angeles	UC Berkeley	UC San Diego	UC Santa Cruz
Female	15,849	13,495	11,535	8,384
Male	12,825	12,456	12,270	7,311

For example, the single cell below tells us that there are 15,849 female undergraduates at UC Los Angeles. The value 15,849 is a joint frequency.

	UC Los Angeles
Female	15,849

▶ Review the table below. All joint frequencies have been removed and the totals have been reinstated. These totals, which are the sum totals of each of the categories, are called **marginal frequencies**:

	UC Los Angeles	UC Berkeley	UC San Diego	UC Santa Cruz	Total
Female					49,263
Male					44,862
Total	28,674	25,951	23,805	15,695	94,125

The marginal frequency for a column or row coresponds to, and may be calculated as, the sum of all the joint frequencies in a given column or row. Below, the total number of undergraduates at UC Los Angeles coresponds to the sum of the number of females and the number of males:

	UC Los Angeles
Female	15,849
Male	12,825
Total	28,674

094 Question Topic

ANALYSIS OF TWO-WAY TABLES

Two–way tables are useful for summarizing large amounts of information and organizing them in purposeful ways. Information is presented in the following ways:

▶ Joint frequencies are the numbers of members that belong at once to two categories.
▶ Marginal frequencies are the totals of the categories named by columns and rows.
▶ Relative frequencies are calculated by dividing joint frequencies by marginal frequencies. For example, the relative frequency of female students at UC Los Angeles is calculated by taking joint and marginal frequencies from the fragment below and doing the subsequent calculation:

	UC Los Angeles
Female	15,849
Male	12,825
Total	28,874

$$\text{Relative Frequency of Females at UCLA} = \frac{\text{Joint Frequency of Females at UCLA}}{\text{Total Students at UCLA}} = \frac{15.849}{28.674} = 0.55$$

▶ Some two-way tables will contain relative frequencies instead of joint frequencies. Tables of this type will list relative frequencies with respect to the total number of members in all categories. The table below is a version of the table on the previous page, but with relative frequencies in place of joint frequencies:

	UC Los Angeles	UC Berkeley	UC San Diego	UC Santa Cruz	Total
Female	0.17	0.14	0.12	0.09	0.52
Male	0.14	0.13	0.13	0.08	0.48
Total	0.31	0.27	0.25	0.17	1.00

Example

According to the table to the right, how many more female undergraduates attend UC Santa Cruz than male undergraduates?

	UC Los Angeles	UC Berkeley	UC San Diego	UC Santa Cruz	Total
Female	15,849	13,495	11,535	8,384	49,263
Male	12,825	12,456	12,270	7,311	44,862
Total	28,674	25,951	23,805	15,695	94,125

Solution :

Locate the number of female undergraduates and male undergraduates at UC Santa Cruz. There are 8,384 female and 7,311 male undergraduates at UC Santa Cruz. To calculate their difference:

$8,384 - 7,311 = 1,073$

There are 1,073 more female than male undergraduates at UC Santa Cruz.

NUMERICAL DATA

▶ **Numerical data** consists of data points that are numerical values. Examples of numerical data include individual test scores and height/weight data for individuals.

095 Question Topic

→ **MEASURES OF CENTER AND SPREAD**

▶ **Mean:** The mean of a set of data is the sum of the numbers in the set divided by the number of members of that set.

▶ **Weighted mean:** A weighted mean is a mean that is calculated from data points that contribute unequally to the mean. In a regular mean, each of the data points is counted once. In a weighted mean, some data points are counted more than others in the calculation of the mean. For example, frequency data and numerical data can be combined to give a weighted mean: data points contribute to the mean proportionally based on how frequently they occur. When calculating a weighted mean, the combined frequency of all data points is used as the divisor.

▶ **Median:** The median of a data set is the middle value when the set is arranged in order of increasing value. If there is an even number of values in the set, the median is the average of the two middle values.

▶ **Mode:** The mode of a set of data is the number that occurs most often in the set.

▶ **Range:** The range is the difference between the greatest and least values of the set.

▶ **Standard deviation:** The standard deviation is a general measure of deviation of data points from the mean. It shows how spread out a data set is; in other words, it is a measure of how concentrated data points are around a certain point (the mean). A small standard deviation indicates that the data are collected around the mean, since the deviations from the mean are small. A large standard deviation indicates that data are spread out from each other, since the deviations from the mean are large. You will not be asked to calculate standard deviation on the SAT—only to make qualitative judgements.

► Consider the following set of integers:

    4, 14, 13, 11, 5, 10, 8, 6, 14

The set contains nine members. Written in ascending order of value, the set becomes:

    4, 5, 6, 8, 10, 11, 13, 14, 14

The statistical measures for this set are calculated below:

$$\text{Mean} = \frac{4+5+6+8+10+11+13+14+14}{9} = 9.4$$

Median = 10

Mode = 14

Range = $14 - 4 = 10$

► Consider the following scenario as an example of the calculation of a weighted mean:

- In a set of data, 30% of data points have a value of 2, 45% of data points have a value of 3, and 25% of data points have a value of 5.

The percentages are frequency data, and as they sum to 100%, the combined frequency of all data points in this case is 1:

$$\text{Weighted Mean} = \frac{(0.3)(2)+(0.45)(3)+(0.25)(5)}{1} = 0.6+1.35+1.25 = 3.2$$

Example

The average score for a class on a biology quiz was 80. If twenty percent of the class scored 90 and thirty percent scored 70, what was the average score for the rest of the class?

    (A) 176   (C) 80

    (B) 78   (D) 82

 **Solution :**

Assume the number of students in the class is one hundred. Assuming a total number of one hundred is a useful way of approaching questions involving percentages. Twenty percent of the class scored 90, so twenty students scored 90.
The total points of these students is (20)(90) = 1800.
Thirty students (thirty percent) scored 70, so their total points is (30)(70) = 2100.
Let x be the average score of the remaining fifty students:

$$\frac{1800+2100+50x}{100} = 80$$

$$\frac{3900+50x}{100} = 80$$

$$50x = 4100$$

$$x = 82$$

The correct choice is (D).

 TEACHER'S TIP

This question could also have been solved by calculating a weighted mean as follows:

$$\frac{(0.2)(90)+(0.3)(70)+(0.5)x}{1} = 80$$

$$39 + 0.5x = 80$$

$$x = 82$$

096 Question Topic

→ **SCATTERPLOTS**

▶ Determine first if the data points are rising or falling as they go from left to right. A rising trend indicates a positive association between the variables; a falling trend indicates a negative association.

▶ Determine if the association is linear (constant slope) or non-linear. If non–linear, determine if the data points represent an exponential or a logarithmic relationship. A logarithmic relationship can be distinguished from an exponential relationship because data points will approach a y-value limit.

▶ To make predictions for values beyond the data set, determine the equation for the line of best fit. Then input the value for which you need to make a prediction. To calculate a line of best fit, sketch a line that follows the course of the data points. Then choose two points that lie on or are very close to this line, and use the coordinates to find the slope and equation of the line.

▶ Outliers are data points that do not follow the pattern of the other data points. If the outlier is much higher in value than expected, it will skew the slope of the line of best fit upwards. If it is lower than expected, it will skew the slope of the line of best fit downwards.

Example

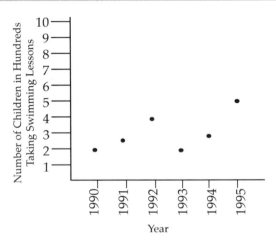

Based on the graph above, the relationship between year and number of students taking swimming lessons is best described as

(A) Positive and linear   (C) Negative and linear

(B) Positive and non-linear   (D) Negative and non-linear

 **Solution :**

The data points rise from left to right. We determine that the relationship between year and students taking lessons is positive. To determine if the relationship is linear or non-linear, consider the two types of non-linear positive relationships between variables: an exponential relationship will show data points curving upwards; a logarithmic relationship will show data points leveling-off to a y-value limit. Neither of those patterns describes the scatterplot above. The data points do, however, increase more-or-less steadily, suggesting a linear relationship between variables.

The correct choice is (A).

097 Question Topic

→ PROBABILITY

▶ An **event** is a set of outcomes. The probability of an event (E) is P(E), and is calculated as follows:

$$P(E) = \frac{number\ of\ outcomes\ in\ E}{total\ number\ of\ possible\ outcomes}$$

▶ If event A and event B are mutually exclusive (that is, the fulfillment of one event excludes the possibility of the other), then the probability of the two occurring is the sum of their individual probabilities:

$$P(A\ or\ B) = P(A) + P(B)$$

Example

In Texas Hold 'Em, players are dealt two "pocket" cards out of a standard 52-card deck. What is the probability that Chris will be dealt two Aces in any given hand?

(A) 0.45   (C) 21

(B) 0.0045   (D) 0.221

 Solution :

To determine the probability of being dealt two Aces in Texas Hold 'Em, first calculate the probability that the first card is an Ace, then multiply that by the probability that the second card is an Ace. Initially, there are four Aces in a 52-card deck. Thus, the probability that Chris' first card is an ace is:

$$Probability = \frac{number\ of\ Aces\ in\ deck}{total\ cards\ in\ deck} = \frac{4}{52} = \frac{1}{13}\ or\ 0.077$$

After one Ace has been dealt, there are only three Aces left in the remaining 51 cards. Therefore the probability that Chris' second card is an Ace is:

$$Probability = \frac{3}{51}\ or\ 0.059$$

The probability that both cards are Aces is the product of the probabilities of each event:

Probability of Pocket Aces = Probability of First Card Ace × Probability of Second Card Ace
= (0.059 × 0.077) = 0.0045

098 Question Topic

INDEPENDENT AND DEPENDENT EVENTS

Independent events

▶ Independent events are events wherein the occurrence of one event does not affect the probability of the other occurring.

▶ For any two independent events A and B, the probability of both occurring together is the product of their individual probabilities:

$$P(A \text{ and } B) = P(A) \cdot P(B)$$

Dependent events

▶ Dependent events change the probability of the other(s) occurring once one event has happened. For any two dependent events, the probability of both occurring together is the product of the probability of event A occurring and the probability of event B occurring given event A has occurred.

$$P(A \text{ and } B) = P(A) \cdot P(B \mid A)$$

▶ An event that is certain to happen has a probability of 1.

▶ An event that is impossible has a probability of 0.

Example

If n and m are positive integers, chosen at random and each less than or equal to 12, what is the probability that $3(n + m) + 5 \leq 19$?

Solution :

Solve the inequality:
$3(n + m) + 5 \leq 19$
$3(n + m) \leq 14$
$n + m \leq 4.667$

Possible values for n and m that may satisfy the equality are 1, 2, and 3. The selections of integers are independent events, so the probability of selecting any given combination of two numbers is $\left(\dfrac{1}{12}\right)\left(\dfrac{1}{12}\right) = \dfrac{1}{144}$. There are a total of 144 possibilities. Of these, there are six combinations that sum to less than or equal to 4.667: 1 and 1; 1 and 2; 1 and 3; 2 and 1; 2 and 2; 3 and 1. The probability that any sum $n + m$ satisfies the inequality is $\dfrac{6}{144}$ (simplified to $\dfrac{1}{24}$) or 0.041.

RATES

▶ **Rates** are a measure of the change in some quantity per unit time.
▶ A commonly seen rate is average speed. It is calculated using the formula:

$$Average\ Speed = \frac{total\ distance}{total\ time}$$

▶ **Uniform Motion**: An object that moves at a constant speed, or rate, is said to be in uniform motion.

099 Question Topic

→ **WORK PROBLEMS**

Work problems deal with the rate of work; that is, they deal with the amount of work that can be completed in a certain period of time. The following formula is the rate formula above rewritten in terms of work:

(rate of work) • (time worked) = amount of work completed

SAT work problems will often have the following form:

• Assume two workers, worker A and worker B, are on the same job. Worker A can finish the job in x hours when working alone and worker B can finish the job in y hours when working alone. This means that worker A completes $\frac{1}{x}$ of the job per hour and worker B completes $\frac{1}{y}$ of the job per hour. If they work together, their rate of work is $\frac{1}{x}+\frac{1}{y}$ of the job per hour. The number of hours they need to complete the job together is given by the following formula:

$$Time\ to\ complete = \frac{1}{\frac{1}{x}+\frac{1}{y}}$$

Example

Peter can build two sand castles in one hour. David can build two sand castles in forty minutes. How long will it take them to make one sand castle together?

Solution :

The job consists of making two sand castles. The time it takes Peter to complete the job is 1 hour and the time it takes David to complete the job is 40 minutes, or $\frac{2}{3}$ hour. Plugging in Peter's time to complete for x and David's time to complete for y in the equation above gives the time it takes for Peter and David to complete the job together:

$$Time\ to\ complete = \frac{1}{\frac{1}{x}+\frac{1}{y}} = \frac{1}{\frac{1}{1}+\frac{1}{\left(\frac{2}{3}\right)}} = \frac{1}{1+\frac{3}{2}} = \frac{1}{\left(\frac{5}{2}\right)} = \frac{2}{5}$$

The time to complete the job is $\frac{2}{5}$ hour, or 24 minutes. As the job consists of making two sand castles, the time to make one sand castle is half this time, 12 minutes.

RATIOS, PROPORTIONS, AND PERCENTAGES

Ratios

▶ A ratio is a quantitative relationship between two numbers and can be written in the following ways:

- $a : b$
- $\dfrac{a}{b}$
- a to b

▶ A ratio between two quantities must express the measures in the same unit. For example, to write a ratio between one quantity in hours and another in seconds, the first quantity must be converted to seconds or the second quantity must be converted to hours, or they both must be converted to a common unit (minutes).

▶ When comparing two ratios to each other, the order in which the ratios are written is crucial. The ratio $a : b$ is not the same as the ratio $b : a$.

Proportions

▶ A proportion is an equation that sets two ratios equal to each other. A proportion is usually written in the following form:

- $\dfrac{a}{b} = \dfrac{c}{d}$

The expression above can be read as "a is to b as c is to d."

Percentages

▶ Percentages are a way of representing parts of a whole in terms of hundredths. For example 85% is equivalent to $\dfrac{85}{100}$, $\dfrac{17}{20}$, and 0.85.

▶ A percent change is calculated as follows:

- Percent change $= \dfrac{amount\ of\ change}{original\ amount} \times 100\%$

MIXTURE PROBLEMS

Mixture problems are similar to rate problems because they involve concentrations, and concentrations are conceptually similar to rates. A **concentration** implies a mixture of at least two different substances. A concentration can be defined as the amount of one substance per unit measure of mixture. This is expressed in the following formula:

$$Concentration\,of\,A = \frac{Amount\,of\,Substance\,A}{Amount\,of\,Mixture}$$

Mixture is almost always present in greater quantity than Substance A.

Example

At a grocery store, nuts are sold at $4.00 per kilogram and raisins are sold at $5.20 per kilogram. How many kilograms of each are in a three kilogram batch sold for $13.56?

 Solution :

The 3-kilogram mixture is sold for $13.65. The cost of the mixture per kilogram is $\frac{\$13.65}{3\,kg}$ = $4.52 per kilogram. Let n be the number of kilograms of nuts, and $3 - n$ be the number of kilograms of raisins. Setting up a table helps keep track of this information (shaded boxes contain information taken directly from the question):

	Kilograms	Price per kilogram	Total Value
Nuts	n	4	$4n$
Raisins	$3 - n$	5.2	$5.2(3 - n)$
Mixture	3	4.52	13.56

 TEACHER'S TIP

Mixture problems are similar to rate problems because concentration is conceptually similar to rate.

The sum of the values of the ingredients is equal to the total value of the mixture:

$4n + 5.2(3 - n) = 13.56$

$4n + 15.6 - 5.2n = 13.56$

$-1.2n = -2.04$

$n = 1.7$

The mixture is made up of 1.7 kilograms of nuts and 1.3 kilograms of raisins.

UNIT CONVERSION

When a question requires you to convert a quantity from one unit to another, use a conversion ratio and dimensional analysis to complete the calculation. Dimensional analysis involves arranging the units in such a way that multiplication cancels out certain units and leaves only the desired units.

101 Question Topic

→ **DENSITY**

Density is a measure of mass per unit volume. The formula for calculating density is

$$Density = \frac{mass}{volume}$$

Example

A metal alloy has a density of 20 g/cm^3. Which of the following represents the mass of a piece of alloy 10 inches long, 3 inches wide, and one inch deep? (one inch = 2.54 centimeters)

(A) $(10)(3)(16.4)(20)$

(B) $(10)(3)(2.54)(20)$

(C) $\frac{(10)(3)(2.54)}{20}$

(D) $\frac{(10)(3)(20)}{2.54}$

 **Solution :**

Sketch the piece of alloy:

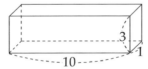

Solution: From the density formula we derive the following formula:

Mass = (density)(volume)

The volume of the piece of alloy is equivalent to the expression $(10)(3)(1)$ in^3. The given density is 20 g/cm^3, but this must be converted to g/in^3 by multiplying the density by a conversion factor. The density is in terms of cm^3, so the conversion factor must also be cubed:

Density = $\left(\dfrac{20g}{cm^3}\right)\left(\dfrac{2.54cm}{in}\right)^3 = \left(\dfrac{20g}{cm^3}\right)\left(\dfrac{16.4cm^3}{in^3}\right) = (20)(16.4)\dfrac{g}{in^3}$

We get an expression for mass by multiplying the expression for volume by the expression for density. This leads us to the expression $(10)(3)(1)(16.4)(20)$, which corresponds to choice (A).

 TEACHER'S TIP

Dimensional analysis involves arranging the units so that multiplication cancels out certain units and leaves only the desired units.

Quick Practice

1. It takes four minutes to raise the temperature of a 10 kilogram iron pot from 4 to 140 degrees Celsius. If mass is directly proportional to heating time, how long will it take to heat a 2.3 kilogram iron pot over the same temperature range using the same heat source?

   (A) 5.8 seconds

   (B) 55 seconds

   (C) 58 seconds

   (D) 6 minutes

2. A person slices a pie into p equal slices and eats three of them. In terms of p, what percentage of the pie is left?

   (A) $100(p-3)\%$

   (B) $\dfrac{100(p-3)}{p}\%$

   (C) $\dfrac{100}{p-3}\%$

   (D) $\dfrac{p-3}{100}\%$

3. A secretary had a typing speed of fifty-five words per minute. After practicing, he raised his typing speed to 4,620 words per hour. By what percent did the secretary's typing speed increase?

   (A) 10%

   (B) 20%

   (C) 30%

   (D) 40%

4. Tickets to a community concert cost three dollars for seniors and five dollars for adults. If a total of 180 tickets are sold for $810, what is the ratio of seniors' tickets to adults' tickets sold?

   (A) 1 to 4

   (B) 1 to 3

   (C) 1 to 2

   (D) 4 to 7

5.

JULIA'S HORSE EXPENSES

	Boarding	Lessons	Total
January		$50	
February		$40	
March		$80	
Total			$260

The table above has information on Julia's expenses for keeping a horse, but it is missing some numbers. If her boarding costs are the same each month, what are her total expenses for February?

   (A) $30

   (B) $50

   (C) $70

   (D) $80

6. Janina handles finances for her band. They are currently touring, and have an arrangement whereby they receive 20% of ticket sales. If tickets are $15 each, and she hopes to make $300 per show, how many people need to attend each show for her to meet her goal?

   (A) 100

   (B) 350

   (C) 400

   (D) 500

7. Due to a particularly dry season, ecologists measured a 25% drop in a local bird population. They attributed this to a concurrent drop in vegetative food sources. If the drop in bird numbers was caused by a 5% drop in vegetation, by what percentage would the bird population drop as a result of an 8% drop in vegetation?

   (A) 16%

   (B) 40%

   (C) 50%

   (D) 62%

8. If a bus averages sixty miles per hour on a certain route, it will arrive at the terminal two hours early. If the bus averages forty miles per hours on the same route, it will arrive two hours late. What is the distance of the trip?

   (A) 9 miles

   (B) 90 miles

   (C) 125 miles

   (D) 480 miles

9. John has twenty milliliters of a 20 percent salt solution. How much salt should he add to make it a 30 percent solution? (Assume that 1 gram of solid is equivalent to 1 milliliter of fluid.)

   (A) 1.8 grams

   (B) 2.0 grams

   (C) 2.7 grams

   (D) 2.9 grams

10. Peter can type a manuscript in three hours. David takes six hours to type the same manuscript. If Peter and David begin working on the manuscript together, how long will they take to finish?

   (A) 1 hour, 54 minutes

   (B) 2 hours

   (C) 2 hours, 10 minutes

   (D) 2 hours, 30 minutes

11.

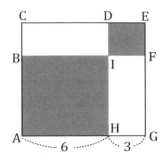

In the figure above, ACEG, DEFI, and ABIH are squares. If a point in ACEG is chosen at random, what is the probability that the point will be in a shaded region?

(A) $\dfrac{1}{3}$

(B) $\dfrac{1}{2}$

(C) $\dfrac{5}{9}$

(D) $\dfrac{2}{3}$

12.

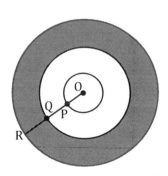

Note: Diagram not to scale

The diagram above shows three circles that share a common origin O. If the lengths of segments $\overline{PQ}$ and $\overline{QR}$ are both equal to the diameter of the smallest circle, what is the probability that a randomly selected point within the diagram falls within the shaded region?

(A) $\dfrac{8}{25}$

(B) $\dfrac{9}{25}$

(C) $\dfrac{1}{9}$

(D) $\dfrac{16}{25}$

13. The shoe sizes of ten men are 8, 10, 9, 12, 7, 10, 10, 11, 6 and 7. How much greater is the mode than the median?

(A) 0

(B) 0.5

(C) 5

(D) 9.5

Questions 14 and 15 refer to the information below.

High Speed Internet Customers
(in thousands)

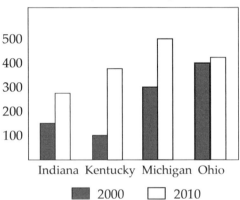

14. The table above is of high speed internet customers for a cable company in four states in the years 2000 and 2010. The number of customers in Kentucky in 2000 was approximately what percent of the number of customers in Ohio in the same year?

(A) 15%

(B) 20%

(C) 25%

(D) 30%

15. From 2000 to 2010, the total number of high speed internet customers in the four states was increased by approximately what percent?

(A) 25%

(B) 33%

(C) 50%

(D) 67%

Questions 17 and 18 refer to the information below.

Poverty data in the United States from 2012 (numbers are in millions)

	Under 18 in families	18-54	55–64	65 and older	All ages
# Poor	15.4	22.5	4.1	3.9	46.5
Total Population	72.4	155.3	38.5	43.3	310.7

17. Which group had the highest percentage of poor in 2012?

(A) Under 18

(B) 18 – 54

(C) 55 – 64

(D) 65 and older

16. **Cellphone Usage for Month Y**

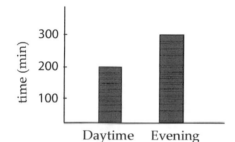

The graph above shows Vivian's cellphone use for the month. Her plan charges her a fee of $20 per month in addition to 10 cents per minute for daytime calls and 5 cents per minute for evening calls after the first 200 minutes (the first 200 evening minutes are included in the fee). What is her cellphone bill for the month?

(A) $25

(B) $40

(C) $45

(D) $70

18. Which of the following best describes the relationship between percentage of people in poverty and age?

(A) Weakly Positive

(B) Strongly Positive

(C) Weakly Negative

(D) No correlation

Quick Practice

Questions 19 and 20 refer to the information below.

Cold-call Success Rate

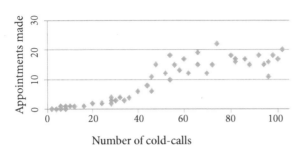

Number of cold-calls

19. For two months, a sales manager tracked the number of cold–calls made per day against the number of appointments set as a result of the call. This data is expressed in the scatterplot above. Which of the following best describes the relationship between number of calls and appointments made?

(A) Linear positive

(B) Linear negative

(C) Exponential

(D) Logistic

20. Shortly after this period, the sales manager decides that she will make 140 cold–calls in a single day. Based on her data, roughly how many appointments can she expect to make?

(A) 10

(B) 20

(C) 30

(D) 40

ANSWERS

&

EXPLANATIONS

1-20

Answers & Explanations...
Mastering Data Analysis

1.	Ⓑ	6.	Ⓐ	11.	Ⓒ	16.	Ⓒ
2.	Ⓑ	7.	Ⓑ	12.	Ⓓ	17.	Ⓐ
3.	Ⓓ	8.	Ⓓ	13.	Ⓑ	18.	Ⓒ
4.	Ⓑ	9.	Ⓓ	14.	Ⓒ	19.	Ⓓ
5.	Ⓒ	10.	Ⓑ	15.	Ⓓ	20.	Ⓑ

1) ➤ B

Convert heating time to seconds:

$$4\,min.(\frac{60\,sec.}{1\,min.}) = 240\,sec.$$

As heating time is proportional to mass, we can write the proportion:

$$\frac{240s}{10kg} = \frac{x}{2.3kg}$$

$$x = \frac{(240s)(2.3kg)}{10kg} = 55s$$

2) ➤ B

The proportion of slices left is: $\frac{p-3}{p}$

To convert this into percentage:

$$\left(\frac{p-3}{p}\right) \times 100\% = \frac{(p-3)100}{p}\%$$

3) ➤ D

$$Typing\ speed = \frac{4,260\,words}{hour} \times \frac{hour}{60\,minute} = \frac{77\,words}{minute}$$

$$Percent\ increase = \frac{22\,words\ per\ minute}{55\,words\ per\ minute} \times 100\% = 40\%$$

4) ➤ B

Let x be the number of senior tickets sold and y be the number of adult tickets sold:

$x + y = 180$

$3x + 5y = 810$

Multiply the first equation by a factor of 3, and subtract from the second:

$$\begin{array}{r} 3x + 5y = 810 \\ -)\ 3x + 3y = 540 \\ \hline 2y = 270 \\ y = 135 \end{array}$$

Therefore, $x + 135 = 180 \rightarrow x = 45$

The ratio $x : y$ is $\frac{45}{135} = \frac{1}{3}$

5) ➤ C

Total spent on lessons = $50 + $40 + $80 = $170

Total spent on boarding = $260 − $170 = $90

As boarding expenses were the same for each of 3 months:

$$Boarding\ expenses\ per\ month = \frac{\$90}{3\,months} = \frac{\$30}{1\,month}$$

Total expenses for February = Boarding + Lessons

= $30 + $40 = $70

6) ➤ A

x = number of tickets sold per show

Revenue = $(0.20)(15)x$

To make at least $300 per show:

$(0.20)(15)x \geq 300$

$$x \geq \frac{300}{(0.20)(15)}$$

$x \geq 100$

7) ➡ B

The drop in the bird ppulation is proportional to the drop in food sources. We can write the proportion:

$$\frac{5\%}{25\%} = \frac{8\%}{x}$$

$$x = (25\%)(\frac{8\%}{5\%}) = 40\%$$

8) ➡ D

Let x be the scheduled time in hours that it takes to make the trip. As the distance is constant regardless of speed, we can use the formula *Distance = (velocity)(time)* and set the two routes equal to each other:

$60(x - 2) = 40(x + 2)$

$60x - 120 = 40x + 80$

$20x = 200$

$x = 10$

Finally, calculate for distance:

Distance = $60(8) = 480$

9) ➡ D

Let x be the number of grams or milliliters of salt that must be added to make a 30% solution (assume grams are equivalent to milliliters). The amount of salt in the 20% solution is:

Amount of salt = $(20mL)(0.2) = 4g$

The volume of the solution increases to 20+x mL:

$$0.3 = \frac{4 + x}{20 + x}$$

$x = 2.86\ g$

10) ➡ B

Peter can type $\frac{1}{3}$ of the manuscript in one hour. David can type $\frac{1}{6}$ of the manuscript in one hour. Let x be the time, in hours, that it takes them to type the manuscript together:

$$\frac{1}{3}x + \frac{1}{6}x = 1$$

$$\frac{1}{2}x = 1$$

$$x = 2$$

11) ➡ C

$$Probability = \frac{Area\ of\ ABIH + Area\ of\ DEFI}{Area\ of\ ACEG}$$

$$= \frac{36 + 9}{81} = \frac{45}{81} = \frac{5}{9}$$

12) ➡ D

Let the radius of the smallest circle, $\overline{OP}$, be r. Then,

$\overline{OQ} = 3r$

$\overline{OR} = 5r$

The areas of the circles are:

Area of circle with radius OQ = $\pi(3r)^2 = 9\pi r^2$

Area of circle with radius OR = $\pi(5r)^2 = 25\pi r^2$

The probability of the point being in the shaded region is:

$$Probability = \frac{25\pi r^2 - 9\pi r^2}{25\pi r^2} = \frac{16}{25}$$

13) ➡ B

In order, the shoe sizes are: 6, 7, 7, 8, 9, 10, 10, 10, 11, 12. The mode is 10. Because there are an even number of sizes, the median is the average of the middle two sizes:

Mode = 10, Median = $\frac{9 + 10}{2} = 9.5$

Therefore,

Mode – Median = $10 - 9.5 = 0.5$

14) ➡ C

Customers in KY in 2000 = 100,000

Customers in OH in 2000 = 400,000

There were 25% as many customers in Kentucky than in Ohio in the year 2000.

15) ⮕ D

Total users in 2000 (thousands)
= 125 + 100 + 275 + 400 = 900
Total users in 2010 (thousands)
= 250 + 350 + 475 + 425 = 1500

Increase from 2000 to 2010(thousands) = 600

% increase = $\dfrac{600}{900} \times 100\% = 67\%$

16) ⮕ C

From the graph, we can see that the number of daytime minutes used is 200, and the number of evening minutes used is 300. The total bill is:

Fee + (Daytime minutes)(0.10) + (Evening minutes − 200)(0.05)
= 20 + (200)(0.10) + (300 − 200)(0.05) = 45

17) ⮕ A

The percentage poor for each age group is calculated by taking the "# Poor" value for that group, dividing it by the "Total Population" for the group, and multiplying the result by "100 percent":

$$\% \text{ Poor} = \dfrac{\# \text{ of Poor}}{\text{Total Population}} \times 100\%$$

Using this formula, it can be shown that the "Under 18" group has the highest percentage poor, with 21.3%.

18) ⮕ C

To answer this question, calculate the percentage poor (according to the formula in the explanation for #17) for each age group, and note whether or not there is a trend in the percentage as age increases:

Under 18: % Poor = 21.3%
18 – 52: % Poor = 14.5%
55 – 64: % Poor = 10.6%
65 and older: % Poor = 9.0%

It is apparent that as age increases, the percentage poor decreases. This result describes a negative relationship between the factors of age and percentage poor. We describe the relationship in this particular case as "weakly negative" because the relationship is not proportional.

19) ⮕ D

A logistic curve demonstrates exponential growth early, followed by a slowing down and plateauing of growth. This pattern most accurately describes the data expressed in the graph.

20) ⮕ B

It is apparent from the scatterplot that if call volume exceeds 70 calls per day, the number of appointments made does not increase with more calls. If the sales manager extended her number of calls in a single day to 140, we would expect the number of appointments to remain around 20.

Math Formulas

▶ The slope of a line containing points (x_1, y_1) and (x_2, y_2):

Slope (m) = $\dfrac{y_2 - y_1}{x_2 - x_1}$

▶ The distance between two points, (x_1, y_1) and (x_2, y_2)

$d = \sqrt{(x_2 - x_1)^2 + (y_2 - y_1)^2}$

▶ *Confidence interval = sample statistic ± margin of error*

▶ The probability of an event P(E):

P(E) = $\dfrac{number\ of\ outcomes\ in\ E}{total\ number\ of\ possible\ outcomes}$

▶ *Average Speed =* $\dfrac{total\ distance}{total\ time}$

▶ *Percent change =* $\dfrac{amount\ of\ change}{original\ amount} \times 100\%$

▶ *Density =* $\dfrac{mass}{volume}$

▶ *Volume of a cylinder or prism = Area of base × Height*

▶ *Volume of a cone or pyramid =* $\dfrac{1}{3}$ *× Area of base × Height*

▶ *Volume of a sphere =* $\dfrac{4}{3} \pi r^3$

▶ Area of a circle: $A = \pi r^2$

▶ Measure of a central angle θ in radians: $\theta = \dfrac{s}{r}$

▶ The standard form for the equation of a circle:
$(x - h)^2 + (y - k)^2 = r^2$

▶ The midpoint between two points (x_w, y_1) and
(x_2, y_2) is the point $\left[\dfrac{x_1 + x_2}{2}, \dfrac{y_1 + y_2}{2} \right]$

▶ Pythagorean Theorem:
$(Hypotenuse)^2 = (side\ 1)^2 + (side\ 2)^2$

▶ Trigonometric Ratios:

$sin\ A = \dfrac{opposite}{hypotenuse}$

$cos\ A = \dfrac{adjacent}{hypotenuse}$

$tan\ A = \dfrac{opposite}{hypotenuse}$

▶ Sine and cosine of complementary angles:

$sin\ x = cos(90° - x)$

$cos\ x = sin(90° - x)$

▶ Converting between radians and degrees:

1 radian = $\dfrac{180}{\pi}$ degrees

1 degree = $\dfrac{\pi}{180}$ radians

▶ The quadratic formula: $x = \dfrac{-b \pm \sqrt{b^2 - 4ac}}{2a}$

KALLIS

SAT® Practice Test #1

IMPORTANT REMINDERS:

1

When you take the official SAT, you will need to use a No. 2 pencil. Do not use a pen or a mechanical pencil.

2

On the official SAT, sharing any of the questions on the test violates the College Board's policies and may result in your scores being canceled.

(This cover is modeled after the cover you'll see when you take the official SAT.)

YOUR NAME (PRINT)

| LAST | FIRST | MI |

TEST CENTER

| NUMBER | NAME OF TEST CENTER | ROOM NUMBER |

TEST BOOKLET

- You may open the booklet to ONLY the section that is currently being tested. You may NOT browse upcoming sections, nor can you review your answers in past sections.
- You MAY write in your test booklet., but you will not receive any credit for answers that you indicate in the booklet. When the time for a section is over, you may NOT transfer answers from your booklet to the answer sheet.
- You may NOT take any part of the test booklet out of the room.

ANSWER SHEET

- Machines will scan your answer sheet by checking your pencil marks. Using a No. 2 pencil, fill in the circles that correspond to your answers completely and darkly.
- Do not make any marks on the answer sheet outside of these circles. If you need to erase anything, make sure to do it thoroughly.

SCORING

- Each correct answer is worth one point.
- There is no penalty for incorrect answers. Even if you are unsure about a particular answer, it is a good strategy to mark one of the choices.

9 | TEST ID
(Copy from back of test book.)

8 | FORM CODE
(Copy and grid as on back of test book.)

Ideas contained in passages for this test, some of which are excerpted or adapted from published material, do not necessarily represent the opinions of KALLIS.

DO NOT OPEN THIS BOOK UNTIL THE TEST ADMINISTRATOR TELLS YOU TO DO SO.

SAT Practice Test
Answer Sheet

Remove (or photocopy) this answer sheet and use it to complete the SAT Practice Test.
See the answer key and explanations following the test when finished.

Start with number 1 for each section.
If a section has fewer questions than answer spaces, leave the extra spaces blank.

SECTION 1

1. Ⓐ Ⓑ Ⓒ Ⓓ	14. Ⓐ Ⓑ Ⓒ Ⓓ	27. Ⓐ Ⓑ Ⓒ Ⓓ	40. Ⓐ Ⓑ Ⓒ Ⓓ
2. Ⓐ Ⓑ Ⓒ Ⓓ	15. Ⓐ Ⓑ Ⓒ Ⓓ	28. Ⓐ Ⓑ Ⓒ Ⓓ	41. Ⓐ Ⓑ Ⓒ Ⓓ
3. Ⓐ Ⓑ Ⓒ Ⓓ	16. Ⓐ Ⓑ Ⓒ Ⓓ	29. Ⓐ Ⓑ Ⓒ Ⓓ	42. Ⓐ Ⓑ Ⓒ Ⓓ
4. Ⓐ Ⓑ Ⓒ Ⓓ	17. Ⓐ Ⓑ Ⓒ Ⓓ	30. Ⓐ Ⓑ Ⓒ Ⓓ	43. Ⓐ Ⓑ Ⓒ Ⓓ
5. Ⓐ Ⓑ Ⓒ Ⓓ	18. Ⓐ Ⓑ Ⓒ Ⓓ	31. Ⓐ Ⓑ Ⓒ Ⓓ	44. Ⓐ Ⓑ Ⓒ Ⓓ
6. Ⓐ Ⓑ Ⓒ Ⓓ	19. Ⓐ Ⓑ Ⓒ Ⓓ	32. Ⓐ Ⓑ Ⓒ Ⓓ	45. Ⓐ Ⓑ Ⓒ Ⓓ
7. Ⓐ Ⓑ Ⓒ Ⓓ	20. Ⓐ Ⓑ Ⓒ Ⓓ	33. Ⓐ Ⓑ Ⓒ Ⓓ	46. Ⓐ Ⓑ Ⓒ Ⓓ
8. Ⓐ Ⓑ Ⓒ Ⓓ	21. Ⓐ Ⓑ Ⓒ Ⓓ	34. Ⓐ Ⓑ Ⓒ Ⓓ	47. Ⓐ Ⓑ Ⓒ Ⓓ
9. Ⓐ Ⓑ Ⓒ Ⓓ	22. Ⓐ Ⓑ Ⓒ Ⓓ	35. Ⓐ Ⓑ Ⓒ Ⓓ	48. Ⓐ Ⓑ Ⓒ Ⓓ
10. Ⓐ Ⓑ Ⓒ Ⓓ	23. Ⓐ Ⓑ Ⓒ Ⓓ	36. Ⓐ Ⓑ Ⓒ Ⓓ	49. Ⓐ Ⓑ Ⓒ Ⓓ
11. Ⓐ Ⓑ Ⓒ Ⓓ	24. Ⓐ Ⓑ Ⓒ Ⓓ	37. Ⓐ Ⓑ Ⓒ Ⓓ	50. Ⓐ Ⓑ Ⓒ Ⓓ
12. Ⓐ Ⓑ Ⓒ Ⓓ	25. Ⓐ Ⓑ Ⓒ Ⓓ	38. Ⓐ Ⓑ Ⓒ Ⓓ	51. Ⓐ Ⓑ Ⓒ Ⓓ
13. Ⓐ Ⓑ Ⓒ Ⓓ	26. Ⓐ Ⓑ Ⓒ Ⓓ	39. Ⓐ Ⓑ Ⓒ Ⓓ	52. Ⓐ Ⓑ Ⓒ Ⓓ

right in Section 1

wrong in Section 1

SECTION 2

1. Ⓐ Ⓑ Ⓒ Ⓓ	12. Ⓐ Ⓑ Ⓒ Ⓓ	23. Ⓐ Ⓑ Ⓒ Ⓓ	34. Ⓐ Ⓑ Ⓒ Ⓓ
2. Ⓐ Ⓑ Ⓒ Ⓓ	13. Ⓐ Ⓑ Ⓒ Ⓓ	24. Ⓐ Ⓑ Ⓒ Ⓓ	35. Ⓐ Ⓑ Ⓒ Ⓓ
3. Ⓐ Ⓑ Ⓒ Ⓓ	14. Ⓐ Ⓑ Ⓒ Ⓓ	25. Ⓐ Ⓑ Ⓒ Ⓓ	37. Ⓐ Ⓑ Ⓒ Ⓓ
4. Ⓐ Ⓑ Ⓒ Ⓓ	15. Ⓐ Ⓑ Ⓒ Ⓓ	26. Ⓐ Ⓑ Ⓒ Ⓓ	38. Ⓐ Ⓑ Ⓒ Ⓓ
5. Ⓐ Ⓑ Ⓒ Ⓓ	16. Ⓐ Ⓑ Ⓒ Ⓓ	27. Ⓐ Ⓑ Ⓒ Ⓓ	39. Ⓐ Ⓑ Ⓒ Ⓓ
6. Ⓐ Ⓑ Ⓒ Ⓓ	17. Ⓐ Ⓑ Ⓒ Ⓓ	28. Ⓐ Ⓑ Ⓒ Ⓓ	40. Ⓐ Ⓑ Ⓒ Ⓓ
7. Ⓐ Ⓑ Ⓒ Ⓓ	18. Ⓐ Ⓑ Ⓒ Ⓓ	29. Ⓐ Ⓑ Ⓒ Ⓓ	41. Ⓐ Ⓑ Ⓒ Ⓓ
8. Ⓐ Ⓑ Ⓒ Ⓓ	19. Ⓐ Ⓑ Ⓒ Ⓓ	30. Ⓐ Ⓑ Ⓒ Ⓓ	42. Ⓐ Ⓑ Ⓒ Ⓓ
9. Ⓐ Ⓑ Ⓒ Ⓓ	20. Ⓐ Ⓑ Ⓒ Ⓓ	31. Ⓐ Ⓑ Ⓒ Ⓓ	43. Ⓐ Ⓑ Ⓒ Ⓓ
10. Ⓐ Ⓑ Ⓒ Ⓓ	21. Ⓐ Ⓑ Ⓒ Ⓓ	32. Ⓐ Ⓑ Ⓒ Ⓓ	44. Ⓐ Ⓑ Ⓒ Ⓓ
11. Ⓐ Ⓑ Ⓒ Ⓓ	22. Ⓐ Ⓑ Ⓒ Ⓓ	33. Ⓐ Ⓑ Ⓒ Ⓓ	

right in Section 2

wrong in Section 2

Remove (or photocopy) this answer sheet and use it to complete the SAT Practice Test.

Start with number 1 for each section.
If a section has fewer questions than answer spaces, leave the extra spaces blank.

SECTION 3

1. Ⓐ Ⓑ Ⓒ Ⓓ   5. Ⓐ Ⓑ Ⓒ Ⓓ   9. Ⓐ Ⓑ Ⓒ Ⓓ   13. Ⓐ Ⓑ Ⓒ Ⓓ
2. Ⓐ Ⓑ Ⓒ Ⓓ   6. Ⓐ Ⓑ Ⓒ Ⓓ   10. Ⓐ Ⓑ Ⓒ Ⓓ   14. Ⓐ Ⓑ Ⓒ Ⓓ
3. Ⓐ Ⓑ Ⓒ Ⓓ   7. Ⓐ Ⓑ Ⓒ Ⓓ   11. Ⓐ Ⓑ Ⓒ Ⓓ   15. Ⓐ Ⓑ Ⓒ Ⓓ
4. Ⓐ Ⓑ Ⓒ Ⓓ   8. Ⓐ Ⓑ Ⓒ Ⓓ   12. Ⓐ Ⓑ Ⓒ Ⓓ

right in Section 3

#wrong in Section 3

16.   17.   18.   19.   20.

SECTION 4

1. Ⓐ Ⓑ Ⓒ Ⓓ   9. Ⓐ Ⓑ Ⓒ Ⓓ   17. Ⓐ Ⓑ Ⓒ Ⓓ   25. Ⓐ Ⓑ Ⓒ Ⓓ
2. Ⓐ Ⓑ Ⓒ Ⓓ   10. Ⓐ Ⓑ Ⓒ Ⓓ   18. Ⓐ Ⓑ Ⓒ Ⓓ   26. Ⓐ Ⓑ Ⓒ Ⓓ
3. Ⓐ Ⓑ Ⓒ Ⓓ   11. Ⓐ Ⓑ Ⓒ Ⓓ   19. Ⓐ Ⓑ Ⓒ Ⓓ   27. Ⓐ Ⓑ Ⓒ Ⓓ
4. Ⓐ Ⓑ Ⓒ Ⓓ   12. Ⓐ Ⓑ Ⓒ Ⓓ   20. Ⓐ Ⓑ Ⓒ Ⓓ   28. Ⓐ Ⓑ Ⓒ Ⓓ
5. Ⓐ Ⓑ Ⓒ Ⓓ   13. Ⓐ Ⓑ Ⓒ Ⓓ   21. Ⓐ Ⓑ Ⓒ Ⓓ   29. Ⓐ Ⓑ Ⓒ Ⓓ
6. Ⓐ Ⓑ Ⓒ Ⓓ   14. Ⓐ Ⓑ Ⓒ Ⓓ   22. Ⓐ Ⓑ Ⓒ Ⓓ   30. Ⓐ Ⓑ Ⓒ Ⓓ
7. Ⓐ Ⓑ Ⓒ Ⓓ   15. Ⓐ Ⓑ Ⓒ Ⓓ   23. Ⓐ Ⓑ Ⓒ Ⓓ
8. Ⓐ Ⓑ Ⓒ Ⓓ   16. Ⓐ Ⓑ Ⓒ Ⓓ   24. Ⓐ Ⓑ Ⓒ Ⓓ

#right in Section 4

#wrong in Section 4

31.   32.   33.   34.   35.

SECTION **4**

36.

37. PART 1

37. PART 2

Remove (or photocopy) this answer sheet and use it to complete the SAT Practice Test.

Section 5 is the Optional Essay test.

SECTION **5**

Reading Test Scoring Guide

Number correct on the SAT Reading Test: _____
(Raw Score)

Raw Score	Scaled Score
52 – 51	400
50 – 49	390
48	380
47	370
46 – 45	360
44 – 43	350
42 – 41	340
40 – 38	330
37	320
36 – 35	310
34 – 33	300
32 – 30	290
29 – 28	280
27	270
26	260
25 – 24	250
23 – 22	240
21	230
20 – 19	220
18	210
17 – 16	200
15	190
14	180
13 – 12	170
11	160
10 – 9	150
8	140
7	130
6	120
5	110
4 – 1	100

Writing and Language Test Scoring Guide

Number correct on the SAT Writing and Language Test: _____
(Raw Score)

Raw Score	Scaled Score
44	400
43	390
42	380
41	370
40 – 38	360
37	350
36	340
35 – 34	330
33 – 32	320
31	310
30 – 28	300
27 – 26	290
25 – 24	280
23 – 22	270
21	260
20	250
19	230 – 240
18	220
17	210
16	200
15	190
14	180
13	170
12	160
11	150
10	140
9	130
8	120
7	110
6 – 1	100

Math Test Scoring Guide

Number correct on the SAT Math Test: _____
(Raw Score)

Raw Score	Scaled Score		Raw Score	Scaled Score
58 – 57	800		25	510
56 – 55	790		24 – 23	500
54	780		22 – 21	490
53	770		20	480
52	750		19	470
51	740		18 – 17	460
50	730		16	450
49	710		15 – 14	440
48	700		13	420 – 430
47	690		12 – 11	400 – 410
46	680		10 – 9	380 – 390
45	670		8 – 6	350 – 370
44	660		5 – 4	310 – 340
43	650		3	290 – 300
42	640		2	250 – 280
41	630		1	210 – 240
40 – 39	620		0	200
38 – 37	610			
36 – 34	600			
33 – 32	590			
31 – 30	570			
29	560			
28 – 27	550			
26	530			

Reading Test Scaled Score: _____

+

Writing Test Scaled Score: _____370_____

+

Math Test Scaled Score: _____

=

Total SAT Practice Test Score: _____

Reading Test 1

 65 MINUTES, 52 QUESTIONS

Turn to Section 1 of your answer sheet to answer the questions in this section.

DIRECTIONS

Each passage or pair of passages is accompanied by 10 or 11 questions. Read each passage or pair of passages, and then select the most appropriate answer to each question. Some passages may include tables or graphs that require additional analysis.

Refer to the passage below to answer questions 1 – 11.

This passage is adapted from P.G. Wodehouse, *Love Among Chickens*, originally published in 1920. The narrator, who is helping his friend with a new chicken farm in the country, has chased a chicken named Aunt Elizabeth into a tall shrub.

line   I was in the middle of it, very hot, tired, and
dirty, when from the other side I heard a sudden
shout of "Mark over! Bird to the right!" and the
next moment I found myself emerging with
5 a black face and tottering knees on the gravel
path of a private garden. Beyond the path was
a croquet lawn, and on this lawn I perceived, as
through a glass darkly, three figures. The mist
cleared from my eyes, and I recognized two of
10 them.
    One was the middle-aged Irishman who had
traveled down with us in the train. The other was
his blue-eyed daughter.
    The third member of the party was a man, a
15 stranger to me. By some miracle of adroitness he
had captured Aunt Elizabeth, and was holding her
in spite of her protests in a <u>workmanlike</u> manner
behind the wing.
    There are moments and moments. The
20 present one belonged to the more painful variety.
    Even to my exhausted mind it was plain
that there was a need here for explanations.
An Irishman's croquet-lawn is his castle, and
strangers cannot plunge in through hedges
25 without inviting comment.
    Unfortunately, speech was beyond me. ...The
conversation was opened by the other man, in
whose restraining hand Aunt Elizabeth now lay,
outwardly resigned but inwardly, as I, who knew
30 her haughty spirit, could guess, boiling with
baffled resentment. I could see her looking out
of the corner of her eye, trying to estimate the
chances of getting in one good hard peck with her

aquiline beak.
    "Come right in," said the man pleasantly.
35 "Don't knock."
    I stood there, gasping. I was only too well
aware that I presented a quaint appearance. I
had removed my hat before entering the hedge,
and my hair was full of twigs and other foreign
40 substances. My face was moist and grimy. My
mouth hung open. My legs felt as if they had
ceased to belong to me.
    "I must apol— ..." I began, and ended the
sentence with gulps.
45   The elderly gentleman looked at me with
what seemed to be indignant surprise. His
daughter appeared to my guilty conscience
to be looking through me. Aunt Elizabeth
sneered. The only friendly face was the man's.
50 He regarded me with a kindly smile, as if I
were some old friend who had dropped in
unexpectedly.
    "Take a long breath," he advised.
    I took several, and felt better.
55   "I must apologize for this intrusion," I said
successfully. "Unwarrantable" would have
rounded off the sentence neatly, but I would
not risk it. It would have been mere bravado to
attempt unnecessary words of five syllables. I
60 took in more breath. "The fact is, I did—didn't
know there was a private garden beyond the
hedge. If you will give me my hen ..."
    I stopped. Aunt Elizabeth was looking
away, as if endeavoring to create an impression
65 of having nothing to do with me. I am told by
one who knows that hens cannot raise their
eyebrows, not having any; but I am prepared
to swear that at this moment Aunt Elizabeth
raised hers. I will go further. She sniffed.
70   "Here you are," said the man. "Though it's
hard to say good-bye."
He held out the hen to me, and at this point a
hitch occurred. He did his part, the letting go,
all right. It was in my department, the taking

75 hold, that the thing was bungled. Aunt Elizabeth
slipped from my grasp like an eel, stood for a
moment eyeing me satirically with her head on
one side, then fled and entrenched herself in some
bushes at the end of the lawn.

80   There are times when the most resolute man
feels that he can battle no longer with fate; when
everything seems against him and the only course
is a dignified retreat. But there is one thing essential
to a dignified retreat. You must know the way out.

1. The words "adroitness" and "workmanlike"
    (lines 15 – 17) help establish the narrator's first
    impression of the stranger as

    (A) a rather harsh person.
    (B) a longtime chicken farmer.
    (C) a person similar to the narrator in tastes.
    (D) at ease with rural life.

2. The statement "There are moments and moments.
    The present one belonged to the more painful
    variety," (lines 19 – 20) serves to

    (A) reveal the nature of the relationship between
        the narrator and the Irishman.
    (B) indicate that the tone of the passage is about to
        change.
    (C) foreshadow the narrator's awkward exchange
        with the man holding Aunt Elizabeth.
    (D) introduce the idea that hard work and
        painstaking efforts are rewarded.

3. The statement "An Irishman's croquet-lawn is
    his castle," (line 23) functions in the passage
    primarily to

    (A) mock the Irishman for valuing his croquet
        lawn so highly.
    (B) cause the reader to associate croquet with wealth
        and royalty.
    (C) describe the circumstances that inspired the
        narrator's apology.
    (D) imply that the Irishman lives on his croquet
        lawn rather than inside his house.

4. As used in line 25, "inviting" most nearly means

    (A) preventing.
    (B) provoking.
    (C) appealing.
    (D) summoning.

5. Based on the passage, the narrator's descriptions
    of Aunt Elizabeth serve primarily to

    (A) depict her as possessing human
        characteristics.
    (B) suggest that she has outsmarted the narrator.
    (C) elicit sympathy for Aunt Elizabeth.
    (D) contrast with the narrator's descriptions of
        himself.

6. Which choice provides the best evidence for the
    answer to the previous question?

    (A) Lines 31 – 34 ("I could see…aquiline beak")
    (B) Lines 37 – 41 ("I stood there…other foreign
        substances")
    (C) Lines 65 – 69 ("I am told…She sniffed")
    (D) Lines 72 – 75 ("He held out…the thing was
        bungled")

7. The sentences "'Unwarrantable' would have…
    words of five syllables" (lines 56 – 59) primarily
    serve to convey the idea that the narrator

    (A) is still exhausted from his physical exertions.
    (B) does not want to seem pretentious.
    (C) enjoys talking to strangers.
    (D) does not want to bore his audience.

8. What is the narrator's attitude toward the Irishman,
    his daughter, and the stranger holding Aunt
    Elizabeth?

    (A) Earnest and mortified
    (B) Resentful and intimidated
    (C) Foolish and presumptuous
    (D) Respectful and demure

9. As used in line 72, "hitch" most nearly means

    (A) barrier.
    (B) interlude.
    (C) setback.
    (D) catch.

10. In regards to the narrator's relationship with Aunt
    Elizabeth, the narrator can be compared to a

    (A) romantic pursuing his unrequited love.
    (B) hunter being outmaneuvered by his prey.
    (C) warrior meeting his opponent on a battlefield.
    (D) clown performing tricks for an audience.

11. The narrator would most likely agree with which of
    the following statements regarding Aunt Elizabeth?

    (A) She is more cooperative than most other chickens.
    (B) She is less intelligent than others believe her to be.
    (C) She eludes the narrator out of resentment and
        obstinacy.
    (D) She would rather live with the Irishman and his
        daughter than with the narrator.

Refer to the passage below to answer questions 12 – 21.

This passage is adapted from Iam Chong (trans. Kristen Chan), "China's Independent Journalists Face High Risks—And are in High Demand," originally published on inmediahk.net in 2016. This English translation was published in Global Voices on May 26, 2016.

line   An experienced Chinese journalist recently told me that nearly all major news stories that captured public attention in the past three years were written by independent
5   journalists who have no legal status in China.

    As propaganda authorities have become increasingly unreasonable and numerous journalists have received jail time for doing journalistic work, more and more professional
10   journalists have either abandoned or transformed their careers. While some have moved into management positions at major online news portals, others have left media outlets and started writing and distributing
15   independent investigative reports by making use of social media.

    Although the people in the latter group are journalists by training and by trade, they do not fit China's legal framework for what
20   constitutes a journalist. Indeed, it is illegal for a person to identify as a journalist if he or she does not hold a press card. All journalists must hold a press identity card issued by registered media outlets, otherwise it is illegal
25   for them to call themselves journalists. The press card must be renewed annually by the journalist's work unit or it will expire.

    At a recent conference, I met a number of independent journalists from mainland China.
30   They identified themselves using terms like "writer", "grassroots historian", "interviewer" and other monikers to avoid using the term "journalist" to describe their work.

    One type among this group is similar to
35   those independent journalists working in Hong Kong. They choose and research topics according to their own liking. Rather than pursuing "hot topics", they typically follow the convention of reportage literature, by researching historical
40   events such as grassroots stories from the anti-Rightist Campaign and Cultural Revolution, or the history and culture of a particular place that has been neglected by the general public….

    …Another common path for independent
45   journalists in China is to work as an informal media outlet sub-contractor. These journalists have close connections with editors or management staff from more established media outlets that cannot initiate their own
50   investigative reports because of internal censorship. However, they do have budgets to buy content like individual interviews, photos, and features from outside writers and

pay famous bloggers to use their platforms.
55   Hence this group of independent journalists can make a living by selling their reports to conventional media outlets or portal sites*.

    According to existing regulations, portal sites cannot conduct original news reports and
60   hence cannot have their own reporter teams. Yet, they have paid columns or paid special features for independent writers to fill in the content. For example, reports from the WeChat public platform "Qianjieyihao" or "No.1 on
65   front street" are frequently quoted by news portals such as Ifeng, QQ and even Xinhua. The platform, which describes itself as "the Eden of a group of oppressed social reporters," publishes posts produced by teams, some of
70   whom may be affiliated with state media.

    There are no reliable figures on how many journalists work in this mode in China, but it is clear that they are walking on a tightrope which carries immense risk, but can also yield
75   opportunities.

    Independent journalists have no institutional protection. The censorship system within media outlets is a form of control, but it also protects journalists from touching
80   sensitive issues that can get them into trouble. The bureaucratic structure makes certain that responsibility is shared at all levels — editors and management staff work to ensure that news coverage will not break local laws or
85   offend state or party officials. This minimizes the part that the journalists have to take on their shoulders.

    Outside the umbrella of the media institution, independent journalists face many
90   more risks. After the introduction of China's Rumor and Libel Regulation in September 2013, which criminalized rumors and defamatory content that has been reposted 500 times or more, reporting on sensitive stories became
95   much more dangerous for them.

    The growth of the independent journalism sector depends on individual courage, but it has also benefited from developing media and communication ecologies. More and
100   more, breaking news circulates first via social media. Similar to other parts of the world, the conventional media sector is withering in the face of competition from online media — this may be even more pronounced in China, where
105   censorship practices have made state-affiliated media increasingly rigid in recent years.

    And in contrast to conventional media outlets, where sensitive content often never makes it to the printed page, sensitive online
110   content is deleted after publication. A popular post that touches on sensitive topics can reach tens or even hundreds of thousands of readers within a few hours on WeChat before the web censor steps in.

115   In the face of rapid growth of capital

investment in the Internet and technology sector in China, content is king and news content is also essential to the development of online platforms. As independent journalists
120 are more flexible and courageous in picking up social topics, including sensitive ones, they are welcomed by Internet portals. Thus their work is high-risk — and in high demand.

Portal sites: Web sites that assimilate information from other sites in a uniform manner. For example, a news portal would connect users to reports from many media outlets.

12. The primary purpose of the passage is to

(A) praise the bravery and ingenuity of independent journalists in China.
(B) explore the relationship between censorship and journalistic reporting in China.
(C) describe recent government regulations that specifically target independent journalists.
(D) explain how the proliferation of news portals has improved journalism in China.

13. As used in line 3, "captured" most nearly means

(A) expressed.
(B) apprehended.
(C) represented.
(D) attracted.

14. The passage is written from the perspective of

(A) a writer who is outside of China.
(B) a Chinese government official.
(C) an independent Chinese journalist.
(D) a foreigner who is working in China.

15. According to the passage, some journalists in China have reacted to increased pressure from authorities with

(A) apathy and indifference.
(B) rebellion and insurrection.
(C) resourcefulness and subterfuge.
(D) understanding and sympathy.

16. The author indicates that some independent journalists in China identify as "writers," "grassroots historians," and "interviewers" (lines 30 – 33) because

(A) the term "journalist" carries negative connotations.
(B) they cannot lawfully call themselves "journalists."
(C) Chinese censorship laws do not apply to writers, historians, or interviewers.
(D) those who call themselves "journalists" tend to make very little money.

17. As used in line 38, "follow the convention" most nearly means

(A) adhere to the practices.
(B) copy the habits.
(C) keep track of the rules.
(D) accompany the customs.

18. According to the passage, the relationship between many registered media outlets and independent journalists in China is best described as

(A) friendly but not collaborative.
(B) intentionally shrouded in mystery.
(C) mercilessly competitive.
(D) one of communication and cooperation.

19. Which choice provides the best evidence for the answer to the previous question?

(A) Lines 20 – 22 ("Indeed…card")
(B) Lines 44 – 49 ("Another…outlets")
(C) Lines 77 – 80 ("The censorship…trouble")
(D) Lines 96 – 99 ("The growth…ecologies")

20. Paragraph 7 (lines 58 – 70) indicates that

(A) the works of independent journalists are frequently published on major news portals.
(B) many portal sites will illegally hire independent journalists for short-term projects.
(C) WeChat is a large, state-sponsored public platform that publishes works by independent journalists.
(D) many Chinese journalists are now hired by news portals rather than conventional media outlets.

21. Which of the following provides the best support for the "immense risk" that many independent journalists take in China?

(A) Lines 81 – 85 ("bureaucratic…officials")
(B) Lines 90 – 95 ("After the…them")
(C) Lines 103 – 106 ("this may…years")
(D) Lines 119 – 122 ("As independent…portals")

Refer to the passage below to answer questions 22 – 32.

This passage is adapted from Henri Bergson, *Dreams*, originally published in 1914. Bergson is describing studies that attempt to discover the physiological processes behind dreaming.

line Thirty or forty years ago, M. Alfred Maury and, about the same time, M. d'Hervey, of St. Denis, had observed that at the moment of falling asleep these colored spots and moving forms
5 consolidate, fix themselves, take on definite outlines, the outlines of the objects and of the persons which people our dreams. But this is an observation to be accepted with caution, since it emanates from psychologists already half asleep.
10 More recently an American psychologist, Professor Ladd, of Yale, has devised a more rigorous method, but of difficult application, because it requires a sort of training. It consists in acquiring the habit on awakening in the morning
15 of keeping the eyes closed and retaining for some minutes the dream that is fading from the field of vision and soon would doubtless have faded from that of memory. Then one sees the figures and objects of the dream melt away little by little
20 into phosphenes, identifying themselves with the colored spots that the eye really perceives when the lids are closed. One reads, for example, a newspaper; that is the dream. One awakens and there remains of the newspaper, whose definite
25 outlines are erased, only a white spot with black marks here and there; that is the reality. Or our dream takes us upon the open sea—round about us the ocean spreads its waves of yellowish gray with here and there a crown of white foam. On
30 awakening, it is all lost in a great spot, half yellow and half gray, sown with brilliant points. The spot was there, the brilliant points were there. There was really presented to our perceptions, in sleep, a visual dust, and it was this dust which served
35 for the fabrication of our dreams.
  Will this alone suffice? Still considering the sensation of sight, we ought to add to these visual sensations which we may call internal all those which continue to come to us from an external
40 source. The eyes, when closed, still distinguish light from shade, and even, to a certain extent, different lights from one another. These sensations of light, emanating from without, are at the bottom of many of our dreams. A candle
45 abruptly lighted in the room will, for example, suggest to the sleeper, if his slumber is not too deep, a dream dominated by the image of fire, the idea of a burning building. Permit me to cite to you two observations of M. Tissié on this subject:
50 "B—— Léon dreams that the theater of Alexandria is on fire; the flame lights up the whole place. All of a sudden he finds himself transported to the midst of the fountain in the public square; a line of fire runs along the chains
55 which connect the great posts placed around the margin. Then he finds himself in Paris at the exposition, which is on fire. He takes part in terrible scenes, etc. He wakes with a start; his eyes catch the rays of light projected by the dark
60 lantern which the night nurse flashes toward his bed in passing. M—— Bertrand dreams that he is in the marine infantry where he formerly served. He goes to Fort-de-France, to Toulon, to Loriet, to Crimea, to Constantinople. He sees lightning, he
65 hears thunder, he takes part in a combat in which he sees fire leap from the mouths of cannon. He wakes with a start. Like B., he was wakened by a flash of light projected from the dark lantern of the night nurse." Such are often the dreams
70 provoked by a bright and sudden light.
  Very different are those which are suggested by a mild and continuous light like that of the moon. A. Krauss tells how one day on awakening he perceived that he was extending his arm
75 toward what in his dream appeared to him to be the image of a young girl. Little by little this image melted into that of the full moon which darted its rays upon him. It is a curious thing that one might cite other examples of dreams where
80 the rays of the moon, caressing the eyes of the sleeper, evoked before him virginal apparitions. May we not suppose that such might have been the origin in antiquity of the fable of Endymion— Endymion the shepherd, lapped in perpetual
85 slumber, for whom the goddess Selene, that is, the moon, is smitten with love while he sleeps?

22. Based on the passage, it can be inferred that the author views dreams as

(A) highly metaphorical and dependent on poetical language.
(B) dependent on the dreamer's cultural and historical environment.
(C) experiences unique to every individual.
(D) phenomena that can be attributed to rational causes.

23. As used in line 7, "people" most nearly means

(A) crowd.
(B) populate.
(C) individualize.
(D) humanize.

24. The author's stance on Maury's and d'Hervey's work—outlined in paragraph 1—is best described as

(A) plainly critical.
(B) generally positive.
(C) deeply intrigued.
(D) highly skeptical.

25. According to paragraph 2 (lines 10 – 35), Professor Ladd's main contention about dreams is that

(A) dreams develop from the colors that we discern during sleep.
(B) dreams consist of muted hues with shining spots.
(C) training can help people remember dreams on awakening.
(D) we visualize materials in dreams that are common in our lives.

26. Which choice provides the best evidence for the answer to the previous question?

(A) Lines 13 – 18 ("It consists in…memory")
(B) Lines 18 – 22 ("Then one sees…closed")
(C) Lines 22 – 26 ("One reads…reality")
(D) Lines 31 – 32 ("The spot…were there.")

27. As used in line 34, the word "dust" most nearly means

(A) feather.
(B) dross.
(C) mist.
(D) trickle.

28. Which choice most clearly states the author's own proposal in the passage about dreams and light?

(A) Dreams are about light-related events that penetrate our eyelids.
(B) People's dreams in the author's era were quite frequently about fire.
(C) External light can combine with memories to create dreams.
(D) Sudden flashes of fire cause nightmares; moonlight is preferable.

29. Which choice provides the best evidence for the answer to the previous question?

(A) Lines 42 – 44 ("These sensations…dreams")
(B) Lines 52 – 57 ("'All of a sudden…fire'")
(C) Lines 64 – 66 ("'He sees lightning…cannon'")
(D) Lines 73 – 76 ("A. Krauss tells…girl")

30. In paragraph 4 (lines 50 – 70), the author quotes descriptions of

(A) the effects of night nurses on two patients.
(B) the terrible memories that two military veterans relive.
(C) two fiery nightmares involving real world events.
(D) two hospital patients' nightmares in settings that are familiar to them.

31. The main rhetorical effect of the phrase "it is a curious thing" (line 78) is to

(A) convey a sense of wonder.
(B) communicate confusion.
(C) express disapproval.
(D) encourage future thinkers.

32. The author refers to the fable of Endymion (lines 82 – 86) primarily to

(A) celebrate a pair of famous lovers.
(B) distinguish between dreams arising from bright and dim light.
(C) demonstrate that dreams represent our deepest longings.
(D) suggest that some dreams may have inspired mythology.

Refer to the passage below to answer questions 33 – 43.

Passage 1 is adapted from Sun Tzu, *The Art of War*, written around 500 BCE and translated in 1910 by Lionel Giles. Passage 2 is adapted from Niccolo Machiavelli, *The Prince*, published in 1532 and translated in 1908 by William K. Marriot.

Passage 1

line
The art of war is of vital importance to the State. It is a matter of life and death, a road either to safety or to ruin. Hence it is a subject of inquiry which can on no account be neglected.

5 All warfare is based on deception. Hence, when able to attack, we must seem unable; when using our forces, we must seem inactive; when we are near, we must make the enemy believe we are far away; when far away, we must make him 10 believe we are near.

Hold out baits to entice the enemy. Feign disorder, and crush him.

If he is secure at all points, be prepared for him. If he is superior in strength, evade him.

15 If your opponent is of choleric* temper, seek to irritate him. Pretend to be weak, that he may grow arrogant.

If he is taking his ease, give him no rest. If his forces are united, separate them. Attack him 20 where he is unprepared, appear where you are not expected.

In war, practice dissimulation, and you will succeed.

Rapidity is the essence of war: take advantage 25 of the enemy's unreadiness, make your way by unexpected routes, and attack unguarded spots. Keep your army continually on the move, and devise unfathomable plans.

Forestall your opponent by seizing what he 30 holds dear, and subtly contrive to time his arrival on the ground.

Walk in the path defined by rule, and accommodate yourself to the enemy until you can fight a decisive battle.

choleric: irritable, angry

Passage 2

35 Every one admits how praiseworthy it is in a prince to keep faith, and to live with integrity and not with craft*. Nevertheless our experience has been that those princes who have done great things have held good faith of little account, and 40 have known how to circumvent the intellect of men by craft, and in the end have overcome those who have relied on their word.

If men were entirely good this precept

45 would not hold, but because they are bad, and will not keep faith with you, you too are not bound to observe it with them. Nor will there ever be wanting to a prince legitimate reasons to excuse this non-observance. Of this endless modern examples could be given, showing how 50 many treaties and engagements have been made void and of no effect through the faithlessness of princes; and he who has known best how to employ the fox has succeeded best.

But it is necessary to know well how to 55 disguise this characteristic, and to be a great pretender and dissembler; and men are so simple, and so subject to present necessities, that he who seeks to deceive will always find someone who will allow himself to be deceived. One recent 60 example I cannot pass over in silence. Alexander the Sixth did nothing else but deceive men, nor ever thought of doing otherwise, and he always found victims; for there never was a man who had greater power in asserting, or who with 65 greater oaths would affirm a thing, yet would observe it less; nevertheless his deceits always succeeded according to his wishes, because he well understood this side of mankind.

And you have to understand this, that a 70 prince, especially a new one, cannot observe all those things for which men are esteemed, being often forced, in order to maintain the state, to act contrary to fidelity, friendship, humanity, and religion. Therefore it is necessary for him to have 75 a mind ready to turn itself accordingly as the winds and variations of fortune force it, yet, as I have said above, not to diverge from the good if he can avoid doing so, but, if compelled, then to know how to set about it.

craft: the skill of deceiving others

33. The author of Passage 1, Sun Tzu, and the author of Passage 2, Machiavelli, could both accurately be described as

(A) advocates trying to start wars.
(B) critics of war and ruthless leadership.
(C) allies devising battle plans for a leader.
(D) pragmatists concerned with longevity.

34. The lack of examples or explanations in Passage 1 primarily serves to

(A) create an impersonal and axiomatic tone.
(B) undermine the passage's central claim.
(C) draw attention to the writer's high status and authority.
(D) emphasize the emotional toughness that is necessary to win wars.

35. As used in line 11, "feign" most nearly means

(A) exaggerate.
(B) conceal.
(C) pretend.
(D) forge.

36. How would Sun Tzu most likely respond to Machiavelli's claim that great leaders "circumvent the intellect of men by craft" (lines 40 – 41)?

(A) With dispassionate concurrence
(B) With some misgivings
(C) With faint praise
(D) With conditional assent

37. Which choice provides the best evidence for the answer to the previous question?

(A) Lines 1 – 2 ("The art…State")
(B) Line 5 ("All warfare…deception")
(C) Lines 13 – 14 ("If he…evade him")
(D) Lines 15 – 16 ("If your…irritate him")

38. In Passage 1, Sun Tzu's advice to "Keep your army continually on the move, and devise unfathomable plans" (lines 27 – 28) most clearly implies that

(A) one's troops will succeed only if they remain in top physical condition.
(B) one's plans for proceeding should be physically and mentally challenging.
(C) one's troops will be more motivated to follow their leader if battle plans are explained.
(D) even one's own troops should be surprised by one's tactics in war.

39. As used in line 46, "observe" most nearly means

(A) commemorate.
(B) pronounce.
(C) maintain.
(D) notice.

40. In paragraph 3 of Passage 2 (lines 54 – 68), Machiavelli identifies which of the following as a reason that people are prone to believing lies?

(A) They want to solve immediate problems.
(B) They tend to be self-centered.
(C) They focus on details rather than seeing the big picture.
(D) They are unsophisticated.

41. Sun Tzu's advice in lines 22 – 23 ("In war… succeed") most closely resembles Machiavelli's advice to

(A) act like Alexander VI.
(B) discern people's motivations.
(C) heed advice from elders.
(D) cultivate a flexible mind.

42. Which choice provides the best evidence for the answer to the previous question?

(A) Lines 43 – 46 ("If men were…them")
(B) Lines 63 – 67 ("for there never…wishes")
(C) Lines 69 – 74 ("And you…religion")
(D) Lines 74 – 79 ("Therefore…about it")

43. On which of the following points would the authors of both passages most likely agree?

(A) Most people are good on a fundamental level.
(B) A leader must always keep in mind the security of future generations.
(C) Leaders must demonstrate courage in order to inspire loyalty.
(D) Maintaining stable government is not always a noble task.

Refer to the passage below to answer questions 44 – 52.

This passage is adapted from "A 'Smoking Gun' for Dinosaur Extinction," Jet Propulsion Laboratory, California Institute of Technology, published in 2003.

line   It is hard to imagine that one of the largest impact craters on Earth, 180 kilometers (112 miles) wide and 900 meters (3,000 feet) deep, could all but disappear from sight, but it did.

5   Chicxulub,* located on Mexico's Yucatán peninsula, eluded detection for decades because it was hidden (and at the same time preserved) beneath a kilometer of younger rocks and sediments. Size isn't the only thing that makes

10   Chicxulub special. Most scientists now agree it's the "smoking gun" – evidence that a huge asteroid or comet indeed crashed into Earth's surface 65 million years ago causing the extinction of more than 70 percent of the living species on

15   the planet, including the dinosaurs. This idea was first proposed by the father and son team of Luis and Walter Alvarez in 1980.

Though the buried giant can't be seen, the impact crater has left subtle clues of its existence

20   on the surface. "When I talk to school children, I describe it like this," says Dr. Gary Kinsland, a geology professor at the University of Louisiana at Lafayette who has been doing research on Chicxulub since 1994. "Put a bowl on your bed,

25   then throw the sheets and blankets over it. All you'll probably see of the bowl now is a subtle depression."

"There is not a big hole anymore," he continues, "but if you look at the rim of the

30   depression on your bed, you'll see that it is still in the same position as the rim of the bowl beneath. That's how surface expression allows us to interpret something about the buried structure."

The view from space lets scientists see some

35   of Chicxulub's surface features that are not nearly so obvious from the ground. Satellite images showing a necklace of sink holes, called cenotes, across the Yucatán's northern tip are what first caught the attention of NASA researchers Drs.

40   Kevin Pope, Adriana Ocampo and Charles Duller in 1990. They were among the first to propose Chicxulub as the impact site linked to the mass extinctions that occurred at the end of the Cretaceous and beginning of the Tertiary

45   geological ages, called the K/T boundary.

"We were ignorant of the existence of a crater," says Pope, now an independent geologist. "We were working on a project on surface water and Mayan archaeology when we saw this

50   perfect semi-circular structure in images from the Landsat* Thematic Mapper. We were fascinated and got the magnetic and gravity data from the area collected earlier by the Mexican petroleum

company, who had been looking for oil. Their

55   data showed a large, remarkably circular structure that they had identified as an impact crater." Pope and his colleagues reasoned that the cenotes resulted from fractures in the buried crater's rim and that the area within the cenote

60   ring corresponded with the crater's floor.

Further studies by other researchers of the magnetic and gravity data plus analysis of rocks and ocean sediments published in 1991 helped convince the scientific world that Chicxulub was

65   the site of the impact that sent life on Earth in a new direction, from the age of dinosaurs to the age of mammals.

Scientists continue to comb through the clues the impact has left behind, some of which show

70   up best from space. "The classic spaceborne synoptic* view," says Pope, "is what you need to see a large structure like this." Maps of the region's wetlands, produced by the spaceborne imaging radar-C (SIR-C) mission in 1994,

75   identified zones of groundwater discharge that correlate with the crater's structure.

Now researchers are getting their first look at detailed, three-dimensional topographical data from the Shuttle Radar Topography Mission.

80   "This new image gives us both corroboration of what we expected and also shows up things we haven't seen before," says Kinsland. "We'll be working to get as much out of the data as possible. Anything we learn at the surface tells us

85   more about the buried crater."

Chicxulub: pronounced "CHICK-sah-lube"
Landsat: satellite program that collect images of Earth
synoptic: taking a thorough view

Deep-Sea Sediment Layers

Layers of sediment below Blake Nose, a spot off the coast of Florida, as indicated by a core sample taken from 370 feet below the sea bed in 1997 by the Joint Oceanographic Institutions for Deep Earth Sampling

textites: glassy condensation from vaporized rock
Cretaceous: last "dinosaur" period
Tertiary: first "mammal" period

44. Which choice best summarizes the passage?

(A) A father-son scientific team amassed evidence of a huge asteroid collision with Earth.
(B) Satellite images of Earth helped researchers deduce an event in geologic history.
(C) An asteroid or comet was responsible for the extinction of the dinosaurs.
(D) Researchers have found a large hole that they had not noticed before.

45. The author's central claim that the Chicxulub crater is a "smoking gun" means that it is

(A) a steaming physical remnant of one of the biggest explosions imaginable.
(B) an exhilarating discovery, yet extremely controversial among researchers.
(C) persuasive evidence, similar to a just-used gun found on a murder suspect.
(D) just a bare physical trace of a violent event, like smoke left behind at a shooting.

46. What function does paragraph 2 (lines 5 – 17) serve in the passage as a whole?

(A) It explains the strange fact that is introduced in the first paragraph.
(B) It places NASA's later findings in a context of earlier discoveries.
(C) It describes Chicxulub's historical background.
(D) It introduces Chicxulub and explains its significance to science.

47. As used in line 32, "expression" most nearly means

(A) form.
(B) face.
(C) iteration.
(D) narrative.

48. In paragraph 3 (lines 18 – 27), the crater is compared to a blanket-covered bowl primarily to

(A) mimic the way ice formed over and obscured the crater.
(B) model the object that formed the crater using simple household objects.
(C) demonstrate how some of the features of the crater were recognized.
(D) provide an exercise the reader can perform to better understand the scenario.

49. In the context of the passage, the author's use of the figurative phrase "a necklace of sinkholes" (line 37) describes

(A) intricate connections among caverns.
(B) the presence of a string of sparkling ponds.
(C) natural wells occurring in an arc.
(D) a ring of land that encircles a lower area.

50. Which choice provides the best evidence for the answer to the previous question?

(A) Lines 48 – 51 ("'We were...Mapper'")
(B) Lines 51 – 54 ("'We were...for oil'")
(C) Lines 57 – 60 ("Pope and his...floor")
(D) Lines 70 – 72 ("'The classic...like this'")

51. According to the author, space technology has supported the Chicxulub hypothesis by recording the

(A) orbits of comets and asteroids.
(B) number of wetlands in the Yucatan.
(C) flow of water underground.
(D) composition of the soil in the region.

52. Does the diagram provide support for the hypothesis that a meteorite struck at Chicxulub?

(A) Yes, because its layers of debris indicate a super-massive impact.
(B) Yes, because it adds to the fossil record on dinosaur-era extinction.
(C) No, because it does not describe sediment composition precisely.
(D) No, because it does not indicate the source for the debris.

STOP

Writing and Language Test 1

 35 MINUTES, 44 QUESTIONS

Turn to Section 2 of your answer sheet to answer the questions in this section.

DIRECTIONS

Each of the following passages is accompanied by approximately 11 questions. Some questions will require you to revise the passages in order to improve coherence and clarity. Other questions will require you to correct grammatical errors. Passages may be accompanied by graphs, charts, or tables that you must consider when making revisions. For most questions, you may select the "NO CHANGE" option if you believe that portion of the passage is clear, concise, and grammatically correct as is.

Within the passages, highlighted numbers followed by underlined text indicate which part of the text corresponds with each question. Bracketed numbers [1] indicate sentence number. These bracketed numbers are only relevant to problems that require you to add or rearrange sentences in a paragraph.

Refer to the passage below to answer questions 1 – 11.

Carpenters

1 Carpentry is one of the **2** most resourceful construction occupations. Unlike electricians or plumbers, carpenters participate in all phases of building construction. Some insulate office **3** buildings; while others install drywall or kitchen cabinets in homes. Carpenters who help construct tall buildings or bridges often install the concrete forms for cement footings or pillars. Some carpenters erect temporary shoring and scaffolding for buildings.

Because they are involved in many types of **4** construction: from building highways to framing doors, carpenters work both indoors and outdoors. Carpenters may work in cramped spaces in which frequent lifting, standing, and kneeling can be tiring. Those who work outdoors are subject to variable weather conditions.

1. (A) NO CHANGE
   (B) A carpenter is one of
   (C) Carpenters are among
   (D) Being a carpenter means that you are one of

2. (A) NO CHANGE
   (B) handiest
   (C) most versatile
   (D) most layered

3. (A) NO CHANGE
   (B) buildings—others
   (C) buildings, or others
   (D) buildings; others

4. (A) NO CHANGE
   (B) construction, from building highways to framing doors, carpenters
   (C) construction. From building highways to framing doors, carpenters
   (D) construction, from building highways to framing doors; carpenters

5 In fact, carpenters have higher rates of injury and illness than national averages. **6**

Most carpenters earn **7** a high school diploma and then learn their trade through 3- or 4-year apprenticeships. For each year of the program, apprentices complete both technical and on-the-job training. In their technical training, apprentices learn carpentry basics, blueprint reading, mathematics, building code requirements, and safety practices. **8** A carpenter, having finished an apprenticeship, is considered a journeyman and may perform tasks on his or her own. Several groups, including unions and contractor associations, sponsor apprenticeship programs, and some contractors have their own carpenter-training programs.

9 Becoming an independent contractor affords greater flexibility and the potential to raise income. General construction supervisors plan, coordinate, budget, and supervise construction projects from development to completion. Carpenters seeking advancement often undergo additional training provided by associations, unions, or employers.

The Bureau of Labor Statistics (BLS) **10** projects a growth in carpentry positions of 24 percent from 2012 to 2022, much faster than the average for all occupations. **11** It predicts that population growth will result in new-home construction—the largest segment employing carpenters—which drives the need for more workers. Home remodeling needs should also spur demand. Construction and maintenance of roads and bridges, though dependent on government spending, is another factor that is expected to contribute to job growth.

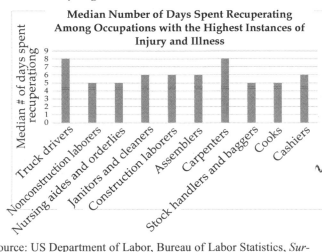

Median Number of Days Spent Recuperating Among Occupations with the Highest Instances of Injury and Illness

Source: US Department of Labor, Bureau of Labor Statistics, *Survey of Occupational Injuries and Illnesses*, 1994.

5. (A) NO CHANGE
   (B) However,
   (C) Ultimately,
   (D) As a result,

6. Which choice most effectively concludes the paragraph with relevant and accurate information based on the graph?
   (A) In fact, carpenters are eight times more likely to become sick or injured while working than the national average.
   (B) Carpenters miss more workdays due to injury and illness than any other profession.
   (C) Surprisingly, working as a cook or cashier can also be quite hazardous.
   (D) Even among high-risk professions, the average recovery period for an injured carpenter is matched only by that of a truck driver.

7. (A) NO CHANGE
   (B) a diploma
   (C) diplomas
   (D) high school diplomas

8. (A) NO CHANGE
   (B) After an apprenticeship is finished by the carpenter, he or she is
   (C) After finishing an apprenticeship, a carpenter is
   (D) The apprenticeship being finished, a carpenter is

9. Which of the following sentences most effectively introduces the topic of paragraph 4?
   (A) Carpentry is a physically demanding job, but most carpenters find the work rewarding.
   (B) Some people mistakenly assume that the rise of technology-oriented careers has reduced interest in manual labor jobs, such as carpentry.
   (C) Because they are exposed to the entire construction process, carpenters often have access to a wide range of specialties.
   (D) Carpenters must know how to use a wide variety of power tools.

10. (A) NO CHANGE
    (B) project
    (C) will project
    (D) projected

11. (A) NO CHANGE
    (B) They predict
    (C) This predicts
    (D) We predict

Refer to the passage below to answer questions 12 – 22.

Antikythera Mechanism

The **12** cyclical motions of the Sun, the Moon, and the planets determined many aspects of **13** normal, everyday life in ancient civilizations. Solar and lunar cycles often regulated communal activities, such as festivals and religious ceremonies; religious authorities **14** expressed certain astronomical events, such as solar and lunar eclipses, as harbingers of either doom or good fortune. As a result, nearly every ancient culture developed remarkably accurate methods for tracking the motions of celestial bodies. Possibly the most **15** impressive (and the most puzzling) astronomical measurement device from the ancient world comes to us from the Greeks.

[1] From 1900 to 1901, **16** artifacts were recovered from a shipwreck off the coast of the Greek island of Antikythera. [2] Among the ruins, they discovered 82 bronze fragments that once made up a single device. [3] For more than half a century, the fragments remained little more than an archaeological curiosity. [4] Appropriately, the device that the fragments once belonged to was named the "Antikythera Mechanism." [5] When they were discovered, the fragments were too corroded for researchers to decipher any of their details. [6] However, beginning in the 1970s, researchers returned to the perplexing fragments armed with x-ray technology. [7] X-ray scans of the fragments revealed that they once belonged to an astronomical measurement device. [8] Essentially, the device measured the movements of a number of noteworthy heavenly bodies. **17**

12. (A) NO CHANGE
    (B) cynical
    (C) seismic
    (D) sinister

13. (A) NO CHANGE
    (B) your life
    (C) daily life
    (D) how people normally lived

14. (A) NO CHANGE
    (B) discovered
    (C) deduced
    (D) interpreted

15. (A) NO CHANGE
    (B) impressive—and the most puzzling astronomical
    (C) impressive; and the most puzzling astronomical
    (D) impressive, and the most puzzling astronomical

16. (A) NO CHANGE
    (B) archaeologists, finding artifacts, recovered them
    (C) archaeologists recovered artifacts
    (D) archaeologists were finding artifacts and recovering them

17. For the sake of the cohesion of paragraph 2, where should sentence 3 be placed?

    (A) Where it is now
    (B) After sentence 4
    (C) After sentence 5
    (D) After sentence 6

[1] However, the x-ray images of the fragments still left many features **18** unclear, whereas inscriptions on the Antikythera Mechanism's fragments remained indecipherable, and its inner workings remained obscured. [2] Then, in 2006, modern technology revealed more of the secrets hidden within the fragments. [3] Researchers at Cardiff University in Wales took CT scans (computerized x-ray scans) of the Antikythera Mechanism's fragments. [4] Analysis of these scans revealed more information about the mechanics and origins of the elusive device. **19**

Thus, after spending over a century shrouded in mystery, the Antikythera Mechanism is finally being recognized as **20** an amazing intricate analog computer. The Antikythera Mechanism was about the size of a jewelry box, and probably **21** looks similar to a modern analog clock. The circular face accommodated at least **22** seven hands, they marked the motions of the Sun, the Moon, and the planets visible to the naked eye (Mercury, Venus, Mars, Jupiter, and Saturn). Thus, each hand rotated at a different rate and moved by means of a series of interconnected bronze gears. The device was powered by winding two dials, which connected to the gears. On the back of the device, small pins followed grooved paths that marked the dates of major athletic festivals. Most researchers suspect that the Antikythera Mechanism was created in the 2nd or 3rd century BCE and was probably based on similar, now-lost devices.

18. (A) NO CHANGE
(B) unclear: inscriptions
(C) unclear, inscriptions
(D) unclear; despite that, inscriptions

19. To maintain the cohesion of paragraph 3, where should the following sentence be placed?

Consequently, most researchers chose to ignore the device rather than stoop to speculation and guesswork.

(A) After sentence 1
(B) After sentence 2
(C) After sentence 3
(D) After sentence 4

20. (A) NO CHANGE
(B) a complex
(C) an incredibly
(D) a remarkable

21. (A) NO CHANGE
(B) had looked
(C) was looking
(D) looked

22. (A) NO CHANGE
(B) seven hands; marking
(C) seven hands, which marked
(D) seven hands, that marked

Refer to the passage below to answer questions 23 – 33.

Leitmotifs

An audience has certain expectations when watching a film. A rousing brass fanfare should accompany a hero's arrival, and sinister strings should **23** underscore a villain's speech. These recurrent musical themes, commonly called "leitmotifs," have pervaded film since its infancy. Leitmotifs are miniature "theme songs" that play whenever a particular character, object, or situation is present on **24** screen. Leitmotifs can provide an audience with information not conveyed directly through dialogue. If an audience wants to know whether a character is good or evil, **25** they need only listen to that character's leitmotif.

The use of leitmotifs begins with 19th century German opera, and one of the most extensive uses of leitmotifs is found in **26** German composer Richard Wagner's, *The Ring Cycle.* **27** Composed over the course of 26 years, *The Ring Cycle* actually consists of four connected operas meant to be performed back-to-back over the course of four days. In total, *The Ring Cycle* takes approximately 15 hours to perform. As the title suggests, the story of *The Ring Cycle* centers on a magical ring that gives its owners the power to dominate the world. Influenced heavily by Norse mythology, the plot **28** includes three generations in which gods, mortals, and mythical creatures vie for possession of the ring. At the center of the struggle is Wotan, **29** ruler and leader of the gods in *The Ring Cycle,* who tries to retrieve the ring from two giants. Over the course of its 15-hour running time, *The Ring Cycle* introduces a huge cast of characters, many of **30** them have leitmotifs.

23. (A) NO CHANGE
   (B) undermine
   (C) undercut
   (D) understand

24. Which choice most effectively combines the sentences at the underlined portion?

   (A) screen, so they
   (B) screen; however, leitmotifs
   (C) screen, and consequently they
   (D) screen, meaning that these leitmotifs

25. (A) NO CHANGE
   (B) a person
   (C) it
   (D) someone

26. (A) NO CHANGE
   (B) German composer, Richard Wagner's *The Ring Cycle.*
   (C) German composer, Richard Wagner's, *The Ring Cycle.*
   (D) German composer Richard Wagner's *The Ring Cycle.*

27. (A) NO CHANGE
   (B) Being composed
   (C) Having been composed
   (D) Composing it

28. (A) NO CHANGE
   (B) traverses
   (C) encloses
   (D) spans

29. (A) NO CHANGE
   (B) ruler of the gods,
   (C) who rules over the rest of the gods,
   (D) who leads the other gods as their ruler,

30. (A) NO CHANGE
   (B) which
   (C) who
   (D) whom

As one would expect, Wagner uses leitmotifs to suggest characters' allegiances. A soaring horn leitmotif introduces Siegfried, Wotan's grandson and a major hero in *The Ring Cycle*, while a lumbering percussive leitmotif announces the presence of the evil giants. [31] Moreover, Wagner occasionally uses leitmotifs to express a character's thoughts or feelings. At the beginning of *The Ring Cycle*, a triumphant-sounding leitmotif introduces the wise and powerful god Wotan. However, by the midpoint of the opera, when his fortunes have turned for the worse, Wotan's leitmotif switches to a minor key, giving it a mournful sound that matches his own despair.

From these examples, one can conclude that Wagner's leitmotifs serve two concurrent functions. Superficially, leitmotifs provide musical cues that help audiences orient themselves to the events of the opera; audiences know which characters to expect on stage based on the leitmotifs that precede their arrival. [32] Consequently, leitmotifs add emotional weight to the events of *The Ring Cycle*. Wotan's despair is heightened by the melancholy reflected in his leitmotif. Thus, it should come as no surprise that the use of leitmotifs has endured for nearly a century and a half: [33] leitmotifs are especially prominent in action and adventure films.

31. Which choice most effectively sets up the information that follows?
   (A) NO CHANGE
   (B) Most composers agree that leitmotifs effectively introduce important themes and characters.
   (C) However, it is fairly uncommon for a minor character to have a leitmotif.
   (D) Furthermore, different instruments may play a leitmotif each time it repeats.

32. (A) NO CHANGE
   (B) Additionally,
   (C) Conversely,
   (D) Quizzically,

33. Which choice most effectively concludes the passage?
   (A) NO CHANGE
   (B) leitmotifs are also employed in literature, where recurrent phrases replace musical themes.
   (C) leitmotifs convey a wealth of information using nothing more than a musical phrase.
   (D) film composer John Williams has created some of the most recognizable leitmotifs.

Refer to the passage below to answer questions 34 – 44.

Planetary Formation

[1] Since the Big Bang, the universe has produced an incredible number of stars and planets. [2] Scientists estimate that, in the Milky Way alone, hundreds of billions of planets orbit approximately one hundred billion stars. [3] Although no two of these heavenly bodies are identical, they all share at least one common **34** feature; their shape. [4] To determine why this is, it helps to understand how stars and planets form. **35**

Most solar systems, including our own, form in a swirling cloud of particles called a nebula. The nebula's gravity **36** draws other nearby particles, causing the nebula to grow. Gradually, particles **37** cluster in the middle of the nebula, drawn together by their mutual gravitational attraction. As more particles gravitate toward the center of the nebula, it begins to spin **38** more faster. This is the same process that causes an ice skater to accelerate when she brings her arms and legs closer to her body while spinning. The center of the nebula continues to spin, accelerating as it **39** has acquired more mass. The center of the nebula becomes a star when the cluster of spinning particles is massive enough— and **40** its gravitational field is strong enough—to undergo nuclear fusion.

34. (A) NO CHANGE
    (B) feature, their shape!
    (C) feature (their shape).
    (D) feature—their shape.

35. To maintain the cohesion of paragraph 1, where should the following sentence be placed?

    Even the largest known star, which is millions of times larger than the Sun, has the same spherical shape as Earth.

    (A) After sentence 1
    (B) After sentence 2
    (C) After sentence 3
    (D) After sentence 4

36. (A) NO CHANGE
    (B) captivates
    (C) evokes
    (D) lures

37. (A) NO CHANGE
    (B) rally
    (C) convene
    (D) assemble

38. (A) NO CHANGE
    (B) rapid.
    (C) more fast.
    (D) faster.

39. (A) NO CHANGE
    (B) acquiring
    (C) acquired
    (D) acquires

40. (A) NO CHANGE
    (B) it's
    (C) its'
    (D) it is

The newly formed star sits at the center of the [41] nebula being surrounded by a spinning cloud of particles that includes gases and space debris. Because they have a greater gravitational pull, the heavier particles in this cloud cluster together, heating up as they form the molten cores of rocky planets. Gas giants, on the other hand, form much like stars, [42] but gas giants never acquire a sufficient amount of mass to undergo the process of fusion.

Ultimately, gravity is the key player in the formation of nebulae, stars, and planets. Gravity ensures that, during formation, every particle tries to get as close to the center as possible, evenly distributing gravitational pull. The only three-dimensional shape that allows for this configuration is a [43] sphere. All points on the outside of a sphere are equidistant, after all. Celestial objects smaller than 100 miles in diameter generally lack sufficient mass, and therefore sufficient gravity, to compress into spheres. [44]

41. (A) NO CHANGE
(B) nebula, surrounded
(C) nebula, surrounding itself
(D) nebula, the star is surrounded

42. (A) NO CHANGE
(B) but gas giants never become massive enough to undergo fusion.
(C) yet, in terms of mass, gas giants never have enough to go through fusion.
(D) but gas giants can never begin the process of fusion because they are not massive enough.

43. Which of the following most effectively combines the sentences at the underlined portion?

(A) sphere, this is because all points
(B) sphere, indicating that the points
(C) sphere, yet every point
(D) sphere; all points

44. Which sentence best concludes the final paragraph of the passage?

(A) This explains why comets and asteroids have irregular, non-spherical appearances.
(B) However, forces other than gravity contribute to the formation of spheres, too.
(C) The strength of an object's gravitational field is proportional to the object's mass.
(D) Without Isaac Newton's pioneering research into the nature of gravity, all this information might remain unknown even today.

STOP

Math Test 1 – No Calculator

 25 MINUTES, 20 QUESTIONS

Turn to Section 3 of your answer sheet to answer the questions in this section.

DIRECTIONS

For questions **1 – 15**, find the solution to each problem and select the most appropriate answer from the choices provided. For questions **16 – 20**, find the solution to each problem and write your answer in the space provided. You may use the blank space in your test booklet for scratch work.

NOTES

1. The use of a calculator on any part of this section is forbidden.
2. Unless otherwise indicated, all variables and expressions used in this test represent real numbers.
3. Unless otherwise indicated, all figures used in this test are drawn to scale.
4. Unless otherwise indicated, all figures used in this test lie on a plane.
5. Unless specified otherwise, a given function, f has the domain the set of all real numbers x for which $f(x)$ is a real number.

REFERENCE

$A = \frac{1}{2}bh$ $c^2 = a^2 + b^2$ Special Right Triangles $A = \pi r^2$ $A = \ell w$
$C = 2\pi r$

$V = \ell w h$ $V = \pi r^2 h$ $V = \frac{4}{3}\pi r^3$ $V = \frac{1}{3}\pi r^2 h$ $V = \frac{1}{3}\ell w h$

The arc of a circle is 360 degrees or 2π radians.
A triangle has angles that sum to 180 degrees.

1. Jenny has a job that pays $8 per hour plus tips ($t$). Jenny worked for 4 hours on Monday and made $65 in all. Which equation could be used to find t, the amount Jenny made in tips?

   (A) $65 = 4t + 8$
   (B) $65 = 8t \div 4$
   (C) $65 = 8t + 4$
   (D) $65 = 8(4) + t$

2. Anna burned 15 calories per minute running for x minutes and 10 calories per minute hiking for y minutes. She spent a total of 60 minutes running and hiking and burned 700 calories. The system of equations shown below can be used to determine how much time Anna spent on each exercise:

$$15x + 10y = 700$$
$$x + y = 60$$

   How many minutes x, did Anna spend running?

   (A) 10
   (B) 20
   (C) 30
   (D) 40

3. Solve $\sqrt{13 - x} = x - 1$.

   (A) $\{4\}$
   (B) $\{4, -3\}$
   (C) $\{-3\}$
   (D) $\{-4, -3\}$

4. A baseball team has $1,000 to spend on supplies. One baseball bat costs $185. New baseballs are $4 each. The inequality $185 + 4b < 1,000$ is used to determine the number of new baseballs b that the team can purchase. What is the maximum number of baseballs that the team can buy?

   (A) 46
   (B) 95
   (C) 185
   (D) 203

5. Which statement best describes the relationship between the graphs of $y = 2$ and $x = 2$?

   (A) The two lines have the same slope.
   (B) The lines are perpendicular.
   (C) The lines are parallel.
   (D) The lines intersect at $(2, 0)$.

6. What is the solution set of this system of equations?

$$x^2 + y - 1 = 0$$
$$x - y + 1 = 0$$

(A) {(−1, −1), (−1, 0)}

(B) {(−1, 0), (−1, 1)}

(C) {(−1, 0), (0, 1)}

(D) {(1, 0), (1, 1)}

7. A set of data has 10 values, no two of which are the same. If the smallest value is removed from the set, which of the following statements MUST be true?

(A) The range of the first data set is greater than the range of the second data set.

(B) The mode of the first data set is greater than the mode of the second data set.

(C) The medians of the two data sets are the same.

(D) The mean of the first data set is greater than the mean of the second data set.

8. Hattie went to a candle store in the mall and saw that all the candles in the store were on sale for 17% off. She had her calculator with her and programmed it to give her the sale price based on the original price. What expression did she use to find the sale price, if the original price in dollars is represented by m?

(A) $m + 0.17m$

(B) $-0.17m$

(C) $0.17m$

(D) $m - 0.17m$

9. Which of the following describes the graph of the function $f(x) = (-x + 3)(x - 5)$?

(A) Opens up with x-intercepts at (−5, 0) and (3, 0)

(B) Opens up with x-intercepts at (5, 0) and (3, 0)

(C) Opens down with x-intercepts at (−5, 0) and (−3, 0)

(D) Opens down with x-intercepts at (5, 0) and (3, 0)

10. A 79-inch-long board is cut into three pieces: A, B, and C. Piece C is twice as long as B, and piece B is 5 inches longer than A. Find the sum of the lengths of pieces B and C.

(A) 21

(B) 42

(C) 59

(D) 63

11.

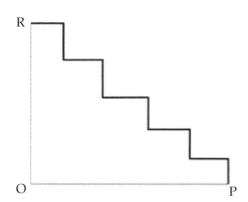

In the figure above, the heavy segmented line from P to R is composed of line segments that are parallel to either $\overline{OR}$ or $\overline{OP}$. If the length of $\overline{OR}$ is x and the length of $\overline{OP}$ is y, what is the total length of the heavy broken line from P to R?

(A) $\sqrt{x^2 - y^2}$

(B) $x + y$

(C) $2(x + y)$

(D) $x^2 + y^2$

12. Copper production increased at a rate of about 4.9% per year between 1988 and 1993. In 1993, copper production was approximately 1.801 billion kilograms. If this trend continues, which equation best models the copper production (P), in billions of kilograms since 1993? (Let $t = 0$ for 1993.)

(A) $P = 1.801(4.900)^t$

(B) $P = 1.801(1.490)^t$

(C) $P = 1.801(1.049)^t$

(D) $P = 1.801(0.049)^t$

$P = 1.801 (1.049)^t$

13. If the range of $f(x) = x^2 + 4$ is all real numbers from 13 to 29, what positive numbers lie in the domain of $f(x)$?

(A) $3 \le x \le 5$

(B) $5 \le x \le 21$

(C) $9 \le x \le 25$

(D) $13 \le x \le 29$

14. Which quadrants contain the solutions to this system of inequalities?

$$y - 2x \le -3$$
$$3y - x \ge -4$$

(A) Quadrants I and IV

(B) Quadrants II and III

(C) Quadrants III and IV

(D) Quadrants II, III, and IV

15. If $i = \sqrt{-1}$, which of the following is equivalent to $\dfrac{2}{5+i}$?

(A) $\dfrac{5-i}{12}$

(B) $\dfrac{5+i}{12}$

(C) $\dfrac{5-i}{13}$

(D) $\dfrac{5+i}{13}$

287

3 Student-Produced Responses

DIRECTIONS

For questions **16 – 20**, find the solution to the problem and enter your answer as demonstrated below.

1. Only the answer that is bubbled in on the answer sheet will be credited. The blank spaces above the bubbles are for you to record your answers for accuracy.
2. Only fill in one bubble in any given column.
3. None of the answers on this portion of the test are negative values.
4. If a problem appears to have more than one answer, only enter one answer. If the answer you enter is one of the correct solutions, you will receive full credit for that question.
5. If the correct answer can be expressed as a mixed number, it must be entered as a decimal or an improper fraction.
6. If the correct answer is a decimal that cannot fit into the grid space, you must fill the grid with enough digits to completely fill the space. The number can be rounded or simply shortened but must fill every blank space.

Answer: $\frac{5}{36}$ Answer: 4.5

Write answer → in boxes.

Grid in result.

← Fraction line
← Decimal point

Acceptable ways to grid $\frac{1}{6}$ are:

Answer: 302 – either position is correct

NOTES

Begin entering answers in any column that accommodates your answer. If you do not need a column do not enter anything in that column.

16.
$$y = 3x + 7$$
The equation for the line above has a y-intercept at the point (a, b). What is b^a?

ANSWER: _____

17. If $h(x + 1) = \dfrac{3h(x) + 4}{3}$ for all positive integers x and $h(1) = -\dfrac{2}{3}$, what is the value of $h(3)$?

ANSWER: _____

18.
$$y = 11x + 3x^2$$
$$y = 11x^2 - 3x$$

Consider the system of equations above for $x > 0$. What is the value of x?

ANSWER: __7/4__

$11x^2 - 3x = 11x + 3x^2$

$8x^2 - 14x = 0$

$4x^2 - 7x = 0$

$x(4x - 7) = 0$

$x = 0, 7/4$

19. The equation $\dfrac{x - 3}{2} = \dfrac{1}{x - 4}$ has two solutions. What is their product?

ANSWER: _____

20. When the polynomial $x^4 - 3x^3 - 7x^2 + 7x + 2$ is divided by $x + 2$, the quotient is $x^3 + Bx^2 + Cx + 1$.

Find the value of $|B + C|$.

ANSWER: __2__

$\begin{array}{r|rrrrr} -2 & 1 & -3 & -7 & \uparrow 7 & 2 \\ & & -2 & & & \\ \hline & 1 & & & & \end{array}$

STOP

Math Test 1 – Calculator

 55 MINUTES, 38 QUESTIONS

Turn to Section 4 of your answer sheet to answer the questions in this section.

DIRECTIONS

For questions **1 – 30**, find the solution to each problem and select the most appropriate answer from the choices provided. For questions **31 – 38**, find the solution to each problem and write your answer in the space provided. You may use the blank space in your test booklet for scratch work.

NOTES

1. The use of a calculator on this section is allowed.
2. Unless otherwise indicated, all variables and expressions used in this test represent real numbers.
3. Unless otherwise indicated, all figures used in this test are drawn to scale.
4. Unless otherwise indicated, all figures used in this test lie on a plane.
5. Unless specified otherwise, a given function, f has the domain the set of all real numbers x for which $f(x)$ is a real number.

REFERENCE

$A = \frac{1}{2}bh$ $c^2 = a^2 + b^2$ Special Right Triangles $A = \pi r^2$ $A = \ell w$
$C = 2\pi r$

$V = \ell wh$ $V = \pi r^2 h$ $V = \frac{4}{3}\pi r^3$ $V = \frac{1}{3}\pi r^2 h$ $V = \frac{1}{3}\ell wh$

The arc of a circle is 360 degrees or 2π radians.
A triangle has angles that sum to 180 degrees.

1.

ANNUAL BUDGET BY DEPARTMENT

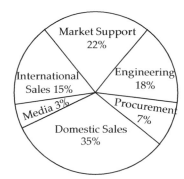

The pie graph above shows the annual budget for the Heavy Equipment Company. If the total budget is $60,000,000, what amount is budgeted for the Market Support and Engineering departments combined?

(A) $18 million

(B) $22 million

(C) $24 million

(D) $28 million

2. A climber measures the oxygen content of the air at 2,000 feet above sea level at 18%. The climber measures it again at 4,500 feet, this time at 14%. By how much does the oxygen content of the air change for every 1,000 feet of elevation?

(A) −1.6%

(B) +1.6%

(C) −2.0%

(D) +2.0%

3. Which of the following expresses the complete solution to the inequality $3x - 5 > 5x - 9$?

(A) $x > -\dfrac{7}{4}$

(B) $x > 2$

(C) $x < 2$

(D) $x > -2$

4. If $f(x) = a(x - 2)^2 + 15$ and $f(1) = 2$, then $a =$

(A) −13

(B) −10

(C) 10

(D) 13

5. A manufacturing company processes raw ore. The number of tons of refined material the company can produce during t days using Process A is $A(t) = t^2 + 2t$ and using Process B is $B(t) = 10t$. The company has only 7 days to process ore and must choose one of the processes. What is the maximum output of refined material, in tons, for this time period?

(A) 10

(B) 51

(C) 63

(D) 70

6. Cynthia is sailing from Florida to Massachusetts and back to Florida. She will make two stops along the way, in North Carolina and at the New Jersey shore. It costs $1.45 per foot to dock in North Carolina, $2.50 per foot to dock in Southern New Jersey, and $300/night to dock at Cape Cod, Massachusetts. Which of the following choices models how much she will spend on docking fees if she plans on spending 3 nights in Massachusetts, making the same stops on the way back, and sails a boat that requires x feet of dockage?

(A) $2x(1.45 + 2.5) + 900$

(B) $x(1.45 + 2.5) + 300$

(C) $x(1.45 + 2.5) - 300$

(D) $\dfrac{1.45 + 2.50}{x} + 900$

7. Which of the following is the equation of the line that passes through the points $(-5, -2)$, $(3, -1)$?

(A) $y = \dfrac{1}{8}x + \dfrac{11}{8}$

(B) $y = \dfrac{1}{8}x - \dfrac{11}{8}$

(C) $y = -\dfrac{1}{8}x - \dfrac{11}{8}$

(D) $y = -\dfrac{1}{8}x + \dfrac{11}{8}$

8. At a banquet of 36 people, each person has the choice of roast beef, chicken divan, and linguine primavera. If 25% choose roast beef and 17 people choose chicken divan, how many people choose linguine primavera?

(A) 7

(B) 8

(C) 9

(D) 10

9. A scientist performs an experiment in which she measures four values two times each, with the following results:

	w	x	y	z
First Measurement	0.2	6	0.5	10
Second Measurement	0.6	3	1	30

Which of the following conclusions is supported by the data?

(A) w and y are directly proportional.

(B) w and z are inversely proportional.

(C) x and y are inversely proportional.

(D) x and z are directly proportional.

10. Martha picked out a pair of shoes that were 30% off the original price. After 5% sales tax, the final cost was $58.80. What was the original price?

(A) $70

(B) $75

(C) $80

(D) $85

11. Of the 126 students who applied for a full scholarship to Kent College, 9 were successful. What is the ratio of students receiving a scholarship to those who are not?

(A) 1 to 11

(B) 1 to 12

(C) 1 to 13

(D) 1 to 14

12. If p percent of 250 is 75, what is 75% of p?

(A) 22.5

(B) 25

(C) 75

(D) 225

13. This semester, Gerry scored an average of 93 on his five history exams. He got the same score on his first two exams, and then a 94, an 85, and a 90 on the remaining exams. What score did he receive on his first two exams?

(A) 95

(B) 96

(C) 97

(D) 98

14. Logan runs x miles per day. Which of the following represents the total distance he runs in a year, if he runs 6 times per week, and takes a week off every 3 months?
(Note: 52 weeks = 1 year)

(A) $(52 - \frac{12}{3})(6)x$

(B) $(52 - \frac{52}{3})(6)x$

(C) $52x(6x) - \frac{12}{3}$

(D) $52x - 6\left(\frac{12}{3}\right)$

15. The owner of a store displays a large jar of nickels and dimes and offers the value of the coins to the person who guesses how many dimes there are. If there are 1,130 coins valued at $100, how many dimes are there?

(A) 130

(B) 260

(C) 870

(D) 970

16. Where are the points (1, 2) and (−1, 1) in relation to the line $3x + 4y = 7$?

(A) Both are on the line.

(B) One is on the line and the other is off the line.

(C) Both are above the line.

(D) One is above the line and the other is below the line.

17. If $f(x) = 3x + 2$, then $f(a + b) =$

(A) $3a + 3b + 2$

(B) $3a + 3b + 4$

(C) $3x + 2 + a + b$

(D) $3x + 4 + 3a + 3b$

Refer to the graph below to answer questions 18 and 19.

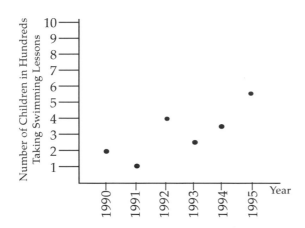

18. Between which years did the largest decrease in children taking swimming lessons occur?

(A) 1990 – 1991
(B) 1991 – 1992
(C) 1992 – 1993
(D) 1993 – 1994

19. What was the approximate average number of children taking swim lessons from 1990 to 1995?

(A) 250
(B) 308
(C) 385
(D) 450

20. What is the length of a line segment drawn from $(-3, 7)$ to $(6, -5)$ on the coordinate plane?

(A) 15
(B) 16
(C) 17
(D) 18

21. A cellphone company produced a faulty device which exploded when overheated. In one country, 190,984 devices were sold, 20 of which exploded. If this ratio is indicative of the ratio of functioning to faulty devices manufactured by the company, which of the following approximates the total number explosive devices, given that 2.5 million devices were sold worldwide?

(A) 152
(B) 262
(C) 343
(D) 1,309

22. David is staying at a hotel that charges $79.50 per night plus tax for a room. A tax of 7.2% is applied to the room rate, and there is an additional one-time untaxed fee of $10.00. Which of the following represents David's total charges, in cents, for a stay of x nights?

(A) $(7950 + 0.072x) + 1000$
(B) $1.072(7950x) + 1000$
(C) $1.072 (7950x + 1000)$
(D) $1.072 (7950 + 1000)x$

23. At 1:00 PM, a car leaves St. Louis for Chicago, traveling at a constant speed of 65 miles per hour. At 2:00 PM, a truck leaves Chicago for St. Louis, traveling at a constant speed of 55 miles per hour. If it is a 305-mile drive between St. Louis and Chicago, at what time the car and truck pass each other?

(A) 2:30 PM

(B) 3:00 PM

(C) 4:00 PM

(D) 4:30 PM

24. To celebrate a colleague's retirement, the coworkers in an office agree to contribute equally to a catered lunch that costs a total of b dollars. If there are a coworkers in the office, and if c coworkers fail to contribute, which of the following represents the extra amount, in dollars, that each of the remaining coworkers must contribute to cover the cost of lunch?

(A) $\dfrac{b}{c}$

(B) $\dfrac{b}{a-c}$

(C) $\dfrac{bc}{a-c}$

(D) $\dfrac{bc}{a(a-c)}$

25. A store charges $39 per pair for a certain type of pants. This price is 30% more than the wholesale price. At a Thanksgiving sale, store employees can purchase any remaining items at 40% off the wholesale price. How much would it cost an employee to purchase a pair of pants of this type at this sale?

(A) $12.00

(B) $14.00

(C) $18.00

(D) $21.00

26.

Quiz Score	Number of Students
0	2
10	4
20	13
30	6

A class of 25 students took a 3-question quiz. The table shows the possible scores on this quiz and the number of students who received each of these scores. What is the average (arithmetic mean) of the scores for this class?

(A) 18.9

(B) 19.1

(C) 19.2

(D) 19.7

4

27. If $y \neq 3$ and $\dfrac{3x}{y}$ is a prime integer greater than 2, which of the following must be true?

    I. $x = y$

    II. $y = 1$

    III. x and y are prime integers.

(A) None

(B) I only

(C) II only

(D) I and III

28. The angle created by an individual's line of vision from sea level to the top of a lighthouse is 60°. The lighthouse is known to rise 180 feet above sea level. What is the distance (to the nearest foot) between the observer and the base of the lighthouse?

(A) 104 feet

(B) 180 feet

(C) 208 feet

(D) 254 feet

29. If $i = \sqrt{-1}$, which of following is equivalent to $\dfrac{2i}{1+i}$?

(A) -2

(B) $-1 + 2i$

(C) $1 - i$

(D) $1 + i$

30. $$f(x) = x^2 - 4x - 21$$

Which of the following is an equivalent factored form of the function above?

(A) $f(x) = (x + 3)(x + 7)$

(B) $f(x) = (x - 3)(x - 7)$

(C) $f(x) = (x - 3)(x + 7)$

(D) $f(x) = (x + 3)(x - 7)$

DIRECTIONS

For questions **31 – 38**, find the solution to the problem and enter your answer as demonstrated below.

1. Only the answer that is bubbled in on the answer sheet will be credited. The blank spaces above the bubbles are for you to record your answers for accuracy.
2. Only fill in one bubble in any given column.
3. None of the answers on this portion of the test are negative values.
4. If a problem appears to have more than one answer, only enter one answer. If the answer you enter is one of the correct solutions, you will receive full credit for that question.
5. If the correct answer can be expressed as a mixed number, it must be entered as a decimal or an improper fraction.
6. If the correct answer is a decimal that cannot fit into the grid space, you must fill the grid with enough digits to completely fill the space. The number can be rounded or simply shortened but must fill every blank space.

Answer: $\frac{5}{36}$

Answer: 4.5

Write answer → in boxes.

← Fraction line
← Decimal point

Grid in result.

Acceptable ways to grid $\frac{1}{6}$ are:

NOTES

Begin entering answers in any column that accommodates your answer. If you do not need a column do not enter anything in that column.

Answer: 302 – either position is correct

31. What is the slope of the line $9x - 3y = 10$?

    ANSWER: _____

32. Angel works part-time as an underwear fit model for $50 an hour, and part-time as a pastry chef for $12 an hour. This past week, he worked for 25 hours and made $718. How many hours did he work as a chef?

    ANSWER: _____

33. At a convenience store, two candy bars and two bags of potato chips cost $4.00, and three candy bars and two bags of potato chips cost $4.75. What is the price, in dollars, of one bag of potato chips?

    ANSWER: _____

34. A two-digit number from 10 to 99, inclusive, is chosen at random. What is the probability that this number is divisible by 5?

    ANSWER: _____

35. If Aaron can do a job in 8 days, and Ben can do the same job in 12 days, how long does it take, in hours, for the two men, working together, to complete the same job? (Round your answer to the nearest hour and assume that an average work day is 8 hours.)

ANSWER: _____

36. The base of a pyramid has the same area as the base of a cylinder, and the cylinder is twice the height of the pyramid. What is the ratio of the volume of the pyramid to the volume of the cylinder?

ANSWER: _____

37. **PART 1**

Karen runs a flower shop. She determines that it takes her two hours of online marketing to bring in five new orders. If each order bills an average of $30, how many hours of marketing are necessary for her business to bill $10,000 a month? (Round your answer to the nearest hour.)

ANSWER: _____

38. **PART 2**

Karen hires a marketing assistant to bolster her online presence, and finds that it now takes only one hour of online marketing to bring in five new orders. If she pays her assistant $15 per hour, and the cost to fill an order is $5, how many hours must her assistant work each month for Karen's business to make a monthly profit of $10,000?

ANSWER: _____

5

Essay Test 1*

 50 MINUTES, Prompt-based essay

Turn to Section 5 of your answer sheet to answer the question in this section.

DIRECTIONS

As you read the passage below, consider how Susanna Heckman uses
- evidence, such as facts or examples, to support claims.
- reasoning to develop ideas and to connect claims and evidence.
- stylistic or persuasive elements, such as word choice or appeals to emotion, to add power to the ideas expressed.

Adapted from "Misusing Personality Tests" by Susanna Heckman. Copyright 2015 KALLIS EDU.

Personality is ephemeral. Yet, humans seem to want to understand personality through sorting and labeling. We would like to borrow the sorting hat from J.K. Rowling's Harry Potter series: it can instantly assess characters' entire past lives and thoughts, and place each one with a group of kindred spirits.

So it is perhaps natural that people have begun to put more stock in computer-based multiple choice "tests." More and more, business and government are adopting such tests with the serious purpose of evaluating someone for a job or an academic program. A person's answers on a multiple choice questionnaire, test, or quiz, supposedly pins down his or her personality traits, laying them out for inspection like butterflies in a glass case.

Of course, personality questionnaires can be useful for self-reflection, and can even be fun. Many people happen to know their own Zodiac "sign," even if they do not believe in astrology. Teen magazines and social media abound with "fun quizzes." Which holiday are you? Discover your shoe personality! What is your candy personality?! What does your coffee order say about you?! Which famous zombie are you?!

Psychological research indicates that assessing personality is actually a complicated, subjective process. As an example, evaluating patients for a personality *disorder* usually involves weighing information from a number of sources, including interviews with the client and the client's family members, not simply multiple-choice questionnaires. One reason is that research has shown that different questionnaires can offer completely different diagnoses. Researchers at Washington University recently summed up their findings regarding questionnaires by saying that "Diagnostic impressions from one instrument [i.e., a single questionnaire] should not be regarded as the only possible option." Anyone who has applied for a position that requires these personal questionnaires has probably been a bit baffled. Some tests ask questions such as, "Which word describes you better, 'orderly,' or 'unique?'" Imagine the thought processes of the nervous test-takers. Some may answer "orderly," reasoning that the employer wants orderly people; some may answer "orderly" because they think that "unique" sounds boastful, or vice-versa; some may answer "unique" because they reason that everyone *is* unique; some may answer "unique" because they think the employer will think that they are only thinking about what the employer is thinking if they answer "orderly." Or vice-versa.

Many questions may blatantly try to discern the applicant's level of honesty. At the same time, they may ask impossible questions, such as, "Which do you prefer: jogging, or volleyball?" although obviously, most people do neither. Questions may ask applicants to agree or disagree with statements such as, "I tend to give up easily." An *honest* answer to that question depends completely and totally on a specific situation. In the abstract, the question is unanswerable.

Adding to the baffling nature of such questions, the companies that sell the tests keep interpretations secret. Exactly how choosing the word "orderly" or the word "unique," or jogging or volleyball, would relate to employment suitability is proprietary information. Thus, it is fair to suspect that the interpretations are highly unscientific.

The heart of the problem is that, as psychological research indicates, it is simply irrational to expect the questionnaires, quizzes, or tests to "work." People are not good sources when it comes to their own traits for three reasons. One is people's "social desirability bias." That is, pretty much everyone chooses the answer that is the most socially desirable; we choose answers that we think are "right." Another factor at work is the "introspection limitation," which means that our self-knowledge has limits.

Finally, there is the bias of the moment. A person's mood, age, gender, health, culture, daily concerns, and many other factors can affect how that person chooses to answer a particular question. Research has shown that people may have completely different results if they take the same tests on different days.

The clear limitations of such questionnaires make it perplexing to me that Human Resources departments are buying them; the personality-test industry rakes in more than $500 million a year. Trying for a moment to imagine being an HR or college admissions officer who must choose one among many qualified applicants, I can see that the magnetic pull of "objective data" must be so strong that one could ignore little things like *the tests do not work*. I would argue that the tests are just as random and complicated as any other measure of human personality.

Write an essay in which you explain how Susanna Heckman builds an argument to persuade her audience that personality tests should not be used for employment or education. In your essay, analyze how the author uses one or more of the features listed in the box above (or features of your own choice) to strengthen the logic and persuasiveness of her argument. Be sure that your analysis focuses on the most relevant features of the passage.

Your essay should not explain whether you agree with the author's claims, but rather explain how the author builds an argument to persuade her audience.

* Sample responses at www.kallisedu.com

KALLIS

SAT® Practice Test #2

IMPORTANT REMINDERS:

When you take the official SAT, you will need to use a No. 2 pencil. Do not use a pen or a mechanical pencil.

On the official SAT, sharing any of the questions on the test violates the College Board's policies and may result in your scores being canceled.

(This cover is modeled after the cover you'll see when you take the official SAT.)

Reading Test 2

65 MINUTES, 52 QUESTIONS

Turn to Section 1 of your answer sheet to answer the questions in this section.

DIRECTIONS

Each passage or pair of passages is accompanied by 10 or 11 questions. Read each passage or pair of passages, and then select the most appropriate answer to each question. Some passages may include tables or graphs that require additional analysis.

Refer to the passage below to answer questions 1 – 10.

This passage is adapted from Mark Twain, *Tom Sawyer*, originally published in 1884.

line
    Saturday morning was come, and all the summer world was bright and fresh, and brimming with life. Tom appeared on the sidewalk with a bucket of whitewash and a long-
5 handled brush. He surveyed the fence, and all gladness left him and a deep melancholy settled down upon his spirit. Thirty yards of board fence nine feet high. Life to him seemed hollow, and existence but a burden. Sighing, he dipped his
10 brush and passed it along the topmost plank; repeated the operation; did it again; compared the insignificant whitewashed streak with the far-reaching continent of unwhitewashed fence, and sat down on a tree-box discouraged.
15   He began to think of the fun he had planned for this day, and his sorrows multiplied. Soon the free boys would come tripping along on all sorts of delicious expeditions, and they would make a world of fun of him for having to work—the
20 very thought of it burnt him like fire. …At this dark and hopeless moment an inspiration burst upon him! Nothing less than a great, magnificent inspiration.
    He took up his brush and went tranquilly
25 to work. Ben Rogers hove in sight presently— the very boy, of all boys, whose ridicule he had been dreading. Ben's gait was the hop-skip-and-jump—proof enough that his heart was light and his anticipations high. He was eating an apple,
30 and giving a long, melodious whoop, at intervals, followed by a deep-toned ding-dong-dong, ding-dong-dong, for he was personating a steamboat.
    Tom went on whitewashing—paid no attention to the steamboat. Ben stared a moment
35 and then said: "*Hi-Yi! You're* up a stump, ain't you!"
    No answer. Tom surveyed his last touch with the eye of an artist, then he gave his brush another

gentle sweep and surveyed the result, as before.
40 Ben ranged up alongside of him. Tom's mouth watered for the apple, but he stuck to his work. Ben said:
    "Hello, old chap, you got to work, hey?"
    Tom wheeled suddenly and said:
45   "Why, it's you, Ben! I warn't noticing."
    "Say—I'm going in a-swimming, I am. Don't you wish you could? But of course you'd druther *work*—wouldn't you? Course you would!"
    Tom contemplated the boy a bit, and said:
50   "What do you call work?"
    "Why, ain't *that* work?"
    Tom resumed his whitewashing, and answered carelessly:
    "Well, maybe it is, and maybe it ain't. All I
55 know, is, it suits Tom Sawyer."
    "Oh come, now, you don't mean to let on that you *like* it?"
    The brush continued to move.
    "Like it? Well, I don't see why I oughtn't to
60 like it. Does a boy get a chance to whitewash a fence every day?"
    That put the thing in a new light. Ben stopped nibbling his apple. Tom swept his brush daintily back and forth—stepped back to note the
65 effect—added a touch here and there—criticized the effect again—Ben watching every move and getting more and more interested, more and more absorbed. Presently he said:
    "Say, Tom, let *me* whitewash a little."
70   Tom considered, was about to consent; but he altered his mind:
    "No—no—I reckon it wouldn't hardly do, Ben. You see, Aunt Polly's awful particular about this fence—right here on the street, you know—
75 but if it was the back fence I wouldn't mind and *she* wouldn't. Yes, she's awful particular about this fence; it's got to be done very careful; I reckon there ain't one boy in a thousand, maybe two thousand, that can do it the way it's got to be
80 done."

"No—is that so? Oh come, now—lemme just try. Only just a little—I'd let *you*, if you was me, Tom."

"Ben, I'd like to, honest injun; but Aunt
85 Polly—well, Jim wanted to do it, but she wouldn't let him; Sid wanted to do it, and she wouldn't let Sid. Now don't you see how I'm fixed? If you was to tackle this fence and anything was to happen to it—"

90 "Oh, shucks, I'll be just as careful. Now lemme try. Say—I'll give you the core of my apple."

"Well, here—No, Ben, now don't. I'm afeard—"

95 "I'll give you *all* of it!"
Tom gave up the brush with reluctance in his face, but alacrity in his heart. And while the late steamer Big Missouri worked and sweated in the sun, the retired artist sat on a barrel in the shade
100 close by, dangled his legs, munched his apple, and planned the slaughter of more innocents.

1. As used in line 11, "operation" most nearly means

   (A) venture.
   (B) maneuver.
   (C) performance.
   (D) process.

2. In paragraph 1 (lines 1 – 14), the narrator conveys Tom's attitude toward whitewashing the fence by

   (A) suggesting that Tom was unknowingly tricked into whitewashing the fence.
   (B) using hyperbole to highlight Tom's despair at the seeming enormity of the fence.
   (C) contrasting the simplicity of the task with Tom's relentlessly negative outlook.
   (D) comparing Tom to a reluctant hero embarking on a long journey.

3. Which choice provides the best evidence for the answer to the previous question?

   (A) Lines 1 –3 ("Saturday morning...with life")
   (B) Lines 3 – 5 ("Tom appeared...a long-handled brush")
   (C) Lines 7 – 9 ("Thirty yards...but a burden")
   (D) Lines 9 – 11 ("Sighing, he dipped...did it again")

4. In context of the passage, paragraph 2 serves to

   (A) contrast Tom's generosity with the other boys' cruelty.
   (B) convey Tom's transformation from despondent to hopeful.
   (C) explain the origins of Tom's mental acuity.
   (D) provide justification for Tom's sorrow.

5. In context of the passage, the author's statement, "Tom surveyed... as before," (lines 37 – 39) is meant to convey

   (A) the idea that Tom's artistic inclinations bleed into all aspects of his daily life.
   (B) Tom's earnest desire to impress Ben with his whitewashing skills.
   (C) Tom's enthusiasm for undertaking tasks with diligence and care.
   (D) Tom's level of commitment in his attempt to deceive Ben.

6. Tom first interests Ben in whitewashing by

   (A) comparing whitewashing to an activity that Ben enjoys.
   (B) offering Ben an apple in exchange for his help.
   (C) pointing out the novelty of the activity.
   (D) claiming that the activity is more fun than swimming.

7. Tom mentions Aunt Polly (lines 71 – 89) primarily to

   (A) explain to Ben why he has so little time to play.
   (B) contrast her laziness with his diligence and determination.
   (C) suggest that meeting her expectations is extremely challenging.
   (D) imply that she will berate Ben if he does not help whitewash the fence.

8. The relationship between Tom and Ben most closely resembles that between

   (A) a con man and his unsuspecting victim.
   (B) an artist and his wealthy patron.
   (C) a child and his disapproving father.
   (D) a detective and a criminal suspect.

9. As used in line 97, "late" most nearly means

   (A) overdue.
   (B) recent.
   (C) tardy.
   (D) deceased.

10. Ben's impersonation of a steamboat and Tom's impersonation of an artist differ in that

   (A) Ben's act is skillful while Tom's is unconvincing.
   (B) Ben's act is playful while Tom's is manipulative.
   (C) Ben's act is harmless while Tom's is hurtful.
   (D) Ben's act is offensive while Tom's is flattering.

Refer to the passage below to answer questions 11 – 21.

This passage is adapted from John Malone, "The Importance of Geothermal Energy," published by The Moderate Voice in 2009.

line   In the world of renewables, most of the attention is on the wind and the sun. Geothermal power just hasn't gotten the same respect. That could be changing, as both the Obama
5   Administration and Silicon Valley are considering the heat under the ground as a potentially huge source of clean, domestic U.S. energy, but recent setbacks are calling into question how much geothermal can contribute. Given the potential
10   benefits, we should be doubling our efforts to make geothermal a viable power source for the U.S.

    Some background: All thermal power plants use the same basic process. A heat source
15   (burning coal or gas, uranium, concentrated solar energy) is used to turn water into steam, and the energy released turns a turbine that produces electricity. What sets geothermal apart is that the steam comes directly from the ground. Water
20   percolates down through cracks in the ground and is heated to the boiling point by hot rocks underground (in some cases coming back up as a geyser — think Old Faithful), and the resulting steam is drawn up via a well to a turbine.

25   This makes for, in principle, the ideal alternative energy source. Geothermal power releases virtually no carbon dioxide or pollutants. Crucially, geothermal provides baseload power— wind and solar power are better suited as peaking
30   technologies, as they are dependent on energy sources that wax and wane over the course of a day. Geothermal power is on 24 hours a day, 365 days a year (geothermal power plants can have utilization rates up to 98 percent). And from a
35   national security angle, the promise of geothermal is obvious: There is no more domestic source of energy than the actual ground underneath us.

    There's one problem, though. There are only a few places in the U.S. where you can find shallow
40   groundwater hot enough to get steam directly from the ground. Engineers and geologists are therefore looking at a new way to tap underground heat. Enhanced Geothermal Systems (EGS) make use of the fact that, if you drill deep
45   enough, any bedrock in the world gets hot enough to boil water. Basically, EGS involves drilling a well into deep, hot, dry rock; drilling a second well nearby to the same depth; fracturing the rock between those two wells enough to allow water
50   to pass between them; and then pumping water down the first well and allowing it to percolate through the hot fractured area to the second well, where it will come back to the surface as superheated steam. The potential for EGS in the

55   U.S. is enormous. A 2006 Massachusetts Institute of Technology report concluded it could provide 100,000 megawatts of power by 2050.

    EGS is not without its drawbacks. Cost is the main hurdle. Oil and gas companies now
60   measure well depths in miles, but these are wells drilled through relatively soft rock, not the hard granites that are best suited for EGS. If not managed properly, rocks could lose their heat — eventually, pumping water through a hot rock
65   system could bring the heat gradient down to the point that new wells need to be drilled. There has also been some concern about earthquakes. In 2006, an EGS pilot project in Switzerland set off a 3.4 magnitude quake.

70   That said, these hurdles are all surmountable, and given the huge benefits it could bring, there is already a surge in investment — both public and private — in EGS. Google laid down an $11 million investment for early-stage research.
75   Perhaps most encouraging is the interest shown in EGS by our Nobel Laureate Secretary of Energy, Steven Chu. Obama's stimulus plan set aside $400 million for pure geothermal research and development. And it's looking like EGS wouldn't
80   need too much more of an investment. A recent New York University study found that as little as $3 billion in R&D development could make EGS cost-competitive with fossil fuel plants.

    The widespread application of EGS is still a
85   ways off. But geothermal, whether traditional or EGS, should be used alongside technologies like wind and solar to diversify our renewable base. There is no silver bullet in renewable energy. It's better to think in terms of silver buckshot, where a
90   collection of solutions add up to a big impact. We should do our best to make sure that one of those solutions is the one right under our feet.

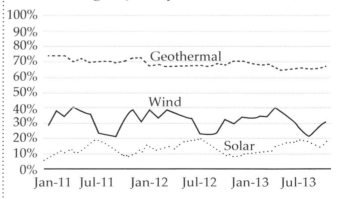

Monthly capacity factors for select fuels and technologies (January 2011 - October 2013)

The net capacity factor of a power plant is the ratio of its actual output over a period of time, to its potential output if it were possible for it to operate at full nameplate capacity continuously over the same period of time.

11. The primary purpose of the passage is to

   (A) describe the potential costs and benefits of an emerging technology.
   (B) compare the effectiveness of EGS to other forms of renewable energy.
   (C) advocate for a viable source of renewable energy.
   (D) challenge the assumption that fossil fuels are the most effective source of energy.

12. According to paragraph 2 (lines 13 – 24), the heat sources for geothermal energy are

   (A) coal and natural gases.
   (B) subterranean rocks.
   (C) underground water reservoirs.
   (D) steam-powered turbines.

13. Based on the passage, it is reasonable to infer that the production of geothermal energy requires

   (A) access to drills owned by gas and oil companies.
   (B) the use of poorly understood technologies.
   (C) global cooperation.
   (D) large reserves of water.

14. As used in line 35, "angle" most nearly means

   (A) perspective.
   (B) gradient.
   (C) direction.
   (D) point.

15. The author indicates that Enhanced Geothermal Systems are beneficial because they

   (A) provide more energy than other methods of geothermal energy production.
   (B) can be effective in places that lack easily accessible heated underground water.
   (C) require less drilling and maintenance than other forms of renewable energy.
   (D) can completely replace wind and solar energy while still proving cost effective.

16. As used in line 87, "silver bullet" most nearly refers to

   (A) a surprising revelation.
   (B) a clear set of instructions
   (C) a short-term plan.
   (D) an all-encompassing solution.

17. In line 91, the phrase "right under our feet" primarily serves to

   (A) underscore the accessibility of geothermal energy.
   (B) suggest that the U.S. should exploit its huge stores of hot underground water.
   (C) reiterate the need to begin producing geothermal energy immediately in the U.S.
   (D) imply that the most effective uses for geothermal energy should be obvious to readers.

18. The author's attitude toward the production of geothermal energy in the U.S. is one of

   (A) anxiety.
   (B) hope.
   (C) surprise.
   (D) criticism.

19. Which choice provides the best evidence for the answer to the previous question?

   (A) Line 9 – 12 ("Given...U.S.")
   (B) Line 34 – 37 ("And from...us")
   (C) Line 38 – 41 ("There's...ground")
   (D) Line 84 – 87 ("But geothermal...energy")

20. Which statement about geothermal energy is best supported by the graph?

   (A) Certain environmental factors affect wind and solar energy production more than they do geothermal energy production.
   (B) The development of solar and wind energies has largely overshadowed that of geothermal energy.
   (C) More energy was produced from geothermal sources than from wind of solar sources durng the period described in the graph.
   (D) Geothermal energy production may never be affordable enough to compete with the production of wind and solar energies.

21. Data from the graph provide most direct support for which claim in the passage?

   (A) Lines 9 – 12 ("Given...U.S.")
   (B) Lines 27 – 32 ("Crucially...day")
   (C) Lines 55 – 57 ("A 2006...2050")
   (D) Lines 87 – 89 ("It's better...impact")

Refer to the passage below to answer questions 22 – 31.

This passage is adapted from Charles Darwin, *On the Origin of Species*, originally published 1859. The book laid the foundation for the study of evolutionary biology.

line   I should premise that I use the term Struggle for Existence in a large and metaphorical sense, including dependence of one being on another, and including (which is more important) not only
5   the life of the individual, but success in leaving progeny. Two canine animals in a time of dearth, may be truly said to struggle with each other which shall get food and live. But a plant on the edge of a desert is said to struggle for life against
10   the drought, though more properly it should be said to be dependent on the moisture. A plant which annually produces a thousand seeds, of which on an average only one comes to maturity, may be more truly said to struggle with the plants
15   of the same and other kinds which already clothe the ground. The mistletoe is dependent on the apple and a few other trees, but can only in a far-fetched sense be said to struggle with these trees, for if too many of these parasites grow on
20   the same tree, it will languish and die. But several seedling mistletoes, growing close together on the same branch, may more truly be said to struggle with each other. As the mistletoe is disseminated by birds, its existence depends on birds; and
25   it may metaphorically be said to struggle with other fruit-bearing plants, in order to tempt birds to devour and thus disseminate its seeds rather than those of other plants. In these several senses, which pass into each other, I use for convenience'

30   sake the general term of struggle for existence.
    A struggle for existence inevitably follows from the high rate at which all organic beings tend to increase. Every being, which during its natural lifetime produces several eggs or seeds,
35   must suffer destruction during some period of its life, and during some season or occasional year, otherwise, on the principle of geometrical increase, its numbers would quickly become so inordinately great that no country could support
40   the product. Hence, as more individuals are produced than can possibly survive, there must in every case be a struggle for existence, either one individual with another of the same species, or with the individuals of distinct species, or with
45   the physical conditions of life. It is the doctrine of Malthus applied with manifold force to the whole animal and vegetable kingdoms; for in this case there can be no artificial increase of food, and no prudential restraint from marriage. Although
50   some species may be now increasing, more or less rapidly, in numbers, all cannot do so, for the world would not hold them.
    It is good thus to try in our imagination to give any form some advantage over another.
55   Probably in no single instance should we know what to do, so as to succeed. It will convince us of our ignorance on the mutual relations of all organic beings; a conviction as necessary, as it seems to be difficult to acquire. All that we can do,
60   is to keep steadily in mind that each organic being is striving to increase at a geometrical ratio; that each at some period of its life, during some season of the year, during each generation or at intervals, has to struggle for life, and to suffer great
65   destruction. When we reflect on this struggle, we may console ourselves with the full belief, that the war of nature is not incessant, that no fear is felt, that death is generally prompt, and that the vigorous, the healthy, and the happy survive and
70   multiply.

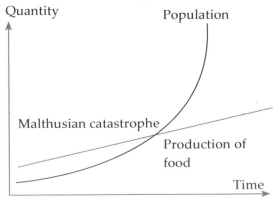

Theory of Human Population Growth by Thomas Robert Malthus (1766 – 1834)

22. The statement in lines 6 – 8 ("Two canine… live") sets up a contrast in the remainder of the paragraph between

    (A) competing for food and depending on other species.
    (B) struggling for individual existence and struggling for success of one's offspring.
    (C) struggling against environmental factors and struggling against other organisms.
    (D) actually fighting over food and a wider definition of the struggle for existence.

23. As used in line 2, the word "sense" most nearly means

    (A) feeling.
    (B) wisdom.
    (C) meaning.
    (D) perception.

24. Darwin's central claim in the passage is that

    (A) every living organism is engaged in a struggle for existence.
    (B) understanding an organism's struggle for existence is impossible.
    (C) all organisms are part of a web of dependence.
    (D) people should be careful to reproduce only in accordance with the food supply.

25. Which choice provides the best evidence for the answer to the previous question?

    (A) Lines 11 – 16 ("A plant which…ground")
    (B) Lines 23 – 28 ("As the mistletoe…plants")
    (C) Lines 40 – 45 ("Hence, as more…life")
    (D) Lines 45 – 49 ("It is the…marriage")

26. Which statement about the struggle for existence is best supported by the graph?

    (A) Lines 1 – 6 ("I should premise…progeny")
    (B) Lines 6 – 8 ("Two canine…live")
    (C) Lines 28 – 30 ("In these several…existence")
    (D) Lines 33 – 40 ("Every being…product")

27. Darwin mentions Malthus primarily to

    (A) argue that Malthus was wrong about animals and plants.
    (B) adapt Malthus's theory to non-human organisms.
    (C) persuade the reader to accept Malthus's conclusions.
    (D) claim that increased food production would benefit all species.

28. As used in line 48, "artificial" most nearly means

    (A) fake.
    (B) cultivated.
    (C) imitation.
    (D) dishonest.

29. In paragraph 3 (lines 52 – 70), Darwin's stance could best be described as

    (A) an advocate seeking supporters for a policy.
    (B) an expert attempting to simplify sophisticated concepts.
    (C) a teacher advising persistence and humility.
    (D) an environmentalist encouraging like-minded readers.

30. What is Darwin's main point about mutual relations of organic beings?

    (A) We can comprehend them, but not fully.
    (B) We must respect and protect them.
    (C) We should think of ourselves as part of the system of mutual relations.
    (D) We ought to double our efforts to study them.

31. The three-part structure of the passage most closely resembles which of the following?

    (A) Thesis-Evidence-Consequence
    (B) Question-Answer-Discussion
    (C) Argument-Counterargument-Synthesis
    (D) Definition-Explanation-Commentary

Refer to the passage below to answer questions 32 – 42.

Passage 1 is adapted from Patrick Henry's speech to the Second Virginia Convention in 1775. Virginia was one of 13 British colonies in America; its leaders were debating whether to join the fight against the British. Passage 2 is adapted from an 1811 speech by Tecumseh, a Shawnee Indian leader from the Northeast. After seeing his own territory overtaken by American colonists, he tried to unite all Native Americans in armed resistance. The following is from a speech he gave in Mississippi to members of the Choctaw and Chickasaw tribes.

Passage 1

line Mr. President,

...Sir, we have done everything that could be done, to avert the storm which is now coming on. We have petitioned; we have remonstrated; we
5 have supplicated... In vain, after these things, may we indulge the fond hope of peace and reconciliation. There is no longer any room for hope. If we wish to be free, if we mean to preserve inviolate those inestimable privileges for which
10 we have been so long contending, if we mean not basely to abandon the noble struggle in which we have been so long engaged, and which we have pledged ourselves never to abandon until the glorious object of our contest shall be obtained,
15 we must fight! I repeat it, sir, we must fight! An appeal to arms and to the God of Hosts is all that is left us!

They tell us, sir, that we are weak; unable to cope with so formidable an adversary. But when
20 shall we be stronger? Will it be the next week, or the next year? Will it be when we are totally disarmed, and when a British guard shall be stationed in every house?...The battle, sir, is not to the strong alone; it is to the vigilant, the active,
25 the brave....There is no retreat but in submission and slavery! Our chains are forged! Their clanking may be heard on the plains of Boston! The war is inevitable and let it come! I repeat it, sir, let it come.
30 It is in vain, sir, to extenuate the matter. Gentlemen may cry, Peace, Peace but there is no peace. The war is actually begun! The next gale that sweeps from the north will bring to our ears the clash of resounding arms! Our brethren are
35 already in the field! Why stand we here idle? What is it that gentlemen wish? What would they have? Is life so dear, or peace so sweet, as to be purchased at the price of chains and slavery? Forbid it, Almighty God! I know not what course
40 others may take; but as for me, give me liberty or give me death.

Passage 2

...The whites are already nearly a match for us all united, and too strong for any one tribe alone to resist; so that unless we support one
45 another with our collective and united forces; unless every tribe unanimously combines to give check to the ambition and avarice of the whites, they will soon conquer us apart and disunited, and we will be driven away from our native
50 country and scattered as autumnal leaves before the wind.

But have we not courage enough remaining to defend our country and maintain our ancient independence? Will we calmly suffer the white
55 intruders and tyrants to enslave us?...The annihilation of our race is at hand unless we unite in one common cause against the common foe. Think not, brave Choctaws and Chickasaws, that you can remain passive and indifferent to the
60 common danger, and thus escape the common fate. Your people, too, will soon be as falling leaves and scattering clouds before their blighting breath. You, too, will be driven away from your native land and ancient domains as leaves are
65 driven before the wintry storms.

Sleep not longer, O Choctaws and Chickasaws, in false security and delusive hopes. Our broad domains are fast escaping from our grasp. Every year our white intruders
70 become more greedy, exacting, oppressive and overbearing.... Before the palefaces* came among us, we enjoyed the happiness of unbounded freedom, and were acquainted with neither riches, wants, nor oppression. How is it now? Wants and
75 oppression are our lot; for are we not controlled in everything, and dare we move without asking, by your leave*? Are we not being stripped day by day of the little that remains of our ancient liberty? Do they not even kick and strike us as
80 they do their blackfaces*? How long will it be before they will tie us to a post and whip us, and make us work for them in their cornfields as they do them? Shall we wait for that moment or shall we die fighting before submitting to such
85 ignominy?

* *palefaces: people of European ancestry*
* *by your leave: with your permission*
* *blackfaces: people of African ancestry*

32. Passage 1 strongly suggests that, given circumstances in the American colonies at the time,

(A) expecting a peaceful solution would be wishful thinking.
(B) a standoff might be possible unless Americans are disarmed.
(C) the British governors are probably ready to negotiate seriously.
(D) Virginians should focus on the goal of building a strong Virginia.

33. Which choice provides the best evidence for the answer to the previous question?

(A) Lines 4 – 5, ("We have...supplicated")
(B) Lines 5 – 7 ("In vain...reconciliation")
(C) Lines 8 – 10 ("If we wish...contending")
(D) Lines 21 – 23 ("Will it be...house?")

34. As used in line 14, "object" most nearly means

(A) recipient.
(B) item.
(C) goal.
(D) protest.

35. In line 26, Henry uses the phrase "Our chains are forged!" primarily to

(A) allude to the work of making weapons to fight the British.
(B) argue that the colonists are already doomed.
(C) encourage a debate in Virginia about whether to own slaves.
(D) suggest that complete political oppression is imminent.

36. Tecumseh's metaphor of autumn leaves blown by wind (lines 49 – 51) primarily conveys the idea that

(A) European people will destroy vital plants and animals.
(B) native people will be forcibly detached from communities.
(C) his listeners' dreams for a better life will be crushed.
(D) everyone involved will be unable to exercise self-restraint.

37. Tecumseh strongly suggests in Passage 2 that, for native tribes,

(A) preparing to defend their own territories is paramount.
(B) a natural strategy would be identifying with African American slaves.
(C) retaining each tribe's unique culture is a major concern.
(D) overcoming their differences is crucial for their survival.

38. Which choice provides the best evidence for the answer to the previous question?

(A) Lines 55 – 57 ("The annihilation...foe")
(B) Lines 58 – 61 ("Think not...fate")
(C) Line 68 – 69 ("Our broad...grasp")
(D) Lines 79 – 80 ("Do they not...blackfaces?")

39. As used in line 74, the word "wants" most nearly means

(A) wishes.
(B) privations.
(C) interests.
(D) objectives.

40. In Passage 2, does Tecumseh base his pro-war argument on the same premise as Patrick Henry does in Passage 1?

(A) Yes, because both refer to their frustration with ineffective written and verbal protests.
(B) Yes, because both predict that courage and vigilance can overcome a stronger enemy.
(C) No, because unlike Henry, Tecumseh claims that the war has already begun.
(D) No, because unlike Henry, Tecumseh warns of the complete loss of communities.

41. One difference between the two speakers' arguments in the passages is that

(A) Tecumseh describes his own experiences in battle.
(B) Henry claims he is ready to die for the cause.
(C) Henry supports unifying the rebels.
(D) Tecumseh warns about literal slavery.

42. Passages 1 and 2 both feature which component?

(A) Evidence in terms of facts and figures
(B) A rhetorical question about dying
(C) A reference to past heroes who prevailed against all odds
(D) A narrative account of a person's suffering

Refer to the passage below to answer questions 43 – 52.

This passage is adapted from Monte Basgall, "A smashing success," 2014 by the Krell Institute. The passage primarily discusses the acquisition and analysis of data from particle colliders, which guide groups of particles into near-light-speed collisions. These collisions can reveal even smaller particles, many of which can only be observed during particle collisions.

line   In 2012, as a worldwide collaboration of
        physicists labored to assemble findings that
        would spawn global headlines, 33 computational
        scientists at Brookhaven National Laboratory
5   were working equally long and tense hours to
        keep many of those particle hunters supplied with
        constantly updated information.
            "Those were probably the most exciting
        moments of my professional career, and this
10   was true for many other people working in
        computing," recalls Michael Ernst about his
        group's role in the discovery of the Higgs boson.
        Ernst directs the RHIC and ATLAS Computing
        Facility (RACF) at Brookhaven, which has served
15   as a key data hub for two massive particle
        accelerators making landmark findings in physics.
            "It was essential for everybody directly
        involved in the analysis to have immediate
        access to the data. Everybody was committed to
20   resolving problems, regardless of what the hour.
        Whenever something was not going as projected
        there were automatic alarms, and people
        got out of their beds to solve these problems
        immediately."
25   Since 2000, RHIC – for Relativistic Heavy
        Ion Collider – has pushed gold ions to near-light
        speeds around a 2.4-mile racetrack at Brookhaven,
        colliding them at energies of up to 500 billion
        electron volts (GeV). That high-energy crash is
30   thought to free an optimal number of quarks
        from their normal bondage to gluons, something
        theoreticians say last happened 100 millionths of a
        second after the Big Bang.
            Researchers anticipated the collisions would
35   result in intensely hot gaseous plasmas of quarks
        and gluons. But RHIC experiments are instead
        showing these extreme conditions create a perfect
        liquid – a substance that flows with virtually no
        viscosity.
40   The RHIC, in essence, is a time machine. So is
        the Large Hadron Collider (LHC), a 17-mile track
        at the French-Swiss border. At intervals since
        2008, the LHC has smashed together beams of
        protons at energy levels of up to 8 trillion electron
45   volts (TeV). Theoretically, that can recreate other
        kinds of physics from just after the Big Bang.
            The LHC's most notable finding to date is the
        apparent discovery of the last major fundamental
        particle needed to complete the Standard Model
50   dictated by quantum mechanics. Theoreticians say

the Higgs boson begat the mass in most states of matter.
    The Tevatron, a 4-mile, 1 TeV proton-and-antiproton smasher at the Fermi National
55 Accelerator Laboratory (Fermilab) near Batavia, Illinois, narrowed down the Higgs search before closing in 2011. That quest then refocused at the higher-energy LHC. Meanwhile, both Fermilab and Brookhaven took on major roles in the
60 European-based mission.
    Seeking particles and states of matter that don't exist in today's world are needles-in-haystacks challenges that demand careful sifting through the many fragments from ferocious
65 matter smashing.
    The Higgs challenge has confronted about 6,000 scientists from 38 nations with byproducts from 600 million proton-proton collisions per second, reports CERN, the laboratory that hosts
70 the LHC. Only one of each trillion such bust-ups would likely create a Higgs, Brookhaven experts say. Caught outside its time zone, each candidate Higgs would instantly decay, in as many as a dozen ways, into other detectable particles.
75   RHIC's gold-gold ion smashups, meanwhile, occur thousands of times a second to generate many more fragments for more than 1,000 other investigators in the U.S. and abroad to analyze.
    These two divergent experiments pose
80 another set of challenges for the information scientists at Ernst's RACF. Besides managing megadata for all RHIC collaborators, Brookhaven and Fermilab also agreed to split the more imposing information management duties for all
85 U.S. collaborators in the LHC.
    That means RACF serves about 600 Americans who analyze fragments logged by the LHC's huge ATLAS particle detector. Fermilab supplies an equal number using LHC's other
90 detector, called CMS.
    RACF is among about 140 data centers sharing the LHC's information-handling duties via a high-speed global fiber optic data grid. PanDA, a special workload management system
95 for ATLAS that draws on disk storage, processors and enabling software, ensures that all of that detector's researchers receive whatever data they need, regardless of where they're working.
    "I think it's fair to say that all these resources
100 combined form a worldwide distributed supercomputer," Ernst says.

43. Over the course of the passage, the focus of the article shifts from

    (A) the benefits of experimentation to the costs of experimentation.
    (B) the production of data to the analysis of data.
    (C) developments in the United States to developments in Europe.
    (D) historic notions of the genesis of the universe to contemporary developments.

44. As used in line 16, "landmark" most nearly means

    (A) geographic.
    (B) visible.
    (C) inspiring.
    (D) seminal.

45. Based on Ernst's description in lines 18 – 25, the atmosphere at the RACF facility is best described as

    (A) pressing and collaborative.
    (B) frantic and competitive.
    (C) frustrated and aggressive.
    (D) open and forgiving.

46. In paragraph 4 (lines 26 – 34), the author mentions "near-light speeds," "energies of up to 500 billion electron volts," and "100 millionths of a second" primarily to

    (A) provide the reader with the sense of the magnitude of the endeavor.
    (B) convince the reader of the wastefulness of the experimental procedures.
    (C) intimidate the reader with difficult concepts.
    (D) encourage the reader to reach out to laboratories and get involved.

47. In paragraph 6 (lines 41 – 47), the author refers to the RHIC and the LHC as time machines primarily to convey the idea that

    (A) they challenge traditional concepts of time and space.
    (B) they were first envisioned by science-fiction writers.
    (C) they allow us to study the origins of the universe.
    (D) they provide glimpses of processes that have not yet occurred.

48. Which choice provides the best evidence for the answer to the previous question?

    (A) Lines 30 – 34 ("That high-energy crash…Big Bang")
    (B) Lines 37 – 40 ("But RHIC experiments…no viscosity")
    (C) Lines 62 – 66 ("Seeking particles and… matter smashing")
    (D) Lines 67 – 71 ("The Higgs challenge…the LHC")

49. According to the passage, the RHIC and LHC produce collisions of

    (A) ions and protons, respectively.
    (B) gluons and quarks, respectively.
    (C) antiprotons and protons, respectively.
    (D) ions and neutral atoms, respectively.

50. In the context of the passage, the author's use of the phrase "needles-in-haystacks" (lines 63 – 64) is primarily meant to convey the

    (A) difficulty and laboriousness of the scientists' task.
    (B) mathematical impossibility of the search.
    (C) necessity of collaboration in science.
    (D) smallness of the Higg's boson compared to an atom or ion.

51. The passage most strongly suggests which of the following about the Higgs boson?

    (A) It does not actually exist.
    (B) It has sparked much controversy among scientists.
    (C) Its existence has been suspected since antiquity.
    (D) It can only be identified indirectly.

52. Which choice provides the best evidence for the answer to the previous question?

    (A) Lines 8 – 12 ("Those were…Higgs boson")
    (B) Lines 46 – 47 ("Theoretically, that…Big Bang")
    (C) Lines 47 – 50 ("The LHC's most…quantum mechanics")
    (D) Lines 61 – 65 ("Seeking particles and… matter smashing")

STOP

Writing and Language Test 2
35 MINUTES, 44 QUESTIONS

Turn to Section 2 of your answer sheet to answer the questions in this section.

DIRECTIONS

Each of the following passages is accompanied by approximately 11 questions. Some questions will require you to revise the passages in order to improve coherence and clarity. Other questions will require you to correct grammatical errors in the passages. Passages may be accompanied by graphs, charts, or tables that you must consider when making revisions. For most questions, you may select the "NO CHANGE" option if you believe that portion of the passage is clear, concise, and grammatically correct as is.

Within the passages, highlighted numbers followed by underlined text indicate which part of the text corresponds with each question. Bracketed numbers [1] indicate sentence number. These bracketed numbers are only relevant to problems that require you to add or rearrange sentences in a paragraph.

Refer to the passage below to answer questions 1 – 11.

The Virtual Office

— 1 —

When I first heard about cloud computing, I thought it was brilliant. The only problem I had with the cloud was **1** this. I'd been using it for years before the term became popular. Since 2007, storage websites, such as Dropbox and Google Drive, have been providing users with basic cloud services including file storage, transfer, and backup. I immediately fell in love with the idea of hosting large amounts of data online and accessing my files from anywhere in the world. I uploaded many of my personal files and created **2** a fake hard drive that I can access from any device connected to the Internet.

1. (A) NO CHANGE
   (B) this;
   (C) this:
   (D) this that

2. (A) NO CHANGE
   (B) an imaginary
   (C) a virtual
   (D) a counterfeit

—2—

Because much of my work is done directly on the cloud, I'm able to work from home most days and only attend formal meetings in a corporate office once a week. In addition, the cloud enables me to work with a much more diverse group of people, many of **3** them live outside the United States. Cloud computing also offers me the flexibility of working from my laptop, tablet, or other device. **4** Because the cloud hosts application as well as file data, I never have to install new **5** software. The cloud automatically updates the programs it hosts, so I'm always working with the most recent release.

—3—

As a consumer, this service is convenient; as a professional, it is invaluable. **6** A collaborator and me can access and edit the same file simultaneously and watch changes made by each other in real time. My documents are saved instantly, backed up multiple times, and can easily be shared with **7** colleagues, and collaborators. I can also leave and reply to comments, creating a conversation about a document right there in the margin. **8** I can even designate privileges when sharing files, so some of my colleagues may be allowed to view, but not edit, a shared document.

3. (A) NO CHANGE
(B) who
(C) whom
(D) they

4. At this point, the writer is considering adding the following information

   I must admit, however, that working from my smartphone has proven rather difficult.

Should the writer make this addition?

(A) Yes, because it provides an important detail that directly supports the main idea of the paragraph.
(B) Yes, because it extends the humorous tone used throughout the passage.
(C) No, because the discussion of smartphones is outside of the scope of this passage.
(D) No, because it distracts from the central focus of the paragraph.

5. Which choice provides the best combination of the two sentences at the underlined portion?

(A) software, so the cloud
(B) software; however, the cloud
(C) software, and the cloud
(D) software, the cloud

6. (A) NO CHANGE
(B) A collaborator and I accesses
(C) A collaborator and me access
(D) A collaborator and I can access

7. (A) NO CHANGE
(B) colleagues and collaborators.
(C) colleagues, and also collaborators.
(D) colleagues and, collaborators.

8. Which choice provides the most relevant detail?

(A) NO CHANGE
(B) Plus, I can easily share stored content on social media.
(C) In addition, I can download a file saved on the cloud and access it offline.
(D) Finally, I can organize files for convenient access later.

—4—

As cloud services become more reliable, more and more businesses are utilizing virtual workplaces. Personally, I'm excited to see the growth and popularity of cloud computing as a business model. **9** In spite of the benefits to employees, the business can expect to see an increase in overall productivity as well as a reduction in operating costs. Since cloud services are typically offered on a pay-per-usage scale, businesses only pay for **10** what I use and can save significant amounts of money compared to conventional data storage methods. These benefits, however, are only the beginning of the next generation of computing systems, and I'm eagerly awaiting the continued development of this promising new field. **11**

9. (A) NO CHANGE
    (B) Because of
    (C) In contrast to
    (D) In regards to

10. (A) NO CHANGE
    (B) what has usage
    (C) what is used
    (D) what they use

11. The most logical placement for paragraph 2 is

    (A) where it is now.
    (B) before paragraph 1.
    (C) after paragraph 3.
    (D) after paragraph 4.

Refer to the passage below to answer questions 12 – 22.

Fermenting Food to Improve Health

Fermentation is the conversion of sugars and starches to alcohols and acids that takes place in yeast and bacteria. Humans have **12** exposed this process for many thousands of years to produce alcoholic beverages as well as nutritionally enhanced food products. These fermented foods typically have a longer shelf life than their traditionally prepared **13** counterparts. They often incorporate new flavors that many people find pleasing. Fermentation can also make food more nutritious by adding vitamins and macronutrients, and by making existing nutrients easier for the body to absorb or use.

In addition, recent research suggests that some fermented foods may have higher quantities of antioxidants, making them good candidates for functional **14** foods—that is, foods which may improve health or help prevent disease. One study in 2016 compared the composition of an unfermented soybean mixture to **15** this of its fermented counterpart. Scientists analyzed extracts of the foods before, during, and after fermentation to determine the concentrations of several antioxidants, notably phenolic and flavonoid compounds. Additionally, samples of the fermented and unfermented mixture were fed to rodents to determine if an antiobesity effect is present.

Researchers discovered that fermented soybeans contained higher levels of phenolic compounds than unfermented ones. In addition, the concentrations of various flavonoids decreased because they were metabolized to aglycones. An aglycone has a similar structure to the flavonoid from which it is derived; however, the aglycone form is more readily available for absorption **16** into the bloodstreams of animals, including humans. The increased concentrations of aglycones and phenolic compounds may account for the postulated health benefits of fermented soybeans. **17** Consequently, researchers analyzed the **18** product's abilities to inhibit pancreatic lipases— enzymes responsible for digesting fats and oils. They were interested in studying lipase inhibition because a decrease in lipase activity could result in an antiobesity effect by preventing the absorption of fatty

12. (A) NO CHANGE
    (B) interrogated
    (C) exploited
    (D) employed

13. Which of the following provides the best combination of the two sentences at the underlined portion?

    (A) counterparts, and
    (B) counterparts and
    (C) counterparts; and they
    (D) counterparts: they

14. (A) NO CHANGE
    (B) foods…
    (C) foods,
    (D) foods

15. (A) NO CHANGE
    (B) that
    (C) those
    (D) these

16. (A) NO CHANGE
    (B) in the bloodstreams of
    (C) in the bloodstreams in
    (D) into the bloodstreams in

17. (A) NO CHANGE
    (B) For instance,
    (C) Furthermore,
    (D) However,

18. (A) NO CHANGE
    (B) products' abilities
    (C) products' ability
    (D) product's ability

317

substances. The scientists found that unfermented soybeans reduced lipase activity moderately, while fermented beans further reduced this activity. In fact, the length of fermentation is directly related to the reduction in lipase activity, and **19** beans which had been fermented for 32 hours or more doubled the concentration of lipase inhibitors.

[1] As expected, mice consuming a high-fat diet showed a significant gain in weight over mice being fed a normal diet. [2] When the soybean mixture was introduced, these effects were **20** attenuated. [3] Further retardation of weight gain was noted when mice were fed the fermented mixture. [4] Researchers took blood and feces samples, and dissected the animals' organs when the experiment was over. [5] They discovered the presence of lipid vacuoles **21** in the mice consuming a high-fat diet only; none were present when the mice were also fed the fermented or unfermented soybean mixture. [6] Finally, the research team fed the soybean mixture (both fermented and unfermented) to mice to determine possible antiobesity effects on mammals. **22**

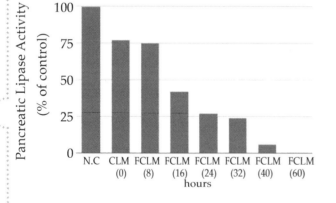

Pancreatic Lipase Activity

19. Which choice provides the most relevant detail based on the information from the graphic?

(A) NO CHANGE
(B) beans which had been fermented for 24 hours reduced lipase function by 25%.
(C) unfermented beans increased lipase activity by 50%.
(D) beans which had been fermented for 60 hours completely inhibited lipase function.

20. (A) NO CHANGE
(B) deflated
(C) immobilized
(D) belittled

21. At this point, the author is considering adding the following information.

—a sign of liver disease—

Should the author make this addition here?

(A) Yes, because it summarizes the research team's findings.
(B) Yes, because it provides context for understanding the experiment.
(C) No, because this information is redundant with the previous statement.
(D) No, because the discussion of liver disease is beyond the scope of the passage.

22. For the sake of logic, sentence 6 should be placed

(A) where it is now.
(B) before sentence 1.
(C) after sentence 1.
(D) after sentence 3.

Refer to the passage below to answer questions 23 – 33.

Living Bridges Span the Roots of Society

Living root bridges are an intriguing architectural feat unique to Meghalaya, a state in Northeast India. These bridges, as the name implies, are formed by manipulating the roots of local rubber trees. The indigenous Khasi people thread root fibers of a young rubber tree over years, sometimes decades, guiding their growth until a bridge is formed. As the tree **23** becomes experienced, the structure becomes more stable; eventually, it grows sturdy enough to support pedestrians.

24 In theory, root bridges can survive for hundreds of years. Root bridges can easily resist the harsh weather common in Meghalaya. They require little to no maintenance once completed and only grow stronger with time. The first historical record of root bridges dates back nearly 200 years, but it is impossible to determine how long the Khasi people have been using them. Many bridges are so old that living villagers no longer remember when they were built or **25** who constructed them. Bridges have been reported up to 50 meters in length, and several multi-level bridges are known to exist. **26**

23. (A) NO CHANGE
    (B) becomes wise,
    (C) matures,
    (D) ripens,

24. Which of the following provides the best combination of the two underlined sentences?

    (A) In theory, root bridges can survive for hundreds of years, so they can easily resist the harsh weather common in Meghalaya.
    (B) Root bridges can easily survive the harsh weather common in Meghalaya, therefore they have been theorized to survive for hundreds of years.
    (C) Because they have been theorized to survive for hundreds of years, root bridges in Meghalaya can resist harsh weather.
    (D) In theory, root bridges can survive for hundreds of years because they can easily resist the harsh weather common in Meghalaya.

25. (A) NO CHANGE
    (B) whom
    (C) whose
    (D) who's

26. At this point, the writer is considering adding the following sentence.

    > Perhaps the most famous living root bridge is the "Double Decker" near the village of Nongriat.

    Should the author include this information?

    (A) Yes, because the "Double Decker" bridge is central to the passage's main idea.
    (B) Yes, because it provides a specific example for the previous statement.
    (C) No, because the audience is likely already familiar with such a famous bridge.
    (D) No, because the village of Nongriat is irrelevant to the discussion.

[1] To build such enduring structures, villagers begin by planting a rubber tree on either bank of a river or stream. [2] The community works together to ensure proper growth and, after many years, the two systems meet in the middle of the river to form a complete bridge. [3] The **27** tree roots and branches are trained to grow along lengths of bamboo as the saplings develop. [4] As the roots and branches continue to grow, stepping stones are inserted into the walkway, and handrails are built through continued manipulation of the plants. **28**

Some bridges appear to be have grown, or at least started to grow, without human intervention. Others are a hybrid between steel cables, bamboo, and **29** they also incorporate living roots. Others still are grown over the ruins of decayed bridges. Many are in various stages of development and may not hold human passengers for years to come.

30 In addition to bridges, some Khasi villages design and grow root ladders and stairways to traverse steep cliffs and gain access to lush farmlands away from the village. To prevent erosion during the monsoon season, some tribes also use roots to develop retaining walls alongside many of the trails and paths through the region. These structures reinforce the soil against floods and reduce landslides. One village even boasts living root bleachers **31** for spectators can observe sporting events. Some living root constructions serve multiple functions; **32** for example, a bridge near Rangthylliang also acts as a **33** ladder, it provides access to the stream which it crosses.

27. (A) NO CHANGE
    (B) tree's
    (C) trees
    (D) trees'

28. To make the paragraph most logical, sentence 3 should be placed

    (A) where it is now.
    (B) before sentence 1.
    (C) after sentence 1.
    (D) after sentence 4.

29. (A) NO CHANGE
    (B) living roots.
    (C) living roots are also used.
    (D) more.

30. Which choice provides the most effective transition from the previous paragraph?

    (A) NO CHANGE
    (B) Although bridges are effective for transporting humans, ladders and stairways are necessary for shipping goods from one village to another.
    (C) Due to the popularity of sites containing root bridges, Khasi villagers have designed additional structures to attract tourists.
    (D) The people of Meghalaya have also developed non-arboreal strategies for coping with the huge amounts of rain that the region receives.

31. (A) NO CHANGE
    (B) to
    (C) which
    (D) where

32. (A) NO CHANGE
    (B) therefore,
    (C) on the other hand,
    (D) furthermore,

33. (A) NO CHANGE
    (B) ladder it provides
    (C) ladder, providing
    (D) ladder. Providing

Refer to the passage below to answer questions 34 – 44.

Antoni Gaudí

Antoni Gaudí was a late-19th and early-20th century architect based in Barcelona, Spain whose work reveals an odd and extremely personal vision. His structures feature curves, color, and complexity. Critics have described some of his buildings as "warped" and "hideous," but **34** they have also been praised as "vivid" and "splendid." **35** Millions of visitors tour Gaudí structures annually, and the United Nations has declared seven of his creations to be World Heritage Sites.

[1] Gaudí was born in 1852 in a village near Barcelona, the capital of Spain's Catalan region. [2] He spent much of his childhood observing the natural world around his home or watching his father, a coppersmith, at work. [3] As a child he was not able to play or go to school with other children because of painful rheumatism. [4] His health improved, yet he retained the passions formed in this quiet childhood — the passion for creating three-dimensional objects as his father had done — and for incorporating shapes from nature. **36**

As a young man, Gaudí moved to Barcelona and earned an architectural degree. His timing was fortunate because Barcelona **37** entered an era of affluence. **38** He designed a display cabinet for a glove factory, and the cabinet was shown at the 1878 Paris World Exhibition. Wealthy clients kept Gaudí busily employed. Soon he was designing and overseeing construction of prominent homes and apartment buildings. Given creative license by his patrons, he devised clever weight-bearing techniques, most notably the use of the parabola for ceilings. He made frequent use of ruled geometrical shapes, which are radiating straight lines that form curves, as in a hand-held fan. Employing the ruled shapes for curves and spirals in staircases, ramps, and balconies, **39** a natural look was achieved. For example, the façade of the Gaudí building *La Pedrera* resembles ocean waves.

34. (A) NO CHANGE
    (B) his buildings have also been praised
    (C) it is also legitimate to praise them
    (D) others have praised them

35. The writer is considering deleting the underlined sentence. Should the sentence be kept or deleted?

    (A) Kept, because it provides supporting evidence of Gaudí's singular talent.
    (B) Kept, because it supplies information to clarify the rest of the passage.
    (C) Deleted, because it does not include explanations for the United Nations' action.
    (D) Deleted, because it blurs the focus on Gaudí's buildings.

36. For the sake of the cohesion of paragraph 2, sentence 3 should be placed

    (A) where it is now.
    (B) before sentence 1.
    (C) after sentence 1.
    (D) after sentence 4.

37. (A) NO CHANGE
    (B) is entering
    (C) was entering
    (D) would enter

38. The writer is considering deleting the underlined sentence. Should the sentence be kept or deleted?

    (A) Kept, because it describes an interesting contextual detail about Gaudí's success.
    (B) Kept, because it explains the reason that Gaudí became an architect.
    (C) Deleted, because it fails to support the proposition that Gaudí quickly became a renowned architect.
    (D) Deleted, because it interferes with the paragraph's focus on Gaudí's opportunities in Barcelona.

39. (A) NO CHANGE
    (B) he achieved a natural look.
    (C) the structures achieved a natural look.
    (D) a natural look was achieved by Gaudí.

Gaudí's **40** principle gift was designing for practical considerations, such as light and ventilation. At the same time, he delighted in ornamentation. He added carefully crafted stained glass, ceramics, wood, stone, and wrought iron. He pioneered the creation of mosaics made from colorful shards of broken dishes. Each building is a personal statement; his style can be described as "baroque" or "Gothic," **41** but in many ways it defies classification. For example, his *Casa Batlló* has been nicknamed the "House of Bones" because of its bone-like window casements. The façade also features glass mosaics that reflect light. The roof curves like a dragon's back, and colorful chimneys **42** adorns it.

In 1926, while working on his masterpiece, the *Sagrada Família* cathedral, Gaudí died in a tram accident. The vast cultural impact of his work was not recognized at first. **43** Today, contemporary architects now make use of Gaudí-style curves and parabolas for space-age bridges and buildings. Gaudí's designs also influenced fine art. **44** He played a big role in the Art Nouveau movement, and Surrealist painter Salvador Dalí said he was influenced by Gaudí's buildings, as did Joan Miró.

40. (A) NO CHANGE
    (B) principal
    (C) princely
    (D) principled

41. (A) NO CHANGE
    (B) but remember, as mentioned above, it is always a personal statement for Gaudí.
    (C) but to be honest, no one can really say what style it is, it is just "Gaudísm."
    (D) but a hallmark of Modernism is its emphasis on using symbols and representations that hold meaning for the individual artist.

42. (A) NO CHANGE
    (B) adorns them.
    (C) adorn it.
    (D) adorn them.

43. (A) NO CHANGE
    (B) Today's architecture now
    (C) Today: architects
    (D) Today, architects

44. (A) NO CHANGE
    (B) Surrealist painters Salvador Dalí and Joan Miró claimed him as an influence, and art critics consider him a major force in the Art Nouveau movement.
    (C) He helped form the Art Nouveau movement in fine art, and he helped Salvador Dalí and Joan Miró get their start as Surrealist painters.
    (D) He had a major impact on Art Nouveau fine art, and also on Surrealism, through the painter Salvador Dalí as well as Joan Miró.

STOP

Math Test 2 – No Calculator

 25 MINUTES, 20 QUESTIONS

Turn to Section 3 of your answer sheet to answer the questions in this section.

DIRECTIONS

For questions **1 – 15**, find the solution to each problem and select the most appropriate answer from the choices provided. For questions **16 – 20**, find the solution to each problem and write your answer in the space provided. You may use the blank space in your test booklet for scratch work.

NOTES

1. The use of a calculator on any part of this section is forbidden.
2. Unless otherwise indicated, all variables and expressions used in this test represent real numbers.
3. Unless otherwise indicated, all figures used in this test are drawn to scale.
4. Unless otherwise indicated, all figures used in this test lie on a plane.
5. Unless specified otherwise, a given function, f, has the domain the set of all real numbers x for which $f(x)$ is a real number.

REFERENCE

$A = \dfrac{1}{2}bh$ $c^2 = a^2 + b^2$ Special Right Triangles $A = \pi r^2$ $C = 2\pi r$ $A = \ell w$

$V = \ell wh$ $V = \pi r^2 h$ $V = \dfrac{4}{3}\pi r^3$ $V = \dfrac{1}{3}\pi r^2 h$ $V = \dfrac{1}{3}\ell wh$

The arc of a circle is 360 degrees or 2π radians.
A triangle has angles that sum to 180 degrees.

1. James rents a car for x days. The rate is $19.95 per day, which includes 20 miles of driving, and $0.40 per mile for each additional mile. If James drives 30 miles per day for the duration of this period, which of the following represents the cost of the rental as a function of x?

   (A) $f(x) = (23.95)x$
   (B) $f(x) = (31.95)x$
   (C) $f(x) = (19.95)x + 4$
   (D) $f(x) = (39.95)x$

2. David and Peter are starting a lawn mowing service. They must buy a lawn mower for $250 and plan to charge $15 per lawn. Which of the following inequalities represents the number of lawns (l) they need to mow to earn at least $800 over the cost of the lawn mower?

   (A) $l \le 54$
   (B) $l \ge 54$
   (C) $l \le 70$
   (D) $l \ge 70$

3. A car travels 125 miles at 60 miles per hour, and then a further 30 miles at 45 miles per hour. What is the total time for the trip?

   (A) 2 hours, 45 minutes
   (B) 3 hours, 15 minutes
   (C) 3 hours, 20 minutes
   (D) 4 hours

4.
$$3x + 2y = -1$$
$$6x + 4y = -2$$

   The system of equations above represents two straight lines. What is true of these lines?

   (A) They meet at the origin.
   (B) They never meet.
   (C) They are perpendicular to each other.
   (D) They are the same line.

5. A cellphone plan charges a $2 monthly fee plus $0.10 per minute of talk time. Which of the following functions represents the cost, in dollars, for a month in which m minutes of talk time are used?

   (A) $C(m) = 10 + 2m$
   (B) $C(m) = 2 + 10m$
   (C) $C(m) = 0.1 + 2m$
   (D) $C(m) = 2 + 0.1m$

6. A massage parlor displays the formula $P = 15 + 45h$, representing the price P as a function of the number of hours h desired by the customer. Which of the following best interprets the number 15 in the expression?

   (A) The hourly rate of a masseuse
   (B) The average amount of time a customer purchases, in minutes
   (C) A convenience fee for paying with a credit card
   (D) The base service fee charged by the establishment

7. The sum of two numbers that differ by 3 is q. What is the the smaller of the two numbers in terms of q?

(A) $\dfrac{q}{2} - 1$

(B) $\dfrac{q}{2}$

(C) $\dfrac{q + 3}{2}$

(D) $\dfrac{q - 3}{2}$

8. A sphere has a surface area of 36π square centimeters. What is the volume of the sphere? (the formula for the surface area of a sphere is $A = 4\pi r^2$.)

(A) 27π cm^3

(B) 36π cm^3

(C) 54π cm^3

(D) 72π cm^3

9.

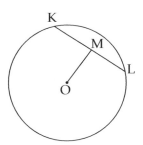

In the figure above, $\overline{KL}$ is a chord of the circle centered at O, with $\overline{KL} \perp \overline{MO}$. If $\overline{KL} = 12$ and $\overline{MO} = 6$, what is the area of the circle?

(A) 36π

(B) 48π

(C) 72π

(D) 96π

10.
$$x + y = 4$$
$$x - y = 0$$

Which of the following corresponds to the system of equations above?

(A)

(B)

(C)

(D)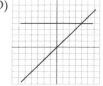

11.

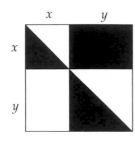

The large quadrilateral above is a square. What is the area of the shaded region in terms of x and y?

(A) $\dfrac{x^2 + y^2}{2}$

(B) $\dfrac{(x + y)^2}{2}$

(C) $\dfrac{\sqrt{x^2 + y^2}}{2}$

(D) $\dfrac{(x^2 + y^2)}{4}$

12. Water is poured from a full 1.5L bottle into an empty glass until the glass and the bottle are $\dfrac{3}{4}$ full. What is the volume of the glass?

(A) 0.5 L

(B) 0.75 L

(C) 1.125 L

(D) 0.4 L

13. If $\dfrac{a}{b} + \dfrac{a+2}{3b} = \dfrac{1}{4}$, what is the value of a in terms of b?

(A) $\dfrac{b + 4}{2}$

(B) $\dfrac{3b + 2}{4}$

(C) $\dfrac{3b - 2}{4}$

(D) $\dfrac{3b - 8}{16}$

14. A car travels 180 km from A to B at 60 km/h and returns from B to A along the same route at 90 km/h. What is the average speed in kilometers per hour for the round trip?

(A) 72

(B) 75

(C) 78

(D) 81

15. If $\dfrac{a^2 + 2ab + b^2}{a^2 - b^2} = 2(a + b)$, what is the value of $a - b$?

(A) 1

(B) $-\dfrac{1}{2}$

(C) 2

(D) $\dfrac{1}{2}$

DIRECTIONS

For questions **16 – 20**, find the solution to the problem and enter your answer as demonstrated below.

1. Only the answer that is bubbled in on the answer sheet will be credited. The blank spaces above the bubbles are for you to record your answers for accuracy.
2. Only fill in one bubble in any given column.
3. None of the answers on this portion of the test are negative values.
4. If a problem appears to have more than one answer, only enter one answer. If the answer you enter is one of the correct solutions, you will receive full credit for that question.
5. If the correct answer can be expressed as a mixed number, it must be entered as a decimal or an improper fraction.
6. If the correct answer is a decimal that cannot fit into the grid space, you must fill the grid with enough digits to completely fill the space. The number can be rounded or simply shortened but must fill every blank space.

Answer: $\frac{5}{36}$ Answer: 4.5

Write answer in boxes. →

Grid in result.

← Fraction line
← Decimal point

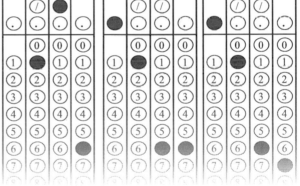

Acceptable ways to grid $\frac{1}{6}$ are:

Answer: 302 – either position is correct

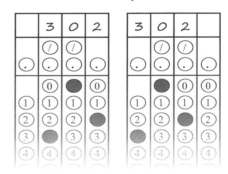

NOTES

Begin entering answers in any column that accommodates your answer. If you do not need a column do not enter anything in that column.

16. If $x^2 + 7x - 33 = 11$, and $x > 0$, what is the value of $x + 11$?

ANSWER: _____

17. Eight men working together can build a house in 12 days. How many days would it take six men working together to build the same house?

ANSWER: _____

18.

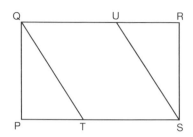

Note: Figure not drawn to scale

PQRS is a rectangle. The length of $\overline{QR}$ is 15, the length of $\overline{QU}$ is 10, and the length of $\overline{SU}$ is 13. What is the area of parallelogram QUST?

ANSWER: _____

19.
$$2x^2 + 5x - 25 = 0$$

If p and q are solutions to the equation above, and $p < q$, what is the value of $\dfrac{p^2}{q^2}$?

ANSWER: _____

20. If $f(n - 1) = 13 + 4n$ for all values of n, what is the value of $f(3)$?

ANSWER: _____

328

Math Test 2 – Calculator

🕐 55 MINUTES, 38 QUESTIONS

Turn to Section 4 of your answer sheet to answer the questions in this section.

DIRECTIONS

For questions **1 – 30**, find the solution to each problem and select the most appropriate answer from the choices provided. For questions **31 – 38**, find the solution to each problem and write your answer in the space provided. You may use the blank space in your test booklet for scratch work.

NOTES

1. The use of a calculator on any part of this section is allowed.
2. Unless otherwise indicated, all variables and expressions used in this test represent real numbers.
3. Unless otherwise indicated, all figures used in this test are drawn to scale.
4. Unless otherwise indicated, all figures used in this test lie on a plane.
5. Unless specified otherwise, a given function, f, has the domain the set of all real numbers x for which $f(x)$ is a real number.

REFERENCE

$A = \frac{1}{2}bh$

$c^2 = a^2 + b^2$

Special Right Triangles

$A = \pi r^2$
$C = 2\pi r$

$A = \ell w$

$V = \ell wh$

$V = \pi r^2 h$

$V = \frac{4}{3}\pi r^3$

$V = \frac{1}{3}\pi r^2 h$

$V = \frac{1}{3}\ell wh$

The arc of a circle is 360 degrees or 2π radians.
A triangle has angles that sum to 180 degrees.

PRACTICE TEST 2

1. There are 200 cookies in a bag, 15% of which are wrapped. If 80% of the cookies are oatmeal, what is the smallest number of wrapped oatmeal cookies that could be in the bag?

   (A) 0
   (B) 15
   (C) 25
   (D) 55

Questions 2 and 3 refer to the following information.

Ellen opened a savings account with an initial balance of $1,000. For the next 8 months, she made one deposit per month, always for the same amount. During that time, she made just one withdrawal.

2. Which of the following graphs accurately describes those transactions over an 8–month period?

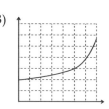
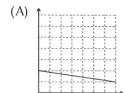

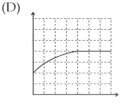
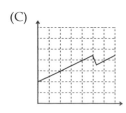

3. If each of Ellen's 8 deposits was for $200, and her withdrawal was for $350, how much money did she have in her account after 8 months?

   (A) $850
   (B) $1,550
   (C) $2,250
   (D) $2,350

4. A clown at an amusement park makes animals from balloons. She sells each animal based on the number of balloons it requires, according to the following chart:

# of Balloons	1	2	3	4	5
Price	$4.00	$4.50	$5.00	$5.50	$6.00

   What is the price, in dollars, of an animal that takes x balloons to make?

   (A) x
   (B) $x + 4$
   (C) $0.5x + 4$
   (D) $0.5x + 3.5$

5. The value of a house increased from $2.0 million to $2.6 million. What was the percent increase in value?

   (A) 15%
   (B) 30%
   (C) 40%
   (D) 50%

6. A bag contains six marbles: two red, one yellow, and three blue. What is the probability of randomly selecting two red marbles in a row, assuming the marbles are not put back in the bag after being drawn?

(A) $\dfrac{1}{15}$

(B) $\dfrac{2}{15}$

(C) $\dfrac{1}{10}$

(D) $\dfrac{1}{10}$

7. For a set of eleven different rational numbers, which of the following CANNOT affect the value of the median?

(A) Doubling each number
(B) Increasing each number by 10
(C) Increasing the smallest number only
(D) Increasing the largest number only

8. Which of the following equations represents the line with the same x-intercept as the line with the equation $y = 2x - 5$?

(A) $y = \dfrac{1}{2}x + 10$

(B) $y = \dfrac{1}{3}x + \dfrac{10}{3}$

(C) $y = -\dfrac{2}{3}x + 5$

(D) $y = -\dfrac{2}{3}x + \dfrac{5}{3}$

9. Rhudopsinol is a new drug designed to treat sleepwalking, and has a half–life of two hours. It is produced in 500mg tablets. If 40% of the orally ingested drug is absorbed into the bloodstream, which of the following functions gives the amount of Rhudopsinol in the bloodstream, in milligrams, t hours after the ingestion of a single tablet?

(A) $f(t) = (400)(0.5)^{2+t}$

(B) $f(t) = (0.4)(500)(0.5)^{\frac{t}{2}}$

(C) $f(t) = (0.4)(500)(0.5t)$

(D) $f(t) = (400)(0.5)^{2t}$

10. Paris and Genevieve are waiting in line to buy tacos. It's Tuesday, and the taqueria has a Taco Tuesday special: all tacos are 50% off. Fish tacos normally sell for $2.50 each, and beef and chicken tacos are normally $1.50. They need exactly 16 tacos, and cannot spend more than $15. What is the most they can spend on fish tacos?

(A) $6
(B) $7.50
(C) $10
(D) $15

11. An isosceles triangle has three angles that measure $40°$, $x°$, and $y°$. Which of the following CANNOT be true?

(A) $x = y$

(B) $x = 50°$

(C) $x - y = 60°$

(D) $x = 70°$

12. According to the chart below, what is the average number of potatoes harvested by the six farms?

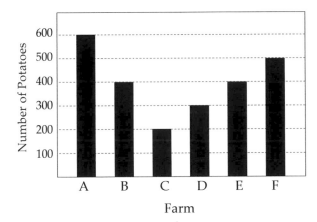

Farm

(A) 200

(B) 400

(C) 500

(D) 600

13. A basketball team had a ratio of wins to losses of 3 to 1. After winning six games in a row, the team's ratio of wins to losses was 5 to 1. How many games had the team won before it won the six games?

(A) 3

(B) 6

(C) 9

(D) 24

Questions 14 and 15 refer to the information below.

An engineer performed strength-tests to measure the durability of a certain plastic. Fifty samples of the plastic were subjected to increasing pressures, and the results are presented below:

Pressure (psi)	# Broken	# Cracked
25	0	1
50	0	1
100	3	6
125	14	30
150	32	18

14. If 10,000 samples were subjected to 100 pounds per square inch (psi) of pressure, based on the results above, how many are expected to break?

(A) 60

(B) 300

(C) 600

(D) 1200

15. At 125 pounds per square inch (psi), the break rate for sample sizes of fifty has a standard error (SE) of 0.06, and a critical value (CV) for a 95% confidence level of 1.96. Using the equation ME = CV × SE, find the margin of error (ME) for the break rate of the entire population of samples at 125 psi.

(A) 0.06
(B) 0.12
(C) 0.68
(D) 0.95

16. Which of the following functions, when graphed, crosses the x-axis three times?

(A) $f(x) = x^3 + 4x^2$
(B) $f(x) = x^3 + 4x^2 - 5x$
(C) $f(x) = 7x^2 - 5x + 75$
(D) $f(x) = x^{\frac{1}{3}}$

17.

Apples Grown by Bob

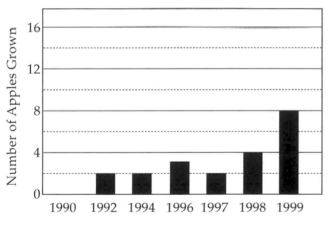

The figure above shows the number of apples grown in Bob's backyard every year. One year, Bob read about a new kind of fertilizer guaranteed to double the number of apples grown the year before. Assuming that the fertilizer works, in which year did Bob first try the fertilizer?

(A) 1995
(B) 1996
(C) 1998
(D) 1999

18. A chemistry student has a 25% solution of acetic acid and a 55% solution of sodium bicarbonate, a base. How much of each solution does the student need to make a 120 milliliters (mL) solution with equal parts acid and base?

(A) 82.5mL of the 25% solution, 37.5mL of the 55% solution
(B) 85mL of the 25% solution, 35mL of the 55% solution
(C) 40.5mL of the 25% solution, 79.5mL of the 55% solution
(D) 60mL of the 25% solution, 60mL of the 55% solution

19. A dessert recipe requires p tablespoons of sugar and q cups of flour. If Peter wants to make a larger batch using $p + 2$ tablespoons of sugar, how many cups of flour does he need to keep the ingredients in the original proportion?

(A) $\dfrac{p}{(p+2)q}$
(B) $\dfrac{p}{q}$
(C) $\dfrac{(p+2)}{q}$
(D) $\dfrac{(p+2)q}{p}$

20. If $f(x) = |x+3| - 7$, which of the following must be true?

(A) $f(x) \le -7$
(B) $f(x) \le 0$
(C) $f(x) \ge -4$
(D) $f(x) \ge -7$

21. A bungee jumper leaps off a cliff 122 meters from the ground. Her cord, when fully stretched, is 72 meters long, and it takes 6 seconds after the jump for it to extend fully. The distance between the jumper and the ground as a function of time can be modeled as a quadratic function. Which equation represents her distance from the ground as a function of time?

    (A) $f(t) = t^2 - 24t + 122$

    (B) $f(t) = 2t^2 - 24t + 122$

    (C) $f(t) = 2t^2 - 28t + 122$

    (D) $f(t) = t^2 - 12t + 122$

22. In 2012, the United States produced 289 million tons of trash, and its total population was 314.1 million. Assume the annual rate of trash produced per U.S. resident stays constant. If x represents the number of millions of U.S. residents in any given year, which variable equation below represents the number of millions of tons of trash produced by the larger population of 2013?

    (A) $289 < x(0.92)$

    (B) $289 \leq x(1.08)$

    (C) $x > \dfrac{289}{0.92x}$

    (D) $x > \dfrac{314.1x}{0.92}$

23. For which real number x will
    $$\frac{2}{x} + \frac{x+2}{x(x-2)} = \frac{4}{x(x-2)}?$$

    (A) -1

    (B) 1

    (C) 2

    (D) No real number

24. If $f(x) = \dfrac{x^2 + 2x + 1}{x + 1}$, what is $f(i)$? $(i = \sqrt{-1})$

    (A) 2

    (B) $\dfrac{2}{i+1}$

    (C) $i - 1$

    (D) $i + 1$

25. In $ABCD$, $\overline{AD}$ and $\overline{BC}$ are parallel and $2 \angle ABC = \angle BAD$. What is the length of $\overline{BC}$?

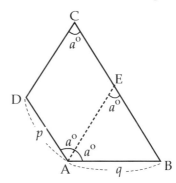

    (A) $2p$

    (B) $p + q$

    (C) $p + 2q$

    (D) $2p + q$

26. The equation of the parabola below is $y = x^2$. If the y-coordinate of A and the y-coordinate of B are both 8, what is the length of $\overline{AB}$?

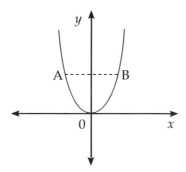

(A) 16

(B) 8

(C) $2\sqrt{2}$

(D) $4\sqrt{2}$

27. If the function $f(x)$ is translated three units to the right, then reflected across the x-axis, a new function is produced. Which of the following is equivalent to the new function?

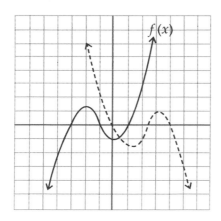

(A) $f(-x) + 3$

(B) $f(-x) - 3$

(C) $-f(x + 3)$

(D) $-f(x - 3)$

28. Sixty cookies were equally distributed to x campers. Eight campers did not want cookies, so their share was redistributed to the other campers, who each received two more. What is the total number of campers?

(A) 12

(B) 20

(C) 32

(D) 40

29. Recent polls indicate that only 15% of those registered to vote in an upcoming election are in the age group 18 to 25. A voter registration drive wants to raise this figure to 20% before the day of the election, so it begins to target this demographic exclusively. If there are currently 51,000 registered voters in the district, and assuming all new registrations are in the target demographic, approximately how many new voters does the drive need to register to meet its goal?

(A) 2,600

(B) 3,200

(C) 6,800

(D) 10,200

30.
$$x^2 = 2y + 8$$
$$2y = 2 - 3x$$

Which of the following is the sum of the x-value solutions for the system of equations above?

(A) 10

(B) 3

(C) –3

(D) –10

PRACTICE TEST 2

DIRECTIONS

For questions **31 – 38**, find the solution to the problem and enter your answer as demonstrated below.

1. Only the answer that is bubbled in on the answer sheet will be credited. The blank spaces above the bubbles are for you to record your answers for accuracy.
2. Only fill in one bubble in any given column.
3. None of the answers on this portion of the test are negative values.
4. If a problem appears to have more than one answer, only enter one answer. If the answer you enter is one of the correct solutions, you will receive full credit for that question.
5. If the correct answer can be expressed as a mixed number, it must be entered as a decimal or an improper fraction.
6. If the correct answer is a decimal that cannot fit into the grid space, you must fill the grid with enough digits to completely fill the space. The number can be rounded or simply shortened but must fill every blank space.

NOTES

Begin entering answers in any column that accommodates your answer. If you do not need a column do not enter anything in that column.

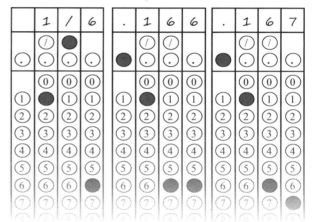

Answer: $\frac{5}{36}$

Answer: 4.5

Write answer → in boxes.

← Fraction line
← Decimal point

Grid in result.

Acceptable ways to grid $\frac{1}{6}$ are:

Answer: 302 – either position is correct

31. Evan and Ricardo spent a combined $399.50 on gasoline in the past month. How many dollars did Ricardo spend on gas if Evan spent $9.50 more than a fourth of what Ricardo did?

ANSWER: _____

32. The force, f, needed to break a board varies inversely with the length, l, of the board. If it takes 5 pounds of force to break a board 2 feet long, how many pounds of force will it take to break a board that is 6 feet long?

ANSWER: _____

33. Two students started walking from the same point in opposite directions. They each walked 12 feet and then one student made a 90 degree turn to her left and walked 5 feet. The other student made a 90 degree turn to his left and walked 5 feet. How many feet apart are two students?

ANSWER: _____

34. A regular polygon is equilateral (it has equal sides) and equiangular (it has equal angles) with an area that is half the product of the perimeter (p) and an apothem (a). A polygon's apothem is a line segment that joins the polygon's center to the midpoint of any side and is perpendicular to that side. How many sides does a polygon with an area of 4,950 units^2 have given a side length and an apothem length of 30 units each?

ANSWER: _____

35. A bookstore has 18,000 books in stock, of which 70% are paperback and 30% are hardcover. The books are either fiction or nonfiction. If 6,800 books are nonfiction, and 4,800 of the nonfiction books are paperback, how many books are both fiction and hardcover?

ANSWER: _____

36. The function f is defined as $f(x) = x^2 - 6$, and the function p is defined as $p(x) = f\left(-\dfrac{x}{2}\right) + 5$. What is the value of $p(-4)$?

ANSWER: _____

Questions 37 and 38 refer to the information below.

Price Summary
U.S Energy Information

	2012	2013	2014	2015 (projected)
WTI Crude Oil	94.12	97.91	93.82	62.75
Brent Crude Oil	111.65	108.64	99.54	68.08
Gasoline	3.63	3.51	3.37	2.60
Diesel	3.97	3.92	3.82	3.07
Natural Gas	10.69	10.30	10.97	10.96
Electricity	11.88	12.12	12.47	12.69

*Crude oil in $ per barrel; 42 gallons per barrel
*Gasoline, and diesel in $ per gallon
*Natural gas in $ per 1,000ft³
*Electricity in cents per kilowatt-hour

37. **Part 1**

What was the average price of natural gas, in dollars per cubic meter (m³), from 2012 to 2014 (1 foot = 0.305 meters)?

ANSWER: _____

38. **Part 2**

The average price of gas per gallon in 2015 was actually $2.40. If the price of crude oil dropped by the same percentage from its price in 2014, how much more expensive was a barrel of Brent Crude Oil than a barrel of WTI Crude Oil in 2015?

ANSWER: _____

Essay Test 2*

 50 MINUTES, Prompt-based essay

Turn to Section 5 of your answer sheet to answer the question in this section.

DIRECTIONS

As you read the passage below, consider how Evan Gerdisch uses
- evidence, such as facts or examples, to support claims.
- reasoning to develop ideas and to connect claims and evidence.
- stylistic or persuasive elements, such as word choice or appeals to emotion, to add power to the ideas expressed.

Adapted from "Earthbound Imagination" by Evan Gerdisch. ©2015 by KALLIS EDU.

Billions upon billions of planets inhabit the observable universe. Although most of them are almost certainly inhospitable, some may harbor life. This is an exciting prospect. What might these exotic beings, intelligent or not, look like? How might they behave? What biological processes might sustain them? If most works of science fiction are to be believed, the answers are simple: human-like, human-like, and the same ones as humans. And that's a shame.

After all, Earth itself is brimming with incredible biodiversity. Hundred-legged millipedes navigate forest floors while sleek, bioluminescent fish lurk in the ocean's depths. Undoubtedly, humans share more genetic information with these strange Earthly beings than *any* extraterrestrial. Yet time and time again, in science fiction films and literature, humans travel trillions of miles through space only to meet human-like aliens.

Don't get me wrong; sometimes an anthropomorphic extraterrestrial (human-like alien) is useful. A skilled science-fiction writer might create an alien society only slightly different from our own in order to explore social, political, or religious issues in or among Earth-bound cultures. But too often, science-fiction writers fall back on the tired trope of the anthropomorphic extraterrestrial for no clear reason. Probably the most egregious offender of this trend just happens to be the most famous science fiction series of all time: *Star Wars*. These films depict aliens from countless planets with wildly varying environments, yet the majority of these aliens have two arms, two legs, and humanoid facial features. What's more, they all seem to share common—and very human-like—cultural practices.

Of course, many will argue that popular culture favors anthropomorphic extraterrestrials because they are relatable. Fair enough. I doubt that Chewbacca, Han Solo's* stalwart companion, would have enjoyed much popularity if he had looked even stranger than Earth's own assortment of bizarre creatures, such as the star-nosed mole, the blobfish, and the aye-aye. But I maintain that this desire to make our extraterrestrials relatable is a major part of the problem: science fiction is meant to challenge, not reassure. Science fiction should cause people to question their preconceptions, not reinforce them.

By depicting aliens as slightly-different-humans, science fiction writers miss opportunities to ask big, important questions about where we came from and where we are going. Life on Earth evolved under unique conditions. For instance, humans' distant ancestors would never have descended from their arboreal habitats had it not been for the extinction event that wiped out many species of dinosaur. A single—albeit very large— meteor impact 65 million years ago drastically altered the trajectory of life on Earth. So even if extraterrestrial life were composed of cells like our own (and that's a big "if"), their appearances and behaviors would have been shaped by their own unique environmental conditions. This is an exciting and humbling concept. So why sacrifice the idea that humans are unique for the reassurance and familiarity of an anthropomorphic extraterrestrial?

Ultimately, I understand that one of science fiction's primary functions is to entertain, but entertainment can still challenge viewers. Stanley Kubrick's 1968 film, *2001: A Space Odyssey*, is an excellent example. The film centers on a crew of astronauts searching for extraterrestrials who leave enigmatic clues throughout the solar system, yet the aliens themselves never appear on screen. Kubrick invites us to consider the possibilities that advanced extraterrestrials take forms incomprehensibly different from our own, or that they have evolved beyond the point of requiring a corporeal form, much as some humans hope to accomplish by downloading their consciousness into computers.

One of science fiction's greatest strengths is its ability to inspire real-world change by stoking the public's imagination. Many of the then-futuristic gadgets depicted in the original *Star Trek* series have inspired real-world innovations. Similarly, the public's interest in space exploration is fueled by imagination. Depicting extraterrestrials as robotic muscle cars (as in the *Transformers* franchise) or small green men with large heads does not challenge the public to stretch its imagination, and it will do no favors for the future of space travel.

Chewbacca and Han Solo are two protagonists from the Star Wars series.

 Write an essay in which you explain how Evan Gerdisch builds an argument to persuade his audience that extraterrestrials have been poorly depicted in science fiction. In your essay, analyze how the author uses one or more of the features listed in the box above (or features of your own choice) to strengthen the logic and persuasiveness of his argument. Be sure that your analysis focuses on the most relevant features of the passage.

Your essay should not explain whether you agree with the author's claims, but rather explain how the author builds an argument to persuade his audience.

---

* Sample responses at www.kallisedu.com

KALLIS

SAT® Practice Test #3

IMPORTANT REMINDERS:

1

When you take the official SAT, you will need to use a No. 2 pencil. Do not use a pen or a mechanical pencil.

2

On the official SAT, sharing any of the questions on the test violates the College Board's policies and may result in your scores being canceled.

(This cover is modeled after the cover you'll see when you take the official SAT.)

Reading Test 3

 65 MINUTES, 52 QUESTIONS

Turn to Section 1 of your answer sheet to answer the questions in this section.

DIRECTIONS Each passage or pair of passages is accompanied by 10 or 11 questions. Read each passage or pair of passages, and then select the most appropriate answer to each question. Some passages may include tables or graphs that require additional analysis.

Refer to the passage below to answer questions 1 – 10.

This passage is adapted from W.E.B. Dubois, *The Souls of Black Folk*, originally published in 1903. Dubois was an African-American sociologist, historian, author, and activist who devoted his life to securing equal rights for African Americans.

line   Between me and the other world there
is ever an unasked question: unasked by
some through feelings of delicacy; by others
through the difficulty of rightly framing it. All,
5   nevertheless, flutter 'round it. They approach me
in a half-hesitant sort of way, eye me curiously
or compassionately, and then, instead of saying
directly, "How does it feel to be a problem?"
they say, "I know an excellent colored man in my
10   town;" or, "I fought at Mechanicsville;*" or, "Do
not these Southern outrages make your blood
boil?" At these I smile, or am interested, or reduce
the boiling to a simmer, as the occasion may
require. To the real question, How does it feel to
15   be a problem? I answer seldom a word.
    And yet, being a problem is a strange
experience, peculiar even for one who has never
been anything else, save perhaps in babyhood
and in Europe. It is in the early days of rollicking
20   boyhood that the revelation first bursts upon one,
all in a day, as it were. I remember well when
the shadow swept across me. I was a little thing,
away up in the hills of New England, where
the dark Housatonic winds between Hoosac
25   and Taghkanic to the sea. In a wee wooden
schoolhouse, something put it into the boys' and
girls' heads to buy gorgeous visiting-cards—ten
cents a package—and exchange. The exchange
was merry, till one girl, a tall newcomer, refused
30   my card,—refused it peremptorily, with a glance.
    Then it dawned upon me with a certain
suddenness that I was different from the others;
or like, mayhap, in heart and life and longing,
but shut out from their world by a vast veil. I
35   had thereafter no desire to tear down that veil,
to creep through; I held all beyond it in common
contempt, and lived above it in a region of
blue sky and great wandering shadows. That
sky was bluest when I could beat my mates at

40   examination-time, or beat them at a foot-race, or
even beat their stringy heads.
    Alas, with the years all this fine contempt
began to fade; for the words I longed for, and
all their dazzling opportunities, were theirs, not
45   mine. But they should not keep these prizes, I
said; some, all, I would wrest from them. Just
how I would do it I could never decide: by
reading law, by healing the sick, by telling the
wonderful tales that swam in my head,—some
50   way. With other black boys the strife was not so
fiercely sunny: their youth shrunk into tasteless
sycophancy, or into silent hatred of the pale world
about them and mocking distrust of everything
white; or wasted itself in a bitter cry, Why did
55   God make me an outcast and a stranger in mine
own house? The shades of the prison-house closed
round about us all: walls straight and stubborn
to the whitest, but relentlessly narrow, tall, and
unscalable to sons of night who must plod darkly
60   on in resignation, or beat unavailing palms
against the stone, or steadily, half hopelessly,
watch the streak of blue above.
    After the Egyptian and Indian, the Greek
and Roman, the Teuton and Mongolian, the
65   Negro is a sort of seventh son, born with a veil,
and gifted with second-sight in this American
world,—a world which yields him no true self-
consciousness, but only lets him see himself
through the revelation of the other world. It is a
70   peculiar sensation, this double-consciousness, this
sense of always looking at one's self through the
eyes of others, of measuring one's soul by the tape
of a world that looks on in amused contempt and
pity. One ever feels his twoness,—an American, a
75   Negro; two souls, two thoughts, two unreconciled
strivings; two warring ideals in one dark body,
whose dogged strength alone keeps it from being
torn asunder.

* *Mechanicsville: a city in Virginia near which several important Civil War battles were fought.*

1. In the context of the passage, the "other world" referred to in line 1 most likely refers to people who

   (A) do not view the narrator as a "problem."
   (B) hope to gain a better understanding of American culture.
   (C) enjoy social privileges that are denied to black Americans.
   (D) refuse to recognize the cultural differences among individuals.

2. The "unasked question" discussed throughout paragraph 1 (lines 1 – 15) is best described as

   (A) the subtext of a conversation between a white and a black American.
   (B) the rhetorical device that the narrator often uses in conversation.
   (C) a puzzling social imbalance that exclusively affects the narrator.
   (D) a serious concern among American writers and orators.

3. As used in line 4, "framing" most nearly means

   (A) presenting.
   (B) establishing.
   (C) drafting.
   (D) placing

4. Which of the following best describes the way that paragraph 2 (lines 16 – 30) functions in the passage as a whole?

   (A) It sets the nostalgic tone that dominates the passage.
   (B) It provides a window into the initial shock of being excluded.
   (C) It emphasizes the importance of the "unasked question" in paragraph 1.
   (D) It establishes the contrast between the author's determination and the laziness of others.

5. The statement "or like, mayhap, in heart and life and longing, but shut out from their world by a vast veil," (lines 33 – 34) primarily serves to

   (A) distinguish the narrator from other black Americans.
   (B) point out specific similarities between different cultures.
   (C) state that black Americans are not inherently different from others.
   (D) suggest that black Americans do not realize that they are viewed as being different from others.

6. By paragraph 4 (lines 42 – 62), the "region of blue sky" introduced by the narrator in paragraph 3 (lines 31 – 41) becomes

   (A) something to be celebrated rather than avoided.
   (B) a useful tool rather than a unattainable goal.
   (C) a manageable nuisance rather than a constant distraction.
   (D) a metaphor for unattainable dreams rather than a viable means of escape.

7. From paragraph 3 (lines 31 – 41) to paragraph 4 (lines 42 – 62), the narrator's attitude toward the opportunities denied to black Americans changes from

   (A) burning jealousy to resignation.
   (B) disdain to defiant desire.
   (C) ambivalence to concern.
   (D) contentment to rebellion.

8. As used in line 54, "bitter" most nearly means

   (A) sharp.
   (B) churlish.
   (C) petulant.
   (D) aggrieved.

9. What does the narrator suggest about the "veil" that separates black Americans from the opportunities available to others?

   (A) It contributes to the formation of a "double-consciousness" in black Americans.
   (B) It creates a rift between the narrator's generation and the preceding one.
   (C) It causes many black Americans to emulate the actions of white Americans.
   (D) It drives many black Americans to work harder than their white counterparts.

10. Which choice provides the best evidence for the answer to the previous question?

    (A) Lines 42 – 45 ("Alas, with…not mine")
    (B) Lines 56 – 58 ("The shades…the whitest")
    (C) Lines 63 – 65 ("After the Egyptian…seventh son")
    (D) Lines 69 – 72 ("It is a peculiar sensation…of others")

Refer to the passage below to answer questions 11 – 21.

Susanna Heckman, "Income Inequality," © 2015 KALLIS EDU.

line
My middle school son, under the spell of pop stars and professional athletes, described a baseball player's signing bonus the other day. After I expressed the appropriate admiration, I
5 added that no one needs that much money. This was dismissed. "Are you really gonna say that a great player, who has worked really hard all his life, and can do what no one else can do, shouldn't get what he *deserves*?"
10 I had just read a newspaper account of a celebrity selling her home, which includes a hall that sounds like a royal ballroom. It made me wonder who *deserves* to earn millions upon millions of dollars. Why isn't one million enough?
15 Maybe even less? Who *needs* a palace? Didn't we once fight a war against the British over this question? We are not supposed to be living in a monarchy. We are not supposed to believe in supporting an entitled class that possesses more
20 money than it could ever spend.
Tax rates that took effect in 2013 have made a small improvement in income inequality. But in truth, there is still an enormous polarization of wealth in the United States. Rappers, athletes, and
25 other celebrities are not even the most affluent, though they are the most visible. American wealth is concentrated in the hands of a relatively tiny group that dwells on fluffy pink clouds of privilege, sometimes with personal jets.
30 On these fluffy clouds, there are no past-due rent notices, no struggle over new shoes for growing kids, no waiting for payday to buy groceries. I don't have to look far for a contrast. In my family's neighborhood of 1950s homes, many
35 people get by on fixed incomes or slim profits from their own tiny businesses. Single teachers and nurses support their children. Work trucks line the street. Multigenerational households are common. Next door to us, three hardworking
40 families with young children squeeze into one small house.
Theirs is not an unusual situation. U.S. Census data indicate that nearly half of all people in the United States qualify as low-income or
45 poor; the figure is a shocking 57 percent for children. Meanwhile, research shows that the top 1 percent of the population possesses 40 percent of the nation's wealth and takes home nearly a quarter of the nation's income each year. These
50 wealthy are not likely to socialize with people like my neighbors—a dozen people who share one bathroom. Instead, the super-wealthy are swaddled by their quiet, green neighborhoods and well-kept schools. Their "normal" is different,
55 and they see no reason why it should change. From childhood on, they meet people like

themselves, and visit friends who live in mansions like theirs.
Economist Robert Reich estimates that if the
60 economic gains of the last three decades had been divided equally among Americans, the typical American would be 60 percent better-off now. Instead, a large portion of the money has gone to the already wealthy. As a group,
65 middle-income earners have actually seen their incomes fall. Admittedly, this dynamic is not simple; its causes certainly include the decline of manufacturing jobs in the U.S., increased automation in the service industry, and the
70 decline of organized labor.
However, one of the causes of the lopsided distribution is clear. In the U.S., according to the non-profit, nonpartisan National Bureau of Economic Research (NBER), companies' top
75 managers regularly help each other take greater proportions of company profits. NBER cites a study showing that top management received 5 percent of their firms' profits in 1995, ballooning to 13 percent by 2002. No matter how chief
80 executive officers (CEOs) perform, NBER says, cronyism results in their getting a bigger piece of the pie. Boards of directors made up of their peers approve salary packages that the CEOs supposedly "deserve," and then shower them
85 with stock options and other benefits that enrich them further.
Many of the super wealthy give to charity, and many people admire them greatly. Bill Gates has famously given away an astounding
90 amount—nearly $40 billion by some accounts— saving millions of lives through vaccine programs. Of course, Gates acquires billions *more* dollars every year through investments; he is still the richest man on Earth, worth nearly $80 billion
95 in 2015. Moreover, Gates' grants and donations give him undue influence in fields such as public education and medical research. He gets to set the priorities. By handing out money, the wealthy claim power that is not theirs by right.
100 But my son was not much convinced by differences in lifestyle or societal influence. Ultimately, what shocked him was that money buys more life. My son and his friends are all familiar with the 2011 science fiction thriller
105 *In Time*. In the film, minutes of life are a form of currency, making the super-rich virtually immortal. In today's United States, life expectancy is increasing much more for the rich than for the poor, according to the Brookings Institute.
110 The average life span of poor women is actually declining. The data show that whatever the specific causes of the longevity gap, the link to income is clear. Rich Americans live to an older age than poor Americans. This blunt, dystopian
115 fact should prod all of us to question the status quo.

Average Federal Tax Rates, by Income Group, 1979 to 2010 and Under 2013 Law

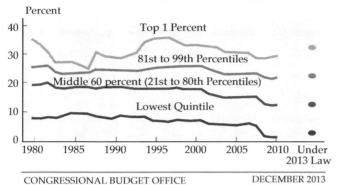

CONGRESSIONAL BUDGET OFFICE   DECEMBER 2013

11. Within the passage, the main purpose of paragraphs 1 and 2 (lines 1 – 9) is to

   (A) provide personal details about the author.
   (B) introduce opposing viewpoints on the topic.
   (C) produce an image of disproportionate wealth.
   (D) criticize the effect of media on the attitudes of young people.

12. In paragraph 3 (lines 10 – 20), the author most strongly implies which of the following?

   (A) Having a house that includes a royal ballroom is unethical.
   (B) America's Revolutionary War against the English king was ultimately meaningless.
   (C) Celebrities in the United States receive too much money and become arrogant.
   (D) Assuming that certain people deserve wealth is a characteristic of monarchies.

13. Which of the author's claims about society is best supported by the graph?

   (A) Lines 12 – 14 ("It made me...of dollars")
   (B) Line 21 – 22 ("Tax rates....income inequality")
   (C) Line 22 – 24 ("But in truth....United States")
   (D) Lines 26 – 29 ("American wealth...personal jets")

14. According to the graph, which statement is true about average tax rates for people with incomes in the top 1 percent?

   (A) In 2013, they returned to about what they were in 1979.
   (B) From 2000 to 2010, they were roughly the same as the other income groups.
   (C) Since 1979, they have varied between 25 and 40 percent of income.
   (D) The top 1 percent receives almost 40 percent of the nation's wealth.

15. In paragraph 5 (lines 30 – 41), the author describes her own neighborhood primarily to

   (A) prove how hard most people work to survive.
   (B) inform readers about an unfamiliar lifestyles.
   (C) explain how her background informs her opinion.
   (D) illustrate in human terms the statistics that follow.

16. The passage strongly suggests that the author shares which assumption?

   (A) Rich people in America actively thwart upward mobility of the less well-off.
   (B) Most affluent Americans do not form emotional bonds with poorer people.
   (C) The very wealthy in the U.S. rarely leave their own neighborhoods.
   (D) The American middle class will disappear within a short time frame.

17. Which choice provides the best evidence for the answer to the previous question?

   (A) Lines 42 – 46 ("U.S. Census...for children")
   (B) Lines 54 – 55 ("Their 'normal' is...change")
   (C) Lines 56 – 58 ("From childhood...like theirs")
   (D) Lines 64 – 66 ("As a group, middle-income... seen their incomes fall")

18. As used in line 66, "dynamic" most nearly means

   (A) motility.
   (B) interaction.
   (C) change.
   (D) upsurge.

19. The author recognizes a counter argument to the position she takes in the passage by

   (A) acknowledging large charitable donations by the affluent.
   (B) admitting a false assumption about charitable funds associated with Bill Gates.
   (C) introducing data about fighting disease, medical research, and public education.
   (D) conceding that the wealthy are usually right about effective aid programs.

20. As used in line 96, "undue" most nearly means

   (A) needless.
   (B) exorbitant.
   (C) unwanted.
   (D) unwarranted.

21. According to the passage, the relationship between the film *In Time* and today's United States is most like

    (A) a stumble compared to a fall.
    (B) hyperbole challenging a flaw.
    (C) a warning regarding a possible outcome.
    (D) an aggregate of multiple concerns.

Refer to the passage below to answer questions 22 – 31.

This passage is adapted from Albert Einstein, *Relativity: The Special and General Theory*, originally published in 1920. In this passage, the German-born physicist discusses the "truth" of fundamental geometric ideas as well as their correspondence to that which is observed in the real world.

line   In your schooldays most of you who read this book made acquaintance with the noble building of Euclid's geometry, and you remember—perhaps with more respect than love—the
5   magnificent structure, on the lofty staircase of which you were chased about for uncounted hours by conscientious teachers. By reason of your past experience, you would certainly regard every one with disdain who should pronounce
10   even the most out-of-the-way proposition of this science to be untrue. But perhaps this feeling of proud certainty would leave you immediately if some one were to ask you: "What, then, do you mean by the assertion that these propositions are
15   true?" Let us proceed to give this question a little consideration.

     Geometry sets out from certain conceptions such as "plane," "point," and "straight line," with which we are able to associate more or
20   less definite ideas, and from certain simple propositions (axioms) which, in virtue of these ideas, we are inclined to accept as "true." Then, on the basis of a logical process, the justification of which we feel ourselves compelled to admit, all
25   remaining propositions are shown to follow from those axioms, i.e. they are proven. A proposition is then correct ("true") when it has been derived in the recognized manner from the axioms. The question of the "truth" of the individual
30   geometrical propositions is thus reduced to one of the "truth" of the axioms. Now it has long been known that the last question is not only unanswerable by the methods of geometry, but that it is in itself entirely without meaning. We
35   cannot ask whether it is true that only one straight line goes through two points. We can only say that Euclidean geometry deals with things called "straight lines," to each of which is ascribed the property of being uniquely determined by

40   two points situated on it. The concept "true" does not tally with the assertions of pure geometry, because by the word "true" we are eventually in the habit of designating always the correspondence with a "real" object; geometry,
45   however, is not concerned with the relation of the ideas involved in it to objects of experience, but only with the logical connection of these ideas among themselves.

     It is not difficult to understand why, in spite
50   of this, we feel constrained to call the propositions of geometry "true." Geometrical ideas correspond to more or less exact objects in nature, and these last are undoubtedly the exclusive cause of the genesis of those ideas. Geometry ought to
55   refrain from such a course, in order to give to its structure the largest possible logical unity. The practice, for example, of seeing in a "distance" two marked positions on a practically rigid body is something which is lodged deeply in our habit
60   of thought. We are accustomed further to regard three points as being situated on a straight line, if their apparent positions can be made to coincide for observation with one eye, under suitable choice of our place of observation.

65   If, in pursuance of our habit of thought, we now supplement the propositions of Euclidean geometry by the single proposition that two points on a practically rigid body always correspond to the same distance (line-interval),
70   independently of any changes in position to which we may subject the body, the propositions of Euclidean geometry then resolve themselves into propositions on the possible relative position of practically rigid bodies. Geometry which
75   has been supplemented in this way is then to be treated as a branch of physics. We can now legitimately ask as to the "truth" of geometrical propositions interpreted in this way, since we are justified in asking whether these propositions are
80   satisfied for those real things we have associated with the geometrical ideas. In less exact terms we can express this by saying that by the "truth" of a geometrical proposition in this sense we understand its validity for a construction with
85   ruler and compasses.

     Of course the conviction of the "truth" of geometrical propositions in this sense is founded exclusively on rather incomplete experience. For the present we shall assume the "truth" of the
90   geometrical propositions, then at a later stage (in the general theory of relativity) we shall see that this "truth" is limited, and we shall consider the extent of its limitation.

22. In lines 1 – 7, the author mentions "Euclid's geometry" and a "lofty staircase" primarily to

    (A) describe a context to which he will later refer as part of his argument.
    (B) highlight the relationship between architecture and geometry.
    (C) emphasize the importance of diligence in the study of geometry.
    (D) relate his topic to a situation with which he believes most of his readers are familiar.

23. The author's use of the phrase "perhaps with more respect than love" (line 4) is primarily meant to convey the sense of

    (A) reverence that most students feel for figures of authority.
    (B) ambivalence that students feel when studying a challenging subject.
    (C) nostalgia about first encountering the principles of geometry.
    (D) formality that marked the relationship between teacher and pupil.

24. According to paragraph 3 (lines 49 – 64), the geometric concepts "plane," "point," and "straight line" probably stem from their

    (A) indisputable truth.
    (B) simplicity and clarity.
    (C) similarity to actual entities.
    (D) cross-cultural acceptance.

25. As used in lines 19 – 20, the phrase "more or less" most nearly means

    (A) concretely.
    (B) quantitatively.
    (C) unreliably.
    (D) approximately.

26. According to the author, the Euclidean definition of a "straight line" is problematic primarily because

    (A) it does not correspond to lived experience.
    (B) it involves two points when it should actually include three.
    (C) it does not sufficiently support the axioms that come from it.
    (D) it is logically connected to other geometric ideas.

27. As used in line 55, "course" most nearly means

    (A) class.
    (B) practice.
    (C) itinerary.
    (D) direction.

28. Based on the passage, which choice best describes the relationship between geometry and physics?

    (A) Geometry overlaps with physics when its concepts are applied to real-world situations.
    (B) Geometry and physics are both important in an educational curriculum.
    (C) Geometry is based in fiction and physics is based in truth.
    (D) Geometry is measured using generalizations whereas physics is studied through experiments.

29. In the final paragraph (lines 86 – 93), the author suggests that the " 'truth' of geometric propositions" is challenged by

    (A) the artificiality of geometry as a system of knowledge.
    (B) humans' limited understanding of physical phenomena.
    (C) humans' inability to confirm geometric truths by measurement.
    (D) the fact that truth actually resides in physics, not geometry.

30. Based on the passage as a whole, the author would most likely agree with the definition of "truth" as

    (A) a concept that corresponds with lived experience.
    (B) a concept that can be experimentally verified.
    (C) a concept that can be applied in a practical setting.
    (D) a notion about which the vast majority would agree.

31. Which choice provides the best evidence to the previous question?

    (A) Lines 7 – 11 ("By reason of...be untrue")
    (B) Lines 40 – 44 ("The concept 'true'...'real' object")
    (C) Lines 51 – 54 ("Geometrical ideas correspond...those ideas")
    (D) Lines 86 – 88 ("Of course the...incomplete experience")

Refer to the passage below to answer questions 32 – 42.

Passage 1 is adapted from Emma Goldman, "Marriage and Love," Mother Earth Publishing Association, 1911. Emma Goldman was a well-known anarchist and feminist writer. Passage 2 is adapted from "Modern Love: Marriage in the 21st Century," originally published in 2015, by KALLIS EDU.

Passage 1

line Marriage and love have nothing in common; they are as far apart as the poles; are, in fact, antagonistic to each other. No doubt some marriages have been the result of love. Not,
5 however, because love could assert itself only in marriage; much rather is it because few people can completely outgrow a convention. There are today large numbers of men and women to whom marriage is naught but a farce, but who submit to
10 it for the sake of public opinion. At any rate, while it is true that some marriages are based on love, and while it is equally true that in some cases love continues in married life, I maintain that it does so regardless of marriage, and not because of it.
15 On the other hand, it is utterly false that love results from marriage. On rare occasions one does hear of a miraculous case of a married couple falling in love after marriage, but on close examination it will be found that it is a
20 mere adjustment to the inevitable. Certainly the growing-used to each other is far away from the spontaneity, the intensity, and beauty of love…
    Marriage is primarily an economic arrangement, an insurance pact. It differs from
25 the ordinary life insurance agreement only in that it is more binding, more exacting. Its returns are insignificantly small compared with the investments. In taking out an insurance policy one pays for it in dollars and cents, always at liberty
30 to discontinue payments. If, however, woman's premium is a husband, she pays for it with her name, her privacy, her self-respect, her very life, "until death doth part." Moreover, the marriage insurance condemns her to life-long dependency,
35 to parasitism, to complete uselessness, individual as well as social. Man, too, pays his toll, but as his sphere is wider, marriage does not limit him as much as woman. He feels his chains more in an economic sense.
40 Behind every marriage stands the life-long environment of the two sexes; an environment so different from each other that man and woman must remain strangers. Separated by an insurmountable wall of superstition, custom,
45 and habit, marriage has not the potentiality of developing knowledge of, and respect for, each other, without which every union is doomed to failure.

Passage 2

    In today's United States, getting married is
50 like tossing a coin. More than half of all marriages end in divorce. The failure rate is even higher for second and third marriages. The number of U.S. homes maintained by married couples is shrinking, dipping below 50 percent in the 2010.
55 Presumably most people are aware of the statistics. Yet, optimism seems to persist. Millions of couples get married each year, vowing to stay together forever. Why do couples believe they will live "happily ever after?" Is the chance of
60 wedded bliss worth the risk of painful divorce?
    It turns out that there may be some solid facts underpinning the popular notion that marriage is blissful. Studies have found that on average, married people claim to be happy more often than
65 their single peers do.
    Claims are all well and good, but there is medical evidence, as well. Since the mid-1800s, researchers have noticed and puzzled over the fact that married people live longer, on average,
70 than never-married, divorced, or widowed people. Research has continually confirmed that married people tend to have lower blood pressure, suffer less from depression, and have more efficient immune systems. Stressful
75 relationships are the exception; people who report conflict-ridden marriages are no healthier than singles. Thus, the evidence points to the conclusion that a loving, supportive relationship reduces stress levels, resulting in the noted health
80 benefits.
    Researchers have collected massive amounts of data on what makes a relationship last. Not surprisingly, among the conclusions is that couples who stay together tend to talk. They talk
85 about more than just household chores; they share hopes, fears, and dreams. They celebrate successes and make each other feel special and cared-for. They maintain a certain level of kindness and consideration, even during arguments.
90 Also, married couples who report high levels of happiness together early in the relationship are more likely to still be married years later.

32. The author of Passage 1 most strongly implies which of the following about marriage?

(A) Keeping love alive in marriage requires work.
(B) Only unconventional people really fall in love.
(C) Some people have to get married so that they can get health insurance.
(D) People frequently get married just to fit into society.

33. Which choice provides the best evidence for the answer to the previous question?

(A) Lines 3 – 7 ("No doubt...convention")
(B) Lines 7 – 10 ("There are...opinion")
(C) Lines 15 – 16 ("On the other...marriage")
(D) Lines 23 – 24 ("Marriage is primarily...pact")

34. In lines 33 – 36, the author of Passage 1 mentions parasitism primarily to

(A) characterize the predicament women found themselves in at the time.
(B) criticize the way health insurance takes advantage of the healthy.
(C) demand equal opportunities for jobs for women.
(D) illustrate the way that unhappy marriages use up the energy of both parties.

35. As used in line 44, "superstition" most nearly means

(A) magic.
(B) belief.
(C) charm.
(D) fear.

36. In Passage 2, the author focuses on which quandary?

(A) Some people get married and divorced multiple times.
(B) Fewer U.S. homes include two adults.
(C) People continue to risk getting married.
(D) Medical researchers still have not been able to explain marriage's effects on health.

37. The author of Passage 2 implies which hypothesis?

(A) People should get married.
(B) Any marriage can become happy.
(C) Marriage can be calming.
(D) Wedded bliss is a fairy tale.

38. Which choice provides the best evidence for the answer to the previous question?

(A) Lines 63 – 65 ("Studies have...peers do")
(B) Lines 67 – 71 ("Since the mid-1800s... people")
(C) Lines 74 – 77 ("Stressful relationships... singles")
(D) Lines 77 – 80 ("Thus, the evidence... benefits")

39. As used in line 89, the word "consideration" most nearly means

(A) sensitivity.
(B) factor.
(C) contemplation.
(D) deliberation.

40. The author of Passage 2 would most likely respond to the life insurance metaphor for marriage in lines 23 – 36 by

(A) criticizing Passage 1 for ignoring medical research on the health benefits of marriage.
(B) pointing out that over the last century, divorce laws and women's status have changed.
(C) agreeing that the "returns" of marriage are much smaller than the "investments."
(D) arguing that the author of Passage 1 was too extreme in her cynical analysis.

41. In Passage 1, is the principle of the "insurmountable wall" (line 44) consistent with conclusions in Passage 2?

(A) Yes, because Passage 2 concludes that communicating (breaking down walls metaphorically) sustains marriages.
(B) Yes, because Passage 1 cites research regarding arguments.
(C) No, because the wall described in Passage 1 has no current equivalent.
(D) No, because Passage 2 focuses more on statistics than relationships.

42. It is reasonable to conclude that the authors of Passage 1 and Passage 2 would both advise that

(A) young couples should avoid marriage due to the stress it causes.
(B) young couples should get married if they really love each other.
(C) getting married will not make a couple love each other more.
(D) the only way to be healthy and happy is to get married.

349

Refer to the passage below to answer questions 43 – 52.

Nick Stockton, "Heat, Pollution, and Skyscrapers Make Cities Have More Thunderstoms," © 2015 by Conde Nast.

line   Ah, city life: The culture! The food! The music! The thunderstorms! Wait, what? Thunderstorms? Yes, that's right: You can add weather to the list of things that are more exciting
5   in the city than in the sticks.

Ok, not all cities. But in regions like the American south, normal urban attributes like heat, pollution, and tall buildings could stir up more storms. New research examined nearly two
10   decades of meteorological data from Georgia and found thunderstorms were slightly more likely to form over Atlanta than the surrounding rural areas. Through modeling and other research, meteorologists have known about the connection
15   between cities and storms for decades, but this is the first time data has shown the phenomena in action.

During the summer, cumulonimbus clouds ripen like peaches over Georgia and Alabama.
20   These moisture-heavy storms appear on radars as dark, pixellated patterns. Alex Haberlie, a geography doctoral student at Northern Illinois University, used a computer program to find these patterns, then crunched 17 years' worth of
25   data. In all, the geographers found that Atlanta is 5 percent more likely to initiate a thunderstorm than the surrounding rural area.

"By our count, that's a couple to three or more storms a year," Haberlie, the study's lead author,
30   says. This doesn't seem like much, but a city's built infrastructure compounds the effects of any storm. For instance, Atlanta's catastrophic 2009 floods probably were worsened because all the asphalt and concrete kept the water from seeping
35   into the soil.

"The discovery that urban environments can create their own storms and rainfall: Not new at all," says J. Marshall Shepherd, a researcher at the University of Georgia who is an expert
40   in urban meteorology. Researchers have long known that cities generally get more rainfall than their surrounding areas. Shepherd says that he and other researchers teased out the relationship between cities and thunderstorms by running
45   models. "Set up studies where you don't include Atlanta, and some where you do, and lo and behold you can see that taking away the city reduces the rainfall," he says. Based on research he's seen, Shepherd says he isn't surprised by
50   the 5 percent difference between Atlanta and its realm. He expected the number to be upward of 20 percent. But despite his misgivings about the degree of difference shown in the current study's results, he says what's really important is that

55   their methods show that these effects are actually happening.

According to Shepherd and Haberlie, these storms are brewed by several factors. First, cities are hotter than surrounding areas. This
60   warm, rising city air creates circulation that mixes with other atmospheric conditions to create thunderheads. Second, tall buildings form a barrier that pushes wind up and around the city. "Upward motion is always good for
65   thunderstorms," says Haberlie. Finally, pollution particles act like nuclei that water glom onto, creating droplets. In essence, cities get more thunder and rain because they are hot, stale, and dirty.

70   But you can't generalize this type of research to every city. Places like New York, Chicago, and Washington D.C. are probably also contributing to their own thunderstorms, but because these cities are so close to large bodies of water, it
75   would be hard to tease this out of radar data the way Haberlie and his co-authors did with Atlanta. Research like this could help city managers plan for bigger influxes of water, either by opening up more reservoirs, or coming up with better
80   strategies for flooding. But perhaps most important, there is no telling if this research will result in a long-awaited new verse to the AC/DC* classic, "Thunderstruck."

* An Australian rock band popular in the 1970s and 1980s. "Thunderstruck" was one of their later hits.

43. The author begins the passage by mentioning aspects of city life primarily to

(A) introduce a specific characteristic of city life about which readers may not be familiar.
(B) imply that he grew up in an urban setting.
(C) demonstrate how these aspects are affected by weather patterns.
(D) point out differences between city and rural life that are just as important as differences in weather.

44. As used in line 13, "modeling" most nearly means

(A) sculpture.
(B) acting.
(C) simulations.
(D) imitations.

45. According to the passage, approximately how many more storms per year can be expected in Atlanta compared to surrounding rural areas?

(A) Two or more
(B) Less than three
(C) Twice as many
(D) Half as many

46. Based on the passage, it can be reasonably inferred that the author shares which of the following assumptions about the experimental technique of modeling weather patterns?

(A) It is as important as data-based methods.
(B) It is ultimately more effective than data-based methods.
(C) It provides insight but is not definitive.
(D) It generates conflicting results.

47. Which choice provides the best evidence for the answer to the previous question?

(A) Lines 9 – 13 ("New research examined… rural areas")
(B) Lines 13 – 17 ("Through modeling…in action")
(C) Lines 25 – 27 ("In all, the…rural area")
(D) Lines 48 – 51 ("Based on research…its realm")

48. Based on the passage, the relationship between Shepherd's and Haberlie's research can best be described as

(A) different approaches to a problem that produce different results.
(B) different approaches to a problem that produce similar results.
(C) similar approaches to a problem that produce similar results.
(D) similar approaches to a problem that produce different results.

49. The author states that cities are "hot, stale, and dirty" (lines 68 – 69) primarily to

(A) summarize the preceding information.
(B) point out similarities between two diverging viewpoints.
(C) express a common opinion.
(D) clarify his purpose in writing the article.

50. The passage strongly suggests that storm effects have a larger impact on cities than on surrounding areas because

(A) the same factors that make storms more likely also make them harder to deal with.
(B) population density in cities makes storm evacuation practices an issue of public safety.
(C) it is more difficult to predict when they will occur due to the challenges of obtaining data.
(D) cities represent greater economic investments and are subject to greater losses.

51. The passage strongly suggests that the difference in weather research between Atlanta and New York is due to

(A) the fundamental ineffectiveness of radar as a research tool.
(B) the unpredictability of the Atlantic Ocean.
(C) geographical factors that obscure results.
(D) a greater concern about flooding effects in cities in the American South.

52. The value of both modeling and interpreting data in verifying weather phenomena is best supported by which choice?

(A) Lines 9 – 13 ("New research examined… rural areas")
(B) Lines 13 – 17 ("Through modeling…in action")
(C) Lines 40 – 42 ("Researchers have… surrounding areas")
(D) Lines 71 – 76 ("Places like New York…with Atlanta")

STOP

Writing and Language Test 3

 35 MINUTES, 44 QUESTIONS

Turn to Section 2 of your answer sheet to answer the questions in this section.

DIRECTIONS Each of the following passages is accompanied by approximately 11 questions. Some questions will require you to revise the passages in order to improve coherence and clarity. Other questions will require you to correct grammatical errors in the passages. Passages may be accompanied by graphs, charts, or tables that you must consider when making revisions. For most questions, you may select the "NO CHANGE" option if you believe that portion of the passage is clear, concise, and grammatically correct as is.

Within the passages, highlighted numbers followed by underlined text indicate which part of the text corresponds with each question. Bracketed numbers [1] indicate sentence number. These bracketed numbers are only relevant to problems that require you to add or rearrange sentences in a paragraph.

Refer to the passage below to answer questions 1 – 11.

Interpreters/Translators

In today's world, globalization has increased the need to overcome language barriers. While computer applications can translate some information from one language to another, computers cannot yet surpass the human brain in terms of processing language meaningfully. Businesses, governments, and many other organizations still rely on multilingual professionals **1** <u>which</u> can interpret or translate languages.

The two skills—interpreting and translating—are actually separate specialties. Interpreting refers to spoken language or sign language. An interpreter listens to someone **2** <u>speak, and an interpreter repeats</u> the message in the language of the listeners. In some cases, interpreters may listen in one language and speak in another simultaneously. However, in most interpretive situations, the interpreter can wait for the speaker to pause before relaying the message.

Translators work with written material; they rewrite text **3** <u>as precise as possible</u> in the target language. The task may involve creative challenges, **4** <u>such as how to express an idiomatic phrase that does not translate literally.</u> Some translators also specialize in business-related "localization," which

1. (A) NO CHANGE
   (B) they
   (C) whom
   (D) who

2. (A) NO CHANGE
   (B) speak and repeats
   (C) who speaks and also repeats
   (D) speak, and he or she repeats

3. (A) NO CHANGE
   (B) as precise as it is possible
   (C) as precisely as possible
   (D) as precisely as it is possible

4. The writer is considering deleting the underlined phrase. Should it be kept or deleted?

   (A) Kept, because it provides a relevant example.
   (B) Kept, because it provides a transition to idiomatic phrases.
   (C) Deleted, because it ignores similar creative challenges faced by interpreters.
   (D) Deleted, because it distracts the reader from the paragraph's focus on written material.

means they help companies **5** <u>adapt</u> products or services to consumers in a particular locale. Localization translators serve as experts on **6** <u>local consumers' language and preferences.</u> They help companies avoid embarrassing cultural missteps and successfully design, package, and advertise products or services.

7 Interpreters and translators may be needed in settings that range from the very humble to the highly prestigious. They may work in local county courtrooms or at meetings of **8** <u>the United Nations. They may work</u> for small rural hospitals or for multinational corporations. Their employers include professional sports teams, publishers, military services, and international aid organizations. Some translators and interpreters work from home via computer, and some travel frequently. Some set up their own freelance businesses.

Becoming a professional interpreter or translator requires earning at least a bachelor's degree, but clearly, the most important skill is complete fluency in at least two languages. **9** <u>Eventual</u> interpreters and translators may also benefit by earning certificates from independent professional organizations in the field. Some employers provide a training period or training materials regarding particular terminology related to a job, such as legal terms used in courtrooms.

Economic forecasters believe that society will experience an increasing need for qualified interpreters and translators in the foreseeable future. The U.S. Bureau of Labor Statistics predicts a 42 percent rise in job opportunities in language interpretation and translation fields between 2012 and 2022. **10** <u>Paradoxically,</u> the biggest need will be for the most commonly spoken languages. **11** <u>Their</u> will also be an increasing need for sign-language interpreters for people with impaired hearing.

5. (A) NO CHANGE
   (B) restore
   (C) transform
   (D) recalibrate

6. (A) NO CHANGE
   (B) local consumer's language and preferences
   (C) local consumers' language, and preferences
   (D) local consumer's language, and preferences

7. Which choice most effectively establishes the main topic of paragraph 4?
   (A) Being a translator or an interpreter is always exciting.
   (B) Fluent bilingualism opens up many opportunities.
   (C) Just think of all the places where people speak different languages.
   (D) Language-related professionals work in extremely diverse fields.

8. Which choice most effectively combines the two sentences at the underlined portion?
   (A) the United Nations, they may work
   (B) the United Nations, also they may work
   (C) the United Nations—they may work
   (D) the United Nations; they may work

9. (A) NO CHANGE
   (B) Prospective
   (C) Attainable
   (D) Feasible

10. (A) NO CHANGE
    (B) Naturally,
    (C) As a result,
    (D) On the other hand,

11. (A) NO CHANGE
    (B) These
    (C) There
    (D) It

Refer to the passage below to answer questions 12 – 22.

Floodplains

Most people consider overflowing rivers to be natural disasters. But incongruously, floods support **12** <u>life, including human life</u> through the creation of floodplains. Floodplains are areas of flat and fertile land stretching out on either side of rivers that have flooded countless times over eons. **13** Governments often build dams and levees to prevent flooding in densely populated floodplains. The dilemma is that **14** <u>from the standpoint of geomorphology, in which "geo" stands for "earth," and "morph" stands for "form,"</u> periodic flooding contributes to the health of the soil as well as the availability of clean water.

Floodplains develop because rivers carry rock and soil downward from mountains. When there is excessive snow or rainfall at the higher elevations, rivers rise above their usual banks and spill over, taking gravel and soil along.

The floodwater spreads out over the land. It sinks into the surface, leaving behind **15** <u>all the stuff</u> that it was carrying. Over the course of time, river floods leave behind so many layers of sediment on either side that wide, flat plains form. The sediment **16** <u>creates rich soil, and supports</u> lush vegetation. Because rivers gradually erode the surfaces over which they flow, **17** <u>floodplains are sometimes located above step-like formations called "terraces."</u>

12. (A) NO CHANGE
    (B) life, including human life,
    (C) life: including human life,
    (D) life including human life

13. The author wants to add a sentence at this point to explain the connection between ideas. Which choice best maintains the paragraph's focus?

    (A) In spite of the danger of flooding, people tend to settle in the floodplains because they can grow healthy crops in the soil.
    (B) People frequently settle in floodplains such as California's Central Valley, Vietnam's Mekong River delta, and Bangladesh's Ganges delta.
    (C) Sometimes ancient cultures adjusted their lives to seasonal, mild flooding, such as in Egypt's Nile River delta.
    (D) Some geologists predict that flooding will threaten more communities due to the effects of global warming and global population growth.

14. (A) NO CHANGE
    (B) with an eye toward the dynamics of change,
    (C) from a very long-term perspective,
    (D) when experts study the situation,

15. (A) NO CHANGE
    (B) the sediment
    (C) things
    (D) the foreign matter

16. (A) NO CHANGE
    (B) creates rich soil, supports
    (C) creates rich soil and
    (D) creates rich soil and supports

17. Which choice accurately and effectively represents the information presented in the diagram?

    (A) NO CHANGE
    (B) floodplains may be surrounded by step-like inclines called "terraces."
    (C) recently formed flood plains may actually form below the surface of a river.
    (D) large floodplains often form at the bases of steep mountains called "terraces."

18 They slow down floods, accommodating water and preventing it from building up even more force downstream. Instead of the excess water tearing up obstacles and charging into the sea, it diffuses calmly over the plains. Gravity slowly pulls the water down, where it replenishes underground aquifers.

An underground aquifer consists of deep layers of permeable rock, sand, and soil that **19** is saturated with drops of water. The water inches through the aquifer, pushed or pulled by natural forces. It is this water that people draw upon when they drill wells. The same mechanisms that cause the water to seep into wells cause it to seep into springs, lake bottoms, and river beds. **20** Geologists estimate that up to 40 percent of the water typically found in rivers and streams comes from underground aquifers.

Therefore, water periodically transfers from rivers to floodplains, from floodplains to underground aquifers, and then back to lakes and rivers. In this cycle, floodplains can improve water quality in two ways. As mentioned, floodplains filter sediment out of the water as it sinks in. Secondly, floodplains can reduce nitrates, which might otherwise contribute to excessive nutrients in aquatic ecosystems. **21** As a result, waterlogged soils harbor types of anaerobic bacteria that break down nitrates. The floodplain's trees and other plants also take up some of the nitrates. The overall result is clear, clean water in the underground aquifer. **22**

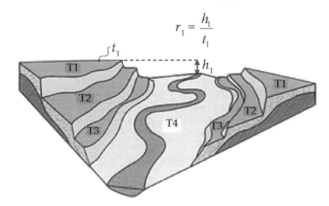

$$r_1 = \frac{h_1}{t_1}$$

T1 – T3: terrace surfaces t_i: age of T1 surface
T4: floodplain surface h_i: height of T1 terrace
                            r_i: average rate of incision

SOURCE: Terranova 274, "A series of paired river terraces"

18. Which choice most effectively establishes the main topic of paragraph 3?

   (A) There are many reasons that floodplains are important.
   (B) Excess water is crucial to maintaining floodplains.
   (C) Floodplains are essentially catch-basins.
   (D) Flooding does not cause damage in the floodplains.

19. (A) NO CHANGE
   (B) might be
   (C) would become
   (D) are

20. The writer is considering deleting the underlined sentence. Should the sentence be kept or deleted?

   (A) Kept, because it successfully summarizes the essay's main point.
   (B) Kept, because it adds supportive and relevant information.
   (C) Deleted, because it adds confusing and unimportant details.
   (D) Deleted, because it strays from the paragraph's main focus and organization.

21. (A) NO CHANGE
   (B) In consequence,
   (C) The reason is that
   (D) For this reason,

22. The writer wants to conclude the passage with a sentence that emphasizes the importance of floodplains. Which choice would best accomplish this goal?

   (A) From this, it is clear to see the importance of floodplains.
   (B) Therefore, floodplains support various habitats that are rich in biodiversity.
   (C) Thus, communities should value floodplains as critical natural resources.
   (D) It is imperative that communities begin to dismantle their dams and levees.

Refer to the passage below to answer questions 23 – 33.

Bedu Culture

[1] Before the 20th century ushered in motorized vehicles, the vast deserts of the Middle East—including those in Egypt, the Arabian Peninsula, and Jordan—were nearly impassable, let alone habitable. [2] The only people who did manage to live there were the Bedu, also known as the Bedouin. [3] Records of their traditional culture, however, provide an intriguing example of humans' ability to adapt to even the most extreme landscapes. [4] For centuries, Bedu people herded camels and served as desert guides. [5] Today, the estimated five million Bedu people have mostly settled in modern towns in the Arab region. **23**

Middle Eastern people typically viewed Bedu people with both fear and admiration. The tough desert **24** dweller's had a reputation for engaging in violent feuds and stealing camels. **25** Nonetheless, they were also known for offering extravagant hospitality to anyone who visited them, and they were held in awe for their poetic way of speaking. Europeans who spent time with Bedu in the desert wrote **26** how you could always hear their lively, loud conversation and recitations from their oral literature. Wilfred Thesiger, a British **27** photographer and author, who traveled with Bedu companions between 1945 and 1950, later wrote that all the Bedu individuals whom he knew were "unflagging talkers." Thesiger said that in his experience they found it "an almost unendurable hardship to keep silent."

23. For the sake of the cohesion of paragraph 1, sentence 3 should go

   (A) where it is now
   (B) before sentence 1
   (C) after sentence 1
   (D) after sentence 5

24. (A) NO CHANGE
   (B) dweller
   (C) dwellers
   (D) dwellers'

25. (A) NO CHANGE
   (B) So far,
   (C) In addition,
   (D) Consequently,

26. (A) NO CHANGE
   (B) some on
   (C) a lot about their
   (D) descriptions of

27. (A) NO CHANGE
   (B) photographer and author
   (C) photographer, and author,
   (D) photographer-author,

Constant communication served a practical purpose **28** in a habitat where resources are thinly spread. Meager water sources could support only small groups of people and camels at a time. Therefore, families often had to camp alone or with just a few other families. Thesiger writes that when visitors **29** were arriving, they would signal from far away their friendly intentions by throwing sand in the air. As soon as visitors arrived, they would be offered a seat and a meal. They were often **30** investigated at length, sometimes overnight. The "news" might include where there was currently grass and water for the camels, where friends and foes were camped, and any current anecdotes or personal news from other camps the guest had visited. **31**

[1] Talking also helped pass the time in barren terrain. [2] These oral traditions were repeated so often that virtually everyone memorized them. [3] Since all the listeners shared knowledge of the same literature and lifestyle, they were able to easily understand metaphors, allusions, and unusual vocabulary. [4] Thus, **32** their elusive poetic speaking gave them a way to creatively engage with a small social circle over a long period of time. **33**

28. (A) NO CHANGE
    (B) in a place like that, with thin resources.
    (C) with thinly spreading resources.
    (D) among the thinly spread resources of the habitat.

29. (A) NO CHANGE
    (B) signaled, they could be seen and known for
    (C) came into sight, they would signal
    (D) were seen, signaling

30. (A) NO CHANGE
    (B) impugned
    (C) queried
    (D) diverted

31. Which choice would most effectively conclude paragraph 3?

    (A) Through such encounters, Bedu people gained up-to-date information about their vast surroundings and far-flung community.
    (B) For example, they might learn about someone acquiring new camels, someone getting married, and so on.
    (C) It was especially important for survival to gain knowledge of places that they could take their goats and camels to graze.
    (D) By talking at length with visitors, Bedu people learned everything they needed to know about their desert home.

32. (A) NO CHANGE
    (B) their spoken literary tradition
    (C) tradition
    (D) a highly developed tradition

33. The writer wants to add the following sentence to the paragraphs.

    From childhood, the Bedu heard thousands of stories, songs, and poems.

    The best placement for this sentence is

    (A) after sentence 1.
    (B) after sentence 2.
    (C) after sentence 3.
    (D) after sentence 4.

Refer to the passage below to answer questions 34 – 44.

Art in the Civil War

--- 1 ---

34 The American Civil War was fought from 1861 to 1865 because the United States' northern and southern regions found it impossible to compromise on a fundamental question: whether the federal government could overrule states. In particular, representatives of the southern states feared that the federal government would overrule them by outlawing **35** slavery. The economy of the South was based on slavery. The resulting war caused the death of at least 600,000 soldiers, and wreaked havoc on civilians through disease and destruction.

--- 2 ---

Ironically, some of the best-known American writers were alive at the time—Ralph Waldo Emerson, Frederick Douglass, Herman Melville, Walt Whitman, Mark Twain, Emily Dickinson, and Henry Wadsworth Longfellow. While some produced elegiac poems, **36** none of them were able to produce a novel or body of poetry that conveyed the turmoil that soldiers and families endured. It was not until 30 years after the war that a young Stephen Crane was able to write such a novel, *The Red Badge of Courage*, based on first-hand **37** accounts that he read, or heard, from veterans.

--- 3 ---

Historians have noted that during the Civil War, **38** American writing was in a transition period away from Victorian romanticism, but not yet free of it. Perhaps it was too difficult to glean insights from the morally ambiguous situation: people on both sides held **39** equivocal views on the issues, yet they also felt disillusioned by the terrifying reality of war.

34. (A) NO CHANGE
(B) People in the north of America and people in the south went to civil war against each other from 1861 to 1865 for the simple reason that they
(C) From 1861 to 1865, the United States' northern and southern regions clashed in the American Civil War. They
(D) The American Civil War, from 1861 to 1865, pitched the South against the North, expressly because, as it turned out, they

35. Which choice most effectively combines the sentences at the underlined portion?

(A) slavery, which sustained the South's economy.
(B) slavery, the main support of the southern economy.
(C) slavery since the southern economy could not do without slavery.
(D) slavery; yet slavery supported the southern economy.

36. (A) NO CHANGE
(B) none of them was
(C) none of the writers were
(D) none of the poems were

37. (A) NO CHANGE
(B) accounts—that he read, or heard,
(C) accounts that he read or heard,
(D) accounts that he read or heard

38. (A) NO CHANGE
(B) American authors published very little that illustrated the war experience.
(C) American authors tended to publish material about travels in Europe or other comforting distractions.
(D) American authors remained largely silent.

39. (A) NO CHANGE
(B) unequal
(C) indefinite
(D) unequivocal

--- 4 ---

Visual artists found it easier to focus on the war even while in its midst. Photography was a recent invention. Cameras still had slow shutter speeds and could not yet capture activity, but photographers documented the gruesome aftermath of battles. **40** Photographers Mathew Brady and Alexander Gardner held photo exhibits in northern cities, providing alarming views of corpse-strewn landscapes. Meanwhile, newspapers and magazines could not yet print photographs, so many hired sketch artists and sent them to the front lines. The artists lived with the troops and risked getting close to battle so they could report accurate images. Probably the most skilled and daring of these artists was Alfred Waud, who excelled at depicting movement. In his images, men and horses run, cannons blast, trains run off bridges, **41** and everywhere there is fire and smoke. War looks anything but glorious.

--- 5 ---

A young Winslow Homer, one of **42** Americas most gifted painters, worked as a sketch artist near the front during the war and also produced a number of paintings. His 1864 painting *Skirmish in the Wilderness* depicts a small group of soldiers engaged in combat in a forest. One of the men is down. The opposing forces cannot be seen through the thickets and shadows. It is impossible to perceive why one soldier is shooting and another **43** runs up with a drawn sword. Consequently, the image conveys panic, disorder, and dread. Homer seems to offer the scene as a metaphor for the larger war. **44**

40. The writer is considering cutting the underlined sentence. Should it be kept or deleted?

(A) Kept, because it supports the previous point about documenting the consequences of battles.
(B) Kept, because it supports the writer's point about the importance of photography as an art.
(C) Deleted, because it is confined to only two examples of photographers.
(D) Deleted, because it blurs the paragraph's focus on the visual arts in general.

41. (A) NO CHANGE
(B) and also fire and smoke are there.
(C) fires blaze, and smoke billows.
(D) fires are threatening, and smoke is everywhere.

42. (A) NO CHANGE
(B) Americans
(C) America's
(D) Americas'

43. (A) NO CHANGE
(B) is running up
(C) ran up
(D) was running up

Think about the previous passage as a whole as you answer question 44.

44. To make the passage most logical, paragraph 3 should be placed

(A) after paragraph 1.
(B) where it is now.
(C) after paragraph 4.
(D) after paragraph 5.

Math Test 3 – No Calculator

25 MINUTES, 20 QUESTIONS

Turn to Section 3 of your answer sheet to answer the questions in this section.

DIRECTIONS

For questions **1 – 15**, find the solution to each problem and select the most appropriate answer from the choices provided. For questions **16 – 20**, find the solution to each problem and write your answer in the space provided. You may use the blank space in your test booklet for scratch work.

NOTES

1. The use of a calculator on any part of this section is forbidden.
2. Unless otherwise indicated, all variables and expressions used in this test represent real numbers.
3. Unless otherwise indicated, all figures used in this test are drawn to scale.
4. Unless otherwise indicated, all figures used in this test lie on a plane.
5. Unless specified otherwise, a given function, f, has the domain the set of all real numbers x for which $f(x)$ is a real number.

REFERENCE

$A = \frac{1}{2}bh$ $c^2 = a^2 + b^2$ Special Right Triangles $A = \pi r^2$ $A = \ell w$
$C = 2\pi r$

$V = \ell w h$ $V = \pi r^2 h$ $V = \frac{4}{3}\pi r^3$ $V = \frac{1}{3}\pi r^2 h$ $V = \frac{1}{3}\ell w h$

The arc of a circle is 360 degrees or 2π radians.
A triangle has angles that sum to 180 degrees.

1. $$x^2(y + 3) = 12$$

If (x, y) is a solution to the equation above, and x and y are both integers, which of the following could NOT be a value of x?

(A) −1
(B) 0
(C) 1
(D) 2

2. A sociologist determines that the population of a city will grow at 3% per year for the next 20 years. If the current population is 850,000, which of the following expressions represents the population x years in the future?

(A) $(850,000)(1.03)^x$
(B) $(850,000) + (1.03)^x$
(C) $\dfrac{850,000}{1.03^x}$
(D) $(850,000)(1.03)x^2$

3. If $10z - 13 = 7$, what is the value of $3z + 14$?

(A) 1
(B) 12
(C) 17
(D) 20

4. Mary wants to print flyers for her fundraising event. Printing costs $0.25 per copy for the first 100 copies, $0.20 per copy for the next 200 copies, and $0.10 per copy for every copy after that. The entire purchase is subject to an 11% sales tax. Which of the following represents the cost of printing, in dollars, as a function of the number of flyers, x, assuming Mary prints at least 500 flyers?

(A) $[(100)(0.25) + (200)(0.2) + (x - 300)(0.1)](1.11)$
(B) $[(100)(0.25) + (100)(0.2) + (x - 200)(0.1)](1.11)$
(C) $(100)(0.25) + (200)(0.2) + (x - 300)(0.1)$
(D) $[(x - 100)(0.25) + (x - 200)(0.2) + (x - 300)(0.1)]$ (1.11)

5. Three boys can paint a fence in 5 hours. How many hours would it take four boys to paint the same fence?

(A) $\dfrac{3}{2}$
(B) 3
(C) $3\dfrac{3}{4}$
(D) 4

6. Angelo makes x dollars for y hours of work. Sarah makes the same amount of money for one less hour of work. Which of the following expressions represents the positive difference between their hourly wages?

(A) $\dfrac{x}{y-1} + \dfrac{x}{y}$

(B) $\dfrac{x}{y} - \dfrac{x}{y-1}$

(C) $\dfrac{x}{y-1} - \dfrac{x}{y}$

(D) $\dfrac{y-1}{x} - \dfrac{y}{x}$

7.
$$\frac{1}{2}x - \frac{1}{4}y = 5$$
$$ax - 3y = 20$$

If the system of linear equations above has no solution, what is the value of the constant a?

(A) $\dfrac{1}{2}$

(B) 2

(C) 6

(D) 12

8. Barbara is planning a lunch for her Sailing Club. It costs $250 to rent the venue, and $15 per guest for food. If the total cost of the lunch is graphed as a function of the number of guests, which of the following represents the slope?

(A) 1

(B) 15

(C) 25

(D) 250

9. If $(x + 1)^2 = 4$ and $(x - 1)^2 = 16$, what is the value of x?

(A) –3

(B) –1

(C) 1

(D) 3

10. An equilateral triangle is inscribed in a circle with a radius of 2 meters. What is the area of this triangle?

(A) $\sqrt{3}$

(B) $2\sqrt{3}$

(C) $3\sqrt{3}$

(D) $\pi\sqrt{3}$

11. Julie, the manager of a tea shop, decides to experiment with a new blend. She mixes some Earl Grey tea at $5 per pound with Orange Pekoe tea at $3 per pound to make 100 pounds of the new blend. The selling price for the new blend is $4.50 per pound, reflecting the prices and proportions of the component teas. How many pounds of the Earl Grey are in the blend?

(A) 70

(B) 75

(C) 80

(D) 85

12. If the radius of a circular cylinder is decreased by 50%, and its height is simultaneously increased by 60%, what is the change in volume?

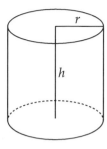

(A) An increase of 40%

(B) A decrease of 40%

(C) An increase of 60%

(D) A decrease of 60%

14.

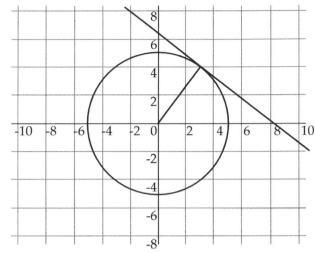

Which of the following equations represents the line tangent to the circle $x^2 + y^2 = 25$ at the point (3, 4)?

(A) $3x + 4y - 25 = 0$

(B) $3x - 4y - 25 = 0$

(C) $4x + 3y + 3 = 0$

(D) $4x - 3y = 0$

13. What is the equation of the line that passes through the point (1, 2) and is perpendicular to the line $x + y = 2$?

(A) $y = 1 - x$

(B) $y = 3 - x$

(C) $y = 1 + x$

(D) $y = 2 + x$

15. If the rational expression $\dfrac{9x^2 - 4}{x + 1}$ is rewritten in the equivalent form $\dfrac{5}{x + 1} + A$, what is A in terms of x?

(A) $x - 1$

(B) $x + 1$

(C) $9x - 9$

(D) $12x - 3$

DIRECTIONS

For questions **16 – 20**, find the solution to the problem and enter your answer as demonstrated below.

1. Only the answer that is bubbled in on the answer sheet will be credited. The blank spaces above the bubbles are for you to record your answers for accuracy.
2. Only fill in one bubble in any given column.
3. There are no negative answers in this portion of the test.
4. If a problem appears to have more than one answer, only enter one answer. If the answer you enter is one of the correct solutions, you will receive full credit for that question.
5. If the correct answer can be expressed as a mixed number, it must be entered as a decimal or an improper fraction.
6. If the correct answer is a decimal that cannot fit into the grid space, you must fill the grid with enough digits to completely fill the space. The number can be rounded or simply shortened but must fill the whole space.

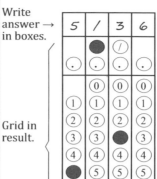

Answer: $\frac{5}{36}$ Answer: 4.5

Write answer in boxes. →   ← Fraction line   ← Decimal point

Grid in result.

Acceptable ways to grid $\frac{1}{6}$ are:

Answer: 302 – either position is correct

NOTES

Begin entering answers in any column that accommodates your answer. If you do not need a column do not enter anything in that column.

16. Daisha bought a car for $15,000, and its value depreciated linearly. After 3 years, the value of the car was $11,250. What is the amount, in dollars, of yearly depreciation?

ANSWER: _____

17. If $\dfrac{z}{y} = 7$, what is the value of $\dfrac{3y}{z}$?

ANSWER: _____

18. If the graph of $y = x^2 + mx + n$ passes through the points (1, 12) and (3, 28), what is the value of the product mn?

ANSWER: _____

19. If $x - 2$ is a factor of $x^3 - kx^2 + kx + 2$, where k is a constant, what is the value of k?

ANSWER: _____

20. If a and b are numbers such that $(a - 4)(b + 6) = 0$, then what is the smallest possible value of $a^2 + b^2$?

ANSWER: _____

STOP

Math Test 3 – Calculator

55 MINUTES, 38 QUESTIONS

Turn to Section 4 of your answer sheet to answer the questions in this section.

DIRECTIONS

For questions **1 – 30**, find the solution to each problem and select the most appropriate answer from the choices provided. For questions **31 – 38**, find the solution to each problem and write your answer in the space provided. You may use the blank space in your test booklet for scratch work.

NOTES

1. The use of a calculator on any part of this section is allowed.
2. Unless otherwise indicated, all variables and expressions used in this test represent real numbers.
3. Unless otherwise indicated, all figures used in this test are drawn to scale.
4. Unless otherwise indicated, all figures used in this test lie on a plane.
5. Unless specified otherwise, a given function, f, has the domain the set of all real numbers x for which $f(x)$ is a real number.

REFERENCE

$A = \frac{1}{2}bh$ $\quad c^2 = a^2 + b^2$ $\quad$ Special Right Triangles $\quad A = \pi r^2$ $\quad A = \ell w$
$\qquad\qquad\qquad\qquad\qquad\qquad\qquad\qquad\qquad\qquad\qquad\qquad C = 2\pi r$

$V = \ell wh$ $\quad V = \pi r^2 h$ $\quad V = \frac{4}{3}\pi r^3$ $\quad V = \frac{1}{3}\pi r^2 h$ $\quad V = \frac{1}{3}\ell wh$

The arc of a circle is 360 degrees or 2π radians.
A triangle has angles that sum to 180 degrees.

1. Economics scholars estimate the 2035 U.S.A. national debt will be x percent of 2035's GDP (Gross Domestic Product). Given that $x \geq 106$, and y is the GDP of 2035 in dollars, which inequality represents the minimum value of Z, the national debt in terms of y?

(A) $106 \geq \dfrac{Z}{y}$

(B) $(1.06)Zy > 0$

(C) $y(1.06) \leq Z$

(D) $x(106) \geq Zy$

2.

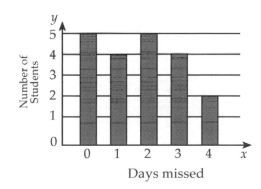

Days missed

According to the bar graph above, what is the average number of days missed by students in the class?

(A) 1.5

(B) 1.7

(C) 3.4

(D) 4

3. If $f(x)$ is a linear function, $f(3) = 1$ and $f(2) = 5$, what is the y-intercept?

(A) –4

(B) 1

(C) 11

(D) 13

Questions 4 and 5 refer to the following information.

The following table shows the results of a survey distributed to thousands of households. Households were asked to select which, if any, forms of public transportation they use regularly. Some households used more than one form of public transportation.

Households Using Public Transport, 2010
(numbers in thousands):
U.S. Census Bureau

	Northeast	Midwest	South	West
Local Public Bus	4595	2365	2853	4501
Subway, Lightrail, Trolley	3487	816	1337	2067
Commuter or Inner-city Train	1296	457	187	457
Total Number of Households Using Public Transportation	6862	3265	4116	5925

4. Which region had the highest proportion of households using public transportation that used the public bus in 2010?

(A) Northeast

(B) Midwest

(C) South

(D) West

5. What percentage of households that used public transport in the Midwest made use of a commuter or inner-city train?

(A) 7.7

(B) 12.6

(C) 14.0

(D) 18.9

6.

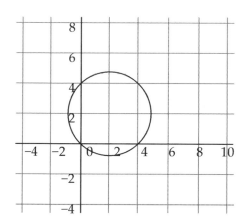

What is the area of the circle that passes through the points (0, 0), (0, 4), and (4, 0), and has a center point at (2, 2)?

(A) 3π

(B) $2\sqrt{2}\pi$

(C) 8π

(D) 16π

7. Larry is driving from Charlotte to Charleston—a distance of 380 miles—with his friend, Omar. Larry and Omar have agreed to split the cost of gas in half. If Omar's car gets 28 miles per gallon, and gas costs x dollars per gallon, which of the following represents the total cost of the trip for Larry?

(A) $\dfrac{380x}{28} \times \dfrac{1}{2}$

(B) $\dfrac{380x}{28}$

(C) $\dfrac{380x}{28} \times \dfrac{1}{28} \times \dfrac{1}{2}$

(D) $\dfrac{190x}{28} \times \dfrac{1}{2}$

8. During a 3-year boom, a government experienced a budget surplus of $15 million per year. An economist predicts that annual revenue will drop to $40 million below current levels and remain at that level for the next 5 years. By how much must the government reduce expenditures yearly to maintain a balanced budget over this period?

(A) $8 million

(B) $16 million

(C) $25 million

(D) $40 million

9. A region is defined by the system:

$$y > 2x + 1$$
$$y \leq -x + 2$$

In which quadrants of the coordinate plane is the region located?

(A) I, II, III only

(B) II, III only

(C) III, IV only

(D) I, II, III, IV

10. If 10 boys averaged 88% on a test on which 15 girls averaged 75%, what was the test average for all 25 students?

   (A) 76.4%

   (B) 80.2%

   (C) 84.6%

   (D) 86.2%

11. The difference of two numbers is 2. If the difference of their squares is 18, what is their sum?

   (A) A number between 16 and 20

   (B) A number between 10 and 16

   (C) A number between 5 and 8

   (D) A number between 8 and 10

12. The function h given by $h(t) = -16t^2 + 48t + 5$ represents the height of a ball, in feet, t seconds after it is thrown. To the nearest foot, what is the maximum height reached by the ball?

   (A) 5

   (B) 23

   (C) 31

   (D) 41

13. Brad and Tom are comparing their classes' scores on a math test. Both of their classes had mean scores of 80 on the test, but Brad's class had a range of 6 while Tom's class had a range of 30. If the highest possible score was 100, which class had the LOWEST score in it?

   (A) Brad's class had the lowest score in it.

   (B) Tom's class had the lowest score in it.

   (C) The lowest score occurred in both classes.

   (D) It cannot be determined from the information.

14. A 2–cup mixture consists of $\frac{1}{3}$ flour and $\frac{2}{3}$ cornmeal. If 1 cup of flour is added to make a 3–cup mixture, approximately what percent of the 3–cup mixture is flour?

   (A) 65%

   (B) 56%

   (C) 50%

   (D) 45%

15. Brian has taken five exams in his biochemistry class and scored 56, 55, 41, 29, and 86 (out of a possible 100). The only exam remaining is the class final, which is worth twice as many points as each of the previous exams. If he must average 65 to pass the course, what is the minimum grade he must receive on the final exam to pass?

   (A) 62

   (B) 94

   (C) 100

   (D) He cannot pass the course.

16. A taxi charges $0.30 for the first mile and $0.15 for each additional mile a passenger travels. If a passenger rides in the taxi for x miles, which of the following expressions describes the cost of this ride in dollars as a function $f(x)$?

(A) $f(x) = 0.30 + 0.15x$

(B) $f(x) = 0.30 + 0.15(1 - x)$

(C) $f(x) = 0.30 + 0.15(x - 1)$

(D) $f(x) = 0.30 + 0.15x - 1$

17. A store received $823.00 for the sales of 5 tape recorders and 7 radios. If the receipts from the tape recorders exceeded the receipts from the radios by $137.00, what is the price of a tape recorder?

(A) $49

(B) $96

(C) $68

(D) $84

18. Car A takes 15 seconds to go once around a circular racetrack, and car B takes 25 seconds to go once around the same track. If the two cars begin racing from the same position at the same time, how many seconds will it take for car A to lap car B?

(A) 1.67 seconds

(B) 10.5 seconds

(C) 31.4 seconds

(D) 37.5 seconds

19. The distance in meters that has been covered by a car at a given time, t (in seconds), after its departure is equal to $35t + 5t^2$. During what time period will the car travel between 75 and 130 meters?

(A) $1.7 \leq t \leq 2.7$

(B) $1.5 \leq t \leq 2.5$

(C) $1.6 \leq t \leq 2.8$

(D) $1.8 \leq t \leq 2.8$

20. Peter has invested $8,000 in stocks and bonds. The stocks pay 4% interest, and the bonds pay 7% interest. If his annual income from both is $500, how much is invested in bonds?

(A) $2,000

(B) $3,500

(C) $4,000

(D) $6,000

21. The cost of a piece of lumber is directly proportionally to its length. A piece of lumber 16 feet long costs $12.00. What is the cost, in dollars, of a piece of lumber x yards long?
(1 yard = 3 feet)

(A) $x - 2$

(B) $3x - 2$

(C) $\dfrac{3}{4}x$

(D) $\dfrac{9}{4}x$

22. Let a and b be numbers such that $a^3 = b^2$. Which of the following is equivalent to $b\sqrt{a}$?

(A) $b^{\frac{2}{3}}$

(B) $b^{\frac{1}{4}}$

(C) $b^{\frac{3}{2}}$

(D) $b^{\frac{4}{3}}$

23.

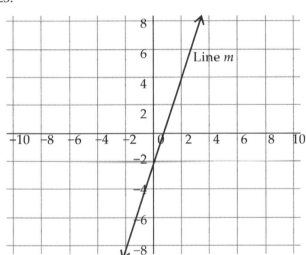

Line m has a positive slope and a negative y-intercept. What happens to the x-intercept if the slope and the y-intercept are doubled?

(A) The x-intercept becomes four times larger.
(B) The x-intercept becomes twice as large.
(C) The x-intercept becomes one-fourth as large.
(D) The x-intercept remains the same.

24.

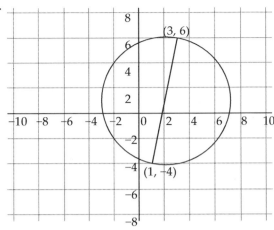

Which of the following is the equation of the circle whose diameter is the line segment connecting points (3, 6) and (1, –4)?

(A) $(x - 2)^2 + (y - 1)^2 = 26$

(B) $(x - 1)^2 + (y + 4)^2 = 104$

(C) $(x + 2)^2 + (y + 1)^2 = 26$

(D) $(x + 2)^2 + (y + 1)^2 = 25$

25.

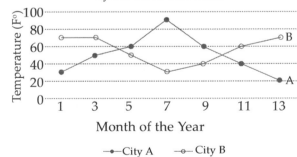

According to the graph, what was City B's average daily high, in Fahrenheit, during the two month period over which City A's average daily temperature increased by the greatest percentage?

(A) 35

(B) 40

(C) 52

(D) 66

371

26.

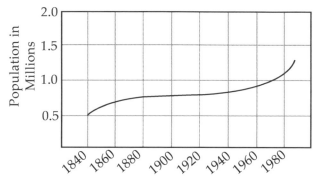

Maine's Population Growth

According to the graph, approximately how many years did it take for Maine's population to double from what it was in 1840?

(A) 25

(B) 40

(C) 70

(D) 130

27.

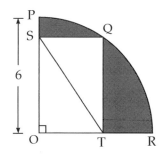

In the figure, arc PQR is one quarter of a circle with center O and radius 6. If $\overline{PS} + \overline{SO} = \overline{OT} + \overline{TR}$, what is the perimeter of shaded region?

(A) $8 + 3\pi$

(B) $12 + 3\pi$

(C) $14 + 3\pi$

(D) $1 + 6\pi$

28. If $(3 + 2i) - (a + 3i) = 10 - i$, what is the real number a?

(A) $2^{\frac{1}{2}}$

(B) $-7 - 2i$

(C) -7

(D) 6

Questions 29 and 30 refer to the following information.

A store's Cyber Monday promotion offers electronics at 28- to 70-percent discounted prices. During the promotion, Ali purchases a laptop that is discounted from \$355.55 to \$165.65. Assume that a 7.5-percent sales tax is included in all prices.

29. Which of the following approximates the percent discount of Ali's Cyber Monday laptop purchase.

(A) 28%

(B) 47%

(C) 53%

(D) 70%

30. What is the difference in sales tax between the laptop's original price and its sale price?

(A) \$11.28

(B) \$13.25

(C) \$14.24

(D) \$24.81

DIRECTIONS

For questions **31 – 38**, find the solution to the problem and enter your answer as demonstrated below.

1. Only the answer that is bubbled in on the answer sheet will be credited. The blank spaces above the bubbles are for you to record your answers for accuracy.
2. Only fill in one bubble in any given column.
3. None of the answers on this portion of the test are negative values.
4. If a problem appears to have more than one answer, only enter one answer. If the answer you enter is one of the correct solutions, you will receive full credit for that question.
5. If the correct answer can be expressed as a mixed number, it must be entered as a decimal or an improper fraction.
6. If the correct answer is a decimal that cannot fit into the grid space, you must fill the grid with enough digits to completely fill the space. The number can be rounded or simply shortened but must fill every blank space.

NOTES

Begin entering answers in any column that accommodates your answer. If you do not need a column do not enter anything in that column.

Answer: $\frac{5}{36}$ Answer: 4.5

Write answer → in boxes.

← Fraction line
← Decimal point

Grid in result.

Acceptable ways to grid $\frac{1}{6}$ are:

Answer: 302 – either position is correct

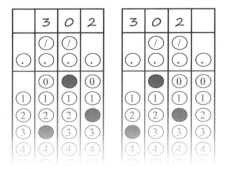

31. On a map, a quarter inch represents 20 actual miles. How many inches on the map separate two towns that are 320 miles apart?

ANSWER: _____

32. A chemistry student has 45 milliliters of a 20% salt solution. How many milliliters of salt are in the solution?

ANSWER: _____

33.

$$y = 4x$$
$$-3x^2 + y^2 = 52$$

If (x, y) is a solution to the system of equations above and $x > 0$, what is the value of x?

ANSWER: _____

34. A ball is dropped from a height of 30 feet. Each time it strikes the ground, it bounces up to $\frac{4}{5}$ of the previous height. How many times does the ball hit the ground before it bounces up less than 6 feet?

ANSWER: _____

35. Linda receives 3% in royalties for every paper copy of her book that is sold. In addition, she receives 20% in royalties for every electronic copy. In the month of February, her book sold 1,200 paper copies at $29.95, and 800 electronic copies at $16.95. How much did she receive from royalties in February? (Round your answer to the nearest dollar.)

ANSWER: _____

36. To measure the height of Lincoln's head on Mt. Rushmore, two sightings 800 feet from the base of the mountain are taken. If the angle of elevation to the bottom of Lincoln's face is 32°, and the angle of elevation to the top is 35°, what is the height, in feet, of Lincoln's face? (Round you answer to the nearest foot.)

ANSWER: _____

Questions 37 and 38 are based on the following information:

A new online music streaming service reached peak volume the previous year with 8-billion songs streamed.

37. **Part 1**
    If volume increased 50% during the second half of the year, what was the average number streams per month, in millions, during this period?

    ANSWER: _____

38. **Part 2**
    The most-streamed single of the year represented 0.3% of all plays during the fifth, sixth, and seventh months of the year. If the song was streamed 7.1 million times during this period, what was the total number of all streams, in billions, during the same three-month period?

    ANSWER: _____

Essay Test 3*

🕐 50 MINUTES, Prompt-based essay

Turn to Section 5 of your answer sheet to answer the question in this section.

DIRECTIONS

As you read the passage below, consider how Susanna Heckman uses
- evidence, such as facts or examples, to support claims.
- reasoning to develop ideas and to connect claims and evidence.
- stylistic or persuasive elements, such as word choice or appeals to emotion, to add power to the ideas expressed.

Adapted from "The Graphic Novel: A Historical Perspective," ©2015 by KALLIS EDU.

Speech balloons have a long and fascinating history. In modern times, they characterize the modes of expression referred to as the comic-book, the cartoon, and the graphic novel. This little device is extremely effective at communicating ideas without taking up much space. As a result, speech balloons imbue their messages with urgency, an important characteristic that has inspired a wide variety of uses. For example, they are often the vehicle of potent political messages, as well as the spring that propels action-packed sequences in superhero comics.

One of the earliest versions of the speech balloon, which dates to 13th century medieval France, is the "banderole" (literally, "small banner"). This term describes flags or banners in general, but also refers to speech scrolls that appear in painting or sculpture. Banderoles denote speech action in the picture, and are often depicted emanating from a person's mouth. An early example is found in the *Postilles de Nic. de Lire sur la Bible*, a 15th century French manuscript. It includes an illustration of clergymen in conference before a crucifix and makes use of banderoles to represent their prayers.

The Yellow Kid, an early newspaper comic by Richard Outcault (considered by some to be the first modern comic), brought the medium unprecedented exposure at the start of the 20th century. Comics and comic-books rose in popularity during The Great Depression as a form of cheap entertainment, and peaked in the 1940s with the advent of the enormously successful superhero comic. As the industry grew, publishers and artists established conventions intended to standardize production and facilitate reading. They capitalized general text and reserved lower-case letters for particular effect. They used detached circles in place of a solid tail for "thought" balloons, and spiky balloons for shouting. Captions also found their place, most often for depicting narration.

Artists and writers began experimenting with the speech balloon as a means of creative expression. Soon there would be "monster" balloons for depicting fear, icicle balloons to indicate a frosty exchange, and colored balloons to express mood. Even *The Yellow Kid* often placed the Yellow Kid's

speech on his oversized smocks instead of in standard bubbles.

Occasionally, speech balloons themselves became a focal point of action. One of the longest-running newspaper comics, Walt Kelly's *Pogo*, often shows characters physically manipulating speech balloons in humorous ways. The novel *Who Censored Roger Rabbit?*, while not a comic book or graphic novel, provided a bridge between comics and animated cartoons when it described a murdered cartoon character whose final words are found in a speech balloon stuffed under its lifeless body.

Many people now consider comic books and graphic novels serious art forms. They have been studied and written about from the perspectives of art history, art theory, and literary criticism. They have even been explored in the context of neurobiology, concerning the effect they have on the visual and language centers of our brains. Even outside of comics, the speech balloon continues to enjoy a life of its own. It is seen in novel forms such as the "speech balloon" interface of text-messaging, and the modern-day rebuses known as "emojis."

Write an essay in which you explain how the author builds an argument to persuade her audience that the addition of visual elements adds complexity to literature. In your essay, analyze how the author uses one or more of the features listed in the box above (or features of your own choice) to strengthen the logic and persuasiveness of her argument. Be sure that your analysis focuses on the most relevant features of the passage.

Your essay should not explain whether you agree with the author's claims, but rather explain how the author builds an argument to persuade her audience.

* Sample responses at www.kallisedu.com

KALLIS

SAT® Practice Test #4

IMPORTANT REMINDERS:

1

When you take the official SAT, you will need to use a No. 2 pencil. Do not use a pen or a mechanical pencil.

2

On the official SAT, sharing any of the questions on the test violates the College Board's policies and may result in your scores being canceled.

(This cover is modeled after the cover you'll see when you take the official SAT.)

Reading Test 4

 65 MINUTES, 52 QUESTIONS

Turn to Section 1 of your answer sheet to answer the questions in this section.

DIRECTIONS

Each passage or pair of passages is accompanied by 10 or 11 questions. Read each passage or pair of passages, and then select the most appropriate answer to each question. Some passages may include tables or graphs that require additional analysis.

Refer to the passage below to answer questions 1 – 10.

This passage is adapted from Mary Shelley, *Frankenstein*, originally published in 1818.

line   It was on a dreary night of November that I beheld the accomplishment of my toils. With an anxiety that almost amounted to agony, I collected the instruments of life around me, that
5 I might infuse a spark of being into the lifeless thing that lay at my feet. It was already one in the morning; the rain pattered dismally against the panes, and my candle was nearly burnt out, when, by the glimmer of the half-extinguished light, I
10 saw the dull yellow eye of the creature open; it breathed hard, and a convulsive motion agitated its limbs.
    How can I describe my emotions at this catastrophe, or how delineate the wretch
15 whom with such infinite pains and care I had endeavored to form? His limbs were in proportion, and I had selected his features as beautiful. Beautiful! Great God! His yellow skin scarcely covered the work of muscles and arteries
20 beneath; his hair was of a lustrous black, and flowing; his teeth of a pearly whiteness; but these luxuriances only formed a more horrid contrast with his watery eyes, that seemed almost of the same color as the dun-white sockets in which they
25 were set, his shriveled complexion and straight black lips.
    The different accidents of life are not so changeable as the feelings of human nature. I had worked hard for nearly two years, for the sole
30 purpose of infusing life into an inanimate body. For this I had deprived myself of rest and health. I had desired it with an ardor that far exceeded moderation; but now that I had finished, the beauty of the dream vanished, and breathless

35 horror and disgust filled my heart.
    Unable to endure the aspect of the being I had created, I rushed out of the room and continued a long time traversing my bed-chamber, unable to compose my mind to sleep.
40   At length lassitude succeeded to the tumult I had before endured, and I threw myself on the bed in my clothes, endeavoring to seek a few moments of forgetfulness. But it was in vain; I slept, indeed, but I was disturbed by the wildest
45 dreams. I thought I saw Elizabeth, in the bloom of health, walking in the streets of Ingolstadt. Delighted and surprised, I embraced her, but as I imprinted the first kiss on her lips, they became livid with the hue of death; her features appeared
50 to change, and I thought that I held the corpse of my dead mother in my arms; a shroud enveloped her form, and I saw the grave-worms crawling in the folds of the flannel.
    I started from my sleep with horror; a cold
55 dew covered my forehead, my teeth chattered, and every limb became convulsed; when, by the dim and yellow light of the moon, as it forced its way through the window shutters, I beheld the wretch—the miserable monster whom I had
60 created. He held up the curtain of the bed; and his eyes, if eyes they may be called, were fixed on me. His jaws opened, and he muttered some inarticulate sounds, while a grin wrinkled his cheeks. He might have spoken, but I did not hear;
65 one hand was stretched out, seemingly to detain me, but I escaped and rushed downstairs. I took refuge in the courtyard belonging to the house which I inhabited, where I remained during the rest of the night, walking up and down in the
70 greatest agitation, listening attentively, catching and fearing each sound as if it were to announce the approach of the demoniacal corpse to which I had so miserably given life.

1.   As used in line 5, "infuse" most nearly means

(A) saturate.
(B) bathe.
(C) imbue.
(D) inspire.

2.   The descriptions in paragraph 2 (lines 13 – 26) indicate that what the narrator despises most about his creation is its

(A) yellow skin.
(B) muscular build.
(C) pale eyes.
(D) black hair.

3.   The statement "The different accidents of life are not so changeable as the feelings of human nature" (line 27 – 28) primarily comments on the

(A) variability of human emotions and attitudes.
(B) methods that people use to cope with misfortune.
(C) narrator's negative outlook toward the concept of fate.
(D) process by which accidental encounters cause people to feel differently.

4.   The narrator leaves his creation alone after giving it life because he

(A) believes that his creation is violent and dangerous.
(B) feels revolted and repulsed by his creation.
(C) wants his creation to become self-sufficient.
(D) is exhausted and leaves to get some rest.

5.   The narrator's actions in lines 36 – 39 ("Unable to endure…compose my mind to sleep") most closely resemble those of

(A) an unwilling father rejecting his child.
(B) a dissatisfied customer returning a product.
(C) an editor revising a manuscript.
(D) a soldier pursuing an enemy.

6.   The narrator recounts his dream (lines 43 – 53) primarily to

(A) emphasize that he can find no relief from the specter of death.
(B) convey his sorrow regarding the death of his mother.
(C) explain why he decided to create life from nonliving matter.
(D) reveal his growing acceptance of his creation.

7.   As used in line 61 – 62, "fixed on" most nearly means

(A) connected to.
(B) focused on.
(C) mended by.
(D) linked to.

8.   Over the course of the passage, the narrator's attitude shifts from

(A) Fear that his experiment will fail to unmitigated joy at its success.
(B) amazement at the beauty of his creation to disappointment in its inability to communicate.
(C) exhaustion due to his physical and mental exertions to exhilaration because of the success of his experiment.
(D) nervous excitement at the prospect of bringing his creation to life to abject horror at his creation's existence.

9.   Which choice provides the best evidence for the answer to the previous question?

(A) Lines 2 – 6 ("With an anxiety…at my feet")
(B) Lines 16 – 18 ("His limbs…Great God!")
(C) Lines 32 – 35 ("I had…filled my heart")
(D) Lines 40 – 43 ("At length…moments of forgetfulness")

10. The main rhetorical effect of the narrator calling his creation a "thing" and a "creature" is to

(A) dehumanize his creation.
(B) confuse and disorient his creation.
(C) hide his true feelings toward his creation.
(D) emphasize his creation's unusual appearance.

Refer to the passage below to answer questions 11 – 20.

This passage is excerpted from U.S. President Bill Clinton's speech, "Remarks to the People of Ghana," which he delivered in Accra, the capital of Ghana, on March 23, 1998.

line   Africa has changed so much in just 10 years. Dictatorship has been replaced in so many places. Half of the 48 nations in sub-Saharan Africa choose their own governments, leading a new
5   generation willing to learn from the past and imagine a future. Though democracy has not yet gained a permanent foothold even in most successful nations, there is everywhere a growing respect for tolerance, diversity, and elemental
10   human rights. A decade ago, business was stifled. Now, Africans are embracing economic reform. Today from Ghana to Mozambique, from Cote d'Ivoire to Uganda, growing economies are fueling a transformation in Africa.
15   For all this promise, you and I know Africa is not free from peril: the genocide in Rwanda; civil wars in Sierra Leone, Liberia, both Congos; pariah states that export violence and terror; military dictatorship in Nigeria; and high levels
20   of poverty, malnutrition, disease, illiteracy, and unemployment. To fulfill the vast promise of a new era, Africa must face these challenges. We must build classrooms and companies, increase the food supply and save the environment, and
25   prevent disease before deadly epidemics break out.
    The United States is ready to help you. First, my fellow Americans must leave behind the stereotypes that have warped our view and
30   weakened our understanding of Africa. We need to come to know Africa as a place of new beginning and ancient wisdom from which, as my wife, our First Lady, said in her book, we have so much to learn. It is time for Americans to put a
35   new Africa on our map.
    Here in Independence Square, Ghana blazed the path of that new Africa. More than four decades ago, Kwame Nkrumah proposed what he called a "motion of destiny" as Ghana stepped
40   forward as a free and independent nation. Today, Ghana again lights the way for Africa. Democracy is spreading. Business is growing. Trade and investment are rising. Ghana has the only African-owned company today on our New York Stock
45   Exchange.
    You have worked hard to preserve the peace in Africa and around the world—from Liberia to Lebanon, from Croatia to Cambodia. And you have given the world a statesman and peacemaker
50   in Kofi Annan to lead the United Nations. The world admires your success. The United States admires your success. We see it taking root throughout the new Africa. And we stand ready to support it.
55   First, we want to work with Africa to nurture democracy, knowing it is never perfect or complete. We have learned in over 200 years that every day democracy must be defended and a more perfect union can always lie ahead.
60   Democracy requires more than the insults and injustice and inequality that so many societies have known and America has known. Democracy requires human rights for everyone, everywhere, for men and women, for children and the elderly,
65   for people of different cultures and tribes and backgrounds. A good society honors its entire family.
    Second, democracy must have prosperity. Americans of both political parties want to
70   increase trade and investment in Africa. We have an "African Growth and Opportunity Act" now before Congress. Both parties' leadership are supporting it. By opening markets and building businesses and creating jobs, we can
75   help and strengthen each other. By supporting the education of your people, we can strengthen your future and help each other. For centuries, other nations exploited Africa's gold, Africa's diamonds, Africa's minerals. Now is the time for
80   Africans to cultivate something more precious, the mind and heart of the people of Africa, through education.
    Third, we must allow democracy and prosperity to take root without violence. We must
85   work to resolve the war and genocide that still tear at the heart of Africa. We must help Africans to prevent future conflicts. Here in Ghana, you have shown the world that different peoples can live together in harmony. You have proved that
90   Africans of different countries can unite to help solve disputes in neighboring countries. Peace everywhere in Africa will give more free time and more money to the pressing needs of our children's future. The killing must stop if a new
95   future is to begin.
    Fourth and finally, for peace and prosperity and democracy to prevail, you must protect your magnificent natural domain. Africa is mankind's first home. We all came out of Africa. We must
100   preserve the magnificent natural environment that is left. We must manage the water and forest. We must learn to live in harmony with other species. You must learn how to fight drought and famine and global warming. And we must share with you
105   the technology that will enable you to preserve your environment and provide more economic opportunity to your people.

Percentages of African Population by Income Category

	Wealthy	Middle Class	Poor
1980	4.8	25.2	69.0
1990	4.3	27.0	68.7
2000	6.5	27.2	66.3
2010	4.8	34.3	60.8

SOURCE: African Development Bank

11. The most prevalent contrast throughout the speech is that between

(A) America's flawed perceptions of Africa and reality.
(B) Africa's troubled past and Africa's hopeful future.
(C) Ghana's peaceful democracy and the violent dictatorships of other African nations.
(D) Ghana's struggling economy and America's thriving economy.

12. Which choice best summarizes paragraphs 1 and 2 (lines 1 – 26)?

(A) African nations now tend to have elected governments, and improved human rights.
(B) Political and economic improvements in Africa have not yet lifted Africans out of danger.
(C) Ghana must help other African nations meet challenges in education, business, food, and so on.
(D) America needs to embrace both the change and the challenge in Africa.

13. As used in line 9, "elemental" most nearly means

(A) fundamental.
(B) rudimentary.
(C) instrumental.
(D) environmental.

14. Throughout the speech, Clinton refers to Ghana as

(A) a social utopia that America should attempt to replicate.
(B) a troubled nation on the brink of social revolution.
(C) a mirror image of America when it was establishing a democracy.
(D) a model that other African nations should aspire to.

15. Which choice provides the best evidence for the answer to the previous question?

(A) Lines 30 – 34 ("We need to…much to learn")
(B) Lines 40 – 43 ("Today, Ghana…are rising")
(C) Lines 55 – 57 ("First, we want…perfect or complete")
(D) Lines 79 – 82 ("Now is the time…through education")

16. The table suggests that in 1998, when Clinton delivered his speech, African nations were experiencing

(A) widespread prosperity.
(B) slightly increasing average incomes.
(C) affluence in a few regions.
(D) a revolution in social mobility.

17. Which trend mentioned in the passage is best supported by the table?

(A) Lines 11 – 14 ("Now, Africans…Africa")
(B) Lines 41 – 42 ("Democracy is spreading")
(C) Lines 77 – 79 ("For centuries…minerals")
(D) Lines 87 – 89 ("Here in Ghana…harmony")

18. As used in line 66, "honors" most nearly means

(A) obeys.
(B) praises.
(C) worships.
(D) respects.

19. The main rhetorical effect of Clinton's use of "we" throughout the passage is to

(A) distinguish Ghana as a fellow democratic nation.
(B) imply a promise of military aid in case of a threat to Ghana.
(C) emphasize the U.S. pledge to help develop a "new Africa."
(D) focus more on the U.S. than on Africa.

20. In the context of the speech, Clinton regards the social, political, and economic future of Africa

(A) with vitriolic pessimism.
(B) with a combination of optimism and pragmatism.
(C) with admiration that borders on jealousy.
(D) with a mixture of resignation and reverence.

Refer to the passage below to answer questions 21 – 30.

This passage is adapted from naturalist John Burroughs, *The Breath of Life*, originally published in 1915.

line   We read our astronomy and geology in the light of our enormous egotism, and appropriate all to ourselves; but science sees in our appearance here a no more significant event than in the foam
5 and bubbles that whirl and dance for a moment upon the river's current. The bubbles have their reason for being; all the mysteries of molecular attraction and repulsion may be involved in their production; without the solar energy, and the
10 revolution of the earth upon its axis, they would not appear; and yet they are only bubbles upon the river's current, as we are bubbles upon the stream of energy that flows through the universe. Apparently the cosmic game is played for us no
15 more than for the parasites that infest our bodies, or for the frost ferns that form upon our window-panes in winter. The making of suns and systems goes on in the depths of space, and doubtless will go on to all eternity, without any more reference
20 to the vital order than to the chemical compounds.

    The amount of living matter in the universe, so far as we can penetrate it, compared with the non-living, is, in amount, like a flurry of snow that whitens the fields and hills of a spring morning
25 compared to the miles of rock and soil beneath it; and with reference to geologic time it is about as fleeting. In the vast welter* of suns and systems in the heavens above us, we see only dead matter, and most of it is in a condition of glowing metallic
30 vapor. There are doubtless living organisms upon some of the invisible planetary bodies, but they are probably as fugitive and temporary as upon our own world. Much of the surface of the earth is clothed in a light vestment* of life, which, back
35 in geologic time, seems to have more completely enveloped it than at present, as both the Arctic and the Antarctic regions bear evidence in their coal-beds and other fossil remains of luxuriant vegetable growths.

40   Strip the earth of its thin pellicle* of soil, thinner with reference to the mass than is the peel to the apple, and you have stripped it of its life. Or, rob it of its watery vapor and the carbon dioxide in the air, both stages in its evolution, and
45 you have a dead world. The huge globe swings through space only as a mass of insensate* rock. So limited and evanescent* is the world of living matter, so vast and enduring is the world of the non-living. Looked at in this way, in the light of
50 physical science, life, I repeat, seems like a mere passing phase of the cosmic evolution, a flitting and temporary stage of matter which it passes through in the procession of changes on the surface of a cooling planet. Between the fiery mist

55 of the nebula, and the frigid and consolidated globe, there is a brief span, ranging over about one hundred and twenty degrees of temperature, where life appears and organic evolution takes place. Compared with the whole scale of
60 temperature, from absolute zero to the white heat of the hottest stars, it is about a hand's-breadth compared to a mile.

    Life processes cease, but chemical and mechanical processes go on forever. Life is as
65 fugitive and uncertain as the bow in the clouds, and, like the bow in the clouds, is confined to a limited range of conditions. Like the bow, also, it is a perpetual creation, a constant becoming, and its source is not in the matter through which
70 it is manifested, though inseparable from it. The material substance of life, like the rain-drops, is in perpetual flux and change; it hangs always on the verge of dissolution and vanishes when the material conditions fail, to be renewed again
75 when they return. We know—do we not?—that life is as literally dependent upon the sun as is the rainbow, and equally dependent upon the material elements; but whether the physical conditions sum up the whole truth about it, as
80 they do with the bow, is the insoluble question. Science says "Yes," but our philosophy and our religion say "No." The poets and the prophets say "No," and our hopes and aspirations say "No."

* welter – a state of disorder or chaos.
* vestment – a garment or piece of clothing
* pellicle – a thin membrane or film
* insensate – unable to perceive or experience physical sensations
* evanescent – quickly fading or disappearing

Elemental Composition of the Human Body

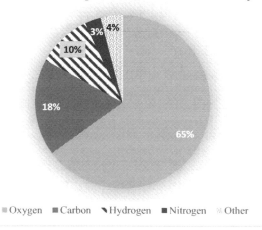

■ Oxygen ■ Carbon ＼ Hydrogen ■ Nitrogen ▨ Other

21. Over the course of the passage, the author presents his argument primarily by

    (A) analogy and reasoning.
    (B) argument and counterargument.
    (C) metaphor and hyperbole.
    (D) appealing to physical laws.

22. As used in line 2, "light" most nearly means

    (A) illumination.
    (B) context.
    (C) ambiance.
    (D) opinion.

23. The author likens living matter to light snow on a "spring morning" (lines 21 – 27) primarily to

    (A) suggest that life is both rare and fleeting on a cosmic scale.
    (B) indicate that spring will always bring new life.
    (C) allude to the conditions that may have created life.
    (D) provide a metaphor for our shallow understanding of life.

24. The author suggests that the amount of life on Earth at present is

    (A) lower than in past geologic periods.
    (B) higher than in past geologic periods.
    (C) comparable to past geologic periods.
    (D) comparable to that on similar planets throughout the universe.

25. As used in line 72, "hangs" most nearly means

    (A) sticks.
    (B) exists.
    (C) prevails.
    (D) depends.

26. According to the chart, the human body is

    (A) comprised of materials not fully understood by scientists.
    (B) composed entirely from only five elements.
    (C) mostly oxygen at the atomic level.
    (D) not unique in terms of elements.

27. Which statement from the passage is best supported by the chart?

    (A) Lines 17 – 20 ("The making…compounds")
    (B) Lines 47 – 49 ("So limited…non-living")
    (C) Lines 54 – 59 ("Between the…place")
    (D) Lines 67 – 70 ("Like the bow…from it")

28. The author would most likely agree that science

    (A) is unable to resolve certain important questions about life.
    (B) has failed the public by not providing answers about life.
    (C) is actually a type of poetic expression.
    (D) consists of an entirely arbitrary set of principles.

29. Which choice provides the best evidence for the answer to the previous question?

    (A) Lines 1 – 6 ("We read our…river's current")
    (B) Lines 33 – 39 ("Much of the…vegetable growths")
    (C) Line 63 – 64 ("Life processes cease…on forever")
    (D) Line 75 – 80 ("We know…question")

30. Based on the passage as a whole, the author's argument is best described as

    (A) an interrogation of traditionally accepted ideals.
    (B) a scientific question approached from a philosophical perspective.
    (C) a poetic treatment of a technical subject.
    (D) a skeptical dismissal based on evidence from the natural world.

Refer to the passage below to answer questions 31 – 41.

This passage is excerpted from the Bill of Rights, which went into effect in 1791. The Bill of Rights is a list of the first ten changes (amendments) to the Constitution of the United States.

line THE Conventions of a number of the
States, having at the time of their adopting the
Constitution, expressed a desire, in order to
prevent misconstruction or abuse of its powers,
5 that further declaratory and restrictive clauses
should be added: And as extending the ground
of public confidence in the Government, will best
ensure the beneficent ends of its institution....

Amendment 1 Congress shall make no
10 law respecting an establishment of religion, or
prohibiting the free exercise thereof; or abridging
the freedom of speech, or of the press; or the right
of the people peaceably to assemble, and to
petition the Government for a redress of
15 grievances.

Amendment 2 A well regulated Militia, being
necessary to the security of a free State, the right
of the people to keep and bear Arms, shall not be
infringed.

20 **Amendment 3** No Soldier shall, in time of
peace be quartered in any house, without the
consent of the Owner, nor in time of war, but in a
manner to be prescribed by law.

Amendment 4 The right of the people to
25 be secure in their persons, houses, papers, and
effects, against unreasonable searches and
seizures, shall not be violated, and no Warrants
shall issue, but upon probable cause, supported
by Oath or affirmation, and particularly
30 describing the place to be searched, and the
persons or things to be seized.

Amendment 5 No person shall be held to
answer for a capital, or otherwise infamous
crime, unless on a presentment or indictment of
35 a Grand Jury, except in cases arising in the land
or naval forces, or in the Militia, when in actual
service in time of War or public danger; nor shall
any person be subject for the same offence to be
twice put in jeopardy of life or limb; nor shall be
40 compelled in any criminal case to be a witness
against himself, nor be deprived of life, liberty, or
property, without due process of law; nor shall
private property be taken for public use, without
just compensation.

45 **Amendment 6** In all criminal prosecutions,
the accused shall enjoy the right to a speedy
and public trial, by an impartial jury of the

State and district wherein the crime shall have
been committed, which district shall have been
50 previously ascertained by law, and to be informed
of the nature and cause of the accusation; to be
confronted with the witnesses against him; to
have compulsory process for obtaining witnesses
in his favor, and to have the Assistance of Counsel
55 for his defense.

Amendment 7 In Suits at common law,
where the value in controversy shall exceed
twenty dollars, the right of trial by jury shall be
preserved, and no fact tried by a jury, shall be
60 otherwise re-examined in any Court of the United
States, than according to the rules of the common
law.

Amendment 8 Excessive bail shall not be
required, nor excessive fines imposed, nor cruel
65 and unusual punishments inflicted.

Amendment 9 The enumeration in the
Constitution, of certain rights, shall not be
construed to deny or disparage others retained by
the people.

70 **Amendment 10** The powers not delegated
to the United States by the Constitution, nor
prohibited by it to the States, are reserved to the
States respectively, or to the people.

31. According to paragraph 1 (lines 1 – 8), Congress included the Bill of Rights primarily to

(A) ensure freedom of speech.
(B) restrict the new government's powers.
(C) ensure that people approve of the government.
(D) halt cases of physical abuse.

32. Based on Amendment 1, the authors wanted to prevent Congress from passing laws that

(A) require people to respect established religions.
(B) ban people from grieving publicly.
(C) ban individuals from owning guns.
(D) ban or establish some religions or religious practices.

33. As used in line 15, "grievances" most nearly means

(A) injustices.
(B) sorrows.
(C) rights.
(D) indignities.

34. In line 27, the authors refer to "Warrants" primarily to

(A) propose a new method for police to keep track of particular searches and seizures.
(B) specify the conditions under which a local judge can authorize a search.
(C) state that official documents must justify and limit searches and seizures beforehand.
(D) emphasize the privacy of homes and belongings, and that authorities should enter respectfully.

35. Amendment 5 strongly suggests that the authors wanted to prevent

(A) civil courts from judging military cases.
(B) arbitrary imprisonment, execution, and confiscation of goods.
(C) government malfunctioning, including mistrials in court cases.
(D) attorneys and bureaucrats from having too much political power.

36. Which choice provides the best evidence for the answer to the previous question?

(A) Lines 35 – 37 ("except in…actual service")
(B) Line 39 – 41 ("nor shall…against himself")
(C) Lines 41 – 42 ("nor be…due process of law")
(D) Line 43 – 45 ("nor shall private property… just compensation")

37. Between Amendment 5 and Amendment 6, the authors' focus shifts from

(A) limits on bringing charges to rights of the accused.
(B) how to form grand juries to the right to have a defense attorney.
(C) exceptions regarding land or naval forces to the importance of juries.
(D) seizing the property of individuals to criminal prosecutions.

38. In Amendment 8, the authors use the words "excessive," "cruel," and "unusual" primarily to

(A) emphasize their strong humanitarian values.
(B) indicate their intent without creating specific rules.
(C) give courts the authority to set bail as well as to fine and punish people.
(D) imply that the new government would be more beneficent than the old.

39. As used in line 68, "construed" most nearly means

(A) deciphered.
(B) interpreted.
(C) simplified.
(D) translated.

40. The passage strongly suggests that the founding document of the new government should

(A) explicitly resolve future grievances.
(B) suggest that an elected government can be trusted.
(C) primarily describe limitations.
(D) serve as a rough draft to be rewritten frequently.

41. Which choice provides the best evidence for the answer to the previous question?

(A) Lines 9 – 15 (Amendment 1)
(B) Lines 20 – 23 (Amendment 3)
(C) Lines 63 – 65 (Amendment 8)
(D) Lines 70 – 73 (Amendment 10)

Refer to the passage below to answer questions 42 – 52.

Passage 1 is adapted from H. W. Conn, *The Story of Germ Life*, originally published in 1915. Passage 2 is adapted from "Guideline for Hand Hygiene in Health-Care Settings," published in 2002.

Passage 1

line   In the study of medicine in the past centuries the only aim has been to discover methods of curing disease; at the present time a large and increasing amount of study is devoted to the
5 methods of preventing disease. Preventive medicine is a development of the last few years, and is based almost wholly upon our knowledge of bacteria. This subject is yearly becoming of more importance. Forewarned is forearmed,
10 and it has been found that to know the cause of a disease is a long step toward avoiding it. As some of our contagious and epidemic diseases have been studied in the light of bacteriological knowledge, it has been found possible to
15 determine not only their cause, but also how infection is brought about, and consequently how contagion may be avoided. Some of the results which have grown up so slowly as to be hardly appreciated are really great triumphs. For
20 instance, bacteriological study has shown that the source of cholera infection in cases of raging epidemics is, in large part at least, our drinking water; and since this has been known, although cholera has twice invaded Europe, and has been
25 widely distributed, it has not obtained any strong foothold or given rise to any serious epidemic except in a few cases where its ravages can be traced to recognized carelessness.

    The study of preventive medicine is yet in its
30 infancy, but it has already accomplished much. It has developed modern systems of sanitation, has guided us in the building of hospitals, given rules for the management of the sick-room which largely prevent contagion from patient to nurse;
35 it has told us what diseases are contagious, and in what way; it has told us what sources of contagion should be suspected and guarded against, and has thus done very much to prevent the spread of disease. Its value is seen in the fact
40 that there has been a constant decrease in the death rate since modern ideas of sanitation began to have any influence, and in the fact that our general epidemics are less severe than in former years, as well as in the fact that more people
45 escape the diseases which were in former times almost universal.

Passage 2

    For generations, handwashing with soap and water has been considered a measure of personal hygiene. The concept of cleansing hands with an
50 antiseptic agent probably emerged in the early 19th century. As early as 1822, a French pharmacist demonstrated that solutions containing chlorides of lime or soda could eradicate the foul odors associated with human
55 corpses and that such solutions could be used as disinfectants and antiseptics.

    In 1961, the U. S. Public Health Service produced a training film that demonstrated handwashing techniques recommended for use
60 by health-care workers (HCWs). At the time, recommendations directed that personnel wash their hands with soap and water for 1–2 minutes before and after patient contact.

    In 1975 and 1985, formal written guidelines on
65 handwashing practices in hospitals were published by CDC (Centers for Disease Control and Prevention). These guidelines recommended handwashing with non-antimicrobial soap between the majority of patient contacts and
70 washing with antimicrobial soap before and after performing invasive procedures or caring for patients at high risk. Use of waterless antiseptic agents (e.g., alcohol-based solutions) was recommended only in situations where sinks were
75 not available.

    In 1988 and 1995, guidelines for handwashing and hand antisepsis were published by the Association for Professionals in Infection Control (APIC). Recommended indications for
80 handwashing were similar to those listed in the CDC guidelines. The 1995 APIC guideline included more detailed discussion of alcohol-based hand rubs and supported their use in more clinical settings than had been recommended
85 in earlier guidelines. In 1995 and 1996, the Healthcare Infection Control Practices Advisory Committee (HICPAC) recommended that either antimicrobial soap or a waterless antiseptic agent be used for cleaning hands upon leaving
90 the rooms of patients with multidrug-resistant pathogens (e.g., vancomycin-resistant enterococci [VRE] and methicillin-resistant *Staphylococcus aureus* [MRSA]). These guidelines also provided recommendations for handwashing and hand
95 antisepsis in other clinical settings, including routine patient care. Although the APIC and HICPAC guidelines have been adopted by the majority of hospitals, adherence of HCWs to recommended handwashing practices has
100 remained low.

42. As used in line 30, "infancy" most nearly means

(A) childhood.
(B) beginnings.
(C) immaturity.
(D) fantasy.

43. Which choice best describes the term "preventive medicine" as it appears in Passage 1?

(A) Lines 1 – 5 ("In the study…preventing disease")
(B) Lines 5 – 8 ("Preventive medicine is…of bacteria")
(C) Lines 9 – 11 ("Forewarned is forearmed… avoiding it")
(D) Lines 11 – 17 ("As some of…be avoided")

44. The reference to the cholera epidemics in lines 19 – 28 primarily serves to

(A) downplay the importance of scientific research to medicine.
(B) warn against the consequences of personal negligence.
(C) demonstrate a major achievement of preventive medicine.
(D) suggest a future free of epidemics.

45. As used in line 54, "foul" most nearly means

(A) avian.
(B) putrid.
(C) illegal.
(D) frightening.

46. The author of Passage 2 mentions "chlorides of lime and soda" (line 53) primarily to

(A) criticize 19th century medicine's crudeness.
(B) describe early forms of disinfectants used by doctors.
(C) update the reader on recent advances in antiseptic technology.
(D) provide an example of a household remedy that was adopted by the scientific community.

47. The progression of hand-washing procedures as outlined in paragraphs 2 and 3 of Passage 2 (lines 57 – 75) is best described as

(A) optional to required.
(B) guidelines to regulations.
(C) disinfectant to antiseptic.
(D) general to specific.

48. The author of Passage 2 strongly suggests that the biggest challenge to improving hand-washing procedures in health-care settings is

(A) providing adequate education.
(B) compelling workers to follow recommendations.
(C) availability of necessary cleaning agents.
(D) opposition from hospital bureaucracies.

49. Which choice provides the best evidence for the answer to the previous question?

(A) Lines 51 – 56 ("As early as…antiseptics")
(B) Lines 72 – 75 ("Use of waterless…not available")
(C) Lines 85 – 91 ("In 1995…pathogens")
(D) Lines 96 – 100 ("Although…remained low")

50. How would the author of Passage 1 most likely respond to the description of the French pharmacist in Passage 2 (lines 51 – 56)?

(A) With surprise, because it refutes the author's assertion that preventive medicine is a 20th century development.
(B) With approval, because he represents an early pioneer in an important movement in public health.
(C) With disdain, because of the crude methods he used to treat disease.
(D) With ambivalence, because it is unrelated to his area of concern.

51. Which choice best states the relationship between the two passages?

(A) Passage 2 provides a public health perspective on a scientific breakthrough described in Passage 1.
(B) Passage 2 describes the failings of a project introduced in Passage 1.
(C) Passage 2 discusses international implications of concerns raised in Passage 1.
(D) Passage 2 criticizes the practicality of the proposals outlined in Passage 1.

52. What information discussed in Passage 1 is represented by Passage 2?

(A) Line 29 – 30 ("The study of…accomplished much")
(B) Lines 32 – 34 ("given rules for…to nurse")
(C) Lines 35 – 39 ("it has told…of disease")
(D) Lines 39 – 44 ("Its value is…former years")

389

Writing and Language Test 4

35 MINUTES, 44 QUESTIONS

Turn to Section 2 of your answer sheet to answer the questions in this section.

DIRECTIONS

Each of the following passages is accompanied by approximately 11 questions. Some questions will require you to revise the passages in order to improve coherence and clarity. Other questions will require you to correct grammatical errors in the passages. Passages may be accompanied by graphs, charts, or tables that you must consider when making revisions. For most questions, you may select the "NO CHANGE" option if you believe that portion of the passage is clear, concise, and grammatically correct as is.

Within the passages, highlighted numbers followed by underlined text indicate which part of the text corresponds with each question. Bracketed numbers [1] indicate sentence number. These bracketed numbers are only relevant to problems that require you to add or rearrange sentences in a paragraph.

Refer to the passage below to answer questions 1 – 11.

Nurse Anesthetist

Most surgeries performed today would not be possible without anesthetic medicine. The medicine blocks **1** pain, and renders patients unconscious, preventing them from going into shock or moving. Although anesthesia has clear benefits, it also carries risks and must be carefully monitored during any instance of use. Thus, the administration of anesthetics has become a specialized field. Medical doctors **2** oversee most anesthetic use in the United States, but increasingly, nurses are taking a share of the responsibility. Doctors in the field are known as "anesthesiologists," while nurses are known as "nurse anesthetists."

1. (A) NO CHANGE
   (B) pain: rendering
   (C) pain, renders
   (D) pain and renders

2. (A) NO CHANGE
   (B) overlook
   (C) watch over
   (D) view

3 Nurse anesthetists can choose to work in diverse settings, from operating rooms or obstetrical wards to **4** emergency rooms. Although they may work under the supervision of a medical doctor, they usually have a high degree of autonomy. Another benefit is that they work with only one patient at a time.

Some nurse anesthetists find personal satisfaction in providing trustworthy care when a patient is most vulnerable. They talk with patients before surgery to **5** ally any anxieties and to determine the best combinations of anesthetics to use. They administer the anesthetic medications and attach patients to necessary machines such as **6** the ventilator, intravenous pumps, and monitoring instruments. They adjust medications and oxygen as needed, and they constantly communicate with the surgeons and surgical nurses. After the procedure, **7** nurse anesthetists must be adept at returning patients to consciousness.

Preparing to take on the responsibilities of a nurse anesthetist takes at least seven years. A candidate must earn a bachelor's degree in nursing and pass a licensing exam to become a registered **8** nurse (RN). Next, he or she must spend at least one year working in an acute care setting. The next step is to return to school and earn a master's degree in nursing anesthetics, and finally **9** passing a national certification exam.

3. Which choice most effectively establishes the main topic of the paragraph?

   (A) The work of administering anesthetics can be stressful.
   (B) Nurses who choose to specialize in anesthetics gain certain advantages.
   (C) Many nurse anesthetists admit that their jobs are occasionally boring.
   (D) Some anesthesiologists object to nurses administering anesthetics.

4. The writer wants to include a setting that provides a strong contrast with the first two examples. Which choice would best accomplish this goal?

   (A) NO CHANGE
   (B) surgery centers
   (C) pediatric hospitals
   (D) specialized dental practices

5. (A) NO CHANGE
   (B) allow
   (C) allay
   (D) purge

6. (A) NO CHANGE
   (B) the ventilator, the intravenous pumps, and the monitoring instruments
   (C) ventilators, intravenous pumps, and monitoring instruments
   (D) a ventilator, an intravenous pump, and a monitoring instrument

7. Which choice maintains the sentence pattern already established in the paragraph?

   (A) NO CHANGE
   (B) they help patients return to consciousness.
   (C) they have been trained to monitor recovery.
   (D) nurse anesthetists are called upon to monitor patients.

8. Which choice most effectively combines the sentences at the underlined portion?

   (A) nurse (RN)—next, he or she must
   (B) nurse (RN), and then he or she
   (C) nurse, known as an "RN," and after that
   (D) nurse (RN), because he or she must

9. (A) NO CHANGE
   (B) passed
   (C) to pass
   (D) to have passed

In the nursing field, anesthesiology is the highest-paid specialty. In fact, nurse anesthetists who earn the median wage for their profession will earn **10** as much as the highest-paid midwives. **11** Already, nurses provide the majority of anesthesia care in rural areas of the U.S. and in U.S. military facilities. The U.S. Bureau of Labor Statistics predicts that the current strong demand for qualified nurse anesthetists will continue to increase. The increase will be driven by the rising median age of the U.S. population, as older people tend to have a greater need for health care services.

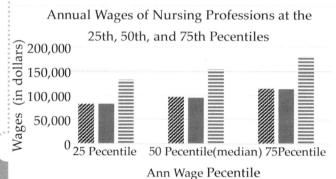

Annual Wages of Nursing Professions at the 25th, 50th, and 75th Pecentiles

Ann Wage Pecentile

⊠Nurse Midwife ■Nurse Practitioner ═Nurse Anethetists

SOURCE: adapted from the Bureau of Labor Statistics, *Occupational Employment Statistics*, "Occupational Employment and Wages, May 2014."

10. Which choice accurately finishes the sentence by interpreting the data in the graph?

(A) NO CHANGE
(B) over 50 percent more than midwives earning the median wage for their profession.
(C) more than the median wages for a midwife and a practitioner combined.
(D) more than double the 25th percentile wages of other nursing professions.

11. The writer is considering deleting the underlined sentence. Should the sentence be kept or deleted?

(A) Kept, because it supports the paragraph's focus on the high demand for nurse anesthetists.
(B) Kept, because it supports the paragraph's focus on places that nurse anesthetists can work.
(C) Deleted, because it does not add information about the job market, the paragraph's focus.
(D) Deleted, because it repeats information previously provided in the passage.

Refer to the passage below to answer questions 12 – 22.

Bat-luring Plants

Flowers have a distinct purpose: to attract wandering organisms that will transfer the flower's pollen for reproduction. Flowering plants need to have pollen carried from anther to stigma, the male and female parts of the flower, **12** in perspective. In some plants, the pollen can be transferred within the flower, but with many it must be carried to another plant's flower. Either way, the plant must attract a mobile assistant, **13** whom it will reward with nectar.

Many flowers have evolved to attract specific assistants. For instance, red, tubular flowers are attractive to hummingbirds, whereas yellow, clustered blossoms appeal to butterflies. **14** Colors in the ultraviolet light spectrum are also visible to butterflies and bees. Once an assistant arrives, it invariably brushes up against sticky pollen while drinking and then **15** transporting pollen whenever it moves to the next source of nectar.

16 A few species of bats drink the nectar of specific flowers with which they have co-evolved. It appears that nectar-drinking in bats developed independently in different hemispheres. In tropical areas of Africa, Asia, and the South Pacific, the trait evolved within the "fruit bat" family Pteropodidae. In the Americas, it evolved within the "leaf-nosed bat" family Phyllostomidae. **17** Across all regions, plants that depend on nectar bats have been developing certain bat-friendly characteristics.

12. (A) NO CHANGE
    (B) respectively
    (C) respectfully
    (D) perceptively

13. (A) NO CHANGE
    (B) who
    (C) that
    (D) him

14. The writer is considering deleting the underlined sentence. Should it be kept or deleted?

    (A) Kept, because it supports the paragraph's topic: colors that attract pollinators.
    (B) Kept, because it adds supporting details about colors that are visible to some pollinators.
    (C) Deleted, because it shifts the focus away from flowers and their adaptations.
    (D) Deleted, because it does not explain how butterflies and bees can see UV light.

15. (A) NO CHANGE
    (B) it transports some pollen as
    (C) transports the pollen when
    (D) it has transported the pollen when

16. Which choice most effectively sets up the information in paragraph 3?

    (A) Hence, plants produce flowers in order to have contact with members of the animal kingdom.
    (B) Nature is replete with surprising species that are the exceptions to the rule.
    (C) What happens when a plant has to compete with too many other flowering plants?
    (D) Most pollinators are insects or birds, but occasionally mammals fill the niche.

17. Which choice maintains the sentence pattern already established in the preceding sentences?

    (A) NO CHANGE
    (B) In both hemispheres, the trait led to the development of bat-friendly flowers.
    (C) Both fruit bats and leaf-nosed bats spurred adaptations in the flowers they visited.
    (D) It appears that nectar-drinking in bats always caused certain flowers to change radically.

Bats are excellent pollinators, **18** giving the plants on which they feed a competitive advantage. Unlike hummingbirds and insects, bats have fur, which holds much larger amounts of **19** pollen, which they use to fly around a wider range than do most other pollinators. Bats also live longer and have more cognitive ability than insects or hummingbirds. They are more likely to remember a flowering plant and return.

On the other hand, flowers must undergo some extreme adaptations to attract bats. The flowers must be sizable to make enough nectar for hungry bats. Bat flowers also bloom at night, when bats are active, so they cannot use reds and yellows to advertise their presence. A more effective way to enhance visibility is to bloom in the open, away from foliage. Flowers might attract bats by protruding above a tree's canopy, or swinging down below it on long stems. As for scent, bats seem to be drawn to musty odors, which many of the flowers have obligingly developed. **20**

A few flowers in the Americas have even adapted to **21** bat's use of echolocation, a process in which bats emit vocalizations and navigate by the echoes they hear. The flowers and leaves of the bats' target plants have developed **22** waxy surfaces and a cupped shape. The dish-like structures reflect sound well, allowing bats to hear the echo of their own soft sound clearly, and to find the flowers with ease.

18. (A) NO CHANGE
    (B) giving plants that depend on bats as pollinators
    (C) so that they can give plants that attract them and provide nectar for them
    (D) which tends to bestow upon their favorite nectar-bearing plants

19. (A) NO CHANGE
    (B) pollen, additionally, bats
    (C) pollen; bats also
    (D) pollen, even though bats

20. Which choice most effectively concludes the paragraph?

    (A) Some researchers describe the odor of bat-attracting flowers as "batty," or smelling like bats.
    (B) All in all, bat-attracting flowers become so highly specialized that butterflies, bees, and even moths are unlikely to find them.
    (C) On the whole, bat-attracting flowers rank among the most unique blossoms on Earth.
    (D) Given all of these constraints, bat-attracting flowers tend to be large, drab, and smelly, but also particularly distinctive.

21. (A) NO CHANGE
    (B) bats' use of
    (C) bats use of
    (D) bats' using

22. (A) NO CHANGE
    (B) a waxy surface and a cupped shape.
    (C) waxy surfaces and cupped shapes.
    (D) surfaces that are waxy and shapes that are cupped.

Refer to the passage below to answer questions 23 – 33.

The Writing of the Ancient Maya

Although there were a number of sophisticated cultures in the Americas before European contact, the culture of the Mayan people stands out in **23** one respect. The Mayans developed a coherent system of reading and writing. Modern scholars suspect that most, if not all, of the Mayans in the elite class **24** were literate.

Mayan culture evolved over many centuries in the rainforests and marshes of Central America, as well as the Yucatán peninsula in what is now Mexico. Early Mayans began forming villages around 2000 BCE. The first evidence of Mayan writing is from around 700 BCE, **25** however it was during the later "Classic Period," from 250 CE to 900 CE, that literacy flourished. During these centuries, culture radiated from powerful, constantly warring city-states. Mayan cities featured pyramids, temples, palaces—and of course a public plaza—all decorated with writing.

23. Which choice most effectively combines the sentences at the underlined portion?

    (A) one respect because the Mayans
    (B) one respect, the Mayans
    (C) one respect: the Mayans
    (D) one respect which is that the Mayans

24. (A) NO CHANGE
    (B) were literary.
    (C) was literary.
    (D) was literate.

25. (A) NO CHANGE
    (B) and literacy flourished during the Mayan Classic Period, from 250 CE to 900 CE.
    (C) but from 250 CE to 900 CE, which was the "Classic Period" for the Maya, was when literacy flourished.
    (D) and by 250 CE to 900 CE, the Mayan Classic Period saw the flourishing of literacy.

[1] The Mayans also produced books that are now referred to as "codices," the plural of "codex." [2] Codices consisted of bark paper folded like an accordion; when unfolded, the pages revealed painted art and text. [3] Unfortunately, the codices were susceptible to mold in the damp **26** climate as the agricultural bounty that had supported an elite class declined. [4] Only three codices survive today **27** because—ironically—Spaniards sent them to Europe. [5] While many Mayan people continued to live in the same territory as their **28** forebears, the unique Mayan writing system was completely forgotten. **29**

[1] During the 19th century, scholars began trying to decode the words of the ancient Maya. [2] But the biggest roadblock for scholars was recognizing that some of the symbols represent phonetic sounds while others represent complete ideas. [3] One challenge was simply learning the ancient Mayan language; today there are 29 modern Mayan languages that have ancient Mayan dialects as their roots. [4] Moreover, scribes seem to have used at least two languages in the texts. [5] Occasionally, Mayan scribes even used symbols in an artistic, nonstandard way, adding yet another mystery **30** for presently working translators to solve now. **31**

26. (A) NO CHANGE
    (B) climate. The agricultural bounty that had supported an elite class declined.
    (C) climate. Slowly the southern lowland city-states' populations outgrew their ability to produce food; water shortages may have contributed to the problem.
    (D) climate. The city-states of the southern lowlands declined after the 8th century CE, and writing appears to have declined with them.

27. (A) NO CHANGE
    (B) ironic because Spaniards sent them to Europe.
    (C) being sent ironically to Europe by Spaniards.
    (D) in Europe because of Spaniards sending them there, ironically.

28. (A) NO CHANGE
    (B) antecedents,
    (C) descendants,
    (D) lineage,

29. The writer wants to add the following sentence to paragraph 3.

    After Spain claimed the continent in the 16th century, a Spanish priest named Diego de Landa began the practice of burning any Mayan codices he could find.

    The most logical placement for the sentence is immediately

    (A) after sentence 2.
    (B) after sentence 3.
    (C) after sentence 4.
    (D) after sentence 5.

30. (A) NO CHANGE
    (B) for modern translators to solve contemporaneously.
    (C) for modern-day translators to solve.
    (D) for current modern-day translators to solve.

31. To make paragraph 4 more logical, sentence 2 should be placed

    (A) where it is now.
    (B) before sentence 4.
    (C) after sentence 4.
    (D) after sentence 5.

Like English, ancient Mayan writing is read from left to right and from top to bottom, but unlike English, each line consists of only two words. Each word is represented by a square that contains up to five glyphs (symbols). The glyphs are either symbols of abstract concepts, or they resemble animals, humans, **32** or objects, and through painstaking work, scholars have identified 800 glyphs, though only about 300 were in use at any one time.

Scholars are finding that much of the text on monuments describes events related to particular leaders, such as birthdates and military conquests. The three surviving books primarily contain almanac-style information about astronomy, agricultural cycles, and religious rituals, indicating that they were resources for priests or other high officials. **33** One can see clearly that Mayans used writing to preserve practical and cultural knowledge.

32. (A) NO CHANGE
    (B) or objects, nevertheless through
    (C) or objects—through
    (D) or objects. Through

33. (A) NO CHANGE
    (B) The translations demonstrate that
    (C) One could say that clearly,
    (D) Therefore, it can be suggested that

Refer to the passage below to answer questions 34 – 44.

The Song of Silence

John Cage's *4'33"* is a unique composition, unprecedented at the time of its first performance. The piece, which contains no notes, lasts for four minutes and thirty-three seconds, during which the performers do not play any instruments. **34** For this reason, many liken the piece to four and a half minutes of silence. However, Cage was convinced that any combination of sounds arranged intentionally could be considered musical. Despite criticism, *4'33"* has become Cage's most famous composition and remains an important part of contemporary art.

The idea for the piece had existed in Cage's previous **35** works, many of them include extended segments of silence. For example, **36** *Concerto for Prepared Piano and Orchestra* has no lyrical component, while *Duet for Two Flutes* lacks rhythm. Some of Cage's other compositions also incorporate silence as an important thematic element. For him, the silences were meant to **37** highlight atmospheric sounds for the listener; he never actually attempted to create the complete absence of sound with any of his songs.

Cage had toyed with the idea of producing an entire song with no score **38** and no recorded notes for many years. However, two events in 1951 prompted him to transform his idea into a performance.

39 Firstly, Cage visited an anechoic chamber—a soundproofed room whose walls absorb all atmospheric noises. Even in this completely "silent" chamber, Cage was aware of the sound of his nervous and circulatory systems. True silence, Cage believed, is impossible for humans to experience, and *4'33"* was meant to convey this idea **40** with the intentional use of environmental sounds as music.

34. The writer is considering deleting the underlined sentence. Should the writer remove this selection?

(A) Yes, because the passage focuses only on praise for *4'33"*.
(B) Yes, because John Cage never intended for *4'33"* to be interpreted in this way.
(C) No, because it reveals John Cage's motivation for writing *4'33"*.
(D) No, because it provides background for the information to follow.

35. (A) NO CHANGE
(B) works, many of them including
(C) works, including
(D) works, many of which include

36. Which choice most effectively illustrates the author's previous statement?

(A) NO CHANGE
(B) *Duet for Two Flutes* includes a complicated melody and unusual time signature.
(C) *Duet for Two Flutes* begins silently, and *Concerto for Prepared Piano and Orchestra* ends with silence.
(D) *Concerto for Prepared Piano and Orchestra* utilizes atypical instrumentation.

37. (A) NO CHANGE
(B) identify
(C) refer
(D) mention

38. (A) NO CHANGE
(B) and no melodies
(C) and no progressions
(D) DELETE the underlined portion.

39. (A) NO CHANGE
(B) First things first,
(C) In the beginning,
(D) Right away,

40. (A) NO CHANGE
(B) through
(C) by
(D) DELETE the underlined portion.

41 Then Cage went to a museum displaying artist Robert Rauschenberg's 1951 "White Paintings." Each painting is not meant to be perceived as a blank canvas, but rather a reflection of the conditions in which it isdisplayed. The appearance of the "blank" paintings **42** changes under different light conditions. This quality inspired Cage to create a musical **43** analogue with *4'33"*, a piece that changes based on the environment in which it is performed.

Although controversial, *4'33"* has greatly influenced modern music. Numerous artists have performed the piece using a variety of instruments. Some, including **44** the rock and jazz icon Frank Zappa, have actually recorded versions of *4'33"* for their albums. One group even created a remix of the work that was broadcast on public radio. This continued interest in the piece ensures its legacy.

41. Which choice provides the best transition to the information in the paragraph?
    (A) NO CHANGE
    (B) Cage was also deeply impressed by.
    (C) Secondly, Cage visited an art exhibit, seeing.
    (D) Could "true silence" occur in a different medium? Cage saw

42. (A) NO CHANGE
    (B) change
    (C) changed
    (D) had changed

43. (A) NO CHANGE
    (B) homologue
    (C) prologue
    (D) monologue

44. (A) NO CHANGE
    (B) a
    (C) one
    (D) DELETE the underlined portion.

Math Test 4 – No Calculator

25 MINUTES, 20 QUESTIONS

Turn to Section 3 of your answer sheet to answer the questions in this section.

DIRECTIONS

For questions **1 – 15**, find the solution to each problem and select the most appropriate answer from the choices provided. For questions **16 – 20**, find the solution to each problem and write your answer in the space provided. You may use the blank space in your test booklet for scratch work.

NOTES

1. The use of a calculator on any part of this section is forbidden.
2. Unless otherwise indicated, all variables and expressions used in this test represent real numbers.
3. Unless otherwise indicated, all figures used in this test are drawn to scale.
4. Unless otherwise indicated, all figures used in this test lie on a plane.
5. Unless specified otherwise, a given function, f, has the domain the set of all real numbers x for which $f(x)$ is a real number.

REFERENCE

$$A = \frac{1}{2}bh$$

$$c^2 = a^2 + b^2$$

Special Right Triangles

$$A = \pi r^2$$
$$C = 2\pi r$$

$$A = \ell w$$

$$V = \ell wh$$

$$V = \pi r^2 h$$

$$V = \frac{4}{3}\pi r^3$$

$$V = \frac{1}{3}\pi r^2 h$$

$$V = \frac{1}{3}\ell wh$$

The arc of a circle is 360 degrees or 2π radians.
A triangle has angles that sum to 180 degrees.

1. David has a total of $3m$ books for sale at n dollars each. He sells all but p books. Which of the following represents the total dollar amount he received in sales?

   (A) $n(3m - p)$

   (B) $n(p - 3m)$

   (C) $pn - 3m$

   (D) $3m - pn$

2. If $6x + 3 = 21$, what is 2^x ?

   (A) 8

   (B) 12

   (C) 16

   (D) 32

3.

$$4Dgh$$

   A bartender uses the formula above to calculate his fee for a party with g guests drinking an estimated 4 drinks per hour for h hours. The constant D is a measurement of the price per drink using a specific label of liquor. Which of the following will change if the bartender is asked to use a more expensive brand of liquor?

   (A) The coefficient 4

   (B) g

   (C) h

   (D) D

4.   TRI–SCHOOL MEET

	Event I	Event II	Event III
1st Place (5 points)	C	A	
2nd Place (3 points)	A		
3rd Place (1 point)	B		

   In a three-school meet, schools A, B, and C each entered one team for each of three events. If the score card above is completed and there are no ties in any event, what is the greatest possible number of points by which B's total score could exceed A's total score?

   (A) 0

   (B) 2

   (C) 4

   (D) 8

5.

$$-6 < 2x + 4 \le 0$$

   What are all the values of x which satisfy the above inequality?

   (A) $-5 < x \le -2$

   (B) $-3 < x \le -2$

   (C) $2 \le x < 3$

   (D) $2 \le x < 5$

6. Given $f(x) = -3x^2 + 5$ for all real numbers x, what is the range of the function?

   (A) All real numbers less than or equal to 5

   (B) All integers less than or equal to 5

   (C) All nonnegative real numbers

   (D) All nonnegative integers

7. If $f(x) = x^2$, and $g(x) = x^2 - 6x + 14$, which of the following best describes the graph of $g(x)$ relative to $f(x)$?

   (A) Raised 5 units and shifted 3 units to the left

   (B) Raised 5 units and shifted 3 units to the right

   (C) Same vertical position shifted 3 units to the left

   (D) Raised 14 units and shifted 6 units to the right

8. Jack and Jill went to Burger King. Jack bought 2 hamburgers and 3 shakes for $4.21 while Jill bought 3 hamburgers and 2 shakes for $5.24. If h is the number of hamburgers and s is the number of shakes purchased, which of the following equations represents the sum of Jack's and Jill's purchases.

   (A) $(2h - 3s) + (3h - 2s) = \$1.03$

   (B) $6h + 6s = \$9.03$

   (C) $5h + 5s = \$9.45$

   (D) $\dfrac{5s}{5h} = \$9.45$

9. Which of the following describes the solution set of the equation $\sqrt{x+4} = x$?

   (A) There is one solution; it is a rational number.

   (B) There are two solutions; they are rational numbers.

   (C) There is one solution; it is an irrational number.

   (D) There are two solutions; they are irrational numbers.

10. An object is fired upward at an initial velocity (v_0) of 240 feet per second. The height, $h(t)$, of the object as a function of time is $h(t) = v_0 t - 16t^2$. How long will it take the object to hit the ground after takeoff?

    (A) 16 seconds

    (B) 15 seconds

    (C) 7.5 seconds

    (D) 4 seconds

11. If $f(x) = x + 3$ and $g(x) = \dfrac{x^2 - 9}{x - 3}$, which of the following statements are true about the graphs of f and g in the coordinate plane?

    I. The graphs are exactly the same.
    II. The graphs are the same except when $x = 3$.
    III. The graphs have an infinite number of points in common.

    (A) I only

    (B) II only

    (C) I and III

    (D) II and III

12. There are 6 people in a room. Each person shakes hands with everyone else in the room. What is the total number of handshakes?

    (A) 6

    (B) 12

    (C) 15

    (D) 30

13. Paul is selling concert tickets at $5 for adults and $2 for students. At the end of the day, he has sold 10 tickets but is unsure if he collected $39 or $41. Can the number of student tickets sold be determined? If so, how many were sold?

(A) Yes, 3 were sold.

(B) Yes, 4 were sold.

(C) Yes, 5 were sold.

(D) No, it cannot be determined.

14. The front, side, and bottom faces of a rectangular solid have areas of 24, 8, and 3 centimeters squared, respectively. What is the volume of the solid in cubic centimeters?

(A) 24

(B) 96

(C) 192

(D) 288

15. What is the equation for the graph below?

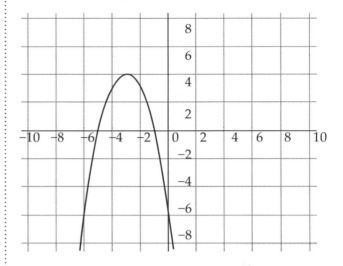

(A) $y = (x + 3)^2 + 4$

(B) $y = -x^2 - 6x - 5$

(C) $y = (x - 3)^2 + 4$

(D) $y = -x^2 - 6x - 9$

DIRECTIONS

For questions **16 – 20**, find the solution to the problem and enter your answer as demonstrated below.

1. Only the answer that is bubbled in on the answer sheet will be credited. The blank spaces above the bubbles are for you to record your answers for accuracy.
2. Only fill in one bubble in any given column.
3. None of the answers on this portion of the test are negative values.
4. If a problem appears to have more than one answer, only enter one answer. If the answer you enter is one of the correct solutions, you will receive full credit for that question.
5. If the correct answer can be expressed as a mixed number, it must be entered as a decimal or an improper fraction.
6. If the correct answer is a decimal that cannot fit into the grid space, you must fill the grid with enough digits to completely fill the space. The number can be rounded or simply shortened but must fill every blank space.

Answer: $\frac{5}{36}$ Answer: 4.5

Write answer → in boxes.

← Fraction line
← Decimal point

Grid in result.

Acceptable ways to grid $\frac{1}{6}$ are:

Answer: 302 – either position is correct

NOTES

Begin entering answers in any column that accommodates your answer. If you do not need a column do not enter anything in that column.

16. The quadratic $x^2 - x = 2$ has two solutions. What is the larger of the two solutions?

ANSWER: _____

17. If $\dfrac{3}{x-3} + \dfrac{5}{2x-6} = \dfrac{11}{12}$, then the value of $2x - 6$ is

ANSWER: _____

18. If $x + y = 11$, $y + z = 14$ and $x + z = 13$, what is the value of $x + y + z$?

ANSWER: _____

19. In a weight-lifting competition, the total weight of Peter's two lifts was 750 pounds. If twice the weight of his first lift was 300 pounds more than the weight of his second lift, what was the weight, in pounds, of his first lift?

ANSWER: _____

20. A baseball team has won 15 games and lost 9. If these games represent $\dfrac{1}{6}$ of all games to be played, how many more games must the team win to achieve a win percentage of 75% by the end of the season?

ANSWER: _____

STOP

Math Test 4 – Calculator

 55 MINUTES, 38 QUESTIONS

Turn to Section 4 of your answer sheet to answer the questions in this section.

DIRECTIONS

For questions **1 – 30,** find the solution to each problem and select the most appropriate answer from the choices provided. For questions **31 – 38,** find the solution to each problem and write your answer in the space provided. You may use the blank space in your test booklet for scratch work.

NOTES

1. The use of a calculator on any part of this section is allowed.
2. Unless otherwise indicated, all variables and expressions used in this test represent real numbers.
3. Unless otherwise indicated, all figures used in this test are drawn to scale.
4. Unless otherwise indicated, all figures used in this test lie on a plane.
5. Unless specified otherwise, a given function, f, has the domain the set of all real numbers x for which $f(x)$ is a real number.

REFERENCE

$A = \frac{1}{2}bh \qquad c^2 = a^2 + b^2 \qquad$ Special Right Triangles $\qquad \begin{array}{l} A = \pi r^2 \\ C = 2\pi r \end{array} \qquad A = \ell w$

$V = \ell wh \qquad V = \pi r^2 h \qquad V = \frac{4}{3}\pi r^3 \qquad V = \frac{1}{3}\pi r^2 h \qquad V = \frac{1}{3}\ell wh$

The arc of a circle is 360 degrees or 2π radians.
A triangle has angles that sum to 180 degrees.

1.

PROPORTIONS SPENT ON RAW MATERIALS BY
FACTORY Y IN 1987

Material	Percent (%)
Paper	28
Wood	32
Metal	40

In the table above, if the total amount spent on wood and paper by Factory Y in 1987 was $277,200, how much was spent on paper?

(A) $77,616

(B) $129,360

(C) $147,840

(D) $184,800

2. Which of the following is the equation of a line with x-intercept $(6, 0)$ and y-intercept $(0, 15)$?

(A) $y = \dfrac{5}{2}x - 15$

(B) $y = -\dfrac{5}{2}x - 15$

(C) $y = \dfrac{5}{2}x + 15$

(D) $y = -\dfrac{5}{2}x + 15$

3. Six peaches of a certain variety weigh collectively 1.5 pounds. Twenty pounds are being sold for $24.00. At this rate, what is the cost, in dollars, of one dozen peaches?

(A) $0.30

(B) $1.80

(C) $3.60

(D) $7.20

4. Seven students played a game. Their scores, from lowest to highest, were as follows: 20, 30, 50, 70, 80, 80, and 90.

Which of the following is true of the scores?

I. The average score is above 70.

II. The median is greater than 70.

III. The mode is greater than 70.

(A) None

(B) III only

(C) I and II only

(D) II and III only

5. Which ordered pair is in the solution set of the system of inequalities $y \leq 3x + 1$ and $x - y > 1$?

(A) $(-1, -2)$

(B) $(1, 2)$

(C) $(2, -1)$

(D) $(-1, 2)$

6. What is the range of the function defined by $f(x) = \dfrac{1}{x} + 2$?

(A) All real numbers

(B) All real numbers except $-\dfrac{1}{2}$

(C) All real numbers except 0

(D) All real numbers except 2

7. The United States' deer population increases 30% every 20 years. If the deer population is x in the year 2000, what factor of x will the deer population be in the year 2080?

(A) 2.197

(B) 2.636

(C) 2.5

(D) 2.856

Question 8 refers to the following information.

Height/Weight Boys age 12

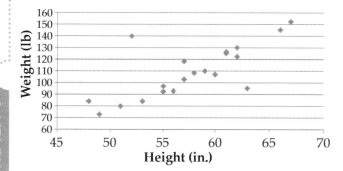

8. Height and weight information was taken for 22 twelve-year-old boys in the same 7th grade class. The data is represented in the scatterplot above. Which of the following best represents the relationship between height (x) and weight (y) in this group?

(A) $y = 4x + b$

(B) $y = 0.1x^2 - 200$

(C) $y^2 = x - 1,000$

(D) $y = -3.5x + b$

9. The IRS has set a standard price of 56 cents per mile driven by any vehicle used for business purposes. Flora, a traveling nurse, calculates the deductible expenses she may claim towards her annual income taxes. After consulting her odometer, Sarah finds that she can deduct $28,224 from her annual income taxes. How many deductible miles did Sarah drive in the past year?

(A) 15,805

(B) 28,224

(C) 50,400

(D) 72,056

10. A student solves the following system of equations using the substitution method:
$$2x - y = 5$$
$$3x + 2y = -3$$

Which of the following expresses the first step in the student's substitution process?

(A) $3x + 2(2x - 5) = -3$

(B) $3x + 2(5 - 2x) = -3$

(C) $3(y + \frac{5}{2}) + 2y = -3$

(D) $3(\frac{5}{2} - y) + 2y = -3$

11. The quadratic equation $2x^2 + 7x + 5 = 0$ has two solutions. What is the sum of these two solutions?

(A) -7

(B) $-\dfrac{3}{2}$

(C) $-\dfrac{7}{2}$

(D) $\dfrac{7}{2}$

12. At how many points do the curves $y = x^2$ and $y = x^{2003}$ intersect?

    (A) 3
    (B) 2
    (C) 1
    (D) 0

13. When Robert was born, his grandfather invested $1,000 in a college education fund for him. The amount of money in the account, A, is given by the formula $A = P(1 + r)^t$, where P is the principal, r is the interest rate, and t is the time in years. At an interest rate of 4.5%, compounded annually, approximately how much money is in the fund when Robert is 18?

    (A) $1,810
    (B) $2,200
    (C) $3,680
    (D) $18,810

14. In 1980, the price of a certain antique car was 30 percent more than in 1975. In 1985 the price of the same car was 50 percent more than in 1980. The price of the car in 1985 is what percent greater than in 1975?

    (A) 40%
    (B) 45%
    (C) 90%
    (D) 95%

15. In 2013, the United States Postal Service charged $0.46 to mail a letter weighing up to 1 ounce and $0.20 per ounce for each additional ounce. Which function represents the cost in dollars, $c(z)$, of mailing a letter weighing z ounces, where z is an integer greater than 1?

    (A) $c(z) = 0.46z + 0.20$
    (B) $c(z) = 0.46(z - 1) + 0.20$
    (C) $c(z) = 0.20z + 0.46$
    (D) $c(z) = 0.20(z - 1) + 0.46$

16. A company decides to give every one of its employees a $1,000 raise. What happens to the mean and median of the salaries as a result?

    (A) The mean stays the same; the median increases by $1,000.
    (B) The mean increases by $1,000; the median stays the same.
    (C) The mean and median are the same.
    (D) The mean and median both increase by $1,000.

17. Which of the following is true of the intersection of the lines $4x - y = 7$ and $x + 3y = 5$?

    (A) They intersect at a point (x, y); both x and y are positive.
    (B) They intersect at a point (x, y); both x and y are negative.
    (C) They intersect at a point (x, y); x is positive, y is negative.
    (D) The lines do not intersect.

18. If $2a = b$, $3b = c$, and $a + c = 70$, what is $a + b + c$?

    (A) 30
    (B) 60
    (C) 70
    (D) 90

19. If $f(x, y) = \dfrac{1}{4}x - y$, which of the following is equal to $f(8, 3)$?

    (A) $f(12, 2)$
    (B) $f(16, 6)$
    (C) $f(2, 1)$
    (D) $f(-12, -2)$

20. If you have 16 milliliters (mL) of a 24% glucose solution, how much of a 50% glucose solution must be added to this solution to get a final mixture with a glucose concentration of 35%?

    (A) 10.7 mL
    (B) 11.7 mL
    (C) 12.3 mL
    (D) 12.7 mL

21.

TRASH COLLECTION BY
DISTRICT IN MAY 2015

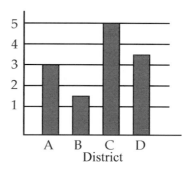

The graph above represents trash collection in four districts in a city in a single month. The total trash collected in the four districts is 130,000 tons. Which of the following could label the vertical axis?

    (A) Trash collected (tons)
    (B) Trash collected (thousands of tons)
    (C) Trash collected (tens of thousands of tons)
    (D) Trash collected (hundreds of thousands of tons)

PRACTICE TEST 4

22. Water is flowing into a basement at a rate of 50 liters per hour. The water can be bailed out at a rate of 60 liters per hour. If the water flows for two hours before anyone begins removing it, how long will it take to bail out all the water in the basement?

    (A) 10 hours

    (B) 20 hours

    (C) 30 hours

    (D) 40 hours

23.

**Investment Portfolio Valued
at $500,000**

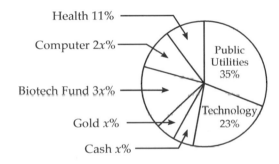

Health 11%

Computer 2x%

Biotech Fund 3x%

Gold x%

Cash x%

Public Utilities 35%

Technology 23%

Note: Figure not to scale

The graph shows how $500,000 is invested. Twenty percent of the amount invested in technology stocks above is reinvested in health stocks. How much total money is invested in health stocks after the transfer?

    (A) $155,000

    (B) $130,000

    (C) $90,000

    (D) $78,000

24. Peter went upstream in a canoe at an average speed of 12 miles per hour. He returned by the same route at an average speed of 18 miles per hour. What was Peter's average speed for the round trip, in miles per hour?

    (A) 14.0

    (B) 14.4

    (C) 15.0

    (D) 15.6

Questions 25 and 26 relate to the information in the table below.

An alien travels to several planets in our solar system and weighs itself on the surface of each with the following results:

	Mercury	Venus	Earth	Mars
Weight (lbs.)	64.2	154.1	170	64

25. Which of the following statements regarding the data above is true?

    (A) Its range is greater than its mean.

    (B) Its range is greater than its median.

    (C) Its mean is greater than its median.

    (D) NONE of the above.

26. Being an admirer of physicist Isaac Newton, the alien decides to calculate how man newtons of force (N) it exerts on Earth. The alien does so using the formula N = kg × 9.80665m/s^2. Given that 1 pound = 0.4536 kilograms (kg.), and that 9.80665 meters/second^2 (m/s^2) is the average gravity of Earth, how many newtons of force does the alien exert on Earth?

(A) 29.6

(B) 756.2

(C) 1,541.3

(D) 3,675.3

27. An equation of the circle with center (2, –3) and diameter 4 is

(A) $x^2 + y^2 - 4x + 6y + 9 = 0$

(B) $x^2 + y^2 - 4x + 6y = 0$

(C) $x^2 + y^2 - 4x + 6y + 13 = 0$

(D) $x^2 + y^2 - 4x - 6y + 9 = 0$

28. If $f(x) = x^3 + x^2 + 2x + 6$, then $f(i) =$

(A) $2i$

(B) $2 + i$

(C) $5 - i$

(D) $5 + i$

29. At Springfield University, there are 10,000 students, half of whom are male and half of whom are female. Each student is enrolled either in the Arts Program or the Science Program, but not in both. Sixty percent of students are in the Arts Program, and 40% of the students in the Science Program are male. Approximately what percent of students in the Arts Program are female?

(A) 26%

(B) 43%

(C) 50%

(D) 52%

30.

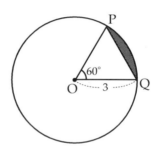

In the figure above, the radius of the circle is 3 and ∠POQ = 60°. What is the perimeter of the shaded region?

(A) $3 + \dfrac{\pi}{2}$

(B) $\sqrt{3} + \pi$

(C) $3 + \pi$

(D) $2\sqrt{3} + \pi$

DIRECTIONS

For questions **31 – 38**, find the solution to the problem and enter your answer as demonstrated below.

1. Only the answer that is bubbled in on the answer sheet will be credited. The blank spaces above the bubbles are for you to record your answers for accuracy.
2. Only fill in one bubble in any given column.
3. None of the answers on this portion of the test are negative values.
4. If a problem appears to have more than one answer, only enter one answer. If the answer you enter is one of the correct solutions, you will receive full credit for that question.
5. If the correct answer can be expressed as a mixed number, it must be entered as a decimal or an improper fraction.
6. If the correct answer is a decimal that cannot fit into the grid space, you must fill the grid with enough digits to completely fill the space. The number can be rounded or simply shortened but must fill every blank space.

Answer: $\frac{5}{36}$ Answer: 4.5

Write answer → in boxes.
← Fraction line
← Decimal point

Grid in result.

Acceptable ways to grid $\frac{1}{6}$ are:

NOTES

Begin entering answers in any column that accommodates your answer. If you do not need a column do not enter anything in that column.

Answer: 302 – either position is correct

31. A jar with a 3-gallon capacity is used to fill a tank with water. The jar is fully filled with water from a faucet, and the jar is then taken to the tank where the water is emptied into the tank. If the tank's capacity is 91 gallons, what is the minimum number of trips needed to fill the tank?

ANSWER: _____

32. To find the image length, L, of a 4–foot–tall object in a spherical mirror with a focal length of 2 feet, the formula $L = 4\left(\dfrac{2}{a-2}\right)^2$ can be used, where a is the distance, in feet, of the object from the mirror. What is the image length, in feet, of the object when it is 1.5 feet away from the mirror?

ANSWER: _____

33. Solve the following for x:
$$\frac{5}{3}(x-3) = \frac{3}{2}(x-2)$$

ANSWER: _____

34. A box contains 4 red balls and 8 white balls. How much greater is the probability of simultaneously drawing 2 white balls at random than simultaneously drawing 2 red balls at random?

ANSWER: _____

35.

$$h = 70 + 5m$$

A runner has a resting heart rate of 70 beats per minute. For every minute he runs, his heart rate increases by a constant number of beats per minute. The runner's heart rate, h, is modeled by the equation above as a function of m minutes of running. On the basis of this equation, what is the increase in heart rate for every five minutes of running?

ANSWER: _____

36. In a car race, David gives Peter a head start of 10 miles. David's car goes 80 miles per hour, and Peter's car goes 60 miles per hour. How long, in minutes, will it take David to catch up to Peter if they leave their starting marks at the same time?

ANSWER: _____

Questions 37 and 38 refer to the information below.

Employment in Brazil, 1997
Total Labor Force: 65.5 million

	% Employed	
	Men	**Women**
Service	42	66
Industry	23	14
Business	15	15
Civil Construction	11	0
Other	9	5

37. **PART 1**
Assuming the workforce is split equally into men and women, how many men, in millions, in Brazil work in Industry?

ANSWER: _____

38. **PART 2**
In reality, men held 61% of all jobs in Brazil in 1997. With this in mind, what is the probability that a worker selected at random will be a woman who is employed in Business? (Round your answer to the nearest percent.)

ANSWER: _____

Essay Test 4*

50 MINUTES, Prompt-based essay

Turn to Section 5 of your answer sheet to answer the question in this section.

DIRECTIONS

As you read the passage below, consider how Ricki Lewis uses
- evidence, such as facts or examples, to support claims.
- reasoning to develop ideas and to connect claims and evidence.
- stylistic or persuasive elements, such as word choice or appeals to emotion, to add power to the ideas expressed.

This passage is adapted from Ricki Lewis, "Dan Brown's Inferno: Good Plot, Bad Science." published in 2014.

When Dan Brown's latest novel, *Inferno*, was published last summer, several people insisted I read it – because it's about an insane geneticist. So when my local library asked me to give a talk about a book with genetics in the plot, I chose *Inferno*. The talk is next week, and I had great fun marking up the book.

Dan Brown gets an A, as usual, for writing style. He keeps the reader turning the pages. But this time, the plot is a stretch, and he gets an F in genetics.

I learned that scientific accuracy shouldn't get in the way of telling a good story at the Catalyst Workshop at the American Film Institute, where every summer a dozen scientists learn screenwriting from the pros. I went in 2005. After a week of dissecting *The Day After Tomorrow*, an exciting end-of-the-world thriller that seems all too possible with the recent crazy weather, we all concluded, as our instructors had said from the outset, that in entertainment, scientific accuracy just doesn't matter. So it's okay if the magnetic poles suddenly switch and a person recovers from septicemia* in a few hours with one shot of penicillin. I love that film.

As anyone who's read Dan Brown's *The Da Vinci Code* and the *Lost Symbol* knows, protagonist Robert Langdon is a Harvard professor specializing in symbology who is summoned for emergencies that require him to rocket through Europe running from bad guys and heading off global disasters, while following clues and cues in art. He's always called "Professor." Many of my friends are professors, and I have an adjunct title myself, and we don't call ourselves Professor. Maybe it's different in the art world.

Having no time for anything other than math and science in college, I admit to being a dunce about the art part of the Dan Brown books. But I can comment on the science.

Early foreshadowing of superficial science is on page 36, where the author confuses cerebellum with cerebrum, and PET scans with CT scans. And he makes the classic trio of errors later on by referring to human cell walls (animals are the only types of organisms without cell walls), "a bacteria," and each of us

having our own genetic codes (the correspondence between RNA codons and amino acids is universal. We have individual genome sequences.)

But the worst illogic comes towards the end.

Tethered beneath the surface of a gloomy underground lagoon lies a bag filled with yellowish-brown goop that holds enough of a mysterious virus to render much of humanity infertile – somehow. The investigators have set up polymerase chain reaction (PCR) devices throughout the area, which all start blinking red to indicate detection of the "never-before-seen viral pathogen." What did they use for primers*? You can't amplify a nucleic acid using the PCR without having a smidgeon of DNA or RNA from known pathogens.

Evolution is also handled oddly, although the protagonist claims to be skilled in matters Darwinian. He and the docs confuse natural selection and survival of the fittest, which deal with reproductive success, with genetic enhancement to "advance the species" and "create better humans." I think Brown means that those who survive to have successful sex after the viral scourge will then, either by the viral DNA or some new genetic treatment, churn out kids who get high SAT scores and humanity will be saved. The long-awaited explanation of the science is delivered in a style I call hand-waving — throw out a bunch of terms that presumably readers won't recognize to make it sound like it makes sense. It doesn't.

It's great that a novelist as acclaimed as Dan Brown would base a plotline around genetics. But he squandered an opportunity to teach the public about the good that geneticists do. Why not a subplot of a sick kid? A family that uses the terrifying "germline genetic engineering" to vanquish a terrible genetic disease?

The last thing our science-phobic world needs is another mad scientist—even a fictional one.

*septicemia—a type of infection in which bacteria enters the bloodstream
*primers—a molecule that induces the creation of a larger molecule

Write an essay in which you explain how Ricki Lewis builds an argument to persuade her audience that the misuse of scientific concepts in literature is problematic. In your essay, analyze how the author uses one or more of the features listed in the box above (or features of your own choice) to strengthen the logic and persuasiveness of her argument. Be sure that your analysis focuses on the most relevant features of the passage.
Your essay should not explain whether you agree with the author's claims, but rather explain how the author builds an argument to persuade her audience.

* Sample responses at www.kallisedu.com

KALLIS

SAT® Practice Test #5

IMPORTANT REMINDERS:

1

When you take the official SAT, you will need to use a No. 2 pencil. Do not use a pen or a mechanical pencil.

2

On the official SAT, sharing any of the questions on the test violates the College Board's policies and may result in your scores being canceled.

(This cover is modeled after the cover you'll see when you take the official SAT.)

Reading Test 5

⏱ **65 MINUTES, 52 QUESTIONS**

Turn to Section 1 of your answer sheet to answer the questions in this section.

DIRECTIONS Each passage or pair of passages is accompanied by 10 or 11 questions. Read each passage or pair of passages, and then select the most appropriate answer to each question. Some passages may include tables or graphs that require additional analysis.

Refer to the passage below to answer questions 1 – 10.

This passage is adapted from Anton Chekhov's short story, "Small Fry," in *The Schoolmistress and Other Stories*, originally published in 1885.

line   "Honored Sir, Father and Benefactor!" a petty clerk called Nevyrazimov was writing a rough copy of an Easter congratulatory letter. "I trust that you may spend this Holy Day even as many
5 more to come, in good health and prosperity. And to your family also I..."
    The lamp, in which the kerosene was getting low, was smoking and smelling. A stray cockroach was running about the table in alarm
10 near Nevyrazimov's writing hand. Two rooms away from the office Paramon the porter was for the third time cleaning his best boots, and with such energy that the sound of the blacking-brush and of his expectorations was audible in all the
15 rooms.
    "What else can I write to him, the rascal?" Nevyrazimov wondered, raising his eyes to the smutty ceiling.
    On the ceiling he saw a dark circle—the
20 shadow of the lamp-shade. Below it was the dusty cornice, and lower still the wall, which had once been painted a bluish muddy color. And the office seemed to him such a place of desolation that he felt sorry, not only for himself, but even for the
25 cockroach.
    "When I am off duty I shall go away, but he'll be on duty here all his cockroach-life," he thought, stretching.
    Nevyrazimov put his ear to the open
30 [window] pane and listened. The Easter chimes floated into the room with a whiff of fresh spring air. The booming of the bells mingled with the rumble of carriages, and above the chaos of sounds rose the brisk tenor tones of the nearest
35 church and a loud shrill laugh.
    He moved away from the window and walked wearily about the rooms. The din of the bells grew louder and louder.... There was no need to stand by the window to hear it. And

40 the better he could hear the bells and the louder the roar of the carriages, the darker seemed the muddy walls and the smutty cornice and the more the lamp smoked.
    "Shall I hook it and leave the office?" thought
45 Nevyrazimov.
    But such a flight promised nothing worth having.... After coming out of the office and wandering about the town, Nevyrazimov would have gone home to his lodging, and in his lodging
50 it was even grayer and more depressing than in the office.... Even supposing he were to spend that day pleasantly and with comfort, what had he beyond? Nothing but the same gray walls, the same stop-gap duty and complimentary letters.
55 Nevyrazimov stood still in the middle of the office and sank into thought. The yearning for a new, better life gnawed at his heart with an intolerable ache. He had a passionate longing to find himself suddenly in the street, to mingle
60 with the living crowd, to take part in the solemn festivity for the sake of which all those bells were clashing and those carriages were rumbling. He longed for what he had known in childhood—the family circle, the festive faces of his own people,
65 the white cloth, light, warmth...! He thought of the carriage in which the lady had just driven by, the overcoat in which the head clerk was so smart, the gold chain that adorned the secretary's chest.... He thought of a warm bed, of the Stanislav order,
70 of new boots, of a uniform without holes in the elbows.... He thought of all those things because he had none of them.
    "Shall I steal?" he thought. "Even if stealing is an easy matter, hiding is what's difficult. Men
75 run away to America, they say, with what they've stolen, but the devil knows where that blessed America is. One must have education even to steal, it seems."
    And Nevyrazimov, racking his brain for a
80 means of escape from his hopeless position, stared at the rough copy he had written. The letter was written to a man whom he feared and hated with his whole soul, and from whom he had for the last ten years been trying to wring a post worth

85 eighteen rubles a month, instead of the one he had at sixteen rubles.

"Ah, I'll teach you to run here, you devil!" He viciously slapped the palm of his hand on the cockroach, who had the misfortune to catch his

90 eye. "Nasty thing!"

The cockroach fell on its back and wriggled its legs in despair. Nevyrazimov took it by one leg and threw it into the lamp. The lamp flared up and spluttered.

95 And Nevyrazimov felt better.

1. The descriptions of "Easter chimes," "spring air," and "the rumble of carriages" (lines 29 – 35) primarily serve to

(A) remind Nevyrazimov of experiences from his childhood.
(B) highlight reasons for Nevyrazimov's distracted demeanor.
(C) inspire Nevyrazimov to make several significant lifestyle changes.
(D) contrast with the miserable conditions in which Nevyrazimov is immersed.

2. As used in line 33, "chaos" most nearly means

(A) tumult.
(B) mayhem.
(C) turmoil.
(D) turbulence.

3. Based on the passage, Nevyrazimov's attitude is best described as

(A) optimistic yet cautious.
(B) fatalistic and resigned.
(C) opportunistic and cunning.
(D) honest and sincere.

4. Which choice provides the best evidence for the answer to the previous question?

(A) Lines 16 – 18 ("What else…smutty ceiling")
(B) Lines 51 – 54 ("Even supposing…letters")
(C) Lines 56 –58 ("The yearning…ache")
(D) Lines 92 – 94 ("Nevyrazimov took…and spluttered")

5. As used in line 60, "solemn" most nearly means

(A) earnest.
(B) dour.
(C) ceremonious.
(D) imposing.

6. It can be inferred from the passage that the intended recipient of Nevyrazimov's letter is

(A) Nevyrazimov's superior at his place of work.
(B) Nevyrazimov's friend who refuses to lend him money.
(C) a wealthy member of Nevyrazimov's family.
(D) a corrupt government official.

7. The irony of the contents of the letter that Nevyrazimov is writing at the beginning of the story is that

(A) the letter focuses on generosity, but its intended recipient is known for his greed.
(B) the letter is flattering and friendly, but Nevyrazimov despises its intended recipient.
(C) the letter is formal and serious, yet Nevyrazimov is a flippant and jocular person.
(D) the letter shows reverence, yet Nevyrazimov has little respect for religious institutions.

8. Which choice provides the best evidence for the answer to the previous question?

(A) Lines 1 – 3 ("'Honored Sir…letter")
(B) Lines 16 – 18 ("What else…smutty ceiling")
(C) Lines 81 – 87 ("The letter…rubles")
(D) Lines 91 – 93 ("The cockroach…lamp")

9. Over the course of the passage, Nevyrazimov's attitude toward the cockroach shifts from

(A) feeling protective of the cockroach to being repulsed by it.
(B) feeling sympathy for the cockroach to feeling contempt toward it.
(C) being unperturbed by the cockroach to becoming obsessed with it.
(D) being disgusted by the cockroach to developing a begrudging sense of camaraderie with it.

10. Nevyrazimov probably kills the cockroach to

(A) convey his desire to keep his workplace clean.
(B) show his disdain toward those whom he perceives as beneath him.
(C) take out his frustrations regarding his station in life.
(D) demonstrate that he is determined to make positive changes to his life.

Refer to the passage below to answer questions 11 – 21.

The following passage is adapted from a speech given by lawyer Andrew Hamilton in 1735. While what is now the east coast of the United States was still a British colony, a newspaper publisher named John Peter Zenger was jailed for printing criticisms of the British colonial governor. In court, Andrew Hamilton (no relation to Alexander Hamilton) defended Zenger. The following is an excerpt of Hamilton's defense in court. (He refers to the prosecutor as "Mr. Attorney.")

line   It is said, and insisted upon by Mr. Attorney, that government is a sacred thing; that it is to be supported and reverenced; it is government that protects our persons and estates; that prevents
5 treasons, murders, robberies, riots, and all the train of evils that overturn kingdoms and states and ruin particular persons; and if those in the administration, especially the supreme magistrates, must have all their conduct censured
10 by private men, government cannot subsist. This is called a licentiousness not to be tolerated. It is said that it brings the rulers of the people into contempt so that their authority is not regarded, and so that in the end the laws cannot be put in
15 execution.
       These, I say, and such as these, are the general topics insisted by men in power and their advocates. But I wish it might be considered at the same time how often it has happened
20 that the abuse of power has been the primary cause of these evils, and that it was the injustice and oppression of these great men which has commonly brought them into contempt with the people. The craft and art of such men are great,
25 and who that is the least acquainted with history or with the law can be ignorant of the specious pretenses which have often been made use of by men in power to introduce arbitrary rule and destroy the liberties of a free people…
30   The loss of liberty to a generous mind is worse than death; and yet we know there have been those in all ages who, for the sakes of preferment or some imaginary honor, have freely lent a helping hand to oppress, nay, to destroy,
35 their country. This brings to my mind that saying of the immortal Brutus, when he looked upon the creatures of Caesar, who were very great men, but by no means good men: "You Romans," said Brutus, "if yet I may call you so, consider what
40 you are doing; remember that you are assisting Caesar to forge those very chains which one day he will make yourselves wear." This is what every man that values freedom ought to consider; he should act by judgment and not by affection or
45 self-interest…
       Power may justly be compared to a great

river; while kept within its bounds, it is both beautiful and useful, but when it overflows its banks, it is then too impetuous to be stemmed; it
50 bears down all before it, and brings destruction and desolation wherever it comes. If, then, this be the nature of power, let us at least do our duty, and, like wise men who value freedom, use our utmost care to support liberty, the only bulwark
55 against lawless power, which, in all ages, has sacrificed to its wild lust and boundless ambition the blood of the best men that ever lived…
       The question before the court, and you, gentlemen of the jury, is not of small nor private
60 concern; it is not the cause of a poor printer, nor of New York alone, which you are now trying. No! It may, in its consequence, affect every free man that lives under a British government on the main continent of America. It is the best cause;
65 it is the cause of liberty; and I make no doubt but your upright conduct, this day, will not only entitle you to the love and esteem of your fellow citizen, but every man who prefers freedom to a life of slavery will bless and honor you as men
70 who have baffled the attempt of tyranny, and, by an impartial and uncorrupt verdict, have laid a noble foundation for securing to ourselves, our posterity, and our neighbors that to which nature and the laws of our country have given us a
75 right – the liberty of both exposing and opposing arbitrary power (in these parts of the world at least) by speaking and writing truth…

11. In the context of the passage, Hamilton's use of the phrase "it is government that protects our persons and estates" (lines 3 – 4) is primarily meant to

(A) explain why people should value and respect the government.
(B) introduce a list of "evils" and crimes.
(C) propose better law enforcement in the colonies.
(D) repeat one of the justifications for the charges.

12. As used in line 9, "censured" most nearly means

(A) censored.
(B) admonished.
(C) evaluated.
(D) sentenced.

13. In lines 26 – 27, Hamilton refers to "specious pretenses" primarily to

(A) describe false reasons commonly given for oppression.
(B) define the types of laws that forbid free speech.
(C) clarify the difference between his stance and his opponent's.
(D) comment on the arrogance of British government officials.

14. Within the passage, paragraph 2 (lines 16 – 29) can best be described as

(A) a rebuke of the prosecution's disrespectful charges.
(B) a partial concession to some of the opponent's points.
(C) a rebuttal of the prosecution's argument.
(D) an introduction to the Roman history that follows.

15. In the third paragraph (lines 30 – 45), Hamilton strongly suggests that people who assist tyrants

(A) do not value liberty.
(B) often expect some kind of promotion in return.
(C) expect the tyrant to promote freedom of speech.
(D) want to destroy their countries.

16. Which choice provides the best evidence for the answer to the previous question?

(A) Lines 16 – 18 ("These, I say...advocates")
(B) Lines 31 – 35 ("and yet we...their country")
(C) Lines 38 – 42 ("'You Romans,'...wear'")
(D) Lines 46 – 51 ("Power may...it comes")

17. In lines 38 – 42 ("'You Romans'...'yourselves wear'"), Hamilton implies that

(A) the British governor plans to enslave everyone.
(B) those who help an oppressive government will go to jail.
(C) the British governor is acting exactly like Caesar did in Rome.
(D) people who assist in denying liberty to others will also lose their liberty.

18. The main rhetorical effect of comparing power to a great river (lines 46 – 57) is to

(A) emphasize its constant potential danger.
(B) remind people that power is always destructive.
(C) predict that the government will be swept away.
(D) place the present struggle in a larger context.

19. In line 54, "bulwark" most nearly means

(A) large weapon.
(B) convincing argument.
(C) defensive wall.
(D) stern warning.

20. In paragraph 5 (lines 58 – 77), Hamilton discusses the possible consequences of the jury's decision in order to

(A) persuade members to take courageous action.
(B) inspire members to speak out themselves.
(C) make sure that members can come to a unanimous decision.
(D) explain details of the case that were confusing.

21. Which choice indicates Hamilton's predictions for the historical importance of the case?

(A) Line 60 – 61 ("it is not...now trying")
(B) Lines 62 – 64 ("It may, in its...of America")
(C) Lines 65 – 68 ("I make...fellow citizen")
(D) Lines 70 – 77 ("by an impartial...truth")

Refer to the passage below to answer questions 22 – 32.

This passage is from Iddo, "Sequencing the frog that can save lives," published on Byte Size Biology on October 1, 2014.

line
        Eighteen people die each day in the United States waiting for an organ transplant. Every ten minutes, a person gets added to the waiting list. The need for improvement in organ donations is
5   real.
        Why are these statistics so grim? Even when a potentially good match is found (which can take months or years), there is a very short window between the time an organ is donated, and
10   the time it can be transplanted. The maximum viability time for a human kidney is estimated at 35 hours; a liver 20, and a lung less than 10. This time constraint also limits the availability of matching organs. Just imagine if we could freeze
15   and thaw organs without the risk of killing them, keeping them viable for months or even years. The time patients need to wait would be shorter, and, also, better matches may be found as the number of frozen organs increase. If we could
20   learn to freeze organs without damaging them, we would revolutionize organ transplant in the same way refrigeration and freezing revolutionized the food industry. Today, however, freezing organs is not an option: once an organ is frozen, there
25   is irreversible and widespread damage from the formation of ice crystals. Cells shrivel and collapse, blood vessels disintegrate, connective tissue rips apart.
        But there are animals that can freeze and
30   re-animate multiple times. In fact, if you live in the northern parts of North America, you have probably seen one, and almost surely heard it: the North American wood frog. The wood frog can freeze solid and then thaw – multiple times
35   – with no ill effect. During this freeze event, the frog dumps glucose (a sugar) and high levels of urea (an acid normally found in urine) into its bloodstream. The glucose pulls water out of the cells and causes ice to freeze outside of the cells
40   – a type of cryo-dehydration. This is to prevent ice forming inside the cells, where it would cause irreparable damage. The urea is thought to do two things – one, it also protects the cell's integrity from damage, and two, it helps slow down the
45   frog's metabolism. The fact that the frog can freeze in and of itself is pretty spectacular – no heartbeat, no brain activity, no movement. When it thaws, the animal spontaneously reanimates.
        What seems even more bizarre about this
50   animal is that once the frog is acclimated to summer, freezing it will simply kill it. We think that there is some sort of seasonal trigger for winter and the possibility of freezing. There must

therefore be a change of gene expression between
55   the summer and winter frogs. One could think of this animal as its own experimental control! So to understand how the wood frog can survive freezing, we just pick frogs from different seasons, and see the difference in RNA expression. This
60   can clue us into what makes a freeze-adapted frog different than a non-freeze adapted one. Unfortunately, we lack a good reference genome. Nothing close to the wood frog has been sequenced yet. Xenopus is a genus of frogs
65   used in laboratories whose genomes have been sequenced. But as a reference for wood frog, the Xenopus genomes aren't good — the two species are too far apart.
        Even more interesting, having the genome
70   of the wood frog will enable studies of the different epigenetic patterns between summer and winter frogs. The control of gene expression is ultimately what some researchers are interested in sorting out, and it's likely that the epigenetics is
75   involved: changes in the DNA that are not in the actual sequence, (like methylation) and affect the production of RNA and proteins. Additionally, because we don't know the wood frog genome yet, we may find gene family expansions and
80   contractions, novel genes that impart the freeze tolerance to the animal that we cannot possibly predict using a hypothesis-driven approach.

Relative contribution of urea and glucose to total cryoprotectant load in several organs of winter and spring wood frogs sampled after freezing.

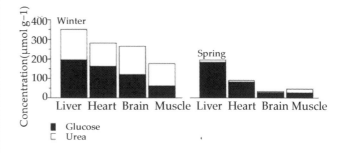

Figure 1

22. Over the course of the passage, the primary focus shifts from

    (A) an assessment of the quality of American healthcare to a description of ecological conservation efforts.
    (B) an explanation of a healthcare-related issue to an exploration of a hypothetical solution.
    (C) an interpretation of healthcare-related statistics to a description of a unique animal species.
    (D) a criticism of a medical practice to praise for a viable alternative.

23. Lines 19 – 23 ("If...industry") primarily serve to

    (A) compare a recent medical discovery to a significant scientific development of the past.
    (B) briefly explore the ethical dilemmas of freezing transplant organs.
    (C) provide an example of the historical benefits of being able to cool or freeze perishable goods.
    (D) emphasize the impact that a theoretical scientific development could have.

24. As used in line 25, "widespread" most nearly means

    (A) predominant.
    (B) extensive.
    (C) ubiquitous.
    (D) sweeping.

25. According to the passage, which choice describes how wood frogs to survive seasonal freezing?

    (A) Their DNA undergoes a radical sequence change every winter.
    (B) Their cells store large amounts of glucose that provides nourishment while the frogs are frozen.
    (C) Their bodies release substances that alter metabolism and cellular composition.
    (D) They possess unique RNA that can heal cells that are damaged when the frogs thaw.

26. The author suggests that protecting "the cell's integrity from damage" (lines 43 – 44) entails

    (A) forming a barrier around the cell to improve its durability.
    (B) extracting potentially harmful urea from the cell before it freezes.
    (C) preventing ice from forming within the cell.
    (D) altering the expression of the frog's RNA to insulate the cell.

27. Which choice provides the best evidence for the answer to the previous question?

    (A) Lines 32 – 35 ("The wood frog...effect")
    (B) Lines 38 – 42 ("The glucose...damage")
    (C) Lines 53 – 55 ("There must...frogs")
    (D) Lines 72 – 75 ("The control...involved")

28. According to the passage, the biggest obstacle for understanding how wood frogs survive prolonged freezing is that

    (A) the roles of glucose and urea in cell preservation remains poorly understood.
    (B) the wood frog genome has not yet been sequenced.
    (C) scientists are unable to distinguish between wood frogs' DNA and their RNA.
    (D) they can only be observed in summer, when freezing damages them.

29. As used in line 80, "novel" most nearly means

    (A) experimental.
    (B) unconventional.
    (C) original.
    (D) unique.

30. The author mentions studying "epigenetic patterns" (line 71) primarily to

    (A) introduce a benefit of sequencing the wood frog's genome.
    (B) emphasize the importance of RNA in the freezing and thawing process.
    (C) differentiate genome sequencing from toehr methods of DNA analysis.
    (D) explain how methylation affects a frog's glucose and urea levels.

31. Which choice best summarizes the information in the graph?

    (A) Lines 35 – 38 ("During...bloodstream")
    (B) Lines 42 – 45 ("The urea...metabolism")
    (C) Lines 49 – 51 ("What...kill it")
    (D) Lines 53 – 55 ("There must...frogs")

32. It can reasonably be inferred from the graph and the passage that

    (A) the genes in wood frogs that regulate urea production disappear in the spring, and reappear in the winter.
    (B) glucose and urea must be present in equal quantities for a wood frog to survive all winter.
    (C) urea is more important than glucose in sustaining wood frogs when they are frozen.
    (D) wood frogs must maintain high levels of urea to prevent cell damage during freezing.

Refer to the passage below to answer questions 33 – 43.

This passage is adapted from a speech given by United States President Ronald Reagan on January 28, 1986. On the morning of January 28, 1986, a NASA space shuttle, the *Challenger*, exploded just after launching. All seven crew members aboard were killed, including Christa McAuliffe, who would have been the first teacher in space. Students in many schools were watching the live coverage when the explosion took place. In the evening, President Reagan addressed the nation with the following televised speech.

line   Ladies and gentlemen, I'd planned to speak to you tonight to report on the state of the Union, but the events of earlier today have led me to change those plans. Today is a day for mourning
5 and remembering. Nancy and I are pained to the core by the tragedy of the shuttle Challenger. We know we share this pain with all of the people of our country. This is truly a national loss.

Nineteen years ago, almost to the day, we
10 lost three astronauts in a terrible accident on the ground. But we've never lost an astronaut in flight; we've never had a tragedy like this. And perhaps we've forgotten the courage it took for the crew of the shuttle. But they, the Challenger
15 Seven, were aware of the dangers, but overcame them and did their jobs brilliantly. We mourn seven heroes: Michael Smith, Dick Scobee, Judith Resnik, Ronald McNair, Ellison Onizuka, Gregory Jarvis, and Christa McAuliffe. We mourn their loss
20 as a nation together.

For the families of the seven, we cannot bear, as you do, the full impact of this tragedy. But we feel the loss, and we're thinking about you so very much. Your loved ones were daring and brave,
25 and they had that special grace, that special spirit that says, "Give me a challenge, and I'll meet it with joy." They had a hunger to explore the universe and discover its truths. They wished to serve, and they did. They served all of us. We've
30 grown used to wonders in this century. It's hard to dazzle us. But for 25 years the United States space program has been doing just that. We've grown used to the idea of space, and perhaps we forget that we've only just begun. We're still
35 pioneers. They, the members of the Challenger crew, were pioneers.

And I want to say something to the schoolchildren of America who were watching the live coverage of the shuttle's takeoff. I know it is
40 hard to understand, but sometimes painful things like this happen. It's all part of the process of exploration and discovery. It's all part of taking a chance and expanding man's horizons. The future doesn't belong to the fainthearted; it belongs to
45 the brave. The Challenger crew was pulling us into the future, and we'll continue to follow them.

I've always had great faith in and respect for our space program, and what happened today does nothing to diminish it. We don't hide our space
50 program. We don't keep secrets and cover things up. We do it all up front and in public. That's the way freedom is, and we wouldn't change it for a minute. We'll continue our quest in space. There will be more shuttle flights and more shuttle
55 crews and, yes, more volunteers, more civilians, more teachers in space. Nothing ends here; our hopes and our journeys continue. I want to add that I wish I could talk to every man and woman who works for NASA or who worked on this
60 mission and tell them: "Your dedication and professionalism have moved and impressed us for decades. And we know of your anguish. We share it."

There's a coincidence today. On this day 390
65 years ago, the great explorer Sir Francis Drake died aboard ship off the coast of Panama. In his lifetime the great frontiers were the oceans, and an historian later said, "He lived by the sea, died on it, and was buried in it." Well, today we can
70 say of the Challenger crew: Their dedication was, like Drake's, complete.

The crew of the space shuttle Challenger honored us by the manner in which they lived their lives. We will never forget them, nor the
75 last time we saw them, this morning, as they prepared for their journey and waved goodbye and "slipped the surly bonds of earth" to "touch the face of God."*

lines from the poem "High Flight," by John Gillespie Magee, Jr.

Space Flights by Shuttle and Date

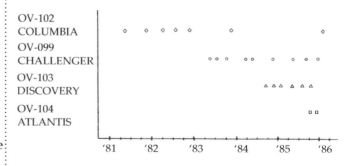

SOURCE: "Shuttle Flights as of Januarry 1986," Space Shuttle Mission STS-51L, Press Kit, January 1986, NASA.

33. What main effect does the phrase "Nancy and I are pained to the core…" (lines 5 – 6) have on the tone of the passage?

    (A) It creates a morbid tone, focusing on the pain experienced by the crew.
    (B) It creates a personal tone, connecting to audience members' emotions.
    (C) It creates a tranquil tone, reminding viewers to turn to family for support.
    (D) It creates an impassioned tone, foreshadowing a description of deep flaws in the system.

34. Reagan says, "This is truly a national loss" (line 8), and "We mourn their loss as a nation together" (line 19 – 20), primarily to

    (A) indicate that he is not speaking for political gain.
    (B) persuade all American viewers to feel devastated.
    (C) promise that the victims will not be forgotten.
    (D) define how history will view the explosion.

35. In the context of the passage, "bear" (line 21) most nearly means

    (A) experience.
    (B) produce.
    (C) convey.
    (D) withstand.

36. The speech strongly suggests that President Reagan believes

    (A) the Challenger's destruction was inexplicable.
    (B) some members of the public will fault the crew members.
    (C) the space shuttle program takes the lives of special people.
    (D) the crew members' lives were not wasted by the explosion.

37. Which choice provides the best evidence for the answer to the previous question?

    (A) Line 11 - 12 ("But we've never…like this")
    (B) Lines 16 – 19 ("We mourn…McAuliffe")
    (C) Lines 28 – 29 ("They wished…all of us")
    (D) Lines 32 – 34 ("We've grown used…begun")

38. According to the chart, at the time of the crash, NASA's space shuttle program

    (A) had used the Challenger more than all the other shuttles combined.
    (B) had begun to phase out the Challenger for newer shuttles.
    (C) relied on the Challenger more than the other shuttles in 1983 and 1984.
    (D) overused the Challenger in 1985, contributing to safety issues in 1986.

39. In the context of the passage, "quest" (line 53) most nearly means

    (A) inquiry.
    (B) search.
    (C) pilgrimage.
    (D) pursuit.

40. In the speech, the president most strongly implies that the accident

    (A) should not cause NASA to lose funding.
    (B) should be investigated to determine fault.
    (C) may have been caused by enemies of democracy and freedom.
    (D) may cause NASA employees to quit their jobs.

41. Which choice provides the best evidence for the answer to the previous question?

    (A) Line 45 – 46 ("The Challenger…follow them")
    (B) Lines 49 – 51 ("We don't hide …in public")
    (C) Lines 56 – 57 ("Nothing ends…continue")
    (D) Lines 62 – 63 ("And we know…share it")

42. President Reagan's mention of Sir Francis Drake in the speech primarily serves as

    (A) an indicator of how long explorers remain famous after their deaths.
    (B) an analogy for the historical contribution of the Challenger crew.
    (C) an example of how often risk-takers die in pursuit of their goals.
    (D) a symbol of a frontier that is easier for viewers to understand.

43. It is reasonable to conclude that the main goal of the speech is to

    (A) put the accident within a historical context.
    (B) comfort the families of the deceased crew members.
    (C) provide inspiration at a discouraging time.
    (D) remind the public that space exploration has just begun.

Questions 44 – 52 are based on the following passages.

Passage 1 is adapted from Carolyn Graybeal, "Did you know 'storm spotters' in your community keep you safe during severe weather?" published in 2015. Passage 2 is from Eva Lewandowski, "Declining monarch population means increased need for citizen scientists," published in 2015.

Passage 1

line   During hazardous weather, we rely on the knowledge, skill and expertise of meteorologists and designated emergency personnel to keep us safe and in the know. They in turn rely on data
5   supplied by not just satellites and Doppler radars but also a network of citizen scientists.
        But wait. With all our sophisticated technology, what could a few volunteers possibly contribute?
10   "Radars can tell us that there is heavy snowfall, but radars don't tell us how much, or if rain is mixing with the snow, or what damage is occurring. Our spotters do," explains Tanja Fransen of the National Weather Service in
15   Glasgow, Montana.
        Skywarn, a national network of more than 350,000 volunteers, was created after a particularly devastating series of tornadoes ripped through Midwestern states in 1965.
20   Overseen by National Oceanic and Atmospheric Administration's (NOAA)'s National Weather Service, the Skywarn program trains citizens to identify severe storms and provide accurate reports of storm developments and effects.
25   During a storm, volunteers send in reports to National Weather Service forecaster offices about what is happening locally. Meteorologists use this valuable 'ground truth' to validate data from their instruments and fill in information gaps, enabling
30   them to make better predictions about what the storm might do next.
        Skywarn storm spotters are a diverse group of people varying in age, background and skill level. What they do have in common is an interest
35   in weather and public service. To be a Skywarn storm spotter, volunteers must attend free training courses which cover the basics of storm formations, accurate reporting techniques and of course, storm safety. Last year alone, NOAA
40   trained over 70,000 storm spotters.
        The Skywarn network includes a subset of licensed amateur radio operators who provide additional assistance during storms. The National Weather Service forecast offices utilize amateur
45   radio to maintain communication between on the ground storm spotters and forecasters. And during especially large storms, which can knock out phone service, amateur radio volunteers help keep their communities informed of new
50   warnings and other critical information.

Passage 2

        The annual estimates of the monarch population are taken at the monarch's overwintering site in central Mexico. Most of the monarchs in North America live east of the Rocky
55   Mountains, and each fall they migrate thousands of miles south to their overwintering location in Mexico, where they cluster together on oyamel fir trees. In the spring those same monarchs fly north, where they produce new generations that
60   spread throughout the United States and Canada. Their vast summer range can make it difficult to get precise estimates of the population size, but in winter the monarchs are bunched tightly together, making population estimates more feasible.
65   Instead of counting individual monarchs, scientists record the amount of land that the overwintering monarch population covers.
        This year, the monarchs covered 1.13 hectares; that's a little more than two football fields' worth
70   of land. That might sound like a staggeringly small size, but it's actually a 69 percent increase over last year's population, which was the smallest on record.
        …Planting native nectar plants and native
75   milkweed, the only plant on which monarchs will lay eggs, is an easy way to help, but people who want to get more involved will find a whole host of monarch citizen science projects in need of volunteers. These projects study monarchs
80   as they migrate and reproduce in the United States and Canada, and provide insight into how disease, climate change, and habitat loss are affecting the monarch population. Citizen science is so important to monarch research that since
85   2000, almost two-thirds of the published results on monarch field research have used citizen science data (Ries, L., and K.S. Oberhauser, in press).

428

44. As used in line 2, "expertise" most nearly means

(A) adroitness.
(B) prowess.
(C) aptitude.
(D) dexterity.

45. In Passage 1, paragraph 3 (lines 16 – 24) is primarily concerned with establishing a contrast between

(A) hazardous weather and damage on the ground.
(B) contributions by individuals and by networks.
(C) heavy snowfall and snow mixed with rain.
(D) information gleaned from different sources.

46. In Passage 1, the central claim about the Skywarn program is that it

(A) provides an opportunity for public service.
(B) educates the public about meteorology.
(C) improves the accuracy of storm predictions.
(D) prevents severe storm damage.

47. Which choice provides the best evidence for the answer to the previous question?

(A) Lines 16 – 19 ("Skywarn, a national…1965")
(B) Lines 20 – 24 ("Overseen by…effects")
(C) Lines 27 – 31 ("Meteorologists use…next")
(D) Lines 34 – 35 ("What they do…service")

48. The author of Passage 1 suggests that amateur radio operators can

(A) radio police units and paramedics in their areas.
(B) provide details that ordinary storm spotters cannot.
(C) take responsibility for emergency evacuations.
(D) function even during phone and power outages.

49. The author of Passage 2 implies that citizen scientists

(A) observe the monarch population when it is most active.
(B) should focus on adding the monarch's host plant in their gardens.
(C) supplant professional naturalists in the study of monarch butterflies.
(D) provide the most reliable data.

50. Which choice provides the best evidence for the answer to the previous question?

(A) Lines 65 – 67 ("Instead of…covers")
(B) Lines 70 – 73 ("That might…record")
(C) Lines 79 – 83 ("Those projects…population")
(D) Lines 83 – 87 ("Citizen science…data")

51. The authors of Passage 1 and Passage 2 would most likely agree that

(A) citizen science data are somewhat useful.
(B) citizen science volunteers must undergo training.
(C) networks of citizens can monitor immense territories.
(D) public enthusiasm for citizen science projects tends to be low.

52. The main purpose of both passages is to

(A) describe a particular case of public participation in science.
(B) encourage readers to become citizen science volunteers.
(C) criticize the science community's dependence on technology.
(D) inform readers about potential environmental crises.

429

Writing and Language Test 5
35 MINUTES, 44 QUESTIONS

Turn to Section 2 of your answer sheet to answer the questions in this section.

Refer to the passage below to answer questions 1 – 11.

Software Developer

Every time a computer user hits a key or clicks on an icon, the user is giving a command to the computer, **1** such as "Open this file." The reason the command brings about the desired result is that a programmer has given the computer precise instructions about how to respond to that command. A person **2** whose job involves writing instructions for computers is called a "software developer."

[1] "Applications" software developers focus specifically on setting up pathways for people to give commands to computers. [2] The applications developers learn programming languages, which they use to create menus of possible actions. [3] Essentially, they tell a computer that if a user does *this*, **3** they must do *that*. [4] A device within the computer translates the code into machine language, and from then on, the computer is programmed to respond appropriately to a user's choice. [5] When the user hits the "x" key, an "x" will appear on the screen, for example. **4**

1. (A) NO CHANGE
   (B) such as "open
   (C) such as: "open
   (D) such as, "Open

2. (A) NO CHANGE
   (B) who's
   (C) where his or her
   (D) that's

3. (A) NO CHANGE
   (B) one
   (C) it
   (D) someone

4. The writer wants to add the following sentence to the paragraph.

   > The developers' series of instructions are referred to as "code."

   The best placement for the sentence is immediately

   (A) after sentence 1.
   (B) after sentence 2.
   (C) after sentence 3.
   (D) after sentence 4.

5 In addition to applications, some software developers focus on "systems," a term which refers to the inner functioning of the computer. Others focus on "networks," or the ways that computers communicate with other computers. Regardless of their specific tasks, all software developers spend their days puzzling out solutions to problems. They must use logic and creativity to craft and **6** ameliorate a section of code until they obtain the desired result. Software developers may find work in public agencies, or in private companies, such as software publishers, financial institutions, and **7** so on.

[1] Working conditions vary greatly for software developers. [2] However, developers commonly must work overtime to meet project deadlines, or be on call during nights and weekends in case there are technical problems. [3] Some developers share offices and collaborate in teams, while some work in cubicles or private offices. [4] Some meet regularly with clients during the business day, and some work from home on their own schedules. [5] Most developers work at least 40 hours a week. **8**

People who work in the software development field often have a bachelor's degree in computer science or a related major, although some employers put more emphasis on experience. Software developers should expect to continually learn new programming languages and other tools. Some employers make a distinction between software developers and software engineers; the latter generally have more responsibility for designing and maintaining systems overall **9** than software developers.

5. (A) NO CHANGE
   (B) Contrary to
   (C) As a result of
   (D) As with

6. (A) NO CHANGE
   (B) renovate
   (C) enhance
   (D) adjust

7. The writer wants to replace the underlined section with a different type of private company that employs software developers. Which choice would best accomplish this goal?

   (A) local governments
   (B) banks
   (C) electronics manufacturers
   (D) police departments

8. To make the paragraph more logical, sentence 5 should be placed

   (A) where it is now.
   (B) before sentence 2.
   (C) before sentence 1.
   (D) after sentence 3.

9. (A) NO CHANGE
   (B) than software developers'.
   (C) than software developers do.
   (D) then software developers.

Software developers are highly valued in today's world economy. According to the U.S. Bureau of Labor Statistics, there are already more than 1 million people working in software development in the United States, **10** with the majority of software developers in the U.S. working from California, Washington, and Texas. Some jobs in the field have been transferred to developing nations, but the unemployment rate among software developers in the U.S. is still a low 2.8 percent. The bureau predicts strong job growth for software developers **11** because of new software being in demand from now on all around the world.

Number of Software Developers by State

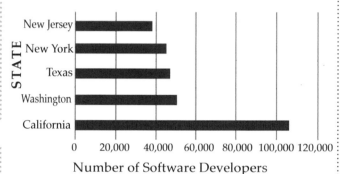

SOURCE: adapted from the Bureau of Labor Statistics, *Occupational Employment Statistics*, "Occupational Employment and Wages, May 2014."

10. Which choice accurately incorporates information from the graph into the passage?

(A) NO CHANGE
(B) and approximately ten percent of software developers in the U.S. work in California.
(C) with California supporting more software developers than Texas, New York, and New Jersey combined.
(D) and California hosts the fastest-growing population of software developers.

11. (A) NO CHANGE
(B) as a consequence of software developers' ability to produce new software, which is going to be in demand more and more.
(C) notwithstanding the growing societal importance of their creative skills.
(D) due to an ever-increasing global demand for new software.

Refer to the passage below to answer questions 12 – 22.

Biology of Hunger

--- 1 ---

12 The complex system for digestion of food and excretion of waste in the human body is always working to break down food for energy and nutrients, but skipping a meal does not give the system a rest. Instead of resting, the system triggers physiological and psychological effects so that a hungry person will not be able to ignore the stomach's emptiness. Indeed, the person may **13** fail concentrating on anything else.

--- 2 ---

14 When the stomach finishes processing and passing along all of the food it has, its walls release a hormone called "ghrelin" into the bloodstream. In response to this and other signals, the hypothalamus—the brain's center for automatic responses—signals the muscular walls of the digestive organs to release digestive fluids and begin contracting. The activity causes hunger pangs and the noise of air bubbles being squeezed. An empty system has none of the contents that would normally muffle the sound.

--- 3 ---

15 If no food enters the digestive system, the body used up its stores of glucose, its main fuel, within about 12 hours. At this point the body begins to rely upon fatty acids from its stored fat. Fatty acids provide fuel to cells effectively, with one exception: brain cells rely almost exclusively on glucose. To keep glucose flowing, the liver is forced **16** to break down protein from the body's muscles and convert it to glucose. The liver also converts some fatty acids into ketone bodies, which are special molecules that serve as an alternative fuel for brain cells. As starvation progresses and the body's stored fat becomes depleted, however, the liver must increase its conversion of protein from muscles and other tissues.

12. (A) NO CHANGE
    (B) The digestive system
    (C) The complex system for digestion in the human body
    (D) The human digestive system

13. (A) NO CHANGE
    (B) find it difficult to concentrate
    (C) be challenged by having to concentrate
    (D) have a problem with concentrating

14. The author wants to add a topic sentence here. Which choice most effectively establishes the main topic of the paragraph?

    (A) It is actually quite accurate to describe an empty stomach as "growling."
    (B) The stomach stretches to accommodate big meals.
    (C) The stomach has two strategies to break down foods: mechanical and chemical.
    (D) Hormones play crucial roles in many bodily processes, including digestion.

15. (A) NO CHANGE
    (B) The body depletes its main fuel, glucose, after about 12 hours with no food.
    (C) The body had used up its stores of glucose, its main fuel, within about 12 hours of no food.
    (D) The body's main fuel, glucose, becomes used up after about 12 hours, if no food is eaten.

16. (A) NO CHANGE
    (B) to break down protein from the body's muscles and converting it
    (C) be breaking down protein from the body's muscles and converting it
    (D) breaking down protein from the body's muscles and to convert it

--- 4 ---

Besides stimulating appetite, the brain has other ways of motivating food-foraging behavior. The brain releases the hormone cortisol, which initiates processes that provide a burst of energy. It also cuts back on its release of serotonin, the "happiness hormone." Therefore, a hungry person usually feels **17** restless and sad, or irritable. This emotional state predisposes **18** them to lose interest in both work and play, and to think only about the next meal.

--- 5 ---

The biochemical processes that occur inside the body during prolonged hunger cause increasingly severe symptoms. These may include **19** low blood pressure, dehydration, weakness, a feeling of being cold, and headache. People at this stage become anxious and depressed. They feel less concern for others, and they may hoard or steal food. As they feel vulnerable, they are more likely to trust strong authority figures. **20** Eventually, starving people become quiet and withdrawn, reserving all remaining energy just to stay alive. Even if food becomes available again, it sometimes takes months to **21** retrieve mental health and sociability, and even longer to recover muscle strength. **22**

Question **22** asks about the previous passage as a whole.

17. (A) NO CHANGE
    (B) restless, and sad and irritable.
    (C) restless, sad, and irritable.
    (D) restless and sad, and irritable.

18. (A) NO CHANGE
    (B) him or her
    (C) one
    (D) us

19. (A) NO CHANGE
    (B) feelings of low blood pressure, dehydration, weakness, cold, and headache.
    (C) low blood pressure, dehydration, feelings of weakness and chilliness, and headache.
    (D) low blood pressure, dehydration, weakness, chilliness, and headache.

20. The writer is considering deleting the underlined sentence. Should it be kept or deleted?

    (A) Kept, because it illustrates the paragraph's focus on increasingly severe symptoms.
    (B) Kept, because it supports the paragraph's emphasis on sociability.
    (C) Deleted, because it blurs the paragraph's focus on physical and mental symptoms.
    (D) Deleted, because it does not provide enough information about reserving energy.

21. (A) NO CHANGE
    (B) regrow
    (C) regain
    (D) revise

Think about the previous passage as a whole as you answer question 22.

22. To make the passage most logical, paragraph 4 should be placed

    (A) after paragraph 1.
    (B) after paragraph 2.
    (C) where it is now.
    (D) after paragraph 5.

Refer to the passage below to answer questions 23 – 33.

Trends in Psychotherapy

A large body of psychiatric research indicates that a combination of medication and psychotherapy can often ease psychological distress in patients. **23** Only medical doctors can prescribe medications, whereas psychotherapy typically involves conversation with a trained therapist. During the conversation, a patient explains troubling thoughts or feelings, and the therapist listens carefully.

Sigmund Freud introduced the concept of psychotherapy in the early 20th century. At that time, people who experienced mental health problems were often isolated and sometimes physically **24** constrained. Freud's basic approach was revolutionary. He correctly predicted that many mental symptoms would eventually be treatable with medications, and he proposed that many symptoms of distress were not innate **25** but rather stemmed from traumatic experiences. He listened to **26** his patients' talk and tried to help them gain insights into why they thought and felt as they did. Although Freud's specific theories about stages of development have been largely rejected, **27** he was still important.

23. (A) NO CHANGE
    (B) Whereas medical doctors only can prescribe medications,
    (C) Only medications can be prescribed by medical doctors, whereas
    (D) Prescribing medications can be done by medical doctors, whereas only

24. (A) NO CHANGE
    (B) restrained
    (C) repressed
    (D) retained

25. The writer is considering deleting the underlined section. Should the section be kept or deleted?

    (A) Kept, because it supports the paragraph's emphasis on the effects of childhood trauma.
    (B) Kept, because it supports the paragraph's focus on Freud's analytical approach.
    (C) Deleted, because it blurs the paragraph's emphasis on innate psychological distress.
    (D) Deleted, because it incorrectly confuses the concepts of trauma and symptoms of distress.

26. (A) NO CHANGE
    (B) his patient's talk
    (C) his patients' talks
    (D) his patients talk

27. The writer wants to conclude the paragraph with a sentence that emphasizes Freud's innovations in therapy. Which choice would best accomplish this goal?

    (A) NO CHANGE
    (B) his theories about stages of development are still taught in college.
    (C) his analytic "talk therapy" approach has proven hugely influential.
    (D) he had the ideas that changed attitudes toward the mentally ill.

Some post-Freudian researchers felt that psychological [28] therapy should be more scientific than Freud. They preferred a "behavioral" approach that focused on changing patients' observable behaviors. Behaviorists propose that all learning is a result of positive or negative consequences. For example, we may learn as toddlers that shouting gets us attention, which is a kind of reward; as a result, we will shout more often. Contrarily, bad experiences dissuade us from continuing a behavior. We may learn to fear swimming because of a [29] childhood experience of being swept off our feet by a strong current, obviously a negative consequence.

[30] Perhaps a child's shouting is causing problems in school; a therapist might teach his parents to praise the child every time he lowers his voice. Due to the rewarding praise, he is likely to begin to speak more softly. Perhaps a patient fears getting in water; a therapist might recommend that she wade in a shallow pool where presumably there will be no waves or currents. [31] Next, to go in a deeper pool. Step by step, due to the water yielding pleasure rather than threat, the patient can overcome her fear.

One popular current therapy focuses on relearning [32] your thought habits. Cognitive Behavioral Therapy (CBT) involves teaching patients to recognize their own "cognitive distortions," or automatic negative thoughts. For example, a young man who tends to regard small problems as [33] catastrophes, may have a disagreement with his girlfriend and automatically assume that their relationship is over. CBT might help him to challenge his catastrophic thinking. Through CBT, he may improve both his moods and his relationships.

28. (A) NO CHANGE
(B) therapies should be more scientific than Freud.
(C) therapy should be more scientific than Freud's was.
(D) therapy should be Freud's.

29. (A) NO CHANGE
(B) negative childhood experience of being swept up by a strong current.
(C) childhood experience in a strong current of water, which was obviously a negative outcome.
(D) childhood experience in which a strong current of water swept us off our feet, a negative consequence.

30. Which choice most effectively establishes the main topic of the paragraph?

(A) Behaviorists look at many possibilities as they begin therapy with patients.
(B) Behaviorists believe that children can learn how to behave by positive reinforcement.
(C) Behaviorism aims to help people learn or unlearn certain behaviors.
(D) Behaviorism holds that all learning is a result of positive or negative consequences.

31. (A) NO CHANGE
(B) Next, a deeper pool would work.
(C) A deeper pool could be gone into next.
(D) Next, the patient could go into a deeper pool.

32. (A) NO CHANGE
(B) his or her thought habits.
(C) thought habits.
(D) their thought habits.

33. (A) NO CHANGE
(B) catastrophes may
(C) catastrophes—may
(D) catastrophes: may

Refer to the passage below to answer questions 34 – 44.

The Krampus

For the approximately 2 billion people who celebrate Christmas each year, Saint Nicholas **34** (you probably know him as Santa Claus) serves as **35** a signal of altruism and kindness. On Christmas Eve, he departs from his home in the North Pole and travels around the world, rewarding virtuous and obedient children with gifts. In most cultures, Santa Claus brings naughty children coal instead of gifts, punishing them for their indiscretions. However, many Germanic cultures believe that something much more **36** menacing, than Santa Claus, visits naughty children in December.

In Germany, Austria, and Hungary, children leave one of their shoes outside their doors on the night of December 5 (their Christmas Eve). The next day, considered Saint Nicholas' Day, children check the shoes they left out. Well-behaved children find shoes filled with toys and food, gifts from **37** Santa Claus; children who have behaved poorly find only a cane rod, a warning from Santa Claus' half-demon, half-goat counterpart, the Krampus. According to folklore, the Krampus beats naughty children with a cane rod before tossing them in a sack and **38** hauling them to the underworld. Clearly, Germanic children have good reason to behave come December.

39 The night of December 5 is Krampus' Night. Around this time, cities and towns host "Krampus Runs," when men dress up as the Krampus and chase people through the streets. Although the Krampus Runs themselves have a Halloween-like air of playfulness, Krampus costumes can be terrifyingly elaborate, often incorporating curved horns, suits of dark fur, cloven feet, and masks depicting fanged goat heads with pointed tongues. For over a century, many Europeans have also sent each other holiday cards featuring the Krampus, who is usually depicted in the process of carrying off children.

34. (A) NO CHANGE
    (B) (usually Santa Claus)
    (C) (commonly referred to as Santa Claus)
    (D) (known internationally as Santa Claus to people around the world)

35. (A) NO CHANGE
    (B) a sign
    (C) a mark
    (D) an emblem

36. (A) NO CHANGE
    (B) menacing than Santa Claus visits naughty children in December.
    (C) menacing than Santa Claus, visits naughty children in December.
    (D) menacing than Santa Claus visits naughty children, in December.

37. (A) NO CHANGE
    (B) Santa Claus, badly behaved children
    (C) Santa Claus; poorly behaved children
    (D) Santa Clause; poor behaved children

38. (A) NO CHANGE
    (B) hauls them
    (C) hauled them
    (D) being hauled

39. Which choice most effectively establishes the main topic of the paragraph?

    (A) The Krampus has been a part of some cultures' Christmas traditions since at least the 17th century.
    (B) Whereas Americans celebrate Christmas at the end of December, many Germanic cultures begin their celebrations at the beginning of the month.
    (C) The Krampus' physical characteristics change slightly depending on who you ask.
    (D) Despite its terrifying appearance and sinister intentions, the Krampus sits at the center of several European traditions.

Many scholars suspect that the Krampus comes from pagan traditions, and that iterations of the Krampus antedate the celebration of Christmas. **40** In Norse mythology, the Krampus is the son of Hel, ruler of the underworld. As Christianity spread throughout Central and Northern Europe during the Middle Ages, **41** they appropriated many pagan traditions and figures, including the Krampus. Over time, the Krampus was conflated with the Devil, another underworld denizen often depicted with goat-like features.

In recent years, the Krampus has seen a sudden rise in popularity, especially in the United States. Many **42** assign this surge to the rise of Christmas "counterculture;" as more people come to regard shopping for Christmas gifts as promoting rampant consumerism, they turn to other, less conventional symbols of the holidays. **43** After all, what subverts the notion of gift giving more than the celebration of the Krampus, a goat-demon with a penchant for snatching **44** children!

40. The writer is considering deleting the underlined sentence. Should the sentence be kept or deleted?

(A) Kept, because it introduces the main topic of Norse mythology in popular culture.
(B) Kept, because it adds relevant information about the Krampus' pagan origins.
(C) Deleted, because it deviates from the paragraph's focus on modern Christian traditions.
(D) Deleted, because it directly contradicts information presented in the previous sentence.

41. (A) NO CHANGE
(B) it
(C) this
(D) these

42. (A) NO CHANGE
(B) equate
(C) attribute
(D) impart

43. (A) NO CHANGE
(B) Thus,
(C) Finally,
(D) However,

44. (A) NO CHANGE
(B) children.
(C) children?
(D) children…

Math Test 5 – No Calculator

25 MINUTES, 20 QUESTIONS

Turn to Section 3 of your answer sheet to answer the questions in this section.

NOTES

1. The use of a calculator on any part of this section is forbidden.
2. Unless otherwise indicated, all variables and expressions used in this test represent real numbers.
3. Unless otherwise indicated, all figures used in this test are drawn to scale.
4. Unless otherwise indicated, all figures used in this test lie on a plane.
5. Unless specified otherwise, a given function, f, has the domain the set of all real numbers x for which $f(x)$ is a real number.

REFERENCE

$A = \dfrac{1}{2} bh$ $c^2 = a^2 + b^2$ Special Right Triangles $A = \pi r^2$ $C = 2\pi r$ $A = \ell w$

$V = \ell wh$ $V = \pi r^2 h$ $V = \dfrac{4}{3}\pi r^3$ $V = \dfrac{1}{3}\pi r^2 h$ $V = \dfrac{1}{3}\ell wh$

The arc of a circle is 360 degrees or 2π radians.
A triangle has angles that sum to 180 degrees.

1. A college dining hall took a survey of 260 students on their favorite meals. One-fifth of students selected macaroni and cheese as their favorite, and 15% selected breakfast sandwiches as their favorite. How many students chose a food other than the two above?

   (A) 52
   (B) 65
   (C) 91
   (D) 169

2. How is the graph of $g(x) = -x^2$ related to the graph of $f(x) = x^2$?

   (A) Reflected vertically
   (B) Reflected horizontally
   (C) Shifted upwards
   (D) Shifted to the left

3. A cell phone provider charges $0.40 for the first minute of a call and $0.20 for each additional minute. The customer is charged at the beginning of each minute. What is the cost of a 12.25-minute call?

   (A) $2.60
   (B) $2.65
   (C) $2.80
   (D) $2.85

4. A linear regression $C = 13.2m + 20.5$ models the relationship between calories burned on a new exercise machine, C, and the number of minutes a person uses the machine, m. Which of the following statements about this model must be true?

   I. A person that spends 22 minutes using the machine burns approximately 311 calories.
   II. C and m are inversely related.

   (A) I only
   (B) II only
   (C) I and II
   (D) Neither I nor II

5. If $S = \dfrac{11(n-2)}{5}$, what is n in terms of S?

   (A) $5S - 9$

   (B) $\dfrac{5(S+2)}{11}$

   (C) $\dfrac{5S}{11} + 2$

   (D) $\dfrac{5S + 2}{11}$

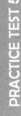

6. A line in the xy-plane that has the equation $x = 3$

   (A) has a point at $(0, 3)$.
   (B) is a line that has a slope of 3.
   (C) is a line that is parallel to $y = 3x$.
   (D) is a line that is parallel to the y-axis.

7. If $x \neq 0$, for what value(s) of x is

   $x + 1 = \dfrac{20}{x}$?

   (A) 4 only
   (B) –5 only
   (C) –4 or 5
   (D) –5 or 4

8. A line with the equation $y = mx + 4$ passes through quadrant IV. What must be true of m?

   (A) $m = 0$
   (B) $m < 0$
   (C) $0 < m < 1$
   (D) $m > 0$

9. The point $(2, 4)$ is on the graph of the function $f(x)$. Which of the following points is on the graph of $f(x + 3)$?

   (A) $(5, 4)$
   (B) $(–1, 4)$
   (C) $(2, 1)$
   (D) $(2, 7)$

10. If $f(x) = 2x + 1$, then $\dfrac{f(x+h) - f(x)}{h}$ is

   (A) $\dfrac{1}{2}$
   (B) 2
   (C) $\dfrac{h-1}{h}$
   (D) $\dfrac{2h+2}{h}$

11. The area of a rectangle is 192 feet squared. If the width of the rectangle is $\dfrac{3}{4}$ of its length, what is the width of the rectangle?

   (A) 12 feet
   (B) 16 feet
   (C) 24 feet
   (D) 144 feet

12. If $f(x) = (x-2)(2-x)^{-1}$ for all values of x except 2, which of the following statements must be true?

I. $f(1) = f(-1)$

II. $f(4) = f(0)$

III. $f\left(\dfrac{1}{2}\right) = f(-2)$

(A) I only

(B) I and II only

(C) II and III only

(D) I, II, and III

13.

$$f(x) = zx^2 - 4z$$

The function above contains the rational number z, and $f(-4) = 18$. What is the value of $f(0)$?

(A) –18

(B) –6

(C) 0

(D) 14

14. A journeyman mechanic works at an auto shop. He services cars, SUVs, and trucks, and he is paid $14 per hour for cars and SUVs, and $36 per hour for trucks. Cars and SUVs take an average of 2 hours to service, whereas trucks require an average of 4 hours each. This past week, he worked 48 hours and made a total of $1,288. If x equals the the number of cars and SUVs serviced, and y equals the number of trucks, which of the following system of equations can be used to determine how many trucks the mechanic serviced?

(A) $2x + 4y = 48$

$2(14x) + 4(36y) = 1,288$

(B) $4x + 2y = 48$

$14x + 36y = 1,288$

(C) $x + y = 48$

$\dfrac{14x}{2} + \dfrac{36y}{4} = 1,288$

(D) $\dfrac{x}{y} = 48$

$\dfrac{14x}{36y} = 1,288$

15. The angle a is an acute angle. If $\sin a = x$, and $b = 90° - a$, what is the value of $\cos b$?

(A) x

(B) $\dfrac{1}{x}$

(C) $90 - x$

(D) Cannot be determined.

DIRECTIONS

For questions **16 – 20**, find the solution to the problem and enter your answer as demonstrated below.

1. Only the answer that is bubbled in on the answer sheet will be credited. The blank spaces above the bubbles are for you to record your answers for accuracy.
2. Only fill in one bubble in any given column.
3. None of the answers on this portion of the test are negative values.
4. If a problem appears to have more than one answer, only enter one answer. If the answer you enter is one of the correct solutions, you will receive full credit for that question.
5. If the correct answer can be expressed as a mixed number, it must be entered as a decimal or an improper fraction.
6. If the correct answer is a decimal that cannot fit into the grid space, you must fill the grid with enough digits to completely fill the space. The number can be rounded or simply shortened but must fill every blank space.

NOTES

Begin entering answers in any column that accommodates your answer. If you do not need a column do not enter anything in that column.

Answer: $\frac{5}{36}$

Answer: 4.5

Write answer in boxes.

Grid in result.

← Fraction line
← Decimal point

Acceptable ways to grid $\frac{1}{6}$ are:

Answer: 302 – either position is correct

16. A bag contains 27 marbles, each of which is either red, green, or blue. The number of blue marbles is double the number of red marbles, and the number of green marbles is three times the number of blue marbles. How many red marbles are in the bag?

    ANSWER: _____

17. If $\dfrac{135}{z^2} = \dfrac{450}{10z}$, then what is the value of z?

    ANSWER: _____

18. If a, b, and c are positive integers and

    $\dfrac{16}{5} = a + \dfrac{1}{b + \dfrac{1}{c}}$, what is the value of $a + b + c$?

    ANSWER: _____

19. If the expression $\dfrac{3x^4 - 2x^2 - 3}{x + 2}$ is written in the equivalent form $A + \dfrac{B}{x + 2}$, what is the value of B?

    ANSWER: _____

20. If a sector of a circle has an arc length of 2π inches and an area of 6π square inches, what is the length of the radius of the circle?

    ANSWER: _____

Math Test 5 – Calculator

55 MINUTES, 38 QUESTIONS

Turn to Section 4 of your answer sheet to answer the questions in this section.

NOTES

1. The use of a calculator on any part of this section is allowed.
2. Unless otherwise indicated, all variables and expressions used in this test represent real numbers.
3. Unless otherwise indicated, all figures used in this test are drawn to scale.
4. Unless otherwise indicated, all figures used in this test lie on a plane.
5. Unless specified otherwise, a given function, f, has the domain the set of all real numbers x for which $f(x)$ is a real number.

REFERENCE

$A = \frac{1}{2}bh$ $c^2 = a^2 + b^2$ Special Right Triangles $A = \pi r^2$ $A = \ell w$
$C = 2\pi r$

$V = \ell wh$ $V = \pi r^2 h$ $V = \frac{4}{3}\pi r^3$ $V = \frac{1}{3}\pi r^2 h$ $V = \frac{1}{3}\ell wh$

The arc of a circle is 360 degrees or 2π radians.
A triangle has angles that sum to 180 degrees.

1. What is the slope of the line m with equation $2x - 5y = 10$?

   (A) $-\dfrac{2}{5}$

   (B) $\dfrac{5}{2}$

   (C) $\dfrac{2}{5}$

   (D) -2

2. The concentration of a substance in a solution is 2×10^{-5} milligrams per milliliter. How many milligrams of the substance are in 3×10^8 milliliters?

   (A) 6×10^{-13}
   (B) 5×10^{-13}
   (C) 5×10
   (D) 6×10^3

3. A train goes from Town A to Town B. If the train averages 50 miles per hour, then it will be 20 minutes late. If it averages 80 miles per hour, then it will be 10 minutes early. When will it arrive with respect to the scheduled arrival time if it goes 60 miles per hour?

   (A) Early by 3 minutes.

   (B) Early by $\dfrac{7}{3}$ minutes.

   (C) Late by 10 minutes.

   (D) Late by $\dfrac{20}{3}$ minutes.

4. Tom deposits $100 into a bank, and the amount in his bank account increases by 5% each year. Christine deposits $100 into a different bank, and the amount in her bank account increases by $5 each year. Which statement is true about the amounts in Tom's and Christine's bank accounts?

   (A) The amount in Tom's bank account can be modeled by an exponential function and the amount in Christine's bank account can be modeled by a linear function.
   (B) The amount in Tom's bank account can be modeled by a linear function and the amount in Christine's bank account can be modeled by an exponential function.
   (C) The amounts in both bank accounts can both be modeled by exponential functions.
   (D) The amounts in both bank accounts can both be modeled by linear functions.

5. John has four more nickels than dimes in his pocket, for a total of $1.25. Which equation could be used to determine the number of dimes, x, in his pocket?

   (A) $0.10(x + 4) + 0.05(x) = \$1.25$
   (B) $0.05(x + 4) + 0.10(x) = \$1.25$
   (C) $0.10(4x) + 0.05(x) = \$1.25$
   (D) $0.05(4x) + 0.10(x) = \$1.25$

6. Two functions, $y = |x - 3|$ and $3x + 3y = 27$, are graphed on the same coordinate plane. Which statement is true about the solution to the system of equations?

   (A) $(3, 0)$ is the solution to the system because it satisfies the equation $y = |x - 3|$.
   (B) $(9, 0)$ is the solution to the system because it satisfies the equation $3x + 3y = 27$.
   (C) $(6, 3)$ is the solution to the system because it satisfies both equations.
   (D) $(3, 0)$, $(9, 0)$, and $(6, 3)$ are the solutions to the system of equations because they all satisfy at least one of the equations.

7. Tim plays a video game five times and achieves the following scores in this order:

   4,526   4,599   4,672   4,745   4,818

   The scores follow a pattern. Which expression could be used to determine his score on playing the game for the nth time?

   (A) $73n + 4,453$
   (B) $73(n + 4,453)$
   (C) $4,453n + 73$
   (D) $4,526n$

8. Anna works out for one hour with a mixture of running and walking. She burns fifteen calories per minute while running and ten calories per minute while walking, and burns 700 calories overall. How many minutes does Anna spend running?

   (A) 10
   (B) 20
   (C) 30
   (D) 40

9. A cetologist wants to estimate the size of a whale population. She observes their migration over several weeks and bases her estimation of the population on her count. The data indicates that there are 3 whales migrating through a particular 5-mile stretch of ocean every hour for 8 weeks. Based on this information, what is the approximate whale population in the area?

   (A) 200
   (B) 3,000
   (C) 4,000
   (D) 20,000

10. When Mike eats at a restaurant, he always tips from eight to twenty percent of the cost of the meal. Which of the following must be true?

   (A) When the cost of the dinner is $10.00, the tip is between $2.00 and $8.00.
   (B) When the cost of the dinner is $15, the tip is between $1.20 and $3.00.
   (C) When the tip is $3.00, the amount of the dinner is between $11.00 and $23.00.
   (D) When the tip is $2.40, the amount of the dinner is between $3.00 and $6.00.

Questions 11 and 12 refer to the information below.

The chart below shows the current enrollment in all social studies classes (Geography, U.S. History, World Cultures, and Government) at Iron Mountain High School.

COURSE TITLE	SECTION	PERIOD	ENROLLMENT
Geography	A	1	23
Geography	B	2	24
U.S. History	A	2	25
U.S. History	B	3	29
U.S. History	C	4	24
World Cultures	A	3	27
Government	A	4	26
Government	B	6	27

11. What is the average number of students enrolled in each course?

    (A) 25
    (B) 26
    (C) 27
    (D) 29

12. Every student in the school is required to read the same book in preparation for a talk that will be given at a school assembly by the author. The school purchases two classroom sets of thirty books each, but shortly afterwards three books go missing from one set and five go missing from the other. If one class period uses both sets at a time, and each student needs his own book, which period(s) will not have enough books for its(their) students?

    (A) Period 2 only
    (B) Period 3 only
    (C) Period 4 only
    (D) Periods 3 and 4

13. Francisco spent ten dollars on hot dogs and hamburgers at a baseball game. Hot dogs are three dollars each, and hamburgers are four dollars each. How many hot dogs and hamburgers did he buy?

    (A) One hot dog and one hamburger
    (B) One hot dog and two hamburgers
    (C) Two hot dogs and one hamburger
    (D) Two hot dogs and two hamburgers

14. If $\dfrac{x+2}{x-5} \geq 0$, then which of the following is true of x?

    (A) $x \geq -2$
    (B) $-2 \leq x \leq 5$
    (C) $x \leq -2$ or $x > 5$
    (D) $x > 5$

Questions 15 – 18 refer to information below.

Types of Wildlife Habitat on Public Lands 2012
(100,000's acres)

	CA	NV	OR	UT
Shrub/Scrub	119	392	125	146
Herbaceous	5.5	20	7.2	17
Evergreen Forest	7.0	44	21	37
Mixed Forest	0	0	1.7	0
Barren Land	16	44	2.9	25
Other	2.3	2.5	3.3	3.0

15. Approximately what percentage of Utah's wildlife habitat is either herbaceous or evergreen forest?

    (A) 7.5
    (B) 24
    (C) 27
    (D) 31

16. Which state has the highest proportion of its wildlife habitat classified as barren land?

    (A) California
    (B) Nevada
    (C) Oregon
    (D) Utah

17. An ecologist projects that 15% of Oregon's herbaceous habitat will be transformed into a shrubby habitat over the next ten years. According to this projection, what will be the total amount of shrubby habitat in Oregon in ten years time?

    (A) 126,000 acres
    (B) 11.8 million acres
    (C) 12.6 million acres
    (D) 13.5 million acres

18. A developer bought 3% of California's public barren lands several years ago at $350 per acre. Since then, the value of the land has increased by 750%. Approximately how much would the land sell for today if sold in its entirety?

    (A) $126 million
    (B) $131 million
    (C) $143 million
    (D) $149 million

19. A band is recording an album. They rent a studio at $200 per day, which gives them access for 12 hours. The day rate cannot be prorated, so studio time must be purchased by the day. Their sound engineer costs $28 per hour, and is needed for half the total recording time. If it will take 50 hours to complete, what is the average cost per hour over the entire course of recording?

    (A) $31.60
    (B) $34
    (C) $44.50
    (D) $48

20. What is the equation of the line that passes through the point (8, –3) and is perpendicular to the line $2x - 3y - 10 = 0$?

    (A) $y = -\dfrac{3}{2}x + 9$

    (B) $y = -\dfrac{2}{3}x + \dfrac{7}{3}$

    (C) $y = -\dfrac{3}{2}x - 15$

    (D) $y = -\dfrac{1}{2}x + 1$

21. In your search for a summer job, you are given the following offers.

Offer 1: At Timmy's Tacos, you will earn $4.50 an hour. However, you will be required to purchase a uniform for $45.00. You will be expected to work 20 hours each week.

Offer 2: At Kelly's Car Wash, you will earn $3.50 an hour. No special attire is required. You must agree to work 20 hours each week.

Before deciding which job offer you wish to take, you consider the factors. Which conclusion below is NOT true?

(A) If I work 8 weeks at Kelly's Car Wash and save all my earnings, I'll be able to save $560.

(B) If I take the job at Timmy's Tacos, I'll have to work 10 hours just to pay for purchasing my uniform.

(C) If I only plan to work for two weeks, I should choose the job at Kelly's Car Wash.

(D) The job at Timmy's Tacos pays more if I work 40 hours.

22. The table below shows the number of words typed by the same student during five timed sessions. Which equation models a line of best fit for this data?

Time (t) in minutes	Number of words Typed (w)
2	122
3	182
4	240
6	368
9	538

(A) $w = -117t + 102$

(B) $w = 102t - 117$

(C) $w = 60t + 3$

(D) $w = 3t + 60$

23.

Student	1st Test Score	2nd Test Score
Amy	25	50
Bill	30	90
Charlie	42	84
Danny	50	75

According to the table above, which two students had the same percent improvement in scores from the first to the second test?

(A) Bill and Charlie

(B) Bill and Danny

(C) Amy and Dora

(D) Amy and Charlie

24.

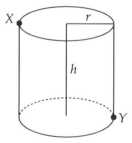

A circular cylinder has a height of 12 and a radius of 3. If X and Y are two points on the surface of the cylinder, what is the maximum possible length of $\overline{XY}$?

(A) $3\sqrt{17}$

(B) 6

(C) $6\sqrt{5}$

(D) $5\sqrt{6}$

450

25. Rebecca is flying from New York to San Francisco. The regular cost of a ticket is $378 plus a tax of 22%. She applies a frequent-flyer discount, which takes 10% off the price of airfare. In addition, there is a flat $25 charge for each checked bag, and a fee of $2.50 per pound over 50 for heavy bags What is the total cost of the flight, in dollars, including bag fees, if she checks two bags that weigh 55 pounds and 62 pounds?

(A) $477.54

(B) $492.04

(C) $504.54

(D) $507.54

26. What is the solution set of this system of equations?

$$x^2 - y = -3$$
$$2x^2 - y = -2$$

(A) $\{(-1, -4), (-1, 4)\}$

(B) $\{(-1, -4), (1, 4)\}$

(C) $\{(-1, 4), (1, -4)\}$

(D) $\{(-1, 4), (1, 4)\}$

27.

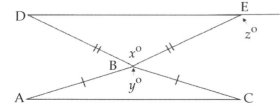

The figure above shows two isosceles triangles, ABC and DBE, where $3z° = x°$, and $z° = y° - x°$. Given that the equal angles in triangle ABC sum to 40°, what is the value of $x + y + z$?

(A) 190

(B) 280

(C) 360

(D) 440

28. Given that $i = \sqrt{-1}$, The expression $\dfrac{3 - 4i}{5 + 3i}$ is equivalent to

(A) $\dfrac{27 - 29i}{34}$

(B) $\dfrac{27 - 29i}{16}$

(C) $\dfrac{3 - 29i}{34}$

(D) $15 - 8i$

29. George Meegan walked 19,019 miles in 2,425 days (1977-1983) from Tierra Del Fuego to the northernmost part of Alaska. If Mr. Meegan walked an average of seven hours per day, what would his average pace, in miles per hour, have been?

(A) 1.12

(B) 1.43

(C) 2.61

(D) 5.4

30.

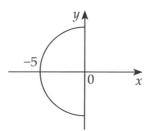

In the semicircle above, the center is at (0, 0). Which of the following are the y-coordinates of two points on this semicircle whose x-coordinates are equal?

(A) $y = 0, -5$

(B) $y = 4, -4$

(C) $y = 1, -3$

(D) $y = 2, -4$

DIRECTIONS

For questions **31 – 38,** find the solution to the problem and enter your answer as demonstrated below.

1. Only the answer that is bubbled in on the answer sheet will be credited. The blank spaces above the bubbles are for you to record your answers for accuracy.
2. Only fill in one bubble in any given column.
3. None of the answers on this portion of the test are negative values.
4. If a problem appears to have more than one answer, only enter one answer. If the answer you enter is one of the correct solutions, you will receive full credit for that question.
5. If the correct answer can be expressed as a mixed number, it must be entered as a decimal or an improper fraction.
6. If the correct answer is a decimal that cannot fit into the grid space, you must fill the grid with enough digits to completely fill the space. The number can be rounded or simply shortened but must fill every blank space.

NOTES

Begin entering answers in any column that accommodates your answer. If you do not need a column do not enter anything in that column.

Answer: $\frac{5}{36}$

Answer: 4.5

Write answer → in boxes.

← Fraction line

← Decimal point

Grid in result.

Acceptable ways to grid $\frac{1}{6}$ are:

Answer: 302 – either position is correct

PRACTICE TEST 5

31.

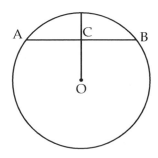

A circle with center O has a radius of five units. The chord $\overline{AB}$ has a length of eight units and is perpendicular to the radius r. What is the length of $\overline{OC}$?

ANSWER: _____

32. Lauren has $80 in her savings account. When she receives her paycheck, she makes a deposit which brings the balance up to $120. By what percent does the total amount in her account increase as a result of this deposit?

ANSWER: _____

33. The oxygen saturation of a lake is calculated by dividing the amount of dissolved oxygen in a liter of lake water by the lake water's dissolved oxygen capacity, and then converting that number into a percentage. If the lake currently has 6.4 milligrams of dissolved oxygen per liter, and the dissolved oxygen capacity is 9.5 milligrams per liter, what is the oxygen saturation level of the lake, expressed as a percentage? (Round your answer to the nearest whole number.)

ANSWER: _____

34. The amount of interest earned on savings is directly proportional to the amount of money saved. If $104 in interest is earned on $1,300, how much in interest, in dollars, will be earned on $1,800 in the same period of time?

ANSWER: _____

35. A number, k, is increased by 10. If the fifth root of the resulting number equals 2, then k is

    ANSWER: _____

36. The selling price of a coat is $91 plus overhead and profit margin. If the overhead is 20% of the selling price and the profit is 10% of the selling price, what is the selling price? (Give your answer to the nearest dollar.)

    ANSWER: _____

Questions 37 and 38 refer to the information below.

A shipping company needs to transport 25 containers. The company has a fleet of five trucks, each of which can carry one container per trip, and each truck can make the trip to the destination in two days. Each truck averages 10 mpg, and the cost of diesel fuel is $2.50/gallon. Once the last container is delivered, trucks stay at their destination until dispatched to their next job.

37. **Part 1:**
    What is the fuel cost associated with the job, to the nearest dollar, if the distance to the destination is 250 miles?

    ANSWER: _____

38. **Part 2:**
    The shipping company adds three trucks to its fleet. In terms of days, how much faster will it be able to complete the same job?

    ANSWER: _____

Essay Test 5*

 50 MINUTES, Prompt-based essay

Turn to Section 5 of your answer sheet to answer the question in this section.

DIRECTIONS

As you read the passage below, consider how Mathew Meyer uses
- evidence, such as facts or examples, to support claims.
- reasoning to develop ideas and to connect claims and evidence.
- stylistic or persuasive elements, such as word choice or appeals to emotion, to add power to the ideas expressed.

Adapted from "The Other Side of American Football," by Mathew Meyer. ©2015 by KALLIS EDU.

A high school boy wants to play in the big game, so he doesn't tell his parents or coaches that he still feels dizzy from an injury weeks ago. After a hard collision in the game, he walks off the field, collapses on the sideline, and dies. A college quarterback wins three national championships, and is dead at age 30. Three National Football League (NFL) superstars earn huge salaries, win Super Bowls, and look forward to long, golden retirements. Instead, all three commit suicide, and are posthumously diagnosed with Chronic Traumatic Encephalopathy (CTE).

CTE is a degenerative brain disease caused by repetitive bruising of the brain. The symptoms include headaches, depression, violent outbursts, memory and motor loss, and dementia. No one knows how many concussions or hard collisions it takes, but it cannot be ignored; the football world must face up to the vulnerability of the human brain.

And fans of football (like myself) must face the question: what kind of country sacrifices the lives of young athletes so it can watch a game? What kind of country spends billions on a sport that kills its heroes? America must ban high school football, restrict football in college, and radically change the professional game, before thousands more men and boys ruin their lives. More than 4,500 retired NFL players are already suing the league over concussion-related illness.

Between 1990 and 2010, 243 high school and college players died. More than 200 were high school players. In the 2005/2006 season, there were more than 500,000 injuries in high school football. More than 50,000 were broken bones or concussions. Already, brain injuries have led high schools in many states, including California, Colorado, and New York, to cancel games, seasons, the sport itself.

Concussions in high school may be more dangerous than those in the NFL, because teenagers' bodies are more vulnerable. Also, high school athletes don't have NFL trainers and doctors. And, many high school boys lie about or hide their brain injuries.

The injuries in college football parallel those in high school. However, an ominous specter looms over the college game. College players suffer much more from CTE than previously thought. In fact, some players diagnosed with CTE were never diagnosed with a concussion. Owen Thomas, a University of Pennsylvania player with no history of concussion, committed suicide in 2010. His autopsy revealed CTE. Cullen Finnerty, a star quarterback who won three NCAA championships, was diagnosed with Stage 2 CTE after dying at age 30. Finnerty had one concussion in college, and none before.

CTE is epidemic in the NFL. When the nation's largest brain bank studied the brains of 79 deceased former players, it found clear evidence of CTE in 76 of them. Last year, the NFL admitted in Federal court that it knows that many retired players will develop long-term cognitive problems.

Some of the NFL's greatest have been ruined by CTE. Andre Waters tackled so hard that the NFL named a rule after him. He suffered at least 15 concussions. After he committed suicide, an autopsy revealed that he had the brain of an 80-90 year old with dementia. "Football killed him," the doctor said. Waters was 44 years old.

Junior Seau was twelve times an All-Star, with six consecutive seasons with more than 100 tackles. Two years after retiring, showing more and more symptoms of CTE, Seau committed suicide. He was 43 years old.

Dave Duerson was a star player for the Super Bowl champion 1985 Chicago Bears. He won two Super Bowls. Duerson also earned an Economics degree from Notre Dame, studied business at Harvard, and was successful in business. Then CTE symptoms began. His business and investments failed. A violent outburst led to a guilty plea for domestic battery. He hid his symptoms, and lied to cover his failing memory. When he shot himself, Duerson left explicit instructions to check for CTE. His autopsy showed clear evidence of disease in the regions of the brain controlling judgement, inhibition, impulse control, mood, and memory. He was 50 years old.

Brain damage is changing the league. After the 2014/2015 season, star rookie Chris Borland retired, walking away from millions of dollars from the San Francisco 49ers. He explained that he wanted to avoid concussions and CTE. Three other young players retired, citing health concerns and leaving tens of millions in salary on the table. Jason Worilds, a Pittsburgh Steelers' linebacker, gave up $15 million.

If football is to survive as a sport, the NFL needs to invest millions in technology and make changes to stop brain injuries. College football needs to do the same, and to limit collisions in practice. American high schools need to stop playing tackle football, and find something safer to do on a Friday night.

Write an essay in which you explain how Mathew Meyer builds an argument to persuade his audience that football-related head injuries are more common and more damaging than people realize. In your essay, analyze how the author uses one or more of the features listed in the box above (or features of your own choice) to strengthen the logic and persuasiveness of his argument. Be sure that your analysis focuses on the most relevant features of the passage.

Your essay should not explain whether you agree with the author's claims, but rather explain how the author builds an argument to persuade his audience.

* Sample responses at www.kallisedu.com

KALLIS

SAT® Practice Test #6

IMPORTANT REMINDERS:

1 When you take the official SAT, you will need to use a No. 2 pencil. Do not use a pen or a mechanical pencil.

2 On the official SAT, sharing any of the questions on the test violates the College Board's policies and may result in your scores being canceled.

(This cover is modeled after the cover you'll see when you take the official SAT.)

Reading Test 6

65 MINUTES, 52 QUESTIONS

Turn to Section 1 of your answer sheet to answer the questions in this section.

DIRECTIONS

Each passage or pair of passages is accompanied by 10 or 11 questions. Read each passage or pair of passages, and then select the most appropriate answer to each question. Some passages may include tables or graphs that require additional analysis.

Refer to the passage below to answer questions 1 – 10.

This passage is adapted from Oscar Wilde, *The Picture of Dorian Gray*, originally published in 1890.

line
"Dorian Gray? Is that his name? " asked Lord Henry, walking across the studio towards Basil Hallward.

"Yes, that is his name. I didn't intend to tell it
5 to you."

"But why not?"

"Oh, I can't explain. When I like people immensely, I never tell their names to anyone. It is like surrendering a part of them. I have grown
10 to love secrecy. It seems to be the one thing that can make modern life mysterious or marvelous to us. The commonest thing is delightful if one only hides it. When I leave town now I never tell my people where I am going. If I did, I would lose
15 all my pleasure. It is a silly habit, I dare say, but somehow it seems to bring a great deal of romance into one's life. I suppose you think me awfully foolish about it?"

"Not at all," answered Lord Henry, "not at
20 all, my dear Basil. You seem to forget that I am married, and the one charm of marriage is that it makes a life of deception absolutely necessary for both parties. I never know where my wife is, and my wife never knows what I am doing. When we
25 meet—we do meet occasionally, when we dine out together, or go down to the Duke's—we tell each other the most absurd stories with the most serious faces. My wife is very good at it—much better, in fact, than I am. She never gets confused
30 over her dates, and I always do. But when she does find me out, she makes no row at all. I sometimes wish she would; but she merely laughs at me."

"I hate the way you talk about your married

35 life, Harry," said Basil Hallward, strolling towards the door that led into the garden. "I believe that you are really a very good husband, but that you are thoroughly ashamed of your own virtues. You are an extraordinary fellow. You never say
40 a moral thing, and you never do a wrong thing. Your cynicism is simply a pose."

"Being natural is simply a pose, and the most irritating pose I know," cried Lord Henry, laughing; and the two young men went out into
45 the garden together and ensconced themselves on a long bamboo seat that stood in the shade of a tall laurel bush. The sunlight slipped over the polished leaves. In the grass, white daisies were tremulous.

50 After a pause, Lord Henry pulled out his watch. "I am afraid I must be going, Basil," he murmured, "and before I go, I insist on your answering a question I put to you some time ago."

"What is that?" said the painter, keeping his
55 eyes fixed on the ground.

"You know quite well."

"I do not, Harry."

"Well, I will tell you what it is. I want you to explain to me why you won't exhibit Dorian
60 Gray's picture. I want the real reason."

"I told you the real reason."

"No, you did not. You said it was because there was too much of yourself in it. Now, that is childish."

65 "Harry," said Basil Hallward, looking him straight in the face, "every portrait that is painted with feeling is a portrait of the artist, not of the sitter. The sitter is merely the accident, the occasion. It is not he who is revealed by
70 the painter; it is rather the painter who, on the colored canvas, reveals himself. The reason I will not exhibit this picture is that I am afraid that I have shown in it the secret of my own soul."

1. As used in line 12, "delightful" most nearly means

   (A) sublime.
   (B) alluring.
   (C) enjoyable.
   (D) distracting.

2. Basil wants to withhold Dorian Gray's name from Lord Henry because

   (A) Basil is ashamed that he is acquainted with Dorian Gray.
   (B) Basil enjoys withholding the names of people whose company he enjoys.
   (C) Basil believes that Lord Henry will be jealous of his friendship with Dorian Gray.
   (D) Basil tries not to talk about his personal life with Lord Henry.

3. Lord Henry talks to Basil about marriage primarily to

   (A) shift the conversation away from Dorian Gray.
   (B) explain why he can relate to Basil's fondness for secrecy.
   (C) provide a description of his wife.
   (D) encourage Basil to get married.

4. Based on paragraph 5 (lines 19 – 33), it can be inferred that Lord Henry's wife

   (A) has a cruel sense of humor.
   (B) is well-respected among her peers.
   (C) is a skillful liar.
   (D) has little respect for Harry.

5. Which contradiction does Basil use to characterize Lord Henry?

   (A) Lord Henry's virtuous actions undermine the immorality he espouses.
   (B) Lord Henry's predictable behaviors belie his supposed love of deception.
   (C) Lord Henry claims to be adventurous but rarely tries new things.
   (D) Lord Henry appears confident but is filled with self-doubt.

6. As used in line 41, "pose" most nearly means

   (A) pretense.
   (B) position.
   (C) posture.
   (D) stance.

7. The passage suggests that Basil wants to keep which secret to himself?

   (A) The personal nature of his artwork
   (B) The reason he rarely paints portraits
   (C) The biggest challenges he faces when painting
   (D) The reason he decided to become an artist

8. Which choice provides the best evidence for the answer to the previous question?

   (A) Lines 39 – 41 ("You never say…a pose")
   (B) Lines 58 – 60 ("I want you…Dorian Gray's picture")
   (C) Line 68 – 69 ("The sitter…the occasion")
   (D) Lines 69 – 71 ("It is not he…reveals himself")

9. In the context of the passage, Basil and Lord Henry differ in that

   (A) Basil values the beauty provided by nature whereas Lord Henry prefers city life.
   (B) Basil encourages social interaction whereas Lord Henry simply begrudgingly accepts it.
   (C) Basil maintains secrecy through silence whereas Lord Henry maintains secrecy through deception.
   (D) Basil appreciates the subjectivity of art whereas Lord Henry prefers rationality and objectivity.

10. The conversation between Basil and Harry most closely resembles that between

    (A) brothers forcing each other to be candid.
    (B) business associates celebrating their successes.
    (C) family members quarreling over trivial matters.
    (D) mortal enemies settling a score.

Refer to the passage below to answer questions 11 – 20.

This passage is adapted from, "Marrying Older, But Sooner." ©2015 by KALLIS EDU.

line   Most developed countries report that more young people are postponing marriage until later in life than has been the case historically. The romantic image of fresh-faced brides and grooms
5 in their early 20s is now largely a myth. In Hong Kong, for example, men tend to be at least 31 years old, and women around 28, when they marry for the first time; in South Korea, the averages are 32 and 29, respectively. Many
10 European countries record even higher average ages, with Sweden topping the charts at 35 for men and 33 for women. North American figures are also rising, with the average age for men in the U.S. being 29, and for women, 27.

15   Grandparents and parents of the current crop of young adults most likely married younger and had more children. These older generations may worry about their offspring "boomeranging" from independent living back to the family home,
20 putting off marriage seemingly forever.

The lack of a healthy income has been a factor in the postponement, according to many economists. Since the global economic recession began in 2008, couples increasingly cannot afford
25 to start a new life together. Even many people with full-time jobs live with their parents. Popular culture has coined many terms to describe this phenomenon. In Brazil, singles living with their parents have been called "the Kangaroo
30 Generation," referring to young kangaroos living in their maternal pouches. In Greece, young people have bitterly called themselves the "700 Euros Generation," referring to the legal minimum wage as all they can hope to earn.

35   The "Sampo Generation" in South Korea, meanwhile, is also a bitter reference to young adults who have reached their 30s without achieving a reliable income that can sustain a family. *Sampo* translates as "give up three,"
40 namely the three goals of attaining a career, getting married, and having children. In Japan, popular perception is even darker, with the "Satori Generation" supposedly not even caring about a successful career or a romantic attachment
45 of any kind, let alone marriage.

Some demographers have encouraged taking a longer-term perspective. They say that comparing today's statistics with those from periods of strong economic growth is misleading.
50 In the U.S., for example, the average ages at first marriage seem high when compared to the period of economic boom after World War II. In 1956, a man typically got married at 23. But looking back to 1890, a man usually waited until his late
55 20s. U.S. Census Bureau blogger Jonathan Vespa points out that, in the U.S., "The 1950s and 1960s stand out as the exception for marriage, not the norm."

Data also indicate that, from a historical
60 perspective, young single people have always tended to live at home with their families, calling into question the current anxiety about generations acting like boomerangs or kangaroos. In the 1940s, more than 70 percent of singles
65 in their 20s lived with their parents. By this standard, the picture looks different; perhaps what has changed are the expectations about what young people *should* be able to achieve in terms of their career. It may be unfair to compare
70 younger generations to their Baby Boomer parents and grandparents, who came of age in the 1960s and 1970s, when economic conditions were more favorable. People's expectations may have also been influenced by watching films or television
75 programs that portray fictional young adults living in enormous apartments and seldom working.

Another way to gain perspective on the data is to look at marriage in terms of historical
80 increases in lifespan. Census experts say that even taking into account the slight skewing of data by higher infant mortality in the 19th century, it is clear that people are marrying earlier in their expected lifespan than ever before. In 1890, an
85 American woman was likely to get married at 22, and to live to be 45. She was marrying nearly halfway into her life. Today, a young woman can expect to live to be 80. If she gets married at around 27, that is only about a third of the way
90 through the typical lifespan. Figures for men are similar.

"Despite marrying at older ages," Vespa writes, "Americans are actually marrying sooner in their lifetime than they did a century ago."

95   Besides economic circumstances, then, it is quite possible that changes in life expectancy have had an effect on individuals' personal decisions. They may feel that they simply have more time to gain an education and job experience before
100 launching into marriage and parenthood.

Marrying Older, but Sooner?

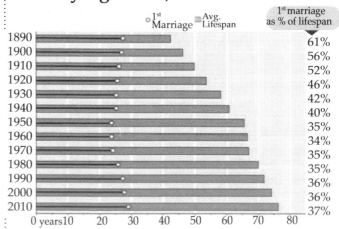

	1st Marriage	Avg. Lifespan	1st marriage as % of lifespan
1890			61%
1900			56%
1910			52%
1920			46%
1930			42%
1940			40%
1950			35%
1960			34%
1970			35%
1980			35%
1990			36%
2000			36%
2010			37%

0 years 10   20   30   40   50   60   70   80

SOURCE: U.S. Census Bureau, *Decennial Censuses, 1890-1940 and Current Population Survey*, Annual Social and Economic Supplements.

11. In paragraph 1, the author most likely mentions "romantic image" (line 4) in order to

(A) draw an analogy with actual circumstances.
(B) provide a realistic context for claims in the text.
(C) indicate the most ideal approach to marriage.
(D) introduce stereotypes that contradict reality.

12. As used in line 15, the word "crop" most nearly means

(A) yield.
(B) coalition.
(C) cutting.
(D) group.

13. The passage strongly suggests that middle-aged and older people

(A) advise younger generations not to move back home.
(B) feel impatient for their adult children to get married.
(C) do not want to support their offspring.
(D) prefer that their children stay at home into their 20s.

14. Which choice best describes the structure of paragraph 3 (lines 21 – 34)?

(A) Description followed by logical analysis
(B) Problem followed by a proposed solution
(C) Claim followed by anecdotal support
(D) Facts followed by an overall conclusion

15. The author most strongly implies which of the following about the "Satori Generation"?

(A) It is based on depressing and indisputable facts.
(B) It may reflect a current stereotype rather than a reality.
(C) It does not describe any actual individuals in Japan.
(D) It probably demonstrates multiple factors at work in Japanese society.

16. The author uses the phrase "by this standard" (lines 65 – 66) primarily to

(A) establish an alternative norm.
(B) refute the statistical evidence.
(C) argue for a new set of ideals.
(D) encourage particular life choices.

17. Which claim about average age at marriage is best supported by the graph?

(A) Lines 56 – 58 ("'The 1950s and 1960s... norm'")
(B) Lines 64 – 65 ("In the 1940s...their parents")
(C) Lines 69 – 73 ("It may be unfair...favorable")
(D) Lines 78 – 80 ("Another way...lifespan")

18. The graph indicates that, based on past trends,

(A) average age at first marriage will gradually catch up to lifespan.
(B) average lifespan will level off at about where it is now.
(C) average age at first marriage will not rise much higher.
(D) average age at first marriage will dip down again in the near future.

19. The main rhetorical effect of the quotation in lines 92 – 94 is to

(A) introduce a new perspective to the discussion.
(B) emphasize the main conclusion from the data.
(C) persuade the reader that the data is accurate.
(D) restate information from the beginning of the article.

20. Based on the passage, it can be inferred that the author's hypothesis about people marrying later is which of the following?

(A) There are more varied opportunities for the current generation.
(B) Young people nowadays tend to be more mature when entering marriage.
(C) Economic factors affect the trend but are not the cause of it.
(D) Longer life expectancy leads people to take their relationships less seriously.

Refer to the passage below to answer questions 21 – 30.

Mary Bates, "Monkey Faces Give Clues to Species and Individual Identity," © 2015 by Conde Nast.

line   In a new study, researchers looked at whether there were clues in certain components or the overall configurations of monkey faces that could reliably send signals to other monkeys —
5 about the species that a face belonged to or the individual identity of a monkey.

William Allen and James Higham, of New York University, previously found that in guenons, a group of Old-World monkeys, species
10 that live near one another tend to look more different from one another, an adaptation that helps prevent hybridization* between species.

In their latest study, Allen and Higham looked at overall face pattern and specific features
15 like eyebrow patches and nose-spots. They examined the performance of a machine learning algorithm to see whether those traits could be used to distinguish between different guenon species or different individuals within a species.
20 "Essentially, we tried to get a computer to do something as similar as possible to what a guenon viewing other guenons' faces would do," says Allen. "This meant taking measurements of visual attributes from photographs of guenon faces and
25 asking a computer to try and separate different groups as accurately as possible on the basis of these measurements. Once it has learnt how to separate groups with one set of data we can then test if its classification 'rules' also work to classify
30 new data that it has not seen before."

Allen and Higham found that across the 12 species of guenon studied, both overall face pattern and differences in eyebrows and nose-spots could be used to reliably categorize species
35 and individuals. These traits did not help classify guenons with respect to age or sex, however.

The researchers say this pattern makes sense, as guenons often form mixed-species groups in which members of the same species can develop
40 complex social relationships, but the presence of other species creates a risk of hybridization.

Higham says that facial patterns do not seem to be different between males and females, and do not seem to change as individuals age, suggesting
45 that facial patterns do not play much of a role in mate choice within specific guenon species.

"Guenons live in stable social groups where they learn and remember things about each other over time," says Higham. "Perhaps if they have
50 individual recognition, and can reliably determine which social partner they are interacting with, then this is sufficient, as other characteristics can then be associated with that individual."

The fact that guenon faces support both
55 species and individual identification has interesting implications for how evolution shapes the design of signals that have conflicting requirements. Guenon faces may represent a compromise, or trade-off, in that they allow
60 individuals within a species to look similar enough so that their species can be ascertained, but also unique enough so that others can tell who a familiar individual is by their face alone.

Animals that can recognize individuals from
65 their facial appearance include humans as well as species as diverse as chimpanzees, sheep, and paper wasps.

Allen says such individual recognition is far from ubiquitous in the animal kingdom.
70 "Generally, it only evolves in species that have complex social systems within which individuals form relatively stable long-term relationships," he says.

Higham and Allen are optimistic about the
75 use of algorithms and machine learning to look at animal visual communication. "We think that machine learning approaches have a really big future in studies of the evolution of animal visual signals, enabling researchers to assess
80 the potential informative content of signals, and hence determine the selective pressures that are likely to have led to their evolution," says Higham.

* hybridization : mating between individuals of different species that
results in offspring with combined genetic material

21. As used in line 3, "configurations" most nearly means

    (A) confluences.
    (B) geometries.
    (C) alignments.
    (D) arrangements.

22. According to the passage, guenon species that live near each other look more different than those that live far from each other because these differences

    (A) assist in the formation of social bonds.
    (B) prevent interspecies breeding.
    (C) reinforce familial structures important in raising offspring.
    (D) allow guenon monkeys to form mixed-species groups, which are favorable to survival.

23. Which choice provides the best evidence for the answer to the previous question?

    (A) Lines 1 – 6 ("In a new...a monkey")
    (B) Lines 31 – 35 ("Allen and Higham...and individuals")
    (C) Lines 37 – 41 ("The researchers say...of hybridization")
    (D) Lines 58 – 63 ("Guenon faces may...face alone")

24. As used in line 14, "features" most nearly means

    (A) presentations.
    (B) secrets.
    (C) highlights.
    (D) characteristics.

25. The experimental procedure outlined in paragraph 4 (lines 20 – 30) is most similar to

    (A) running a mouse through a maze using positive and negative reinforcement.
    (B) programming a computer to redraw photographs of human faces.
    (C) teaching monkeys to form simple words using blocks that have letters on them.
    (D) training a police dog to sniff contraband.

26. Based on the passage, the computer algorithm was able to identify an individual guenon's

    (A) social status.
    (B) species affiliation.
    (C) sex.
    (D) approximate age.

27. Based on the passage, the work of Allen and Higham is primarily concerned with

    (A) the computer modeling of recognition processes.
    (B) the similarities between monkey and human behaviors.
    (C) the evolution of facial recognition across species.
    (D) the role of facial recognition in mating behaviors.

28. The author uses the phrase "trade-off" (line 59) primarily to

    (A) clarify a technical concept using a phrase from common speech.
    (B) make an analogy between biology and economics.
    (C) inject humor into a serious discussion.
    (D) suggest that scientists and non-scientists interact more.

29. The passage strongly suggests that Allen and Higham share which assumption?

    (A) There are still many Old-World monkey species to be discovered.
    (B) Interbreeding between species produces offspring that have lower rates of survival.
    (C) Guenon monkeys recognize other species to avoid mating with them.
    (D) Computer programs can perfectly mimic biological processes.

30. According to the last paragraph (lines 74 – 83), Higham and Allen suggest that their studies in animal recognition are significant because

    (A) they produce important data regarding mate selection across all species.
    (B) they may provide insight into the nature and development of animal communication.
    (C) they address questions of human evolution from primate ancestors.
    (D) they can be used to improve recognition technologies for human faces.

Refer to the passage below to answer questions 31 – 41.

This passage is adapted from "Palm Oil." ©2015 by KALLIS EDU.

line   In zoos around the world, some of the most popular animals among visitors are the shaggy, red-haired apes—the orangutans. Young orangutans endearingly chase, play, and roll
5 around their enclosures. Older orangutans sit quietly and treat visitors to soulful gazes.
    In 2008, the Singapore Zoo held a memorial service for a female orangutan named Ah Meng, and 4,000 people attended. At the zoo in
10 Houston, Texas, people pay hundreds of dollars for paintings created by orangutans, including "Doc," who was also known as one of the most doting ape dads ever. At the San Diego Zoo, Ken Allen, another male orangutan, inspired his own
15 fan club in the 1980s. He became iconic because he repeatedly outwitted his keepers by breaking out of his enclosure, apparently so that he could peacefully wander around the zoo and look at the other animals.
20   Celebrity status for orangutans in zoos notwithstanding, wild orangutans struggle to remain in existence today. They are one of countless species threatened by deforestation of their tropical habitat in Indonesia and Malaysia.
25 Unfortunately for orangutans and other wildlife, the same equatorial conditions which support lush rainforests—year-round warmth, humidity, and rain—are ideal for cultivating a wildly popular product: palm oil.
30   The forests of Malaysia and Indonesia have long been logged for timber. But increasingly, the forests are cleared completely out of the way to make way for oil-producing palm trees. In Malaysia, tidy rows of cultivated palm trees
35 already cover an estimated 14 percent of the total land area. A report by the United Nations Environment Program, "Last Stand of the Orangutan," predicted that Indonesia's national parks would be 98 percent destroyed by 2022
40 due to illegal clearing, mostly for large palm oil plantations.
    The constant pressure to expand the palm oil industry comes from its profitability. The oil comes from the fruit of particular palm trees,
45 which produce for around 25 years. Therefore, the trees are more stable sources of income than annual crops. They also have a much higher yield per acre than other vegetable oil crops, making them efficient in terms of land use. Not
50 surprisingly, local governments tend to support palm plantations because they have the potential to lift many of the rural poor out of poverty. This is especially true in Indonesia, where millions live on less than two dollars per day.
55   Meanwhile, global demand for palm oil has skyrocketed. The oil is solid at room temperature, similar to butter. Thus it is useful not only for cooking, but for packaged foods such as cookies. It is also a common ingredient in cosmetics, soaps,
60 and detergents.

    Environmental groups have attempted to educate consumers in the United States and Europe about the oil's impact. The research group Earthwatch Institute has called palm oil
65 "one of the main reasons for massive rainforest destruction in some of the most wildlife-rich places on Earth." Some zoos have urged visitors to avoid buying products containing palm oil. And the group SumOfUs.org drew millions
70 of social network viewers when it parodied a commercial for a popular snack in the U.S. that contains palm oil. The parody reveals the source of the snack as a burned-out, barren field in the midst of a rainforest.
75   The media has also aired claims that profits from the industry are enriching a small elite. Human rights groups say that, in general, laborers earn very little, and the industry is rife with abusive labor practices. Meanwhile,
80 members of indigenous forest tribes lose their livelihoods altogether when forests are bulldozed. The Rome-based Inter-Press Service (IPS) quotes one indigenous activist, Mina Setra, as direly predicting that the industry "will expand until it
85 pushes us into the ocean."
    The bad press has created a niche market for palm oil that is grown in a more responsible manner. Some palm oil producers have teamed up with environmental groups and consultants to
90 create a system of certifying oil so that it can be labeled "sustainable."
    The certification system gathers environmental groups including the World Wildlife Fund with investors, growers,
95 producers, traders, buyers, and governments. These "stakeholders" form the Roundtable on Sustainable Palm Oil (RSPO), which certifies as "sustainable" any oil that is not from illegally cleared forest land. About 15 percent of all palm
100 oil produced is now RSPO-certified. However, companies say that it is not yet possible for them to trace the source of all palm fruit that they use. Several multinational food companies have vowed to make every part of the supply chain
105 transparent. They are in a race against time; environmentalists using satellite data report the widespread continuation of illegal burning and clearing of rainforests in the archipelago.

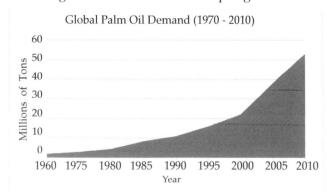

Global Palm Oil Demand (1970 - 2010)

SOURCE: USDA report "Indonesia: Rising Global Demand Fuels Palm Oil Expansion," 2010.

31. The passage strongly suggests that

    (A) orangutans could become extinct fairly soon.
    (B) logging rainforests for timber is decreasing.
    (C) a benefit of palm oil is the tidiness of palm plantings.
    (D) the United Nations is helping to enforce laws in Indonesia.

32. Which choice provides the best evidence for the answer to the previous question?

    (A) Lines 22 – 24 (They are one…Malaysia.")
    (B) Line 30 – 31 ("The forests…for timber.")
    (C) Lines 33 – 36 ("In Malaysia, tidy… land area.")
    (D) Lines 36 – 41 ("A report by the… plantations.")

33. What function does paragraph 3 (lines 20-29) serve in the passage as a whole?

    (A) It supports claims made in the first two paragraphs.
    (B) It illustrates an important example.
    (C) It provides important background information.
    (D) It transitions to the main topic.

34. As used in line 46, the word "stable" most nearly means

    (A) settled.
    (B) reliable.
    (C) inflexible.
    (D) sturdy.

35. In paragraph 5 (lines 42 – 54), the author implies that

    (A) there is no other land-use in the region that could turn such a profit.
    (B) palm oil plantations have already improved the lives of poor Indonesians.
    (C) equivalent yields from other vegetable oil crops would require more land.
    (D) it is nearly impossible for local governments to enforce laws about land use.

36. The author refers to poverty in Indonesia (lines 52 – 54) primarily to

    (A) persuade the reader to support palm oil in spite of its environmental impact.
    (B) introduce a discussion about jobs and the environment.
    (C) argue that annual crops cannot adequately feed populations in the region.
    (D) help explain one reason that policymakers allow palm oil plantations.

37. Paragraph 8 (lines 75 – 85) is primarily concerned with establishing a contrast between

    (A) the media vs. palm oil growers and manufacturers.
    (B) a thriving few vs. many who are impoverished.
    (C) job opportunities vs. the rights of local villages.
    (D) agriculture lifestyles vs. hunting and gathering lifestyles.

38. As used in line 86, "press" refers to

    (A) weights.
    (B) a pushing crowd.
    (C) reports.
    (D) machinery.

39. What is the author's main point about palm oil certification?

    (A) The RSPO process generally cannot be trusted.
    (B) Some food companies are more transparent than others.
    (C) Consumers may be able to decrease rainforest destruction.
    (D) Laws may be able to decrease rainforest destruction.

40. Which choice provides the best evidence for the answer to the previous question?

    (A) Lines 86 – 88 ("The bad press…manner")
    (B) Lines 92 – 95 ("The certification system… governments")
    (C) Lines 99 – 100 (About 15…RSPO-certified")
    (D) Lines 105 – 108 ("They are in…archipelago")

41. Do the data in the graph provide support for the author's claim that "global demand for palm oil has skyrocketed" (lines 55 – 56)?

    (A) Yes, because between 2000 and 2010, demand increased substantially.
    (B) Yes, because it shows global demand growing from near zero to over 50 million tons.
    (C) No, because there is no way to tell if the demand was actually met.
    (D) No, because the term "skyrocketed" is misleading, as demand has risen steadily since 1970.

Refer to the passage below to answer questions 42 – 52.

Passage 1 is adapted from Jean-Baptiste Lamarck, *Zoological Philosophy*, originally published in 1809. In this passage, Lamarck is outlining a theory that accounts for physiological variations between and within species. Passage 2 is adapted from Charles Darwin, *On the Origin of Species*, originally published in 1859.

Passage 1

line   But changed circumstances produce changed wants, [and] changed wants [produce] changed actions. If the new wants become constant, the animals acquire new habits, which are no less
5   constant than the wants which gave rise to them. And such new habits will necessitate the use of one member rather than another, or even the cessation of the use of a member which has lost its utility.
10   The frequent use of an organ, if constant and habitual, increases its powers, develops it, and makes it acquire dimensions and potency such as are not found among animals which use it less. Of this principle, the web-feet of some birds,
15   the long legs and neck of the stork, are examples. Similarly, the elongated tongue of the ant-eater, and those of lizards and serpents.
    The effect of use is curiously illustrated in the form and figure of the giraffe. This animal,
20   the largest of mammals, is found in the interior of Africa, where the ground is scorched and destitute of grass, and has to browse on the foliage of trees. From the continual stretching thus necessitated over a great space of time in all the
25   individuals of the race, it has resulted that the fore legs have become longer than the hind legs, and that the neck has become so elongated that the giraffe, without standing on its hind legs, can raise its head to a height of nearly twenty feet.
30   Observation of all animals will furnish similar examples.

Passage 2

    Naturalists continually refer to external conditions, such as climate, food, etc., as the only possible cause of variation. In one limited sense,
35   as we shall hereafter see, this may be true; but it is preposterous to attribute to mere external conditions the structure, for instance, of the woodpecker, with its feet, tail, beak, and tongue, so admirably adapted to catch insects under the
40   bark of trees. In the case of the mistletoe, which draws its nourishment from certain trees, which has seeds that must be transported by certain birds, and which has flowers with separate sexes absolutely requiring the agency of certain insects
45   to bring pollen from one flower to the other, it is equally preposterous to account for the structure of the [plant], with its relations to several distinct organic beings, by the effects of external

50   conditions, or of habit, or of the volition of the plant itself.
    How have all the exquisite adaptations of one part of the body to another part, and to the conditions of life, and of one organic being to
55   another being, been perfected? For everywhere we find these beautiful adaptations.
    The answer is to be found in the struggle for life. Owing to this struggle, variations, however slight, and from whatever cause proceeding, if
60   they be in any degree profitable to the individuals of a species in their infinitely complex relations to other organic beings and to their physical conditions of life, will tend to the preservation of such individuals, and will generally be inherited
65   by the offspring. The offspring, also, will thus have a better chance of surviving, for, of the many individuals of any species which are periodically born, but a small number can survive. I have called this principle, by which each slight
70   variation, if useful, is preserved, by the term Natural Selection, in order to mark its relation to man's power of selection. But the expression, often used by Mr. Herbert Spencer, of the Survival of the Fittest, is more accurate.
75   We have seen that man, by selection, can certainly produce great results, and can adapt organic beings to his own uses, through the accumulation of slight but useful variations given to him by the hand of Nature. Natural Selection
80   is a power incessantly ready for action, and is as immeasurably superior to man's feeble efforts as the works of Nature are to those of Art.

**Lamarck's and Darwin's
Ideas of Evolution**

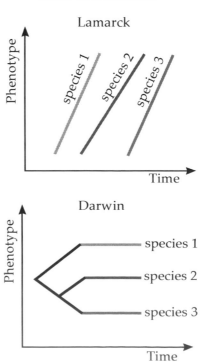

42. As used in line 7, "member" most nearly means

(A) participant.
(B) appendage.
(C) element.
(D) supporter.

43. The author mentions "scorched" ground that is "destitute of grass" (lines 21 – 22) as an example of

(A) conditions that compel a species to move to another area.
(B) scarcity that provokes competition within a species.
(C) the distribution of resources evoking certain behaviors.
(D) displays of dominance in the food chain.

44. Which choice provides the best evidence for the answer to the previous question?

(A) Lines 1 – 3 ("But changed…actions")
(B) Lines 3 – 5 ("If the new…them")
(C) Lines 10 – 13 ("The frequent…less")
(D) Lines 23 – 30 ("From the…feet")

45. As used in line 38, "structure" most nearly means

(A) organization.
(B) design.
(C) anatomy.
(D) edifice.

46. Based on Passage 2, the "struggle for life" introduced in line 57 – 58 most probably includes

(A) competition among individuals for food.
(B) various uses of the term "Natural Selection."
(C) destructive conditions imposed by human society.
(D) rivalry among siblings for their parents' affection.

47. Which choice provides the best evidence for the answer to the previous question?

(A) Lines 36 – 46 ("but it is…the other,")
(B) Lines 58 – 65 ("Owing to…the offspring.")
(C) Lines 68 – 72 ("I have…selection.")
(D) Lines 75 – 79 ("We have seen…Nature.")

48. An example of the process described in lines 75 – 79 ("We have seen…Nature.") is

(A) the environmental impact of humanity's overuse of natural resources.
(B) the hunting of an endangered species to the point of extinction.
(C) the creation of different dog breeds to fill various practical roles.
(D) the use of rats and mice in cancer-related research.

49. According to the graphs, a major disagreement between the authors is whether

(A) organisms should be divided into two or three kingdoms.
(B) phenotype is important when categorizing species.
(C) species can become extinct under certain conditions.
(D) life on Earth originated once or multiple times.

50. The author of Passage 2 (Darwin) would most likely claim that the author of Passage 1 (Lamarck)

(A) relies too heavily on casual observation to formulate a valid argument.
(B) overlooks the importance of predation in determining physiological variations.
(C) incorrectly assesses the function of the giraffe's long neck.
(D) misinterprets the role of environmental factors in determining variation among species.

51. Which claim from Passage 2 most effectively undermines Passage 1's claim in lines 6 – 13?

(A) Lines 33 – 35 ("Naturalists…variation")
(B) Lines 52 – 55 ("How have all…been perfected?")
(C) Lines 58 – 65 ("Owing to…the offspring")
(D) Lines 75 – 79 ("We have seen…Nature")

52. The first paragraph of Passage 2 effectively serves to

(A) refute the thesis of Passage 1.
(B) contrast woodpeckers and mistletoes.
(C) expand on the discussion of the giraffe in Passage 1.
(D) introduce the "struggle for life" outlined later in the passage.

STOP

Writing and Language Test 6

35 MINUTES, 44 QUESTIONS

Turn to Section 2 of your answer sheet to answer the questions in this section.

Refer to the passage below to answer questions 1 – 11.

Wind Turbine Technicians

As interest in **1** <u>renewable</u> energy continues to rise, many utility companies are opening power plants to exploit alternative means of producing electricity. Wind energy is one of the most promising alternatives to fossil fuels because of the low cost of converting wind to electrical energy. Though the industry is still in its infancy, rapid growth is expected; with this growth comes an increased demand for wind turbine service technicians—professionals capable of servicing wind turbines and their components. **2** <u>Since the number of wind farms in the U.S. is expected to double, service technicians may be required to move several times throughout their careers.</u>

1. (A) NO CHANGE
   (B) free
   (C) recyclable
   (D) DELETE the underlined portion.

2. Based on the information from the graph (see following page), which choice provides the most relevant detail?

   (A) NO CHANGE
   (B) Because wind energy is experiencing such rapid growth, the number of jobs available to service technicians is expected to double over the next ten years.
   (C) Because they are in such high demand, technicians can expect to see a doubling of their salary over the next ten years.
   (D) Due to the shortage of workers, technicians may be expected to work twice as many hours.

3 Technicians spend the majority of their time working outdoors and during inclement weather. In addition, wind turbine service technicians work on underground transmission lines and other auxiliary components of the system. They also run tests, collect data, and analyze results to ensure devices continue to operate efficiently. Though most maintenance occurs regularly, technicians are expected to work on-call to handle after-hours emergencies. **4**

Because of the many dangers associated with this type of work, wind turbine service technicians make extensive use of safety equipment **5** to protect themselves. Harnesses, **6** for example, protect technicians while they maintain and repair equipment hundreds of feet above the ground. Technicians often rappel from the tops of turbines to damaged sections, and must rely on these harnesses, ropes, and helmets to ensure safety on the job. As an added safety measure, many technicians work with a **7** partner whom provides support during more strenuous activities.

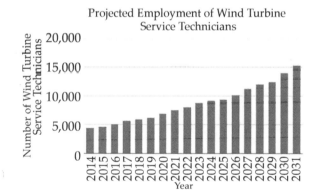

Projected Employment of Wind Turbine Service Technicians

3. Which choice provides the best introduction to the paragraph?

   (A) NO CHANGE
   (B) Typical work for a technician includes installing new equipment and maintaining existing turbines.
   (C) Many wind turbine technicians acquire the skills necessary to switch careers to any number of technical or manufacturing fields.
   (D) Work for technicians is expected to change drastically as wind energy becomes more popular.

4. At this point, the writer is considering adding the following sentence.

   > They may get called to help in cases of fires or accidents at the site, for example.

   Should the writer make this addition?

   (A) Yes, because it provides a better transition to the next paragraph.
   (B) Yes, because it provides more detail about the type of maintenance service technicians perform.
   (C) No, because responding to emergencies is not likely to be a major part of the job.
   (D) No, because it distracts from the passage's focus on the rapid growth of alternative energy sources.

5. (A) NO CHANGE
   (B) for personal protection.
   (C) to prevent bodily injury.
   (D) DELETE the underlined portion and put a period after "equipment."

6. (A) NO CHANGE
   (B) however,
   (C) therefore,
   (D) DELETE the underlined portion.

7. (A) NO CHANGE
   (B) partner who
   (C) partner. Who
   (D) partner, he or she

To perform under these stressful conditions, service technicians must be comfortable working at great heights. They must also possess physical strength and dexterity in order to effectively manipulate the machinery inside turbines. **8** Therefore, wind turbine service technicians must develop keen spatial awareness and the ability to visualize the results of their tinkering. Many have a background in another technical trade, such as maintenance or automotive repair. The best technicians are sensitive to the systems they oversee and can anticipate problems before they arise.

To become proficient at working with wind turbines, **9** a technical school is attended where technicians take courses about installing and repairing turbine equipment. Many other courses are necessary to become a successful technician, and students often elect to learn electrical systems maintenance, hydraulic systems maintenance, basic computer programming, as well as **10** first aid and CPR. Apprenticeships are also available for technicians to learn their trade on the job. Certificates are not necessary for employment but can be attained to lend credibility to technicians with **11** fewer work experience. In some states, the demand for workers is so high that many companies will hire technicians without credentials or formal work experience.

8. (A) NO CHANGE
   (B) However,
   (C) For example,
   (D) Moreover,

9. (A) NO CHANGE
   (B) technicians attend a technical school where they
   (C) a technical school educates technicians who
   (D) DELETE the underlined portion

10. (A) NO CHANGE
    (B) first aid, and CPR.
    (C) first, aid, and CPR.
    (D) first, aid and CPR.

11. (A) NO CHANGE
    (B) less
    (C) lower
    (D) lesser

Refer to the passage below to answer questions 12 – 22.

Influenza Research

Medical research institutions usually have policies requiring their scientists' studies to be reasonably safe. They must balance any risks with **12** potential, meaningful results. But even within the scientific community, researchers can fervently disagree about **13** both qualities.

Recent research into the influenza (flu) virus has provoked particularly heated debate about risks versus benefits. The stakes are high because, although most cases of the flu are fairly mild, as **14** people's immune systems can offer swift resistance, more deadly flu outbreaks do occur periodically. **15** Many of these outbreaks begin on poultry or livestock farms where animals carry strains of the flu that become transmissible to humans. Due to the ever-present possibility of such epidemics, researchers would like to be able to track flu strains that are always circulating in birds and mammals. Ideally, **16** scientists identify hazardous strains, predict when and how they could threaten humans, and stockpile an effective vaccine.

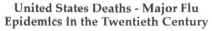

United States Deaths - Major Flu Epidemics in the Twentieth Century

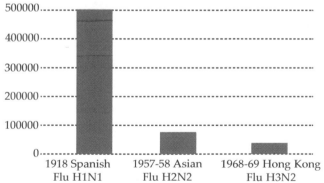

SOURCE: Adapted from National Institute of Allergy and Infectious Diseases, "Timeline of Human Flu Pandemics."

12. (A) NO CHANGE
    (B) potentially meaningful
    (C) potential and meaningful
    (D) DELETE the underlined portion.

13. The writer wants to finish the sentence with a phrase that emphasizes the scientists' basic disagreements. Which choice would best accomplish this goal?

    (A) NO CHANGE
    (B) the two judgments.
    (C) most things.
    (D) what is safe and what is meaningful.

14. (A) NO CHANGE
    (B) a person's
    (C) peoples'
    (D) personal

15. The author wants to add a sentence here. Which choice adds relevant and accurate information based on the chart?

    (A) The deadliest of these outbreaks, the Spanish Flu, killed up to half of the U.S. population in 1918.
    (B) Half of all deaths in the United States in the past century can be attributed to devastating flu outbreaks.
    (C) For instance, in the last century alone, three flu outbreaks have killed over half of a million people in the United States.
    (D) For example, the leading cause of death in the United States in 1918 was the Spanish Flu.

16. (A) NO CHANGE
    (B) scientists would have identified
    (C) scientists can identify
    (D) scientists could identify

In pursuit of that ideal, some researchers have taken a controversial approach called "gain-of-function." In the laboratory, they produce new strains of the flu virus that have "gained" abilities, or **17** functions. In other words, they **18** got more efficient and capable at infecting and harming the human body. The purpose of creating these tiny enemies is to understand the types of genetic mutations that occur in them. These researchers claim that, by knowing which strains have particular mutations and how the strains **19** may evolve— scientists may be able to prevent pandemics.

[1] However, critics decry gain-of-function teams' efforts to create virulent flu strains. [2] Lab workers repeatedly selected resistant strains for reproduction until they created versions that cannot be neutralized by human antibodies. [3] For example, critics question why one laboratory has replicated the "Spanish flu," the strain that was responsible for a 1918 global pandemic that killed at least 50 million people. [4] The same lab also produced a more lethal version of a deadly strain that erupted in 2009. [5] That is, the lab created a strain that can overcome all human immune responses. **20**

17. Which choice most effectively combines the sentences at the underlined portion?

   (A) functions, so, in other words, they
   (B) functions, they
   (C) functions; specifically, they
   (D) functions, but they

18. (A) NO CHANGE
   (B) gained a lot of ability to infect and harm
   (C) became more able to infect and harm
   (D) could do a better job of infecting and harming

19. (A) NO CHANGE
   (B) may evolve, scientists may be
   (C) may evolve, scientists may be,
   (D) may evolve: scientists may be

20. To make the paragraph more logical, sentence 2 should be placed

   (A) where it is now.
   (B) before sentence 1.
   (C) before sentence 5.
   (D) after sentence 5.

Gain-of-function researchers say that their samples are not dangerous because they can be treated with common antiviral medications and deactivated by soap and water. Critics remain unconvinced about the strains' harmlessness. They argue that the strains should not be stored. **21** Nor should researchers create new ones.

Furthermore, critics challenge the usefulness of such research. Lab-created specimens do not provide information about how strains might evolve in natural settings. Critics add that the work is impractical because strains of the influenza virus exist in countless animals worldwide and are highly unpredictable. **22** Thus, opponents and proponents of the research remain starkly polarized regarding its risks and benefits.

21. Which choice most effectively supports the argument stated in the previous sentence?

(A) NO CHANGE
(B) They simply create too high of a risk, which does not guarantee safety.
(C) High-security labs have accidentally released dangerous germs in the past.
(D) They claim that a flu strain has escaped from at least one laboratory in the past—from somewhere in China in 1977—causing a pandemic.

22. Which choice most effectively concludes the passage?

(A) NO CHANGE
(B) As the information above demonstrates, however, the research is perfectly safe.
(C) Opponents also point out the risk of terrorist groups copying the research.
(D) Thus, opponents of the research continue to influence the scientific community worldwide.

Refer to the passage below to answer questions 23 – 33.

Mancala

Mancala may be the oldest and most widely played board game on Earth. It is known across many cultures and appears in many **23** languages; besides the name "mancala," the game has an estimated 800 other names. It has so many variations in procedures and rules that it is more accurate to think of mancala as a family of games.

The word "mancala" stems from an Arabic word meaning "to move or transfer." **24** Consequently, the common procedure of all mancala games is to transfer game pieces, dropping them one by one, simulating sowing seeds in the ground. To begin the game, rows of shallow pits are filled with equal numbers of pebbles or other small objects that serve as playing pieces. Two players face each other across the board. They take turns scooping up the pieces in one pit and "sowing" them in the subsequent pits until they run out. A player has some choices about which pits to scoop out first, and has **25** a ton of opportunities to "capture" playing pieces. Usually, **26** the player, who collects the most pieces wins the game.

27 The exact origin and the diffusion of mancala spreading across the ancient world remain mysterious. Mancala's origins may be northern or eastern Africa, the eastern Mediterranean, or the Persian Gulf. Archaeological evidence in these areas sometimes includes game-sized rows of shallow pits. Without finding written or pictorial evidence, however, **28** it is impossible to know how the pits were actually used. **29** By around 500 CE, people in East Africa were playing mancala games. Regardless of exactly how or where it developed, mancala spread widely, probably through trade and migration. It has flourished ever since in many African, Arab, Asian, and European cultures.

23. (A) NO CHANGE
    (B) languages, besides the name "mancala"
    (C) languages besides the name "mancala,"
    (D) languages, besides, the name "mancala"

24. (A) NO CHANGE
    (B) Concurrently,
    (C) Significantly,
    (D) Indeed,

25. (A) NO CHANGE
    (B) a lot of
    (C) multiple
    (D) maximum

26. (A) NO CHANGE
    (B) the player who collects the most pieces
    (C) the player, who collects the most pieces,
    (D) the player who collects the most pieces,

27. (A) NO CHANGE
    (B) The game's dissemination across the ancient world remains
    (C) The way that mancala ended up all over the ancient world remains
    (D) The origin of mancala and its diffusion by spreading across the ancient world remain

28. (A) NO CHANGE
    (B) it is uncertain
    (C) it is impossible to determine
    (D) archaeologists cannot determine

29. (A) NO CHANGE
    (B) It is clear to everyone that by around 500 CE,
    (C) Pottery shards do indicate that by around 500 CE,
    (D) There is a claim that by around 500 CE,

Researchers speculate that one reason for the enduring popularity of mancala-style games has been its accessibility. Kings and sultans can play, but so can peasants. All manner of elegant mancala boards exist, but a patch of dirt will also do. Playing pieces **30** can be any materials. The simple motions of scooping and distributing the pieces seem to be enjoyable to all people.

31 Mancala games may fascinate people due to their continual challenges, because **32** they become gradually more complex as players grow and learn. Psychological researchers believe that with practice, mancala players tend to increase their abilities to evaluate visual information, such as how many pieces are in which pits, and to recognize **33** circumstances. This recognition helps players draw on a store of learned strategies as they plan their next move.

30. Which choice maintains the sentence pattern already established in the paragraph?

(A) NO CHANGE
(B) can be made of precious materials or almost anything else.
(C) can be smoothed glass, dried beans, river pebbles, or cowrie shells.
(D) can be jewels, but dried beans will serve equally well.

31. The author wants to add a sentence here. Which choice results in the most effective transition to the information that follows in the paragraph?

(A) However, why would people play mancala their whole lives, and pass it on to their children?
(B) Children can play mancala from a young age.
(C) Beyond its simple pleasures, however, mancala has an inexplicable draw.
(D) Mancala games are particularly conducive to socializing, as onlookers gather to watch.

32. (A) NO CHANGE
(B) the games
(C) the challenges
(D) people

33. (A) NO CHANGE
(B) contexts
(C) patterns
(D) generalizations

Refer to the passage below to answer questions 34 – 44.

Shakespeare's "Problem Plays"

William Shakespeare wrote at least 37 plays between 1590 and 1612. He had an unerring ability to mesmerize audiences. Even today, audiences love his moving tragedies, such as *Romeo and Juliet*; his historical plays, such as *Henry V*; and his romantic comedies, such as *A Midsummer Night's Dream*. However, **34** the last few plays that Shakespeare wrote tend to be unappreciated: *Cymbeline, Winter's Tale,* and *The Tempest*. Directors and literary critics often refer to them as "problem plays."

One reason it is hard to appreciate the three plays is **35** their ambiguous mood. They **36** precede with betrayal and loss, but they end with reunions and weddings. Shakespeare wrote them during **37** the reign of King James I, who was an enthusiastic sponsor of Shakespeare's troupe. The "tragicomedies" create suspense by revealing powerful characters' evil schemes and dangerous misconceptions. However, unlike all of Shakespeare's classic tragedies, the villains realize their errors and make amends. Nearly every character lives; **38** many deliver extra lines.

34. (A) NO CHANGE
    (B) *Cymbeline, The Winter's Tale,* and *The Tempest,* which tend to be unappreciated, were the last few plays that Shakespeare wrote.
    (C) the unappreciated last few plays of Shakespeare are *Cymbeline, The Winter's Tale,* and *The Tempest.*
    (D) Shakespeare's last few plays, *Cymbeline, The Winter's Tale,* and *The Tempest,* tend to be unappreciated.

35. Which choice most effectively establishes the main topic of the paragraph?

    (A) NO CHANGE
    (B) that they have too many characters.
    (C) that they make use of dramatic irony.
    (D) their constantly shifting settings.

36. (A) NO CHANGE
    (B) proceed
    (C) prevaricate
    (D) propel

37. (A) NO CHANGE
    (B) just before retiring from the constant pressure of producing new scripts for his theatre troupe.
    (C) his mid-40s and seemed interested in characters who become wiser over time.
    (D) a time when he had reason for optimism: England was at peace.

38. The writer wants to complete the sentence with another example of conclusions that would be surprising in a tragic play. Which choice would best accomplish this goal?

    (A) NO CHANGE
    (B) they vow to go back to the lives they were living before the conflict.
    (C) the truth does not arrive too late.
    (D) all the characters go home.

To a greater extent than in other Shakespeare plays, the problem **39** plays have followed convoluted plots and subplots, involving betrayals, deceit, errors, and unbelievable coincidences. For example, in the midst of *Cymbeline*, a princess disguises herself as a male servant in order to travel and find her **40** exiled husband. She seeks shelter along the way with foresters whom she does not realize are her long-lost brothers. Through several twists in the story, she ends up waking up from a sleeping potion and finding herself next to a corpse, which is actually the body of the **41** princesses enemy whom the foresters have killed, but whom she thinks must be her husband because he is dressed in her husband's clothes. Many more plot twists ensue before all of the characters explain, confess, and restore order.

The problem plays can also provoke a sense of unease in audience members. In the above-mentioned scene in *Cymbeline* in which the princess wakes up and thinks the headless corpse next to her is her beloved husband's, the audience is aware of the true identity of the corpse. Thus, people may not know exactly how to react to **42** her grief, unlike Juliet when she sees the lifeless body of her beloved in *Romeo and Juliet*.

Therefore, Shakespeare's last plays push the boundaries of drama and comedy in a way that still seems unconventional. Shakespeare's focus on forgiveness may still surprise **43** the audience because they may expect that bad behavior will be punished. But Shakespeare may have been contemplating his own desire for grace and forgiveness regarding what he perceived as his own faults. In *The Tempest*, the main character, a magician who controls events on an island— just like a playwright controls events in a play— directly addresses the audience at the end. He requests that the audience show him forgiveness for his tyranny, as his goal was only "to please." He says he will be stuck on the island unless the audience frees him by clapping. **44**

39. (A) NO CHANGE
(B) plays will follow convoluted plots
(C) plays are following convoluted plots
(D) plays follow convoluted plots

40. (A) NO CHANGE
(B) excommunicated
(C) expatriated
(D) extradited

41. (A) NO CHANGE
(B) prince's enemy
(C) princess' enemy
(D) princess is enemy

42. (A) NO CHANGE
(B) her grief, unlike the scene with Juliet
(C) her grief, unlike that of Juliet
(D) her, unlike Juliet's feelings

43. (A) NO CHANGE
(B) people because they may
(C) all audiences because they may
(D) one because it may

44. Which choice most effectively concludes the paragraph?

(A) Many critics believe that Shakespeare wrote the character to represent himself, as a way of saying farewell to the theater with humility.
(B) What the character really wants, as Shakespeare makes clear in this speech, is to escape the island on which he has been stuck for 12 years.
(C) Thus, as in an aside, Shakespeare's character reaches through the so-called "fourth wall" that usually separates actor from audience.
(D) Hopefully, audiences will someday look upon Shakespeare's "problem plays" more favorably.

STOP

Math Test 6 – No Calculator

25 MINUTES, 20 QUESTIONS

Turn to Section 3 of your answer sheet to answer the questions in this section.

DIRECTIONS

For questions **1 – 15**, find the solution to each problem and select the most appropriate answer from the choices provided. For questions **16 – 20**, find the solution to each problem and write your answer in the space provided. You may use the blank space in your test booklet for scratch work.

NOTES

1. The use of a calculator on any part of this section is allowed.
2. Unless otherwise indicated, all variables and expressions used in this test represent real numbers.
3. Unless otherwise indicated, all figures used in this test are drawn to scale.
4. Unless otherwise indicated, all figures used in this test lie on a plane.
5. Unless specified otherwise, a given function, f, has the domain the set of all real numbers x for which $f(x)$ is a real number.

REFERENCE

$$A = \frac{1}{2}bh$$

$$c^2 = a^2 + b^2$$

Special Right Triangles

$$A = \pi r^2$$
$$C = 2\pi r$$

$$A = \ell w$$

$$V = \ell wh$$

$$V = \pi r^2 h$$

$$V = \frac{4}{3}\pi r^3$$

$$V = \frac{1}{3}\pi r^2 h$$

$$V = \frac{1}{3}\ell wh$$

The arc of a circle is 360 degrees or 2π radians.
A triangle has angles that sum to 180 degrees.

1. Find all values of x that satisfy following inequality:

$$\frac{x}{2} - 1 \le 1 - \frac{x}{2}$$

(A) $x \le -2$

(B) $x \le 0$

(C) $x \le 2$

(D) All real numbers

2. George is mailing a Christmas gift to each member family. Three family members live in California, and eight live in New York. If the cost of sending a package to California, x, is three times the cost of sending a package to New York, which of the following represents the total cost of shipping?

(A) $\frac{11}{3}x$

(B) $\frac{17}{3}x$

(C) $9x$

(D) $11x$

3. If $f(x) = ax^2 + bx + c$ is concave downward, which of the following must be true?

(A) $a < 0$

(B) $a > 0$

(C) $b^2 - 4ac > 0$

(D) $b^2 - 4ac < 0$

4. It takes about 4 joules of energy to raise the temperature of 1 milliliter of water by one degree Celsius. How many joules of energy will it take to raise the temperature of 3 liters of water by 8 degrees Celsius? (1 liter = 1,000 milliliters)

(A) 9.6

(B) 960

(C) 9,600

(D) 96,000

5. Four consecutive integers are summed, and the total is assigned the variable x. What is the sum of the next four consecutive integers in terms of x?

(A) $x + 16$

(B) $x + 4$

(C) $4x + 4$

(D) $4x + 16$

6. Carol is catering an office Super Bowl party. She plans to serve macaroni and cheese as well as pizzas. She figures that one pizza will feed two people, and one pan of macaroni and cheese will feed six people. If she expects at least 30 and at most 60 attendees, and cannot exceed a ratio, in favor of either food, of 2 to 1, what is the maximum number of pizzas she can order?

(A) 4

(B) 6

(C) 12

(D) 15

7. Kim's Fruit Market prices fruit by the piece. A small bag of three apples and two pears costs $3.30. A large bag of nine apples and five pears costs $9.15. What is the cost of a pear?

(A) $0.60

(B) $0.75

(C) $0.80

(D) $1.05

8. The current population of a town is 10,000. If the population, P, increases by 20% each year, which equation could be used to find the population after t years?

   (A) $P = 10,000(0.2)^t$

   (B) $P = 10,000(1.2)^t$

   (C) $P = 10,000(0.8)^t$

   (D) $P = 10,000(1.8)^t$

9. Solve for x : $\dfrac{5}{x+1} \geq 1$

   (A) $x \leq -4$ or $x > 1$

   (B) $-1 < x \leq 4$

   (C) $x \leq -1$ or $x > 4$

   (D) $-4 < x \leq 1$

10. Which of the following is equal to $x^{\frac{3}{2}}$ for all values of x?

    (A) $x^3 - x^2$

    (B) $\dfrac{x^3}{2x}$

    (C) $\sqrt[3]{x^2}$

    (D) $\sqrt{x^3}$

11. What is the range of $f(x) = \sqrt{4 - x^2}$?

    (A) $y \geq 0$

    (B) $y \geq 2$

    (C) $-2 \leq y \leq 2$

    (D) $0 \leq y \leq 2$

12. If a is any positive integer, then which of the following is NOT a true statement?

    (A) $2a + 1$ is always an odd integer.

    (B) $\sqrt{a}$ is always a real number.

    (C) $\sqrt{-a}$ is always an imaginary number.

    (D) a^3 is always an odd integer.

13. Which of the following is NOT true concerning the line containing the points (4, 3) and (–2, –6)?

    (A) It has an x-intercept greater than its slope.

    (B) It is parallel to the line $y = \dfrac{3}{2}x + 10$.

    (C) It is perpendicular to $2x + 3y = 10$.

    (D) It has y-intercept 3.

14. Which of the following has the greatest absolute value of x for $y = 0$?

    (A) $y = |x - 9|$

    (B) $y = x^2 - 6$

    (C) $y = \left(\dfrac{2x}{3}\right)^2$

    (D) $x^3 = y$

15. $f(x) = \dfrac{rx}{4} + x^2 - 16$

    If r is a real number coefficient, and $f(4) = 4$, which value is equal to $f(2)$?

    (A) 24

    (B) 8

    (C) –10

    (D) –16

DIRECTIONS

For questions **16 – 20**, find the solution to the problem and enter your answer as demonstrated below.

1. Only the answer that is bubbled in on the answer sheet will be credited. The blank spaces above the bubbles are for you to record your answers for accuracy.
2. Only fill in one bubble in any given column.
3. None of the answers on this portion of the test are negative values.
4. If a problem appears to have more than one answer, only enter one answer. If the answer you enter is one of the correct solutions, you will receive full credit for that question.
5. If the correct answer can be expressed as a mixed number, it must be entered as a decimal or an improper fraction.
6. If the correct answer is a decimal that cannot fit into the grid space, you must fill the grid with enough digits to completely fill the space. The number can be rounded or simply shortened but must fill every blank space.

Answer: $\frac{5}{36}$ Answer: 4.5

Write answer → in boxes.

← Fraction line
← Decimal point

Grid in result.

Acceptable ways to grid $\frac{1}{6}$ are:

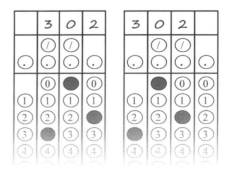

Answer: 302 – either position is correct

NOTES

Begin entering answers in any column that accommodates your answer. If you do not need a column do not enter anything in that column.

16. The sum of two numbers is $2\frac{1}{2}$. The sum of twice the first number plus three times the second number is seven. What is their product?

ANSWER: _____

17. The lines of $x + 2y = 7$ and $2x - ky = 5$ are perpendicular if the value of k is

ANSWER: _____

18.

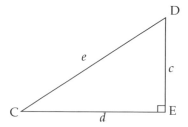

NOTE: figure not drawn to scale

For the right triangle $\triangle CDE$ above, $\cos C = \frac{1}{2}$. If the hypotenuse is 10 centimeters long, what is the length of side d?

ANSWER: _____

19. An opinion poll asked which of two candidates, A or B, would make a good mayor. Of respondents, 70% chose candidate A and 60% chose candidate B. Each person polled chose at least one candidate, and 900 of them chose both candidates. How many people were polled?

ANSWER: _____

20.

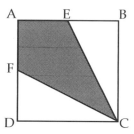

In the figure, ABCD is a square with side of length 2. If E is the midpoint of line segment AB and F is the midpoint of line segment AD, the area of quadrilateral CFAE, in units squared, is

ANSWER: _____

STOP

Math Test 6 – Calculator

55 MINUTES, 38 QUESTIONS

Turn to Section 4 of your answer sheet to answer the questions in this section.

DIRECTIONS

For questions **1 – 30**, find the solution to each problem and select the most appropriate answer from the choices provided. For questions **31 – 38**, find the solution to each problem and write your answer in the space provided. You may use the blank space in your test booklet for scratch work.

NOTES

1. The use of a calculator on any part of this section is allowed.
2. Unless otherwise indicated, all variables and expressions used in this test represent real numbers.
3. Unless otherwise indicated, all figures used in this test are drawn to scale.
4. Unless otherwise indicated, all figures used in this test lie on a plane.
5. Unless specified otherwise, a given function, f, has the domain the set of all real numbers x for which $f(x)$ is a real number.

REFERENCE

$A = \frac{1}{2}bh$ $c^2 = a^2 + b^2$ Special Right Triangles $A = \pi r^2$ $A = \ell w$
$C = 2\pi r$

$V = \ell wh$ $V = \pi r^2 h$ $V = \frac{4}{3}\pi r^3$ $V = \frac{1}{3}\pi r^2 h$ $V = \frac{1}{3}\ell wh$

The arc of a circle is 360 degrees or 2π radians.
A triangle has angles that sum to 180 degrees.

1. A band wants to distribute its music on CDs. The recording equipment costs $250, and blank CDs cost $5.90 for a package of 10. Which of the following represents the total, in dollars, it costs to produce n CDs, if n is a multiple of 10?

   (A) $(250 + 0.59)n$

   (B) $250 + 0.59n$

   (C) $(250 + 5.90)n$

   (D) $250n + 5.90$

2.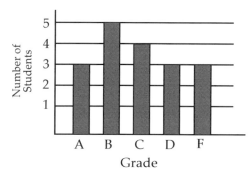

The bar graph above shows the grades in a mathematics class for the last grading period. If A, B, C and D are satisfactory grades, what fraction of grades shown in the graph are satisfactory?

   (A) $\dfrac{1}{6}$

   (B) $\dfrac{2}{3}$

   (C) $\dfrac{3}{4}$

   (D) $\dfrac{5}{6}$

3. A man 5 feet 8 inches tall casts a shadow of 8 feet. What is the height, in feet, of a pole that casts a shadow of 96 feet? (1 foot = 12 inches)

   (A) $4\dfrac{1}{2}$

   (B) 13

   (C) 39

   (D) 68

4.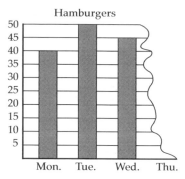

A bar graph above shows the number of hamburgers sold by a fast food chain over 4 days. However, the information on the hamburgers sold on Thursday was lost. If exactly 25% of the chain's hamburgers were sold on Wednesday, how many hamburgers were sold on Thursday?

   (A) 40

   (B) 45

   (C) 50

   (D) 55

5. Find the value of x if $\dfrac{x}{12} - \dfrac{x+2}{4} < 0$.

   (A) $x < -3$

   (B) $x > -3$

   (C) $x < 3$

   (D) $x > 3$

6. Which of the following is TRUE about the line whose equation is $4x - 2y - 10 = 0$?

   (A) The x-intercept is 4 and the y-intercept is -2.

   (B) The x-intercept is $\dfrac{5}{2}$ and the y-intercept is 5.

   (C) The x-intercept is $\dfrac{5}{2}$ and the y-intercept is -5.

   (D) The x-intercept is 5 and the y-intercept is $\dfrac{5}{2}$.

7. A problem from the Rhind papyrus (1650 BCE) states: "A quantity and its $\frac{1}{2}$, its $\frac{2}{3}$, and its $\frac{1}{7}$, added together, becomes 388." What is this quantity?

   (A) 42
   (B) 84
   (C) 126
   (D) 168

8. The function f is defined by $f(x) = x^2 + ax + a$ where a is a constant. What is $f(5)$ in terms of a?

   (A) $25 + a$
   (B) $25 + 2a$
   (C) $5 + a^2$
   (D) $25 + 6a$

9. During 100 minutes of playing time, each of 5 teams plays each of the other 4 teams exactly once. Only 2 teams play at any given time. If the total playing time for each team is the same, what is the total number of minutes that each team plays?

   (A) 50
   (B) 40
   (C) 36
   (D) 30

10.

Age (in weeks)	2	3	4	5	6
Length (cm)	6	15	20	22	23

The measurements of a fish at different ages are given in the table above. Which of the following graphs could represent the information in the table?

(A)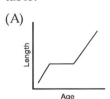

(B)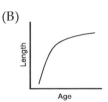

(C)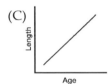

(D)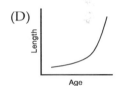

11. Two classes were given a math test. The first class has 25 students and the average test score was 86%. The second class had 15 students and its average score was 94%. If the teacher combined the test scores of both classes, what is the average of both classes together?

   (A) 88%
   (B) 89%
   (C) 90%
   (D) 91%

12.

SALES OF WILDLIFE TOURS

Price of Tour	$5.00	$10.00	$20.00
Number of Purchased Tours	120,000	95,000	65,000

A wildlife company offered tours for three different prices during a single year. Based on the information above, how much more money did the company make when the price was $20.00 than when the price was $5.00?

(A) $35,000

(B) $70,000

(C) $350,000

(D) $700,000

13. Peter wants to purchase 2 dozen pencils and a pen. Those items cost $8.45, and he does not have enough money. Instead, he decides to purchase 8 fewer pencils and pays $6.05. How much does the pen cost?

(A) $0.33

(B) $1.15

(C) $1.25

(D) $1.65

14. A student is asked to add two numbers, A and B. However, the student accidentally subtracted B from A and got 4. This number differs from the correct answer by 12. Which of the following is A?

(A) 4

(B) 5

(C) 6

(D) 10

15. Jane types at 100 words per minute, but wants to improve her words-per-minute by another 100. If she practices and accomplishes her improvements in the last 12 weeks of the school year, which of the following expressions represents her words-per-minute at any x weeks after she begins improving?

(A) $4 + \dfrac{x}{3}$

(B) $\left(200 - \dfrac{x}{12}\right) + 100$

(C) $12x + 100$

(D) $100 + \dfrac{25}{3}x$

Questions 16 – 17 refer to the following information.

Number of Poor in U.S, 1990 – 2010 (millions)

	Number of Poor by Age Group				**Total**
	< 18	**18 – 54**	**55 – 64**	**≥ 65**	
1990	13.3	14.6	2.1	3.7	248.6
1995	14.4	16.5	2.2	3.3	263.7
2000	11.1	14.1	2.2	3.4	275.9
2005	12.3	18.0	2.7	3.6	293.1
2010	15.7	22.6	3.7	3.5	305.7

16. How many people in the United States were not poor in 2010?

(A) 22.6 million

(B) 48.5 million

(C) 260.2 million

(D) 305.7 million

17. Approximately what percentage of poor people in 1995 were 65 and older?

(A) 15%

(B) 9%

(C) 6%

(D) 1%

18. Ximena earns an average of $2,127 per month, and is budgeting her income. Ximena pays $2x + 10$ dollars for internet and phone bills, $4x + \dfrac{4}{5}x$ dollars for fuel, $3x$ on groceries, $4x$ dollars for student loans, $4x$ dollars for savings, and a whopping $20x$ dollars on her rent every month. How much is Ximena left for pocket money if she spends $240 on gas per month?

(A) $154

(B) $227

(C) $354

(D) $427

19. A tennis player needs to win 60% of her matches to qualify for a post-season tournament. She currently has 10 wins. If there are 30 matches in total, and the season is two–thirds over, what percentage of her remaining matches must she win in order to qualify for the post–season tournament?

(A) 15%

(B) 50%

(C) 80%

(D) 100%

20. What is the solution set of this system of equations?

$$y - x = 3$$
$$x^2 - 7y + 31 = 0$$

(A) {(2, 5), (5, 2)}

(B) {(2, 5), (5, 8)}

(C) {(5, 8), (8, 5)}

(D) {(8, 5), (8, 8)}

21. Which quadrants contain the solutions to this system of inequalities?

$$y - 2x \leq -3$$
$$3y + x \geq -4$$

(A) Quadrants I and IV

(B) Quadrants II and III

(C) Quadrants III and IV

(D) Quadrants II, III, and IV

22. Checking Account Activity for Peter

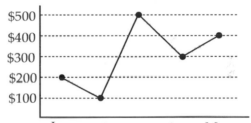

Month

According to the chart, what was the difference in Peter's account from the beginning of the 5–month period to the end of the 5–month period?

(A) –$200

(B) –$100

(C) $200

(D) $300

23. Connor wants to attend the town carnival. The price of admission to the carnival is $4.50, and each ride costs an additional 79 cents. If he can spend at most $16.00, which of the following inequalities can be used to represent the number of rides he can go on, r, and what is the maximum value of r?

(A) $0.79 + 4.50\, r \le 16.00$; 3 rides

(B) $0.79 + 4.50\, r \le 16.00$; 4 rides

(C) $4.50 + 0.79\, r \le 16.00$; 14 rides

(D) $4.50 + 0.79\, r \le 16.00$; 15 rides

24. Some banks charge a fee on savings accounts that are left inactive for an extended period of time. The equation $y = 5000(0.98)^x$ represents the value, y, of one account that was left inactive for a period of x years. What is the y-intercept of this equation and what does it represent?

(A) 0.98; the percent of money in the account initially

(B) 0.98; the percent of money in the account after x years

(C) 5000; the amount of money in the account initially

(D) 5000; the amount of money in the account after x years

25. Pat can inspect a case of watches in 5 hours. James can inspect the same case of watches in 3 hours. After inspecting a case of watches alone for one hour, Pat stops for lunch. After lunch, Pat and James work together to inspect the remaining watches. How long do Pat and James work together after lunch to complete the job?

(A) 1 hour, 30 minutes

(B) 1 hour, 45 minutes

(C) 2 hours

(D) 2 hours, 15 minutes

26. Ansel throws a basketball whose path can be modeled by the equation $y = -4x^2 + 16x + 6$, where x represents time and y represents the height of the basketball. Which of the following is the maximum height of the ball?

(A) 18

(B) 20

(C) 22

(D) 24

27.

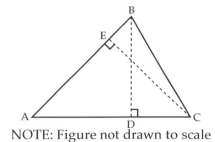

NOTE: Figure not drawn to scale

In △ABC above, BD is the altitude to side AC and CE is the altitude to side AB. If BD = 7, AB = 8, and CE = 9, what is the length of AC?

(A) $5\dfrac{1}{7}$

(B) $6\dfrac{2}{9}$

(C) $7\dfrac{7}{8}$

(D) $10\dfrac{2}{7}$

28. Two companies produce equivalent e-readers at the same production cost. They sell the same number of units in each 6-month period at the current selling price of $100. The first company plans to reduce its selling price by 5% at the end of each 6-month period, and the second company plans to reduce its price by 11% after each year. What will be the difference in their prices five years from now?

(A) $4.03
(B) $6.07
(C) $21.53
(D) $30.13

29. An open box was formed from a square sheet of metal by cutting smaller squares with sides measuring 4 centimeters from each of the corners of the sheet and folding up the edges. The volume of the box was 576 cubic centimeters. What is the area, in square centimeters, of the original sheet?

(A) 80
(B) 144
(C) 256
(D) 400

30. JumboTron Pizzeria offers small, medium, and large pizza pies at $10, $14, and $18 respectively. Given that the pizza diameters are 12 inches, 16 inches, and 18 inches, which of the following represents the best pie surface area per dollar ratio offered at JumboTron's?

(A) 3.6π inches²/dollar

(B) 3.67π inches²/dollar

(C) 4.5π inches²/dollar

(D) 4.57π inches²/dollar

DIRECTIONS

For questions **31 – 38**, find the solution to the problem and enter your answer as demonstrated below.

1. Only the answer that is bubbled in on the answer sheet will be credited. The blank spaces above the bubbles are for you to record your answers for accuracy.
2. Only fill in one bubble in any given column.
3. None of the answers on this portion of the test are negative values.
4. If a problem appears to have more than one answer, only enter one answer. If the answer you enter is one of the correct solutions, you will receive full credit for that question.
5. If the correct answer can be expressed as a mixed number, it must be entered as a decimal or an improper fraction.
6. If the correct answer is a decimal that cannot fit into the grid space, you must fill the grid with enough digits to completely fill the space. The number can be rounded or simply shortened but must fill every blank space.

NOTES

Begin entering answers in any column that accommodates your answer. If you do not need a column do not enter anything in that column.

Answer: $\frac{5}{36}$ Answer: 4.5

Write answer → in boxes.

← Fraction line
← Decimal point

Grid in result.

Acceptable ways to grid $\frac{1}{6}$ are:

Answer: 302 – either position is correct

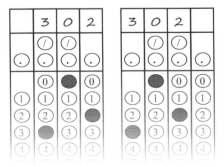

PRACTICE TEST 6

31. If $f(x) = x^2 + 1$, then $f(f(4))$

ANSWER: _____

32. Two-thirds of the sum of eight and a number x results in the number ten. What is the value of x?

ANSWER: _____

33. Line l passes through the origin and is parallel to the line $y = \dfrac{2}{3}x - 6$. If line l intersects the line $y = \dfrac{1}{2}x - 4$ at the point (x, y), what is the value of the product xy?

ANSWER: _____

34. The function $f(x) = \pi x^2 - 4\pi x + 5\pi$ has a vertex wat point $(2, k)$. What is the nearest integer value of $\dfrac{113k}{355}$?

ANSWER: _____

35. The probability that it will snow tomorrow is 23%, and the probability that it will snow the day after tomorrow is 20%. These probabilities are independent of each other. What is the probability that it will snow tomorrow but not the day after tomorrow? (Express your answer as a percent rounded to the nearest integer.)

ANSWER: _____

36. Peter found a battery-powered drill for 25% off the original price. At the checkout counter, the clerk enters the sale price, adds a 5% sales tax, and then tells Peter he owes $189. What was the original (pre-sale) price of the drill, in dollars? (Round your answer to the nearest dollar.)

ANSWER: _____

Questions 37 and 38 refer to the following information below.

A shoe company produces batches of leather shoes and boots. Each batch is made from a starting material of 2000 square feet of leather. A pair of boots requires 10 square feet of leather to produce, and a pair of shoes requires 3 square feet.

37. **PART 1**
The company needs to produce a batch of exactly 500 pairs. How many pairs of boots are in this batch?

ANSWER: _____

38. **PART 2**
The company receives one order for a single batch consisting ONLY of boots and another order for a single batch consisting ONLY of shoes, Given that boots cost $300 per pair and shoes cost $90 per pair, what is the price difference, in dollars, of the two orders?

ANSWER: _____

Essay Test 6*

 50 MINUTES, Prompt-based essay

Turn to Section 5 of your answer sheet to answer the question in this section.

DIRECTIONS

As you read the passage below, consider how Chloe Medosch uses
- evidence, such as facts or examples, to support claims.
- reasoning to develop ideas and to connect claims and evidence.
- stylistic or persuasive elements, such as word choice or appeals to emotion, to add power to the ideas expressed.

This passage is adapted from Chloe Medosch, "Out on a Limb: Dwindling Trees in Cities," published in 2015.

Of all the environmental resources we take for granted, large, older trees might be near the top of the list. Not only do we rely on trees for oxygen and wood products, but about 180 different animal species rely on the hollow-bearing features of these trees for shelter, roosting, and nesting. Unfortunately, rapid urbanization poses an enormous threat to the existence of these trees.

Large old trees take centuries to mature, and scientists are paying particular attention to the changes in wooded areas as urbanization spreads. The authors of a recent study published in *PLOS ONE* utilized a simulation model to determine the future of older trees in and around Canberra, Australia. In this urban area of Australia where the population is projected to double from 375,000 people by 2056, the authors found that dramatic changes to the terrestrial environment could occur.

The simulation model developed by the authors calculated the average number of trees in a given area using pre-defined rates of tree mortality and existing data for trees they had catalogued and measured. The data collection included the total number of trees, how fast new ones were growing, and how quickly existing ones were dying or being removed. By extrapolating from this data, they were able to assess tree population changes in the coming years.

Unfortunately, building for a growing human population means clearing out these older trees that may pose a safety threat or may simply be in the way. By projecting the current rate of decline for existing trees in the next 300 years, the researchers found that these trees die or are removed at a rate so rapid that it could lead to their eventual disappearance. To put that threat into numbers, it seems that the population of these hollow-bearing trees will decline by nearly 87% over the next 300 years. In a worst case scenario, we could lose all old, hollow-bearing trees within 115 years. That's a terrifying thought.

According to the authors' review of tree population changes, several policies may need to change to reverse the decline of these trees. Only with a combined management strategy, including planting more trees and forming more hollow-bearing habitats, would the population of the trees increase over 250 years after a short period of decline. A decline in older, hollow-bearing trees, including some endangered Eucalyptus varieties, means a decline in shelter for the birds, bats, squirrels, and invertebrates that inhabit them.

Luckily, urbanization brings new innovation, and innovation inspires new solutions to important problems. Environmental consciousness in the public requires a discussion about improving tree management, community engagement, conservation strategies, and biodiversity offsets. For example, we now have the technology to give hollow-bearing features to trees in urban areas by using other hollow-structures or artificial nest boxes.

If large older trees are facing almost certain decline due to urbanization, we need to put forth significant efforts to develop conservation and management strategies to change that. With the research available today, we can develop strategies to protect the large trees in existence, improve regeneration for ones we lose, and develop plans to build structures for animals who are displaced. We are not the only living beings on Earth, and we need to take into consideration how we effect change in our environments.

Write an essay in which you explain how Chloe Medosch builds an argument to persuade her audience that urbanization is leading to a decline of older trees. In your essay, analyze how the author uses one or more of the features listed in the box above (or features of your own choice) to strengthen the logic and persuasiveness of her argument. Be sure that your analysis focuses on the most relevant features of the passage.

Your essay should not explain whether you agree with the author's claims, but rather explain how the author builds an argument to persuade her audience.

* Sample responses at www.kallisedu.com

ANSWERS

&

EXPLANATIONS

1- 6

SAT Practice Test 1: Answers & Explanations

Reading Test

1. Ⓓ	6. Ⓒ	11. Ⓒ	16. Ⓑ	21. Ⓑ	26. Ⓑ	31. Ⓐ	36. Ⓐ	41. Ⓐ	46. Ⓓ	51. Ⓒ
2. Ⓒ	7. Ⓐ	12. Ⓑ	17. Ⓐ	22. Ⓓ	27. Ⓒ	32. Ⓓ	37. Ⓑ	42. Ⓑ	47. Ⓐ	52. Ⓐ
3. Ⓒ	8. Ⓐ	13. Ⓓ	18. Ⓓ	23. Ⓑ	28. Ⓒ	33. Ⓓ	38. Ⓓ	43. Ⓓ	48. Ⓒ	
4. Ⓑ	9. Ⓒ	14. Ⓐ	19. Ⓑ	24. Ⓓ	29. Ⓐ	34. Ⓐ	39. Ⓒ	44. Ⓑ	49. Ⓒ	
5. Ⓐ	10. Ⓑ	15. Ⓒ	20. Ⓐ	25. Ⓐ	30. Ⓓ	35. Ⓒ	40. Ⓐ	45. Ⓒ	50. Ⓒ	

1) ➡ D

Concept(s) Tested: Inference, Implication, and Suggestion

The claim that the man handled Aunt Elizabeth skillfully suggests that the man has a level of experience in the countryside that the narrator does not, so (D) is the correct choice. (A) is incorrect because holding a hen in a "workmanlike manner" does not indicate harsh treatment. (B) is incorrect because no direct information is given about the man's longtime profession. Finally, (C) is incorrect because the words "adroit" and "workmanlike" relate to ability, not to taste.

2) ➡ C

Concept(s) Tested: Purpose

The narrator speaks in general about the painfulness of the moment, and this can be taken to indicate the narrator's embarrassment about having burst into the garden chasing a chicken. The narrator's statement is about feeling foolish, and thus (C) is the answer. (A) is incorrect because the moments of which the narrator is speaking do not clarify the nature of the relationship between the narrator and the Irishman; the dynamic between the two is not what is being highlighted here. (B) is incorrect because the tone of the passage before and after the narrator's statement is realtively light-hearted and humorous. Finally, (D) is incorrect because the narrator's statement is not meant to introduce a general claim that hard work and effort are inevitably rewarded; the narrator's efforts have ended in failure up to this point, and will culminate in a failure to successfully take the bird from the man.

3) ➡ C

Concept(s) Tested: Purpose

The statement, "An Irishman's croquet-lawn is his castle" implies that a lawn is an important extension of personal living space for any Irishman who has one. As such, trespassers on the lawn would not be welcome. Since the narrator is trespassing on the Irishman's croquet-lawn, he feels that he has made a serious social mis-step, so (C) is the correct choice. (A) is incorrect because the tone of the narrator is humorously self-deprecatory, and does not imply criticism or mockery of others. (B) is incorrect because the narrator does not associate a croquet-lawn with literal wealth and royalty. Finally, (D) is incorrect because it is inconsistent with the information presented in the passage.

4) ➡ B

Concept(s) Tested: Words in Context

As used in the passage, to "invite" something is to elicit a particular reaction or response, generally to an action, such as the narrator running out of the hedge. Choice (B), "provoking," is correct because it highlights this action-response dynamic. (A) is incorrect because it is inconsistent with the usage in the passage. (C) is incorrect because "appealing a response" does not have clear meaning. Finally, (D) is incorrect because to summon a response would mean to urgently call for it or demand it, but the narrator's actions are an accident, not a demand or a summons.

5) ➡ A

Concept(s) Tested: Purpose

Throughout the passage, the narrator describes Aunt Elizabeth using terms that normally describe a person's mood, feelings, and behavior. He states that she is "resentful," that she "raises her eyebrows," and that she eyes the narrator "satirically." The narrator attributes human qualities and characteristics to Aunt Elizabeth, so (A) is correct. (B) is incorrect because Aunt Elizabeth escapes, not because she is cleverer than the narrator, but because the narrator himself is so inexperienced at working with chickens. (C) is incorrect because while the narrator does describe Aunt Elizabeth in terms normally reserved for people, the effect of this language is not to elicit sympathy for Aunt Elizabeth, but to make her behavior and "moods" clearer to the reader while adding humor to the passage. Finally, (D) is incorrect because the narrator's descriptions of Aunt Elizabeth do not set up a clear and direct contrast with the narrator: descriptions are *not* of a clumsy narrator and a clever hen, but of a clumsy narrator and an angry hen.

6) **⟹ C**

Concept(s) Tested: Citation

The most conspicuous example of the seemingly "human" characteristics of Aunt Elizabeth is when she "raised her eyebrows" at the narrator and "sniffed" at him. The hen is responding in a typically human fashion to the narrator, so (C) is correct. (A) is incorrect because the description of Aunt Elizabeth wanting to peck the man holding her does not indicate that she possesses human emotions so much as that she wants to get free of the man, which is natural for any animal being held against its will. The description in choice (B) serves to highlight the disheveled appearance and general incompetence of the narrator, but it does not indicate that Aunt Elizabeth possesses human characteristics. Finally, (D) is incorrect because the lines focus on the narrator, not Aunt Elizabeth.

7) **⟹ A**

Concept(s) Tested: Purpose

The narrator indicates that he is breathless when he claims, "I stood there, gasping." Thus, it makes sense that he cannot speak well because of his breathlessness, making (A) correct. (B) is incorrect because the context of the narrator's assertion at lines 56 - 59 does not suggest that he is worried about seeming pretentious, but rather that he feels foolish. (C) is incorrect because we cannot determine whether the narrator enjoys talking to strangers simply based on his hesitance to utter a five-syllable word. Finally, (D) is incorrect because the inability to articulate a long word is a humorous detail, not a means of skipping boring information.

8) **⟹ A**

Concept(s) Tested: Attitude and Tone

The narrator says that he is "only too well aware" of his disheveled appearance, and that his legs "felt as if they had ceased to belong to" him. We can infer that he is deeply embarrassed, so (A) is the correct choice. (B) is incorrect because there is no indication that the narrator feels frightened by the other characters. (C) is incorrect because there is no indication that the narrator "presumes" or expects special treatment or privileges. He is, rather, apologetic for his blunder. (D) is incorrect because, although the narrator is embarrassed, he is not shy and reserved; he is willing to engage with the other characters and speak up to explain himself.

9) **⟹ C**

Concept(s) Tested: Words in Context

The context in which the word "hitch" occurs suggests that the narrator had a problem taking hold of the hen, and that he "bungled" it. A "hitch" is a problem or interruption to a process. Thus, (C) is the correct answer. (A) is incorrect because a barrier prevents something from happening, and there is no indication that there was anything stopping the narrator from taking hold of the hen. (B) is incorrect because an interlude is an intervening period of time between two events, and there is no indication that there was one. Finally, (D) is incorrect because "catch" means a built-in problem or trap. There was no catch to the attempted handover of Aunt Elizabeth to the narrator; he simply bungled it by accident.

10) **⟹ B**

Concept(s) Tested: Analogies

The correct choice is (B) because the narrator is "hunting" Aunt Elizabeth by chasing her, and she is "outmaneuvering" him by running into hedges. (A) is incorrect because the narrator appears to dislike, not love, Aunt Elizabeth, imagining that she wants to peck him. (C) is incorrect because Aunt Elizabeth and the narrator are not actually opponents. Rather, the narrator is simply trying to capture her. Finally, (D) is incorrect because the narrator is not performing tricks for an audience.

11) **⟹ C**

Concept(s) Tested: Inference, Implication, and Suggestion

Aunt Elizabeth's refusal to be caught hints at her stubbornness, or obstinacy, and the narrator characterizes her as possessing "baffled resentment." Thus, choice (C) is correct. (A) is incorrect because the narrator's descriptions of Aunt Elizabeth, such as when he says that "she slipped from my grasp like an eel," indicate that she is exceptionally uncooperative. (B) can be eliminated because the narrator indicates that Aunt Elizabeth is fairly shrewd, as she eyes the narrator "satirically," an action that requires a degree of intelligence. There is not evidence to support choice (D), as Aunt Elizabeth's attitude toward the Irishman is not mentioned in the passage.

12) **⟹ B**

Concept(s) Tested: Primary purpose

Choice (B) is correct; throughout the passage, the author describes ways in which journalists circumvent China's "increasingly unreasonable" censorship laws, which effectively summarizes the passage's purpose, making (B) the best choice. Choice (A) is incorrect; while the author does characterize independent journalists in China as "flexible and courageous," he does so infrequently, so praising Chinese journalists is not the primary purpose of the passage. Choice (C) is incorrect because the author only describes general censorship laws in China, not ones that "target independent journalists." Choice (D) is incorrect because news portals are a minor point in the passage, not the primary focus.

13) **▶ D**

Concept(s) Tested: Words in Context

Choice (D) is correct because "to capture attention" is an English idiom that means to attract or draw interest from the public, making "attract" the most appropriate choice given the context. Choice (A) is incorrect because a news story cannot "express" attention, it draws, or attracts, it. Choice (B) is incorrect because "to apprehend" is to physically catch or stop a person, which does not make sense in the context of a sentence discussing a story's ability to attract interest. Choice (C) is incorrect; "to represent" has many meanings, none of which fit the context of the sentence or mean "to attract" or "to capture."

14) **▶ A**

Concept(s) Tested: Inference, Implication, and Suggestion

Choice (A) is correct because the writer suggests that most of his information on this topic comes from interviews and discussions with Chinese journalists, not from firsthand experience. Thus, it is reasonable to conclude that he is researching this topic from outside of China. The other choices are incorrect because they state that the author is in or from China, assertions for which there is no evidence.

15) **▶ C**

Concept(s) Tested: Summary

Choice (C) is correct because the passage discusses numerous ways that Chinese independent journalists have been "resourceful" in circumventing Chinese regulations (see paragraphs 2, 4, 5, 6, and 8) by using "subterfuge," or deception (see paragraph 4). Choice (A) is incorrect because, in lines 117 and 118, the author characterizes Chinese independent journalists as "flexible and courageous," which disproves choice (A). Choice (B) is incorrect because describing the actions of Chinese independent journalists as "insurrection" is too strong—although these journalists are finding ways to circumvent Chinese law, they are not staging an all-out revolt or "rebellion" against the Chinese government. Choice (D) is incorrect because the author reveals that Chinese independent journalists are finding subtle ways of defying Chinese censorship laws, so these journalists' actions are not characterized by "sympathy."

16) **▶ B**

Concept(s) Tested: Summary

Choice (B) is correct because paragraph 3 reveals that, in China, one can only call him/herself a "journalist" if he or she holds a press card, which must be issued by a registered media outlet. Thus, by nature of being "independent," independent journalists cannot call themselves "journalists" because they do not hold press cards. For this reason, they identify by various other professional titles to circumvent the law. Choice (A), (C), and (D) are incorrect because they are not supported by any of the passage information.

17) **▶ A**

Concept(s) Tested: Words in Context

Choice (A) is correct; "follow the convention" describes how independent journalists approach reportage literature. Because reportage literature is a profession or practice, we can infer that journalists "adhere to," or keep to, the "practices," or ways of doing things, within this field. Choice (B) is incorrect because it is unconventional to claim that a professional field has "habits," as habits are usually reserved for sentient being (humans and possibly animals). Choices (C) and (D) are incorrect because, in the context of the sentence, "follow" does not mean "keep track" or "accompany."

18) **▶ D**

Concept(s) Tested: Inference, Implication, and Suggestion

Choice (D) is correct because lines 44 – 51 describes a system in which Chinese independent "journalists have close connections with editors or management staff from more established media outlets," which implies that registered media outlets and independent journalists "communicate and cooperate" to create news. Choice (A) is incorrect because lines 44 – 51 disprove the claim that the two groups are "not collaborative." Choices (B) and (C) are incorrect because the passage provides no evidence supporting either choice.

19) **▶ B**

Concept(s) Tested: Citation

Choice (B) is correct because it succinctly summarizes the relationship between independent and registered journalists in China: independent journalists may work as "sub-contractors" for "more established media outlets," proving that the two groups "communicate" and "cooperate" with one another. All other choices are incorrect because they do not accurately characterize the relationship between independent journalists and established media outlets.

20) ➡ **A**

Concept(s) Tested: Summary

Choice (A) is correct because paragraph 7 reveals that "independent writers "produce content for public platforms such as "Qianjieyihao," and that the content on these platforms is "frequently quoted by news portals," providing thorough support for choice (A). Choice (B) is incorrect because the passage states that "portal sites cannot conduct original news reports," and does not indicate that portals "illegally hire independent journalists." Choice (C) is incorrect because paragraph 7 does not indicate that WeChat is "state-sponsored." Choice (D) is incorrect because paragraph 7 states that portals cannot "have their own reporter teams," disproving (D).

21) ➡ **B**

Concept(s) Tested: Citation

Choice (B) is correct because it describes recent Chinese legislation that has made "reporting on sensitive stories...much more dangerous" for independent journalists. All other choices are incorrect because they do not support the claim that Chinese independent journalists take "immense risks" in their line of work.

22) ➡ **D**

Concept(s) Tested: Inference, Implication, and Suggestion

Throughout the passage, the author states that different phenomena can influence the production of different dreams. The author mentions that a flickering lamp of a night nurse can produce dreams of fire, and that the light of the moon can produce feelings of love. This suggests that dreams are produced by identifiable causes, so (D) is correct. (A) is incorrect because the author does not indicate that dreams are necessarily metaphorical and poetical. Though they may involve these elements, the main thrust of the author's claims is that dreams are connected to external reality. (B) is incorrect because the author does not state that dreams are determined by culture or history. Finally, (C) is incorrect because the author is concerned with those aspects of dreams that are common across individuals, not unique to them.

23) ➡ **B**

Concept(s) Tested: Words in Context

In line 7, the author uses the word "people" as a verb. (B) is closest in meaning, because to populate means to fill with people, which is an accurate way to describe the images of people that appear in one's dreams. (A) overstates the meaning; people appearing in our dreams does not necessarily mean that they crowd, or overpopulate, them. (C) is incorrect because to individualize means to change something to fit someone's needs, which does not

make sense in the sentence. Finally, (D) is incorrect because humanizing involves making something seem more humane and civilized, and the author does not suggest that dreams need to become more humane.

24) ➡ **D**

Concept(s) Tested: Attitude and Tone

In paragraph 1 the author states that the observations of Maury and d'Hervey should be taken with caution, because they are literally "half asleep." This suggests that the author is skeptical of their work. (D) is the correct choice. (A) is incorrect because the author does not plainly disagree with or criticize Maury and d'Hervey. He instead counsels caution when considering their claims. (B) is incorrect because, if the author had a generally positive outlook toward Maury's and d'Hervey's work, he would not advise being cautious toward their claims. Finally, (C) is incorrect because the author does not display a deep fascination with Maury's and d'Hervey's work, and he does not discuss it in great detail.

25) ➡ **A**

Concept(s) Tested: Summary

The author says that once people are trained to keep their eyes closed and retain dreams, "one sees the figures and objects of the dream melt away little by little into phosphenes, identifying themselves with the colored spots that the eye really perceives when the lids are closed." In other words, we construct our dreams based on colors that our eyes discern when closed, so (A) is correct. (B) is incorrect because the muted hues and shining spots associated with an ocean dream were meant to be an example, not applicable to every dream. (C) is incorrect because the author mentions training only in order to understand dreams, not as a goal in itself. (D) is incorrect because it is overly general; the passage does not include discussion about why we visualize particular objects or materials in dreams beyond claims that their colors are from external stimuli.

26) ➡ **B**

Concept(s) Tested: Citation

Choice (B) is correct because it states that dreams include "the colored spots that the eye really perceives" even in sleep, which is the paragraph's main contention. (A) is incorrect because lines 13 – 18 describe a procedure, not a contention or conclusion. Neither (C) nor (D) are the correct choices because lines 22 – 26 and 31 – 32 describe examples, not main points.

27) ➡ **C**

Concept(s) Tested: Words in Context

The best choice is (C) because it fits most closely with the metaphorical meaning of "dust" in line 33. The "visual dust" the author mentions refers to colors that appear, like dust motes in the air or water particles in a mist. (A) is incorrect because it does not fit the context of the sentence. (B) and (D) are incorrect because neither "dross" nor "trickle" describes floating particles.

28) C
Concept(s) Tested: Summary
In paragraph 4 (lines 50 – 70), the author describes two dreams that are set in places where the dreamers remember seeing fire. Their memories are evoked in dreams by an external light source. Thus, (C) is the answer. The answer cannot be (A) because the author contends that light contributes in an abstract way to dreams, but not directly; in other words, the men did not dream about the passing lamp. (B) is incorrect because the author is discussing specific examples, not making general statements about fire in dreams. (D) is incorrect because the author is not making recommendations.

29) A
Concept(s) Tested: Citation
Choice (A) provides direct support to the answer to the previous question, because in lines 42 – 44, the author writes that external light "is at the bottom of many of our dreams." (B), (C), and (D) all describe specific examples, so they are incorrect answer choices.

30) D
Concept(s) Tested: Summary
Choice (D) is correct because it is the best summary of the descriptions in paragraph 4. (A) is incorrect because the night nurses' lanterns, not the night nurses themselves, affect the patients' dreams. (B) is incorrect because the passage does not say or even imply that the patients in the hospital are military veterans reliving real experiences in their dreams. (C) is incorrect because the author does not say or imply that the dreams are about actual experiences or real-world events.

31) ━━▶ A
Concept(s) Tested: Purpose
The author uses the adjective "curious" in the sense of "strange or odd." Thus, (A) is the answer because the purpose of pointing out something odd is often to convey a sense of interest or wonder. (B) is incorrect because there is no indication that the author is confused, merely that he is pointing out something he regards to be an odd phenomenon. (C) is incorrect because there is no indication that the author feels disapproval. (D) is incorrect because the author is not using "curious" in the sense of "eager to learn," nor mentioning anything about the need for further thought.

32) ━━▶ D
Concept(s) Tested: Purpose
The author suggests that moonlight causes men to dream of young women, and that the experience is so common that it may be "the origin" of the fable of a shepherd and a moon goddess. Thus, (D) is correct. (A) is incorrect because the author's topic is dreams, not myths. (B) is incorrect because the author mentions the fable in order to present a theory about the moon's influence on dreams, not to distinguish between levels of light. Finally, (C) is incorrect because, in mentioning the fable of Endymion, the author does not establish a connection between dreams and our deepest longings.

33) ━━▶ D
Concept(s) Tested: Inference, Implication, and Suggestion; Multiple-Text Synthesis
The authors of Passage 1 and Passage 2 are largely unconcerned with the morality of the actions they advocate as long as state stability is maintained. Morality plays little or no role in either author's analysis. This in turn suggests that each author is offering practical advice about how to win and survive. Thus, (D) is the correct answer. (A) is incorrect because neither author appears interested in starting war for its own sake. (B) is incorrect because Passage 1's author, Sun Tzu, supports rather than opposes war when necessary to maintain the state; and the author of Passage 2, Machiavelli, advises the new prince to take any action to secure power. (C) is incorrect because both authors present general strategies for winning, not plans for a specific battle.

34) ━━▶ A
Concept(s) Tested: Purpose
The answer is (A) because Sun Tzu's short, imperative statements are not directed at any one particular person, situation, place, or time. They can be thought of as "axioms"–statements to be taken as true. Because they can apply to any competitive circumstance, they are impersonal in tone. (B) is incorrect because the statements do not seem weak or unlikely due to a lack of explanation; just the opposite, they seem to be more obviously true, more axiomatic. (C) is incorrect because the writer remains mysterious; the reader has no idea about what his status or authority may be. (D) is not the best choice because while the axiomatic statements sound like stark truths and stern commands, the author emphasizes the importance of shrewdness, not necessarily emotional toughness.

35) ➤ C

Concept(s) Tested: Words in Context

Choice (C) is correct because "pretend" is closest in meaning to the more antiquated term "feign." Sun Tzu's advice here is to pretend to be disorganized in order to trap an attacking army. (A) is not as close in meaning, although feigning likely involves exaggeration. (B) and (D) are incorrect because Sun Tzu is advising neither the covering up of nor the "forging" of actual disorder, but the opposite: pretending to be disordered to appear vulnerable.

36) ➤ A

Concept(s) Tested: Attitude and Tone, Multiple-Text Synthesis

The correct choice is (A). Machiavelli is describing his observation that powerful men often hold onto power by tricking others—circumventing or "going around" peoples' better judgment. Sun Tzu advises holding onto power by playing tricks on the enemy. He even writes that "All warfare is based on deception." Therefore, it is likely that he would be unsurprised and dispassionate about Machiavelli's advice. (B) is incorrect because Sun Tzu seems to have no qualms about deception. (C) is incorrect because it is reasonable to suspect that Sun Tzu would be completely satisfied with Machiavelli's contention, not with the hesitancy suggested by "faint praise." (D) is wrong because there is no indication that Sun Tzu would set limitations or conditions for tricking others.

37) ➤ B

Concept(s) Tested: Citation

Choice (B) is correct because Sun Tzu's statement that "All warfare is based on deception," is consistent with Machiavelli's assertion that great men stay powerful by tricking others. (A) is incorrect because while it says that the "art of war" is important to the state, it does not specifically address the topic of deception. (C) and (D) are incorrect because they describe strategies in war, but do not specifically discuss deception.

38) ➤ D

Concept(s) Tested: Inference, Implication, and Suggestion

In the context of Sun Tzu's advice about ways to gain the advantage of surprise over the enemy, the statement about unfathomable plans—plans that no one can predict—suggests that the plans remain unpredictable even to one's own troops. Thus, (D) is the correct choice. (A) and (B) are incorrect because the juxtaposition of "keeping troops on the move" with "devising unfathomable plans" indicates that the topic is surprise, not the fitness of the troops. (C) is incorrect because "unfathomable" means "mysterious" and implies secrecy, the opposite of explaining one's strategies to the troops.

39) ➤ C

Concept(s) Tested: Words in Context

While "observe" can refer to seeing something happen, another meaning is to comply with something, as in "observe the rules." Because the context in which "observe" is used suggests the latter meaning, the correct choice is (C). (A) is incorrect because "to commemorate" an event means remembering it with a marker or ritual, which would not makes sense in the context. (B) and (D) are incorrect because neither "pronounce" nor "notice" would make sense in the context of the passage.

40) ➤ A

Concept(s) Tested: Summary

Choice (A) is correct; Machiavelli notes that, in his experience, princes can fool people easily because "men are so simple, and so subject to present necessities." A paraphrase of the sentence is that people are ruled by what they need at the moment, or by solving immediate problems. (B) and (C) are incorrect because there is no indication in the passage that Machiavelli is saying that people cannot look outside of themselves or that they cannot see the "big picture." (D) is incorrect because Machiavelli clarifies that by "simple" he means short-sighted, not necessarily stupid or unsophisticated.

41) ➤ A

Concept(s) Tested: Multiple-Text Synthesis

The correct choice is (A) because Sun Tzu's advice to "dissimulate," or pretend to feel or think differently than one actually does is similar to Machiavelli's instructive description in lines 59 – 68 of Alexander VI. Machiavelli says that Alexander "did nothing else but deceive men, nor ever thought of doing otherwise," and that there was never anyone who "with greater oaths would affirm a thing, yet would observe it less…" (B), (C), and (D) are all incorrect because they do not reflect the meaning of "dissimulate," and also because the concepts they represent are not mentioned in the passage.

42) ➤ B

Concept(s) Tested: Citation

Choice (B) is correct because in lines 63 – 67, Machiavelli is using Alexander VI as an example of someone who succeeded through dissimulation—pretending to think and feel differently than he did. (A) is incorrect because the statement in lines 43 – 46 is not specifically about Alexander. (C) and (D) are both incorrect because they do not directly address dissimulation and because they are not focused on Alexander.

43) ➤ D

Concept(s) Tested: Inference, Implication, and suggestion; Multiple-Text Synthesis

Both authors are concerned with maintaining stable governments, and both authors discuss the deception and trickery they feel is required to do so. Therefore, the correct choice is (D). (A) is incorrect because neither author seems to think that people are fundamentally good; Machiavelli even states that they are bad. (B) is incorrect because neither author mentions future generations; they both seem concerned with their own. Finally, (C) is incorrect because in these excerpts, neither author addresses ways to inspire loyalty.

44) ➤ B

Concept(s) Tested: Summary

Choice (B) most accurately summarizes the passage. It mentions the main technology that led to the original hypothesis about Chicxulub (satellite technology), the process that led to the theory (deduction), and the conclusion (a geological event occurred at the site). Choices (A) and (C) are minor points in the passage. Choice (D) is incorrect because, as the passage points out in line 18, there is no longer a big hole at Chicxulub.

45) ➤ C

Concept(s) Tested: Inference, Implication, and Suggestion

Generally, a "smoking gun" is a metaphor that refers to compelling evidence, as in a murder suspect holding a gun that is still smoking from being fired. Thus, (C) is the correct choice. (A) is incorrect because there is no indication in the passage that the crater is still steaming or "smoking" 65 million years after the impact. (B) is incorrect because the passage does not identify the theory as "controversial." (D) is incorrect because it mentions the smoke but not the gun.

46) ➤ D

Concept(s) Tested: Organization

Choice (D) is correct because paragraph 2 provides the crater's name, location, condition (buried under a kilometer of rocks), and importance as the suspected site of the asteroid event proposed by the Alvarez team. Thus, it introduces Chicxulub and its scientific significance. (A) is incorrect because it is a partial answer; paragraph 2 does explain how the crater disappeared (by being buried), but it also includes other important information as well. (B) is incorrect because the paragraph does not provide descriptions of earlier discoveries. (C) is incorrect because it is too broad to describe paragraph 2.

47) ➤ A

Concept(s) Tested: Words in Context

In line 32, the "surface expression" of the buried crater is being compared to the rim of a blanket-covered bowl. One cannot see the bowl, just the shape, or "form," of its rim where it pushes up the blanket. Thus, (A) is correct. Choice (B) does not make sense in the context of the sentence since faces are unrelated to the topic of the passage. (C) is incorrect because an iteration is a repetition of a motion or an action, which could not be applied sensibly to a blanket-covered bowl. (D) is incorrect because the blanket-covered bowl in question could not be called a narrative.

48) ➤ C

Concept(s) Tested: Purpose

Choice (C) is correct because, before the crater is compared to a blanket-covered bowl, the author says, "the impact crater has left subtle clues of its existence on the surface." Thus, the blanket-covered bowl is an example of the "subtle clues" that helped scientists identify the crater. (A) is incorrect because the blanket mimics rocks and sediment, not ice. (B) is incorrect because the blanket-covered bowl models the geography of the the crater, not the object that formed it. (D) is incorrect because neither the professor nor the passage's author recommends that readers create the model.

49) ➤ C

Concept(s) Tested: Summary

Choice (C) is correct because the surface feature is later described (lines 49 – 50) as water sources in a "perfect semi-circular structure" (i.e., an arc). Because the water is in "sink holes," (is sunk into the ground), the structures could be thought of as natural wells. (A) is incorrect because there is no mention in the passage of connections among sink holes. (B) is incorrect because the term "necklace" refers to the "perfect arc," not to jewel-like sparkling water; the water deep in the sink holes cannot be expected to sparkle in the sunlight. (D) is incorrect because a smooth ring of raised land does not fit the analogy of "a necklace of sink holes."

50) ➤ C

Concept(s) Tested: Citation

Choice (C) is correct; it describes the figurative "necklace" as cenotes (wells) occurring in a natural arc due to the asteroid's impact. Choice (A) is incorrect because it does not describe the sinkholes, but rather part of the discovery process. (B) and (D) are incorrect because they refer to aspects of the research other than geological evidence.

51) ➡ C

Concept(s) Tested: Summary

In lines 72 — 76, Pope states that satellite "maps of the region's wetlands...identified zones of groundwater discharge that correlate with the crater's structure." Thus, satellite images of underground water flow ("groundwater discharge") supported the Chicxulub hypothesis, making choice (C) correct. (A) is incorrect because celestial orbits are not mentioned in the passage. (B) is incorrect because the quantity of wetlands is not linked to the Chicxulub hypothesis. Choice (D) is incorrect because soil composition is not mentioned.

52) ➡ A

Concept(s) Tested: Graph and Text Synthesis

Because the diagram illustrates that some natural event produced layers of "impact debris" and "iron asteroid particles," we can infer that it supports the hypothesis that a large celestial object struck the Earth at the end of the Cretaceous period, making (A) correct. (B) is incorrect because the diagram makes no mention of new dinosaur fossil discoveries. (C) and (D) are incorrect because neither of these shortcomings are relevant enough to disprove or challenge the Chicxulub hypothesis.

SAT Practice Test 1: Answers & Explanations

Writing and Language Test

1. Ⓐ	5. Ⓓ	9. Ⓒ	13. Ⓒ	17. Ⓒ	21. Ⓓ	25. Ⓒ	29. Ⓑ	33. Ⓒ	37. Ⓐ	41. Ⓑ	
2. Ⓒ	6. Ⓓ	10. Ⓐ	14. Ⓓ	18. Ⓑ	22. Ⓒ	26. Ⓓ	30. Ⓓ	34. Ⓓ	38. Ⓓ	42. Ⓑ	
3. Ⓓ	7. Ⓓ	11. Ⓐ	15. Ⓐ	19. Ⓐ	23. Ⓐ	27. Ⓐ	31. Ⓐ	35. Ⓒ	39. Ⓓ	43. Ⓓ	
4. Ⓑ	8. Ⓒ	12. Ⓐ	16. Ⓒ	20. Ⓒ	24. Ⓐ	28. Ⓓ	32. Ⓑ	36. Ⓐ	40. Ⓐ	44. Ⓐ	

1) ➡ A
Concept(s) Tested: Noun Agreement
The sentence is discussing a "construction occupation." Carpentry is an occupation, so the correct answer must be (A). The other choices are incorrect because they equate "a carpenter" or "carpenters" to an occupation, which is illogical.

2) ➡ C
Concept(s) Tested: Precise Diction
The second sentence of the passage states, "carpenters participate in all phases of building construction," which means a carpenter must possess many skills. Using this information, we can infer that the most appropriate choice is (C) because "versatile" can mean "multipurpose," or possessing many skills. (A) is incorrect because a person, not an occupation, can be resourceful. (B) is inappropriate because describing something or someone as "handy" is too colloquial for a passage with a formal tone. (D) can be eliminated because it would not make sense in context.

3) ➡ D
Concept(s) Tested: In-Sentence Punctuation
If two independent clauses appear in the same sentence, they must be separated using a comma and a coordinating conjunction or a semicolon. (D) uses a semicolon to connect the two independent clauses, and is therefore the correct choice. (A) is incorrect because beginning a clause with "while" makes it a subordinate clause, which cannot be separated from an independent clause using a semicolon. We can eliminate choice (B) because an em dash cannot be used to separate two independent clauses, and (C) is incorrect because the conjunction "or" implies that only one of two choices can be true, which is not the case with the sentence at 3.

4) ➡ B
Concept(s) Tested: In-Sentence Punctuation, Sentence Boundaries
The phrase "from building highways to framing doors" is a non-essential prepositional phrase describing the range of construction that carpenters may undertake. Generally, non-essential phrases are separated from the rest of a sentence using a pair of commas, parentheses, or em dashes. The only choice that does so is choice (B), which separates the phrase from the rest of the sentence with commas. The other choices are incorrect because they do not separate the phrase properly.

5) ➡ D
Concept(s) Tested: Transition Words and Phrases
The transition word at 5 must accurately convey the relationship between the physically demanding work environments of carpenters and the high rates of injury and illness among carpenters. (D) is the correct choice because it clearly illustrates that the high rates of carpentry-related illness and injury result from the difficulty working conditions. (A) can be eliminated because the phrase "In fact" implies that the claim that follows it might be surprising based on previous information, which is not the case here. (B) is incorrect because "However" indicates contrast, which does not fit the context, and (C) is wrong because "Ultimately" generally signifies that what follows concludes or summarizes a main idea of a passage.

6) ➡ D
Concept(s) Tested: Graph Analysis
The graph reveals that the median number of days that truck drivers and carpenters spend recuperating from injuries or illnesses is 8 days per year, more days than any other profession listed in the table. The only choice that accurately conveys this information is (D). Because the y-axis of the graph displays number of days, not how much more likely someone in a certain profession is to become sick or injured, (A) and (C) are incorrect. (B) can be eliminated because truck drivers miss as many days as carpenters due to injury or illness, so the claim that carpenters miss "more workdays... than any other profession" is inaccurate.

7) ➡ D
Concept(s) Tested: Noun Agreement

Because the author wants to explain what type of diploma most carpenters earn (high school diplomas), and because "diplomas" must be plural to correspond with the plural subject of the sentence, "carpenters," the correct choice is (D). (A) is incorrect because it is singular; "a…diploma" does not agree in number with the plural noun "carpenters." (B) and (C) are both incorrect because they do not provide a sufficient amount of information; there are many types of diplomas, so the correct choice must explain what type of diploma most carpenters earn before attending trade school.

8) ➡ C
Concept(s) Tested: Voice, Concision

Choice (C) is the clearest and most concise option because it is phrased using the active voice, and it conveys the idea that the carpenter is the one who finishes the apprenticeship. (A) is incorrect because it incorrectly implies that "having finished an apprenticeship" is nonessential to the meaning of the sentence. (B) can be eliminated because it relies on the passive voice ("an apprenticeship is finished by the carpenter") to convey an idea that can easily be explained using the active voice ("the carpenter finishes an apprenticeship"). (D) is incorrect because it does not make clear who finishes the apprenticeship.

9) ➡ C
Concept(s) Tested: Passage Development

The focus of paragraph 4 is that carpenters can advance their careers by becoming independent contractors or general construction supervisors. The only choice that focuses on carpenters advancing their careers is (C), making it the most appropriate answer.

10) ➡ A
Concept(s) Tested: Verb Tense

The subject of the sentence is the Bureau of Labor Statistics, which is a singular noun. The nearest verb in the paragraph (predicts) is in the present tense and refers to the BLS. Thus, we can conclude that the correct form of the verb is present tense, third-person singular, making (A) the correct choice. (B) is incorrect because "project" does not correspond with third-person singular nouns. (C) and (D) can be eliminated because they are in incorrect tenses.

11) ➡ A
Concept(s) Tested: Pronoun Use

To determine the correct answer, we must determine the subject of the sentence. We can reasonably infer that the subject of the previous sentence (The Bureau of Labor Statistics) is the subject of the sentence at 11. Because "The Bureau" is singular, "it" is the appropriate pronoun, making (A) the correct choice. (B) and (D) are incorrect because they contain plural pronouns, which cannot accurately refer to "The Bureau," and (C) is incorrect because "this" is a demonstrative pronoun that serves to "point" to a particular preceding noun or concept, which is inaccurate here.

12) ➡ A
Concept(s) Tested: Precise Diction

Celestial bodies such as the Sun and Moon appear to humans in regular cycles of days and nights. Thus, their motions appear to be cyclical, making (A) the correct choice. (B) is incorrect because cynical means skeptical or distrustful. (C) can be eliminated because seismic relates to earthquakes or, more generally, vibrations of the earth's surface, and (D) is inappropriate because sinister refers to something disturbing or evil.

13) ➡ C
Concept(s) Tested: Concision

Of the choices at 13, (C) is the most concise. It does not contain any redundancies or ambiguous pronouns and is therefore the correct answer. (A) is incorrect because "everyday life" is assumed to be "normal," making choice (A) redundant. We can eliminate (B) because the sentence describes "ancient civilizations," which logically cannot describe "your life." (D) is incorrect because the phrase "how people normally lived" is a less concise way of saying "daily life."

14) ➡ D
Concept(s) Tested: Precise Diction

A "harbinger" is a sign or indication of things to come. If religious authorities used astronomical event as harbingers, we can infer that they interpreted visible astronomical events in order to make predictions. Thus, (D) is the correct choice. The other choices do not make sense in the context of the sentence.

15) ➡ A
Concept(s) Tested: In-Sentence Punctuation

The phrase "and the most puzzling" provides nonessential information, which must be set apart from the rest of the sentence using a pair of commas, em dashes, or parentheses. The correct choice is (A) because it is the only choice that uses a pair of the aforementioned punctuation to separate the interjection from the rest of the sentence. (B) and (D) fail to punctuate the end of the interjection, and (C) incorrectly uses a semicolon, which should only be used to separate two independent clauses.

16) ➡️ C

Concept(s) Tested: Voice, Concision

Generally, using the active voice (placing the subject before the action it performs) conveys information more effectively than using the passive voice (placing the subject after the verb or omitting the subject altogether). Choice (A) can be eliminated because it does not say who recovered artifacts (omitting the subject). (B) and (D) are incorrect because saying that something was found *and* recovered is redundant. (C) is the correct answer because it uses the active voice, and it is concise.

17) ➡️ C

Concept(s) Tested: Passage Organization

Sentence 5 indicates that the fragments of the recovered device were too corroded to be deciphered. It naturally would follow that the device remained an "archeological curiosity" for a half-century. Because the information in sentence 5 sets up the context for the information in sentence 3, (C) is the answer. (A) is incorrect because the sentence as it is now placed breaks up the logical flow about where the device was found and what it was named. (B) is incorrect because it breaks up the chronological order of the discovery. Finally, (D) is incorrect because the information in sentence 6 logically comes after the information in sentence 3; sentence 6 indicates why researchers can now "decode" the device.

18) ➡️ B

Concept(s) Tested: In-Sentence Punctuation

This question requires one to determine the relationship between the first two clauses of the paragraph. The second clause elaborates on the information of the first clause by describing which features remained unclear. Thus, we can eliminate (A) and (D) because they signal contrast, not elaboration. The use of a colon in choice (B) shows that the second clause defines, describes, or elaborates on the first clause, making (B) the correct choice. A comma cannot be used to combine two independent clauses in a single sentence unless the comma is followed by a coordinating conjunction, making (C) incorrect.

19) ➡️ A

Concept(s) Tested: Passage Organization

Sentence 1 of paragraph 3 describes the unclear inscriptions and obscure inner working of the mechanism uncovered in the 1970s, and sentence 2 jumps to the year 2006, when more was discovered about the mysterious mechanism. Thus, we can infer that the added sentence should be placed after sentence 1 because it explains that "researchers chose to ignore the device" for decades until more information about it could be gathered in 2006.

20) ➡️ C

Concept(s) Tested: Sentence Modifiers

The underlined portion at 20 modifies the adjective "intricate." Adjectives must be modified, or described, using an adverb. Most adverbs are easily identifiable because they end in "-ly." Thus, (C) is the correct answer because it contains the adverb "incredibly," which makes sense both grammatically and when placed in the context of the sentence. All other choices contain an adjective rather than an adverb, making them grammatically incorrect.

21) ➡️ D

Concept(s) Tested: Verb Tense

The verb that precedes the underlined portion at 21 is the past tense verb "was," and the verb that comes immediately after the underlined portion at 21 is the past tense verb "accommodated." Moreover, using the simple past tense makes sense in the context of the sentence. The Antikythera Mechanism is no longer fully intact, so the author must be referring to how the mechanism looked when it was intact in the past. Using these clues, we can infer that the correct answer is (D). Choices (A), (B), and (C) are incorrect because they each break the simple past tense pattern established by "was" and "accommodated."

22) ➡️ C

Concept(s) Tested: Relative Clauses

The correct choice is (C) because it uses the correct relative pronoun (which) to add additional information about the seven hands. (A) is incorrect because two independent clauses connected by a comma must include a conjunction, such as "and." (B) is incorrect because semicolons can only connect independent clauses, and "marking" begins a phrase. (D) is incorrect because using the restrictive pronoun "that" might confuse readers. If the seven hands are "the ones that marked," the reader is left wondering if there were additional hands that marked other things.

23) ➡️ A

Concept(s) Tested: Precise Diction

The correct answer is (A) because to underscore is to highlight or emphasize. Thus, "underscore" makes sense in context because "sinister" (evil-sounding) strings would logically serve to highlight a villain's speech. (B) and (C) are both incorrect because "undermine" and "undercut" both mean to weaken, which is the opposite of the intended meaning. "To understand" is to comprehend or recognize, which does not make sense in context, so (D) is incorrect.

24) ➡ A
Concept(s) Tested: Combining Sentences
The relationship between the two sentences is one of cause and effect. (A) nicely illustrates this cause-effect relationship by using "so." (B) is incorrect because "however" indicates a contrast, which is not the case here. (C) is incorrect because it is a less-direct way of saying what (A) says succinctly. (D) is incorrect for the same reason: it is too wordy.

25) ➡ C
Concept(s) Tested: Pronoun Use
The pronoun at 25 refers to the subject of the sentence, "an audience." Although an audience is made up of many individuals, the word "audience" itself is singular. Thus, the singular pronoun "it" is appropriate, making (C) correct. (A) is incorrect because "they" is plural whereas "an audience" is singular. (B) can be eliminated because "a person" cannot accurately stand in for an audience (a group of people), and (D) is incorrect because "someone" refers to a particular individual whereas an audience is a group of people.

26) ➡ D
Concept(s) Tested: Appositives and Titles
The underlined portion at 26 gives Richard Wagner's title (German composer), which should not be followed by a comma. The title serves as an adjective, which should not be separated from the noun it precedes and modifies. Likewise, a possessive noun (Wagner's) should not be separated from the noun it describes (*The Ring Cycle*) with a comma, making (D) the only appropriate choice. Other choices use one or more commas to inappropriately separate Richard Wagner from his title or his work.

27) ➡ A
Concept(s) Tested: Participial Phrases
The phrase "Composed over the course of 26 years" does not require any additional information to be comprehensible or grammatically correct, so (A) is the most concise, and therefore correct, answer. Other choices add unnecessary participles to the phrase, making the phrase more convoluted and wordy.

28) ➡ D
Concept(s) Tested: Precise Diction
(D) is the best choice because the verb "to span" suggests that something begins and ends within a certain period of time. Thus, to claim that the plot *spans* three generations means "the plot of *takes place* over three generations." (A) is incorrect because logically, a plot can include events over three generations, but it cannot "include" the generations themselves. (B) is incorrect because "to traverse" means to cross or travel, which is not close in meaning to "take place."

(C) can be eliminated because "enclose" is illogical when discussing plots.

29) ➡ B
Concept(s) Tested: Concision
The correct choice is (B) because it serves as an appositive that summarizes the same information as all the other choices using fewer words and without redundancies. (A) contains a redundancy, as ruler and leader mean the same thing. (C) and (D) both unnecessarily turn the appositive phrase "ruler of the gods" into a relative clause, making the choices needlessly wordy.

30) ➡ D
Concept(s) Tested: Pronoun Use/Case
Choice (A) is incorrect because the clause "many of them have leitmotifs" is an independent clause, so it cannot be separated from the preceding independent clause by just a comma. Instead, a relative clause is needed to further describe the characters. "Which" is the relative pronoun used to refer to things, and "who" and "whom" refer to people. Since the pronoun refers to "a huge cast of characters" (people), we can eliminate (B). The pronoun follows the preposition "of," so the pronoun must be the object of a preposition. Thus, the answer must be (D) because "whom" is the objective case form of "who."

31) ➡ A
Concept(s) Tested: Passage Development
Choice (A) is correct because it prepares for the claim that Wotan's leitmotif changes based on how he is feeling. (B) is too general to clearly relate to the rest of the paragraph. (C) is incorrect because the rest of the paragraph discusses Wotan's leitmotif, not the relationship between minor characters and leitmotifs. (D) can be eliminated because the paragraph does not mention instrumentation.

32) ➡ B
Concept(s) Tested: Transition Words and Phrases, Sentence Modifiers
This question requires you to recognize the relationship between the ideas that "leitmotifs provide musical cues" and that they "add emotional weight to" the opera. Both ideas focus on the ways leitmotifs help an audience understand the opera, with the second idea simply adding to the discussion. Thus, (B) is the most appropriate answer. Although the two sentences discuss the same topic, the second idea is not a consequence or result of the first idea, so (A) is incorrect. (C) can be eliminated because the two ideas do not contrast with or contradict each other, making "Conversely" inappropriate. (D) is incorrect because the second idea, that leitmotifs "add emotional weight to" the opera, should not come as a surprise or cause confusion based on the first idea, as implied by the adverb "Quizzically."

33) ➡ C
Concept(s) Tested: Passage Development
As written, the paragraph inappropriately concludes by offering specific information about the use of leitmotifs in action and adventure films, information that demands further elaboration. (B) and (D) are incorrect because, like (A), they require elaboration, making them inappropriate conclusions. (C) is correct because it supports the information in the first part of the sentence—that leitmotifs have survived for well over a century. (C) provides a statement that succinctly summarizes the paragraph as well as the entire passage.

34) ➡ D
Concept(s) Tested: In-Sentence Punctuation
Choice (A) is incorrect because a semicolon separates two independent clauses, and the phrase "their shape" is not an independent clause. (B) is incorrect because an exclamation point breaks the tone of the passage, which is one of academic neutrality. (C) is incorrect because parentheses are generally used to set aside nonessential interjections; because the phrase "their shape" adds essential information to the sentence, it should not be set aside in parentheses. The correct choice is (D) because the em dash can separate a description (*a common feature*) from what it describes (*their shape*).

35) ➡ C
Concept(s) Tested: Passage Organization
The information in the sentence elaborates on the writer's point about shape in sentence 3, and should therefore go after it. (C) is the correct choice. (A) is incorrect because sentence 1 only states that the universe has produced a large number of stars and planets. This information is not logically connected to the added sentence. Likewise, (B) only includes a statement that there are hundreds of billions of stars and planets in the Milky Way. At this point, the paragraph has not yet mentioned anything about the spherical shape of stars and planets. Finally, (D) is incorrect because it would interrupt sentence 4, which sets up the information that follows, from concluding the paragraph..

36) ➡ A
Concept(s) Tested: Precise Diction
The correct choice will convey the idea that gravity pulls particles toward a nebula. The verb closest in meaning to "pull toward" is "draw," because one meaning of "to draw something" is to pull it in a specific direction. (B) is incorrect because "to captivate" is to interest, which, in the context of nebulae formation, is unrelated to "pull toward." To evoke is to bring something to mind, which cannot be applied to nebulae, making (C) incorrect.

Although "to lure" someone or something means to attract or draw, luring is a conscious act. Because nebulae cannot consciously do anything, choice (D) is incorrect.

37) ➡ A
Concept(s) Tested: Precise Diction
All the choices mean approximately the same thing: to group together. However, only (A) is accurate based on the context in which the word is used. Inanimate objects (particles in this case) can "cluster" because clustering is not necessarily a conscious action. The other choices are incorrect because they describe conscious acts.

38) ➡ D
Concept(s) Tested: Sentence Modifiers
Choice (D) is correct because one-syllable comparative modifiers such as "fast" take "-er" and "-est" endings. They do not use "more." Choice (A) is incorrect because it uses both "more" and an "-er" ending, which is redundant. (B) is incorrect because "rapid" is an adjective, and an adverb is needed here. The correct form is "more rapidly." (C) is incorrect because, like (A), it places "more" with "fast."
NOTE: the modifier "faster" may be used as an adjective or an adverb. However, most adverbs will have an "-ly" ending.

39) ➡ D
Concept(s) Tested: Verb Tense
Choice (D) is correct because the present tense is appropriate to describe an ongoing process. There are also present-tense verbs before and after the underlined portion, meaning the present tense is used consistently in the paragraph. (A) is incorrect because it is in the present perfect tense, which breaks the pattern established by the surrounding verbs "continues" and "becomes." (B) can be eliminated because "acquiring" is not a verb at all: words ending in "-ing" function as adjectives or nouns, depending on context. (C) is incorrect because "acquired" is in the past tense, which is inconsistent with the present-tense verbs "continues" and "becomes."

40) ➡ A
Concept(s) Tested: Commonly Confused Words
The underlined portion at 40 is showing possession, or ownership, over the phrase "gravitational field." Thus, the correct choice is (A) because "its" is the possessive form of the pronoun "it." (B) is incorrect because "it's" is a contracted form of "it is." (C) can be eliminated because, much like the possessive pronouns "his" or "hers," the possessive pronoun "its" does not need an apostrophe. And (D) is

incorrect because "it is" does not make sense in the context of the sentence.

41) ➡ B

Concept(s) Tested: Participial Phrases

Choice (B) is correct because the participial phrase "surrounded by..." should be separated by a comma to avoid confusion. We can eliminate (A) because the inclusion of the participle "being" muddies the meaning of the sentence while making it less concise. (C) is incorrect because the use of the reflexive pronoun "itself" adds nothing of value to the sentence and implies a conscious act. Choice (D) makes the second clause of the sentence into an independent clause, which creates a run-on sentence.

42) ➡ B

Concept(s) Tested: Concision

Choices (A) and (D) can be eliminated because they use unnecessarily convoluted phrasing to get their points across. Phrases such as "acquire a sufficient amount of mass" and "the process of fusion" can be made less wordy without any loss of meaning. (B) is correct because it conveys the same information as (A) using fewer words. (C) is incorrect because it moves the subject of the clause (gas giants) to the middle of the sentence, muddying the meaning of the sentence.

43) ➡ D

Concept(s) Tested: Combining Sentences

The information in the second clause elaborates on the information on the first clause. Choices (A), (B), and (C) are incorrect because they include words that imply that the second clause is an effect of or a contrast to the previous clause, which is incorrect. Only choice (D) appropriately separates the two independent clauses by using a semicolon, which suggests that the two ideas are closely related without explicitly illustrating the nature of the relationship.

44) ➡ A

Concept(s) Tested: Passage Development

The last paragraph discusses the role of gravity in the formation of spheres, with the last sentence explaining why only some celestial objects are spherical. Thus, it makes sense that the final sentence will elaborate on this concept, so (A) is the correct answer. (B) is incorrect because it introduces a topic that is unrelated to the discussion of gravity, the main focus of the paragraph. (C) is incorrect because it introduces a law of gravity that would require further elaboration. Finally, (D) is incorrect because it abruptly transitions to a general claim about Isaac Newton, which, again, would require further elaboration.

SAT Practice Test 1: Answers & Explanations

Math Test

No Calculator Portion

1. Ⓓ	7. Ⓐ	13. Ⓐ		18.	$\frac{7}{4}$
2. Ⓑ	8. Ⓓ	14. Ⓐ			
3. Ⓐ	9. Ⓓ	15. Ⓒ	19.	10	
4. Ⓓ	10. Ⓓ	16.	1	20.	2
5. Ⓑ	11. Ⓑ	17.	2		
6. Ⓒ	12. Ⓒ				

Calculator Portion

1. Ⓒ	7. Ⓑ	13. Ⓓ	19. Ⓑ	25. Ⓒ	31.	3	
2. Ⓐ	8. Ⓓ	14. Ⓐ	20. Ⓐ	26. Ⓒ	32.	14	36. $\frac{1}{6}$
3. Ⓒ	9. Ⓒ	15. Ⓒ	21. Ⓑ	27. Ⓐ	33.	1.25	37. 133
4. Ⓐ	10. Ⓒ	16. Ⓓ	22. Ⓑ	28. Ⓐ	34.	0.2	38. 91
5. Ⓓ	11. Ⓒ	17. Ⓐ	23. Ⓒ	29. Ⓓ	35.	38	
6. Ⓐ	12. Ⓐ	18. Ⓒ	24. Ⓓ	30. Ⓓ			

No Calculator Portion

1) ➡ D

Concept(s) Tested: Problem Solving, Algebra
Jenny's earnings can be modeled as a linear function, dependent on hourly wage, time worked, and tips. Hourly wage is set at $8 per hour, and tips are not dependent on hours worked; the independent variable is hours worked. This relationship is modeled as the equation $65 = (8)4 + t$.

2) ➡ B

Concept(s) Tested: Problem Solving, Algebra
To solve the system of equations for x, multiply the second equation by 10:

$10(x + y) = 10(60)$
$10x + 10y = 600$

Subtracting this equation from the first equation gives the following equation: $5x = 100$

The amount of time spent running, x, is 20 minutes.

3) ➡ A

Concept(s) Tested: Algebra
Taking the square of both sides of the equation gives:

$\left(\sqrt{13 - x}\right)^2 = (x - 1)^2 \rightarrow 13 - x = x^2 - 2x + 1$

Move all terms to one side of the equation, setting them equal to zero: $x^2 - x - 12 = 0$
Factor: $(x - 4)(x + 3) = 0$
$x = 4, -3$
After finding these possible solutions of $x = 4, -3$, we plug both values into our original equation to ensure which of these is correct.

$$\sqrt{13 - x} = x - 1$$

$x = 4 \rightarrow \sqrt{13 - 4} = 4 - 1 \rightarrow \sqrt{9} = 3 \text{ (O)}$

The primary square root of 9 is 3.

$x = -3 \rightarrow \sqrt{13 + 3} = -3 - 1 \quad \sqrt{16} = -4 \text{ (✗)}$
The primary square root of 16 is 4.

Since our original equation concerns the square root expression on the left, the expression on the right must be positive to reflect the primary root of the quantity under our radical, therefore only answer choice (A) is correct.

4) ➡ D

Concept(s) Tested: Problem Solving, Algebra
The answer choices describe the number of baseballs that can be purchased. Solve the inequality:

$185 + 4b < 1000 \rightarrow 4b < 815 \rightarrow b < 203.75$

The inequality states that the number of baseballs that can be purchased is 203.75. Since baseballs cannot be purchased in parts, the maximum number of baseballs that can be purchased is 203. The only choice consistent with this result is (D).

5) ➡ B

Concept(s) Tested: Graphs and Functions

The line $y = 2$ is a horizontal line, and line $x = 2$ is a vertical line, so they are perpendicular to each other.

6) ➡ C

Concept(s) Tested: Graphs and Functions

Moving y to the other side of the first equation gives:
$x^2 - 1 = -y \rightarrow -1(1 - x^2) = -1(y) \rightarrow 1 - x^2 = y$

Similarly, the second equation gives: $y = x + 1$
Set these two equations equal to each other and solve:

$1 - x^2 = x + 1 \rightarrow x^2 + x = 0 \rightarrow x(x+1) = 0$

$x = 0, -1$

$x = 0, y = 1; x = -1, y = 0.$

The only choice that includes both of these x values as solutions is (C).

7) ➡ A

Concept(s) Tested: Problem Solving, Measures of Center and Spread

The range of a set is the difference between the smallest and largest values. Since no two values of the set are the same, removing the smallest value of the set will alter the difference between the smallest and largest values.

8) ➡ D

Concept(s) Tested: Problem Solving, Ratios and Percentages

The sale price is the original price minus 17% of the original price; 17% can also be written, in decimal form, as 0.17m. The final price is modeled in choice (D).

9) ➡ D

Concept(s) Tested: Graphs and Functions

Determine the intercepts by setting the function equal to zero:

$(-x + 3)(x - 5) = 0$

$x = 3, 5$

If the function is written in the form $f(x) = ax^2 + bx + c$, a is a negative number. This indicates that the parabola opens downward.

10) ➡ D

Concept(s) Tested: Problem Solving

$A + B + C = 79$, $B = 5 + A$, and $C = 2B$. Therefore, $C = 2(5 + A)$, and we can rewrite the lengths of the board in terms of A:

$A + (5 + A) + 2(5 + A) = 79$

Solving for A gives:

$A + 5 + A + 10 + 2A = 79$

$4A + 15 = 79$, so $A = 16$

Plugging the value of A into $B = 5 + A$ gives $B = 21$, and therefore $C = 42$. Thus, the sum of B and C is $21 + 42 = 63$, so (D) is correct.

11) ➡ B

Concept(s) Tested: Problem Solving, Geometry

The horizontal components of the heavy lines sum to y and the vertical components of the same line sum to x. The total length is the sum of x and y.

12) ➡ C

Concept(s) Tested: Problem Solving

The annual increase is 4.9%, so the amount at the end of each year can be determined by multiplying the previous year's production by a factor of 1.049. This factor must be raised to an exponent equal to the number of years of increase.

13) ➡ A

Concept(s) Tested: Graphs and Functions

The range of the function can be expressed in the following inequality:

$13 \leq x^2 + 4 \leq 29$

$9 \leq x^2 \leq 25$

Since we are only looking for positive numbers in the domain, we take the square root of all values in the inequality but consider only positive roots:
$3 \leq x \leq 5$

14) ➡ A

Concept(s) Tested: Graphs and Functions

To determine the region bounded by the system of inequalities, graph the two inequalities as lines. For ease of graphing, convert the inequalities to equations in slope-intercept form:

$y = 2x - 3$

$y = \frac{1}{3}x - \frac{4}{3}$

Examine the inequalities to determine if the regions are below or above the lines. The first inequality opens to the right, so the region is below the line; the second opens to the left, so the region is above the line. The region bounded by the system is restricted to quadrants I and IV.

15) ➡ C

Concept(s) Tested: Number Rules

To simplify this expression, begin by rationalizing the denominator:

$$\frac{2}{5+i} \cdot \frac{(5-i)}{(5-i)} = \frac{2(5-i)}{25-i^2}$$

Making use of the identity $i^2 = -1$:

$$\frac{2(5-i)}{25-(-1)} = \frac{2(5-i)}{26}$$

$$= \frac{5-i}{13}$$

$$(x-3)(x-4) = 2$$
$$x^2 - 7x + 12 = 2$$
$$x^2 - 7x + 10 = 0$$

Factor and solve:

$$(x-5)(x-2) = 0$$
$$x = 2, 5$$

The product of the two solutions is 10.

16) 1

Concept(s) Tested: Graphs and functions
Since the point (a, b) is a y-intercept, the x-value (a) must be equal to 0. Any value raised to the 0th power is 1.

17) 2

Concept(s) Tested: Graphs and Functions
Since $h(1) = -\frac{2}{3}$,

$$h(2) = \frac{3\left(-\frac{2}{3}\right)+4}{3} = \frac{2}{3}, \text{ and}$$

$$h(3) = \frac{3\left(\frac{2}{3}\right)+4}{3} = \frac{6}{3} = 2$$

18)  $\frac{7}{4}$, 1.75

Concept(s) Tested: Algebra
Set the two equations equal to each other and solve:
$$11x + 3x^2 = 11x^2 - 3x$$
$$14x - 8x^2 = 0 \rightarrow x(14 - 8x) = 0$$

$x = 0$ and $(14 - 8x) = 0$
Since $x > 0$, x cannot be equal to zero. To find the second solution:

$$14 - 8x = 0 \rightarrow 8x = 14$$

$$x = \frac{14}{8} = \frac{7}{4}$$

19) 10

Concept(s) Tested: Algebra
Simplify the expression:

$$\frac{x-3}{2} = \frac{1}{x-4}$$

20) 2

Concept(s) Tested: Algebra

$$\begin{array}{r} x^3 - 5x^2 + 3x + 1 \\ x+2 \overline{)\, x^4 - 3x^3 - 7x^2 + 7x + 2} \\ -)\,\underline{x^4 + 2x^3} \\ -5x^3 - 7x^2 \\ -)\,\underline{-5x^3 - 10x^2} \\ 3x^2 + 7x \\ -)\,\underline{3x^2 + 6x} \\ x + 2 \\ -)\,\underline{x + 2} \\ 0 \end{array}$$

$B = -5$
$C = 3$
$|B + C| = |-5 + 3|$
$= |-2| = 2$

Calculator Portion

1) C

Concept(s) Tested: Data Analysis
Market Support is 22% of the budget, and Engineering is 18%. The combined amount is 40% of the total budget:

$(0.4)(60{,}000{,}000) = 24{,}000{,}000$

2) A

Concept(s) Tested: Problem Solving, Ratios and Percentages
To apply a ratio, note that oxygen content falls 4% (from 18% to 14%) as elevation increases 2500 feet (from 2000 feet to 4500 feet). The variable x is the change in oxygen content per 1000 feet of elevation:

$$\frac{4}{2500} = \frac{x}{1000}$$

$$x = \frac{4000}{2500}$$

$$x = 1.6$$

The oxygen content falls 1.6% per 1000 feet of elevation.

3) ➡ C

Concept(s) Tested: Algebra

Solve the inequality: $3x - 5 > 5x - 9$

$$4 > 2x$$

$$x < 2$$

4) ➡ A

Concept(s) Tested: Functions and Graphs

To find a, replace x with 1 and set the function equal to 2:

$$2 = a(1 - 2)^2 + 15$$

$$2 = a + 15$$

$$a = -13$$

5) ➡ D

Concept(s) Tested: Problem Solving, Graphs and Functions

If the company uses Process A for seven days, the output is:

$$A(7) = 7^2 + 14 = 63 \text{ tons}$$

If the company uses Process B for seven days, the output is:

$$B(t) = 10(7) = 70 \text{ tons}$$

Maximum output is achieved with Process B and is 70 tons.

6) ➡ A

Concept(s) Tested: Problem Solving

On her way to Florida, Cynthia spends $1.45x$ dollars to dock her boat in North Carolina and $2.50x$ dollars to dock her boat in New Jersey. She pays $300 per night to dock for three nights in Massachusetts, a total of $900. To model total docking fees, the amount spent in North Carolina and New Jersey are doubled to account for the trip back to Florida:

$$2(1.45x) + 2(2.50x) + 900$$

$$2x(1.45 + 2.50) + 900$$

7) ➡ B

Concept(s) Tested: Graphs and Functions

The slope-intercept form of a line is $y = mx + b$. To calculate slope:

$$m = \frac{y_2 - y_1}{x_2 - x_1}$$

$$m = \frac{(-1) - (-2)}{3 - (-5)}$$

$$m = \frac{1}{8}$$

To find the y-intercept, substitute x and y values of the point $(-5, -2)$:

$$y = \frac{1}{8}x + b$$

$$-2 = \frac{1}{8}(-5) + b$$

$$b = -\frac{11}{8}$$

8) ➡ D

Concept(s) Tested: Problem Solving, Ratios and Percentages

Roast beef + Chicken divan + Linguine primavera = 36

Linguine primavera = 36 − Roast beef − Chicken divan

L.P. = 36 − (0.25)(36) − 17

L.P. = 36 − 9 − 17 = 10

9) ➡ C

Concept(s) Tested: Data Analysis

The following is a directly proportional relationship (also called "direct variation"), where x and y are variables and k is a constant:

Direct Variation: $y = kx$, $k = \frac{y}{x}$ (k is a constant.)

The following is an inversely proportional relationship (also called "inverse variation"), where x and y are variables and k is a constant:

Inverse Variation: $xy = k$, $y = \frac{k}{x}$ (k is a constant.)

Since $k = \frac{(w)}{(y)} = \frac{(0.2)}{(0.5)} \neq \frac{(0.6)}{(1)}$, w and y are not directly proportional and (A) is incorrect.

Since $k = wz$; $(0.2)(10) \neq (0.6)(30)$ w and z are not inversely proportional, and (B) is incorrect.

Since $k = xy$; $6(0.5) = 3(1) = 3$, x and y are inversely proportional. Therefore, (C) is correct.

10) ➡ C

Concept(s) Tested: Problem Solving, Ratios and Percentages

Let the variable x be the original price of the shoes. The sale price is 30% off the original price, or 70% of the original price. The 5% sales tax is applied to the sale price:

$(0.7x)(1.05) = 58.50$

$$x = \frac{58.50}{(0.7)(1.05)}$$

$x = 80$

11) C

Concept(s) Tested: Problem Solving, Ratios and Percentages

There are 126 applicants, 9 successful applicants, and 117 non-successful applicants. The ratio of successful to unsuccessful applicants is:

$$\frac{successful}{unsuccessful} = \frac{9}{117} = \frac{1}{13}$$

12) A

Concept(s) Tested: Percentages and Ratios

P percent of 250 is 75; let p percent be represented by the variable p:

$p(250) = 75$
$p = 0.3$, or 30%

To find 75% of p: $(0.75)p = (0.75)(30) = 22.5$

13) D

Concept(s) Tested: Problem Sovling, Measures of Center and Spread

Let the variable x represent the student's scores on the first and second exams. The sum of all scores divided by the number of scores is the average score, 93:

$$\frac{x + x + 94 + 85 + 90}{5} = 93$$

$$\frac{2x + 269}{5} = 93$$

$2x = 196$

$x = 98$

14) A

Concept(s) Tested: Problem Solving

Logan runs x miles per day, 6 days per week. To determine how many weeks he runs, note that he takes off a full week every three months:

Weeks off = 12 months $\times \dfrac{1\ week}{3\ months} = \dfrac{12}{3}$

With 52 weeks in a year, the number of weeks that Logan runs is:

Week on = $52 - \dfrac{12}{3}$

To model the total number of miles for the year,

multiply the number of weeks on by six (running days per week) and miles per day (x):

$$\left(52 - \frac{12}{3}\right)(6)x$$

15) C

Concept(s) Tested: Problem Solving, Algebra

Set the variable x as the number of nickels in the jar, and y as the number of dimes. There are 1,130 coins total, valued at $100:

$$x + y = 1130 \rightarrow x = 1130 - y$$

$$0.05x + 0.1y = 100$$

Use substitution to solve for y:

$0.05(1130 - y) + 0.1y = 100$
$56.5 - 0.05y + 0.1y = 100$
$0.05y = 43.5$
$y = 870$

There are 870 dimes in the jar.

16) D

Concept(s) Tested: Graphs and Functions

This question can be solved by graphing the line on the coordinate plane and comparing it to the positions of the two points. Algebraically, it can be solved by substituting the x-values into the equation of the line and comparing the y-values of points on the line to the y-values of the points given. Begin with the point (1, 2), which has x-coordinate 1:

$$3(1) + 4y = 7 \rightarrow 4y = 4 \rightarrow y = 1$$

At $x = 1$, the point on the line is (1, 1). The point (1, 2) is above the line.

The second point is (−1, 1). Substituting $x = -1$ into the equation of the line:

$$3(-1) + 4y = 7 \rightarrow 4y = 10 \rightarrow y = \frac{10}{4} = \frac{5}{2}$$

At $x = -1$, the point on the line is (−1, 2.5). The point (−1, 1) is below the line.

17) A

Concept(s) Tested: Graphs and Functions

$f(x) = 3x + 2$
$f(a + b) = 3(a + b) + 2$
$f(a + b) = 3a + 3b + 2$

18) C

Concept(s) Tested: Data Analysis

The period 1990 – 1991 decreases 100 lessons. The

period 1992 – 1993 decreases 150 lessons. Thus, the answer is (C).

19) ➡ B

Concept(s) Tested: Data Analysis, Measures of Center and Spread

By year, the number of children taking swim lessons is: 200 in 1990, 100 in 1991, 400 in 1992, 250 in 1993, 350 in 1994, 550 in 1995. To find the average per year:

$$\frac{200 + 100 + 400 + 250 + 350 + 550}{6} = 308.3$$

This is closest to choice (B).

20) ➡ A

Concept(s) Tested:

The distance between two points on the coordinate plane is:

$$d = \sqrt{(x_2 - x_1)^2 + (y_2 - y_1)^2}$$

The distance between the points $(-3, 7)$ and $(6, -5)$ is:

$$d = \sqrt{(6-(-3))^2 + (-5-7)^2}$$

$$d = \sqrt{81 + 144} \to d = \sqrt{225} \to d = 15$$

21) ➡ B

Concept(s) Tested: Problem Solving, Ratios and Percentages

Because the ratio of faulty to functioning devices in one country $\left(\dfrac{20}{190,984}\right)$ is proportional to the total number of faulty to functioning device, we can create the following expression:

$$\frac{20}{190,984} = \frac{x}{2,500,000}$$

Solve for x to find the number of explosive devices worldwide:

$20(2,500,000) = 190,984x \to 50,000,000 = 190,984x$

$x \approx 262$

22) ➡ B

Concept(s) Tested: Problem Solving

The nightly rate is $79.50 plus 7.2% of that rate. Including tax, the nightly rate is written as $(79.50)(1.072)$ dollars. Including the one-time fee, the cost of staying x nights is: $(79.50)(1.072)x + 10.00$

In cents, the cost can be written as

$1.072(7950x) + 1000$

23) ➡ C

Concept(s) Tested: Problem Solving, Algebra

The vehicles will meet when their combined distance equals the distance between the cities, 305 miles. Set t as the time, in hours, that has passed since 2:00 pm; the distance traveled by the car is $65t + 65$, with the additional 65 miles accounting for the one hour head-start. The distance traveled by the truck is simply its speed, 55 miles per hour, multiplied by t. These distances sum to 305 miles:

$(65t + 65) + 55t = 305$

$120t = 240$

$t = 2$

The two cars pass each other two hours after 2:00 pm, at 4:00 pm.

24) ➡ D

Concept(s) Tested: Problem Solving

To determine the additional amount certain coworkers must pay as a result of other coworkers not contributing to the lunch, we require expressions for the amount paid if all coworkers contributed and the actual amount contributed only by those coworkers that participated. The first expression, the amount expected if all coworkers contributed, is the total cost divided by the total number of coworkers: $\dfrac{b}{a}$

The actual amount paid is equivalent to the expression: $\dfrac{b}{a-c}$

The difference between the expressions is the additional amount that must be contributed by the coworkers that participated:

$$\frac{b}{a-c} - \frac{b}{a} = \frac{ba - b(a-c)}{a(a-c)}$$

$$= \frac{ba - ba + bc}{a(a-c)} = \frac{bc}{a(a-c)}$$

25) ➡ C

Concept(s) Tested: Problem Solving, Percentages and Ratios

The selling price is the cost price marked up 30%. Let the cost price be x:

$(1.3)x = 39$

$x = 30$

The employee price is 40% off, or 60% of the cost price:

Employee price $= (30)(0.6) = 18$

26) ➡ C

Concept(s) Tested: Problem Solving, Measures of

Center and Spread

$$\text{Average score} = \frac{Sum\ of\ all\ scores}{Number\ of\ students}$$

$$\text{Average score} = \frac{2(0) + 4(10) + 13(20) + 6(30)}{25} = \frac{480}{25}$$

$$= 19.2$$

27) ➡ A

Concept(s) Tested: Number Rules

Examine Roman numeral I. If x and y are equal, $\frac{3x}{y}$ is reduced to 3, which is a prime integer. There exist, however, values of x and y which are not equal to each other that will produce a prime integer greater than 2; for example, the values $x = 14$, $y = 6$ also satisfy the requirement. Roman numeral I is not always true, thus choices (B) and (D) are eliminated. Roman numeral II is not always true, as demonstrated above. Thus, the correct choice is (A).

28) ➡ A

Concept(s) Tested: Geometry, Trigonometry

The question should be diagrammed:

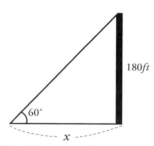

Note: Figure not drawn to scale

The thick black line to the right represents the lighthouse, and x is the distance from the observer to the lighthouse. To calculate the distance to the lighthouse, use the trigonometric identity:

$$\tan 60^{\circ} = \frac{opposite\ side}{adjacent\ side}$$

$$\tan 60^{\circ} = \frac{180}{x}$$

$$x = \frac{180}{\tan 60^{\circ}}$$

$$x = 104$$

29) ➡ D

Concept(s) Tested: Number Rules

Rationalize the denominator:

$$\frac{2i}{1+i} \cdot \frac{(1-i)}{(1-i)} = \frac{2i - 2i^2}{1 - i^2}$$

Taking $i^2 = -1$,

$$\frac{2i - 2(-1)}{1 - (-1)} = \frac{2i + 2}{2} = i + 1$$

30) ➡ D

Concept(s) Tested: Graphs and functions, Algebra

To factor $f(x) = x^2 - 4x - 21$, you must find two number whose sum is –4 (so as to give –4x when factored) and whose product is –21.

Since –7 × 3 = 21 and –7 + 3 = –4, the factored form is $f(x) = (x + 3)(x - 7)$

31) ➡ 3

Concept(s) Tested: Graphs and Functions

Convert the equation into the slope–intercept form, $y = mx + b$:

$$9x - 3y = 10 \rightarrow 3y = 9x - 10$$

$$y = 3x - \frac{10}{3}$$

The slope, m, of the line is 3.

32) ➡ 14

Concept(s) Tested: Problem Solving, Algebra

Let x be the number of hours worked as a model, and y be the number of hours worked as a chef. Angel's total hours are 25:

$$x + y = 25$$

He works for \$50 per hour as a model and \$12 per hour as a chef, and makes a total of \$718 for the week:

$$50x + 12y = 718$$

Multiply both sides of the first equation by 50 and subtract the second equation from the multiplied form of the first equation:

$$50x + 50y = 1,250$$

$$\underline{-)\ 50x - 12y = 718}$$

$$38y = 532$$

33) ➡ 1.25 or $\frac{5}{4}$

Concept(s) Tested: Problem Solving, Algebra

Let b be the price of one candy bar and c be the

price of one bag of chips.

$2b + 2c = 4$

$3b + 2c = 4.75$

Subtracting the first equation from the second gives: $b = 0.75$

According to the first equation, the cost of one candy bar, in dollars, is

$c = 2 - b$

$c = 1.25$

34)  $0.2 \ or \ \dfrac{1}{5}$

Concept(s) Tested: Problem Solving, Ratios and Percentages

One way to answer this question is to count the number of two-digit numbers divisible by five and divide by the total number of two-digit numbers. We can also calculate the numbers divisible by five by noting that there are twenty such numbers between 1 and 100. Excluding the numbers 5 and 100, which are not included in the set, leaves 18 two-digit numbers divisible by five. As there are 90 two digit numbers in the set, the probability of picking a number divisible by 5 at random is:

$P = \dfrac{18}{90} = \dfrac{1}{5}$

35) 38

Concept(s) Tested: Problem Solving, Algebra

Aaron is able to complete one-eighth of the job in a single day, and Ben is able to complete one–twelfth of the job in a single day. Let x be the time in days it takes the two men, working together, to complete the job:

$\dfrac{1}{8}x + \dfrac{1}{12}x = 1$

$\dfrac{5}{24}x = 1$

$x = \dfrac{24}{5}$

To calculate the number of hours:

$\dfrac{24}{5} \ \text{days} \times \dfrac{8 \ \text{hours}}{1 \ \text{day}} = 38.4 \ \text{hours}$

Rounded to the nearest hour: 38 hours.

36) $\dfrac{1}{6}$, 0.166, 0.167

Concept(s) Tested: Geometry

The volume of a general cylinder is: $V = bh$

where b is the area of the base of the cylinder. The volume of a general cone is: $V = \dfrac{1}{3}bh$

where b is the area of the base of the cone. A pyramid is a type of general cone that has a polygonal base. The area of the base of this cylinder is the same as the area of the base of the cone. The cylinder has a height twice the height of the pyramid: $h_c = 2h_p$

The ratio of the volume of the pyramid to the volume of the cylinder is:

$\dfrac{Volume \ of \ pyramid}{Volume \ of \ cylinder} = \dfrac{\dfrac{1}{3}bh_p}{bh_c} = \dfrac{\dfrac{1}{3}h_p}{2h_p} = \dfrac{1}{6}$

37) 133

Concept(s) Tested: Problem Solving, Algebra

Two hours of marketing bring in five orders at $30 each; for every two hours of marketing, Karen bills $150. If x is the number of marketing hours needed to bill $10,000, then

$x = 2 \cdot \left(\dfrac{10,000}{150}\right)$

$x = 133.3$

Rounded to the nearest hour: 133

38) 91

Concept(s) Tested: Problem Solving, Algebra

Each hour worked by the assistant costs $15 in wages and $25 to fill orders (five orders at $5 each). Each hour worked by the assistant brings in $150 in billings (five orders at $30 each). The profit to the business per hour is:

Profit by hour = $150 - (15 + 25) = 110$

To bill $10,000 in a month:

$Hours \ worked = \dfrac{10,000}{110} = 90.9$

Rounded to the nearest integer, hours worked = 91

Reading Test

1. ⓓ	6. ⓒ	11. ⓒ	16. ⓓ	21. ⓑ	26. ⓓ	31. ⓓ	36. ⓑ	41. ⓓ	46. ⓐ	51. ⓓ
2. ⓑ	7. ⓒ	12. ⓑ	17. ⓐ	22. ⓓ	27. ⓑ	32. ⓐ	37. ⓓ	42. ⓑ	47. ⓒ	52. ⓓ
3. ⓒ	8. ⓐ	13. ⓓ	18. ⓑ	23. ⓒ	28. ⓑ	33. ⓑ	38. ⓐ	43. ⓑ	48. ⓐ	
4. ⓑ	9. ⓑ	14. ⓐ	19. ⓐ	24. ⓐ	29. ⓒ	34. ⓒ	39. ⓑ	44. ⓓ	49. ⓐ	
5. ⓓ	10. ⓑ	15. ⓑ	20. ⓐ	25. ⓒ	30. ⓐ	35. ⓓ	40. ⓓ	45. ⓐ	50. ⓐ	

1) ➡ D
Concept(s) Tested: Words in Context
The word "operation" refers to the process of dipping the brush in the whitewash and painting the fence, which Tom repeats over and over, so (D) is correct. Choice (A), "venture," does not refer to a process; it is a risky adventure or journey. Choice (B), "maneuver," refers to a carefully executed series of movements; the word implies a level of skill that does not fit the context of painting the fence as well as "operation" and "process" do. Choice (C) is incorrect because Tom is not giving a performance for anyone by painting the fence; he is simply going about his work for the day.

2) ➡ B
Concept(s) Tested: Summary
The author speaks of the "far-reaching continent" of fence that Tom is required to paint. The author also speaks of life being "hollow" and a "burden" for Tom. These are exaggerations meant to convey Tom's child-like discouragement at having to paint such a large fence. (B) is correct because "hyperbole" refers to exaggerated speech or writing. (A) is incorrect because there is no evidence that Tom was tricked into painting the fence. In fact, the passage later reveals that Tom tricks another into painting the fence for him. (C) is incorrect because, although it is true that the job is simple and that Tom is negative, the answer choice implies a note of judgment; the author, in contrast, simply conveys Tom's childish feelings, creating ironic humor as a result. (D) is incorrect because it is *too* hyperbolic; Tom's attitude does not extend to thinking of himself as a hero.

3) ➡ C
Concept(s) Tested: Citation
In lines 8 – 9, the author writes that life seems "hollow" to Tom and existence a "burden." These terms are meant to convey the depth of Tom's discouragement at having to paint the fence by using hyperbole. Thus, (C) is correct. Choice (A) is incorrect because it does not establish Tom's mood, instead making a general comment on the day appearing "bright" and "fresh." Choice (B) is incorrect because it simply explains that Tom appeared with a brush and a bucket of whitewash, which does not convey Tom's attitude toward painting the fence. Finally, while (D) does convey a slight sense of discouragement and weariness in Tom, the statement does not convey the depth of Tom's discouragement.

4) ➡ B
Concept(s) Tested: Organization
Paragraph 2 starts out by discussing Tom's sorrow at having to paint the fence. Yet the paragraph transitions to a moment of "magnificent inspiration" that encourages Tom and brightens his mood. Thus, choice (B) is correct. (A) is incorrect because the paragraph does not mention Tom's generosity, only that he has a plan that cheers him up. (C) is incorrect because paragraph 2 does not discuss Tom's background or intelligence. (D) is incorrect because the paragraph describes Tom's feelings but does not justify them.

5) ➡ D
Concept(s) Tested: Organization
The statement in lines 37 – 39 indicates that Tom is fascinated with his painting task. Yet the reader understands that Tom is pretending: the reader knows that Tom does not want to paint the fence and that he was suddenly struck by an idea. Thus, (D) is correct. (A) and (B) are incorrect because one can infer that Tom's motivation is neither artistic expression nor making a good impression on one of his peers. (C) is incorrect because the reader knows that moments before, Tom was unenthusiastic about the task, and there is no indication that he has changed his mind.

6) ➡ C
Concept(s) Tested: Summary
Choice (C) is correct because Tom interests Ben by saying, "Does a boy get a chance to whitewash a fence every day?" (lines 61 – 62), implying that it is a rare opportunity. (A) is incorrect because Tom does not mention any other activities; rather, he pretends to focus all attention on whitewashing. (B) is incorrect because it is Ben who offers Tom an apple, not the other way around. (D) is incorrect because Tom does not mention swimming.

7) ➡ C
Concept(s) Tested: Purpose
The correct choice is (C) because Tom speaks of Aunt Polly as an authority figure who is "awful particular," and that painting the fence "has got to be done very careful." He implies that Aunt Polly has privileged him by asking him to take on a task that only "one boy in a thousand, maybe two thousand," could do. (A) is incorrect because Tom does not blame Aunt Polly for depriving him of play time; he instead speaks of her with what appears to be reverence. (B) is incorrect because, while Tom pretends to be diligent for the sake of his ruse, he never suggests that Aunt Polly is lazy. (D) is incorrect because the opposite it true; Tom implies that Aunt Polly would not want Ben to help.

8) ➡ A
Concept(s) Tested: Analogy
Tom's despondence changes when he has the idea to manipulate Ben into painting the fence for him. Thus, Tom is similar to a con man who wants to deceive Ben into thinking that whitewashing the fence is enjoyable and requires the talents of an expert, so (A) is correct. (B) is incorrect because a patron hires an artist to produce art, but in this case neither boy is paying the other to create anything for him; rather, Ben is "paying" Tom for the privilege of doing the work. (C) is incorrect because neither boy has authority over the other, and neither boy disapproves of the other. (D) is incorrect because Tom is not trying to find or catch Ben, and vice versa. Tom's principal aim is to get Ben to take over his chore.

9) ➡ B
Concept(s) Tested: Words in Context
Lines 97 – 99 discuss "the late steamer" and "the retired artist." Ben was *recently* "personating (impersonating) a steamboat," and the reader can understand that Tom was pretending to be an artist, so (B) is correct. (A), (C), and (D) are incorrect because they do not make sense in the context of the story.

10) ➡ B
Concept(s) Tested: Inference, Implication, and Suggestion
Choice (B) is correct because the passage indicates that Ben is being playful when impersonating a steamboat, revealing that "his heart was light" as he committed to his impersonation. On the other hand, Tom's impersonation of an artist is designed to interest Ben in painting the fence through manipulation. (A) is incorrect because there is little indication that Ben's impersonation of a steamboat evinces any skill while Tom's impersonation of an artist is apparently convincing. (C) is incorrect because, while Ben's impersonation of a steamboat may be harmless, saying that Tom is hurting Ben by impersonating an artist is not entirely true. (D) is incorrect because there is no indication in the passage that Ben's impersonation offends Tom, and Tom is not offering artificial compliments to Ben.

11) ➡ C
Concept(s) Tested: Primary Purpose
Choice (C) is correct because, in both the first and the last paragraphs, the author makes the claim that "we should be doubling our efforts to make geothermal a viable power source," (lines 10 – 11). Choice (C) is also supported throughout the passage, as the author spends the majority of the passage espousing the benefits of geothermal energy and advocating for more geothermal-related research. Choice (A) is incorrect because there is no indication that geothermal energy production is "controversial." Choice (B) is incorrect; although the passage occasionally compares geothermal energy to other renewable energies, these comparisons primarily serve to support the passage's main argument. Choice (D) is incorrect because fossil fuels are not discussed in the passage.

12) ➡ B
Concept(s) Tested: Summary
Choice (B) is correct because lines 19 – 24 reveal that underground water "is heated to the boiling point by hot rocks underground," so the heat sources for geothermal energy can be described as "subterranean (underground) rocks." Choices (A) and (D) are incorrect because they are unsupported by the passage, and choice (C) is incorrect because "underground water" is what is heated by the rocks, so the reservoirs are not the sources of heat, but rather the medium through which heat is converted into energy.

13) ➡ D
Concept(s) Tested: Inference, Implication, and Suggestion
Choice (D) is correct because all forms of geothermal energy production described in the passage

(traditional and EGS) require large amounts of aboveground or belowground water for conversion into steam for energy. Therefore, it is reasonable to assume that geothermal energy production requires access to water reserves.

14) ■■■▶ A
Concept(s) Tested: Words in Context
Choice (A) is correct because, as used in the passage, "angle" is describing the point-of-view of U.S. "national security," and "perspective" is closest in meaning to point-of-view, making (A) the most appropriate choice. All other choices are incorrect because they do not fit the context of the sentence.

15) ■■■▶ B
Concept(s) Tested: Summary
Choice (B) is correct because paragraph 4 explains that the U.S. lacks hot shallow groundwater, and that the use of EGS can compensate for this because it allows one to drill into any hot rock and then connect the hot rock to a water source, thus supporting the claim in choice (B). Choice (A) is incorrect because the passage does not claim that EGS is more efficient than other forms of renewable energy. Choice (C) is disproven by the passage: lines 58 – 69 imply that EGS might require more drilling and maintenance than other renewable energy sources. Choice (D) is also disproven by the passage: lines 84 – 86 state that geothermal energy (including EGS) "should be used alongside…wind and solar" energies.

16) ■■■▶ D
Concept(s) Tested: Words in Context
Choice (D) is correct; in the final paragraph, the "silver bullet" is contrasted with "silver buckshot," which is defined as "a collection of solutions [that] add up to a big impact." Because the "silver bullet" is contrasted with "silver buckshot," we can infer that a "silver bullet" is the opposite of "a collection of solutions," which can be summarized as "an all-encompassing solution." All other choices are incorrect because they do not contrast with the definition of "silver buckshot," and therefore do not fit the context of the sentence.

17) ■■■▶ A
Concept(s) Tested: Purpose
Choice (A) is correct; throughout the passage, the author espouses the benefits of geothermal energy, one of which is its accessibility (see lines 34 – 37). The phrase "right under our feet" serves to emphasize, or "underscore," this accessibility by explaining the geothermal energy comes from a source that is easily accessible and close by. Choice (B) is incorrect because it is disproven

by lines 38 – 41, which reveal that the U.S. lacks accessible underground water. Choices (C) and (D) are incorrect because they do not fit the meaning of the phrase "right under our feet," which relates to geothermal energy's accessibility more than its production or uses.

18) ■■■▶ B
Concept(s) Tested: Attitude and Tone
Choice (B) is correct because both the first and last paragraphs advocate for widespread geothermal energy production, implying that the author is "hopeful" that geothermal energy will be more widely adopted in the future. Choice (A) and (D) are incorrect because the passage takes a positive view towards geothermal energy production, so the negative attitudes in (A) and (D) are unsupported. Choice (C) is incorrect because the author presents numerous statistics which demonstrate that he understands geothermal energy production, so he does not seem "surprised" in the passage.

19) ■■■▶ A
Concept(s) Tested: Citation
Choice (A) is correct because, in this excerpt, the author mentions "potential benefits" of geothermal energy production and advocates for making it "a viable power source for the U.S.," thus summarizing his hopeful and optimistic attitude toward U.S. geothermal energy production. All other choices are incorrect; although they provide information about geothermal energy production, they do not provide any information that would support the author's hopeful attitude.

20) ■■■▶ A
Concept(s) Tested: Graph and Text Synthesis
Choice (A) is correct because the graph illustrates that wind and solar energy production is much more variable than geothermal energy production is, which implies that environmental factors (such as total sunlight and wind) affect wind and solar energy production more than they do geothermal energy production. This choice is further supported by lines 28 – 32 of the passage.

21) ■■■▶ B
Concept(s) Tested: Graph and Test Synthesis
Choice (B) is correct; these lines explain that geothermal energy can be produced more consistently than wind or solar energies, and they are supported by the graph, which illustrates that geothermal produces energy at a rate that is closer to maximum capacity that wind or solar energies.

22) ■■■▶ D
Concept(s) Tested: Summary
Darwin states at the beginning of the paragraph

that he uses the term "struggle for existence" in a "large and metaphorical sense," then sets that against the example of the "two canine animals," such as wolves or dogs, fighting for food when there is a dearth (shortage) of it. His point is that the struggle for existence extends beyond the out-and-out fight to eat between two animals. Thus, the answer is (D). Choices (A), (B), and (C) are incorrect because they do not describe the author's basic contrast in the paragraph.

23) ➡ C
Concept(s) Tested: Words in Context
The correct choice is (C) because in line 2, the author explains in what sense he is using a term—that is, what *meaning* he intends. Choices (A), (B), and (D) are incorrect because the author is not discussing the feeling, wisdom, or perception of what he intends, but rather, the meaning.

24) ➡ A
Concept(s) Tested: Summary
Choice (A) is correct because Darwin is painting a new world-view for readers of his era in which nature is not gentle, and large-scale "destruction" is normal. (B) is incorrect because, although Darwin does make the claim that such understanding is ultimately impossible, it is not the passage's main focus. (C) is incorrect because, while Darwin does mention dependence among organisms, it is, again, not his main topic. (D) is incorrect because Darwin does not mention anything about human reproduction levels.

25) ➡ C
Concept(s) Tested: Citation
Choice (C) is correct because lines 40 – 45 support the claim that all organisms struggle to survive because more are produced than can survive. (A) is incorrect because it is a specific example, not a statement that summarizes the main point of the passage. (B) is incorrect because, again, it is only one example of an organism's competitive challenge. (D) is incorrect because it refers to a theory that helps explain the point; it is not in and of itself a central claim.

26) ➡ D
Concept(s) Tested: Citation, Graph and Text Synthesis
Choice (D) is correct because the graph depicts the "principle of geometric increase" in population that Darwin mentions in lines 37 – 38, as well as the way that a population inevitably exceeds its food supply such that "no country could support" it. Choices (A), (B), and (C) are incorrect because they describe aspects of the struggle for existence but only relate to the graph indirectly.

27) ➡ B
Concept(s) Tested: Purpose
The correct choice is (B). In lines 45 – 49, after Darwin makes his main claim about the struggle for existence, he explains that he has been describing Malthus's population theory, but in relation to animals and plants. (A) is incorrect because Darwin is using, not rejecting, Malthus's theory. (C) is incorrect because Darwin does not provide evidence or reasoning to support Malthus; he assumes the reader already accepts Malthus's conclusions. (D) is incorrect because Darwin is not discussing artificial food production.

28) ➡ B
Concept(s) Tested: Words in Context
Choice (B) is correct because in line 48, Darwin mentions that plants and animals must rely on a natural food supply, presumably as opposed to humans, who have an "artificial" food supply in the sense that we can grow crops and raise animals; in other words, we can *cultivate* food. (A) and (C) are incorrect because Darwin clearly is not referring to fake or imitation food, but simply to food that is not wild. (D) is incorrect because there is no indication that Darwin considers cultivating food to be dishonest.

29) ➡ C
Concept(s) Tested: Attitude and Tone
The correct choice is (C). In paragraph 3, Darwin says that it is good to try to understand why some species or individuals have advantages, but to keep in mind that it will be impossible to completely succeed, because of limitations in our perceptions. He is most like a teacher encouraging his students to persist in a difficult task. (A) is incorrect because Darwin does not propose any policies in the passage. (B) is incorrect because Darwin is not simplifying concepts but commenting on them. (D) is incorrect because Darwin does not promote any action except research and study.

30) ➡ A
Concept(s) Tested: Summary
Choice (A) is correct because Darwin points out that when we try to comprehend the vast number connections ("mutual relations") between an organism and its environment, we will inevitably fail, and that we should be aware of that, even though it is difficult to accept. (B) is incorrect because Darwin does not advocate respect or protection for organisms or habitats in the passage. (C) is incorrect because Darwin does not claim that humans are part of these relationships. Finally, (D) is incorrect because Darwin does not explicitly advocate more study.

31) ➡ D
Concept(s) Tested: Organization

In paragraph 1, Darwin defines several senses of the term "Struggle for Existence." In paragraph 2 he explains why this struggle takes place: the high reproduction rate of species. He sums up these ideas in the last paragraph and adds some commentary about how to approach the study of organisms. Thus, the passage as a whole has a Definition—Explanation—Commentary structure, and choice (D) is correct. (A) is incorrect because the author is not presenting a thesis in paragraph 1, but is instead defining and giving examples of a term. Likewise, paragraph 3 does not provide any consequences of the discussion in the previous two paragraphs. (B) is incorrect because none of the information in paragraph 1 is stated in the form of a question. Finally, (C) is incorrect because the second paragraph is not in the form of a counterargument—the author does not argue against anything he stated in the first paragraph.

32) ➡ A
Concept(s) Tested: Inference, Implication, and Suggestion

The correct choice is (A) because in line 4, Henry says that after so many failed attempts, it would be useless ("vain") to "indulge in fond hopes (wishful thinking) of peace and reconciliation." (B) is incorrect because Henry is not arguing for a standoff with the British, but for war. (C) is incorrect because Henry's point is not that the British may be ready to negotiate, but that the time for negotiating with the British has passed. (D) is incorrect because Henry is not speaking specifically about the state of Virginia, but about the colonies as a whole.

33) ➡ B
Concept(s) Tested: Citation

Choice (B) is correct because, in lines 5 – 7, Henry describes hopes for peace as being "in vain," or futile. (A) is incorrect because lines 4 – 5 merely provide the context for Henry's claim about wishful thinking. (C) and (D) are incorrect because they are both part of Henry's exhortations to the assembly to go to war, and they do not speak clearly and directly to the idea that peace is impossible under the present circumstances.

34) ➡ C
Concept(s) Tested: Words in Context

Henry uses the phrase "the glorious object of our contest" to refer to the objective, or *goal*, of American independence. Thus, choice (C) is correct. Choice (A) is incorrect because a recipient is someone who receives something, and Henry is not talking about a "recipient" of the aim or goal of independence, but the goal itself. (B) is incorrect because an "item" is a thing, which does not make sense in the context of the sentence. (D) is also incorrect: although the colonies are protesting their treatment by the British, their protests are meant to achieve a specific *goal*—independence.

35) ➡ D
Concept(s) Tested: Purpose

The answer is (D). In line 26, Henry warns that if colonists do not fight, they will end up "in submission and slavery," and he adds the metaphor "our chains are forged!" to imply that the British have prepared oppressive laws and policies for the colonies, presumably to prevent further rebellion. (A) is incorrect because Henry is speaking metaphorically about political oppression, not about making weapons to fight the British. (B) is incorrect because Henry does not use the metaphor of the chains to imply that people are doomed; rather, he is using it to warn about what could happen if colonists try to avoid war. (C) is incorrect because the threat of the chains is not addressing actual slavery, but rather a metaphor for political oppression.

36) ➡ B
Concept(s) Tested: Inference, Implication, and Suggestion

In lines 42 – 50, Tecumseh warns that Native Americans must unite or they all will be "driven from" their native country, or *forcibly detached* and "blown away" like leaves blown from trees in autumn. Thus, (B) is correct. Since Tecumseh is only speaking metaphorically, and not literally, about autumn leaves being "blown by wind," (A) is incorrect. (C) is incorrect because it articulates a more general consideration than what Tecumseh is speaking about. Finally, (D) is incorrect because Tecumseh is not discussing self-restraint; he is instead trying to provoke action.

37) ➡ D
Concept(s) Tested: Inference, Implication, and Suggestion

Choice (D) is correct because Tecumseh speaks of the need for the different Native American tribes to unite and collectively face the danger that is upon them. (A) is incorrect because it encompasses part of Tecumseh's message, but not its overall focus on uniting forces. (B) is incorrect, because while Tecumseh does state that whites "kick and strike" them as they do African Americans (lines 79 – 80), Tecumseh does not imply that Native American tribes should unite with African Americans. Finally, (C) is incorrect because Tecumseh's focus is on the tribes' need to unite and see themselves as one group; he is not discussing how to preserve unique tribal cultures.

38) ➡️ A
Concept(s) Tested: Citation
(A) is the correct choice because in lines 55 – 57, Tecumseh clearly states his fear that the very survival of native tribes is at stake, and that their only hope is to combine forces to fight. (B) is incorrect because it is more of a general warning to the audience than an articulation of his overall message. (C) is incorrect because it is one of the reasons to fight, not Tecumseh's overall call to arms. Choice (D) contains a rhetorical question that Tecumseh is using to motivate Native Americans to unite, so it is not a direct message.

39) ➡️ B
Concept(s) Tested: Words in Context
Usually "want" is used as a verb that is similar in meaning to "desire." The noun form of "want" refers to a lack of something, as in a "need." Tecumseh is saying here that the Native American tribes had neither riches nor wants—they were not rich but they did not lack anything that they needed. Only choice (B)—"privations"—means the same thing as "want" in this context. (A) is incorrect because having a "wish" is having a desire for something, while having a "want" is having an unmet need. (C) is incorrect because an "interest" is a desire to know something or learn something. This is conceptually different from a want. Finally, (D) is incorrect because an "objective" is an aim or goal, not quite the same as an unmet need.

40) ➡️ D
Concept(s) Tested: Multiple-Text Synthesis
The correct choice is (D). The two passages differ in that Henry warns about political oppression while Tecumseh warns of being evicted and scattered—a "complete loss of communities." (A) is incorrect: although Tecumseh accuses the Choctaws and Chickasaws of having "false security and delusive hopes" of peace, he does not explicitly describe peaceful yet ultimately ineffective protests. (B) is incorrect because neither writer predicts victory; only that war is inevitable. (C) is incorrect because both men, not just Tecumseh, state that war has begun or been ongoing.

41) ➡️ D
Concept(s) Tested: Multiple-Text Synthesis
Choice (D) is correct. In Passage 1, Henry speaks metaphorically of the colonists' chains being forged, but the colonists are not in danger of being literally enslaved. This fact distinguishes Henry's argument from Tecumseh's argument in Passage

2, because Tecumseh warns of literal slavery if the Native American tribes do not unite to face the whites. (A) is incorrect because neither Henry nor Tecumseh describe their own experiences in battle. (B) is incorrect because Tecumseh expresses his willingness to die for his cause, asking rhetorically whether tribes should wait for slavery, or die fighting against it. Similarly, (C) is incorrect because both men speak of the need for unity; Henry exhorts his audience to join others to the north by saying "Our brethren are already in the field!" while Tecumseh also calls for tribes to combine forces.

42) ➡️ B
Concept(s) Tested: Multiple-Text Synthesis
Choice (B) is the correct answer because both speakers ask questions that are intended to motivate their audiences to risk their lives in battle. Henry asks, "Is life so dear, or peace so sweet, as to be purchased at the price of chains and slavery?" Tecumseh warns of slavery and asks, "Shall we wait for that moment, or shall we die fighting before submitting to such ignominy?" (A) is incorrect because neither passage uses "facts and figures." (C) is incorrect because neither passage mentions heroes. Finally, (D) is incorrect because both passages speak of the plight that their audiences face, and not specifically about the suffering of any one individual.

43) ➡️ B
Concept(s) Tested: Organization
Paragraphs 1 and 2 discuss the roles of computational scientists and the role of Brookhaven in managing the vast quantities of data from the collision experiments that physics researchers around the world sort through. In paragraphs 10 and 12, the author discusses the task of analyzing the enormous amount of data generated by particle colliders. Thus, (B) is correct. (A) is incorrect because the author does not speak about benefits and costs of experimentation. (C) is incorrect because the author shifts throughout the article from discussing the work of teams in the United States to discussing the work of teams in Europe. There are no places in the article where the focus is exclusively on the United States, and then exclusively on Europe. Finally, (D) is incorrect because although the passage briefly mentions current ideas about the genesis of the universe, there is no mention of past theories.

44) ➡️ D
Concept(s) Tested: Words in Context
A "landmark" finding is one that is so significant that it marks a change or a turning point in thinking. Thus, (D) is the correct choice because only the term "seminal" conveys a similar significance; "seminal" refers to new, influential ideas. Choice (A), "geographic," is incorrect because "landmark"

is not being used in a literal sense to refer to a structure or natural feature. (B) is incorrect because "visible" does not make sense in the context. In addition, (C) is incorrect because it adds a subjective evaluation of the findings and therefore is not a precise substitute.

45) ➤ A
Concept(s) Tested: Inference, Implication, and Suggestion
Choice (A) is correct because the author quotes Ernst as saying that all of the individuals involved were committed to solving problems with the work, regardless of the time of day or night. This suggests that workers felt both collaborative and pressed for time. (B) is incorrect because although the atmosphere may have been stressful, to say that it was "frantic" is too strong; there is also no indication that it was competitive. (C) is incorrect because there is no evidence that the scientists involved were frustrated. The fact that problems were tackled head-on whenever they arose speaks to their dedication, not to frustration or aggression. Finally, (D) is incorrect because the quotes refer to the professional working atmosphere at the facility, not to the emotional atmosphere.

46) ➤ A
Concept(s) Tested: Purpose
The extraordinary factors described in the work indicate the magnitude of the experiments. Thus, (A) is correct. (B) is incorrect because it conflicts with the author's positive tone toward the experiments being conducted, and there is no evidence that the author thinks the experimental procedures are wasteful. Likewise, (C) is incorrect because the author does not use jargon or references to concepts that might undermine the reader's self-confidence, and instead takes a neutral, explanatory tone. Finally, (D) is incorrect because at no point in paragraph 4 or in the passage as a whole does the author encourage the reader to get involved in the experiments.

47) ➤ C
Concept(s) Tested: Inference, Implication, and Suggestion
The author mentions that the RHIC allows collision experiments to free quarks from gluons, which last occurred 100 millionths of a second after the Big Bang—the explosion that created the universe. Taken in conjunction with the claim that both the RHIC and LHC are "time machines," this suggests that both of these experiments allow physicists to better understand the Big Bang. Thus, (C) is correct. (A) is incorrect because no mention is made in the passage about challenges

to traditional notions of time and space. (B) is incorrect because the passage does not anywhere mention science-fiction. (D) is incorrect because the passage explicitly states that colliders provide information about how the universe began, not about what might occur in the future.

48) ➤ A
Concept(s) Tested: Citation
Choice (A) is correct because in lines 30 – 34, the author explicitly states that research from the colliders provides information about the Big Bang. (B) does not directly support the connection between the research and the Big Bang, but rather provides a brief description of an apparent discovery from the research. (C) and (D) both provide information about the research process, but do not support the concept that the colliders are "time machines" because they give us a glimpse of the Big Bang.

49) ➤ A
Concept(s) Tested: Summary
Lines 27 – 28 mentions that the RHIC smashes gold ions at speeds close to the speed of light; line 43 mentions that the LHC smashes protons into each other. Thus, (A) is the correct answer. (B), (C), and (D) are incorrect because they are not mentioned as colliding particles.

50) ➤ A
Concept(s) Tested: Purpose
The phrase "needle in a haystack" is meant to convey the difficulty of finding something that is hidden among countless similar things. Thus, (A) is correct. (B) is incorrect because the passage nowhere mentions the mathematical impossibility of finding what the experimenters are looking for. Similarly, (C) is incorrect because the author does not use the image of the needle in the haystack to convey an idea about collaboration, but rather about the task itself. (D) is incorrect because the passage never discusses the size of the Higgs boson relative to an atom or ion.

51) ➤ D
Concept(s) Tested: Inference, Implication, and Suggestion
In lines 73 – 75, the author states that even if the colliders created a Higgs boson, it would "instantly" decay into particles that are "detectable." Similarly, lines 62 – 63 state that the search for "particles and states of matter that don't exist in today's world" is challenging. These statements strongly suggest that the Higgs boson can only be detected indirectly, so (D) is correct. (A) is incorrect because the passage nowhere states that the Higgs boson does not exist, or that

scientists suspect that it does not exist. Likewise, (B) is incorrect because there is no indication that the search for the Higgs has generated controversy. Finally, (C) is incorrect because the passage offers no claim or evidence that the existence of the Higgs boson has been suspected since ancient times.

52) ➡ D
Concept(s) Tested: Citation
The correct choice is (D), because lines 61 – 65 point out that the Higgs boson is a particle that does not exist today, and that it must be made by the colliders. The implication is that the Higgs boson can only be detected through indirect evidence. (A) is incorrect because it describes the researchers' excitement, not the method for identifying the Higgs boson. (B) is incorrect because it focuses on the possible results of particle collision experiments, but does not specify whether the results would be obtained directly or indirectly. (C) does focus on the Higgs boson discovery, but it is incorrect because it describes the significance of finding the particle, not the method used to find it.

Writing and Language Test

1. Ⓒ	5. Ⓒ	9. Ⓑ	13. Ⓑ	17. Ⓒ	21. Ⓑ	25. Ⓐ	29. Ⓑ	33. Ⓒ	37. Ⓒ	41. Ⓐ
2. Ⓒ	6. Ⓓ	10. Ⓓ	14. Ⓐ	18. Ⓑ	22. Ⓑ	26. Ⓑ	30. Ⓐ	34. Ⓓ	38. Ⓓ	42. Ⓒ
3. Ⓒ	7. Ⓑ	11. Ⓒ	15. Ⓑ	19. Ⓓ	23. Ⓒ	27. Ⓓ	31. Ⓓ	35. Ⓐ	39. Ⓑ	43. Ⓓ
4. Ⓓ	8. Ⓐ	12. Ⓒ	16. Ⓐ	20. Ⓐ	24. Ⓓ	28. Ⓒ	32. Ⓐ	36. Ⓒ	40. Ⓑ	44. Ⓑ

1) ➡ C

Concept(s) Tested: In-Sentence Punctuation
The information after the underlined portion provides clarification. Therefore, (C) is the best choice, as a colon often serves to introduce a clarification or elaboration. (A), (B), and (D) are incorrect because the information after the underlined pronoun defines it, which is only indicated by (C).

2) ➡ C

Concept(s) Tested: Precise Diction
The correct choice should emphasize the fact that cloud-based storage is primarily an online platform, and (C) is the correct choice because "virtual" can be used to describe a system embedded in a computer.

3) ➡ C

Concept(s) Tested: Pronoun Case
Choice (C) is correct because the underlined pronoun is the object of the preposition "of," so it must be in the objective case. (A) is incorrect because it creates an independent clause after "people," which cannot be separated from the rest of the sentence by a comma alone.

4) ➡ D

Concept(s) Tested: Passage Development
The added sentence is not essential to the passage and breaks noticeably from the academic tone establishes in the passage, so (D) is the correct choice. (B) is incorrect because the passage is not written in a humorous tone.

5) ➡ C

Concept(s) Tested: Combining Sentences
There is an independent clause on either side of the underlined portion. Combining two independent clauses requires either a comma and coordinating conjunction or a semicolon. Because the second sentence adds another detail, (C) is the best choice. (A) is incorrect because the relationship between the two sentences is not one of cause and effect, so "so" is not an appropriate conjunction.

6) ➡ D

Concept(s) Tested: Pronoun Case, Verb Tense
The pronoun in the underlined portion is acting as a subject, so it should be in the subjective form ("I"). The verb in the underlined portion should be plural, because the subject is a plural noun ("a collaborator and I"). Therefore, (D) is the best choice.

7) ➡ B

Concept(s) Tested: In-Sentence Punctuation
Because there are only two items in the list, a comma is unnecessary, so (B) is the correct choice.

8) ➡ A

Concept(s) Tested: Passage Development
The paragraph focuses on the collaborative nature of cloud computing. Since (A) provides an additional detail related to working with files on the cloud, it is the best choice. (B) is incorrect because sharing content on social media does not directly pertain to collaboration.

9) ➡ B

Concept(s) Tested: Transition Words and Phrases
The relationship between the information in the two clauses of this sentence can best be described as one of cause and effect. Therefore, (B) is the correct answer.

10) ➡ D

Concept(s) Tested: Pronoun Use, Verb Tense and Voice
The pronoun in the underlined portion replaces "businesses," so (D) is the best choice. (C) is incorrect because it is written in the passive voice, which makes the meaning of sentence less clear.

11) ➡ C

Concept(s) Tested: Passage Organization
Paragraph 2 describes many details about cloud computing technology and how cloud services operate. Therefore, it belongs in the middle of the passage; paragraph 1 and paragraph 4 already provide an adequate introduction and

conclusion, respectively. (C) is the best choice because paragraph 3 provides a more logical transition from the introduction to the passage's focus on using the cloud for work.

12) ➡ C
Concept(s) Tested: Precise Diction
The correct choice should emphasize the fact that humans are taking advantage of a natural process. Thus, (C) is the best choice. (A) and (B) are incorrect because these words are typically associated with taking advantage of other people, not using or utilizing natural occurrences.

13) ➡ B
Concept(s) Tested: Combining Sentences
The two sentences have the same subject, so the subject can be eliminated from the second sentence when combining them. In this case, a coordinating conjunction is still necessary, but a comma is not. Therefore, (B) is the best choice.

14) ➡ A
Concept(s) Tested: In-Sentence Punctuation
The information after the underlined portion serves as an explanation of an unfamiliar term. Therefore, an em-dash or a colon is the best way to separate this information from the rest of the sentence, and (A) is the correct choice.

15) ➡ B
Concept(s) Tested: Pronoun Use
Choice (B) is correct because the underlined pronoun is replacing "composition," so it must be singular. (A) is incorrect because the sentence provides a comparison between the quality of two food products, and "that" is necessary for the second of the two items ("this" is only appropriate for the first term mentioned).

16) ➡ A
Concept(s) Tested: Preposition Use
The first preposition should be "into" to indicate the movement of chemicals into an animal's bloodstream. The second preposition shows ownership over "bloodstreams," so it should be "of." Thus, (A) is the correct choice.

17) ➡ C
Concept(s) Tested: Transition Word and Phrases
Choice (C) is correct because the information in this paragraph adds details to the experiment. The remaining choices create relationships between the paragraphs that are not present in the passage (consequence, example, and contrast, respectively).

18) ➡ B
Concept(s) Tested: Possession
In the experiment, researchers are testing multiple products (ie. fermented and unfermented soybeans), so the noun needs to be plural, with the apostrophe on the outside to show ownership by the group.

Because "products'" is a plural noun, "abilities" must also be plural, making (B) the correct choice.

19) ➡ D
Concept(s) Tested: Graph Analysis
The graph displays the amount of lipase function as a percentage of the control for each of the products tested (including the control, unfermented beans, and beans at a variety of fermentation times). At 60 hours, fermented beans show zero percent lipase activity, making (D) the correct choice. (A) is incorrect because the graph does not comment on the concentration of lipase inhibitors. (B) is incorrect because beans which had been fermented for 24 hours reduced lipase activity by close to 70 percent. (C) is incorrect because none of the products tested increased lipase activity.

20) ➡ A
Concept(s) Tested: Precise Diction
The correct answer will illustrate a decrease in the amount of weight gained by the mice studied. The only choice that accurately demonstrates this reduction is (A). Choice (B) is incorrect because "deflated" refers to a drain in one's mood, or the loss of air from inside a tire or balloon, with does not fit the context.

21) ➡ B
Concept(s) Tested: Passage Development
The correct answer is (B), because the added information is essential to the passage, as most readers would not understand the significance of lipid vacuoles without it.

22) ➡ B
Concept(s) Tested: Passage Organization
Sentence 6 describes the final stage in the experiment's methodology. The remainder of the paragraph discusses the results of this last step, so sentence 6 should be used to introduce the paragraph, making (B) the correct choice.

23) ➡ C
Concept(s) Tested: Precise Diction
The correct word should express the idea that root bridges become sturdier as the tree grows and develops. The choice that most accurately indicates growth or development is (C), "matures." Choices (A) and (B) are incorrect because they imply the acquisition of knowledge, which does not apply to trees, and (D) is incorrect because "ripens" refers to the maturation of fruit, not trees.

24) ➡ D
Concept(s) Tested: Passage Organization
The information in the second sentence provides a cause, while the information in the first sentence explains its effect. When combining these sentences, we want to ensure that this relationship is maintained and that the items are introduced in the proper order. The only choice that accurately describes the

relationship between the two sentences without inverting the cause and effect is (D).

25) ➡ A
Concept(s) Tested: Pronoun Case
The pronoun in this sentence is acting as a subject, telling us who performed an action. Of the choices presented, only "who" can act as the subject of a sentence, making (A) the correct answer.

26) ➡ B
Concept(s) Tested: Passage Development
The added sentence provides a minor detail, which illustrates the author's point about multi-level bridges. The comment is not essential, but it is not entirely irrelevant, either, providing an example of a "multi-level" tree bridge. Thus, (B) is the best choice.

27) ➡ D
Concept(s) Tested: Possession
The correct choice is (D), because the author is showing possession over the roots of multiple trees.

28) ➡ C
Concept(s) Tested: Passage Organization
Sentence 3 describes the second step in the formation of root bridges and should be placed directly after the first step, which is described in the first sentence of the paragraph. Therefore, (C) is the correct choice.

29) ➡ B
Concept(s) Tested: parallel structure, concision
The underlined portion breaks from the pattern established by the nouns "steel cables" and "bamboo"; to maintain the pattern, the final item in the list must use the same structure as earlier elements. (B) continues the pattern established and is therefore the correct choice.

30) ➡ A
Concept(s) Tested: Passage Development
The correct answer will link the two paragraphs and logically express the relationship between them. The final paragraph discusses additional root structures that Khasi villagers have developed to improve daily life. Therefore, (A) is the best choice; the remaining choices fail to focus on root bridges, making them incorrect.

31) ➡ D
Concept(s) Tested: Preposition Use
The correct choice should be a spatial preposition to express the fact that bleachers are a location where people can watch sporting events. (B) and (D) are both spatial prepositions. However, "to" is only used to discuss motion to a location, while "where" conveys information about what happens at that location. Thus, (D) is the correct choice.

32) ➡ A
Concept(s) Tested: Transition Words and Phrases
The information following the semicolon serves as an example of the author's previous statement. Therefore, (A) is the best choice as it accurately expresses this relationship.

33) ➡ C
Concept(s) Tested: Participial Phrases
The information after the comma is a participial phrase that modifies the noun "ladder." Only (C) uses the participle correctly and with proper punctuation to form an appropriate participial phrase, making it the best choice.

34) ➡ D
Concept(s) Tested: Pronoun Use
The word "but" introduces a contrast between what some critics think and what others think. Given this, (D) is the correct choice because it maintains parallel structure with the first part of the sentence, namely subject–verb–object. (A) is incorrect because it is unclear whether "they" refers to the buildings or the critics. (B) is incorrect because it uses the passive voice in a roundabout way and fails to mention who is praising Gaudí's buildings. (C) is incorrect because it does not answer the question: "Legitimate according to whom?"

35) ➡ A
Concept(s) Tested: Passage Development
The previous sentence introduces information that includes both criticism and praise of Gaudí's work. The sentence at 35 highlights the fact that there is much positive regard for Gaudí's work, and that several of his creations have been recognized by the United Nations. Thus, the underlined sentence conveys the significance of Gaudí's work and should be kept, making (A) correct. (B) is incorrect because the information does not clarify anything else in the passage. (C) is incorrect primarily because no explanation for the United Nations' action is needed. The statement merely indicates that the United Nations recognizes the importance of Gaudí's work, which is a testament to its value. (D) is also incorrect because the sentence does not blur the focus on Gaudí's buildings, but provides evidence of their special qualities.

36) ➡ C
Concept(s) Tested: Passage Organization
Choice (C) is correct because sentence 3 provides needed context for understanding why and how Gaudí was able to spend time in his childhood observing the natural world around him and the work of his father. It is also for this reason that (A) is incorrect. (B) is incorrect because the information about Gaudí's birth is logically prior to his childhood, and the passage is organized to provide information about Gaudí's life in roughly

chronological order. (D) is likewise incorrect because sentence 3 mentions information about his poor health, which precedes his recovery, and since, again, the paragraph is in chronological order, this information should be mentioned before sentence 4.

37) ➡ C
Concept(s) Tested: Verb Tense
Based on the context of the sentence, Barcelona was going through something of an economic boom by the time Gaudí arrived. Since this boom was not something that was completed before Gaudí's arrival, but was ongoing when Gaudí arrived, (C) is the correct choice. (A) is incorrect because it implies that the process had been completed before Gaudí's arrival, which is not the intention of the sentence. (B) is incorrect because it makes it sound as if Barcelona is undergoing an economic upturn in the present, which is not the intended meaning. (D) makes Barcelona's revival either conditional upon some unstated fact or happen at some point after Gaudí arrived, which is not the intention of the sentence.

38) ➡ D
Concept(s) Tested: Passage Development
The sentence mentions one isolated project designed by Gaudí—a display cabinet. Considered within the context of the whole paragraph, this information does not fit well with the emphasis on the opportunities provided to Gaudí by his wealthy patrons. Thus, (D) is the correct choice. (A) is incorrect because the sentence mentions one fact about Gaudí that exists in isolation from the central focus of the paragraph. (B) is incorrect because there is no evidence that the design of the display cabinet was the reason that Gaudí became an architect. (C) is also incorrect because the paragraph does not focus on how fast Gaudí became a renowned architect, but on the fact that Gaudí had many opportunities in Barcelona to develop his ideas.

39) ➡ B
Concept(s) Tested: Voice, Concision
As written, the sentence is missing a subject; it is not clear who is employing ruled shapes. This is called a dangling modifier. Therefore, (A) is incorrect, and (B) is correct because it includes the subject "he." (C) is incorrect because it is not the structures that "employed" and "achieved," but the architect. (D) is incorrect because it is a convoluted use of the passive voice.

40) ➡ B
Concept(s) Tested: Precise Diction
The author is discussing Gaudí's *main* gift. Yet as written, it refers to a belief, and not the idea of centrality. Thus, (A) is incorrect. The correct spelling of the term is "principal," so choice (B) is correct. (C) is incorrect because "princely" describes someone with prince-like qualities and therefore has nothing to do with the topic of the sentence.

(D), "principled," suggests someone who acts based on moral principles, and this is not the intended meaning in this case.

41) ➡ A
Concept(s) Tested: Concision, Passage Tone
The sentence as written appropriately uses the term "but" to indicate a contrast with something said previously. Although Gaudí's style incorporates elements of baroque and gothic architecture, it is ultimately not easy to classify. Thus, the sentence is correct as written and (A) is the answer. (B) and (C) are both long-winded and informal ways of rewriting the clause that confuse more than clarify. (D) mentions Modernism as though the term and its significance have already been discussed, which is not the case.

42) ➡ C
Concept(s) Tested: Subject-Verb Agreement, Pronoun Use
The subject of the phrase is "chimneys," which is plural. Thus, a plural verb, "adorn," is needed, and choice (C) is correct. Since (A) and (B) use the third-person singular form of the verb, they are incorrect. (D) is incorrect because the pronoun refers to the singular noun "roof."

43) ➡ D
Concept(s) Tested: In-Sentence Punctuation, Concision
Choice (D) is correct because it is the most concise choice that maintains appropriate punctuation. (A) is grammatically correct, but "contemporary" and "now" are redundant to "today." (B) is incorrect for the same reason—"now" is redundant. (C) is incorrect because a colon indicates that an explanation or an explanation of the previous information is to follow, which is not the case here.

44) ➡ B
Concept(s) Tested: Syntax, Concision
As written, the sentence contains awkward phrasing and unnecessary wordiness, so (A) is incorrect. (B) is the best answer because it conveys its point clearly and concisely. (C) changes the sentence's basic meaning by making it sound as if Gaudí purposefully "formed" the Art Nouveau movement and sponsored Dalí and Miro, which is not the intended connotation. Finally, (D) is incorrect because it is wordy and its meaning is imprecise.

Math Test

✓ No Calculator Portion

1. (A)	7. (D)	13. (D)	19. 4
2. (D)	8. (B)	14. (A)	20. 29
3. (A)	9. (C)	15. (D)	
4. (D)	10. (A)	16. 15	
5. (D)	11. (B)	17. 16	
6. (D)	12. (A)	18. 120	

✓ Calculator Portion

1. (A)	7. (D)	13. (C)	19. (D)	25. (B)	31. 312	36. 3
2. (C)	8. (D)	14. (C)	20. (D)	26. (D)		37. 0.38
3. (C)	9. (B)	15. (B)	21. (B)	27. (D)	32. $\frac{5}{3}$	38. 4.07
4. (D)	10. (B)	16. (B)	22. (A)	28. (B)	33. 26	
5. (B)	11. (B)	17. (C)	23. (D)	29. (B)	34. 11	
6. (A)	12. (B)	18. (A)	24. (D)	30. (C)	35. 3,400	

No Calculator Portion

1) A

Concept(s) Tested: Problem Solving

James drives 30 miles a day, so the daily cost of rental is:

Daily cost = 19.95 + (30 − 20)(0.4)
Daily cost = 23.95

The cost of the rental as a function of days rented is: $f(x) = (23.95)x$

2) D

Concept(s) Tested: Problem Solving, Inequalities

The money earned mowing lawns less the cost of the mower must be equal to or greater $800:

$15l − 250 \geq 800$
$15l \geq 1050$
$l \geq 70$

3) A

Concept(s) Tested: Problem Solving, Algebra

$$Travel\ time = \frac{125\ miles}{60\ miles\ per\ hour} + \frac{30\ miles}{45\ miles\ per\ hour}$$

$$Travel\ time = 2\frac{1}{12}\ hours + \frac{2}{3}\ hours = 2\frac{3}{4}\ hours$$

4) D

Concept(s) Tested: Graphs and Functions

The second line is equivalent to the first line multiplied by a factor of 2; a simple transformation shows that they are the same line:

$2(3x + 2y) = 2(−1)$
$6x + 4y = −2$

5) ➡ D

Concept(s) Tested: Problem Solving

The monthly cost can be modeled as a function of minutes of talk time (0.1m) with the monthly fee (2) as the constant: $C(m) = 0.1m + 2$

6) ➡ D

Concept(s) Tested: Problem Solving

We can infer that the constant 45 represents the hourly rate for a massage because it is being multiplied by h, the number of hours per appointment. Thus, (A) is incorrect. The question does not state how long customers generally spend receiving massages, disproving (B). Moreover, credit card fees are no mentioned, making (C) incorrect. Thus, by process of elimination, the most reasonable choice is (D) because the constant 15 is applied regardless of how many hours a customer purchases.

7) ➡ D

Concept(s) Tested: Problem Solving, Algebra

Let the smaller of the two numbers be a.

The larger of the two numbers is then $a + 3$.

$q = a + (a + 3)$

$q = 2a + 3$

$a = \dfrac{q - 3}{2}$

8) ➤ B
Concept(s) Tested: Geometry

The radius of the sphere can be determined from the formula for surface area:

$4\pi r^2 = 36\pi$

$r^2 = 9$

$r = 3$

The volume of the sphere is:

$V = \dfrac{4}{3}\pi r^3$

$V = \dfrac{4}{3}\pi (3)^3$

$V = 36\pi \text{ cm}^3$

9) ➤ C
Concept(s) Tested: Geometry

A radius perpendicular to a chord bisects the chord, therefore $\overline{KM} = \overline{ML} = 6$. If we consider the right triangle ΔLMO, with the hypotenuse of the triangle equivalent to the radius of the circle:

$\overline{OM}^2 + \overline{ML}^2 = \overline{OL}^2$

$6^2 + 6^2 = r^2$

$72 = r^2$

The area of the circle is 72π.

10) ➤ A
Concept(s) Tested: Data Analysis, Graphs and Functions

The second equation is equivalent to the line $x = y$. Eliminate answer choice (B), which does not contain this line. The first line can be written as $y = -x + 4$, which has a negative slope. Of the remaining choices, only (A) has a line with negative slope.

11) ➤ B
Concept(s) Tested: Geometry

Area of small triangle $= \dfrac{x^2}{2}$

Area of large triangle $= \dfrac{y^2}{2}$

Area of rectangele $= xy$

The sum of these areas is the area of the shaded region:

Area of shaded region $= \dfrac{x^2}{2} + \dfrac{y^2}{2} + xy$

$= \dfrac{x^2 + y^2 + 2xy}{2} = \dfrac{(x = y)^2}{2}$

12) ➤ A
Concept(s) Tested: Problem Solving, Geometry

One fourth of the volume of the bottle constitutes three fourths of the volume of the glass (V_g):

$\dfrac{1}{4}(1.5\text{L}) = \dfrac{3}{4}V_g$

$V_g = \dfrac{4}{3} \cdot \dfrac{1}{4}(1.5\text{L})$

$V_g = 0.5\text{L}$

13) ➤ D
Concept(s) Tested: Algebra

$\dfrac{a}{b} + \dfrac{a+2}{3b} = \dfrac{1}{4} \rightarrow \left(\dfrac{3}{3}\right)\left(\dfrac{a}{b}\right) + \dfrac{a+2}{3b} = \dfrac{1}{4}$

$\dfrac{3a + a + 2}{3b} = \dfrac{1}{4} \rightarrow 4a + 2 = \dfrac{3b}{4}$

$a = \dfrac{3b - 8}{16}$

14) ➤ A
Concept(s) Tested: Problem Solving, Algebra

$Time\ driving\ A \rightarrow B = \dfrac{180km}{60km / hr} = 3hrs$

$Time\ driving\ B \rightarrow A = \dfrac{180km}{90km / hr} = 2hrs$

$Average\ speed = \dfrac{Total\ distance}{Total\ time}$

$Average\ speed = \dfrac{360km}{5\ hr} = 72\ km/hr$

15) ■➤ D

Concept(s) Tested: Algebra

$$\frac{a^2 + 2ab + b^2}{a^2 - b^2} = 2(a+b)$$

$$\frac{(a+b)^2}{(a-b)(a+b)} = 2(a+b)$$

$$(a-b) = \frac{1}{2}$$

16) ■➤ 15

Concept(s) Tested: Algebra

$x^2 + 7x - 33 = 11$

$x^2 + 7x - 44 = 0$

$(x + 11)(x - 4) = 0$

Since $x > 0$,

$x = 4$

Therefore, $x + 11 = 15$.

17) ■➤ 16

Concept(s) Tested: Problem Solving, Algebra

Eight men build one-twelfth of a house in one day. One man builds one-eighth of one-twelfth of a house in one day:

Work done by one man in one day

$= \left(\frac{1}{8}\right)\left(\frac{1}{12}\right) = \frac{1}{96}$ of a house

In one day, six men can build $\frac{6}{96}$, or $\frac{1}{16}$ of a house. Six men take 16 days to build a house.

18) ■➤ 120

Concept(s) Tested: Geometry

The formula for the area of a parallelogram is:

$A = bh$

The base of the parallelogram is the length of $\overline{QU}$, which is 10. The height of the parallelogram is the length of $\overline{RS}$. The right triangle $\triangle RSU$ is a 5–12–13 right triangle, with $\overline{RS} = 12$. The area of the parallelogram is: $A = (10)(12) = 120$

19) ■➤ 4

Concept(s) Tested: Graphs and Functions

$2x^2 + 5x - 25 = 0$

$(2x - 5)(x + 5) = 0$

$x = \frac{5}{2}, -5$

As $p < q$, $p = -5$ and $q = \frac{5}{2}$.

$$\frac{p^2}{q^2} = \frac{(-5)^2}{\left(\frac{5}{2}\right)^2} = 4$$

20) ■➤ 29

Concept(s) Tested: Algebra

If $f(n-1) = f(3)$, then n must equal 4.

For $n = 4$, $f(n-1) = f(3) = 13 + 4(4) = 29$.

Calculator Portion

1) ■➤ A

Concept(s) Tested: Problem Solving

Fifteen percent of the cookie pieces are wrapped, and 85% of the pieces are not wrapped. Since only 80% of the pieces are oatmeal, it is possible that none of oatmeal pieces are wrapped.

2) ■➤ C

Concept(s) Tested: Data Analysis

Ellen's account balance increases by a constant amount each month, so the slope of the line that represents her balance is a straight line with positive slope. Her single withdrawal is visible as region of the function with negative slope.

3) ■➤ C

Concept(s) Tested: Problem Solving, Algebra

Account Balance

= Initial Deposit + Additional Deposits – Withdrawals

Account balance = 1000 + 8(200) – 350 = 2250

4) ➤ D

Concept(s) Tested: Data Analysis
If $x = 1$, the price is $4.00.
Only choice (D) meets this requirement:
If $x = 1$, then $0.5x + 3.5 = 4$.

5) ➤ B

Concept(s) Tested: Problem Solving, Ratios and Percentages
The increase in price is $600,000. The percentage increase is:

$$\% \text{ increase} = \frac{amount\ increase}{initial\ amount} \times 100\%$$

$$\% \text{ increase} = \frac{600,000}{2,000,000} \times 100\% = 30\%$$

6) ➤ A

Concept(s) Tested: Problem Solving, Probability
There are two red marbles and six marbles total. The probability of selecting one red marble from the bag is $\frac{2}{6}$, which simplifies to $\frac{1}{3}$.
After one red marble has been selected, there is one red marble in the bag and five marbles total. The probability of selecting a second red marble is $\frac{1}{5}$.
The probability of both events happening together is the product of their individual probabilities:
$$\frac{1}{3} \cdot \frac{1}{5} = \frac{1}{15}$$

7) ➤ D

Concept(s) Tested: Measures of Center and Spread
The median will only be affected if the number of values or sequence of values is changed. If the largest number is increased, it remains the largest number and does not affect the sequence of the other numbers in increasing value, so it does not affect the median.

8) ➤ D

Concept(s) Tested: Graphs and Functions
Calculate the x-intercept by setting $y = 0$:

$$0 = 2x - 5$$

$$x = \frac{5}{2}$$

The line in choice (D) has the same x-intercept. Verify this by setting $y = 0$:

$$0 = -\frac{2}{3}x + \frac{5}{3} \rightarrow \frac{2}{3}x = \frac{5}{3} \rightarrow x = \frac{5}{2}$$

9) ➤ B

Concept(s) Tested: Problem Solving, Ratios and Percentages
One tablet contains 500mg of Rhudopsinol, of which 40% is absorbed into the bloodstream, that is, (0.4) $(500mg)$.

The half-life of the drug is two hours, so the number of half-lives in t hours is $\frac{t}{2}$.

The amount of Rhudopsinal in the bloodstream after t hours is: $f(t) = (0.4)(500)(0.5)^{\frac{t}{2}}$

10) ➤ B

Concept(s) Tested: Problem Solving, Algebra
Let x be the number of fish tacos they purchase, and y be the number of beef or chicken tacos. On Tuesdays, all tacos are 50% off; fish tacos are $1.25 and beef and chicken tacos are $0.75.

$$x + y = 16$$
$$(1.25)x + (0.75)y \leq 15$$

Combine the two equations by substitution:

$$(1.25)x + (0.75)(16 - x) \leq 15$$
$$1.25x + 12 - 0.75x \leq 15$$
$$x \leq 6$$

Paris and Genevieve buy 6 fish tacos at $1.25 each:
Most spent on fish tacos $= (6)(1.25) = \$7.50$

11) ➤ B

Concept(s) Tested: Geometry
Two angles must be equal in an isosceles triangle. If $x = 50°$, then $y = 180° - 40° - 50° = 90°$, which is not possible for an isosceles triangle.

12) ➤ B

Concept(s) Tested: Data Analysis, Measures of Center and Spread

$$\text{Average harvest} = \frac{\text{Total harvest}}{\text{Number of farms}}$$

$$\text{Average harvest} = \frac{600 + 400 + 200 + 300 + 400 + 500}{6}$$

$$= 400$$

13) ➡ C

Concept(s) Tested: Problem Solving, Ratios and Percentages

Let x be the number of wins before the streak. The number of losses is $\frac{x}{3}$. After the streak:

$$\frac{x+6}{\frac{x}{3}} = \frac{5}{1}$$

$$x + 6 = \frac{5x}{3}$$

$$3x + 18 = 5x$$

$$x = 9$$

14) ➡ C

Concept(s) Tested: Data Analysis

At 100psi, 3 of 50 samples broke. Let x be the number of samples that break in a group of samples:

$$\frac{x}{10,000} = \frac{3}{50}$$

$$x = 600$$

15) ➡ B

Concept(s) Tested: Problem Solving, Data Analysis

Margin of Error = Critical Value × Standard Error
Margin of Error = (0.06)(1.96) = 0.12

16) ➡ B

Concept(s) Tested: Graphs and Functions

Choices (A) and (B) are polynomials of order three, but only choice (B) has three distinct roots, or solutions, making it the only choice that will cross the x-intercept 3 times.

17) ➡ C

Concept(s) Tested: Data Analysis

According to the bar graph, the first year in which the number of apples doubled from the previous year was 1998.

18) ➡ A

Concept(s) Tested: Problem Solving, Unit Conversion

Let x by milliliters of acetic acid solution, and y be milliliters of sodium bicarbonate solution.

Amount of acetic acid = $0.25x$
Amount of sodium bicarbonate = $0.55y$

$$x + y = 120$$

The final solution has equal parts acetic acid and sodium bicarbonate:

$$0.25x = 0.55y$$

$$y = \frac{0.25}{0.55}x$$

$$= \frac{5}{11}x$$

Substitute this equation into the equation above:

$$x + \frac{5}{11}x = 120$$

$$\frac{16}{11}x = 120$$

$$x = 82.5, \text{ and } y = 37.5$$

19) ➡ D

Concept(s) Tested: Problem Solving, Ratios and Percentages

Let x be the amount of flour needed for the adjusted recipe:

$$\frac{p}{q} = \frac{p+2}{x}$$

$$x = \frac{(p+2)q}{p}$$

20) ➡ D

Concept(s) Tested: Graphs and Functions

The expression $|x + 3|$ is greater than or equal to zero for all values of x. Therefore, $f(x) \geq -7$.

21) ➡ B

Concept(s) Tested: Problem Solving, Graphs and Functions

At $t = 6$, the cord is fully extended. The cliff is 122 meters high, and the cord is 72 meters long, so when the cord is fully extended, the jumper is 50 meters from the ground. Recall that the quadratic function is $y = a(x - h)^2 + k$, where a represents the stretching factor of the parabola. It follows that

$$f(t) = a(t - 6)^2 + 122 - 72$$
$$f(0) = 122 \rightarrow a = 2$$

22) ➡ A

Concept(s) Tested: Problem solving, Graphs and functions

First, calculate how much trash was produced per U.S. resident (z) in 2012:

289 million tons = 314.1 million residents × z

$z = 0.92$

Since the trash production per resident (z) is a constant, and since 2013's population is greater than 2012's, we can use the inequality

$289 < x(0.92)$ to indicate that a greater amount of

trash that will be produced in 2013 than was in 2012.

23) ➡ D

Concept(s) Tested: Algebra, Number Rules

$$\frac{2}{x} + \frac{x+2}{x(x-2)} = \frac{4}{x(x-2)}$$

$$\frac{2}{x} = \frac{4 - (x+2)}{x(x-2)}$$

$$\frac{2}{x} = \frac{2-x}{x(x-2)} \rightarrow \frac{2}{x} = \frac{-(x-2)}{x(x-2)}$$

$$\frac{2}{x} = -\frac{1}{x}$$

There is no real number for which this equation is true.

24) ➡ D

Concept(s) Tested: Number Rules

$$f(x) = \frac{x^2 + 2x + 1}{x+1}$$

$$f(i) = \frac{i^2 + 2i + 1}{i + 1}$$

$$= \frac{-1 + 2i + 1}{i + 1}$$

$$= \frac{2i}{i + 1}$$

Rationalize the denominator:

$$f(i) = \frac{2i}{i+1} \cdot \frac{(1-i)}{(1-i)}$$

$$= \frac{2i - 2i^2}{1 - i^2} \rightarrow \frac{2(i - (-1))}{1 - (-1)} = \frac{2(i+1)}{2}$$

$$= i + 1$$

25) ➡ B

Concept(s) Tested: Geometry

$\triangle AEB$ is an isosceles triangle, and the length of $\overline{EB} = q$. The quadrilateral formed by the bisector, ADCE, is a parallelogram, so the length of $\overline{CE}$ = p. The length of $\overline{CB}$ is:

$$\overline{CB} = \overline{CE} + \overline{EB} = p + q$$

26) ➡ D

Concept(s) Tested: Graphs and Functions

For $y = 8$,

$$x^2 - 8 = 0 \rightarrow x^2 = 8$$

$$\sqrt{x^2} = \pm\sqrt{8} = \pm 2\sqrt{2}$$

The distance between the points $(2\sqrt{2}, 8)$ and $(-2\sqrt{2}, 8)$ is $4\sqrt{2}$.

27) ➡ D

Concept(s) Tested: Graphs and Functions

A horizontal translation of a function $f(x)$ by a units is the new function $f(x - a)$. A reflection of the function $f(x)$ across the y-axis is the transformation $-f(x)$. If the function $f(x)$ is translated three units to the right and reflected across the y-axis, the function produced is $-f(x - 3)$.

28) ➡ B

Concept(s) Tested: Problem Solving, Algebra

This is a complex word problem to be approached step-by-step. To set up the equation, note that the initial share is $\dfrac{60}{x}$ cookies per camper. Eight returned their share, which were distributed two each to the remaining campers:

$$8\left(\frac{60}{x}\right) = 2(x - 8)$$

$$\frac{480}{x} = 2x - 16$$

$$2x^2 - 16x - 480 = 0$$

$$2(x^2 - 8x - 240) = 0$$

$$2(x - 20)(x + 12) = 0 \rightarrow x = 20, -12$$

There are 20 campers in total.

29) ➡ B

Concept(s) Tested: Problem Solving, Ratios and Percentages

The number of voters age 18 to 25 is:

Voters = (0.15)(51,000) = 7650

Let x be the number of new voters added to this group:

$$\frac{7650 + x}{51,000 + x} = 0.2$$

$$7650 + x = 10,200 + 0.2x$$

$$0.8x = 2250$$

$$x = 3188$$

30) ➡ C

Concept(s) Tested: Algebra

Recognize that, based on the relationship in the second equation, we can substitute $2 - 3x$ for $2y$ in the first equation, giving $x^2 = 2 - 3x + 8$

Simplify and solve for x by factoring:

$$x^2 = -3x + 10$$

$$x^2 + 3x - 10 = 0$$

$$(x + 5)(x - 2) = 0$$

$$x = -5, 2$$

The sum of the x-values is $-5 + 2 = -3$.

31) ➡ 312

Concept(s) Tested: Problem solving, Algebra

Let e be Evan's spending on gas and r be Ricardo's spending on gas. Expressed mathematically, the problem reads:

Total spending: $e + r = 399.5$

Evan's spending: $e = 9.5 + \dfrac{1}{4}r$

Use substitution to find the value of r:

$$9.5 + \frac{1}{4}r + r = 399.5$$

$$1\frac{1}{4}r = 390$$

$$r = 312$$

32) ➡ $\dfrac{5}{3}$, 1.66, 1.67

Concept(s) Tested: Problem Solving, Ratios and Percentages

Force and length are inversely related. Let x be the force needed to break a board 6 feet long:

$$(5\ lb)(2\ ft) = x(6\ ft) \rightarrow x = \frac{5\ lb \cdot 2\ ft}{6\ ft}$$

$$x = \frac{5\ lb}{3}$$

33) ➡ 26

Concept(s) Tested: Problem Solving, Geometry

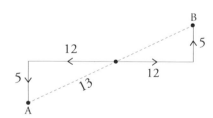

The path taken by each student marks a 5–12–13 right triangle. Since they walk parallel paths, the distance between them is 26 feet.

34) ➡ 11

Concept(s) Tested: Problem solving, Geometry

Use the information provided to determine the polygon's perimeter (p):

$$\text{Area} = \frac{1}{2}pa$$

$$4{,}950 = \frac{1}{2}p(30)$$

$$p = 330$$

If a side is equal to 30 units, and if the polygon is equilateral, the number of sides is determined by dividing the perimeter by a side length: $\frac{330}{30} = 11$. Thus, the polygon has 11 sides.

35)  3,400

Concept(s) Tested: Problem Solving, Algebra
The number of hardcover books is:
$(18{,}000)(0.3) = 5400$

There are 6800 nonfiction books, of which 4800 are paperback, and 2000 are hardcover. The remaining hardcover books must be fiction:

Hardcover fiction = $5400 - 2000 = 3400$

36) ➡ 3
Concept(s) Tested: Graphs and Functions
$$p(x) = f\left(-\frac{x}{2}\right) + 5 \rightarrow p(-4) = f\left(-\frac{-4}{2}\right) + 5$$

$$\rightarrow p(-4) = f(2) + 5 \rightarrow f(2) = 2^2 - 6$$

$$p(-4) = (2^2 - 6) + 5 = 3$$

37) ➡ 0.38, 0.375

Concept(s) Tested: Data Analysis, Unit Conversion

The average price of natural gas from 2012 to 2014 is:

$$\frac{10.69 + 10.30 + 10.97}{3} = \$10.65/1000\ ft^3$$

Convert to dollars per cubic meter:

$$Price = \frac{\$10.65}{1000\ ft^3} \cdot \frac{ft^3}{\left(0.305\ meter\right)^3} = \frac{\$10.65}{(1000)\left(0.305^3\right) meter^3}$$

$$= \$0.38$$

38) ➡ 4.07

First, find the percent decrease in the price of gasoline from 2014 to 2015:

Change in price = $3.37 - $2.40 = $0.97

% Change = $\dfrac{\$0.97}{\$3.37} = 0.2878$ or 28.78%

Next, find the actual 2015 values for Brent and WTI Crude Oil and subtract WTI from Brent to find the difference in price:

WTI (2015): $93.82 - (0.2878 * $93.82) = $66.82
Brent (2015): $99.54 - (0.2878 * $99.64) = $70.89

Difference in price:
Brent - WTI = $70.89 - $66.82 = $4.07

Reading Test

1. Ⓒ	6. Ⓓ	11. Ⓑ	16. Ⓑ	21. Ⓑ	26. Ⓐ	31. Ⓑ	36. Ⓒ	41. Ⓐ	46. Ⓒ	51. Ⓒ
2. Ⓐ	7. Ⓑ	12. Ⓓ	17. Ⓒ	22. Ⓓ	27. Ⓑ	32. Ⓓ	37. Ⓒ	42. Ⓒ	47. Ⓑ	52. Ⓑ
3. Ⓐ	8. Ⓓ	13. Ⓑ	18. Ⓒ	23. Ⓑ	28. Ⓐ	33. Ⓑ	38. Ⓓ	43. Ⓐ	48. Ⓑ	
4. Ⓑ	9. Ⓐ	14. Ⓐ	19. Ⓐ	24. Ⓒ	29. Ⓑ	34. Ⓐ	39. Ⓐ	44. Ⓒ	49. Ⓐ	
5. Ⓒ	10. Ⓓ	15. Ⓓ	20. Ⓓ	25. Ⓓ	30. Ⓐ	35. Ⓑ	40. Ⓑ	45. Ⓐ	50. Ⓐ	

1) ➤ C
Concept(s) Tested: Inference, Implication, and Suggestion

The answer is (C) because throughout the passage, Dubois describes what it feels like to live outside the dominant culture—a "world" that he cannot enter. He speaks of himself as a "Negro" existing "behind a veil" that separates him from this world of white privilege. (A) is incorrect because the "other world" is one that Dubois defines as peopled by those who *do* consider him to be a problem. (B) is incorrect because the narrator is referring to people who exclude him, not to people who want to understand American culture. (D) is incorrect because the "other world" is people who emphasize, rather than disregard, perceived differences, cultural as well as ethnic.

2) ➤ A
Concept(s) Tested: Inference, Implication, and Suggestion

Choice (A) is correct because the passage implies that the "unasked question," which we learn is, "How does it feel to be a problem?" is being asked of him in one way or another by people in "the other world." (B) is incorrect because it is an "unasked question," so it is implicit by nature. (C) is incorrect because throughout the passage, the narrator assumes that readers understand that he is not talking about an experience that is unique to himself, but rather is experienced from childhood by him and by "other black boys." (D) is likewise incorrect because Dubois does not mention the intellectual concerns of other writers and orators.

3) ➤ A
Concept(s) Tested: Words in Context

The correct answer is (A) because "framing" is used to refer to the best way of stating or *presenting* some information, i.e. what exactly to say and which words to use to have one's meaning understood. (B) is incorrect because it

would not make sense within the context. Choice (C) is incorrect because the question is not about trying out a phrase, as in writing a first draft, but rather in carefully expressing it. Choice (D) is incorrect because the question is not about where in a conversation to mention something, as in where to place it, but rather how best to express it.

4) ➤ B
Concept(s) Tested: Organization

The correct answer is (B) because in paragraph 2 the narrator is recounting how, during a "rollicking boyhood," a "shadow swept across me." (A) is incorrect because the narrator is recounting the dawn of a painful realization, not feelings of nostalgia. (C) is incorrect because the personal experiences recounted in the second paragraph do not emphasize the importance of the "unasked question" so much as they elaborate on it by describing the narrator's first experience of exclusion and its effect on his attitudes. (D) is incorrect because paragraph 2 does not discuss work ethics.

5) ➤ C
Concept(s) Tested: Purpose

Choice (C) is correct because the phrase functions as a claim that Dubois was not different from his white classmates, but rather the same in "life and love and longing." (A) is incorrect because the reader can infer that the narrator's classmates are white, and that he is made to feel different from them because he is black. (B) is incorrect because Dubois is not pointing out similarities between any cultures, but between himself and his classmates. (D) is incorrect: by using his own experiences as a black child, Dubois indicates the subtle instruction that informs black children that they are viewed as "different."

6) ➤ D
Concept(s) Tested: Summary

Choice (D) is correct because in paragraph 3, Dubois uses the "blue sky" to symbolize his mental strategy; it was a "region" in which he could feel successful as he played and competed with his white classmates. But in paragraph 4, he suggests that such a bright feeling is nearly impossible for black adults to attain because they are trapped by barriers from which they cannot escape. (A) is incorrect because the "blue sky" is a positive image, but not one to be celebrated in itself. (B) is incorrect because the "blue sky" is not spoken of as a means to accomplish something (i.e. as a tool). (C) is incorrect because the "blue sky" is never merely a distraction or a nuisance.

7) ➡ B
Concept(s) Tested: Attitude and Tone
Choice (B) is correct because in paragraph 3, the narrator describes coping with prejudice by adopting a disdainful attitude toward his white classmates, holding them and others on the other side of the "veil" in "common contempt." In paragraph 4, he has realized that he will not have the same opportunities that they will, and defiantly decides to out-compete them in some way. (A), (C) and (D) are inaccurate descriptions of the narrator's emotions.

8) ➡ D
Concept(s) Tested: Words in Context
Choice (D) is correct because the word occurs in the midst of a sentence about how some African American boys coped with discrimination; some respond with a "bitter cry" against God for making them an "other" in their own country. Thus, Dubois is using "bitter" in the sense of "aggrieved," or anger at being wronged. Choice (A), "sharp," is incorrect because it does not convey the emotional meaning of "bitter." (B) is incorrect because "churlish" implies "mean," which does not convey the author's intended meaning. (C) is incorrect because "petulant" conveys a sense of childishness or a bad mood, which does not fit the serious context of the sentence.

9) ➡ A
Concept(s) Tested: Inference, Implication, and Suggestion
The answer is (A) because the narrator indicates that the veil symbolizes racism; it symbolizes the divide between being like others and being identified as "different." Black people's "double-consciousness" stems from the "peculiar sensation" of always seeing oneself as different through the eyes of others. (B) is incorrect because, although Dubois describes his own changing attitudes as he matures, there is no mention of different generations' views on racism. (C) and (D) are incorrect because, for the narrator,

the veil symbolizes general racist views, not specific consequences of those views.

10) ➡ D
Concept(s) Tested: Citation
Choice (D) is correct because it provides specific evidence to support the narrator's connection of the veil—a symbol of the racism experienced by black Americans—to the sense of "twoness" felt by blacks. (A) is incorrect because it does not address the symbolism of the veil or the "double-consciousness." (B) is incorrect because it does not directly address issues of identity. (C) is incorrect because the "seventh son" is an allusion to folklore in which a seventh son may possess special powers (in this case, second-sight). However, the connection between the veil and a "double-consciousness" is not clear and direct, as it is in (D).

11) ➡ B
Concept(s) Tested: Organization
Choice (B) is correct because paragraph 1 depicts admiration for a baseball player's signing bonus. Next, the author contrasts that admiration with the comment that no one needs that much money. This establishes the two opposing viewpoints in the passage. (A) is incorrect because the purpose of the paragraphs is not to introduce the author but to introduce an argument. (C) is incorrect because the author mentions the athlete's large signing bonus but does not at this point attempt to describe an image of the wealthy. (D) is incorrect because, although the author's son may be demonstrating the influence of the media, that is not mentioned as a focus of the paragraphs.

12) ➡ D
Concept(s) Tested: Inference, Implication, and Suggestion
The best answer is (D), because the author alludes to the Revolutionary War ("a war against the British"), which challenged the assumption that it is the birthright of royalty—kings, queens, and nobles—to make the rules and own the land. The author is implying that such an assumption is echoed in the belief that some people deserve to have enough money to build modern-day "palaces," such as the celebrity whose home included "a royal ballroom." (A) is not the best answer, because the author's focus is not on the ethics of a particular house or type of house, but on the overall attitude about deserving excessive wealth. (B) is not the answer because the author does not make or imply sweeping statements about the Revolutionary War itself. (C) is incorrect because the mention of celebrities in paragraph 3 is designed to serve as a springboard for the questions

the author subsequently asks, and not to open a discussion of celebrities as such.

13) ➤ B
Concept(s) Tested: Citation, Graph and Text Synthesis
The graph indicates that tax rates increased for the nation's top earners in 2013. This is consistent with the author's statement about improving income inequality, so (B) is the correct choice. (A) and (D) are incorrect because they highlight the author's opinion with rhetorical devices rather than discussing tax rates. (C) is incorrect because the graph does not display information about the polarization of wealth in the United States.

14) ➤ A
Concept(s) Tested: Graph and Text Synthesis
The graph shows that under the 2013 tax law, the tax rate of people with incomes in the top 1 percent should return to approximately where it was in 1979. (B) is incorrect because the tax rate of the top 1 percent fell in similar fashion as other tax rates during the decade, but it was not itself the *same* as rates for other income groups. Choice (C) is incorrect because tax rates for the wealthiest 1 percent consistently remained below 40 percent. (D) is incorrect because the graph does not illustrate the distribution of wealth in the United States.

15) ➤ D
Concept(s) Tested: Purpose
Choice (D) is correct because the images of working families who struggle financially immediately precede the information that nearly half of Americans are considered low-income or poor. (A) is incorrect because the author does not describe how hard people work. (B) is incorrect because the description of the neighborhood serves as a rhetorical device to compare with other neighborhoods; the author's purpose is not to inform the reader more completely about a "way of life." (C) is incorrect because the author does not mention how she formed her opinion.

16) ➤ B
Concept(s) Tested: Inference, Implication, and Suggestion
Choice (B) is correct because the author explicitly states that wealthy Americans generally do not socialize with individuals who are not wealthy. She states that instead, wealthy Americans tend to "meet people like themselves." (A) is incorrect because there is no evidence that the author believes that wealthy Americans actively thwart

the upward mobility of those less well-off. (C) is incorrect because, while the passage says that wealthy Americans are "swaddled" in their own neighborhoods, there is no suggestion that wealthy Americans never leave. (D) is incorrect because the author does not discuss the fate of the middle class in America.

17) ➤ C
Concept(s) Tested: Citation
Choice (C) is correct because it implies that affluent people mainly befriend other affluent people. (A) is incorrect because the author's discussion of the poverty rate for children is a separate and distinct point from the discussion of the insulated social life of wealthy Americans. Choice (B) is incorrect because it primarily speaks about assumptions about "normal" life, not specifically how the assumptions form. Choice (D) mentions an economic fact—that middle-income Americans' incomes have fallen. But again, this factual evidence does not pertain to affluent people's social and emotional bonds.

18) ➤ C
Concept(s) Tested: Words in Context
The answer is (C) because, as used here, a "dynamic" is a change that requires explanation. The author uses it to refer to an economic phenomenon—the falling incomes of the middle class—that the author admits is "not simple." (A) is incorrect because "motility" refers to the ability to move, which would not make sense in the context. (B) is incorrect because the author is not merely referring to an interaction, but a measurable change. (D) is incorrect because the author is not describing an upsurge, or increase in wealth, but an actual decrease in income for middle-class Americans.

19) ➤ A
Concept(s) Tested: Summary
The author agrees with the counter-argument that many wealthy Americans have given enormous sums of money to charity. Thus, choice (A) is correct. (B) is incorrect because the author does not say that she made any false assumptions. (C) is incorrect because the author does not present any statistics about fighting disease, medical research, or public education. Rather, these are mentioned as areas in which wealthy donors contribute. (D) is incorrect because the author does not concede that wealthy donors are usually right about aid programs—in contrast, she complains that the wealthy have excessive influence in setting public priorities.

20) ➡ D
Concept(s) Tested: Words in Context
Something that is "undue" is unearned or unjustified. In this paragraph the author is implying that wealthy Americans should not have excessive influence in setting societal priorities. Choice (A) is incorrect because "needless" means unnecessary. The author is not saying that Bill Gates' influence is unnecessary, but unjustified. Answer choice (B), "exorbitant," would not make sense in the context because it primarily refers to prices that are very high. (C) is incorrect because the author does not make the case that wealthy donors do not want influence.

21) ➡ B
Concept(s) Tested: Analogy
The answer is (B) because the film depicts an exaggerated dystopian scenario that serves as a segue into a discussion of wealth inequality and life expectancy in the United States. (A) is incorrect because the author does not imply that the country's circumstances are even worse than in the film, as falling is to stumbling. (C) is incorrect because the author does not argue that the film might become reality. (D) is incorrect because the author does not indicate that there are multiple concerns relevant to both the film and today's American society. The author's use of the film is to dramatize the single fact that life expectancy is tied to income level.

22) ➡ D
Concept(s) Tested: Purpose
Choice (D) is correct because Einstein uses the notion of a "structure" with "staircases" as a metaphor for describing the process of building proofs, one based upon another, that comprise Euclidean geometry. He assumes that the experience is shared with readers. (A) is incorrect, because once Einstein uses the metaphor of a staircase in the first paragraph, he does not use it subsequently. (B) is incorrect because it misinterprets the architectural metaphor as representing an actual relationship between geometry and architecture. (C) is incorrect because the notion that geometry must be studied with diligence is separate and distinct from the discussion of geometry as a "structure."

23) ➡ B
Concept(s) Tested: Purpose
Choice (B) is correct because the phrase "perhaps more respect than love" is meant to suggest that readers would remember geometry as something they respected, but not something they enjoyed. (A) is incorrect because "reverence" implies warm feelings, while "more respect than love" implies the opposite. (C) is incorrect because a nostalgic memory would be a generally positive one, the opposite of what Einstein implies. (D) is incorrect because the phrase "more respect than love" refers to readers' attitudes toward geometry, not toward their teachers.

24) ➡ C
Concept(s) Tested: Inference, Implication, and Suggestion
Choice (C) is correct because Einstein says that the ideas' apparent correspondence to objects in nature is "undoubtedly the exclusive cause of the genesis of those ideas." (A) is incorrect because Einstein does not say that the geometrical principles under discussion are "indisputable;" rather, he is preparing to dispute them. (B) is incorrect because Einstein made no mention of how simple or clear these concepts are. Similarly, (D) is incorrect because the author does not discuss the concepts in terms of cultures.

25) ➡ D
Concept(s) Tested: Words in Context
Choice (D) is correct because "more or less definite ideas" means that the ideas are nearly, or *approximately*, definite. (A) is incorrect because "concretely definite" is redundant, and the phrase does not fit conceptually in the passage, which challenges the certainty of the concepts. (B) is incorrect because Einstein is not discussing concepts quantitatively, i.e., with numbers. (C) is incorrect because it is not clear what it would mean to say that an idea is "unreliably definite."

26) ➡ A
Concept(s) Tested: Summary
Choice (A) is correct. In paragraph 2, Einstein says that "the concept 'true' does not tally with the assertions of pure geometry" because geometry is not based on real objects that people experience in their lives, but only on the logical connections of certain ideas. (B) is incorrect because Einstein's point is that it is impossible to prove the definition of "straight line," not that the definition itself needs to change. (C) sounds like the answer, but on closer examination, Einstein is saying that the definition of a straight line *does* support the geometric axioms that come from it, which does not make it problematic. (D) is incorrect because the definition of a straight line is not problematic because it is connected to other ideas in geometry, but because it is unverifiable.

27) ➡ B
Concept(s) Tested: Words in Context
A "course" is a way of proceeding, or in this case, the usual *practices* in geometry of considering propositions to be "true." Thus, (B) is the answer.

(A) is incorrect because a "class" is a category or classification, and it would not make sense to say that geometry should refrain from such a class. (C) is incorrect because "itinerary" typically refers to a planned route of a journey, and the author is not talking about a journey in this sentence. (D) incorrectly implies that geometry is just beginning to engage in the practices, as in "heading in that direction."

28) ➡ A
Concept(s) Tested: Inference, Implication, and Suggestion
Choice (A) is correct because in paragraph 3, Einstein discusses how humans habitually think of points on a rigid object as representing a straight line, even if one of the points is farther away and even seems to "coincide" with the others and appear to be one point. For example, looking at the end of a string of beads, one might see only one bead. In paragraph 4, Einstein says that such real-world experiences can form the basis for legitimate questions about the "truth" of geometric propositions, interpreted as physics problems. (B) is incorrect because Einstein does not provide an opinion in the passage about whether geometry and physics are both important in an educational curriculum; rather, he describes a new perspective on geometry itself. (C) is incorrect because Einstein says only that geometric principles are limited in their truth, not that they are fiction. (D) is not the answer because Einstein is not drawing a contrast between generalizations and experiments.

29) ➡ B
Concept(s) Tested: Inference, Implication, and Suggestion
The answer is (B) because Einstein points out that, when physicists examine the fundamental truth of geometric propositions, even the notion of "real things" is based on "rather incomplete experiences." In other words, humans have a limited understanding of the phenomena around them. (A) is incorrect because Einstein does not call geometry an "artificial" system of knowledge. (C) is incorrect because Einstein does not mention measurement. (D) is incorrect because Einstein does not say that geometrical propositions are untrue, but that the theory of relativity in physics can demonstrate that their truth is limited.

30) ➡ A
Concept(s) Tested: Inference, Implication, and Suggestion
Choice (A) is correct because, in lines 40 – 44 and lines 76 – 81, Einstein implies that it is only

meaningful to consider the truth of geometric propositions in terms of "objects of experience," or in other words, "real things." (B) is incorrect because Einstein does not mention experiments. (C) is incorrect because Einstein does not discuss applying concepts for practical purposes. (D) is incorrect because there is no indication that Einstein would consider something to be true simply because it is what most people think is true. Instead, Einstein is questioning readers' "proud certainty" that geometric propositions are true.

31) ➡ B
Concept(s) Tested: Citation
Choice (B) is correct because in lines 40-44, Einstein points out that people believe something is true if it corresponds with a real object. (A) is incorrect because it is not a statement by Einstein about a definition of truth, but about people remembering as "true" what they learned in school. (C) simply critiques geometry because its ideas are based on "more or less exact objects," so it does not directly address Einstein's concept of "truth." (D) is incorrect because again, Einstein is pointing out a problem with the notion of "truth," not a definition of truth that he supports.

32) ➡ D
Concept(s) Tested: Inference, Implication, and Suggestion
Choice (D) is correct because in paragraph 1, Goldman implies that many marriages are not the result of love, but rather of people wanting to take part in a societal convention and gain public approval. (A) is not the answer because the author does not mention working on love in a marriage; in fact, she suggests that love rarely continues in married life. (B) is incorrect because Goldman does not claim that all people in love are "unconventional." (C) is incorrect because in the passage, Goldman uses insurance as an analogy to marriage; she does not discuss getting health insurance via marriage.

33) ➡ B
Concept(s) Tested: Citation
Choice (B) most clearly and directly confirms the author's assertions about marriage, namely that couples get married in order to gain approval from society. (A) is incorrect because it does not address the reason that most people get married, according to Goldman. Instead, it addresses the reason that some people who are truly in love get married. (C) is incorrect because it comprises Goldman's view that getting married never causes couples to fall in love, which does not directly address marrying

for convention's sake. (D) is incorrect because it focuses on economic rather than social pressures to get married.

34) ➡️ A
Concept(s) Tested: Purpose
Choice (A) is the answer because when she mentions parasitism, Goldman is commenting on married woman in her era (she published the article in 1911). She implies that they are not allowed to work outside the home, and thus their "predicament" is that they are subjected to "life-long dependency" on their husbands. (B) is incorrect because the only role health insurance plays in the paragraph is as an analogy to marriage. (C) is incorrect because the passage focuses on the effects of marriage, with only an indirect suggestion about equality in the job market. (D) is incorrect because the metaphor of the parasite refers only to the wife being financially dependent on the husband; the metaphor does not address energy.

35) ➡️ B
Concept(s) Tested: Words in Context
Choice (B) is correct because in paragraph 4, Goldman argues that society keeps men and women strangers to each other by means of an "insurmountable wall;" the wall comprises the undramatic factors of "custom and habit," so that the reader can infer that "superstition" simply means unfounded beliefs about the opposite gender. (A), C), and (D) are incorrect because there is nothing in the rest of the sentence or the passage to suggest that Goldman is referring to magic, charm, or fear keeping the genders from knowing and respecting each other.

36) ➡️ C
Concept(s) Tested: Summary
According to the author of Passage 2, it is intriguing that, despite the fact that half of all marriages end in divorce, people continue to get married and remain optimistic. Thus, (C) is the answer. (A) is incorrect because the main focus of the passage is on why people get married. (B) is incorrect because the author does not focus on analyzing why fewer homes include two adults. (D) is incorrect because, while the author mentions research from the mid-1800s, she does not focus on it in the passage.

37) ➡️ C
Concept(s) Tested: Inference, Implication, and Suggestion
Choice (C) is correct because in paragraph 4, the author says that that married people tend to have lower blood pressure and suffer less from depression than their single counterparts. This indicates the

hypothesis that marriage can have a calming effect. (A) is incorrect because the author does not offer any recommendations, namely that people should or should not get married. (B) is incorrect because there is no evidence that the author is suggesting that any marriage can be happy; rather, she provides figures indicating that more than half of them end in divorce. At the same time, (D) is incorrect because the author does not imply that happy marriage is only a fantasy.

38) ➡️ D
Concept(s) Tested: Citation
Choice (D) is correct because it most directly links healthy marriage and reduced stress levels, so it provides the best evidence that "marriage can be calming." (A) is incorrect because its focus is the happiness of married people, not their calmness. (B) is incorrect because it discusses married people living longer without attributing that to any cause. (C) is incorrect; although it reports that, as a group, people in stressful marriages do not tend to exhibit better health than singles, that is only indirect evidence that marriage can be calming.

39) ➡️ A
Concept(s) Tested: Words in Context
Choice (A) is the answer because, as used here, "consideration" means the act of considering or being sensitive to another person's feelings, in this case even during an argument. (B), C), and (D) are incorrect; although they can all serve as synonyms of consideration in other contexts, none of them makes sense in the context of "maintaining a level of kindness and consideration…"

40) ➡️ B
Concept(s) Tested: Multiple-Text Synthesis
The answer is (B); the author of Passage 1 is writing in 1911, more than 100 years before the author of Passage 2. Thus, whereas Goldman says that women who get married become trapped in a state of economic dependence until death, the author of Passage 2 would be likely to point out that the status of American women has changed so much that marriage is no longer a form of dubious "insurance" in the same way. (A) is incorrect because there is no indication that research on the health benefits of marriage was available in 1911. (C) is incorrect because the author of Passage 2 cites research showing that marriage can have substantial "returns." (D) is incorrect because the author of Passage 2 is not offering a personal evaluation of marriage as an institution, so she would not likely critique Goldman's analysis.

41) ▶ A

Concept(s) Tested: Multiple-Text Synthesis

Choice (A) is correct because in Passage 1, Goldman uses the image of a wall to symbolize the barriers to men and women becoming close in marriage; she says that they "remain strangers." In Passage 2, the author describes "massive amounts of data" that conclude that marriages are more successful if couples talk to each other "about more than just household chores." Based on the data, it is likely that she would agree with Goldman that, if there is an "insurmountable wall" blocking communication, the "union is doomed to failure." (B) is incorrect because the principle of the "insurmountable wall" is not focused on questions of arguments, but on communication. (C) is incorrect because the "insurmountable wall" is a metaphor for barriers to communication, a timeless problem. (D) is incorrect because Passage 2 incorporates more than just statistics; it includes researchers' conclusions about relationships.

42) ▶ C

Concept(s) Tested: Inference, Implication, and Suggestion; Multiple-Test Synthesis

Choice (C) is correct; in Passage 1, Goldman states her view that "it is utterly false that love results from marriage." The author of Passage 2 cites research findings in paragraph 5 that married couples who are happiest at the beginning of the marriage are the most likely to stay together. Thus, it is likely that both authors would agree that couples should not expect to fall more in love or to become happier in a relationship just by getting married. (A) is incorrect because neither author says that marriage causes stress. (B) is incorrect because neither author recommends marriage; Goldman describes a negative view of it, and the author of Passage 2 does not make any recommendations. (D) is incorrect because neither author implies that the only way to be healthy and happy is to get married; Goldman, in fact, believes that in her era (1911), marriage causes unhappiness.

43) ▶ A

Concept(s) Tested: Purpose

The answer is (A) because the author begins by listing well-known aspects of city life, and then adds weather to the list, something readers would not normally expect to be different in cities. (B) is incorrect because the passage is not about the author and where he grew up; it is about research on weather. (C) is incorrect because the author does not address the ways that weather affects

urban culture, such as its food and music. (D) is incorrect because the passage that follows is not about general differences in city life and rural life; rather, the opening sentence sets up the following discussion about unexpected weather patterns in cities.

44) ▶ C

Concept(s) Tested: Words in Context

Choice (C) is correct because in the context, the author means that meteorologists have studied thunderstorm patterns by creating replicas, or *simulating* the conditions and patterns that they have observed. (A) is incorrect because a sculpture is a work of art, which does not fit the scientific context. (B) is incorrect because there is no indication that anyone or anything is "acting." (D) is incorrect because *modeling* the weather implies creating a small image or digital depiction and simulating possible activity, whereas to imitate something is to act like it, which is impossible in terms of atmospheric conditions.

45) ▶ A

Concept(s) Tested: Summary

In paragraph 4, Haberlie says that a difference of 5 percent in the number of storms per year amounts to "a couple to three" more storms per year. Thus choice (A) is correct. (B) is incorrect because Haberlie specifically states that three or more extra storms per year are possible. (C) is incorrect because "twice as many" storms is more than a 5 percent increase. (D) is incorrect because it contradicts what Haberlie says: that there are more storms per year, and not half as many.

46) ▶ C

Concept(s) Tested: Inference, Implication, and Suggestion

Choice (C) is the answer because in paragraph 2, the author says that modeling made researchers aware of the phenomena of increased rainfall in cities, but that the new research verifies the models by showing actual effects over time. Thus, modeling provides ideas about how things work, but not proof. (A) and (B) are both incorrect because the author is not evaluating the relative importance of modeling vs. data collection. If anything, the passage indicates that both are important. (D) is incorrect because the author not does address the question of models generating conflicting results.

47) ▶ B

Concept(s) Tested: Citation

The answer is (B) because it supports the notion

that, in this case, modeling was verified by data, indicating a practical relationship between the two methods. (A) is incorrect because it describes the new research, but does not mention models. (C) is incorrect because it reports results, but does not compare them to models. (D) is incorrect because it is merely a researcher's reaction to data, and is too indirect to serve as evidence.

48) B
Concept(s) Tested: Summary
Choice (B) is correct because the passage describes how Haberlie's data and Shepherd's models both showed that cities experience an increased number of thunderstorms compared to their rural surroundings. (A) is incorrect because the researchers both had similar, not different, findings. (C) and (D) are incorrect because Shepherd created simulations, and Haberlie compiled measured data; therefore, their approaches were different, not similar.

49) A
Concept(s) Tested: Purpose
Choice (A) is correct because the adjectives "hot, stale, and dirty" conclude a paragraph that begins by laying out "several factors" that cause storms over cities. Another clue is that the adjectives follow the phrase "in essence," which indicates that the previous information is about to be compressed and summed up. (B) is incorrect because the passage does not compare "two diverging viewpoints." The two scientists quoted in the passage both agree that cities "brew up" more thunderstorms. (C) is incorrect because, while it may be common opinion that cities are hot, stale, and dirty, the author's purpose is to explain the consequences of those factors. (D) is incorrect because the author is not explicitly addressing heat and pollution as problems; instead, he is discussing a related phenomenon and the research methods used to identify it.

50) A
Concept(s) Tested: Inference, Implication, and Suggestion
Choice (A) is the answer because in paragraph 4, the author points out that the asphalt and concrete in cities block the soil from absorbing water, leading to increased run-off and flooding. The same materials presumably cause cities to be hotter (paragraph 6) and thus create conditions for more thunderstorms and rain. (B) is incorrect because the passage mentions neither population density, nor evacuation. (C) is incorrect because there is no indication that data for cities is difficult to obtain. (D) will not work because the author does not address

the topic of thunderstorms' economic impact on either cities or their surrounding areas.

51) C
Concept(s) Tested: Inference, Inference, Implication, and Suggestion
Choice (C) is correct because paragraph 7 explains that the radar-data research method cannot be applied to every city; as an example, it would be too difficult to separate out effects caused by a city and those caused by a large body of water (like New York and the Atlantic Ocean.) (A) is incorrect because the author never states that radar is ineffective. (B) is incorrect because the author does not state that the Atlantic Ocean is unpredictable, only that large bodies of water near cities make weather patterns more complicated. (D) is incorrect because the author does not address public concern regarding flooding in one place or another.

52) B
Concept(s) Tested: Citation
Choice (B) is correct because it summarizes the concept that recent data analysis has supplemented previous meteorological models to confirm the connection between cities and storms. Choices (A) and (C) are incorrect because they focus solely on either modeling or data interpretation, but they do not mention any synthesis between the topics. (D) is incorrect because it addresses the limitations, not value, of modeling and data interpretation.

SAT Practice Test 3: Answers & Explanations

Writing and Language Test

1. Ⓓ	5. Ⓐ	9. Ⓑ	13. Ⓐ	17. Ⓑ	21. Ⓒ	25. Ⓐ	29. Ⓒ	33. Ⓐ	37. Ⓓ	41. Ⓒ
2. Ⓑ	6. Ⓐ	10. Ⓑ	14. Ⓒ	18. Ⓒ	22. Ⓒ	26. Ⓓ	30. Ⓒ	34. Ⓒ	38. Ⓑ	42. Ⓒ
3. Ⓒ	7. Ⓓ	11. Ⓒ	15. Ⓑ	19. Ⓓ	23. Ⓓ	27. Ⓑ	31. Ⓐ	35. Ⓐ	39. Ⓓ	43. Ⓑ
4. Ⓐ	8. Ⓓ	12. Ⓑ	16. Ⓓ	20. Ⓑ	24. Ⓒ	28. Ⓐ	32. Ⓑ	36. Ⓑ	40. Ⓐ	44. Ⓐ

1) ➡ D

Concept(s) Tested: Pronoun Use/Case

"Multilingual professionals" immediately precedes the pronoun "which" in the sentence. Since "multilingual professionals" refers to a group of *people*, it is necessary to use the relative pronoun "who," so (D) is the answer. Choice (B) is not a relative pronoun; it is incorrect because "they" does not properly connect the definition to the term it defines, and it would confuse the reader. Choice (C), "whom," uses the objective case of "who," making it incorrect in the context of the sentence.

2) ➡ B

Concept(s) Tested: Concision

Although (A) and (D) are grammatically correct, they repeat the subject of the sentence, making the sentence unnecessarily lengthy. (B) is the answer because it is concise and grammatically correct. (C) is incorrect because it sounds as if the "person who speaks" also does the repeating.

3) ➡ C

Concept(s) Tested: Correlative Conjunction Use

Choices (A) and (B) both incorrectly use the adjective "precise." Choice (C) is correct because "precise" functions as an adverb that modifies "rewrite," so it needs to be written with an "-ly" ending. (D) uses "precisely," but the words "it is" are superfluous, making (D) incorrect.

4) ➡ A

Concept(s) Tested: Passage Development

The underlined phrase provides a meaningful example to illustrate the author's point. It should be kept, so (A) is correct. (B) is incorrect because the sentence does not transition to the topic of idiomatic phrases; they are not discussed in the following material. (C) is incorrect because, while the example is applied to translators, it does not necessarily exclude interpreters. And we can

eliminate (D) because the underlined phrase does not distract the reader from the paragraph's focus on written material. In contrast, it provides an example of the very challenges translators face when writing.

5) ➡ A

Concept(s) Tested: Precise Diction

Choice (A) is correct because "to adapt" means to change something to make it more suitable for a context, situation, or circumstance. The word is correct within this context because companies are adapting their products and services to fit local environments. Choice (B) is incorrect because "to restore" something means to bring it back to a prior or original state, which would not make sense in the sentence. (C) is incorrect because "to transform" indicates a more significant and thorough change than an adaptation. But the passage does not indicate the change is as significant as a transformation. (D) is incorrect because "to recalibrate" means to check an instrument or gauge for accuracy, so the word is not appropriate in this context.

6) ➡ A

Concept(s) Tested: In-Sentence Punctuation, Possession

No change is necessary, so (A) is the best answer choice. "Consumers" should have an apostrophe after the "s" because it is referring to more than one consumer, so we can eliminate (B) and (D) on this account. (C) is incorrect because a comma is not necessary between "language" and "preferences," as it would be were the author citing three or more items in a list.

7) ➡ D

Concept(s) Tested: Passage Development

The first sentence of paragraph 4 states that translators and interpreters' work settings "range from the very humble to the highly prestigious," suggesting that they work in a diversity of settings. Because (D) sets up this same focus, it is the correct choice. (A) is incorrect because the paragraph emphasizes the diversity of scenarios in which translators and interpreters work, so it would not be appropriate to begin with a blanket statement that the jobs are "always exciting." (B) can be eliminated because it implies that the focus of the paragraph is "fluent bilingualism" rather than language-related professions. (C) is incorrect because it makes an inappropriate shift to a more informal style by addressing the reader.

8) ➡ D
Concept(s) Tested: Combining Sentences
The punctuation at the underlined portion must connect two independent clauses (clauses that can act as complete sentences). Only (D) does so correctly; a semicolon can replace a period when the clauses to either side of the semicolon contain closely related information, as is the case here. (A) is incorrect because a comma cannot separate two independent clauses unless the comma is followed by a coordinating conjunction. (B) is incorrect for the same reason, as "also" is not a coordinating conjunction such as "and." (C) can be eliminated because, like a comma, an em dash alone cannot separate two independent clauses.

9) ➡ B
Concept(s) Tested: Precise Diction
In English when a writer or speaker wishes to state that a person will eventually attain a professional level or position, the word "prospective" is most often used. "Prospective" most clearly indicates that a person is working toward attaining a certain professional stature or position. Thus, (B) is correct. Choice (A), "eventual," is awkward because it usually indicates something that will happen in the distant future. (C) and (D) are incorrect because it would not make sense to use "attainable" or "feasible" for people, only for goals, plans, and targets.

10) ➡ B
Concept(s) Tested: Transition Words and Phrases
The answer will be the word or phrase that is most logical. (B) is correct because it is "natural" that the highest volume of work for interpreters and translators would involve the most commonly spoken languages. (A) is incorrect because "paradoxically" would imply a contradiction; yet there is no apparent contradiction in the idea that the biggest market for language interpretation and translation would involve the most widely spoken languages, and no such contradiction is elaborated

upon in the paragraph. (C) is incorrect because "as a result" would refer to the preceding sentence and would imply that the biggest need being for the most commonly spoken languages is the result of the US Bureau of Labor Statistics predicting a rise in job opportunities, which does not make sense. Similarly, (D) implies a contrast with the preceding sentence, which is also incorrect.

11) ➡ C
Concept(s) Tested: Pronoun Use
Choice (A) is incorrect because "their" describes ownership whereas the sentence indicates something happening in the future. Therefore, the answer is (C) because the homonym "there" is an existential pronoun showing that something simply exists, or in this case, will exist. Choices (B) and (D) are incorrect because they are pronouns that refer to specific entities.

12) ➡ B
Concept(s) Tested: In-Sentence Punctuation
Choice (B) is correct because a pause or break is needed to separate off the part of the sentence that mentions human life. The information is not essential to the sentence; it is simply an elaboration of the previous statement. Moreover, a natural pause occurs on either side of the phrases beginning with "including," as in "(x), including (y)," so they always take a pair of commas. (A) is incorrect because the second comma is missing. (C) is incorrect because a colon can introduce items or lists of items or an independent clause elaborating on the concept; neither applies here. (D) is incorrect because it creates a run-on sentence.

13) ➡ A
Concept(s) Tested: Passage Development
As the two sentences on either side of 13 stand now, there is a gap between the discussion of floodplains and governments building dams to prevent flooding. A connecting sentence is needed to reveal that people often settle in floodplains, making the building of dams necessary. (A) makes this connection most clearly. (B) is incorrect because it is not as important that people settle in the specific floodplains mentioned, only that they generally tend to settle in floodplains, wherever they are located. (C) presents a historical fact that does not fit the context of the present discussion. (D) is incorrect because it raises topics that are not discussed further in the passage.

14) ➡ C

Concept(s) Tested: Passage Development

Choice (C) is correct because it provides the most relevant information to further the author's purpose. The clause connects the idea of people trying to control flooding to the "dilemma" that flooding is beneficial *from a very long-term perspective.* (A) is incorrect because the clause becomes sidetracked into an explanation of the term "geomorphology." (B) and (D) are incorrect because they do not add any relevant information to the sentence.

15) ➡ B

Concept(s) Tested: Passage Tone

Choice (B) is correct because "sediment" is the most precise word for geological material deposited by water. (A) is incorrect because "all the stuff" is an informal phrase, which does not fit the academic tone of the passage. (C) is incorrect because it is unnecessarily vague. (D) is incorrect because its meaning is unclear from the context.

16) ➡ D

Concept(s) Tested: In-Sentence Punctuation

As written, the sentence incorrectly introduces a pause by using a comma. Generally, when two verbs connected by "and" refer to the same subject, no comma is needed between them, so (A) is incorrect. (D) removes the comma while effectively preserving the rest of the sentence, making it the correct choice. (C) incorrectly states that sediment creates vegetation rather than that it supports the growth of such vegetation. (B) incorrectly implies that the author is about to list several things that sediment does. A comma is not needed to separate a list of two things, only three or more.

17) ➡ B

Concept(s) Tested: Graph Analysis

Choice (A) is incorrect because the diagram indicates that the river flows below the terraces, not above. (B) is the correct choice because it explains that the river is flanked by terraces, which, based on the diagram, are both "inclined" and "step-like." (C) is incorrect because the diagram illustrates newly formed floodplains as being level with the river, not below it. (D) can be eliminated because the diagram does not suggest any relationship between terraces and mountains.

18) ➡ C

Concept(s) Tested: Passage Development

Choice (C) is correct because it is the best topic sentence for the paragraph. It describes floodplains

as "catch-basins," which sets up the paragraph's explanations about floodplains diffusing and absorbing flood water. (A) incorrectly implies that the paragraph that follows will list many reasons that floodplains are important. (B) incorrectly implies that the paragraph will focus on how floodplains are maintained. (D) is incorrect because the paragraph does not support a general statement that floods do not cause damage to floodplains.

19) ➡ D

Concept(s) Tested: Verb Tense/Mood

Choice (D) is correct because the subject of the verb is "deep layers," which is plural and requires a plural verb. Choice (A) is incorrect because "is" requires a singular subject; while "aquifer" is singular, it is not the subject of the phrase (and it determines the verb "consists"). The clause "that *are* saturated with drops of water" describes the "deep layers," not the aquifer or the "rock, sand, and soil." Choices (B) and (C) incorrectly change the meaning of the phrase, so the saturation with water becomes dependent on some factor that is not stated.

20) ➡ B

Concept(s) Tested: Passage Development

Choice (B) is correct because the sentence at 20 provides information that helps explain the significance of underground aquifers. (A) is incorrect because the sentence focuses on underground aquifers, which are the main topic of the paragraph but not the main topic of the passage. (C) is incorrect because the data cited is clear, simple, and relevant to the point made in the previous sentence. (D) is likewise incorrect because the sentence at 21 rightly keeps the focus on aquifers and does not take the paragraph in another direction.

21) ➡ C

Concept(s) Tested: Transition Words and Phrases

Choice (A) is incorrect because it wrongly indicates consequence—one thing following from another—when it should indicate an explanation: the reason that floodplains are able to reduce the amount of nitrates in water. Thus, (C) is the correct answer. (B) and (D) are both incorrect because they indicate that the sentence at 21 is explained by the previous sentence. As in (A), they wrongly indicate consequence.

22) ➡ C

Concept(s) Tested: Passage Development

An effective concluding sentence will state in a

general way that floodplains are valuable. (C) most clearly and effectively accomplishes this task by suggesting the relationship between communities and floodplains, which is implied by the passage's focus on flood prevention, rich soil, and clean water. Thus, the sentence sums up the passage by referring to "natural resources." (A) is incorrect because it is vague and wordy; the phrase "it is clear to see" is unnecessary. (B) limits the value of floodplains to richness in biodiversity, and does not include a reference to floodplains supporting human life, as mentioned in paragraph 1. (D) requires further argumentation and support. It is clear from the passage that floodplains are important, but it is not clear that communities should thereby begin dismantling their dams and levees.

23) ➡ D
Concept(s) Tested: Passage Organization

Sentence 3 includes the word "however," which is usually used to indicate a contrast with something that was said previously. Since sentence 3 talks about the ability of the Bedu to survive in the harsh desert climate, it most appropriately goes after sentence 5, which mentions that most Bedu now live in towns. Thus, (D) is correct. Choices (A), (B), and (C) place the sentence in awkward and incohesive positions, so they are incorrect.

24) ➡ C
Concept(s) Tested: Possession

Choice (C) is correct because the noun "dwellers" must be plural and has no need for a possessive apostrophe. The noun serves as a substitute for "Bedu people" in the previous sentence. Choices (A), (B), and (D) are therefore incorrect.

25) ➡ A
Concept(s) Tested: Transition Words and Phrases

The preceding sentence states that the Bedu were once known for violence and stealing. The next sentence describes positive aspects of their reputation, setting up a contrast with what was stated earlier. The term "Nonetheless" is appropriate because it clearly indicates a qualification of what was said in the previous sentence. Therefore (A) is correct. (B) is incorrect because "So far" is typically used to indicate progress up to a point in time, which is not being discussed here. (C), "In addition," is incorrect because it does not include the required element of contrast with what was said before. (D) is incorrect because the two sentences contrast with each other whereas "consequently" implies a cause and effect relationship.

26) ➡ D
Concept(s) Tested: Passage Tone

The phrase should fit the formal tone of the rest of the passage. Therefore, (D) is correct because it appropriately and concisely conveys the information. (A) is incorrect because it uses "you," which reflects informal spoken English. (B) is incorrect because claiming "Europeans...wrote some on" is unclear and informal. (C) can be eliminated because the term "a lot" is generally avoided in formal written English.

27) ➡ B
Concept(s) Tested: In-Sentence Punctuation

Choice (B) is correct because it does not have a comma separating the two essential phrases that identify Wilfried Thesiger. He is "a British photographer... who traveled with..." Choice (A), (C), and (D) add the unnecessary comma.

28) ➡ A
Concept(s) Tested: Concision, Syntax

The phrase is appropriate as written, because it clearly indicates that resources are thinly spread in the given area. (B) is too choppy and includes the vague phrase "a place like that." (C) does not make sense, since it is not clear how resources could currently be "spreading." (D) incorrectly shifts the focus from the habitat onto the resources and makes the meaning of the sentence unclear.

29) ➡ C
Concept(s) Tested: Concision, Syntax

Choice (C) is correct because it describes the traditional custom clearly and simply. (A) is incorrect because it contains awkward syntax; it separates the verb ("would signal") from the object of the sentence ("their friendly intentions") with a prepositional phrase ("from far away"). It also creates a redundancy, as the next sentence also mentions the visitors arriving. (B) is incorrect because its word order and its use of the passive voice ("could be seen") make it confusing. (D) is incorrect because it lacks a subject, so it is not clear who is signaling.

30) ➡ C
Concept(s) Tested: Precise Diction

To "query" someone is to question them in an attempt to find out information. This is the most appropriate word to describe what the Bedu were doing when they spoke with their guests, so (C) is correct. Choice (A) is incorrect because to "investigate" someone is to scrutinize and research him or her, often in relation to a crime; it is more than simply asking questions and trying to gain information from people. (B) is incorrect because the Bedu would only be "impugning" their visitors if they disputed the validity of what the visitors were telling them. But the context of the sentence seems to suggest the Bedu were more interested in simply acquiring whatever information they could from their guests. (D) is incorrect because to "divert" is to change course or change direction, or to entertain, neither of which makes sense in this sentence.

31) ➡ A
Concept(s) Tested: Passage Development
The concluding sentence of this paragraph should sum up the purpose and meaning of the encounters the Bedu had with visitors. (A) accomplishes this by stating what the Bedu gained from these encounters about their physical and social environment. (B) would be more appropriate to continue the paragraph, not to end it, because it includes details that elaborate on what was said previously. (C) is incorrect because it narrowly focuses on one aspect of social interaction with others—the need to find grazing areas for goats and camels—at the expense of the larger value and utility of such interaction. (D) is incorrect because it neglects to mention that the Bedu also learned about their own people through their interactions with visitors, and not just their desert surroundings.

32) ➡ B
Concept(s) Tested: Concision
As written, the phrase is an elaborate and slightly confusing way of referring to the literature of the Bedu. Thus, (A) is incorrect and (B) is correct. (C) will not work because it is not the traditions of the Bedu that allow them to socialize among a small group, but their literature, which serves as the basis for discussion and communication. For the same reasons, (D) will not work. In addition, (D) needlessly incorporates several modifiers that do not convey any essential information.

33) ➡ A
Concept(s) Tested: Organization
Because of the use of the pronoun "these," which is used to indicate to something mentioned previously, the phrase "These oral traditions," located in sentence 2, is awkward and unclear unless information is added before sentence 2 that describes or defines the oral traditions. Thus, the added sentence should be placed after sentence 1 because "thousands of stories, songs, and poems" is an appropriate antecedent for the pronoun "these." The sentence also belongs at the beginning of the discussion about literature

because it introduces and describes the topic. (B), (C), and (D) create disorganization and are therefore incorrect.

34) ➡ C
Concept(s) Tested: Syntax
In writing, it is often preferable to use the active voice over the passive voice. Choice (A) is incorrect because it uses the passive voice, stating that the American Civil War "was fought." (C) is correct because it uses the more direct and easier to understand active voice. (B) uses redundant and awkward phraseology. People do not "go to civil war against each other," they fight a civil war. (D) is incorrect because it is wordy and awkwardly personalizes.

35) ➡ A
Concept(s) Tested: Combining Sentences
Choice (A) is correct because "which" is an effective way to introduce additional information, in this case about slavery. (B) is incorrect because the phrase "the main support of the southern economy" is unclear and awkward. (C) is incorrect because it creates an overly long sentence and because it uses the word "slavery" twice, which is redundant. Similarly, (D) uses the word "slavery" twice and joins the sentences using the word "yet," which implies contrast and therefore does not fit the context.

36) ➡ B
Concept(s) Tested: Subject-Verb Agreement
Choice (B) is correct because, in standard English grammar, "none" is treated as if it were "not one." Thus, it is a singular subject and requires a singular form of the verb. (A), (C), and (D) are each incorrect for that reason. In (C), it is also not necessary to state "the writers," since it is clear from the context of the sentence that the author is speaking about the writers mentioned. Also, (D) is incorrect because it wrongly places emphasis on the poems. It was not the case that the poems were unable to produce good writing, but that the authors themselves were unable to do so.

37) ➡ D
Concept(s) Tested: In-Sentence Punctuation
As written, the two commas after "read" and "heard" interrupt the flow of the sentence. When using "or" to indicate two alternatives, it is not necessary to place a comma before each alternative. Therefore (D) is correct and (A) is incorrect. (B) uses an em dash, which should primarily be used to indicate an interjection or interruption in the

middle of a sentence. Since there is no interruption here, the "—" symbol is not necessary. (C) also incorrectly places a break in the sentence by placing a comma where one is not needed.

38) ➡ B
Concept(s) Tested: Passage Development
Choice (A) is incorrect because it strays from the author's focus on the Civil War. It also fails to introduce the "morally ambiguous situation" that is mentioned in the next sentence. (B) rectifies this situation by mentioning American authors and their failure to capture experiences of the Civil War. This sentence provides context for the sentences that follow. (C) has a less direct connection to the main point of the paragraph. It is less relevant that American authors wrote about travels in Europe or other distractions than that they failed to illustrate the war. (D) is incorrect because the passage does not support the idea that American authors remained silent during the Civil War, only that they failed to publish material that portrayed the realities of war.

39) ➡ D
Concept(s) Tested: Precise Diction
The entire sentence at 39 sets up a contrast. (D) is correct because "unequivocal" (absolute) maintains that contrast. It makes sense that the moral ambiguity was caused by people having *absolute* opinions on the issues, but also hating the war. (A) is incorrect because "equivocal" (uncertain) views would not contrast with disillusionment about the war. (B) is incorrect because as in (A), the word would create an illogical sentence; "indefinite" views would be views that were not very strongly held and would not contrast with negative feelings about the war.

40) ➡ A
Concept(s) Tested: Passage Development
Choice (A) is correct because the sentence at 40 elaborates on the previous point: photographers documented the carnage of the Civil War. (B) is incorrect because the author is not making a statement about the overall importance of photography, but about its role in documenting the Civil War. (C) is incorrect because listing famous photographers is superfluous and interrupts the paragraph's flow. (D) is incorrect because the focus is not on the visual arts "in general," but on the visual arts as a means for conveying the graphic nature of Civil War battles.

41) ➡ C
Concept(s) Tested: Parallel Structure

Choice (C) is correct because it maintains parallel structure. If men and horses *run*, and trains *run off* bridges, then it sounds best if fires *blaze* and smoke *billows*. (A) is incorrect because in mid-sentence it shifts to a structure using "there is." (B) is incorrect because it also shifts structure in mid-sentence ("also fire and smoke are there.") (D) is incorrect; it contains a different verb tense (fires "are threatening") and a less active verb (smoke "is") compared to the series' other phrases.

42) ➡ C
Concept(s) Tested: Possession
Choice (C) is correct because the sentence indicates America's ownership of "most gifted painters." Thus, the word requires an apostrophe. Since "America" is referring to the country, it is a singular noun that requires an apostrophe before the "s." (A) is incorrect because it has no apostrophe to indicate the possessive. (B) wrongly mentions Americans, which does not make sense. Winslow Homer is a product of America, not Americans. (D) is incorrect because "America" is a singular noun, and the apostrophe belongs before the "s."

43) ➡ B
Concept(s) Tested: Verb Tense
Choice (B) is correct because it maintains consistent verb forms in the sentence. One soldier "is shooting," so it is appropriate to say another "is running." (A) is incorrect because it shifts the sentence's verb tense from present progressive ("is shooting") to simple present ("runs"). (C) and (D) are incorrect because each creates a mid-sentence shift into past tenses. The shift is awkward, and activity within images is normally described in the present tense.

44) ➡ A
Concept(s) Tested: Passage Organization
Choice (A) is correct because it creates a cohesive flow of information. Paragraph 1 provides historical context for the American Civil War. Yet paragraph 2 begins with the word "ironically," which is confusing because no irony has been introduced. Paragraph 3, however, explains that very few contemporary American authors depicted the war experience. Thus, it makes sense to place paragraph 3 before paragraph 2 because paragraph 2 introduces a legitimate irony: few American authors wrote about the Civil War, so it is ironic that "some of the best-known American writers were alive at the time."

Math Test

✓ No Calculator Portion

1. (B)	7. (C)	13. (C)	19. 5		
2. (A)	8. (B)	14. (A)	20. 16		
3. (D)	9. (A)	15. (C)			
4. (A)	10. (C)	16. 1,250			
5. (C)	11. (B)	17. $\frac{3}{7}$			
6. (C)	12. (D)	18. 28			

✓ Calculator Portion

1. (C)	7. (A)	13. (B)	19. (A)	25. (B)	31. 4	37. 800
2. (B)	8. (B)	14. (B)	20. (D)	26. (D)	32. 9	38. 2.37
3. (D)	9. (A)	15. (B)	21. (D)	27. (B)	33. 2	
4. (D)	10. (B)	16. (C)	22. (D)	28. (C)	34. 8	
5. (C)	11. (D)	17. (B)	23. (D)	29. (B)	35. 3,790	
6. (C)	12. (D)	18. (D)	24. (A)	30. (B)	36. 60	

No Calculator Portion

1) B

Concept(s) Tested: Graphs and Functions
It must be true that $x^2 \neq 0$ and $(y + 3) \neq 0$.

2) ▶ A

Concept(s) Tested: Problem Solving, Ratios and Percentages
Every year, the population grows by a factor of 1.03—an increase of 3%. Over the course of x years, the factor of increase is $(1.03)^x$.

3) ▶ D

Concept(s) Tested: Algebra
Solve for z:

$10z - 13 = 7$

$10z = 20$

$z = 2$

Plug in z's value to $3z + 14$: $3(2) + 14 = 20$

The correct choice is (D).

4) ▶ A

Concept(s) Tested: Problem Solving
If Mary prints at least 500 flyers, the first 100 are charged at $0.25 each, 200 at $0.20, and the remaining flyers, $(x - 300)$, at $0.10. The entire purchase is multiplied by a factor of 1.11 to account for the 11% sales tax.

5) ▶ C

Concept(s) Tested: Problem Solving, Algebra
In one hour, three boys paint $\frac{1}{5}$ of a fence, so one boy is able to paint $\frac{1}{15}$ of a fence per hour.
Therefore:

$$\text{Four boys} = 4 \times \frac{\frac{1}{15}\text{fence}}{\text{hour}} = \frac{4}{15} \text{ fence per hour}$$

It takes $\frac{15}{4}$ hours for four boys to paint a fence.

6) ▶ C

Concept(s) Tested: Problem Solving
Angelo's hourly wage = $\frac{x}{y}$

Sarah's hourly wage = $\frac{x}{y - 1}$

As $y > y - 1$, the positive difference between hourly wages is:

$$\frac{x}{y - 1} - \frac{x}{y}$$

7) ▶ C

Concept(s) Tested: Graphs and Functions
A system of equations has no solution if the equations contradict each other. To verify that this is the case, multiply the first equation by 12:

$$12\left(\frac{1}{2}x - \frac{1}{4}y\right) = (5)12 \rightarrow 6x - 3y = 60$$

If $a = 6$ in the second equation, the system has no solution.

8) ➡ B

Concept(s) Tested: Problem Solving, Graphs and Functions

The cost of the lunch can be written as a function of the number of guests (x):

$$C(x) = 250 + 15x$$

The slope of this graph is 15.

9) ➡ A

Concept(s) Tested: Algebra

Solve for x in the first equation:

$$(x + 1)^2 = 4$$
$$x + 1 = \pm 2$$
$$x = -3, 1$$

Only $x = -3$ satisfies the second equation.

10) ➡ C

Concept(s) Tested: Geometry

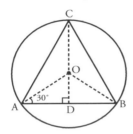

The central angle inscribed by each of the sides of the triangle (for example, $\angle COB$) is twice the measure of the angles of the equilateral triangle ($\angle CAB$), that is, 120°. This implies that the radii to the vertices divide the circle into equivalent thirds, and also bisect the angles of the triangle. The angle $\angle OAD = 30°$. If a line is drawn from O to $\overline{AB}$ at D, a 30–60–90 triangle is created. According to the ratio of lengths of a 30–60–90 triangle, $\overline{OD} = 1$ and $\overline{AD} = \sqrt{3}$. The area of $\triangle AOB$ is:

$$\text{Area} = \frac{1}{2}(1)(2\sqrt{3}) = \sqrt{3}$$

As the equilateral triangle is made up of three triangles all equivalent to $\triangle AOB$, the area of the equilateral triangle is:

Area of $\triangle ABC = 3\sqrt{3}$

11) ➡ B

Concept(s) Tested: Problem Solving, Algebra

Let x be pounds of Earl Grey, and y be pounds of Orange Pekoe:

$$x + y = 100$$

$$5x + 3y = (100)(4.50)$$

Multiplying the first equation by factor of 3 and subtracting from the second gives:

$$2x = 150$$
$$x = 75$$

12) ➡ D

Concept(s) Tested: Problem Solving, Geometry

The volume of a circular cylinder is: $V = \pi r^2 h$

The radii of the cylinder before (r_1) and after (r_2) the change are expressed in the relationship: $r_2 = \frac{r_1}{2}$

The heights of the cylinder before (h_1) and after (h_2) the change are expressed as: $h_2 = 1.6 h_1$

The ratio of the volume of the initial cylinder (v_1) to the volume of the new cylinder (v_2) is:

$$\frac{V_2}{V_1} = \frac{\pi r_2^2 h_2}{\pi r_1^2 h_1} = \frac{\left(\frac{r_1}{2}\right)^2 (1.6 h_1)}{r_1^2 h_1} = 0.4$$

The volume of the new cylinder is 40% of the volume of the initial cylinder, a decrease of 60%.

13) ➡ C

Concept(s) Tested: Graphs and Functions

Convert the equation of the line to slope–intercept form to determine slope:

$$y = -x + 2$$

The slope of the line is −1. The slope of the line perpendicular to this line is 1. To determine the equation of the line, use the coordinates of the point through which the line passes:

$$y = (1)x + b$$

Since $x = 1$ and $y = 2$:

$$2 = 1 + b$$
$$b = 1$$

14) ➡ A

Concept(s) Tested: Graphs and Functions

Because the radius includes the points (0, 0) and (3, 4), the slope of the radius to the tangent is $\frac{4}{3}$.

The tangent line, which is perpendicular to the radius at the point of contact, is $-\frac{3}{4}$. The equation of the tangent line is:

$$y = -\frac{3}{4}x + b$$

$$4 = -\frac{3}{4}(3) + b$$

$$b = \frac{25}{4}$$

The equation is:

$$y = -\frac{3}{4}x + \frac{25}{4}$$

$$3x + 4y - 25 = 0$$

15) ➡ C

Concept(s) Tested: Algebra

Set the expression as a long-division:

$$\begin{array}{r} 9x - 9 \\ x+1\overline{)9x^2 + 0x - 4} \\ -)\underline{9x^2 + 9x} \\ -9x - 4 \\ -)\underline{-9x - 9} \\ 5 \end{array}$$

The quotient is $9x - 9 + \dfrac{5}{x+1}$.

16) ➡ 1,250

Concept(s) Tested: Problem Solving, Algebra
The price depreciation per year is:

$$\text{Depreciation} = \frac{\text{Total decrease in value}}{\text{Number of years}} = \frac{15,000 - 11,250}{3 \text{ years}}$$

$$= 1,250/\text{year}$$

17) ➡ $\dfrac{3}{7}$

Concept(s) Tested: Algebra

Transform the first equation to isolate z:

$$\frac{z}{y} = 7$$

$$z = 7y$$

Note that we can now substitute "$7y$" for z in the second expression, giving $\dfrac{3y}{7y}$.

The y variables in the numerator and denominator cancel out, leaving you with $\dfrac{3}{7}$.

18) ➡ 28

Concept(s) Tested: Graphs and Functions
Plug in values for the point (1, 12):

$$12 = (1)^2 + (1)m + n$$

$$11 = m + n$$

Plug in values for the point (3, 28):

$$28 = (3)^2 + 3m + n$$

$$19 = 3m + n$$

Subtract the first equation from the second:

$$\begin{array}{r} 19 = 3m + n \\ -)\underline{11 = m + n} \\ 8 = 2m \\ 4 = m \rightarrow n = 7 \end{array}$$

Thus, $mn = 4 \times 7 = 28$

19) ➡ 5

Concept(s) Tested: Algebra
If $x - 2$ is a factor, $f(2) = 0$:

$$2^3 - (2^3)k + 2k + 2 = 0$$

$$10 - 2k = 0$$

$$k = 5$$

20) ➡ 16

Concept(s) Tested: Data Analysis, Graphs and Functions

For the equation to be true, either $a = 4$ or $b = -6$
If $a = 4$ and $b = 0$, then $a^2 + b^2 = 4^2 + 0 = 16$

If $a = 0$ and $b = -6$, then $0 + 36 = 36$

Calculator Portion

1) ➡ C

Concept(s) Tested: Problem Solving, Inequalities
Because $x \geq 106$, the value of Z (the minimum national debt value for 2035) must be greater than or equal to the product of x and y, so $Z \geq xy$.
Since $x \geq 106$ <u>percent</u>, x must be expressed as the decimal 1.06 in the inequality, giving $y(1.06) \leq Z$ as the correct choice.

2) ➡ B

Concept(s) Tested: Data Analysis, Mesaures of Center and Spread

$$\text{Average days missed} = \frac{\text{Total days missed}}{\text{Number of students}}$$

$$= \frac{5(0) + 4(1) + 5(2) + 4(3) + 2(4)}{20}$$

3) ➡️ D

Concept(s) Tested: Graphs and Functions

The question provides the coordinates (3, 1) and (2, 5), so the slope of the linear function $f(x)$ is:

$$m = \frac{5-1}{2-3} = -4$$

Use the slope-intercept form of the equation of a line to determine the y-intercept:

$$y = mx + b \rightarrow y = -4x + b \rightarrow 1 = -4(3) + b$$

$$b = 13$$

4) ➡️ D

Concept(s) Tested: Data Analysis, Ratios and Percentages

$$Northeast = \frac{4595}{6862} = 0.67$$

$$Midwest = \frac{2365}{3265} = 0.72$$

$$South = \frac{2853}{4116} = 0.69$$

$$West = \frac{4501}{5925} = 0.76$$

5) ➡️ C

Concept(s) Tested: Data Analysis, Ratios and Percentages

Percentage using train in Midwest:

$$\frac{457}{3,265} \times 100\% = 14\%$$

6) ➡️ C

Concept(s) Tested: Graphs and Functions, Geometry

The center of the circle is (2, 2), and the radius of the circle is the line segment from (2 , 2) to (0 , 0) and has length $2\sqrt{2}$ according to the 45–45–90 right triangle.

The area is: Area $= \pi r^2 = \pi(2\sqrt{2})^2 = 8\pi$

7) ➡️ A

Concept(s) Tested: Problem Solving

Cost for Larry:

$$Distance\ of\ trip \times \frac{Gallon}{Distance} \times \frac{Cost}{Gallon} \times Larry's\ share$$

$$= (380)\left(\frac{1}{28}\right)(x)\left(\frac{1}{2}\right)$$

$$= \frac{380x}{28} \times \frac{1}{2}$$

8) ➡️ B

Concept(s) Tested: Problem Solving, Algebra

For the preceding 3-year period:

$$Total\ Surplus = \left(\frac{\$15\ million}{year}\right)(3\ years) = \$45\ million$$

If revenue drops to $40 million below current levels, expenditure will drop $25 million per year (from a point of a $15 million surplus) for the government to break even:

$$Cut\ in\ expenditures = \left(\frac{\$25\ million}{year}\right)(5\ years) = \$125\ million$$

Taking the existing surplus into account, we can determine the yearly reduction in expenditures:

$$Yearly\ reduction = \frac{\$125\ million - \$45\ million}{5\ years} = \frac{\$16\ million}{year}$$

9) ➡️ A

Concept(s) Tested: Graphs and Functions

Graph the two inequalities. Note that the two lines intersect in quadrant I:

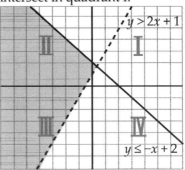

10) ➡️ B

Concept(s) Tested: Problem Solving, Mesaures of Center and Spread

$$Class\ average = \frac{Total\ points\ for\ boys + Total\ points\ for\ girls}{Number\ of\ boys + Number\ of\ girls}$$

$$= \frac{10(88) + 15(75)}{25} = 80.2$$

11) ➡️ D

Concept(s) Tested: Problem Solving, Algebra

Let the two numbers be represented by variables x and y, and $x > y$:

$$x - y = 2$$
$$x^2 - y^2 = 18$$

Factor the difference of square and solve for the sum of the two numbers:

$$(x - y)(x + y) = 18$$
$$2(x + y) = 18$$
$$x + y = 9$$

12) ➡ D

Concept(s) Tested: Problem Solving, Graphs and Functions

Convert the quadratic into vertex form:

$h(t) = -16t^2 + 48t + 5 = -16t^2 + 48t - 36 + 5 + 36$

$= -16(t^2 - 3t + \frac{9}{4}) + 41$

$= -16(t - \frac{3}{2})^2 + 41$

Since $a < 0$, the parabola is inverted and the vertex $(\frac{3}{2}, 41)$ is the highest point of the arc.

13) ➡ B

Concept(s) Tested: Problem Solving, Measures of Center and Spread

The range of scores is the difference between the highest and lowest scores; the mean must be between these scores. This necessitates that in Brad's class the lowest score is within 6 points of the mean. In Tom's class, a range of 30 points requires that the lowest score be equal to or less than 70, as the highest possible score is 100 points. This places the lowest score in Tom's class below the lowest possible score in Brad's class: $70 < 80 - 6$.

14) ➡ B

Concept(s) Tested: Problem Solving, Ratios and Percentages

In the 2–cup mixture, the amount of flour is:

$Amount\ of\ flour = \left(\frac{1}{3}\right)(2\,cups) = \frac{2}{3}\ cup$

After one cup of flour is added, the percentage of flour in the mixture is:

$Percent\ flour = \dfrac{\left(\frac{2}{3} + 1\right)cups}{3\,cups} \times 100\%$

$= \frac{5}{9} \times 100\% = 55.6\%$ which is approximately 56%.

15) ➡ B

Concept(s) Tested: Problem Solving, Measures of Center and Spread

Let x be Brian's score on the final, and because the final is worth two tests, let the total number of tests be the 5 Brian has already taken plus 2 additional tests representing the final:

$\dfrac{56 + 55 + 41 + 29 + 86 + 2x}{7} \geq 65$

$267 + 2x \geq 455 \rightarrow x \geq 94$

16) ➡ C

Concept(s) Tested: Problem Solving

The cost of the first mile is $0.30, and the remainder of the trip, $x - 1$ miles, is charged at $0.15 per mile:

$f(x) = 0.30 + 0.15(x - 1)$

17) ➡ B

Concept(s) Tested: Problem Solving, Algebra

Let x be the price of one tape recorder and y be the price of one radio:

$5x + 7y = 823$
$5x - 7y = 137$

Add the two equations:

$10x = 960$
$x = 96$

18) ➡ D

Concept(s) Tested: Problem Solving, Algebra

Because the racetrack is circular, the distance once around the racetrack is $2\pi r$ where r represents the radius of the circular track. The velocities of A and B are $\dfrac{2\pi r}{15\,sec}$ and $\dfrac{2\pi r}{25\,sec}$ respectively. If A passes B at time t, at this time B has traveled a distance x, and A has traveled a distance $x + 2\pi r$:

Time for A to travel $x + 2\pi r$ = Time for B to travel x

Time expressed in terms of velocity and distance is:

Therefore, $Time = \dfrac{Distance}{Velocity}$

$\dfrac{Distance_A}{Velocity_A} = \dfrac{Distance_B}{Velocity_B}$

$\dfrac{x + 2\pi r}{\left(\frac{2\pi r}{15}\right)} = \dfrac{x}{\left(\frac{2\pi r}{25}\right)}$

$15(x + 2\pi r) = 25x$

$x = 3\pi r$

The time at which A passes B is:

$Time = \dfrac{3\pi r}{\left(\frac{2\pi r}{25}\right)} = 37.5\,sec$

19) ➡ A

Concept(s) Tested: Problem Solving, Inequalities

$75 \le 35t + 5t^2 \le 130$

To determine the lower limit of t:

$5t^2 + 35t \le 75$

$5t^2 + 35t - 75 \le 0$

$5(t^2 + 7t - 15) \le 0$

From this inequality was can infer that

$t^2 + 7t - 15 \le 0$

Use the quadratic formula to determine the solutions for t:

$t = \dfrac{-7 \pm \sqrt{(-7)^2 - 4(-15)}}{2}$

$t = \dfrac{-7 \pm \sqrt{109}}{2}$

$t = 1.7, -8.7$

The value of t must be positive, so the car has traveled 75 meters at 1.7 seconds.

20) ➡ D

Concept(s) Tested: Problem Solving, Ratios and Percentages

Let x be the amount invested in stocks and y be the amount invested in bonds:

$x + y = 8000 \rightarrow x = 8000 - y$

$(0.04)x + (0.07)y = 500$

Substitute the first equation into the second:

$(0.04)(8000 - y) + (0.07)y = 500$

$320 - 0.04y + 0.07y = 500$

$0.03y = 180$

$y = 6000$

21) ➡ D

Concept(s) Tested: Problem Solving, Algebra

The cost per yard of lumber, in dollars, is:

$\text{Cost} = \dfrac{12}{\frac{16}{3} \$/\text{yard}} = \dfrac{36}{16} = \dfrac{9}{4} \$/\text{yard}$

The cost of x yards of lumber is $\dfrac{9}{4}x$ dollars.

22) ➡ D

Concept(s) Tested: Number Rules

$a^3 = b^2$

The structure of the answer choices indicate that we need to find b in terms of a.

$(a^3)^{\frac{1}{6}} = (b^2)^{\frac{1}{6}}$

$a^{\frac{1}{2}} = b^{\frac{1}{3}}$

Because $a^{\frac{1}{2}} = \sqrt{a}$, substitute $b^{\frac{1}{3}}$ for $\sqrt{a}$ in $b\sqrt{a}$:

$b\sqrt{a} = b \cdot b^{\frac{1}{3}} = b^{\frac{4}{3}}$

23) ➡ D

Concept(s) Tested: Graphs and Functions

Using the intercepts $(x , 0)$ and $(0 , y)$, calculate the slope of line m:

$slope = \dfrac{(y - 0)}{(0 - x)} = -\dfrac{y}{x}$

$x = -\dfrac{y}{slope}$

If the y-intercept is doubled, the new y-intercept is $(0 , 2y)$. If the slope is also doubled, the new x-intercept $(x_a , 0)$ can be calculated as:

$2(slope) = \dfrac{2y - 0}{0 - x_a}$

$x_a = -\dfrac{y}{slope}$

The x-intercept is unchanged.

24) ➡ A

Concept(s) Tested: Graphs and Functions, Geometry

The length of the diameter is the distance between the points $(3, 6)$ and $(1, -4)$:

$d = \sqrt{(x_2 - x_1)^2 + (y_2 - y_1)^2}$

$= \sqrt{(3 - 1)^2 + (6 - (-4))^2}$

$= \sqrt{104}$

The radius is:

$r = \dfrac{1}{2} diameter = \dfrac{\sqrt{104}}{2}$

and the square of the radius is:

$r^2 = \left(\dfrac{\sqrt{104}}{2}\right)^2 = \dfrac{104}{4} = 26$

Two answer choices, (A) and (C), have a value for r^2 of 26. To determine the correct choice, observe that circle represented in (C) would have a center at the point $(-2, -1)$. The diameter of a circle must pass through its center, and because the diameter of the circle in the diagram does not pass through quadrant III, the center of the circle cannot be in this quadrant.

25) ➡ B

Concept(s) Tested: Data Analysis

City A experiences its greatest increase in average daily temperature by percentage from month 5 to month 7. During this period, the average daily high in City B drops from 50 degrees to 30 degrees. The average daily high in City B over this two month period is:

$$Average = \frac{50 + 30}{2} = 40$$

26) ➡ D

Concept(s) Tested: Data Analysis

The population of Maine in 1840 is 500,000. The population reaches 1 million at some point between 1960 and 1980, that is, between 120 and 140 years after 1840.

27) ➡ B

Concept(s) Tested: Geometry

The length of the curve is one–fourth the circumference of the circle, and $r = 6$:

$$\text{Length of curve} = \frac{2\pi r}{4} = \frac{12\pi}{4} = 3\pi$$

It can be seen that $\overline{PS} + \overline{SO} = \overline{PO} = 6$.

As OSQT is a rectangle, $\overline{SO} = \overline{QT}$.

It follows that $\overline{PS} + \overline{QT} = 6$.

In a similar fashion it can be seen that $\overline{SQ} + \overline{TR} = 6$

The perimeter of the shaded region is:

$$\text{Perimeter} = \overparen{PQR} + \left(\overline{SQ} + \overline{TR}\right) + \left(\overline{PS} + \overline{QT}\right)$$
$$= 3\pi + 6 + 6$$
$$= 3\pi + 12$$

28) ➡ C

Concept(s) Tested: Algebra, Number Rules

$(3 + 2i) - (a + 3i) = 10 - i$

$(3 - a) - i = 10 - i$

$a = -7$

29) ➡ B

Concept(s) Tested: Problem Solving, Ratios and Percentages

Let x be the percent discount offered on the

$355.55 laptop expressed as a decimal, given that its discounted price is $165.65:

$355.55x = 165.65$

$x = 0.466$, or approximately 47 percent.

30) ➡ B

Concept(s) Tested: Problem Solving, Algebra

Because sales tax is included in the listed price, solve for the original price then subtract that from the listed price:

$355.55 = 1.075 \times \text{original price}$
Original price = 330.74

Taxes = $355.55 - 330.74 = 24.81$

$165.65 = 1.075 \times \text{original price}$
Original price = 154.09

Taxes = $165.65 - 154.09 = 11.56$

Subtracting the two values gives the difference in taxes:

$24.81 - 11.56 = 13.25$

31) ➡ 4

Concept(s) Tested: Problem Solving, Ratios and Percentages

$$\frac{0.25 \ inches}{20 \ miles} = \frac{x}{320 \ miles}$$

$$x = \frac{(0.25)(320)}{20} \ inches$$

$x = 4$ inches

32) ➡ 9

Concept(s) Tested: Problem Solving, Ratios and Percentages

$mL \ of \ salt = (0.2)(45 \ mL) = 9 \ mL$

33) ➡ 2

Concept(s) Tested: Graphs and Functions

$-3x^2 + (4x)^2 = 52$

$-3x^2 + 16x^2 = 52$

$x^2 = 4$

$x = 2, -2$

34) ➡ 8

Concept(s) Tested: Problem Solving, Algebra

The height that the ball reaches after x bounces is:

Height $= (30)(0.8)^x$

To determine x for which height is below 6 feet—that is, below 20% (0.2) of its original bounce:

$(30)(0.8)^x < 6$
$(0.8)^x < 0.2$

For $x = 7$, the bounce is: $(0.8)^7 = 0.21$

For $x = 8$, the bounce is: $(0.8)^8 = 0.16$

35) ➡ 3790

Concept(s) Tested:Problem Solving, Algebra

Royalties $= (1200)(29.95)(0.03) + (800)(16.95)(0.2)$

$\qquad = 3790$

36) ➡ 60

Concept(s) Tested: Trigonometry, Geometry

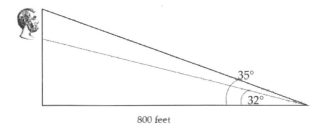

Let h_1 be the height of the top of Lincoln's face and h_2 be the height of the bottom of Lincoln's face. Because we are given two angle measurements (32 and 35 degrees) and the length of a side adjacent to the angles (800 feet), and because we are trying to find the length(s) of the side opposite these angles (h_1 and h_2), we must use tangent:

$h_1 = 800 \tan 35$
$h_2 = 800 \tan 32$

The height of his face is $800(\tan 35 - \tan 32) = 60.27$

37) ➡ 800

Concept(s) Tested: Problem Solving, Ratios and Percentages

Let x be the number of streams during the first half of the year:

$x + 1.5x = 8\ billion$
$x = 3.2\ billion$

During the second half of the year, the service streamed 4.8 billion songs. To determine the monthly streams:

$Monthly\ average = \dfrac{4.8\ billion}{6} = 800\ million$

38) ➡ 2.37 or 2.36

Concept(s) Tested: Problem Solving, Ratios and Percentages

Let x be the total streams in the three-month period:

$(0.003)x = 7.1\ million$

$x = 2.366\ billion$

Rounded and truncated answer are both acceptable

Reading Test

1. Ⓒ	6. Ⓐ	11. Ⓑ	16. Ⓑ	21. Ⓐ	26. Ⓒ	31. Ⓑ	36. Ⓒ	41. Ⓓ	46. Ⓑ	51. Ⓐ
2. Ⓒ	7. Ⓑ	12. Ⓑ	17. Ⓐ	22. Ⓑ	27. Ⓓ	32. Ⓓ	37. Ⓐ	42. Ⓑ	47. Ⓓ	52. Ⓑ
3. Ⓐ	8. Ⓓ	13. Ⓐ	18. Ⓓ	23. Ⓐ	28. Ⓐ	33. Ⓐ	38. Ⓑ	43. Ⓓ	48. Ⓑ	
4. Ⓑ	9. Ⓒ	14. Ⓓ	19. Ⓒ	24. Ⓐ	29. Ⓓ	34. Ⓒ	39. Ⓑ	44. Ⓒ	49. Ⓓ	
5. Ⓐ	10. Ⓐ	15. Ⓑ	20. Ⓑ	25. Ⓑ	30. Ⓑ	35. Ⓑ	40. Ⓒ	45. Ⓑ	50. Ⓑ	

1) ➤ C

Concept(s) Tested: Words in Context

Choice (C) is correct because the narrator wants to give the body a "spark of being," or fill it with life, and "imbue" means to cause someone or something to absorb feelings or qualities. (A) is incorrect because "pervade" is not something that can be done to another person or object; while life could pervade the body, it would not make sense to say that the doctor "pervaded" the body with life. (B) is incorrect because "bathe" most nearly means to immerse, which would be an exterior treatment only. Finally, (D) is incorrect because "inspire" means to give someone the will to do something, which does not fit the context.

2) ➤ C

Concept(s) Tested: Summary

Choice (C) is correct because the narrator says that the creature's otherwise beautiful features "formed a more horrid contrast with his watery eyes," which were almost as white as his eye sockets. (A) is incorrect because, although the narrator mentions the creature's yellow skin, he specifically calls the eyes "horrid." (B) is incorrect because the only comment the narrator makes about the creature's build is positive— that his "limbs were in proportion." Finally, (D) is incorrect because the narrator mentions the creature's "lustrous" hair as one of its positive features.

3) ➤ A

Concept(s) Tested: Inference, Implication, and Suggestion

This statement means that the different circumstances and events of life do not change as much as feelings change; in other words, a person's feelings frequently undergo transformations. Thus, (A) is correct. (B) is incorrect because the narrator is not specifically speaking of misfortune, but instead about all kinds of circumstances. (C)

is incorrect because the narrator is not focusing on fate and does not express an outlook on it. Finally, (D) is incorrect because the narrator is not commenting on the effects of accidents. Rather, he is explaining how drastically his feelings changed.

4) ➤ B

Concept(s) Tested: Summary

Choice (B) is correct because, at the end of paragraph 3, the narrator states that "horror and disgust" filled his heart. In other words, he was "revolted and repulsed." (A) is incorrect because the narrator does not specifically mention in the passage that he is afraid that the creature is violent. (C) is incorrect because the narrator does not leave the creature in order to help it gain self-sufficiency, but because of his own overwhelming emotions. (D) is not the best answer because in paragraph 4 the narrator says that he rushed out of the room because he was "unable to endure the aspect of the being I had created"; thus, although he may have been tired, he did not leave because of it.

5) ➤ A

Concept(s) Tested: Analogy

Choice (A) is correct, as the narrator leaves his creation because he cannot stand to look at it, and sleeplessly paces in his bedroom. This behavior strongly suggests that the narrator—the creator—rejects the monster—his own creation. (B) is incorrect because a customer is able to return a product at will, but the monster cannot be returned, which is the cause of the narrator's agitation. (C) is incorrect because an editor generally revises manuscripts written by others; in this case, not only is the narrator unable to change the creature, but he himself created it, and thus has responsibility for it. Finally, (D) is incorrect because the narrator is not pursuing the creature; rather, he is fleeing it.

6) ➤ A

Concept(s) Tested: Purpose

Choice (A) is correct because the narrator's dream is about the death and decay of his loved ones. The horrific images indicate that even in sleep, he is not able to forget what he has brougth to life. (B) is incorrect because the main focus of the narrator's dream is not sorrow at the death of his mother, but his preoccupation with death now that he has created life from death. (C) is incorrect because the narrator's dream hints at, but does not fully explain, his reasons for undertaking the experiment. Finally, (D) is incorrect because the dream indicates the narrator's disgust and regret, not his acceptance, of his creation.

7) **B**

Concept(s) Tested: Words in Context

The correct choice is (B) because the narrator says that when the creature held up the bed curtain, the creature's eyes were fixed on him. When eyes "fix on" something it means they are staring; in other words, the creature's eyes were focusing on the narrator and nothing else. (A), (C), and (D) are incorrect because these other meanings of "fixed" would not make sense in this context.

8) **D**

Concept(s) Tested: Attitude and Tone

Choice (D) is correct because in the opening paragraph, the narrator speaks of his "anxiety that almost amounted to agony." By paragraph 3, he says that what he had desired "with an ardor that far exceeded moderation" horrified him as soon as he accomplished it. (A) is incorrect because, while the narrator may have felt fear that the experiment would fail, he feels horror, not joy, when it succeeds. (B) is incorrect because the narrator does not feel that the creature is beautiful; moreover, he does not attempt to communicate with it. Finally, (C) is incorrect because the narrator does not start out feeling tired. Also, by the end of the passage, he indicates regret, not exhilaration.

9) **C**

Concept(s) Tested: Citation

The answer is (C) because it captures the hopeful excitement that the narrator had for his experiment—"the beauty of the dream"—and the "breathless horror" he felt the instant the creature came to life. (A) is incorrect because it expresses only the nervous feelings of the narrator before he brings his creation to life. (B) is incorrect because reveals only the shock and horror the narrator feels when the creature opens his eyes. Finally, (D) is incorrect because it does not support the narrator's major shift from excitement to horror; rather, it describes his desire to escape his feelings for awhile with sleep.

10) **A**

Concept(s) Tested: Purpose

Choice (A) is correct because, by calling his creation a "thing" and a "creature," the narrator identifies it as an object or an animal, not as a human with thoughts and feelings. Thus, the narrator's descriptions "dehumanize" it. (B) is incorrect because the narrator is not attempting to disorient his creation; he is too caught up in his own feelings of revulsion to be concerned with confusing his creation. (C) is incorrect because the narrator does not attempt to hide his feelings toward his creation. Finally, (D) is incorrect because the terms "thing" and "creature" have a more general rhetorical effect; they emphasize the creature's non-human status, not just its unusual appearance.

11) **B**

Concept(s) Tested: Organization

Choice (B) is correct because Clinton says in line 1 that "Africa has changed so much in just 10 years," and the rest of the passage is about how to reinforce positive changes in Africa, contrasting the troubled past with the hopeful future. (A) is incorrect because although paragraph 3 states that Americans must change their stereotypes of Africa, that contrast is not a focus of the speech. (C) is incorrect; although Clinton praises Ghana's democratic movement by saying that "Ghana blazed the path of that new Africa," he does not dwell on the differences between Ghana's government and those of other African nations. Finally, (D) is incorrect because Clinton only mentions Ghana's economy to point out a firm from Ghana that is traded on the New York Stock Exchange.

12) **B**

Concept(s) Tested: Summary

Choice (B) best summarizes the points made in the first two paragraphs: (1) Africa has changed politically and economically over the last decade, and (2) Africa is not "free from peril." (A) is incorrect because Clinton says that "democracy has not yet gained a foothold even in most successful nations" in Africa (lines 6 – 8), not that African nations tend to have elected governments now. (C) is incorrect because paragraphs 1 and 2 talk about the African continent in general, not about Ghana in particular. (D) is incorrect because Clinton does not mention the United States in the first two paragraphs of the passage; rather, he provides a general overview of African nations' positive shifts and continuing challenges.

13) **A**

Concept(s) Tested: Words in Context

Choice (A) is correct because the term "elemental" refers to parts of something that cannot be broken down further. Within the context of the speech, "elemental" refers to the basic rights of every human; in other words, "fundamental" rights. (B) is incorrect because "rudimentary" carries the connotation of undeveloped, which does not make sense in Clinton's reference to human rights. (C) is incorrect because "instrumental" connotes something that is helpful or useful, which does not make sense in the context. Finally, (D) is incorrect because "environmental" refers to the conditions surrounding something, which would not make sense in terms of human rights.

14) ➡ D
Concept(s) Tested: Summary
Choice (D) is correct because Clinton praises Ghana for blazing "the path of that new Africa" through political and peacekeeping efforts (lines 36 – 51), implying that Ghana is a progressive African nation. Thus, (D) is correct. (A) is incorrect because Clinton praises Ghana, but he never refers to it as a "utopia": a perfect, idealized society. (B) is incorrect because Clinton's speech focuses largely on Ghana's social and political progress in recent years; (D) is incorrect because, although Clinton relates the establishment of democracy in Ghana to democracy in America, he does not imply that Ghana *mirrors* America.

15) ➡ B
Concept(s) Tested: Citation
Choice (B) is correct because it clearly establishes Ghana as a model for other African nations by stating, "Ghana again lights the way for Africa." (A) is incorrect because it focuses on Americans' perceptions of Africa, not on Ghana's relationship with Africa. (C) and (D) are incorrect because they do not focus on Ghana's potential as a model for the rest of the continent.

16) ➡ B
Concept(s) Tested: Graph and Text Synthesis
Choice (B) is correct because, when Clinton gave the speech in 1998, the middle class was experiencing slight growth while the number of poor people was gradually decreasing, indicating slightly higher incomes for many Africans. (A) is incorrect because even with the positive changes, around two-thirds of Africans could still be classified as "poor," which is the opposite of "widespread prosperity." (C) cannot be supported because the table is not differentiated by region. (D) is incorrect because the changes are slight, which does not indicate a sudden change, or "revolution."

17) ➡ A
Concept(s) Tested: Citation

Choice (A) is correct because it refers to the trend toward "growing economies" in Africa, which is supported by the slight rise in the middle class and slight decrease in poor people throughout Africa, as indicated by the table. (B) is incorrect because it refers to political change, which cannot be supported by the information in the table. (C) is incorrect because it refers to economic exploitation of resources, which is not reflected in the contents of the table. (D) is incorrect because it refers to the trend of peace and tolerance within Ghana, not to economic trends indicated by the table.

18) ➡ D
Concept(s) Tested: Words in Context
Choice (D) is correct because in lines 65 – 66 Clinton refers to society metaphorically as a family, and says that a good society "honors," or *respects*, each family member. The overall emphasis is on respect for individuals' human rights. (A) is incorrect because it would not make sense to suggest that society should obey each member. (B) is incorrect because Clinton is not referring to praising each member of society, but to recognizing that each member has basic rights. (C) is incorrect because "worship" refers to demonstrating reverence, typically for a deity; there is no indication that Clinton is making such an implication.

19) ➡ C
Concept(s) Tested: Attitude and Tone
Choice (C) is correct because in the passage Clinton uses the term "we" when proposing various measures that must be taken to put Africa on a path to prosperity and democracy. The use of "we" coming from the leader of the United States indicates the U.S. commitment, or pledge, to help set Africa on a new course. (A) is incorrect because Clinton does not use "we" to distinguish Ghana from other nations, but to encourage Ghana and other nations to see themselves as unified by common political and social goals. (B) is incorrect because Clinton does not mention military assistance. (D) is incorrect because the passage consistently focuses on African society, and the U.S. is only mentioned in passing.

20) ➡ B
Concept(s) Tested: Inference, Implication, and Suggestion
Clinton expresses optimism in Africa's political future when he says that the U.S. sees Ghana's success "taking root throughout the new Africa." Yet Clinton remains pragmatic, acknowledging that Africa still has many hurdles to overcome, and that democracy "is never perfect or complete."

(A) is incorrect because while Clinton does say in the paragraph that war and genocide still "tear at the heart of Africa" (line 86), he does not elaborate on the horrifying outcomes, so pessimism is not his dominant attitude. (C) is incorrect because Clinton never mentions jealousy, even though he does claim that "the United States admires your [Ghana's] success." And (D) is incorrect because Clinton never shows resignation. Rather, he consistently expresses optimism and determination.

21) ➤ A
Concept(s) Tested: Organization
Choice (A) is correct because the author uses analogy to help explain his perspective: he likens humans' cosmic significance to that of "foam and bubbles upon the river's current." He also uses logic and reasoning to emphasize his points: he uses reasoning to conjecture that life elsewhere in the universe must be as fleeting as life on Earth. (B) is incorrect because the passage is a philosophical musing, not a structured argument containing counterarguments. (C) is incorrect because it is too limited; the passage does use metaphor, but the passage is primarily philosophical in nature, so the author makes use of reasoning as well and uses no exaggeration or hyperbole. Finally, (D) is incorrect because the author does not appeal to specific physical laws to present his views.

22) ➤ B
Concept(s) Tested: Words in Context
The correct choice is (B). If we use the idiom "in light of (x), we have decided (y)" we mean "considering (x), we think (y);" in other words, the idiom "in light of" refers to pieces of information that help one interpret other pieces of information. In this case, humans think highly of themselves, and in this *context* interpret the universe as theirs. Thus, "context" is close to "in light of" because it refers to circumstances that lead to a particular interpretation. (A), (C), and (D) do not make sense in the sentence.

23) ➤ A
Concept(s) Tested: Purpose
The answer is (A) because the author's point is that living matter in the universe is minuscule and short-lived compared to nonliving matter. Life is analogous to a thin layer of snow that melts quickly on a warm spring morning, insignificant when compared to the miles of rock upon which it briefly exists. (B) is incorrect because the analogy does not include any mention of life recurring in spring; the point of the "spring morning" is the idea that the warm sunlight will quickly melt the snow. (C) and (D) are incorrect because the author says he is comparing the amount of living matter to non-living matter, so his purpose

is neither to speculate on the conditions that created life, nor to describe a shallow understanding of life.

24) ➤ A
Concept(s) Tested: Inference, Implication, and Suggestion
The answer is (A) because, according to the information available in the author's era (he published the passage in 1915), it appeared that in past geological periods life "seems to have more completely enveloped" the Earth (lines 33 – 39). (B) and (C) are incorrect because they contradict the author's assertion in lines 33 – 39. Finally, (D) is incorrect because the author says that other planets likely contain life, but he does not compare the amount of life on Earth to the amount on other planets.

25) ➤ B
Concept(s) Tested: Words in Context
Choice (B) is correct; when the author states that life "hangs on the verge of dissolution," he means that life exists on the verge of termination. Thus, "hangs" means "exists precariously," or simply "exists." (A) is incorrect because the author is not implying that life is attached or stuck in the universe in any way; rather, he is emphasizing that it is in constant danger of disappearing. (C) is incorrect because "dangles" implies that life is literally hanging over a precipice. In the passage, however, "hangs" is used metaphorically, not literally. Finally, (D) is incorrect because to say that life "depends" on the verge of dissolution would not have a clear meaning, as dependence involves relying upon something.

26) ➤ C
Concept(s) Tested: Graph and Text Synthesis
Choice (C) is correct, because the chart shows that the element oxygen makes up 65 percent of a human body. The chart shows proportions of materials at the level of (elemental) atoms, rather than compounds made up of molecules, such as water. (A) is incorrect because there is no information in the chart about how well understood the composition of the human body is. (B) is incorrect because the chart lists four elements and one "other" category, which consists of an unknown number of additional elements. (D) is incorrect because the chart does not compare the elements in humans to the elements in other species, so it does not address whether the human composition is unique.

27) ➤ D
Concept(s) Tested: Citation
The answer is (D) because it refers to the mystery of life that is evident in the chart: living things such as humans are made up of nonliving elements (as shown in the chart) without which they cannot

live. Yet, if one were to mix those same elements together in a laboratory, the result would not be a living thing. (A), (B), and (C) are incorrect because the chart shows only the proportions of elements that make up the human body; there is no direct connection to the insignificance of life in the universe or the limited conditions in which life can exist.

28) ➡ A

Concept(s) Tested: Inference, Implication, and Suggestion

Choice (A) is correct because the author states that, when it comes to life, we do not know "whether the physical conditions sum up the whole truth about it." The author calls the question "insoluble," meaning that science may never be able to answer it. (B) is incorrect because the author does not criticize science. (C) is incorrect because, although the author uses poetic analogies to articulate his points, these are not meant to indicate that science itself is poetry. Finally, (D) is incorrect because the author never indicates that he considers science to consist of an arbitrary or meaningless set of principles. Rather, the author seeks to draw attention to scientific facts.

29) ➡ D

Concept(s) Tested: Citation

Choice (D) is correct because lines 75 – 80 provide the clearest evidence of the author's belief that there are certain questions that science is not equipped to answer. (A) is incorrect because it focuses on humans lacking perspective on their own place in the universe, which by itself does not address science's limitations. (B) is incorrect because it focuses on the amount of life present on Earth over the course of time; it does not comment on scientific limitations. Finally, (C) is incorrect because it is a straightforward factual claim; life ends, but the universe's chemical and mechanical process seem to be without end. The statement does not address the deeper questions of whether science can determine what creates life, what life is, or whether it matters.

30) ➡ B

Concept(s) Tested: Summary

Choice (B) is correct because the author considers whether life originates from materials only, and whether life is a phenomenon that science can ever explain. Thus, he is exploring a scientific question, but at the same time, his approach is philosophical; he predicts that the question is "insoluble," meaning that we will never be able to solve the problem. (A) is incorrect because the author is not interrogating, or asking

questions; he is providing perspective on human understanding. (C) is incorrect because, although the author uses poetic analogies (bubbles, snow, cliffs, apples, rainbows, etc.), he is not primarily concerned with either poetry or technical subjects. Finally, (D) is incorrect because the author does not demonstrate personal skepticism, or disbelief, about anything.

31) ➡ B

Concept(s) Tested: Summary

Choice (B) is correct because the authors say that their purpose is to "prevent misconstruction or abuse of powers." (A) is incorrect because, although freedom of speech is mentioned in the First Amendment, the Bill of Rights addresses the larger purpose of limiting government powers. (C) is incorrect because although the introduction does mention that the Bill of Rights is designed to increase public confidence in the government, the way to do so is to prevent abuses by the government. Finally, (D) is incorrect because although the authors mention "abuse," they are referring specifically to government exceeding its rightful powers.

32) ➡ D

Concept(s) Tested: Summary

Choice (D) is correct because in paragraph 2— the First Amendment—the authors state that Congress does not have the power to make any law regarding setting up any religion, nor to prohibit people from freely exercising religion. Thus, it cannot favor, sponsor, or ban any religion. (A) is incorrect because it has the opposite meaning. (B) is incorrect because a "redress of grievances" refers to compensation/recognition for being wronged or harmed; thus, the passage does not mention "grieving." (C) is incorrect because a discussion of "arms," in the sense of guns and other weapons, occurs in the Second Amendment, not the First Amendment.

33) ➡ A

Concept(s) Tested: Words in Context

Choice (A) is correct because a "grievance" is a complaint about a wrong or an injustice that was committed. The "redress of grievances" means that citizens will have the right to petition the government to acknowledge and address their complaints. (B) is incorrect because although "grievance" shares the same root as "grief," which means "sorrow," a grievance is a complaint, not a feeling of sadness. (C) is incorrect because a "right" is an entitlement to something, not a complaint. Finally, (D) is incorrect because an "indignity" refers to a situation that makes a person feel embarrassed or ashamed; an indignity might cause someone to have a grievance—a feeling of anger at having been wronged—but it is not the same as a grievance.

34) ➤ C
Concept(s) Tested: Purpose
Choice (C) is correct because the Fourth Amendment describes the only conditions under which representatives of the government (such as the police) can undertake searches. A "Warrant" (justification) to search must include a specific explanation of purpose. (A) is incorrect because the purpose of the amendment is to protect people from "unreasonable searches and seizures" by authorities, not to keep records. (B) is incorrect because the amendment does not provide details about exactly what would justify searches; that is left open to interpretation. (D) is incorrect because while the amendment does emphasize the privacy of homes and belongings, it is not enough for officials to enter respectfully. Rather, officials must have formal permission for a justifiable search.

35) ➤ B
Concept(s) Tested: Inference, Implication, and Suggestion
Choice (B) is correct because the Fifth Amendment states that no one can be "deprived of life, liberty, or property, without due process of law"; in the context of the amendment, this provides protection from being executed, imprisoned, or having property taken without fair legal procedures. (A) is incorrect because lines 35 – 37 make a fairly minor point, which is that in times of crisis, members of the military may not have access to the same grand jury protection regarding being charged with a crime that they would have in civilian life. (C) is incorrect because the focus of the amendment is on the rights of people accused of wrongdoing, not on preventing government problems. Finally, (D) is incorrect because Amendment 5 is quite general, and does not discuss the role of attorneys or bureaucrats.

36) ➤ C
Concept(s) Tested: Citation
The answer is (C) because lines 41 – 42 summarize the major concern of the authors here, which is to limit the government's power to accuse people, bring them to trial, and so on. Choices (A) and (B) are incorrect because they include details rather than a summary of the purpose of the amendment. Finally, (D) is incorrect because it concerns the separate matter of the right to compensation if the government takes one's property, as in claiming someone's land to make room for a road.

37) ➤ A
Concept(s) Tested: Organization
The correct choice is (A) because the Fifth

Amendment restricts the government from accusing and imprisoning people without the "due process of law," while the Sixth Amendment focuses on the rights of people who have been accused and are being tried in court. (B) is incorrect because it is inaccurate; the Fifth Amendment does not provide details about forming grand juries, and the right to having an attorney is not the major focus of Amendment 6. (C) is incorrect because it does not capture the overall focus of either amendment. (D) is incorrect because seizing the property of individuals is an aspect, but not an overall focus, of Amendment 6.

38) ➤ B
Concept(s) Tested: Purpose
Choice (B) is correct because the authors indicate that they intend that bail, fines, and punishments be reasonable and standard. The authors do not provide specifics, leaving open the interpretation of their words. (A) is incorrect because the authors' purpose is not exactly to emphasize humanitarian values, but rather to set limits on government powers. (C) is incorrect because the authors are not establishing the power of the courts in this amendment, but rather, limiting it. (D) is incorrect because Amendment 8 has a narrower purpose: keeping the treatment of accused and convicted criminals within bounds.

39) ➤ B
Concept(s) Tested: Words in Context
The correct choice is (B). To "construe" something is to interpret it a particular way; in line 68, the authors are warning that their words should not be *misconstrued*—they have listed certain rights, but readers should not *interpret* that to mean they have listed the *only* rights guaranteed to people. (A) is incorrect because to "decipher" something means to figure it out, and the act of listing rights does not need to be figured out. (C) is incorrect because simplifying someone else's action is not necessarily the same as interpreting it. Finally, (D) is incorrect because "translated" also would be an imprecise synonym for "construed."

40) ➤ C
Concept(s) Tested: Inference, Implication, and Suggestion
The correct choice is (C) because the authors state in the introductory paragraph that they are adding the Bill of Rights to the Constitution to satisfy critics who want more "declaratory and restrictive clauses" to be added regarding governmental powers. Most of the wording in the amendments is about what the government "shall not" do. (A) is incorrect because the authors do not appear to think that the founding document should try to resolve all future problems that people will have with the government. (B) is incorrect because the restrictions on government power outlined in the passage suggest that the

government cannot necessarily be trusted. Finally, (D) is incorrect because the authors do not suggest or imply in the Bill of Rights that any of the amendments should be altered in the future.

41) ➡ D

Concept(s) Tested: Citation

The correct choice is (D). In the Tenth Amendment, the authors make a sweeping statement about the Constitution: the federal government holds *only* those powers that the document gives to it. This best supports the authors' view that the founding document should primarily describe limitations on power. Choices (A), (B), and (C) are incorrect because they describe specific restrictions rather than general purpose.

42) ➡ B

Concept(s) Tested: Words in Context

Choice (B) is correct because generally, when a field of study (preventative medicine, in this case) is in its infancy, it is just beginning, like an infant just beginning life. (A) is incorrect because it would be awkward and unclear to say that the study of preventive medicine is "in its childhood." (C) is incorrect because it is a less precise synonym than (B); "immature" can convey a critical tone, which would not match the author's attitude, and in addition, it is not logical to say that something is "in its immaturity." Finally, (D) is incorrect because "fantasy" refers to imaginary ideas, which would not make sense in the context.

43) ➡ D

Concept(s) Tested: Citation

Choice (D) is correct because it describes preventive medicine thoroughly, encompassing the study of how different bacteria cause infectious diseases and how to prevent their spread. (A) is incorrect because it describes the increasing interest at the time (1915) in preventing rather than just trying to cure disease but does not describe the concept of preventive medicine in any detail. (B) is incorrect because it says that preventive medicine is based on the knowledge of bacteria but does not explain the connection. (C) is incorrect because it is simply a general statement about avoiding disease by knowing what causes it; the statement does not describe any specific aims of preventive medicine.

44) ➡ C

Concept(s) Tested: Purpose

The answer is (C) because the author says that stemming the spread of cholera is one instance of the "really great triumphs" of preventive medicine (lines 18 – 19). (A) is incorrect because the author's purpose is to highlight, not downplay, the importance of scientific research. (B) is incorrect because the author is not addressing personal responsibility or negligence regarding cholera. (D) is incorrect because the author discusses triumphs over cholera but does not speculate about a disease-free future.

45) ➡ B

Concept(s) Tested: Words in Context

Choice (B) is correct. In lines 51 – 56, the author discusses the "foul odors associated with human corpses"; The reader can infer that "foul" here means "disgusting" and "repulsive," similar meanings to "putrid." (A) is incorrect because "avian" refers to "fowl"—birds—a homonym to the word "foul" which would not make sense in the context. (C) and (D) are incorrect because it does not make sense to say that an odor is "illegal" or "frightening."

46) ➡ B

Concept(s) Tested: Purpose

The answer is (B). In lines 47 – 56, the author of Passage 2 is pinpointing a time when "the concept of cleansing hands with an antiseptic agent probably emerged": he mentions that around 1822, "chlorides of lime and soda" became known as disinfectants. (A) is incorrect because the author is not criticizing 19th century medicine as primitive; rather, his diction suggests that he admires people for understanding hygiene "as early as 1822." (C) is incorrect because the author of Passage 2 is not talking about "recent advances;" rather, he is writing in 2002 about events taking place in 1822. Finally, (D) is incorrect because the author does not indicate whether chlorides of lime and soda were a household remedy.

47) ➡ D

Concept(s) Tested: Organization

The correct choice is (D) because lines 57 – 63 describe the government recommending washing hands with soap before and after contact with patients; but lines 64 – 75 describe more recent and more specific federal recommendations about what kinds of soaps to use in which situations. In other words, recommendations went from general to more specific. (A) and (B) are incorrect because both paragraphs 2 and 3 describe the guidelines as recommendations, not requirements or regulations. (C) is incorrect because "disinfectant" generally refers to cleansers for non-living surfaces, while "antiseptic" refers to cleansers for living tissue, such as the skin. The paragraphs do not discuss the difference.

48) ➡ B

Concept(s) Tested: Inference, Implication, and Suggestion

Choice (B) is correct because the author of Passage 2 mentions in paragraph 4 that despite most hospitals adopting more specific guidelines for hand washing procedures, "adherence of HCWs (health care workers) to recommended handwashing practices has remained low" (lines 96 – 100). Thus, the challenge is getting workers to cooperate. (A) is incorrect because the author does not mention challenges regarding educating people in health care settings, although such a problem is indirectly implied. (C) and (D) are incorrect because the author does not mention either topic.

49) ➡ D

Concept(s) Tested: Citation

Choice (D) is correct because it directly mentions the biggest challenge to improving hand washing procedures in health-care settings: getting people to do what they should. (A), (B), and (C) are incorrect because they describe historical facts or specific hand-washing recommendations; they do not precisely address improving hand-washing procedures in today's health care settings.

50) ➡ B

Concept(s) Tested: Multiple-Text Synthesis

The answer is (B) because the author of Passage 1 is describing the triumphs of preventive medicine; his positive attitude indicates that he would approve of the 1822 discovery of disinfectants and antiseptics. (A) is incorrect because the author of Passage 1 states that the practice of preventive medicine arose over the past few years, not that all related discoveries only took place within the 20th century. (C) is incorrect because it does not match the tone of Passage 1, and because the French pharmacist is not described as treating disease. Finally, (D) is incorrect because the French pharmacist's discovery is directly related to the author's area of concern: preventing the spread of harmful bacteria.

51) ➡ A

Concept(s) Tested: Multiple-Text Synthesis

Choice (A) is correct. The "scientific breakthrough" described in Passage 1 is the study of "contagious and epidemic diseases in the light of bacteriological knowledge" (lines 11 – 17), which provided a clear understanding of how to prevent diseases such as cholera. Passage 2's "public health perspective" shows how that understanding has furthered the practice of hand washing recommendations in health-care settings. (B) is incorrect because Passage 1 describes a successful trend in medical research, not a failed project. (C) is incorrect because Passage 2 does not discuss any international concerns, but rather focuses on U.S. health care settings.

(D) is incorrect because Passages 1 and 2 do not make direct proposals or criticisms; they report information neutrally.

52) ➡ B

Concept(s) Tested: Citation, Multiple-Text Synthesis

The correct choice is (B). Passage 2 provides an overview of the development of hand-washing, especially hand-washing expectations for health-care workers in hospitals and other health-care settings. Thus Passage 2 most directly relates to the mention in Passage 1 about the effect of preventive medicine research on "rules for the management of the sick-room which largely prevent contagion from patient to nurse" (lines 31 – 34). (A) is incorrect because it is a general statement that preventive medicine has "accomplished much," and the author of Passage 2 does not discuss the accomplishments of preventive medicine. (C) is incorrect because it concerns learning about sources of contagion, and the connection between this topic and Passage 2 is indirect. Finally, (D) is incorrect because it addresses preventive medicine's importance, which is not mentioned in Passage 2.

Writing and Language Test

1. Ⓓ	5. Ⓒ	9. Ⓒ	13. Ⓐ	17. Ⓑ	21. Ⓑ	25. Ⓑ	29. Ⓑ	33. Ⓑ	37. Ⓐ	41. Ⓑ
2. Ⓐ	6. Ⓒ	10. Ⓑ	14. Ⓒ	18. Ⓐ	22. Ⓒ	26. Ⓓ	30. Ⓒ	34. Ⓓ	38. Ⓓ	42. Ⓐ
3. Ⓑ	7. Ⓑ	11. Ⓐ	15. Ⓒ	19. Ⓒ	23. Ⓒ	27. Ⓐ	31. Ⓒ	35. Ⓓ	39. Ⓐ	43. Ⓐ
4. Ⓓ	8. Ⓑ	12. Ⓑ	16. Ⓓ	20. Ⓓ	24. Ⓐ	28. Ⓐ	32. Ⓓ	36. Ⓒ	40. Ⓑ	44. Ⓓ

1) ➡ D
Concept(s) Tested: In-Sentence Punctuation
(D) is correct because it separates the two main verbs of the sentence with a conjunction ("and") and does not include any inappropriate punctuation. Choice (A) is incorrect because the subject of the sentence, "the medicine," is not repeated between the verbs "blocks" and "renders," so no comma is needed. Colons are commonly used to separate a statement from an elaboration or definition of that statement. Because the information following the colon in (B) is neither an elaboration nor a definition of the first part of the sentence, (B) is incorrect. When a subject corresponds with two main verbs in a sentence, the verbs must be separated by a conjunction. (C) lacks any such conjunction and is therefore incorrect.

2) ➡ A
Concept(s) Tested: Precise Diction
Choice (A) is correct because to "oversee" an activity means to supervise it, so doctors "supervise anesthetic use in the United States." To overlook is to fail to notice, and the sentence does not indicate that doctors ignore anesthetic use, so (B) is incorrect. Although choice (C) conveys the correct idea, the phrase "watch over" is not as precise as "oversee," making (C) less appropriate than (A). Saying that "doctors view most anesthetic use" implies that doctors always watch nurses as they administer anesthetics, which contradicts the intended meaning of the passage; thus, (D) is incorrect.

3) ➡ B
Concept(s) Tested: Passage Development
The paragraph focuses on the benefits that come with working as a nurse anesthetist, so (B) is correct. (A) is incorrect because the tone of the paragraph is positive in that it focuses on the aforementioned benefits rather than pointing out a negative aspect of the work. (C) is incorrect because the paragraph does not mention that the work of nurse anesthetists is boring. the paragraph focuses on the benefits of being a nurse anesthetist, not the drawbacks. Finally, (D) is incorrect because the paragraph does not mention anesthesiologists objecting to nurses administering anesthetics.

4) ➡ D
Concept(s) Tested: Passage Development
The sentence describes "diverse settings," and then operating rooms and obstetrical wards, both of which would be found in a hospital, along with emergency rooms. A contrast would include an area of medicine that is not found in a hospital. Only (D) is a place other than a hospital setting. (A) is incorrect because an emergency room is located in a hospital. (B) is incorrect because surgery centers are either located in or connected with hospitals, and surgery is similar to operating rooms. (C) is incorrect because pediatric hospitals have operating rooms and emergency rooms, so they do not constitute a contrast.

5) ➡ C
Concept(s) Tested: Precise Diction
We can infer that the purpose of talking to patients before a surgery is to *lessen* any anxieties a patient might have. Choice (C) means to alleviate or dispel, so (C) is the correct answer. Although (A) looks similar to (C), "ally" means "friend" or "supporter," which is unrelated to "lessen." Choice (B) is unrelated to lessening anxieties and is therefore incorrect. Choice (D) is incorrect because to "purge" is to clean or remove something undesirable, which does not fit the context.

6) ➡ C

Concept(s) Tested: Parallel Structure

The items in a list must be presented using the same word pattern. The list at 6 refers to "necessary machines." Because "machines" is plural, the items in the list should also be plural. (A), (B), and (D) can be eliminated because one or more of the items are singular and include unnecessary articles. Thus, (C) is the correct answer.

7) ➡ B

Concept(s) Tested: Parallel Structure, Passage Development

The sentences that precede the underlined portion begin with the pronoun "they," so the correct choice will maintain this subject pattern. Choice (B) is correct because it does so. (A) and (D) can be eliminated because they use "nurse anesthetist" as a subject instead of "they." Additionally, the preceding sentences in the paragraph are written using the active voice—the subject of the sentence (they) is performing an action. For this reason, we can eliminate (C), as it uses the passive voice.

8) ➡ B

Concept(s) Tested: Combining Sentences

Joining the two sentences would require indicating a succession relationship, as one step comes after another. Only choice (B) combines both sentences using "and then" to indicate that one qualification follows upon another. (A) is incorrect because an em dash is not grammatically correct here and is usually used to indicate nonessential information in a sentence. (C) is incorrect because it introduces an unnecessary and superfluous phrase—"known as an 'RN,'"—which makes the sentence wordy. Finally, (D) is incorrect because it indicates a relationship of cause and effect, when the correct relationship is one of succession.

9) ➡ C

Concept(s) Tested: Parallel Structure

Sentences must maintain parallel structure. In other words, phrases or clauses on either side of a coordinating conjunction ("and" in this case) must use verb forms consistently. The phrase before 9 uses the infinitive verb "to return," so the second part of the sentence, which describes the next step in the same process, should also use an infinitive verb. Thus, (C) is the correct choice because it uses the infinitive verb "to pass." Choice (A) is not a parallel structure, while choices (B) and (D) introduce past-tense verb forms, which do not make sense in the sentence.

10) ➡ B

Concept(s) Tested: Graph Analysis

The correct choice is (B) because, according to the graph, the median income for an anesthetist is just over 150,000 dollars, and the median income for a midwife is just under 100,000 dollars. Therefore, the median wage for an anesthetist is just over 50,000 dollars—about 50 percent—more than that of a midwife. (A) is incorrect because the graph only includes data for wages at the 25th, 50th, and 75th percentiles, so we cannot say what the highest-paid midwives earn in the 100th percentile. We can eliminate (C) because the combined median incomes for a practitioner and a midwife is just under 200,000 dollars, 50,000 more than the median income for an anesthetist. And (D) is incorrect because the graph does not reflect all other nursing professions, only midwives and practitioners.

11) ➡ A

Concept(s) Tested: Passage Development

Choice (A) is correct because the paragraph mainly discusses the high demand for nurse anesthetists. Because the added sentence contributes to this discussion by reporting the trend toward using nurse anesthetists in place of medical doctors, it should be kept. (B) is incorrect because the paragraph focuses on anesthetist job prospects, not where nurse anesthetists can work. (C) and (D) are incorrect because the underlined sentence is relevant to the paragraph, so it should not be deleted.

12) ➡ B

Concept(s) Tested: Precise Diction

The second half of the sentence is a definition; it needs to convey the idea that "anther" and "stigma" correspond to the male and female parts of a plant *in the order that they are listed*. The term with that meaning is "respectively," making (B) the correct choice. (A) is incorrect because to put something "in perspective" is to realize its importance, which does not make sense in the context of the sentence. Similarly, (C) and (D) are is incorrect because "respectfully" means doing something with respect, and "perceptively" means wisely, so neither provides the necessary meaning of "corresponds to."

13) ➡ A

Concept(s) Tested: Pronoun Use/Case

The underlined portion at 13 must be a pronoun that refers to "a mobile assistant." Because the pronoun refers to the object of the sentence, the correct answer must be (A), which is the *objective* case of the pronoun "who." (B) is incorrect because "who" is the subjective case, so it can only refer to the subject of a sentence or clause. The gender of the assistant cannot be determined based on the sentence, so (D) is incorrect. The demonstrative pronoun "that" is very rarely preceded by a comma, so we can eliminate (C).

14) ➡ C

Concept(s) Tested: Passage Development

The paragraph's focus is flowers' adaptations to attract specific assistants. However, the sentence at 14 wrongly shifts the paragraph's focus to the perceptions of bees and butterflies. This information appears to be unrelated to the information about flowers attracting assistants and breaks the continuity of the paragraph. Thus, answer choice (C) is correct. (A) is incorrect because the paragraph focuses on flowers attracting assistants while colors that attract pollinators is only a detail. (B) is incorrect because the sentence adds details that do not directly support the paragraph's main topic. Finally, (D) is incorrect because explaining how butterflies and bees can see UV light would only further distract from the focus of the paragraph, so the sentence does not offer a good reason for deletion.

15) ➡ C

Concept(s) Tested: Parallel Structure, Subject-Verb Agreement

In the sentence containing 15, the assistant (it) "brushes up against pollen" and "transports pollen." Because the verb "transports" must agree with "brushes" in terms of number and tense, we can eliminate (A), which uses "transporting", and (D), which uses "has transported." (B) incorrectly adds a subject ("it"), thereby creating an independent clause that does not fit. The sentence does not have a comma after "while drinking," so an independent clause cannot begin there. Thus, the correct choice is (C) because it does not repeat the subject of the sentence—"it"—and conjugates "transports" to match "brushes."

16) ➡ D

Concept(s) Tested: Passage Development

Up to this point, the passage has indicated that insects and birds are attracted to specific flowers. Yet the paragraph beginning at 16 changes the focus from insects and birds to bats, which are mammals. Thus, a sentence is needed to set up the change. Only choice (D) accomplishes this. (A) is incorrect because it inappropriately sets up

a focus on reasons that plants produce flowers rather than the relationship between some bats and flowers. (B) is incorrect because it sets up a focus on how unusual it is for bats to serve as pollinators rather than the actual focus of the paragraph. Finally, (C) is incorrect because it sets up a discussion about competitive pressures among different plants. It therefore fails to set up the paragraph's information about bat and flower coevolution.

17) ➡ B

Concept(s) Tested: Parallel Structure, Passage Development

The sentences that precede 17 follow a certain pattern: each sentence starts, "In (place), the trait…" Thus, the sentence at 17 should maintain this word pattern and begin with the prepositional phrase "In (place), it…" Because (B) is the only choice to maintain this word pattern, it is the correct choice. Other choices begin differently than preceding sentence and/or use a different verb tense than previous sentences.

18) ➡ A

Concept(s) Tested: Concision

Choice (A) is correct because it is concise and clear. (B) is relatively clear, but it includes redundancies ("bats," "pollinators"). (C) also contains redundancies ("them"). (D) includes archaic language ("bestow upon"). Thus, (B), (C), and (D) are incorrect because they are not as clear and concise as (A).

19) ➡ C

Concept(s) Tested: Sentence Boundaries, In-Sentence Punctuation

Semicolons function to connect two related independent clauses in the same sentence. Because the two ideas in the sentence containing 19 are independent clauses with closely related ideas, (C) is correct. (A) is incorrect because the pronoun "which" traditionally refers to the noun that immediately precedes it. Because pollen does not "fly around a wider range…" we can infer that the pronoun "which" is being misused. (B) is incorrect because the adverb "additionally" is generally used to transition between two sentences, not between two ideas within the same sentence. (D) is incorrect because "even though" implies contrast, yet the sentence does not suggest that any contrast is intended.

20) ➤ D

Concept(s) Tested: Passage Development

An appropriate concluding sentence would sum up the types of traits that flowers must develop in order to attract bats. Only choice (D) does this effectively by acknowledging all of the constraints previously mentioned, and concluding with an insight into how bat-attracting flowers appear. (A) is incorrect because it invites further discussion by commenting on the odors of bat-attracting flowers. It does not summarize the information presented. (B) is incorrect because it shifts the focus of the paragraph onto butterflies, bees, and moths, when the focus should be the subject of the paragraph—bat-attracting flowers. Finally, (C) is incorrect because it makes a general statement about the uniqueness of bat-attracting flowers that, like (A), invites further discussion rather than neatly and succinctly concluding the paragraph.

21) ➤ B

Concept(s) Tested: Possession

The phrase attributes the use of echolocation to bats. Thus, "bats'" must be plural and possessive, eliminating (A) and (C). (D) makes the sentence somewhat unclear: the use of the present participle "using" implies that some flowers have adapted to bats that *currently* use echolocation. However, we can infer that the flowers have adapted over time to the use of echolocation by bats.

22) ➤ C

Concept(s) Tested: Noun Agreement

The descriptions contained in the underlined portion refer to "flowers and leaves." Because both flowers and leaves are plural, the corresponding descriptions must also be plural. Choices (A) and (B) are incorrect because one or both of the descriptions are singular. Although (D) is grammatically correct, it is unnecessarily wordy and can be eliminated. Thus, the correct choice is (C).

23) ➤ C

Concept(s) Tested: Combining Sentences

Choice (C) is correct because a colon is appropriate when combining two independent clauses if the second clause defines the information in the first clause, as is the case here. (A) is incorrect; "because" is used to explain causes rather than to further define. (B) is incorrect because a comma cannot separate two independent clauses unless the comma is followed by an appropriate coordinating conjunction. Finally, (D) is incorrect because the phrase "which is that" is unnecessarily wordy.

24) ➤ A

Concept(s) Tested: Subject-Verb Agreement, Precise Diction

The plural subject "most of the Mayans" requires the plural noun "were," so (C) and (D) are incorrect. the word "literary," when applied to people, means well-read or intellectual, yet the passage clearly focuses on people having a system of writing and being able to read, or being "literate," so (B) is incorrect, and (A) is the correct choice.

25) ➤ B

Concept(s) Tested: Syntax

Choice (B) is correct because it is the most clear and concise choice. (A) is incorrect because it uses the transition word "however" as a coordinating conjunction even though there is no contrast in ideas. (C) is incorrect because of its awkward phrasing, such as "from 250 CE to 900 CE…was when literacy flourished." (D) can also be eliminated because of unnecessary wordiness, such as using "the flourishing of literacy" instead of "literacy flourished."

26) ➤ D

Concept(s) Tested: Passage Development

The main goal when answering this question is to determine the relationship between Mayan codices and the decline of Mayan civilization. Only choice (D) does so by stating that writing declined with the Mayan "city-states of the southern lowlands." Choice (A) uses "as" to imply a connection between the two, but it does not elaborate on this connection, so it can be eliminated. (B) makes no attempt to connect the codices and agriculture, so it is incorrect. (C) is incorrect because it explains why agriculture declined, but it does not clarify the relationship between literacy and agriculture.

27) ➤ A

Concept(s) Tested: Syntax

Choice (A) is correct because it clearly indicates that it is ironic that the ancient books survived only because they were taken away by the Spaniards. (B) is incorrect because the word "ironic" appears to begin a casual, informal aside, but the elliptical sentence leaves the reader unsure. (C) is incorrect because its syntax implies that the Spaniards sent the books ironically, which is inaccurate. (D) is incorrect because it is unclear whether the three books are the only surviving ones, or the only surviving ones in Europe.

28) ➡️ A

Concept(s) Tested: Precise Diction

Choice (A) is correct because a "forebear" is an ancestor, or someone or something that came before the current generation. It makes sense to say that Mayan people continue to live in the same territory as their *ancestors* did. (B) is incorrect because an antecedent is something that came before a current version, but "antecedent" is used to reference things or events. "Descendants" refers to offspring, or individuals who come *after* the current generation, so (C) is incorrect. Finally, (D) can be eliminated because a "lineage" refers to one's ancestry in the abstract (as in one's origins or genealogy), not to actual people.

29) ➡️ B

Concept(s) Tested: Passage Organization

Choice (B) is correct because sentence 4 mentions that "only three codices survived" because they were sent to Spain. The added sentence should precede sentence 4 in order to introduce the Spanish conquest and its effect on the codices. Choices (A), (C), and (D) would not create a coherent flow of information.

30) ➡️ C

Concept(s) Tested: Concision

Choice (C) is correct because it is concise. Choices (A), (B), and (D) all contain redundant terms, making them unnecessarily wordy. Additionally, the word "contemporaneously" in (B) is illogical because it means "existing or occurring at the same time."

31) ➡️ C

Concept(s) Tested: Passage Organization

The paragraph focuses on the difficulties of decoding the Mayan language. Sentence 2 mentions the biggest hurdle, so it should go after sentences 3 and 4, which mention two additional problems. Thus, (C) is correct and (A) is incorrect. (B) is incorrect because it would interrupt the topic of Mayan languages in sentences 3 and 4. Finally, (D) is incorrect because sentence 2 is not appropriate as a concluding sentence of the paragraph. It does not sum up the information in the previous sentences and instead invites further comment.

32) ➡️ D

Concept(s) Tested: In-Sentence Punctuation, Sentence Boundaries

The correct answer must convey the relationship (if any) between the two independent clauses using punctuation. (A) is incorrect because the ideas joined by a comma are distinct. They need to be separated into two sentences. (B) and (C) consist of further attempts to join the two distinct thoughts. Both lack a conjunction such as "and," making them doubly incorrect. Choice (D) clearly transitions between clauses by creating separate sentences, making it correct.

33) ➡️ B

Concept(s) Tested: Passage Tone

The underlined portion should link the rest of the sentence to information in the paragraph. The only answer that makes a connection between the surviving Mayan books and the final sentence is (B) because it shows how the surviving texts have affected scholars' understanding of Mayan culture. The other choices are wordy and less effective than (B).

34) ➡️ D

Concept(s) Tested: Passage Development

The underlined sentence explains a major criticism of 4'33" and is necessary for the contrast that follows, making (D) the best choice.

35) ➡️ D

Concept(s) Tested: Relative Clauses

The information after the comma is a relative clause and must be introduced by a relative pronoun, making (D) the correct choice. (A) is incorrect because two independent clauses cannot be separated by a comma alone. (B) and (C) are incorrect because, without a relative pronoun, they are unclear in meaning.

36) ➡️ C

Concept(s) Tested: Passage Development

Choice (C) is correct because the paragraph focuses on Cage's use of silence in many of his compositions, and this is the only choice that emphasizes silence in his music.

37) ➡️ A

Concept(s) Tested: Precise Diction

Based on the context of the sentence, the underlined word should be close in meaning to "emphasize." Only (A) captures this connotation, making it the correct choice. The other choices most nearly means "acknowledge," which is not as emphatic as "highlight," making them incorrect.

38) ➤ D

Concept(s) Tested: Concision

The correct choice is (D) because the underlined portion contains a redundancy (it is repetitive to say that the song had "no score" and "no notes") and the remaining answer choices repeat this error.

39) ➤ A

Concept(s) Tested: Transition Words and Phrases

(A) is the best choice, because the sentence following the underlined portion describes the *first* of Cage's aforementioned two influences. (B) is incorrect, because this is a phrase used to emphasize the need to deal with important issues before minor ones. (C) is incorrect, because the paragraph describes the first of two experiences, not as "beginning." (D) is incorrect, because this choice refers to an action taking place immediately.

40) ➤ B

Concept(s) Tested: Preposition Use

The underlined preposition indicates the use of art to express ideas. Only (B) signifies this relationship, so it is the correct choice. (A) is incorrect because "with" usually indicates accompaniment. (C) is incorrect because "by" indicates nearness in space or authorship. (D) is incorrect because a preposition is necessary to clarify the relationship between each of the ideas presented in the sentence.

41) ➤ B

Concept(s) Tested: Passage Development

(B) is correct because it is the only choice that maintains the passage's focus on Cage's thought process regarding *4'33"*. Choices (A) and (C) emphasize irrelevant chronological details. Meanwhile, (D) is incorrect because the rhetorical question is not clearly connected to Cage.

42) ➤ A

Concept(s) Tested: Verb Tense, Subject-Verb Agreement

The verb in the underlined portion describes a work of art, so it must use the simple present tense. The verb must also agree in number with the subject of the sentence ("appearance"), which is a singular noun. Therefore, (A) is the correct choice.

43) ➤ A

Concept(s) Tested: Precise Diction, Commonly Confused Words

In the context of the sentence, the underlined word should explain that *4'33"* is analogous, or that it corresponds, to the white paintings. Thus, (A) is

the best choice. (B) is incorrect because homology refers to similar body parts, chemical compounds, or words, and is not typically associated with works of art. (C) is incorrect because a prologue is an introduction. (D) is incorrect, because a monologue is a speech.

44) ➤ D

Concept(s) Tested: Appositives and Titles

Because the descriptive phrase that identifies Frank Zappa does not use punctuation, it is being treated as a title, not an appositive. Therefore, an article is unnecessary, and (D) is the best choice.

SAT Practice Test 4: Answers & Explanations

 Math Test

☑ No Calculator Portion

1. Ⓐ	7. Ⓑ	13. Ⓐ	19. *350*
2. Ⓐ	8. Ⓒ	14. Ⓐ	20. *93*
3. Ⓓ	9. Ⓓ	15. Ⓑ	
4. Ⓐ	10. Ⓑ	16. *2*	
5. Ⓐ	11. Ⓓ	17. *12*	
6. Ⓐ	12. Ⓒ	18. *19*	

☑ Calculator Portion

1. Ⓑ	7. Ⓓ	13. Ⓑ	19. Ⓓ	25. Ⓒ	31. *31*	36. *30*
2. Ⓓ	8. Ⓐ	14. Ⓓ	20. Ⓑ	26. Ⓑ	32. *64*	37. *7.53*
3. Ⓒ	9. Ⓒ	15. Ⓓ	21. Ⓒ	27. Ⓐ	33. *12*	38. *0.06*
4. Ⓑ	10. Ⓐ	16. Ⓓ	22. Ⓐ	28. Ⓓ	34. $\frac{1}{3}$	
5. Ⓒ	11. Ⓒ	17. Ⓐ	23. Ⓓ	29. Ⓑ		
6. Ⓓ	12. Ⓑ	18. Ⓓ	24. Ⓑ	30. Ⓒ	35. *25*	

No Calculator Portion

1) A

Concept(s) Tested: Problem Solving

The number of books sold is $3m - p$ and books are sold at n dollars each.

2) A

Concept(s) Tested: Algebra

Solve the first equation for x:

$6x + 3 = 21 \rightarrow 6x = 18 \rightarrow x = 3$

Then plug in the value of x for $2^x : 2^3 = 8$.

Thus, (A) is correct.

3) D

Concept(s) Tested: Data analysis, Word problems

Because the value of the variable D will increase if the price per drink increases, the correct choice is (D).

4) ➡ A

Concept(s) Tested: Data Analysis

Calculate the lowest possible score for A and the highest possible score for B. If A is in 3rd place in Event III, its total is:

Total points for A = $3 + 5 + 1 = 9$

If B comes in 2nd place in Event II and 1st place in Event III, its total is:

Total points for B = $1 + 3 + 5 = 9$

It is apparent that B cannot exceed A in points.

5) ➡ A

Concept(s) Tested: Inequalities

$-6 < 2x + 4 \leq 0$

$-10 < 2x \leq -4$

$-5 < x \leq -2$

6) ➡ A

Concept(s) Tested: Graphs and Functions

If x is a real number, the term $-3x^2$ is always negative, the largest value for the function is $f(0) = 5$. All values of $f(x)$ must be less than or equal to 5.

7) ➡ B

Concept(s) Tested: Graphs and Functions

Rewrite the function $g(x)$ in vertex form:

$g(x) = x^2 - 6x + 14$

$g(x) = x^2 - 6x + 9 + 14 - 9$

$\quad = (x - 3)^2 + 5$

The vertex of the parabola that is the graph of $g(x)$ is (3, 5). The vertex of $f(x) = x^2$ is (0, 0).

8) ➡ C

Concept(s) Tested: Problem Solving, Algebra

If h is the cost of one hamburger and s is the cost of one shake: $2h + 3s = 4.21$, $3h + 2s = 5.24$

Adding these equations gives: $5h + 5s = 9.45$

9) D

Concept(s) Tested: Algebra, Number Rules

$$\sqrt{x+4} = x$$
$$x + 4 = x^2$$
$$x^2 - x - 4 = 0$$

Solve for x:

$$x = \frac{-(-1) \pm \sqrt{(-1)^2 - 4(-4)}}{2}$$
$$x = \frac{1 \pm \sqrt{17}}{2}$$

Both solutions are irrational. Approximating the value of $\sqrt{17}$: $x = 2.56, -1.56$

Both of these values satisfy the original equation, so (D) is correct.

10) B

Concept(s) Tested: Problem Solving, Graphs and Functions

The object hits the ground when $h(t) = 0$:

$$240t - 16t^2 = 0$$
$$t(240 - 16t) = 0$$

Therefore,

$$240 - 16t = 0$$
$$t = 15$$

11) ➤ D

Concept(s) Tested: Graphs and Functions

The function $g(x)$ can be rewritten as:

$$g(x) = \frac{x^2 - 9}{x - 3} = \frac{(x-3)(x+3)}{x-3} = x + 3 \text{ for } x \neq 3$$

The graph of $g(x)$ is the same as the graph of $f(x)$ except for $x = 3$.

12) ➤ C

Concept(s) Tested: Problem Solving, Combinations and Permutations

Person 1 shakes five times with each of the others.
Person 2 shakes four times with Persons 3, 4, 5, and 6.
Person 3 shakes three times with Persons 4, 5, and 6.
Person 4 shakes twice with Persons 5 and 6.
Person 5 shakes with Person 6.
The total number of handshakes is:

$$5 + 4 + 3 + 2 + 1 = 15$$

13) ➤ A

Concept(s) Tested: Problem Solving, Algebra

Let x be the number of adult tickets sold and y be the number of student tickets sold: $x + y = 10$

This equation is equivalent to: $5x + 5y = 50$

As the total could have been $39 or $41, there are two equations that could express the total:

$$5x + 2y = 39 \quad \text{OR} \quad 5x + 2y = 41$$

By using the subtraction method on the equations we have created, we can determine that only the second of these gives an integer value for y when subtracted from $5x + 5y = 50$:

$$\begin{array}{r} 5x + 5y = 50 \\ - \,) \ 5x + 2y = 41 \\ \hline 3y = 9 \\ y = 3 \end{array}$$

14) ➤ A

Concept(s) Tested: Problem Solving, Geometry

The dimensions of the rectangular solid are 8 centimeters by 3 centimeters by 1 centimeter. The volume of the solid is:

$$V = l \times h \times w$$
$$V = 8 \text{ cm} \times 3 \text{ cm} \times 1 \text{ cm} = 24 \text{ cm}^3$$

15) ➤ B

Concept(s) Tested: Graphs and Functions

The vertex of the parabola is $(-3, 4)$. We can write the equation for the parabola in vertex form, for which $a < 0$ because the parabola is inverted:

$$y = a(x - h)^2 + k$$
$$y = -(x + 3)^2 + 4$$
$$y = -(x^2 + 6x + 9) + 4$$
$$y = -x^2 - 6x - 5$$

16) ➤ 2

Concept(s) Tested: Algebra, Graphs and Functions

$$x^2 - x = 2$$
$$x^2 - x - 2 = 0$$
$$(x - 2)(x + 1) = 0$$
$$x = 2, -1$$

17) ➡ 12

Concept(s) Tested: Algebra

$$\frac{3}{x-3} + \frac{5}{2x-6} = \frac{11}{12}$$

$$\frac{6}{2x-6} + \frac{5}{2x-6} = \frac{11}{12}$$

$$\frac{11}{2x-6} = \frac{11}{12} \rightarrow 2x - 6 = 12$$

18) ➡ 19

Concept(s) Tested: Algebra

Add all three equations:

$$x + y = 11$$
$$y + z = 14$$
$$+)\ x + z = 13$$
$$\overline{2x + 2y + 2z = 38}$$

Therefore, $x + y + z = 19$

19) ➡ 350

Concept(s) Tested: Problem Solving, Algebra

Let x be the weight, in pounds, of the first lift and y be the weight of the second lift. We can write the following two equations:

$$x + y = 750$$
$$2x - 300 = y$$

Substitute the second equation into the first:

$$x + (2x - 300) = 750$$
$$x = 350$$

20) ➡ 93

Concept(s) Tested: Problem Solving, Ratios and Percentages

The team has played a total of 24 games, with 15 wins and 9 losses. This constitutes $\frac{1}{6}$ of all games in the season. Let x be the number of games in the season:

$$\frac{x}{6} = 24$$
$$x = 144$$

In order to achieve a 75% win percentage:
Total wins needed = $(0.75)144 = 108$
The number of additional wins needed is:
Additional wins needed = $108 - 15 = 93$

Calculator Portion

1) ➡ B

Concept(s) Tested: Data Analysis

Paper and wood, together, make up 60% of the budget. If x represents total expenditures:

$$(0.6)x = 277,200 \rightarrow x = 462,000$$

To determine the share of this portion that is spent on paper:

$$462,000 \times 0.28 = 129,360$$

2) ➡ D

Concept(s) Tested: Graphs and Functions

The y-intercept is given. To determine slope:

$$m = \frac{15 - 0}{0 - 6}$$
$$m = -\frac{5}{2}$$

The equation of the line is: $y = -\frac{5}{2}x + 15$

3) ➡ C

Concept(s) Tested: Problem Solving, Algebra

$$\frac{12\ peaches}{1\ dozen} \times \frac{1.5\ lb}{6\ peaches} \times \frac{\$24.00}{20\ lb}$$
$$= \frac{(12)(1.5)(24)}{(6)(20)} \$ / dozen$$
$$= \$3.60 / dozen$$

4) ➡ B

Concept(s) Tested: Problem Solving, Measures of Center and Spread

Begin by evaluating III: the mode is the value that appears most often. Looking at the list, it is clear that the mode is 80, so III is true. Eliminate choices (A) and (C). Next, evaluate II: as there are seven scores, the median score is 70. II is not true.

5) ➡ C

Concept(s) Tested: Graphs and Functions

Test the ordered pairs with the inequalities. The second inequality is the easier to work with:

$$x - y > 1$$

Only choice (C) satisfies this inequality:

$$2 - (-1) > 1 \rightarrow 3 > 1$$

6) ⬛➤ D

Concept(s) Tested: Graphs and Functions

The graph of the function $f(x) = \dfrac{1}{x} + 2$ is the

graph of $f(x) = \dfrac{1}{x}$ translated vertically 2 units:

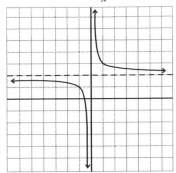

The only value of $f(x)$ that is excluded is $f(x) = 2$.

7) ⬛➤ D

Concept(s) Tested: Problem Solving, Ratios and Percentages

Let n be the number of years that have passed since 2000. The increase in the deer population is:

Factor of increase $= (1.3)^{\frac{n}{20}}$

In the year 2080:

Factor of increase $= (1.3)^{\frac{80}{20}} = (1.3)^4 = 2.856$

8) ⬛➤ A

Concept(s) Tested: Data Analysis, Graphs and Functions

The points on the scatterplot indicate a positive linear relationship between height and weight. Only choice (A) represents this type of relationship.

9) ⬛➤ C

Concept(s) Tested: Problem solving, Algebra

Let x be the number of tax-deductible miles that Sarah drove:

$0.56x = 28{,}224$

$x = 50{,}400$

Sarah drove 50,400 tax-deductible miles.

10) ⬛➤ A

Concept(s) Tested: Algebra

The first equation can be rewritten as:

$y = 2x - 5$

Substituting into the second equation gives:

$3x + 2(2x - 5) = -3$

11) ⬛➤ C

Concept(s) Tested: Graphs and Functions

$2x^2 + 7x + 5 = 0$

$(2x + 5)(x + 1) = 0$

$x = -\dfrac{5}{2}, -1$

The sum of the solutions is: $-\dfrac{5}{2} + (-1) = -\dfrac{7}{2}$

12) ⬛➤ B

Concept(s) Tested: Graphs and Functions

The two functions have the same values at only two points, $x = 0$ and $x = 1$.

13) ⬛➤ B

Concept(s) Tested: Problem Solving, Algebra

Use the formula $A = P(1 + r)^t$, where A is the amount in the fund, P is the principal, r is the interest rate, and t is the time in years. Here, the principal is \$1000, the interest rate is 4.5%, and the term is 18 years:

$A = P(1 + r)^t \longrightarrow A = 1000(1.045)^{18} \approx 2200$

14) ⬛➤ D

Concept(s) Tested: Problem Solving, Ratios and Percentages

Let x be the price of the car in 1975:

Price in 1980 $= (1.3)x$

Price in 1985 $= (1.5)(1.3x) = 1.95x$

The price of the car in 1985 is 95% greater than the price in 1975.

15) ⬛➤ D

Concept(s) Tested: Problem Solving, Graphs and Functions

The cost of mailing is a linear function. The y-intercept is the baseline cost, \$0.46. The slope is the cost per additional ounce, \$0.20: $c(z) = 0.2(z - 1) + 0.46$

16) ⬛➤ D

Concept(s) Tested: Problem Solving, Measures of Center and Spread

As all salaries increase by the same amount, the median will increase by this amount. If a is the number of employees and x is the mean before the raises:

Adjusted mean $= \dfrac{xa + 1000a}{a} = x + 1000$

17) ➡ A

Concept(s) Tested: Graphs and Functions

Solve the system of equations by multiplying the second equation by a factor of 4 and subtracting the two equations:

$$4x - y = 7$$
$$-) \; 4x + 12y = 20$$
$$\overline{\qquad -13y = -13}$$
$$y = 1$$

Solve for x:

$$x + 3(1) = 5$$
$$x = 2$$

18) ➡ D

Concept(s) Tested: Algebra

Write the equation $a + c = 70$ in terms of b:

$$a = \frac{b}{2}, \; c = 3b$$

$$\frac{b}{2} + 3b = 70$$

$$\frac{7}{2}b = 70$$
$$b = 20$$

Therefore, $a = 10, \; c = 60$
$$a + b + c = 90$$

19) ➡ D

Concept(s) Tested: Graphs and Functions

$$f(8, 3) = \frac{1}{4}(8) - 3 = -1$$
$$f(-12, -2) = \frac{1}{4}(-12) - (-2) = -1$$

20) ➡ B

Concept(s) Tested: Problem Solving, Ratios and Percentages

Let x be the amount of 50% glucose solution that is added:

$$(0.24)(16) + (0.5)(x) = (0.35)(16 + x)$$
$$3.84 + 0.5x = 5.6 + 0.35x$$
$$x = 11.7$$

21) ➡ C

Concept(s) Tested: Data Analysis

The axis lines indicate that the total amount of trash collected across districts is "13." The unit of measurement indicated by the axis lines can be represented by x:

$$13x = 130,000 \; tons \rightarrow x = 10,000 \; tons$$

22) ➡ A

Concept(s) Tested: Problem Solving, Rate

Let x be number of hours it takes to remove the water. 50 liters of water enter the basement for 2 hours before removal begins, and for x hours of removal: $50(2 + x)$. We can set this expression equal to the amount of water removed per hour: 60 liters $\times x$.

Therefore:

$$50(2 + x) = 60x \rightarrow 100 + 50x = 60x \rightarrow x = 10$$

23) ➡ D

Concept(s) Tested: Data Analysis

23% of the portfolio is invested in Technology. Twenty percent of this portion is:

$$(0.2)(23\%) = 4.6\%$$

The percent invested in Health after the transfer is: $11\% + 4.6\% = 15.6\%$

The dollar amount invested in Health is:

$$(0.156)(500,000) = 78,000$$

24) ➡ B

Concept(s) Tested: Problem Solving, Rate

Let x be the distance of the one-way trip. The times to travel up and down the route are:

$$Time_{up} = \frac{x \; mile}{12 \frac{mile}{hr}} = \frac{x}{12} hr$$

$$Time_{down} = \frac{x \; mile}{18 \frac{mile}{hr}} = \frac{x}{18} hr$$

The time for the round trip is: $\frac{x}{18} + \frac{x}{12} = \frac{5x}{36} hours$

The average speed for the round trip ($2x$) is:

$$\frac{2x}{\left(\frac{5x}{36}\right)} = \frac{72}{5} = 14.4 \frac{miles}{hour}$$

25) ➡ C

Concept(s) Tested: Data analysis, Measures of Center and Spread

Arrange the data set and calculate the mean, median, and range:

Mean: $\frac{64 + 64.2 + 154.1 + 170}{4} = \frac{452.3}{4} = 113.075$

Median: $\frac{64.2 + 154.1}{2} = 109.15$

Range: $\quad 170 - 64 = 106$

Thus, the mean is the greatest value, and (C) is correct.

ANSWER KEY – TEST 4

26) ▬▶ B

Concept(s) Tested: Problem solving, Unit conversion

Convert 170 pounds (the alien's weight on Earth) to kg.

$$\frac{170}{1} lbs. = \frac{x}{0.4536} kg.$$

$x = 170(0.4536)$

$x = 77.112$ kg.

Thus,

$N = 77.112 \times 9.80665 m/s^2$

$N = 756.2$

27) ▬▶ A

Concept(s) Tested: Graphs and Functions, Geometry

The equation of a circle with center (2, −3) and diameter of 4 units—radius 2 units—is:

$(x - 2)^2 + (y + 3)^2 = 4$

Expanding the expressions in brackets:

$x^2 - 4x + 4 + y^2 + 6y + 9 = 4$

$x^2 + y^2 - 4x + 6y + 9 = 0$

28) ▬▶ D

Concept(s) Tested: Number Rules

$f(i) = i^3 + i^2 + 2i + 6$

$= i(i^2) + i^2 + 2i + 6$

$= -i - 1 + 2i + 6$

$= 5 + i$

29) ▬▶ B

Concept(s) Tested: Problem Solving, Ratios and Percentages

As sixty percent of students are in the Arts Program, 40% of students—or 4000 students—are in the Science program. The Science program is forty percent male and sixty percent female:

Female students in Science program = (4000)(0.6)

= 2400

The remaining female students are in the Arts program:

Female students in the Arts program = 5000 − 2400

= 2600

The percentage of students in the Arts program that are female is:

% of students in Arts that are female

$= \frac{2600}{6000} \times 100\% = 43\%$

30) ▬▶ C

Concept(s) Tested: Geometry

The perimeter of the shaded region is made up of one side of the triangle and a portion of the circumference of the circle. Beginning with the side of the triangle: $\overline{PO} = \overline{OQ}$ so ΔPOQ is an isosceles triangle.

$\angle OPQ = \angle PQO$ and $\angle OPQ + \angle PQO = 120^0$

Therefore, $\angle OPQ = \angle PQO = \angle POQ = 60°$

ΔPOQ is an equilateral triangle, and $\overline{PQ} = 3$

Next, consider the arc. The length of the arc is proportional to the central angle:

$$\frac{60^0}{360^0} = \frac{\overparen{PQ}}{2\pi r}$$

$$\overparen{PQ} = \frac{6\pi}{6} = \pi$$

The perimeter of the shaded region is $3 + \pi$.

31) ▬▶ 31

Concept(s) Tested: Problem Solving, Algebra

Number of trips $= \frac{91\,gallons}{3\frac{gallons}{trip}} = 30.3\,trips$

The minimum number of trips is 31. There are 30 trips where the jar is filled, and the last trip, when the jar is filled to 1 gallon.

32) ▬▶ 64

Concept(s) Tested: Problem Solving, Algebra

The distance of the object from the mirror is 1.5 *feet*:

$L = 4\left(\frac{2}{1.5 - 2}\right)^2 = 4(-4)^2 = 64$

33) **➡ 12**

Concept(s) Tested: Algebra

$$\frac{5}{3}(x-3) = \frac{3}{2}(x-2)$$

$$\frac{5}{3}x - 5 = \frac{3}{2}x - 3$$

$$\frac{10x - 9x}{6} = 2$$

$$x = 12$$

34) **➡ $\frac{1}{3}$ or 0.33**

Concept(s) Tested: Problem Solving, Probability

Although the question asks about the probability of drawing two balls simultaneously, we get the same result if we think of drawing the balls one at a time.

For red balls:

$P(one\ red\ ball) = \frac{4}{12} = \frac{1}{3}$

$P(second\ red\ ball) = \frac{3}{11}$

$P(drawing\ two\ red\ balls) = \frac{1}{3} \cdot \frac{3}{11} = \frac{3}{33}$

For white balls: $P(one\ white\ ball) = \frac{8}{12} = \frac{2}{3}$

$P(second\ white\ ball) = \frac{7}{11}$

$P(drawing\ two\ red\ balls) = \frac{2}{3} \cdot \frac{7}{11} = \frac{14}{33}$

The difference in probabilities is: $\frac{14}{33} - \frac{3}{33} = \frac{11}{33} = \frac{1}{3}$

35) **➡ 25**

Concept(s) Tested: Problem Solving, Graphs and Functions

The heartrate is modeled as a linear function, with slope of the function representing the change in beats per minute and equal to 5. The increase in beats per five minutes of running is 25.

36) **➡ 30**

Concept(s) Tested: Problem Solving, Algebra

Let the distance that Peter has traveled when David catches up to him be x. The time it takes for David to catch Peter is:

$$\frac{x\ miles}{60\frac{miles}{hour}} = \frac{x+10}{80\frac{miles}{hour}}$$

$$80x = 60x + 600$$

$$20x = 600$$

$$x = 30\ miles$$

David will catch Peter at time t:

$$t = \frac{30\ miles}{60\frac{miles}{hour}} = \frac{1}{2}\ hour = 30\ minutes$$

37) **➡ 7.53**

Concept(s) Tested: Data Analysis, Ratios and Percentages

Men in workforce
= (0.5)(65.5 million) = 32.75 million

Men in Industry
= (0.23)(32.75 million) = 7.53 million

38) **➡ 0.06**

Concept(s) Tested: Ratios and Percentages

If 61% of the workforce is male, 39% of the workforce is female. Among females, 15% work in business:

P(woman in business) = (0.39)(0.15) ≈ 0.06

Reading Test

1. (D)	6. (A)	11. (D)	16. (B)	21. (D)	26. (C)	31. (A)	36. (D)	41. (C)	46. (C)	51. (C)
2. (A)	7. (B)	12. (B)	17. (D)	22. (B)	27. (B)	32. (D)	37. (C)	42. (B)	47. (C)	52. (A)
3. (B)	8. (C)	13. (A)	18. (A)	23. (D)	28. (B)	33. (B)	38. (C)	43. (C)	48. (D)	
4. (B)	9. (B)	14. (C)	19. (C)	24. (B)	29. (D)	34. (A)	39. (B)	44. (B)	49. (A)	
5. (A)	10. (C)	15. (B)	20. (A)	25. (C)	30. (A)	35. (A)	40. (A)	45. (D)	50. (C)	

1) ➡ D
Concept(s) Tested: Purpose
Choice (D) is correct because Nevyrazimov does not react with pleasure to the sounds of festivities and the spring air from outdoors, and in the following paragraph, the narrator implies that the sounds only make the room seem darker and dirtier in contrast. (A) is incorrect because the character's childhood does not factor into his thoughts at this point in the story. (B) is incorrect because, although the joyful noises outside do serve to distract Nevyrazimov, they in themselves do not explain the reasons for his "distracted demeanor." (C) is incorrect because there is no indication in the story that the festivities outside inspire Nezyrazimov to make any lifestyle changes; they merely deepen his negative feelings.

2) ➡ A
Concept(s) Tested: Words in Context
Choice (A) is correct because "tumult" precisely conveys the idea of a "chaos of sound" caused by excited crowds of people outside Nevyrazimov's window. (B) and (C) both refer to confusing disturbances and conflicts, thus they do not make sense in the context of festivities. (D) is incorrect because "turbulence" refers to violent or unsteady movement of air or water, or to violent confusion, so it does not fit with the context of the passage.

3) ➡ B
Concept(s) Tested: Attitude and Tone
The answer is (B) because, while the holiday seems to provoke the character to consider several ways that he might change his evening, and even his life, in the end, he has resigned himself to the fatalistic belief that none of these plans will work and that he is trapped by his circumstances. (A) is incorrect because the character never appears optimistic. For instance, when he considers stealing and running away to America, he rejects the entire idea because he has no idea where America is (lines 75 – 77). (C) is incorrect because the reader does not know enough to appraise the character as opportunistic or cunning; we learn nothing of his behavior in the past. Finally, (D) is incorrect because the passage begins with Nevyrazimov writing a formal but friendly letter to his employer, even though he has contempt for him. Therefore, the reader cannot consider the character to be honest and sincere.

4) ➡ B
Concept(s) Tested: Citation
Choice (B) is correct because, in these sentences, the character decides not to leave the office for the Easter festivities after all because he probably would not have a good time, and that even if he did, it would not change his life. This illustrates that he is discontented with his life and feels powerless to change it. (A) is incorrect because it indicates only a difficult relationship with his "Honored Sir, Father and Benefactor." (C) is incorrect because it indicates only the character's desire for a better life, but not his feelings that it is impossible for him to have one. Finally, (D) is incorrect because, though the act of killing the cockroach shows Nevyrazimov's bitterness and callousness, it does not clearly demonstrate a sense of resignation.

5) ➡ A

Concept(s) Tested: Words in Context

Choice (A) is correct in the context of the passage. It forms a phrase, "solemn festivities," which combines two words that appear to be opposite in meaning, unless "solemn" is taken in the sense of "serious" or "earnest." The phrase then has the meaning that the celebrants are sincere and serious, which is consistent with the descriptions in the passage. Choices (B), (C), and (D) are incorrect because they do not describe this sentiment.

6) ➡ A

Concept(s) Tested: Inference, Implication, and Suggestion

The correct choice is (A). In line 1, Nevyrazimov starts his letter with "Honored Sir, Father and Benefactor!"—all of which indicate that he is writing to a superior. Later the reader learns that Nevyrazimov has been trying to get a promotion from the man to whom he is writing, providing definitive evidence that the man is his boss (line 80 – 86). (B) is incorrect because it is unlikely that the character would call a friend by such titles, and there is no indication that he is trying to get a loan from the recipient. (C) is incorrect because Nevyrazimov begins writing greetings "to your family," indicating that the recipient is not related to him. Finally, (D) is incorrect because there are no indications that the recipient is corrupt or engages in criminal activity of any kind.

7) ➡ B

Concept(s) Tested: Inference, Implication, and Suggestion

The correct choice is (B) because it is ironic that Nevyrazimov addresses the man as "Honored Sir" in the letter, and then privately calls him a "rascal" (line 16). This inference is confirmed later in the story, when it is revealed that Nevyrazimov despises the man "with his whole soul" (lines 82 – 83). (A) is incorrect because, although Nevyrazimov dislikes the recipient, there is no direct indication of either generosity or greed on his part. (C) is incorrect because, although the letter is formal and serious, it is clear from the context of the entire passage that Nevyrazimov is not a high-spirited person, or in any way "flippant" or "jocular." Finally, (D) is incorrect because it appears that Nevyrazimov has respect for religious institutions, as he longs to take part in the religious festivities (lines 57 – 61).

8) ➡ C

Concept(s) Tested: Citation

The correct choice is (C) because it captures the irony of the letter, which is written with warmth in spite of the character's true feelings. (A) is incorrect because, while it includes the honorific titles the character is using to address his recipient, it does not indicate anything about his actual feelings. (B) is incorrect because although the character calls the recipient a "rascal" in this sentence, it does not reveal the extent of his negative feelings for him. (D) is incorrect because it does not concern the letter.

9) ➡ B

Concept(s) Tested: Organization, Attitude and Tone

Choice (B) is correct; in lines 22 – 28, the reader learns that Nevyrazimov feels sorry for the cockroach because it cannot leave the office, but in lines 90 – 93, Nevyrazimov calls it a "nasty thing" and throws it into the flame. (A) is incorrect because it is not true to say that the character ever felt protective of the cockroach. (C) is incorrect because, although the character does seem "unperturbed" by the cockroach, he does not become obsessed by it. (D) is incorrect because it is in the wrong order; it is correct to say that the character felt camaraderie and then disgust, but not the other way around.

10) ➡ C

Concept(s) Tested: Purpose, Inference, Implication, and Suggestion

Choice (C) is correct because the character's anger grows as he contemplates his "hopeless situation," a feeling which is mirrored by the cockroach wriggling its legs "in despair." (A) is incorrect because Nevyrazimov is concerned with his situation, not his office. (B) is incorrect because the passage does not portray Nevyrazimov's attitude toward anyone he might consider to have an inferior position. Finally, (D) is incorrect because the character appears to kill the cockroach out of anger, not due to optimism about making positive changes.

11) ➡ D

Concept(s) Tested: Purpose

Choice (D) is correct because the phrase is part of a longer sentence that begins, "It is said, and insisted upon by Mr. Attorney, that…" (lines 1 – 2) in which Hamilton lists the justifications put forth by the other side. Answer choices (A), (B), and (C) fail to correctly convey the meaning of Hamilton's long sentence.

12) ➡ B

Concept(s) Tested: Words in Context
The correct choice is (B) because, according to the prosecution's claims (in Hamilton's paraphrase), government cannot be effective if the "supreme magistrates" have their actions criticized—i.e., if they are admonished— "by private men." (A) is incorrect because "censor" has a different meaning than "censure." In this sentence, Hamilton is not referring to people censoring (suppressing) governmental actions, but rather, criticizing them. (C) is incorrect because evaluating is a private mental process, not necessarily an outward expression. Finally, (D) is incorrect because the paragraph does not discuss "sentencing" anyone for a crime; rather, its topic is the open criticism of the government.

13) ➡ A

Concept(s) Tested: Purpose
Choice (A) is correct because in paragraph 2 Hamilton says that leaders have historically used "specious pretenses," or tricky excuses, for totalitarian rule. (B) is incorrect because Hamilton is not discussing types of laws, but abuses of power. (C) is incorrect because it is not the primary, specific purpose of the phrase "specious pretenses." (D) is incorrect because Hamilton is not singling out British officials, but talking about leaders in general.

14) ➡ C

Concept(s) Tested: Organization
The correct choice is (C). In paragraph 1, Hamilton describes his opponent's view, namely that the people must respect authority. In paragraph 2, Hamilton responds to these charges, arguing that if people do not respect leaders' authority, it is due to the leaders themselves and their abuse of power, not because people are criticizing them. (A) is incorrect because in paragraph 2 Hamilton does not focus on issues of respect for himself or his client. (B) is incorrect because Hamilton does not concede any points in paragraph 2. (D) is incorrect because, although Hamilton does use an example from Roman history later in his speech, paragraph 2 does not introduce details or themes that directly relate to it.

15) ➡ B

Concept(s) Tested: Inference, Implication, and Suggestion
The correct choice is (B). In paragraph 3, Hamilton states that many people throughout history have lent a hand in destroying their own countries "for the sake of preferment or some imaginary honor," that is, for some benefit or favorable status. (A) is incorrect because those who have a hand in oppression may or may not value liberty, but act primarily out of their own self-interest. (C) is incorrect because Hamilton does not suggest that people who help tyrants expect them to restore freedoms. Finally, (D) is incorrect because Hamilton does not suggest that certain people want to destroy their countries. Instead, they want to secure certain advantages for themselves.

16) ➡ B

Concept(s) Tested: Citation
Choice (B) is correct because it provides direct support of the idea that people assist oppressive leaders out of self-interest. They help "for the sakes of preferment or some imaginary honor." (A), (C), and (D) are incorrect because none of them explains the probable motivations of the people who have "freely lent a helping hand" to oppressors (lines 33 – 34).

17) ➡ D

Concept(s) Tested: Inference, Implication, and Suggestion
The correct choice is (D). In lines 35 – 45, Hamilton quotes Brutus, a senator in ancient Rome, as he warns other senators that when they help set up the means of oppression, they should remember that they themselves will be among the oppressed. (A) and (B) are incorrect because Hamilton is speaking of enslavement or imprisonment metaphorically, not literally. Choice (C) is incorrect because Hamilton is using Caesar as an example for a specific point, not an extended comparison.

18) ➡ A

Concept(s) Tested: Purpose
The correct choice is (A). According to Hamilton, power is similar to beautiful and useful rivers that nevertheless occasionally overflow their banks; potential danger is always present. (B) is incorrect because the river metaphor does not imply that power is always destructive, only that it always

carries the potential to become destructive. (C) is incorrect because Hamilton's river metaphor is not a prediction about particular governments or people. (D) is incorrect because the imagery of a river creates a specific effect; it is not merely an indication of a larger context.

19) **═➤ C**

Concept(s) Tested: Words in Context

Choice (C) is correct. In lines 54 – 55, Hamilton urges listeners to "support liberty, the only bulwark against lawless power" in the sense that the only "wall" that protects against the abuse of power is liberty. (A) is incorrect because Hamilton is talking about containing and managing power, not attacking it with a weapon. (B) and (D) are incorrect because it does not make sense to say that liberty is a convincing argument; nor does it make sense to say that liberty is a stern warning. Liberty is an abstract concept, which cannot be described as a type of statement.

20) **═➤ A**

Concept(s) Tested: Purpose

The correct choice is (A); Hamilton focuses on the impact that jury members can have by laying a "noble foundation" for liberty, not just in their state, but throughout the colonies. (B) is incorrect because there is no indication that Hamilton wishes the jury members to speak out. (C) is incorrect because it can be assumed that all lawyers want to persuade all juries to vote unanimously in their favor, so that alone cannot explain Hamilton's action. Finally, (D) is incorrect because Hamilton is not clarifying details, and there is no indication that the case was confusing.

21) **═➤ D**

Concept(s) Tested: Citation

Choice (D) is correct because here Hamilton says that ruling in favor of his client will lay a foundation of liberty for "ourselves, our posterity, and our neighbors…" Specifically, the decision will secure the right to oppose and expose "arbitrary power…by speaking and writing truth." In other words, Hamilton is predicting that the case will make history as a victory for freedom of speech. (A), (B), and (C) are incorrect because they describe the importance of the case to the colonies, but not its historical significance.

22) **═➤ B**

Concept(s) Tested: Main Argument,

Organization

Choice (B) is correct because paragraph 1 and 2 (lines 1 – 28) describe a "healthcare-related issue" (our inability to store organ donations for long periods of time), and the rest of the passage describes an animal that can freeze its organs without damaging them, and implies that being able to apply this ability to organ transplants would be revolutionary (a "hypothetical solution"). Choice (A) is incorrect because the passage does not focus on the overall "quality of American healthcare," but rather on one specific healthcare issue. Moreover, the author's discussion of wood frogs does not mention "conservation efforts." Choice (C) is incorrect; although paragraphs 1 and 2 do provide some "healthcare-related statistics," these statistics support the main focus of organ donations—the statistics themselves are not the focus. Choice (D) is incorrect because paragraphs 1 and 2 reveal a healthcare-related issue, but the author does not imply that he is criticizing the issue, only that he is explaining it.

23) **═➤ D**

Concept(s) Tested: Purpose

Choice (D) is correct because in these lines, the author claims that freezing organs without damaging them could "revolutionize organ transplant," so we can conclude that he is praising the "impact" of a "theoretical scientific development." Choice (A) is incorrect because organ freezing is not yet possible, so it is not a "recent medical discovery." Choice (B) is incorrect because these lines do not mention or imply any "ethical dilemmas." Choice (C) is incorrect because these lines are making a comparison, not "providing an example."

24) **═➤ B**

Concept(s) Tested: Words in Context

Choice (B) is correct because, in the context of the sentence, "widespread" describes the damage done to cells as a result of freezing; thus, "extensive," which means "considerable," fits the context best, as lines 26 – 28 describe the extensiveness of the damage done by freezing. Choice (A) is incorrect because "predominant" means "primary" or "superior," neither of which fit the context of the sentence. Choice (C) is incorrect because "omnipresent" means "found everywhere" or "common," which is too broad to be applicable to the passage. Choice (D) is incorrect because "sweeping" usually describes something that is spread out over a broad area, which does not fit a conversation about cell damage.

25) C

Concept(s) Tested: Summary

Choice (C) is correct because it provides an accurate summary of lines 35 – 45, which explains the process that allows wood frogs to survive freezing and thawing. Choice (A) is incorrect because the passage states that wood frogs likely have a seasonal "difference in RNA expression" (line 60), but it does not indicate that wood frogs' DNA undergoes any seasonal changes. Choice (B) is incorrect because lines 38 – 39 explain that the glucose draws water out of wood frogs' cells, so it does not "provide nourishment" for the frogs. Choice (D) is incorrect because the passage does not indicate that wood frogs' RNA "can heal cells"; rather, wood frogs' RNA expression allows it to survive freezing in winter.

26) C

Concept(s) Tested: Inference, Implication, and Suggestion

Choice (C) is correct because paragraph 3 states that wood frogs release glucose into their system to pull "water out of the cells," which protects them from ice formation during a freeze. Since urea "also protects the cell's integrity," we can infer that urea also "pulls water out of the cells" to prevent "ice from forming within" them. Choice (A) is incorrect because the glucose and urea draw water out of cells, but the passage does not indicate that they improve a cell's durability. Choice (B) is incorrect because paragraph 3 states that wood frogs release urea into their bloodstream, which implies that urea is helpful, not "potentially harmful." Choice (D) is incorrect because the passage indicates that a change in RNA expression induces the release of certain chemicals, not that it "insulates the [wood frog's] cell."

27) B

Concept(s) Tested: Citation

Choice (B) is correct because it explains that glucose prevents ice from forming in wood frog cells, and it adds that the formation of ice within cells causes "irreparable damage," thus fully supporting the answer to the previous question. All other choices are incorrect

because they fail to associate the freezing of a cell with cellular damage.

28) B

Concept(s) Tested: Summary

Choice (B) is correct because it provides an effective summary of lines 60 – 64, and is therefore fully supported by the passage. Choice (A) is incorrect because paragraph 3 provides a thorough explanation of the roles of glucose and urea in wood frog preservation, disproving (A). Choices (C) and (D) are incorrect because they are entirely unsupported by the passage.

29) D

Concept(s) Tested: Words in Context

Choice (D) is correct because "novel" describes genes that perform specific functions and can only be detected using certain gene-sequencing methods. Thus, you can infer that, in the context of the sentence, "novel" means "previously unknown" and "specialized," which can be effectively summarized by the word "unique." All other choices are incorrect because, based on the passage, it is unclear what an "experimental," "unconventional," or "original" gene would be.

30) A

Concept(s) Tested: Summary

Choice (A) is correct because, in paragraph 5, the author explains that "having the genome of the wood frog" (so "sequencing the wood-frog genome") will allow scientists to study "epigenetic patterns. Choices (B) and (D) are incorrect because neither RNA nor methylation is mentioned in reference to the freezing or thawing process, and choice (C) is unsupported by the passage, which does not discuss DNA-analysis methods beyond sequencing.

31) A

Concept(s) Tested: Graph Synthesis

The graph shows that the amount of glucose and urea in a wood frog's body increases significantly in winter, and this information is effectively summarized in lines 35 – 38. Choice (B) is incorrect because it only describes the effects of an increase in urea, and it does not mention an increase in glucose, which is depicted in the graph. Choices (C) and (D) are unrelated to the graph and therefore incorrect.

32) ➡ D
Concept(s) Tested: Graph and Text Synthesis
Choice (D) is correct because lines 49 – 51 reveal that freezing wood frog in summer (when, we can infer from the graph, urea levels in the animal are low) will kill it. Thus, we can infer that urea helps preserve the frogs during their winter freezing. Choice (A) is unsupported by the passage and therefore incorrect. Choices (B) and (C) are incorrect because neither the graph nor the passage provides support for them.

33) ➡ B
Concept(s) Tested: Attitude and Tone
The correct choice is (B). By mentioning his wife, Nancy, and talking about the couple's emotional response to the explosion, Reagan is responding on a personal level and identifying with the feelings of many of the people who are watching the speech. (A) is incorrect because Reagan does not focus on the morbid details of the explosion. (C) is incorrect because the description "pained to the core" is not a tranquil, or calm, one. (D) is incorrect because Reagan's statement that he and his wife are feeling deep pain does not serve as an introduction to impassioned criticism of the system.

34) ➡ A
Concept(s) Tested: Purpose
Choice (A) is correct because Reagan's statements emphasize a sense of shared grief as a whole nation, not as a political group. (B) is incorrect because Reagan does not attempt to persuade viewers to feel sadness. Rather, his statements assume that the feeling already exists. (C) and (D) are incorrect because the short phrases describe a sense of grief and unity and do not address the larger ideas of the explosion's legacy.

35) ➡ A
Concept(s) Tested: Words in Context
Choice (A) is correct because as used here, "bear" implies carrying a heavy load, or (metaphorically) experiencing grief. (B), (C), and (D) are incorrect because they are different meanings for "bear," which do not make sense in the context of the sentence.

36) ➡ D
Concept(s) Tested: Inference, Implication, and Suggestion
Choice (D) is correct because the president calls the crew members "heroes" (line 17), saying that "they wished to serve, and they did. They served all of us" (lines 28 – 29). These statements imply the crew members' lives were meaningful to the whole nation and even the world. (A) is incorrect because Reagan does not mention anything about the cause of the explosion. Instead, the tone suggests that the nation is in shock ("Today is a day for mourning," lines 4 – 5), and that it is too early for explanations. (B) is incorrect because Reagan says the crew members did their jobs "brilliantly," and there is no indication that anyone is blaming or faulting them. (C) is incorrect because Reagan does not speak in a critical tone regarding the space shuttle program. In fact, in paragraph 5 (lines 47 – 63), Reagan vows to continue the shuttle program.

37) ➡ C
Concept(s) Tested: Citation
Choice (C) is correct because it provides the most direct evidence to support the suggestion that crew members' lives were meaningful because they served the public. (A) is incorrect because it does not focus on the lives of the crew members. Choice (B) is incorrect because, while Reagan calls the crew members "heroes," in this sentence he does not explain the significance of their lives. Finally, (D) is incorrect because it does not focus solely on the astronauts.

38) ➡ C
Concept(s) Tested: Graph and Text Synthesis
Choice (C) is correct. The chart shows that Challenger had six flights in 1983 and 1984, whereas all other shuttles had a combined three flights during the same period. Choices (A) and (B) are incorrect according to the information in the chart. (D) is incorrect because there is no information about safety issues in the chart.

39) ➡ B
Concept(s) Tested: Words in Context
Choice (B) is correct because when Reagan says that "We'll continue our quest in space," the context suggests an adventurous journey in *search* of something, like the Medieval knights' "quests" for the Holy Grail. (A) is incorrect because "inquiry" does not incorporate the sense of an ongoing journey. (C) is incorrect because a pilgrimage is a regular, usually religious, journey to a known location, unlike the exploration of space. (D) is incorrect because "pursuit" implies an attempt to catch or achieve a specified objective, which would not fit in a general statement about space exploration.

40) ➡ A

Concept(s) Tested: Inference, Implication, and Suggestion

Choice (A) is correct because in lines 55 – 59, Reagan explicitly states that the space shuttle program will continue. These statements make clear Reagan's stance on funding NASA's missions. (B) is incorrect because Reagan does not mention an investigation in the speech. (C) is incorrect because Reagan never implies that the accident was caused by enemies of democracy and freedom. Reagan's tone here is not accusatory. Finally, (D) is incorrect because Reagan seeks to reassure "every man and woman who works for NASA" (lines 60 – 64) that the nation has been moved and impressed by them "for decades," but this encouragement does not imply that the accident might cause them to quit their jobs.

41) ➡ C

Concept(s) Tested: Citation

Choice (C) is correct because it is the most comprehensive statement in which Reagan says that he wants NASA to continue in spite of the accident. (A) is incorrect because it is vague and does not directly refer to NASA. (B) is incorrect because it is a positive description of NASA's transparency but does not address its future. Finally, (D) is incorrect because it expresses sympathy to NASA employees, but like (B), it does not address the agency's future.

42) ➡ B

Concept(s) Tested: Purpose

Choice (B) is correct because Reagan implies that the space shuttle crew were like Sir Francis Drake: they explored the unknown frontiers of their time, right up until their deaths. (A) is incorrect because, even though the implication is that we still remember Drake after 390 years and that the shuttle crew will also be remembered, it is not the primary purpose of mentioning Drake. (C) is incorrect because Reagan's focus is the astronauts' lifelong dedication, not the dangers of risk-taking in general. Finally, (D) is incorrect because mention of Drake's sea explorations does not serve to clarify any difficult concepts.

43) ➡ C

Concept(s) Tested: Primary Purpose

Choice (C) is correct because the speech's main focus is on the crew's courage and dedication to discovery. One can infer that these words are meant to comfort viewers and to inspire viewers to follow the crew's example. (A) is incorrect because history is only mentioned at a few points in the speech. (B) is incorrect because Reagan's main audience is television viewers, and his remarks are mainly directed to them. Finally, (D) is incorrect because the speech is primarily about the admirable traits of the crew members, not space exploration.

44) ➡ B

Concept(s) Tested: Words in Context

The author points out that the public relies on meteorologists' "skill, knowledge, and expertise." Thus, "expertise" here indicates experience that surpasses skills and knowledge. (B) is the correct choice because "prowess" connotes a superior ability, which is similar to expertise. (A) and (D) are incorrect because both of these words simply suggest a quick reaction or physical skill, while (C) is incorrect because "aptitude" refers to natural ability, not mastery of a field of knowledge.

45) ➡ D

Concept(s) Tested: Organization

The paragraph quotes an employee of the National Weather Service explaining what types of information only radar can provide and what types trained storm spotters can provide. Thus, (D) correctly identifies the contrast described in the paragraph. Choice (A) is incorrect because it does not describe contrasting elements, and, like (B) and (C), it does not reflect the main point that the speaker makes in the quotation.

46) ➡ C

Concept(s) Tested: Summary

The introductory sentences in Passage 1 describe how the community relies on meteorologists, who in turn rely on community volunteers, to "keep us safe and in the know." Thus, the passage is mainly about contributions that improve weather forecasting, and (C) is correct. The passage does suggest that Skywarn provides the public with information and opportunities, but these are minor points, thus (A) and (B) are incorrect. (D) is incorrect because the passage focuses on making better predictions, not on preventing damage once a storm arrives.

47) ➡ C

Concept(s) Tested: Citation

Choice (C) is correct because the sentence fully articulates the passage's central claim: that "ground truth" provided by volunteers helps meteorologists predict storm activity. (A) and (B) are incorrect because, although they describe the Skywarn program, neither of them describes the program's ultimate value. (D) is incorrect because it describes basic characteristics of volunteer storm spotters, which does not convey the passage's central claim.

48) ➡ D

Concept(s) Tested: Inference, Implication, and Suggestion

Choice (D) is correct because Passage 1 describes professional forecasters' frequent reliance on amateur radio operators who "provide additional assistance during storms." The radio operators can "maintain communication" between forecasters and communities during large storms that "knock out phone service." These statements suggest that radio operations can occur even when telephones and the Internet are disabled, and thus (D) is correct. Meanwhile, there is no textual support for choices (A), (B), or (C).

49) ➡ A

Concept(s) Tested: Inference, Implication, and Suggestion

In Passage 2, the author describes the butterflies clustering in Mexico in winter. After the monarchs' winter of inactivity, they disperse all over the northern areas of the continent, where citizen scientists are called upon to study them. Thus, (A) is correct. The author does not state that citizen scientists should grow host plants, that they take the place of professional naturalists, or that they provide more reliable data than any other source. Therefore, (B), (C), and (D) are incorrect.

50) ➡ C

Concept(s) Tested: Citation

Choice (C) is correct because it states that citizen scientists participate when the monarchs migrate and reproduce throughout the United States and Canada. The reader can infer that citizen scientists are not needed to observe the population while it overwinters (and is inactive) in Mexico. Choices (A) and (B) are incorrect because they do not address the work of citizen scientists; (D) is incorrect because it does not indicate anything about when citizen scientists participate in data collection.

51) ➡ C

Concept(s) Tested: Multiple-Text Synthesis

The author of Passage 1 describes citizen scientists reporting from specific locations within areas covered by "satellites and Doppler radars." The author of Passage 2 describes citizen scientists contributing information from the monarch's "vast summer range." Thus, (C) is correct because both authors emphasize the practical effect of far-flung volunteers. (A) and (D) are incorrect because neither author addresses the quality of the data from volunteers, nor do they address the skills required within the fields that they discuss. (B) is incorrect because, while Passage 1 mentions required training, Passage 2 does not, so it is impossible to predict the author's attitude toward it.

52) ➡ A

Concept(s) Tested: Primary Purpose, Multiple-Text Synthesis

The answer is (A) because each passage primarily describes a particular case where non-scientists provide valuable assistance to scientists. Meanwhile, the tone of both passages is neutral, allowing readers to eliminate choices (B) and (C). Choice (D) is incorrect because in a precise sense neither passage's focus is on environmental issues, but rather on scientific research.

SAT Practice Test 5: Answers & Explanations

Writing and Language Test

1. Ⓓ	5. Ⓐ	9. Ⓒ	13. Ⓑ	17. Ⓒ	21. Ⓒ	25. Ⓑ	29. Ⓑ	33. Ⓑ	37. Ⓒ	41. Ⓑ
2. Ⓐ	6. Ⓓ	10. Ⓑ	14. Ⓐ	18. Ⓑ	22. Ⓑ	26. Ⓓ	30. Ⓒ	34. Ⓒ	38. Ⓐ	42. Ⓒ
3. Ⓒ	7. Ⓒ	11. Ⓓ	15. Ⓑ	19. Ⓓ	23. Ⓐ	27. Ⓒ	31. Ⓓ	35. Ⓓ	39. Ⓓ	43. Ⓐ
4. Ⓒ	8. Ⓑ	12. Ⓓ	16. Ⓐ	20. Ⓐ	24. Ⓑ	28. Ⓒ	32. Ⓒ	36. Ⓑ	40. Ⓑ	44. Ⓒ

1) **➡ D**
Concept(s) Tested: In-Sentence Punctuation
When starting a quotation within a sentence, the first letter of the sentence in quotes must be capitalized, and a comma must be placed immediately before the first quotation mark. The correct choice is (D) because all other choices fail to include one or both of these elements.

2) **➡ A**
Concept(s) Tested: Pronoun Use, Relative Clauses
Relative pronouns, such as who, which, where, and when, serve to link a noun to additional information about that noun. In the sentence containing 2, the noun "a person" is being linked to information about that person's job. The appropriate relative pronoun for referring to people is a form of "who." Therefore, choices (C) and (D) can be eliminated because they use relative pronouns that are used to refer to places (where) or things (that). Moreover, (B) is incorrect because "who's" is a contracted form of "who is," and plugging "who is" into the sentence makes it grammatically incorrect. Thus, (A) is the correct answer because the possessive relative pronoun "whose" accurately shows that "a person" is showing ownership over the "job" he or she performs.

3) **➡ C**
Concept(s) Tested: Pronoun Use
The pronoun at 3 refers to "a computer." This can be determined using the context of the sentence: it makes sense that a software developer tells "a computer that if a user does this, a computer must do that" in response. "A computer" is a singular noun, meaning we can eliminate (A) because "they" can only refer to plural nouns. Additionally, because "a computer" is a thing whereas the pronouns "one" and "someone" refer to people, (B) and (D) can be eliminated. Therefore, (C) is the correct answer.

4) **➡ C**
Concept(s) Tested: Passage Organization
Sentence 3 outlines the process by which a developer gives a computer a "series of instructions," and sentence 4 uses the term "code" (which is introduced in the added sentence) as if the term has already been introduced. Thus, the best place for the added sentence is after sentence 3 because it builds upon the topic of sentence 3 while defining a term used in sentence 4.

5) **➡ A**
Concept(s) Tested: Transition Words and Phrases
The paragraph containing the underlined portion is primarily talking about specializations that developers can pursue other than applications, which was discussed in the previous paragraph. Therefore, this paragraph is adding information on the same topic, making (A) the most appropriate choice. (B) is incorrect because it suggests that the topics of paragraphs 2 and 3 contrast with each other, which is not the case. (C) can be eliminated because "As a result" implies a cause-and-effect relationship, yet paragraphs 2 and 3 simply provide examples of developer career specializations. (D) is incorrect because "As with" suggests a comparison, which does not make sense in the context.

6) **➡ D**
Concept(s) Tested: Precise Diction
Choice (D) is correct. In the current and previous sentences, the passage states that software developers must solve problems, and that they do so by working on code until they "obtain the desired result." This process suggests trial-and-error and is best described as "adjusting." Choice (A) is incorrect because "to ameliorate" means to make a negative situation better, whereas making adjustments to code is described as a normal part of software development. Choice (C) is

incorrect for a similar reason: "to enhance" is to add to something or otherwise increase it, whereas the process being described here involves small changes, and not necessarily additions. Choice (B) is incorrect because "to renovate" is used in the context of physical structures such as buildings.

7) ➡ C

Concept(s) Tested: Passage Development

The question asks for "a different type of private company." Choice (C) is correct because electronics manufacturers are different from software publishers and financial institutions, so the term provides the most contrast for the list. (A) is incorrect because a "local government" is not a private employer. It refers to a city or county. (B) is incorrect because the author already mentions financial institutions, which by definition would include banks. Finally, (D) is incorrect because a police department is a public agency.

8) ➡ B

Concept(s) Tested: Passage Organization

Sentence 5 discusses the hours that are a minimum for most software developers. Since sentence 2 makes a claim about overtime, it is logical that sentence 5 should be placed before it, so (B) is correct. (A), (C), and (D) are incorrect because they do not result in an organized and logical flow of ideas.

9) ➡ C

Concept(s) Tested: Logical Comparison

When forming a comparison between two things, you must ensure that you are comparing two of the same type of thing. Thus, (A) is incorrect because it compares the responsibility of software engineers to developers. To form a logical comparison, we must ensure that the responsibility of software engineers is being compared to the responsibility of developers. Although no choice makes this comparison directly, (C) does an acceptable job by claiming that software engineers have more *responsibility* than software *developers* do. Here, the word "do" serves as a substitute for what the developers have (in this case, responsibility). Like (A), choices (B) and (D) incorrectly compare responsibility to software developers.

10) ➡ B

Concept(s) Tested: Graph Analysis

Choice (A) is incorrect because the passage states that there are over 1 million software developers in the U.S. Since there are only about 200,000 working in California, Washington, and Texas, it is inaccurate to claim that the majority (more than 50 percent) come from these three states. The correct choice

is (B) because 10 percent of 1 million is 100,000, and just over 100,000 software developers work in California. (C) is incorrect because, based on the graph, approximately 42,000 software developers work in Texas and Washington, and just under 40,000 work in New Jersey. Thus, at least 120,000 software developers work in these three states, more than the approximately 105,000 who work in California. (D) can be eliminated because the graph shows the number of software developers, not the rate of growth by state. Thus, even if (D) were true, it would be impossible to determine based on the graph.

11) ➡ D

Concept(s) Tested: Concision

The correct choice will concisely summarize why strong job growth is predicted for software developers. All choices provide valid reasons for this job growth, but only (D) does so concisely. Other choices convey the same information as (D) but use more words and convoluted phrasing.

12) ➡ D

Concept(s) Tested: Concision

Choices (A) and (C) can be eliminated because they are wordy and convoluted. (D) is the correct choice because it specifies that the passage's focus is the human digestive system. Because the digestive systems of other organisms may function differently, choice (B) is too general to be the correct choice.

13) ➡ B

Concept(s) Tested: Syntax, Concision

Choice (A) is incorrect because the verb "fail" is generally followed by an infinitive verb (e.g. "to concentrate") and not a participle, as is the case in (A). (C) and (D) can be eliminated because they convey the same meaning as (B), but are less concise. Thus, (B) is correct because it is the most concise, grammatically correct choice.

14) ➡ A

Concept(s) Tested: Passage Development

The paragraph primarily talks about what happens in the stomach shortly after a person stops eating. One of the main effects, explained in detail throughout the paragraph, is that the stomach begins to produce loud noises. Choice (A) is correct because it introduces the topic of stomach noises by mentioning the idiom of "growling" stomachs. Choice (B) focuses on the consumption of "big meals," which distracts from the passage's focus on starvation. (C) is incorrect because it introduces the processes of breaking down food, whereas the focus of the paragraph is the stomach's response to a lack of food. And (D) is incorrect because, although the passage briefly mentions a hormone called ghrelin, this hormone is by no means the main focus of the paragraph.

15) ➡ B
Concept(s) Tested: Syntax, Verb Tense
Because the passage describes the process of starvation in humans, it is written in the present tense (the present tense is usually preferred for general processes). Thus, choice (B) is correct because it maintains the passage's use of the present tense with the verb "depletes." (B) is also the most concise choice, further solidifying its position as the correct choice. (A) is incorrect because it uses the past-tense form "used" in an otherwise present-tense sentence. Similarly, (C) is written in the past-perfect tense, breaking the passage's pattern of using present-tense verbs. Finally, (D) can be eliminated because it unnecessarily uses the passive voice ("becomes used up"), and it uses too many phrases, making it wordy.

16) ➡ A
Concept(s) Tested: Parallel Structure
The verb "forced" is generally followed by an infinitive verb. For this reason, we can eliminate choices (C) and (D); after all, one would not say, "the liver is forced breaking down protein." When choosing between (A) and (B), we can determine that (A) is correct because (B) does not maintain parallel structure. The sentence must maintain the infinitive-verb word pattern established by "to break." (A) maintains parallel structure when it claims, "the liver is forced to break…and convert."

17) ➡ C
Concept(s) Tested: Parallel Structure
A proper list will separate each item in the list using a comma (or a semicolon in the case of complex lists), and it will include either "and" or "or" between the last two items in the list. The correct choice is (C) because it fulfills both of the aforementioned requirements. (A), (B), and (D) are incorrect because they incorporate too many conjunctions ("ands" and "ors"), which muddies the meaning of the sentence. If the author wanted to say that hunger causes one to become either restless and sad *or* irritable, (A) could be correct, but there is no indication that doing so was the author's intention.

18) ➡ B
Concept(s) Tested: Pronoun Use
The pronoun in the underlined portion at 18 is referring back to "a hungry person" mentioned in the previous sentence. Because "a hungry person" is a singular noun phrase that refers to a particular (though theoretical) individual, the correct answer must be (B). (A) and (D) are incorrect because "them" and "us" refer to more than one person or thing. (C) can be eliminated because "one" refers to an individual in general. Because we are referring to a specific person, the singular "him or her" is preferable.

19) ➡ D
Concept(s) Tested: Parallel Structure
Choice (D) is correct because it maintains parallel structure within the list of nouns, increasing clarity and concision. (A), (B), and (C) are incorrect because each of them includes the phrase "feelings of" at some point, making the list inconsistent and awkward. Moreover, (B) indicates that low blood pressure and dehydration are feelings, whereas more precisely, they are physical conditions.

20) ➡ A
Concept(s) Tested: Passage Development
The paragraph's introduction reveals that the focus of the paragraph is the "increasingly severe" symptoms of starvation. Because the underlined portion reveals that one symptom is becoming "quiet and withdrawn," we can determine that the sentence includes valuable information that adds to the paragraph's focus. Thus, (A) is the correct answer. Although the underlined sentence itself focuses on sociability, this is not the paragraph's primary focus, so (B) is incorrect. (C) is incorrect because the underlined sentence focuses, rather than blurs the focus, on mental symptoms, and (D) can be eliminated because reserving energy is not the focus of the paragraph, so there is no need for the underlined sentence to provide detailed information on this topic.

21) ➡ C
Concept(s) Tested: Precise Diction
To regain something is to get it back, and "regain" can apply to physical objects or mental processes. Thus, (C) fits in the context of the sentence and is the correct choice. Because the underlined verb refers to mental health, which is not something that can be physically manipulated, (A) is incorrect. Similarly, to regrow something is generally a physical process, making (B) incorrect. To revise is to review or change something that was created, such as a document, statement, or work of art. Because mental health is not created in this sense, (D) is incorrect.

22) ➡ B
Concept(s) Tested: Passage Organization
Paragraph 2 discusses how the brain triggers the release of hormones that stimulate a person's appetite. Because paragraph 4 begins by saying "Besides stimulating appetite," we can infer that it should follow the information in paragraph 2, which discusses the brain's role in increasing appetite. Thus, (B) is the correct choice.

23) ➡ A
Concept(s) Tested: Syntax, Voice
Although each choice is technically grammatically correct, only (A) conveys the intended meaning clearly using the active voice. Because "medical doctors" perform the action of the clause (they "prescribe"), "medical doctors" should come first in the sentence. Because (C) and (D) move the subject to the end of the clause, they can be eliminated. (B) is incorrect because it is unclear whether "only" modifies "doctors" or what doctors are able to prescribe.

24) ➡ B
Concept(s) Tested: Precise Diction
The underlined portion should convey the idea that some people with mental health issues were tied down. To "constrain" generally means to limit options, not to physically hold down. So although "constrain" is close in meaning, (A) is incorrect. To "restrain" is to physically hold in place, making (B) the correct choice. To "repress" is to psychologically block or suppress something, so (C) fails to convey the physical action suggested by the context of the sentence. (D) is incorrect because to "retain" is to keep, which would not make sense in the context.

25) ➡ B
Concept(s) Tested: Passage Development
The underlined portion of the paragraph is important because it notes a relevant aspect of Freud's psychotherapy: symptoms of distress were often due to traumatic experiences. This fact in turn shaped how Freud spoke with his patients to analyze and understand the source of their distress. Thus, (B) is the correct answer. (A) is incorrect because the paragraph does not focus specifically on childhood trauma, but instead focuses on Freud's attitude that mental illness could be treated. (C) is incorrect because the paragraph does not focus on psychological distress and does not claim that it is innate. Rather, it focuses on Freud's insights about its causes and treatment. Finally, (D) is incorrect because the paragraph does not confuse any concepts. It clearly notes that Freud believed that symptoms of distress often resulted from prior trauma.

26) ➡ D
Concept(s) Tested: Possession
Choice (D) is correct because, in this case, it is unnecessary for the noun "patients" to show ownership, or possession, over "talk." Thus, any answer with an apostrophe in patients is incorrect.

27) ➡ C
Concept(s) Tested: Passage Development
An appropriate concluding sentence for the paragraph would explain why his "basic approach was revolutionary." Thus, (C) is the correct answer. (A) is incorrect because it provides no information about Freud's significance. (B) is incorrect because it changes the focus to Freud's theories about stages of development rather than his "revolutionary" approach. Finally, (D) is incorrect because it mentions only Freud's "ideas," without specifying which ideas changed attitudes toward the mentally ill. In contrast, (C) briefly articulates how Freud's approach revolutionized psychotherapy.

28) ➡ C
Concept(s) Tested: Logical Comparison
When making a comparison, the things being compared must be of the same type. In other words, you must compare a person to another person or a concept to another concept. Because choices (A) and (B) compare psychological therapy (a practice) to Freud (a person), they are illogical comparisons and therefore incorrect. (D) fails to make a comparison at all because it excludes the word "more," which serves as a common marker that a comparison is being made. (C) is the correct answer because, although it does not explicitly say "Freud's *psychological therapy* was," such a meaning is implicit.

29) ➡ B
Concept(s) Tested: Concision, Syntax
Although each choice conveys approximately the same meaning, only (B) does so clearly and concisely, making it the correct choice. (A) is too wordy, as "being swept off our feet by a strong current" includes no more information than "being swept up by a strong current." (C) and (D) are also less concise than (B), and both of these choices include convoluted phrasing.

30) ➡ C
Concept(s) Tested: Passage Development
The paragraph beginning at line 30 gives specific examples of how behavioral therapists change patients' behaviors through teaching. Only answer

choice (C) focuses on teaching and learning, so it is the correct choice. (A) is vague and not supported by the examples that follow. (B) is incorrect because its focus is too narrow and specific. The paragraph does not focus only on children, nor does it focus on only positive reinforcement. Finally, (D) is incorrect because it merely repeats a sentence from the preceding paragraph. Moreover, the focus of the paragraph is not precisely on how behavior is the result of positive or negative consequences but how behavior can be learned or unlearned.

31) ➡️ D

Concept(s) Tested: Style and Tone, Sentence Boundaries

The correct choice is (D) because it follows the active subject-predicate construction established as a pattern in the paragraph. (A) lacks a subject and uses an infinitive verb where a verb with tense would be more appropriate. (B) is unclear, as it does not clarify for whom or why "a deeper pool would work." (C) can be eliminated because it excludes the subject, leaving the reader wondering who, exactly, would go into a deeper pool.

32) ➡️ C

Concept(s) Tested: Pronoun Use

The sentence containing 32 does not specify who "focuses on relearning thought habits." Thus, the use of a pronoun at the underlined portion is unnecessary—it has no one to refer to. (C) is the correct answer because all other choices incorrectly use a personal pronoun or pronouns. The use of "you" and "your," when referring to a general audience, is more common in casual spoken English, but it is not appropriate in most formal writing.

33) ➡️ B

Concept(s) Tested: In-Sentence Punctuation

The information after the underlined portion at 33 describes a consequence of regarding small problems as catastrophes. Since this consequence is essential to the coherence of the sentence, no punctuation is necessary after the word "catastrophes," making (B) the correct choice. Other choices introduce an unnecessary break in the sentence and are therefore incorrect.

34) ➡️ C

Concept(s) Tested: Concision, Sentence Boundaries

Because the passage is written in a fairly neutral, academic tone, choice (A) can be eliminated.

Generally, academic written English does not include direct addresses to the audience. (B) is incorrect because it does not provide enough information. It fails to tell the reader what is "usual" about Santa Claus. (C) is the correct answer because it is consistent with the academic tone of the passage, and it provides a sufficient amount of information. From (C), we can determine that Saint Nicholas is commonly called Santa Claus. (D) is incorrect because it contains a redundancy. If something is described as international, it goes without saying that it applies "around the world."

35) ➡️ D

Concept(s) Tested: Precise Diction

Based on the context of the sentence, Santa Claus is a symbol, or representation, "of altruism and kindness," so the correct choice will be the one that most closely means "a symbol." (A) is incorrect because a signal generally refers to a gesture or cue that is used to convey instructions, which does not make sense in the context. (B) is incorrect because a sign is either a physical marker or supernatural indication; Santa Claus is a fictional person, not a marker or indication. (C) can be eliminated because a mark is a physical indication, which does not apply to Santa Claus. (D) is the correct answer because an "emblem" is often a person or thing that represents an idea, which applies to Santa Claus in the context of the sentence.

36) ➡️ B

Concept(s) Tested: In-Sentence Punctuation

In the underlined phrase, "something much more menacing than Santa Claus" is the subject and "visits" is the verb; subjects should not be separated from their main verbs by commas. Because (B) is the only choice that avoids excessive comma usage, it is the correct choice.

37) ➡️ C

Concept(s) Tested: In-Sentence Punctuation, Sentence Modifiers

As written, the clauses to either side of the semicolon are independent clauses. Moreover, the clauses to either side of the semicolon should maintain parallel structure by containing similar grammatical structures. Because choice (C), "poorly behaved children," maintains the same word order as "well-behaved children," and because a semicolon can separate two related independent clauses, (C) is correct. (A) does not maintain parallel structure, as "children who have behaved poorly" is structured differently than the preceding phrase "well-behaved children," and it is less concise than choice (C). (B) is incorrect because a comma cannot separate two independent clauses unless the comma is followed by a coordinating conjunction. And (D) can be eliminated because the word "poor" must modify the adjective "behaved," and therefore should be an adverb, "poorly."

38) ➡ **A**
Concept(s) Tested: Verb Tense
Actions that are separated by a coordinating conjunction ("and" in this case) must maintain parallel structure. Because the participle "tossing" is used first, we must ensure that the participle "hauling" comes after the conjunction, so (A) is correct. Other choices fail to maintain parallel structure by using present-tense verbs, as in the case of (A), or past-tense verbs/participles, as in the case of (C) and (D).

39) ➡ **D**
Concept(s) Tested: Passage Development
The paragraph just prior to 39 notes the tradition of the Krampus in Germany, Austria, and Hungary. The paragraph beginning at 39 also notes that today cities and towns host "Krampus Runs." Thus, an appropriate transition should focus on Krampus traditions in European culture. Only (D) does this. (A) is incorrect because the paragraph beginning at 39 does not focus on the historical lineage of Krampus-inspired Christmas traditions. It instead focuses on Krampus traditions in the present. (B) is incorrect because it wrongly focuses on the time of the month that Germanic cultures celebrate Christmas. Though the paragraph does mention December 5 as Krampus night, the entire paragraph does not focus on the date. Finally, (C) is incorrect because neither the paragraph prior to 39, nor the one beginning at 39, speak of the Krampus's physical characteristics.

40) ➡ **B**
Concept(s) Tested: Passage Development
The information at 40 provides relevant information about the origins of the Krampus. Specifically, it provides an example of the previous statement that the Krampus comes from pagan mythology. Thus, it should be kept, and (B) is the correct answer. (A) is incorrect because the main topic of the paragraph is not Norse mythology, but rather the pagan origins of the Krampus and its appropriation by Christianity. (C) is incorrect because the paragraph is not focused on modern Christian traditions, but instead on the origins of the Krampus. Finally, (D) is incorrect because the sentence at 40 does not contradict the information in the previous sentence. It instead provides information that adds detail to

the previous sentence.

41) ➡ **B**
Concept(s) Tested: Pronoun Use
Choice (B) is correct because "it" can stand for the subject of the sentence, "Christianity," which is a singular noun. Choices (A) and (D) are incorrect because "they" and "these" are plural pronouns. Moreover, (C) is incorrect because "this" is a demonstrative pronoun, and demonstrative pronouns are used to "point" toward a certain noun to give that noun emphasis or to avoid confusion, which is not necessary here.

42) ➡ **C**
Concept(s) Tested: Precise Diction
The verb at 42 must convey the idea that many people think the rise in the Krampus' popularity *is caused by* the rise of Christmas "counterculture." In other words, they *attribute* the surge to the rise of a Christmas "counterculture," and (C) is correct. (A) is incorrect because "to attain" is to achieve, which does not convey the same meaning as "caused." (B) and (D) are incorrect because they do not make sense in the context of the sentence. "To equate" is to associate or compare two or more things, and "to impart" is to inform or tell.

43) ➡ **A**
Concept(s) Tested: Transition Words and Phrases
The correct answer will properly communicate the relationship between the sentence preceding 43 and the sentence containing it. The sentence containing 43 is reconfirming the statements made in the preceding sentence. When used as a transition, "After all" often indicates that a summary of or an elaboration on previous information will follow, so (A) is the most appropriate choice. (B) is incorrect because "thus" implies that one thing is a consequence of another, which is not the case here. "Finally" usually introduces a new, concluding idea. Because the information in the sentence containing 43 does not introduce a new idea, (C) is incorrect. (D) can be eliminated because "however" implies contrast, which does not occur here.

44) ➡ **C**
Concept(s) Tested: End-of-Sentence Punctuation
Generally, a sentence that begin with an interrogative (question words such as "what," "why," and "where") is a question and therefore must end with a question mark. The sentence containing 44 asks a question, making (C) the correct answer.

SAT Practice Test 5: Answers & Explanations

 Math Test

☑ **No Calculator Portion**

1. Ⓓ	7. Ⓓ	13. Ⓑ	19. 37	
2. Ⓐ	8. Ⓑ	14. Ⓐ	20. 6	
3. Ⓒ	9. Ⓑ	15. Ⓐ	.	
4. Ⓐ	10. Ⓑ	16. 3		
5. Ⓒ	11. Ⓐ	17. 3		
6. Ⓓ	12. Ⓓ	18. 8		

☑ **Calculator Portion**

1. Ⓒ	7. Ⓐ	13. Ⓒ	19. Ⓑ	25. Ⓓ	31. 3	37. 2,813
2. Ⓓ	8. Ⓑ	14. Ⓒ	20. Ⓐ	26. Ⓓ	32. 50	38. 4
3. Ⓓ	9. Ⓒ	15. Ⓑ	21. Ⓓ	27. Ⓑ	33. 67	
4. Ⓐ	10. Ⓑ	16. Ⓓ	22. Ⓒ	28. Ⓒ	34. 144	
5. Ⓑ	11. Ⓑ	17. Ⓒ	23. Ⓓ	29. Ⓐ	35. 22	
6. Ⓒ	12. Ⓑ	18. Ⓒ	24. Ⓒ	30. Ⓑ	36. 130	

No Calculator Portion

1) ⟹ D

Concept(s) Tested: Problem Solving, Ratios and Percentages

Students that did not select macaroni or breakfast sandwich

$$= 260 - \left(\frac{1}{5}\right)260 - (0.15)260 = 169$$

2) ⟹ A

Concept(s) Tested: Graphs and Functions

The graphs of functions $f(x)$ and $-f(x)$ are reflections of each other across the x-axis. The graph of function $g(x) = -x^2$ is the vertical reflection of the graph of function $f(x) = x^2$.

3) ⟹ C

Concept(s) Tested: Problem Solving, Algebra

The caller is charged for 13 minutes:
First minute = 0.40
12 minutes = 0.20 per minute
Cost = 0.40 + 12(0.20) = 2.80

4) ⟹ A

Concept(s) Tested: Problem Solving, Graphs and Functions

To verify I:
Calories = (13.2)(22) + 20.5 ≈ 311
I is true. The slope of the linear function is positive, so the relationship between calories and minutes is directly proportional, and II is not true.

5) ⟹ C

Concept(s) Tested: Algebra

$$S = \frac{11(n-2)}{5} \rightarrow n = \frac{5S}{11} + 2$$

6) ⟹ D

Concept(s) Tested: Graphs and Functions

The line $x = 3$ represents all points in the xy-plane at which the value of x is 3. This is a vertical line (parallel to the y-axis).

7) ⟹ D

Concept(s) Tested: Algebra

Solve for x:

$$x + 1 = \frac{20}{x} \rightarrow x^2 + x = 20 \rightarrow x^2 + x - 20 = 0$$

$$\rightarrow (x + 5)(x - 4) = 0 \rightarrow x = -5, 4$$

Both solutions satisfy the equation.

8) ➡ B

Concept(s) Tested: Graphs and Functions

The y-intercept is the point $(0, 4)$. For the line to pass through quadrant IV, it must slope downwards when $x > 0$. This implies that the slope, m, must be negative.

9) ➡ B

Concept(s) Tested: Graphs and Functions

For the function $f(x)$, $f(2) = 4$. This implies that $f(x + 3) = 4$ when $x = -1$. We can conclude that the point $(-1, 4)$ is on the graph of $f(x + 3)$.

10) ➡ B

Concept(s) Tested: Graphs and Functions

$$\frac{f(x + h) - f(x)}{h} = \frac{2(x + h) + 1 - (2x + 1)}{h}$$

$$= \frac{2x + 2h + 1 - 2x - 1}{h}$$

$$= \frac{2h}{h} = 2$$

11) ➡ A

Concept(s) Tested: Geometry

Let x be the length of the rectangle:

Width $= \left(\dfrac{3}{4}\right)x$

Area $= (x)\left(\dfrac{3}{4}x\right) \to \dfrac{3x^2}{4} = 192 \to x^2 = 256 \to x = 16$

Calculate width: $\left(\dfrac{3}{4}\right)(16) = 12$

12) ➡ D

Concept(s) Tested: Graphs and Functions

We can rewrite the function as: $f(x) = (x - 2) \times \dfrac{1}{(2 - x)}$

$$f(x) = \frac{x - 2}{2 - x} = \frac{x - 2}{-1(x - 2)} = -1 \text{ for } x \neq 2$$

As $f(2)$ is not included in any of the Roman numerals, all values of the function listed are equal to each other and to -1.

13) ➡ B

Concept(s) Tested: Algebra, Functions and graphs

Start by plugging in the known values of $f(x)$ and x to find the value of z:

$$18 = z(-4)^2 - 4z \to 18 = 16z - 4z \to 18 - 12z \to z = \frac{3}{2}$$

Given the value of z, plug in $x = 0$ and solve for $f(0)$

$$f(0) = \frac{3}{2}(0)^2 - 4\left(\frac{3}{2}\right)$$

$$f(0) = 0 - 6 \to f(0) = -6$$

Thus, the correct choice is (B).

14) ➡ A

Concept(s) Tested: Problem Solving

Let x be the number of cars and SUVs, and y be the number of trucks. Since he worked 48 hours:

$2x + 4y = 48$

As it takes 2 hours to service a car and 4 hours to service an SUV:

$2(14x) + 4(36y) = 1288 \to 28x + 144y = 1288$

15) ➡ A

Concept(s) Tested: Trigonometry

For all acute angles (angles between $0°$ and $90°$), the sine of the angle is equal to the cosine of the complementary angle.

16) ➡ 3

Concept(s) Tested: Problem Solving, Probability

Let r be the number of red marbles, g be the number of green marbles, and b be the number of blue marbles. Thus, $r + g + b = 27$.

Using the information in the question, we can determine that: $b = 2r$ and $g = 3b$

And using substitution, we get $g = 3(2r)$.
Now that g and b have been substituted for a form of r, solve for r:

$r + 2r + 3(2r) = 27 \to 9r = 27 \to r = 3$

17) ➡ 3

Concept(s) Tested: Algebra

Start by cross-multiplying:

$$\frac{135}{z^2} = \frac{450}{10z}$$

$$450z^2 = 1,350z$$

Then simplify for z:

$$z^2 = \frac{1,350z}{450} \rightarrow z^2 = 3z \rightarrow z = 3$$

18) ➡ 8

Concept(s) Tested: Algebra

$$\frac{16}{5} = a + \frac{1}{b + \dfrac{1}{c}}$$

$$16 = 5a + \frac{5}{b + \dfrac{1}{c}}$$

The fraction on the right side of the equation will

be easy to manage if it can be set equal to 1. This

can be accomplished if $a = 3$. Thus, $\dfrac{5}{b + \dfrac{1}{c}} = 1$.

By inspection, this equation is satisfied if $b = 4$ and
$c = 1$. Therefore, $a + b + c = 8$

19) ➡ 37

Concept(s) Tested: Algebra

Set up and complete the long division:

$$\begin{array}{r}
3x^3 - 6x^2 + 10x - 20 \\
x + 2 \overline{) 3x^4 + 0x^3 - 2x^2 + 0x - 3} \\
-) 3x^4 + 6x^3 \\
\hline
-6x^3 - 2x^2 \\
-) -6x^3 - 12x^2 \\
\hline
10x^2 + 0x \\
-) 10x^2 + 20x \\
\hline
-20x - 3 \\
-) -20x - 40 \\
\hline
37
\end{array}$$

We can write the quotient as:

$$\frac{3x^4 - 2x^2 - 3}{x + 2} = 3x^2 - 6x^2 + 10x - 20 + \frac{37}{x + 2}$$

20) ➡ 6

Concept(s) Tested: Geometry

As both the area and the arc length of the segment
are proportional to central angle, we can set these
proportions equal to each other:

$$\frac{6\pi}{\pi r^2} = \frac{2\pi}{2\pi r} \rightarrow r = 6$$

Calculator Portion

1) ➡ C

Concept(s) Tested: Graphs and Functions

Convert the equation of the line into the slope-
intercept form $y = mx + b$:

$$2x - 5y = 10$$
$$2x - 10 = 5y$$
$$\frac{2}{5}x - 2 = y$$

Therefore, $m = \dfrac{2}{5}$

2) ➡ D

**Concept(s) Tested: Problem Solving, Unit
Conversion**

$$\frac{2 \times 10^{-5}\, mg}{mL} = \frac{x}{3 \times 10^8\, mL}$$

$$x = \frac{\left(2 \times 10^{-5}\, mg\right)\left(3 \times 10^8\, mL\right)}{mL}$$

$$x = 6 \times 10^3 mg$$

3) ➡ D

Concept(s) Tested: Problem Solving, Algebra

Let x be the distance in miles from Town A to
Town B, and y be the 'scheduled' time it takes, in
hours, to travel the distance x. When traveling 50
miles per hour:
When traveling at 80 miles per hour:

$$\frac{x}{50\, miles/hour} = y + \frac{1}{3}\, hour$$

Solve for y:

$$\frac{x}{80\, miles/hour} = y - \frac{1}{6}\, hour$$

$$30y = \frac{180}{6}$$

$$y = 1$$

Solve for x: $x = 50 + \frac{50}{3} = \frac{200}{3}$ miles

At 60 miles per hour, the time it takes to travel x is:

$$\frac{\left(\frac{200}{3} \text{ miles}\right)}{\left(60 \frac{miles}{hour}\right)} = \frac{200}{180} \text{ hours} = 1\frac{1}{9} \text{ hours}$$

Thus, the train is hours late when traveling at 60 miles per hour. In minutes:

$$\left(\frac{1}{9} \text{ hour}\right)\left(\frac{60 \text{ minutes}}{hour}\right) = \frac{20}{3} \text{ minutes}$$

4) ➡ A

Concept(s) Tested: Problem Solving, Data Analysis

The amount in Tom's bank account can be modeled as the following exponential function, where t is number of years that have passed since the initial deposit:

Amount in Tom's account $= 100(1.05)^t$

The amount in Christine's bank account is modeled as a linear function, as the amount increases by the same amount each year:

Amount in Christine's account $= 100 + 5t$

5) ➡ B

Concept(s) Tested: Problem Solving

If x is the number of dimes, then the number of nickels is $x + 4$. The total amount in terms of coins can be written as:

$$0.10x + 0.05(x + 4) = 1.25$$

6) ➡ C

Concept(s) Tested: Graphs and Functions

A solution to a system of equations must satisfy all equations. Only (6, 3) satisfies both equations.

7) ➡ A

Concept(s) Tested: Data Analysis

Each score is 73 points higher than the previous score. The first time Tim plays the game, which corresponds to $n = 1$, he achieves a score of 4526. This is expressed in choice (A):

Points $= 73n + 4{,}453$

8) ➡ B

Concept(s) Tested: Problem Solving, Algebra

Let r be the number of minutes spent running, and s be the number of minutes spent walking: $r + s = 60$
Calories burned are $15r + 10s = 700$
Multiply the first equation above by 10, and subtract from the second equation:

$$\begin{array}{r} 15r + 10s = 700 \\ -)10r + 10s = 600 \\ \hline 5r = 100 \\ r = 20 \end{array}$$

9) ➡ C

Concept(s) Tested: Problem Solving, Algebra

Whale population =

$$\left(\frac{3 \text{ whales}}{hour}\right)\left(\frac{(24)(7)hours}{week}\right)(8 \text{ weeks})$$
$$= (3)(24)(7)(8) \approx 4{,}000$$

10) ➡ B

Concept(s) Tested: Problem Solving, Data Analysis

If x is the cost of the meal, the tip is:

$0.08x \le tip \le 0.20x$
For $x = 15$,
$1.2 \le tip \le 3.0$

11) ➡ B

Concept(s) Tested: Data Analysis, Measures of Center and Spread

There are three sections in U.S. History: sections A, B, and C. The average number of students is:

$$Average = \frac{25 + 29 + 24}{3} = 26$$

12) ➡ B

Concept(s) Tested: Problem Solving, Data Analysis

There are 27 books in one set and 25 in the other, and 52 books in both sets. Only Period 3 has more than 52 students with 56 students.

13) ➡ C

Concept(s) Tested: Problem Solving, Algebra

Let x be the number of hot dogs, and y be the number of hamburgers:

$3x + 4y = 10$

The answer choices indicate that he bought *at most* 4 items in total. Thus, we can plug in the values 1 and 2 for x and y to determine which combination totals 10. The only combination that equals ten is:

$x = 2, y = 1$

14) ➡ C

Concept(s) Tested: Algebra, Inequalities

For the inequality to be true, the numerator and denominator of the rational expression on the left must be either both positive or both negative. This is true when:

$x > 5$ (both positive) OR $x \leq -2$ (both negative)

15) ➡ B

Concept(s) Tested: Data Analysis, Ratios and Percentages

Percent herbaceous or evergreen

$$= \frac{Acres\ herbaceous\ and\ evergreen}{Total\ acres} = 100\%$$

$$= \frac{17 + 37}{146 + 17 + 37 + 25 + 3} \times 100\% = 24\%$$

16) ➡ D

Concept(s) Tested: Data Analysis, Ratios and Percentages

The proportion of wildlife habitat that is barren land by state:

$$CA : \frac{16}{149.8} = 0.107$$

$$NV : \frac{44}{502.5} = 0.088$$

$$OR : \frac{2.9}{161.1} = 0.018$$

$$UT : \frac{25}{228} = 0.110$$

17) ➡ C

Concept(s) Tested: Problem Solving, Data Analysis, Ratios and Percentages

In 2012, there are 12,500,000 acres of shrubby habitat in Oregon. In ten years:

Shrubby habitat = 12,500,000 + (0.15)(720,000)

= 12.6 million

18) ➡ C

Concept(s) Tested: Problem Solving, Data Analysis, Ratios and Percentages

Begin by determining how many acres the developer purchased (3 percent of 1,600,000 acres):

1,600,000(0.03) = 48,000

Then multiply the number of acres purchased by the purchase price per acre:

48,000(350) = 16,800,000

We can determine today's selling price by multiplying the original purchase price by 850 percent (8.5 in decimal form):

16,800,000(8.5) = 142,800,000, or approx. 143 million dollars.

19) ➡ B

Concept(s) Tested: Problem Solving, Algebra

$$Days\ of\ studio\ time = \frac{50\ hours}{12\ \dfrac{hour}{day}} = 4.2\ days$$

As studio time must be purchased by the day, the band must pay for 5 full days of studio time. The engineer is hired for half the recording time: 25 hours. The total cost of recording is:

$$Total\ cost = \left(\frac{\$200}{day}\right)(5\ days) + (25\ hours)\left(\frac{\$28}{hour}\right)$$

$$= \$1,700$$

The cost per hour over the course of recording is:

$$Cost\ Per\ hour = \left(\frac{\$1,700}{50\ hours}\right) = \$34\ per\ hour$$

20) ➡ A

Concept(s) Tested: Graphs and Functions

Convert the equation into slope-intercept form:

$2x - 3y - 10 = 0$

$y = \dfrac{2}{3}x - \dfrac{10}{3}$

The slope m of the line perpendicular to this line is:

$m\left(\dfrac{2}{3}\right) = -1$

$m = -\dfrac{3}{2}$

Substitute the coordinates of the point $(8, -3)$:

$y = -\dfrac{3}{2}x + b$

$-3 = -\dfrac{3}{2}(8) + b$

$b = 9$

The equation of the line perpendicular to the given line is: $y = -\dfrac{3}{2}x - 9y$

21) ➡ D

Concept(s) Tested: Problem Solving

If you work 40 hours at Timmy's Tacos, earnings are:

$(40 \text{ hours})\left(\dfrac{\$4.50}{\text{hour}}\right) - \$45.00 = \$135$

If you work 40 hours at Kelly's Carwash, earnings are:

$(40 \text{ hours})\left(\dfrac{\$3.50}{\text{hour}}\right) = \$140$

22) ➡ C

Concept(s) Tested: Data Analysis, Graphs and Functions

The number of words typed increases with time spent typing, so the slope of the line of best fit is positive. When the time increases by one minute, from 2 minutes to 3 minutes, the number of words typed increases 60 words, from 122 to 182. When the time increases by one minute from 3 minutes to 4 minutes, the number of words typed increases 58 words. When the time increases two minutes, from 4 minutes to 6 minutes, the number of words typed increases 128 words, or 64 words per minute. We conclude that the slope of the line of best fit is approximately 60.

23) ➡ D

Concept(s) Tested: Data Analysis

Amy and Charlie both doubled their first test score in the second test, an increase of 100%.

24) ➡ C

Concept(s) Tested: Geometry

The length of $\overline{XY}$ is maximum when the points X and Y are 180° from each other on the circle. The cross-section of the cylinder with points X and Y at opposite ends of the circle is a right triangle with one side equal to the diameter of the base (6 units), one side equal to the height of the cylinder (12 units), and hypotenuse $\overline{XY}$:

$\overline{XY}^2 = 12^2 + 6^2$

$\overline{XY} = \sqrt{180} = \sqrt{36 \cdot 5} = 6\sqrt{5}$

25) ➡ D

Concept(s) Tested: Problem Solving, Algebra

Price of airfare $= (378)(1.22)(0.9) = 415.04$

Baggage fees $= (25 + 5(2.5)) + (25 + 12(2.5)) = 92.50$

Total cost $= 415.04 + 92.50 = 507.54$

26) ➡ D

Concept(s) Tested: Graphs and Functions

Solve for x using the elimination method:

$$\begin{array}{r} x^2 - y = -3 \\ -\,)\,2x^2 - y = -3 \\ \hline -x^2 \quad\;\; = -1 \\ x \quad\quad = \pm 1 \end{array}$$

The only y-value that satisfies both x-values is 4, so (D) is correct.

27) ➡ B

Concept(s) Tested: Geometry

Since $z = 140 - x$ and $3z = x$, substitute $140 - x$ for z in the second equation, and solve for x:

$3(140 - x) = x$

$420 - 3x = x$

$4x = 420$

$x = 105$

Therefore, $3z = 105$, and $z = 35$.

$x + y + z = 105 + 140 + 35 = 280$.

28) ➤ C

Concept(s) Tested: Number Rules

Rationalize the denominator (Note: $i^2 = -1$):

$$\frac{3-4i}{5+3i} \cdot \frac{5-3i}{5-3i} = \frac{15-9i-20i+12i^2}{25-9i^2}$$

$$= \frac{15-29i+12(-1)}{25-9(-1)} = \frac{3-29i}{34}$$

29) ➤ A

Concept(s) Tested: Problem Solving, Rate

To calculate his average pace in miles per hour, we must determine for how many hours George walked:

$$2,425 \, \text{days} \times \frac{7 \, \text{hours}}{\text{day}} = 16,975 \, \text{hours}$$

Thus, George walked

$$\frac{19,019 \, \text{miles}}{16,975 \, \text{hours}} = 1.12 \, \text{miles/hour}$$

30) ➤ B

Concept(s) Tested: Graphs and Functions, Geometry

The circle has center $(0, 0)$ and radius 5. The equation is: $x^2 + y^2 = 25$

From the equation, we see that when two points share the same x-coordinate, the y-coordinates of these points must be the same or related by a factor of -1.

31) ➤ 3

Concept(s) Tested: Geometry

The radius perpendicular to a chord bisects the chord, so ΔOCB is a right triangle with hypotenuse equal to the radius (5 units) and side $\overline{CB} = 4$. This is a 3–4–5 right triangle, and $\overline{OC} = 3$.

32) ➤ 50

Concept(s) Tested: Problem Solving, Ratios and Percentages

Increase = $40

% increase $= \dfrac{\$40}{\$80} \times 100\% = 50\%$

33) ➤ 67

Concept(s) Tested: Problem Solving, Ratios and Percentages

$$\text{Oxygen saturation} = \frac{Dissolved\ oxygen}{Oxygen\ capacity} \times 100\%$$

$$\text{Oxygen saturation} = \frac{6.4\frac{mg\ O_2}{L}}{9.5\frac{mg\ O_2}{L}} \times 100\% = 67.4\%$$

34) ➤ 144

Concept(s) Tested: Problem Solving, Rate, Ratios and Percentages

Let x be the interest, in dollars, earned on $1800:

$$\frac{104}{1300} = \frac{x}{1800}$$

$$x = 144$$

35) ➤ 22

Concept(s) Tested: Problem Solving, Algebra

$(k+10)^{\frac{1}{5}} = 2$

$k + 10 = 2^5$

$k + 10 = 32$

$k = 22$

36) ➤ 130

Concept(s) Tested: Problem Solving, Ratios and Percentages

Let x be the selling price, in dollars, of the coat:

$x = 91 + 0.2x + 0.1x$

$0.7x = 91$

$x = 130$

37) 2,813

Concept(s) Tested: Problem Solving, Algebra

The cost of one truck making a one-way trip is:

$$\text{Cost of one trip} = \frac{250\,miles}{10\,\dfrac{miles}{gallon}} \times \frac{\$2.50}{gallon} = \$62.50$$

For five trucks to deliver 25 containers, they need to take a combined 45 trips (the fleet goes back and forth once to deliver 5 containers, amounting to 10 trips for 5 containers and 40 trips for 20 containers, but the trucks do not return after delivering the final 5 containers). The total cost to deliver all 25 containers is:

$$\text{Total cost} = 45\,trips \times \frac{\$62.50}{trip} \approx \$2,813$$

38) 4

Concept(s) Tested: Problem Solving, Algebra

It takes two days to make a one way trip, and four days to make a round trip.

With five trucks:

4 round trips = 16 days (20 containers)
1 one way trip = 2 days (5 containers)
Total time with 5 trucks = 18 days

With eight trucks:

3 round trips = 12 days (24 containers)
1 one way trip = 2 days (1 container)
Total time with 8 trucks = 14 days

It takes four days less to deliver the containers with eight trucks than it does with five.

1. ⓒ	6. Ⓐ	11. Ⓓ	16. Ⓐ	21. Ⓓ	26. Ⓑ	31. Ⓐ	36. Ⓓ	41. Ⓑ	46. Ⓐ	51. ⓒ
2. Ⓑ	7. Ⓐ	12. Ⓓ	17. Ⓐ	22. Ⓑ	27. Ⓐ	32. Ⓐ	37. Ⓑ	42. Ⓑ	47. Ⓐ	52. Ⓐ
3. Ⓑ	8. Ⓓ	13. Ⓑ	18. ⓒ	23. ⓒ	28. Ⓐ	33. Ⓓ	38. ⓒ	43. ⓒ	48. ⓒ	
4. ⓒ	9. ⓒ	14. ⓒ	19. Ⓑ	24. Ⓓ	29. ⓒ	34. Ⓑ	39. ⓒ	44. Ⓐ	49. Ⓓ	
5. Ⓐ	10. Ⓐ	15. Ⓑ	20. ⓒ	25. Ⓓ	30. Ⓑ	35. ⓒ	40. Ⓐ	45. ⓒ	50. Ⓓ	

1) **➡ C**

Concept(s) Tested: Words in Context

Choice (C) is correct because the character is claiming that secrecy can make life "mysterious" and "marvelous," and even the "commonest thing" can be enjoyable if hidden; for example, going out without telling anyone where he is going. (A) is incorrect because "sublime" is closer in meaning to "glorious" or "majestic." (B) is incorrect because "alluring" means powerfully attractive, which would not make sense in the context. (D) is incorrect because "distracting" can mean "amusing" but more often has a negative connotation.

2) **➡ B**

Concept(s) Tested: Summary

Choice (B) is correct because Basil says in lines 7 – 8 that he enjoys withholding names of friends: "When I like people immensely, I never tells their names to anyone. It is like surrendering a part of them." Choices (A) and (C) are incorrect because there is no implication of a sense of shame or concerns about jealousy in the excerpt. (D) is incorrect because the reader can infer from the rest of the passage that Basil usually shares personal news with Lord Henry.

3) **➡ B**

Concept(s) Tested: Purpose

Choice (B) is correct because Lord Henry begins talking about his marriage in order to assure Basil that he empathizes with his need to keep secrets: "The one charm of marriage is that it makes a life of deception absolutely necessary for both parties." (A) is incorrect because there is no indication that Lord Henry does not want to discuss Dorian Gray. (C) and (D) are incorrect because Lord Henry does not provide a description of his wife or suggest that Basil should get married.

4) **➡ C**

Concept(s) Tested: Inference, Implication, and Suggestion

Choice (C) is correct because Lord Henry explains that his wife is much better at the "absurd stories" they tell each other about where they have been and does not get confused about her own lies. Thus, clearly she is a skillful liar. (A) is incorrect because there is no indication that Lord Henry's wife is truly cruel; Lord Henry says that when she catches him in his lies, she "makes no row at all," and merely laughs at him. (B) and (D) are incorrect because there are no indications of how Lord Henry's wife is regarded by her peers or how she truly regards Lord Henry.

5) **➡ A**

Concept(s) Tested: Summary

Choice (A) is correct because Basil tells Lord Henry, "You never say a moral thing, and you never do a wrong thing. Your cynicism is simply a pose" (lines 39 – 41). (B) is incorrect because Basil does not claim that Lord Henry is predictable. (C) is incorrect because Lord Henry does not lie about having adventures, except as a kind of game with his wife. Furthermore, Basil does not comment on whether his friend is adventurous or tries new things. (D) is incorrect because the topic of self-confidence does not appear in the passage.

6) **➡ A**

Concept(s) Tested: Words in Context

Choice (A) is correct because the way that Lord Henry presents himself is "simply a pose;" this is similar to the meaning of a "pretense"—an attempt to make something appear true when it is not. (B), (C), and (D) are incorrect because none of them implies deception, as does (A).

7) ➡ A

Concept(s) Tested: Summary

Choice (A) is correct because Basil explains in the last paragraph that when portraits are painted with feeling, they reveal the artist's true self; he says he may have disclosed "the secret of my own soul" (line 73) with his portrait of Dorian Gray. (B), (C), and (D) are incorrect because the passage does not address how often Basil paints portraits, what challenges he faces when painting, nor the reason that he decided to become an artist.

8) ➡ D

Concept(s) Tested: Citation

Choice (D) is correct because it most directly expresses the personal nature of Basil's portrait of Dorian Gray, saying that the painter reveals himself on the canvas. (A) is incorrect because its focus is on Lord Henry, not on Basil's artwork. (B) is incorrect because it is a request for Basil's explanation, not the explanation itself. (C) is incorrect because it describes what the artwork is not, rather than what it is.

9) ➡ C

Concept(s) Tested: Inference, Implication, and Suggestion

Choice (C) is correct because Basil says that he had not intended to reveal the name of the subject of his painting, and he does not want to exhibit the painting. Lord Henry pretends to be worse than he is; for him it is normal to keep secrets through deception. (A) and (B) are incorrect because no mention is made of nature, city life, or social interaction. (D) is incorrect because Lord Henry's opinions on subjectivity do not appear in the passage.

10) ➡ A

Concept(s) Tested: Analogy

Choice (A) is correct because there are several indications that the two characters are old friends: they call each other by their first names, "Basil" and "Harry;" they each share details of their inner lives; and they seem to have known each other for a long time. (B) is incorrect because they do not discuss business matters in the passage. (C) and (D) are incorrect because there is no indication that the two are quarreling or that they are enemies; rather, they speak in a friendly manner and sit down together on a garden bench (lines 45 – 46).

11) ➡ D

Concept(s) Tested: Purpose

Choice (D) is correct because the "romantic image" in question is brides and grooms in their early 20s; the author states that such an image is "now largely a myth;" in other words, it contradicts reality. (A) is incorrect because the "romantic image" is meant to contradict actual circumstances, not serve as an analogy for them. (B) is incorrect because the point of the "romantic image" is that it is not realistic. (C) is incorrect because the author uses the term "romantic" to describe how people tend to see marriage rather than how it is. The author does not imply that there is an ideal approach to marriage.

12) ➡ D

Concept(s) Tested: Words in Context

Choice (D) is correct because the author uses the word "crop" in its metaphorical sense to refer to a generation or a cohort of people. (A) and (C) are incorrect because they both indicate a more literal sense of the word—a season's agricultural planting, as in "this year's crop of corn." These meanings do not make sense in the context of the passage. (B) is incorrect because a coalition is a set of cooperating groups with a shared goal; this meaning does not make sense in reference to young adults as a whole.

13) ➡ B

Concept(s) Tested: Inference, Implication, and Suggestion

Choice (B) is correct because in paragraph 2 the author says that older generations might worry that their adult children are putting off marriage "seemingly forever." (A) is incorrect because the passage does not precisely address whether older generations are advising younger generations not to move home. (C) is incorrect because the passage addresses parents' specific feelings and expectations regarding their adult children or grandchildren becoming independent, not their general feelings about supporting their children. (D) is incorrect because the passage does not imply that parents want their adult children to stay home, but the opposite—that older generations may be impatient for their adult children to move out and establish their own homes and families.

14) ➡ C

Concept(s) Tested: Organization

Choice (C) is correct because paragraph 3 begins with the claim that "a major factor" of marriage at older ages is that incomes are not high enough. To show that the phenomenon is real and widespread, the author then describes two cultural terms that describe it in two different countries. Rather than data, the terms serve as anecdotal evidence. (A) is incorrect because the author does not provide logical analysis of the claim that people cannot afford to marry and establish homes. (B) is incorrect because the phenomenon is not presented as a problem, and popular terms such as "kangaroo generation" serve as descriptions, not solutions. (D) is incorrect because there is no "overall conclusion" about not being able to afford to establish a household.

15) ➡ B

Concept(s) Tested: Inference, Implication, and Suggestion

Choice (B) is correct. In paragraph 4, the author states that the popular perceptions of the "Satori Generation" are "even darker" than the Korean perception of having lost the chance to ever marry. The author's use of the word "supposedly" implies doubt that the extreme attitude is actually pervasive in Japan. (A) is incorrect because the author only mentions the popular term, and does not back it up with facts. (C) is incorrect because though the stereotype of the "Satori Generation" may be exaggerated, it is also unlikely that it describes no one. Finally, (D) is incorrect because the author mentions the "Satori Generation" term only briefly, and does not analyze the societal factors behind it.

16) ➡ A

Concept(s) Tested: Purpose

Choice (A) is correct because the author uses "standard" here to indicate a means of measuring, a different way of deciding what is normal. (B) is incorrect because the author is not seeking to argue against statistical evidence, but rather to draw different conclusions from it. (C) and (D) are incorrect because the author's tone is neutral; she does not attempt to argue for a new set of ideals or to encourage particular life choices.

17) ➡ A

Concept(s) Tested: Citation

The correct choice is (A). The graph shows that

for both men and women in the United States, age at first marriage dipped in the 1950s and 1960s. Therefore, it makes sense to say that the age of first marriage during those decades is not the norm. (B) is incorrect because the graph does not indicate the number of adult children living with their parents. (C) is incorrect because the graph does not provide information about economic conditions in any of the time periods. (D) is incorrect because it describes the graph's objective but does not make a claim based on its data.

18) ➡ C

Concept(s) Tested: Graph and Text Synthesis

Choice (C) is correct because the graph indicates that average lifespan for men and women in the U.S. has grown continually since 1890, and that average age at first marriage has stayed more consistent over time. (A) is incorrect for the same reason: the graph indicates that age of first marriage is not catching up to increased lifespan. (B) is incorrect because the graph shows that average lifespan has been increasing over the entire time period documented by the graph, so it is not reasonable to predict that it will level off. Finally, (D) is incorrect because there is no pattern established by the graph from which we can infer that average age at first marriage will drop lower in the future. Rather, the dip in the 1950s and 1960s appears to be an anomaly.

19) ➡ B

Concept(s) Tested: Inference, Implication, and Suggestion

Choice (B) is correct. In the preceding paragraph, the author says that "Census experts say…people are marrying earlier in their expected lifespan than ever before," and provides an example. After the example, the direct quotation serves to summarize and restate the conclusion drawn from the data. (A) is incorrect because the quotation does not provide a new perspective. (C) is incorrect because there is no attempt to persuade the reader that the data is accurate. (D) is incorrect because the quotation is not restating information from the beginning of the passage. Rather, the quotation describes the U.S. average from the perspective of average lifespan.

20) ➡ C

Concept(s) Tested: Inference, Implication, and Suggestion

The correct choice is (C). The author suggests

that a strong economy may have lowered the age of first marriage in the 1950s and 1960s, and a weaker economy may be raising it now. However, she also suggests that the real cause may be a longer expected lifespan, as people now may "feel that they simply have more time." (A), (B), and (D) are incorrect because the author makes no mention of varied opportunities, maturity, or the quality of relationships.

21) ➡ D

Concept(s) Tested: Words in Context

Choice (D) is correct because a "configuration" is a specific arrangement of a group of elements—in this case, how the face looks in terms of nose, eyes, mouth, and so on. (A) is incorrect because "confluence" refers to the merger of two things, which does not make sense in the context of the sentence. (B) is incorrect because "geometries" does not include the concept of "arrangement" which is central to "configuration. Finally, (C), "alignments" is incorrect because an alignment refers to an arrangement that is in a straight line, which does not fit the meaning in this case.

22) ➡ B

Concept(s) Tested: Summary

Choice (B) is correct because the researchers suggest that neighboring monkey species' different appearances are "an adaptation that helps prevent hybridization between species" (lines 11 – 12). (A) is incorrect because the author does not claim that species' different appearances help them form social bonds, although it is implied that it makes it possible for them to live together in social groups. (C) is incorrect because the passage does not address the effect of appearance on raising offspring. Finally, (D) is incorrect because the passage does not speculate about whether different appearances provide an adaptive advantage gained from living in mixed-species groups.

23) ➡ C

Concept(s) Tested: Citation

The correct choice is (C). The author is reporting on the researchers' interpretation of their findings. They state that differing appearances between species that live near each other makes sense because otherwise, there would be "a risk of hybridization." (A), (B), and (D) are incorrect because none of them describes the study's findings in terms of the prevention of interbreeding; (A) is an introduction, (B) is a factual statement about the study results, and (D) is an

extended discussion of the implications.

24) ➡ D

Concept(s) Tested: Words in Context

Choice (D) is correct. In line 7, the author says that the researchers looked at "specific features like eyebrow patches and nose-spots;" she is using the word "features" in the sense of "parts of the face," making "characteristics" the best answer. Choices (A) and (B) are incorrect because it would not make sense to refer to eyebrow patches and nose-spots as "presentations" or "secrets." (C) is incorrect because a "highlight" is a main or outstanding feature; the author does not indicate that eyebrow patches and nose-spots are highlights of the face.

25) ➡ D

Concept(s) Tested: Analogy

The correct choice is (D) because the method used in the study involves programming a computer to discern facial features; it is analogous to training a dog to pinpoint the smell of contraband among other smells. (A) is incorrect because training a mouse to memorize a pathway through a maze is not complex enough to be an analogy for training a computer to recognize and distinguish between configurations. (B) is incorrect because the goal of the study is not to reproduce single images, but to recognize and categorize different images. (C) is incorrect because the study is not analogous to teaching a pattern, such as forming words with letters on blocks.

26) ➡ B

Concept(s) Tested: Summary

Choice (B) is correct because in lines 34 – 35, the author reports that the computer was able to "reliably categorize species and individuals." (A) is incorrect because the passage does not discuss the social status of monkeys within their groups. (C) and (D) are incorrect because lines 35 – 36 say that the computer was *not* able to determine an individual guenon's age or sex based on its facial features.

27) ➡ A

Concept(s) Tested: Summary

The correct choice is (A). In lines 15 – 19, the author says that the study "examined the performance of a machine learning algorithm" to see if it could classify monkeys based on particular facial traits. In lines 74 – 82, the researchers are quoted as concluding that algorithms and machine learning can help researchers study the evolution of visual signals in animals. (B) is incorrect because the study did not address monkey or human behaviors.

(C) is incorrect because, while the researchers clearly have an interest in the evolution of visual communication in species, it is not their primary interest. (D) is incorrect because the study in the passage did not focus on mating behaviors, but rather on facial recognition abilities.

28) ➡ A

Concept(s) Tested: Purpose

The correct choice is (A) because the author uses the term "trade-off" to indicate that selective pressures favor guenon faces looking distinctive in terms of species, yet still uniquely individual. The term "trade-off" therefore simplifies a more complex set of processes within evolution. (B), (C), and (D) are incorrect because the passage does not address economics, humor, or the relationship between scientists and non-scientists.

29) ➡ C

Concept(s) Tested: Inference, Implication, and Suggestion

The correct choice is (C) because the author reports that Allen and Higham found that guenon monkeys can recognize other individual monkeys by their faces and can discern members of their own species. The researchers interpret the recognition ability as "an evolutionary adaptation that helps prevent hybridization between species" (line 17). (A) is incorrect because there is no indication within the passage that the authors assume there are more Old-World monkey species to be discovered. (B) is incorrect because the passage does not mention unhealthy offspring or any other reason that selective pressures would favor the prevention of interbreeding with other species. (D) is incorrect because the author does not report that the researchers expected the computer program to "perfectly mimic" biological recognition processes. Rather, the researchers wanted to design a program that could "do something as similar as possible" (lines 20 – 22) to what an actual guenon could do in terms of recognition.

30) ➡ B

Concept(s) Tested: Inference, Implication, and Suggestion

The correct choice is (B). In lines 74 – 83, the author reports that Higham and Allen believe that machine learning approaches "have a really big future" in the study of animal visual communication; machine learning approaches such as the one they tested in the study will help researchers understand "the informational content" of signals. Thus, their study may unlock information about the nature of the signals that animals send and receive, and how the signals developed. (A) is incorrect because the study does not attempt to produce data regarding "all species." (C) and (D) are incorrect because the author does not mention either topic in the passage.

31) ➡ A

Concept(s) Tested: Inference, Implication, and Suggestion

The correct choice is (A) because in lines 21 – 22, the author says that "wild orangutans struggle to remain in existence today" due to the destruction of their natural habitat; in other words, they could become extinct. (B) is incorrect because the author does not imply that the problem of logging the rainforests for timber has disappeared, only that it has been overshadowed as "forests are cleared completely" for palm-oil plantations (line 32). (C) is incorrect; in line 34 the author does contrast the "tidy rows" of palm plantations with wild forests, but the implication is that the tidiness is not beneficial to wild species. (D) is incorrect because there is no indication that the UN is helping to enforce laws in Indonesia.

32) ➡ A

Concept(s) Tested: Citation

The correct choice is (A) because it refers directly to extinction when it describes orangutans as a species that is "threatened" by habitat destruction. (B), (C), and (D) are incorrect because, although they each address habitat destruction, the connection to species loss is only indirect.

33) ➡ D

Concept(s) Tested: Organization

Choice (D) is correct because the third paragraph serves as a transition from the opening paragraphs' focus on orangutans in zoos to the plight of wild orangutans in the rainforests of Indonesia and Malaysia, and to the passage's main topic of palm oil production. (A) is incorrect because the third paragraph does not contain or support information about zoo orangutans, the topic of the first two paragraphs. (B) is incorrect because the third paragraph describes general facts, and does not present a specific example. (C) is incorrect because, while the third paragraph does provide background information—i.e., the location of the habitat, the conditions that support palm oil—its purpose is to transition between the passage's introductory paragraphs and its main topic.

34) ➡️ B

Concept(s) Tested: Words in Context

Choice (B) is correct. The author says that palm trees are "stable sources of income" because they produce palm fruits for about 25 years; in other words, they are not subject to the ups and downs of annual crops. Thus for growers, the trees are "reliable." (A), (C), and (D) are incorrect because although presumably the trees are "settled" in their spots, and are somewhat "inflexible" and "sturdy," these words do not quite makes sense when placed with "sources of income."

35) ➡️ C

Concept(s) Tested: Inference, Implication, and Suggestion

The correct choice is (C) because the author says in lines 47–49 that palm trees have a much higher yield per acre than other vegetable oil crops; it follows that if growers wanted to get similar yields from a different vegetable oil crop, they would need to use more land. (A) is incorrect because, although the author states that palm oil plantations are profitable, she does not imply that there are no other possible uses of the land that could generate a comparable profit. (B) is incorrect because in paragraph 5 the author mentions that palm oil plantations have the potential to lift many poor people out of poverty. The reader can infer that this "potential" has not yet been realized. Finally, (D) is incorrect because the author does not address the issue of land use in the passage.

36) ➡️ D

Concept(s) Tested: Purpose

The correct choice is (D). In paragraph 5, the author explains that palm oil plantations are profitable, reliable, and efficient, and that there are many poor people in the region, so it is "not surprising" that local governments approve plantations to help ease poverty. (A) is incorrect because the author does not attempt to persuade the reader to support palm oil. (B) is incorrect because the author does not make general comments about jobs and the environment. (C) is incorrect because the author does not address the question of how best to meet the food needs of the region's population.

37) ➡️ B

Concept(s) Tested: Summary, Organization

The correct choice is (B). In line 75 – 76, the author reports claims that the palm oil plantations are

"enriching a small elite" group of people. In contrast, the people who actually work on the plantations have small wages and suffer from abusive labor practices. (A) is incorrect because the paragraph does not mention growers' responses. (C) is incorrect because the author does not refer to conflicts between laborers and villagers. (D) is incorrect because the paragraph does not focus on contrasting "lifestyles."

38) ➡️ C

Concept(s) Tested: Words in Context

The correct choice is (C). In line 82, the author refers to a quotation from the "Inter-Press Service," and in line 86, the author refers to the palm oil industry getting "bad press." The reader can infer that "press" here refers to media reports, and that the "Inter-Press Service" must be a news publisher. Choices (A), (B), and (D) are incorrect because it would not make sense in the context for the industry to suffer from bad "weights," "crowds," or "machinery."

39) ➡️ C

Concept(s) Tested: Summary, Primary Purpose

The correct choice is (C) because the author introduces the concept of the RSPO by saying that "the bad press has created a niche market for palm oil that is grown in a more responsible manner." By this, she implies that some consumers are demanding "sustainable" palm oil, creating a market force that is changing the practices of some companies. (A) is incorrect because the author does not claim that the RSPO certification process cannot be trusted. (B) is incorrect because, while some companies may be more transparent than others about ingredient sources and other matters, such discrepancies are not the author's main focus. (D) is incorrect because the author does not describe the RSPO as a government organization, but rather, a private cooperative. Therefore, it is not concerned with creating laws.

40) ➡️ A

Concept(s) Tested: Citation

Choice (A) is correct because it provides the most direct support for the author's main point about palm oil certification—when consumers learned about the effects of palm oil production through the media (i.e., the industry got "bad press,") some formed a consumer base ("niche market") for differently produced oil. (B) is incorrect because it simply describes the participants in the certification system and does not mention the role of consumers. (C) is incorrect because it describes the effects of the RSPO on the industry—changes in about 15 percent of the market—but again, it does not mention consumers. (D) is incorrect because it describes the urgent need for market pressures to halt clear-cutting, but does not refer directly to the role that consumers can play.

41) ➡ B

Concept(s) Tested: Graph-Text Synthesis

The correct choice is (B). The graph shows that since 1970, the demand for palm oil has more than doubled during every 10-year period. (A) is incorrect because while demand did grow more quickly between 2000 and 2010 than during previous decades, the term "increased substantially" is a vague description of its rise. (C) is incorrect because it raises a question that is not relevant to supporting the author's characterization of demand for palm oil. (D) is incorrect because it presents a subjective interpretation of a word but does not support it convincingly. "Rising steadily" is not necessarily incompatible with "skyrocketing."

42) ➡ B

Concept(s) Tested: Words in Context

The correct choice is (B) because Lamarck claims in lines 6 – 9 that animals' changing habits cause "the use of one member rather than another," and that some "members" might cease to be useful at all. Thus, the reader can infer that the author was using diction more common to his era (1809) for "limb" or "appendage." (A), (C), and (D) are incorrect because they would not make sense in the context of discussing physical development in animals.

43) ➡ C

Concept(s) Tested: Summary

Choice (C) is correct. Lamarck states that since the ground in "the interior of Africa" is "scorched and destitute of grass," the giraffe has to eat leaves from trees. The leaves have made "continual stretching" necessary "over a great space of time in all the individuals of the race" (lines 23 – 25). Thus, Lamarck says that the distribution of resources has evoked the behavior of stretching the neck. (A) is incorrect because the author does not claim that the conditions cause the giraffe to relocate, but rather to reach up. (B) and (D) are incorrect because the author does not imply that the giraffes must compete with each other or establish dominance.

44) ➡ A

Concept(s) Tested: Citation

Choice (A) is correct because it most directly supports Lamarck's use of "scorched" bare ground as an example of a "changed circumstance," that produces wants and needs that in turn produce "changed actions," such as the behavior of reaching up to the trees to eat leaves. (B), (C), and (D) are incorrect because in them, the author elaborates upon his theory. (A) is the only choice that focuses solely on distribution of resources changing animals' behaviors.

45) ➡ C

Concept(s) Tested: Words in Context

Choice (C) is correct. In lines 38 – 41, Darwin mentions "the structure…of the woodpecker, with its feet, tail, beak, and tongue, so admirably adapted to catch insects under the bark of trees." Thus by "structure," Darwin is referring to composition or "anatomy" of the woodpecker's body. (A) is incorrect because "organization" connotes the way that various parts are arranged, not how they are formed and adapted. (B) is incorrect because a "design" is a plan or blueprint for something, whereas Darwin is referring to actual birds. (D) is incorrect because "edifice" refers to buildings, not animals.

46) ➡ A

Concept(s) Tested: Inference, Implication, and Suggestion

The correct choice is (A). In lines 58–64, Darwin says that because of the "struggle for life," individuals tend to survive if they have variations that are "in any way profitable" in their environments. Based on the examples Darwin uses in lines 38 – 42, the reader can infer that obtaining food is "profitable" to an animal and is a major part of the "struggle for life." (B) and (C) are incorrect because neither makes sense as a component of the "struggle for life." (D) is incorrect because the "struggle for life" in organisms would not generally include a struggle for parental affection.

47) ➡ A

Concept(s) Tested: Citation

The correct choice is (A) because it provides two examples of obtaining food that Darwin uses to introduce the term "struggle for life." Choices (B), (C), and (D) are incorrect because they do not directly connect the Darwinian "struggle for life" with "competition among individuals for food."

48) ➤ C

Concept(s) Tested: Inference, Implication, and Suggestion

Choice (C) is correct. In lines 75 – 79, Darwin explains that people have been able to "produce great results" in adapting organisms (such as "dog breeds") to become more useful to them ("fill practical roles"). Darwin says that people have achieved these results by accumulating variations provided by "the hand of Nature;" i.e., selectively breeding plants or animals to emphasize various traits. (A) is incorrect because it refers to humanity's overuse of natural resources, not its manipulation of natural selection. (B) is incorrect because hunting an animal to the point of extinction destroys it, rather than adapts it for human uses. (D) is incorrect because the use of rats and mice in cancer research refers to observing individuals subjected to certain conditions, not to selective breeding.

49) ➤ D

Concept(s) Tested: Graph-Text Synthesis

Because the graphs include only three unnamed species, the reader can infer that the graphs are meant to convey basic concepts rather than precise information. The correct answer is (D) because the graph depicting Lamarck's theory shows species being generated spontaneously over time, while Darwin's theory shows species branching out from one origin in time. (A), (B), and (C) are incorrect because the graphs do not supply information regarding the two theories' stance on these topics.

50) ➤ D

Concept(s) Tested: Multiple-Text Synthesis

The correct choice is (D) because the author of Passage 2 (Darwin) would most likely claim that his predecessor (Lamarck) misinterpreted the way in which conditions influence the development of organisms. Lamarck writes that changes in organisms come about when they change their habits in response to changing conditions; Darwin criticizes such an interpretation when he says it is "preposterous" to think that animals and plants decide to change their habits based on external conditions (lines 33 – 51). (A) is incorrect because there is no indication that Lamarck is relying on casual observations. (B) is incorrect because neither Darwin nor Lamarck mentions predation in the passages. (C) is incorrect because Lamarck indicates that the function of the giraffe's long neck is to enable it to browse on tree leaves; it is unlikely that Darwin would disagree.

51) ➤ C

Concept(s) Tested: Citation, Multiple-Text Synthesis

Choice (C) is correct. In lines 6 – 13, Lamarck claims that, if an organism uses a part of its body more, it will become larger and more powerful. Darwin most clearly refutes this hypothesis in lines 58 – 65, where he explains the principle of Natural Selection—that certain variations in individuals tend to help them survive, and that their offspring will be more likely to possess the same variations. Darwin's explanation of the mechanism for acquiring different traits thus undermines Lamarck's. (A) and (B) are incorrect because they are not precise claims. (D) is incorrect because it focuses on how humans have altered the development of some organisms to become more useful to them; it does not explain how differences among organisms develop.

52) ➤ A

Concept(s) Tested: Organization, Multiple-Text Synthesis

The correct choice is (A). In the first paragraph of Passage 2, Darwin describes as "preposterous" the belief that "mere external conditions" cause differences among organisms. He points to both a bird and a plant that have unique abilities for getting food from trees. Darwin argues that the two species could not have developed such complicated adaptations simply by means of habitual practice. (B) is incorrect; Darwin mentions the woodpecker and mistletoe not to compare the two organisms to each other, but to give two examples of complexity. (C) and (D) are incorrect because Darwin does not mention either giraffes or the struggle for life in the first paragraph of Passage 2.

Writing and Language Test

1. Ⓐ	5. Ⓓ	9. Ⓑ	13. Ⓓ	17. Ⓒ	21. Ⓓ	25. Ⓒ	29. Ⓒ	33. Ⓒ	37. Ⓒ	41. Ⓒ
2. Ⓑ	6. Ⓐ	10. Ⓐ	14. Ⓐ	18. Ⓒ	22. Ⓐ	26. Ⓑ	30. Ⓓ	34. Ⓓ	38. Ⓒ	42. Ⓒ
3. Ⓐ	7. Ⓑ	11. Ⓑ	15. Ⓒ	19. Ⓑ	23. Ⓐ	27. Ⓑ	31. Ⓐ	35. Ⓐ	39. Ⓓ	43. Ⓑ
4. Ⓐ	8. Ⓓ	12. Ⓐ	16. Ⓓ	20. Ⓒ	24. Ⓓ	28. Ⓓ	32. Ⓑ	36. Ⓑ	40. Ⓐ	44. Ⓐ

1) ➡ A
Concept(s) Tested: Precise Diction
Choice (A) is correct because it accurately emphasizes the sustainable nature of wind energy. (D) is incorrect because a modifier is necessary to highlight the "alternative" quality mentioned later in the sentence.

2) ➡ B
Concept(s) Tested: Graph Analysis
The graph relates the number of job opportunities for wind turbine service technicians over nearly two decades. (B) is the only choice that comments on job availability, making it the correct answer. The remaining answer choices make statements about information not provided in the graph, making them irrelevant.

3) ➡ A
Concept(s) Tested: Passage Development
Choice (A) is correct because the paragraph discusses the typical duties of a wind turbine service technician. (B) and (C) are incorrect because they focus on the conditions under which technicians work and how much training they receive respectively, and (D) is incorrect because the passage never mentions changes in technicians' duties, nor does it compare and contrast any changes in this field.

4) ➡ A
Concept(s) Tested: Passage Development
The added sentence provides a minor detail about emergencies that is neither crucial nor irrelevant to the passage. However, it serves as an effective transition to the discussion of job safety presented in the next paragraph, so (A) is the correct choice.

5) ➡ D
Concept(s) Tested: Concision
Choice (D) is correct because safety equipment serves one purpose: to protect people. Therefore, it is unnecessary to restate this in the passage,

especially given the context of the discussion.

6) ➡ A
Concept(s) Tested: Transition Words and Phrases
The discussion of harnesses serves to illustrate the author's point about safety equipment. Thus, it acts as an example, and (A) is the best choice.

7) ➡ B
Concept(s) Tested: Pronoun Case
Choice (B) is correct because the information after the underlined portion is a relative clause and requires a relative pronoun, in this case "who." (A) and (D) are incorrect because "whom" is an objective pronoun and "he or she" is a subjective pronoun; neither of these acts as a relative pronoun. (C) is incorrect because a relative clause cannot stand alone as a complete sentence.

8) ➡ D
Concept(s) Tested: Transition Words and Phrases
Choice (D) is correct because the information after the underlined portion adds another detail regarding the skills necessary to be a successful wind turbine service technician, and "moreover" effectively expresses that additional relevant information will follow.

9) ➡ B
Concept(s) Tested: Voice
The correct choice is (B) because it is structured using the active voice. Choices (A) and (C) are incorrect because they are written in the passive voice. Choice (D) is incorrect because it changes the sentence from third- to second-person, which is not an appropriate shift.

10) ➡ A
Concept(s) Tested: In-Sentence Punctuation
Choice (A) is correct because a grouped element within a list does not require a comma to separate its components. All remaining answer choices use

unnecessary punctuation.

11) ➡️ B
Concept(s) Tested: Countable/Uncountable Pronouns and Modifiers
Choice (B) is correct because "work experience" is uncountable and can only be modified with "less." (A) is incorrect because "fewer" modifies countable nouns only. (C) is incorrect because "lower" compares elevation or status. (D) is incorrect because "lesser" is used to compare values to each other.

12) ➡️ A
Concept(s) Tested: In-Sentence Punctuation, Sentence Boundaries
The phrase "and that any risk is outweighed" corresponds with "policies requiring," which comes earlier in the sentence. It is grammatically correct to say "policies requiring…that any risk is outweighed…" and doing so connects "policies" to "risks," making (A) the correct answer. Although (B) is grammatically correct, the inclusion of a period muddies the relationship between "policies" and "any risk," meaning (B) can be eliminated. Similarly, the lack of "that" in (C) disassociates the phrase that begins "any risk is outweighed" from the "policies" to which it refers. (D) is grammatically incorrect because the phrase that follows the semicolon is not an independent clause.

13) ➡️ D
Concept(s) Tested: Passage Tone
As written, the claim that researchers can and do disagree about "both qualities" is too vague, as the reader cannot determine which specific qualities is the author talking about. The answer has to be explicitly related to what the author says in the previous sentence. Only choice (D) mentions the specific qualities that cause disagreement among researchers: defining what is safe and what is meaningful. (B) is incorrect because it does not specify what the two judgments in question are, and (C) is incorrect because it is far too broad and vague. Academic writing should be clear and concise, and that often means being specific as well.

14) ➡️ A
Concept(s) Tested: Precise Diction, Possession
The underlined noun is showing possession over "immune systems." Because immune systems is plural, we can conclude that we need to use the plural form of person, which is people. We can eliminate (B) and (D) because they fail to use this plural form. Generally, a plural possessive is formed by adding an apostrophe to the end of the word, but in the case of plural nouns that do not already end in "s," the possessive is formed by adding an 's to the

end of the plural noun. Thus, the possessive form of "people" is "people's," making (A) the correct choice.

15) ➡️ C
Concept(s) Tested: Graph Analysis
Choice (C) is correct because the graph shows the number of deaths in the U.S. that resulted from various flu outbreaks, and only (C) describes the number of deaths related to these flu outbreaks. (A) and (B) incorrectly assume that the graph displays the number of deaths as a proportion of the U.S. population, which it does not. (D) is incorrect because the graph shows that many people died from these outbreaks, but it does not suggest that these outbreaks were the *leading* causes of death. There is simply not enough information in the graph to make this assumption.

16) ➡️ D
Concept(s) Tested: Verb Tense/Mood
Because the sentence begins with "Ideally," we can conclude that it is describing a desirable, hypothetical situation. Thus, we must use a conditional auxiliary verb to show that this is an ideal yet nonexistent situation. (A) and (C) are incorrect because both of these imply that the situation exists, which conflicts with the word "Ideally." (B) is incorrect because saying "scientists *would have* identified" implies that something in the past has prevented them from identifying, which we cannot confirm based on the context of the passage. Thus, (D) is correct because "could" suggests possibility, which is also suggested by the adverb "Ideally."

17) ➡️ C
Concept(s) Tested: Combining Sentences
The sentence containing 17 mentions that scientists produce new strains of the flu virus that have gained abilities, or functions. Thus, an appropriate combination of both sentences would include a term that indicates the transition from a general explanation to a more detailed one. Only (C) accomplishes this by including the word "specifically;" in addition, since the two sentences can stand alone, a semicolon is needed to separate them. (A) is incorrect because the author is adding new information, not rewording. (B) is incorrect because it would create a run-on sentence. Finally, (D) is incorrect because "but" indicates a contrast; yet the information contained in the two sentences does not contrast.

18) ➡️ C
Concept(s) Tested: Concision, Passage Tone
The tone of the passage is academic and informative, so the underlined portion at 18 should maintain this

academic tone. The correct choice is (C) because it conveys the same information as the other choices but uses a more academic tone while remaining clear and concise. Choice (A) is incorrect because it uses colloquial diction ("got more"), and it contains a redundancy (in the context of the sentence, capable and efficient mean nearly the same). (B) can be eliminated because the phrase "a lot" is rarely, if ever, used in academic English writing, as the term fails to add useful, quantifiable information. (D) is incorrect because the phrase "do a better job" is too colloquial for the tone of the passage as a whole.

19) ➡ B

Concept(s) Tested: In-Sentence Punctuation
The phrase "by knowing...evolve" interrupts the main idea of the sentence, which is that "researchers claim that...scientists may be able to prevent pandemics." Generally, interruptions are separated from the rest of a sentence with a pair of commas. Thus, (B) is the most appropriate choice because it places a single comma at the end of the interjection, signaling the interjection's end.

20) ➡ C

Concept(s) Tested: Passage Organization
Choice (C) is correct because it places sentence 2 logically between sentences 4 and 5. Sentence 2 describes one lab's creation of a flu strain that humans cannot "neutralize." That explains sentence 4's "more lethal" strain. Sentence 5 begins with "That is," and reiterates the information about the human immune system. (A), (B), and (D) do not create a logical flow.

21) ➡ D

Concept(s) Tested: Passage Development
An appropriate supporting claim for the sentence at 21 would clearly state a reason or example showing why the different strains of flu should not be kept. Since the sentence as written does not do this, (A) is incorrect. (B) is incorrect because it includes the mere speculative possibility that the flu virus could escape and cause a pandemic. (C) is stronger than (B), but it does not specify any concrete negative effects of the labs having accidentally released the most dangerous pathogens. Only (D) clearly indicates that there are real dangers to genetically modifying flu viruses, since an outbreak of the flu virus in China actually did cause a pandemic that made many people ill.

22) ➡ A

Concept(s) Tested: Passage Development
The passage as a whole has represented the pros and cons of creating "gain of function"

flu viruses. The sentence at 22 includes a fitting general summation by noting that supporters and opponents of this research continue to disagree strongly. It is not necessary to substitute another sentence, so (A) is the correct answer. (B) is incorrect because it advocates one side of the debate, whereas the author's tone is neutral throughout the passage. (C) will not work as a conclusion because it adds new information to the discussion. Finally, (D) is incorrect because it is vague and unsupported by evidence. The reader has no information about the influence of either side on the scientific community. Overall, (D) fails to conclude the issue in a neutral tone.

23) ➡ A

Concept(s) Tested: In-Sentence Punctuation
The clauses to either side of the semicolon are independent clauses. Because these independent clauses contain closely related ideas, a semicolon is the appropriate punctuation, making (A) the correct choice. (B) is incorrect because a comma alone is not sufficient to separate independent clauses. (A comma must be followed by a coordinating conjunction to do so.) (C) can be eliminated because it lacks any punctuation, forming a run-on sentence. Like (B), (D) is incorrect because it replaces the semicolon with a comma without adding a conjunction. Moreover, the comma after "besides" is unnecessary.

24) ➡ D

Concept(s) Tested: Transition Words and Phrases
The sentence containing the underlined portion expresses the idea that "mancala" (to transfer) is appropriate because it accurately reflects the goal of the game. Thus, the transition word at 24 should show that the rest of the sentence emphasizes the validity of the previous sentence. (D) is the correct choice because "Indeed," when used as a transition, serves to strengthen or validate a previous claim. (A) is incorrect because the rules of the game are not likely a consequence of the game's name. "Concurrently" means that two things take place at the same time. Because the chronology of mancala is not discussed in these two sentences, (B) must be incorrect. The transition word "Significantly" serves to emphasize that the information that follows is of greater importance than previous statements. Because there is no indication that the sentence containing the underlined portion is any more important than preceding or following sentences, (C) can be eliminated.

25) ➡ C

Concept(s) Tested: Passage Tone, Precise Diction
Choices (A) and (B) can be eliminated because

the passage is written using an academic and somewhat formal tone, and the terms "a ton" and "a lot" are generally avoided in academic writing because these terms add little in the way of useful, quantifiable information. Choice (D) is incorrect because, as used in the sentence, "maximum" has no clear meaning: the reader is not told what this "maximum" is. Usually, one should avoid unclear or ambiguous terms. Thus, (C) is the correct choice because "multiple" and "many" are acceptable replacements for "a lot" in academic writing.

26) ➤ B
Concept(s) Tested: In-Sentence Punctuation
If the information that follows "who" in a sentence is not essential to the meaning of the sentence (if the sentence would make perfect sense without that information), then the clause beginning with "who" should begin and end with commas. But if the information is necessary to the coherence of the sentence, no commas are necessary. Here, the information "who collects the most pieces" is necessary to understanding *how* to win the game. Thus, the "who" clause contains necessary information and should not be set aside using commas, making (B) the correct choice. Other choices add superfluous commas, making the sentence choppy, unclear, and ungrammatical.

27) ➤ B
Concept(s) Tested: Concision, Passage Tone
The correct answer to a SAT Writing and Language Test question will always be the clearest, most concise choice. We can eliminate (A) because it contains a redundancy: "diffusion" and "spreading across" mean the same thing. (B) is the most concise, so it is the correct choice. (C) is not as concise as (B), and it contains overly colloquial terms such as "ended up all over," so it is incorrect. (D) can be eliminated because, like (A), it contains redundancies.

28) ➤ D
Concept(s) Tested: Dangling Modifier
The correct choice is (D) because it is the only choice that explicitly states *who* is trying to determine how the pits were used. Although the term "it is" is an acceptable way to begin a phrase, clause, or sentence, it should only be used when the subject is unknown or nonexistent. But (D) tells us that archaeologists are performing the action, making it the choice containing the most relevant information.

29) ➤ C
Concept(s) Tested: Concision
Although (A) is concise, it leaves out information that helps connect the previous sentence to the sentence containing the underlined portion; we can eliminate

(A). Only (C) adds necessary information that reveals that archaeological evidence has provided clues as to mancala's development, linking it to the previous sentence. Thus, (C) is the correct choice. Like (A), choices (B) and (D) fail to mention the archaeological evidence of "pottery shards."

30) ➤ D
Concept(s) Tested: Passage Tone, Parallel Structure
The sentences comprising the paragraph establish a pattern of contrasts using "but." To maintain this sentence structure, the sentence at 30 should contain a "but" as well. Only sentence (D) does, by indicating that playing pieces can be jewels, *but* dried beans will serve equally well. Each of (A), (B), and (C) are incorrect because do not follow the established pattern.

31) ➤ A
Concept(s) Tested: Passage Development
An appropriate transition sentence for the paragraph beginning at 31 would likely acknowledge and sum up the general characteristics that make mancala so attractive, but would also note that there are additional features that draw people to play it. Choice (A) does this effectively, by pointing out that, in addition to the features mentioned in the previous paragraph, mancala has an additional draw. (B) is incorrect because it is too wordy, and it refers to the preceding features vaguely as "that." (C) is incorrect because it contains a question that is not answered by the paragraph at 31, which describes additional reasons why mancala is attractive, without stating why people should pass it on to their children. Finally, (D) is incorrect because the paragraph at 31 does not specifically discuss or mention the social aspects of mancala, but only the continual challenges that the game presents.

32) ➤ B
Concept(s) Tested: Pronoun Use
A personal pronoun should always *clearly* refer to a specific noun, noun phrase, or pronoun mentioned elsewhere in a sentence or paragraph. (A) is incorrect because it is unclear whether "they" refers to "Mancala games," "people," or "challenges." The correct choice is (B), as it clarifies the meaning of the sentence. Choices (C) and (D) are incorrect because they substitute inaccurate nouns for the pronoun.

33) ➤ C
Concept(s) Tested: Precise Diction
The sentence containing the underlined portion states that mancala helps people "evaluate visual information," so the word at the underlined portion should demonstrate that mancala helps people process visual information. Because "patterns" is

the only choice that suggests a visual element, we can infer that (C) is the correct choice. (A) is incorrect because "circumstances" relate to situations, not generally to visual information. Similarly, contexts usually refer to the information surrounding something, making (B) inappropriate. (D) is incorrect because "generalizations" are thoughts or statements, and therefore not directly related to mancala.

34) ➡ D

Concept(s) Tested: Voice, Syntax

Generally, when a term is elaborated on with descriptions or examples, the descriptions or examples should come immediately after the term they describe. Choices (A), (B), and (C) can be eliminated because they separate mention of Shakespeare's "last few plays" from a list of the plays themselves. Only (D) places the phrase "Shakespeare's last few plays" immediately before a list of these plays. Doing so is the clearest and most concise way to illustrate the relationship between the "last few plays" and the list of plays provided in the sentence.

35) ➡ A

Concept(s) Tested: Passage Development

As it is written, the sentence containing 35 is acceptable because "their ambiguous mood" clearly identifies a specific feature of the plays that makes them difficult to appreciate and understand. The rest of the paragraph appropriately develops and expands upon this point. (B), (C), and (D) are incorrect because the author does not state or imply that the plays are tedious, outdated, or have too many characters. It is rather the emotional dynamics of the plays that make them difficult to appreciate.

36) ➡ B

Concept(s) Tested: Precise Diction

Based on the context of the sentence, the verb at the underlined portion should convey the idea that the plays *begin*, or *progress* as tragedies before ending happily. To precede means to come before, which does not make sense based on the sentence, making (A) incorrect. To proceed means to progress or begin, so (B) works well in the context of the sentence and is the correct choice. To prevaricate is to stall or evade, making (C) incorrect. And (D) can be eliminated because to propel is to push something forward, which does not make sense in the context of the sentence.

37) ➡ C

Concept(s) Tested: Passage Development

The preceding sentence introduces the opposing genres in Shakespeare's last plays. The most appropriate choice will retain the paragraph's focus on Shakespeare's creative choices and also transition to elaborations on them. (C) is correct because it implies that, as a maturing person, Shakespeare had become interested in characters that mature. Thus, it retains the focus on Shakespeare, and transitions to details about the maturing characters. (A) and (B) are incorrect because the writer does not clearly connect them to the opposing genres. (D) correctly maintains a focus on Shakespeare, but the connection to the plays in question is not made clear in the sentences that follow.

38) ➡ C

Concept(s) Tested: Passage Development

(C) provides the biggest contrast to tragedy, and thus supports the description of the three tragicomedies' untragic conclusions. It is the opposite of tragedies in which characters' deaths could be prevented if only some message or confession arrived in time. Choice (A) is incorrect because it shifts away from plot description and thus fails to support the paragraph's main claim. The endings described in (B) and (D) would be more neutral than that in (C).

39) ➡ D

Concept(s) Tested: Verb Tense

The SAT Writing and Language Test may test your understanding of the literary present tense: use the present tense when describing the events of a literary work, such as a book, play, or movie. Thus, even though Shakespeare's plays were written in and take place in the past, people refer to the events of the play using present-tense verbs. For this reason, (D) is the correct choice. Although (C) uses a form of the present tense, this choice's structure is incorrect because it makes it seem as though the plays are *currently in the process of* following convoluted plots, which is inaccurate. (A) and (B) are in past-perfect or future tenses, not the literary present tense, making these choices incorrect.

40) ➡ A

Concept(s) Tested: Precise Diction, Commonly Confused Words

The paragraph itself provides few clues as to the most appropriate choice, except that the princess must travel to find her husband. Therefore, we can infer that her husband has been exiled (forced to leave for political reasons), making (A) correct. (B) and (D) are incorrect because they describe specific processes that would have been elaborated on by the author were they true of the play. To excommunicate someone is to exclude that person from participation in a church; to extradite someone is to hand him or her over to the authorities of a foreign state for a crime committed in that state. (C) is incorrect because to be expatriated is to be sent out of one's native country altogether, and the princess would have had to travel much father than the local forest.

41) **▶ C**

Concept(s) Tested: Possession

Here, "princess" must show ownership, or possession, over "enemies" in order to establish that they are, in fact, her enemies. There are two ways to make a singular noun that ends in "s" show possession: add an apostrophe to the end of the word, or add an apostrophe and then an "s," as you would for other singular possessive nouns. (C) is the only choice that follows one of these rules, making it the correct choice. (A) is incorrect because "princesses" is the plural of "princess" and is not inflected to show possession. (B) can be eliminated because the context of the paragraph makes it clear that the underlined portion is discussing the princess's actions, not those of a prince. And (D) is incorrect because the underlined portion must show possession, not state of being, as is the case with (D).

42) **▶ C**

Concept(s) Tested: In-Sentence Punctuation

The underlined portion should compare the audiences' reaction to "her [the princess's] *grief*, unlike [the *grief* of] Juliet." Because no option explicitly mentions Juliet's grief, we must select the choice that suggests it; the choice that most clearly does so is (C), as the pronoun "that" refers to the grief mentioned earlier in the sentence. (A) is incorrect because it compares "grief" to "Juliet." (B) is incorrect because it compares "grief" to a "scene." Although (D) mentions Juliet's "feelings," this choice illogically compares "the princess" to Juliet's feelings.

43) **▶ B**

Concept(s) Tested: Pronoun Use

Choice (A) is incorrect because of a pronoun-antecedent disagreement. The pronoun "they" must refer to a plural pronoun, but in (A), it refers to "the audience," a singular pronoun. (C) is incorrect because "all audiences" is too specific in this context. (D) is incorrect because, based on the

context of the sentence, the pronoun "it" wants to refer to "one," but "it" refers to non-human nouns whereas "one" refers to a person. Thus, "it" cannot refer to "one," making (D) ungrammatical. Only (B) is grammatically correct, as it uses the plural pronoun "they" to refer to the plural noun "people."

44) **▶ A**

Concept(s) Tested: Passage Development

The paragraph begins by talking about forgiveness and how its appearance in Shakespeare's plays may signal Shakespeare's own desire for forgiveness. The author then provides a specific example of this in *The Tempest*, when the main character addresses the audience directly. An appropriate concluding sentence would tie in this speech with the earlier focus on Shakespeare's own desire for forgiveness by concluding that the main character represents Shakespeare himself asking for forgiveness. Thus, (A) is correct. (B) is incorrect because it stays focused on *The Tempest* rather than serving as an effective conclusion. (C) is incorrect because, while it may be true that Shakespeare's character reaches through the "fourth wall," (C) does not explain exactly why the character is doing this and what the significance of his action is. Finally, (D) is incorrect because it makes a statement that is disconnected from the discussion of the deeper meaning of the character's speech, as well as shifting the passage's tone away from neutrality to one of advocacy.

Math Test

✓ No Calculator Portion

1. Ⓒ	7. Ⓑ	13. Ⓓ	19. *3000*
2. Ⓑ	8. Ⓑ	14. Ⓐ	20. *2*
3. Ⓐ	9. Ⓑ	15. Ⓒ	
4. Ⓓ	10. Ⓓ	16. *1*	
5. Ⓐ	11. Ⓓ	17. *1*	
6. Ⓒ	12. Ⓓ	18. *5*	

✓ Calculator Portion

1. Ⓑ	7. Ⓓ	13. Ⓒ	19. Ⓒ	25. Ⓐ	31. *290*	37. *71*
2. Ⓓ	8. Ⓓ	14. Ⓓ	20. Ⓑ	26. Ⓒ	32. *7*	38. *60*
3. Ⓓ	9. Ⓑ	15. Ⓓ	21. Ⓐ	27. Ⓓ	33. *384*	
4. Ⓑ	10. Ⓑ	16. Ⓒ	22. Ⓒ	28. Ⓐ	34. *1*	
5. Ⓑ	11. Ⓑ	17. Ⓑ	23. Ⓒ	29. Ⓓ	35. *18*	
6. Ⓒ	12. Ⓓ	18. Ⓑ	24. Ⓒ	30. Ⓓ	36. *240*	

No Calculator Portion

1) **➡ C**

Concept(s) Tested: Algebra, Inequalities

$$\frac{x}{2} - 1 \le 1 - \frac{x}{2} \rightarrow \frac{x}{2} + \frac{x}{2} \le 1 + 1 \rightarrow x \le 2$$

2) **➡ B**

Concept(s) Tested: Problem Solving

Cost of shipping to CA = x

Cost of shipping to NY = $\frac{x}{3}$

Total cost = $3x + 8\left(\frac{x}{3}\right) = \frac{17x}{3}$

3) **➡ A**

Concept(s) Tested: Graphs and Functions

A value of $a < 0$ for a general quadratic function $f(x) = ax^2 + bx + c$ indicates that the graph of the function is a parabola that opens downward. NOTE: choices (C) and (D) are the discriminant; (C) indicates that the function has real number solutions, and (D) indicates that the function has no real number solutions.

4) **➡ D**

Concept(s) Tested: Problem Solving, Ratios and Percentages

$$\text{Energy} = 3L \times \frac{1000\ mL}{L} \times \frac{4\ J}{ml \cdot {}^\circ C} \times 8{}^\circ C$$

$$= (3)(1000)(4)(8)\ J$$

$$= 96{,}000\ J$$

5) **➡ A**

Concept(s) Tested: Problem Solving

Let a, b, c, and d represent four consecutive integers. The next four integers can be represented as $a + 4$, $b + 4$, $c + 4$, and $d + 4$. If the sum $a + b + c + d = x$,

then

$$(a + 4) + (b + 4) + (c + 4) + (d + 4)$$
$$= (a + b + c + d) + 16 = x + 16$$

6) **➡ C**

Concept(s) Tested: Problem Solving, Inequalities

Let x be the number of pizzas that Carol orders, and y be the number of pans of macaroni and cheese:

$$30 \le 2x + 6y \le 60$$

Because the ratio of one food to another cannot exceed 2 to 1, the most pizzas that Carol can order is: $\frac{x}{y} \le 2$, $y \ge \frac{x}{2}$

Substitute this relation into the inequality above:

$$30 \le 2x + 6\left(\frac{x}{2}\right) \le 60$$

$$30 \le 5x \le 60$$

$$6 \le x \le 12$$

7) ➡ **B**

Concept(s) Tested: Problem Solving, Algebra

Let a be the cost of one apple, and p be the cost of one pear. The costs of a small bag and large bag, respectively, are:

$3a + 2p = 3.30$

$9a + 5p = 9.15$

Multiplying the first equation by 3, and then subtracting the second equation from the first will then give us the price of one pear:

$3(3a + 2p) = 3(3.30)$

$9a + 6p = 9.90$

$9a + 6p = 9.90$

$\underline{-)\ 9a + 5p = 9.15}$

$p = 0.75$

8) ➡ **B**

Concept(s) Tested: Problem Solving, Ratios and Percentages

A population increase of 20% is equivalent to multiplying the current population by a factor of 1.2. As a function of the number of years, t, then, the population is: $P(t) = 10,000(1.2)^t$

9) ➡ **B**

Concept(s) Tested: Algebra, Inequalities

$$\frac{5}{x+1} \geq 1$$

$5 \geq x + 1$

$x \leq 4$

$x + 1$ must be a positive number, so,

$x + 1 > 0$

$x > -1$

10) ➡ **D**

Concept(s) Tested: Algebra

When an expression is raised to a fraction, the denominator of the fraction indicates to what power you must raise a radical, and the numerator indicates to what power you should raise the expression itself.

Since the denominator is "2," we must take the square root of the expression, and since the numerator is "3," we must raise the value to the third power.

Thus, $x^{\frac{2}{3}} = \sqrt{x^3}$ and the answer is (D).

11) ➡ **D**

Concept(s) Tested: Graphs and Functions

The restrictions on the range of the function are:

1. The value of the function must be positive because it is a square root.
2. The value of the function must be less than or equal to 2 because the radicand $(4 - x^2)$ must be less than or equal to 4.

This implies that the range of the function is

$0 \leq y \leq 2$.

12) ➡ **D**

Concept(s) Tested: Number Rules

Choice (D) is not a true statement, as a^3 will always be an odd number if a is an odd integer and an even number if a is an even integer. Choices (A), (B), and (C) are all necessary consequences of the fact that a is a positive integer.

13) ➡ **D**

Concept(s) Tested: Graphs and Functions

Calculate the slope of the line: $m = \dfrac{-6 - 3}{-2 - 4} = \dfrac{3}{2}$

Because the slope is the same as that in (B), (B) is true and therefore incorrect. Because the slope above is the opposite reciprocal of that in (C), (C) is true and therefore incorrect.

Calculate the y-intercept using the point $(-2, -6)$:

$$y = \frac{3}{2}x + b$$

$$-6 = \frac{3}{2}(-2) + b$$

$$b = -3$$

Choice (D) is not true, and is the correct answer. To confirm that choice (A) is incorrect:

$$y = \frac{3}{2}x - 3$$

$$0 = \frac{3}{2}x - 3$$

$$\frac{3}{2}x = 3$$

$$x = 2$$

The x-intercept is $x = 2$, which is greater than the slope.

14) ➤ A

Concept(s) Tested: Algebra
Plug in $y = 0$ to each choice and solve for x to determine the largest absolute value for x:

For (A): $0 = |x - 9| \rightarrow x = 9$

For (B): $0 = x^2 - 6 \rightarrow 6 = x^2 \rightarrow x = \pm\sqrt{6}$

For (C): $0 = \left(\dfrac{2x}{3}\right)^2 \rightarrow x = 0$

For (D): $0 = x^3 \rightarrow x = 0$

Thus, the correct choice is (A).

15) ➤ C

Concept(s) Tested: Graphs and Functions
Plug in $f(4) = 4$ into the equation provided:

$4 = \dfrac{4r}{4} + 4^2 - 16$

$4 = r + 16 - 16$, so $r = 4$

Then plug $r = 4$ and $x = 2$ into the equation to determine $f(2)$:

$f(2) = \dfrac{4 \times 2}{4} + 2^2 - 16$

$f(2) = 2 + 4 - 16 = -10$

16) ➤ 1

Concept(s) Tested: Problem Solving, Algebra
Represent the first number as x, and the second number as y:

Their sum is: $x + y = \dfrac{5}{2}$

This is equivalent to: $2x + 2y = 5$

The second relation is: $2x + 3y = 7$

Subtract these two equations to give: $y = 2$

Therefore,

$x = \dfrac{1}{2} \rightarrow xy = 1$

17) ➤ 1

Concept(s) Tested: Graphs and Functions
Rewrite the equation of the first line in slope-intercept form:

$x + 2y = 7 \rightarrow 2y = 7 - x \rightarrow y = \dfrac{7}{2} - \dfrac{x}{2}$

The slope of this line is $-\dfrac{1}{2}$, and the line perpendicular to this line will have slope $m = 2$. Rewrite the second equation in slope-intercept form:

$2x - ky = 5$

$ky = 2x - 5$

$y = \dfrac{2}{k}x - \dfrac{5}{k}$

For $m = 2$ for this line, $k = 1$.

18) ➤ 5

Concept(s) Tested: Geometry, Trigonometry

$\cos C = \dfrac{adjacent\ side}{hypotenuse}$

$\cos C = \dfrac{1}{2} = \dfrac{d}{e} = \dfrac{d}{10}$

$d = 5$

19) ➤ 3000

Concept(s) Tested: Problem Solving, Ratios and Percentages
The participants of a poll must total 100%.

70% for A + 60% for B = 130%, so 30% of those polled must have voted for both. Thus, the numbers of people who chose each or both candidates are:

Candidate A only = 30%
Candidate B only = 40%
Candidate A and B = 30%

Let x be the total number of people that were polled: $0.3x = 900$

$\qquad\qquad x = 3000$

20) ➤ 2

Concept(s) Tested: Geometry
The length of $\overline{EB}$ is 1. The triangle $\triangle EBC$ has a base of 1 unit, a height of 2 units, and an area equal to $\dfrac{1}{2} \cdot 2 \cdot 1 = 1$

The same is true of $\triangle CDF$. The area of the shaded region is:

Area of CFAE
= Area of ABCD − (Area of $\triangle EBC$ + Area of $\triangle CDF$)
= 4 − (1 + 1) = 2

Calculator Portion

1) ➡ B

Concept(s) Tested: Problem Solving

The cost to produce CDs can be written as a linear function, with the y-intercept being the cost of recording equipment and the slope being the cost per CD:

The cost per CD is $0.59.

$Cost = 250 + 0.59n$

2) ➡ D

Concept(s) Tested: Data Analysis

A, B, C, and D are considered satisfactory grades:

$$\frac{Number\ of\ satisfactory\ grades}{Total\ number\ of\ grades}$$

$$= \frac{3+5+4+3}{3+5+4+3+3} = \frac{15}{18} = \frac{5}{6}$$

3) ➡ D

Concept(s) Tested: Problem Solving, Ratios and Percentages

At the same time of day, the ratio of the height of the man to the length of his shadow will be the same as the height of the pole to the length of its shadow. The ratio of the man's height to his shadow in inches is:

$$\frac{5\ feet\ 8\ inches}{8\ feet} = \frac{68\ inches}{96\ inches}$$

Conveniently, this is the same ratio we encounter with the pole:

$$\frac{68\ inches}{96\ inches} = \frac{height\ of\ pole}{96\ feet}$$

$height\ of\ pole = 68\ feet$

4) ➡ B

Concept(s) Tested: Problem Solving, Data Analysis

Let the total number of burgers sold be x. On Wednesday, 45 burgers, or 25% of burgers were sold:

$0.25x = 45$

$x = 180$

The number of burgers sold on Thursday is:

Burgers sold on Thursday

5) ➡ B

Concept(s) Tested: Algebra

$$\frac{x}{12} - \frac{x+2}{4} < 0$$

$$\frac{x - (3x+6)}{12} < 0$$

$$\frac{-2x-6}{12} < 0$$

The denominator is always positive, so,

$-2x - 6 < 0 \rightarrow -2x < 6 \rightarrow x > -3$

6) ➡ C

Concept(s) Tested: Graphs and Functions

Convert the equation of the line to slope-intercept form:

$4x - 2y - 10 = 0 \rightarrow 2y = 4x - 10 \rightarrow y = 2x - 5$

Only choice (C) has the correct value for the y-intercept.

7) ➡ D

Concept(s) Tested: Problem Solving, Algebra

$$x + \frac{1}{2}x + \frac{2}{3}x + \frac{1}{7}x = 388$$

$$\frac{42x + 21x + 28x + 6x}{42} = 388$$

$$\frac{97x}{42} = 388$$

$x = 168$

8) ➡ D

Concept(s) Tested: Graphs and Functions

$f(x) = x^2 + ax + a$

$f(5) = 5^2 + 5a + a = 25 + 6a$

9) ➡ B

Concept(s) Tested: Problem Solving, Algebra

If each of the five teams plays every other team once, there are ten matches total:

–Team A plays Teams B, C, D, and E : 4 matches

–Team B plays Teams C, D, and E : 3 matches

–Team C plays Teams D and E : 2 matches

–Team D plays Team E : 1 match

The time per match is:

$$Time\ per\ match = \frac{100\ minutes}{10\ matches} = 10\ minutes\ per\ match$$

As each team plays four matches, each team plays for 40 minutes.

10) **➡ B**

Concept(s) Tested: Data Analysis, Graphs and Functions

As age increases, the growth per week decreases and length approaches a plateau.

11) **➡ B**

Concept(s) Tested: Problem Solving, Measures of Center and Spread

Combined average

$$= \frac{Sum\ of\ scores\ in\ A + Sum\ of\ scores\ in\ B}{Total\ number\ of\ students}$$

$$= \frac{(25)(86)+(15)(94)}{40} = \frac{3,560}{40} = 89$$

12) **➡ D**

Concept(s) Tested: Data Analysis, Problem Solving

$$Revenue\ at\ \$20 = \left(\frac{\$20}{tour}\right)(65,000\ tours) = \$1,300,000$$

$$Revenue\ at\ \$5 = \left(\frac{\$5}{tour}\right)(120,000\ tours) = \$600,000$$

The difference is $700,000.

13) **➡ C**

Concept(s) Tested: Problem Solving, Algebra

The cost of 8 pencils is the difference between the totals:

Cost of 8 pencils = 8.45 − 6.05 = 2.40

Cost of 1 pencil = 0.30

Let y be the cost of the pen:

$y = 6.05 − 16(0.30) = 1.25$

14) **➡ D**

Concept(s) Tested: Problem Solving, Algebra

$A − B = 4$, $A + B = 16$

Adding these two equations gives:

$2A = 20$

$A = 10$

15) **➡ D**

Concept(s) Tested: Problem solving, Algebra

After 12 weeks, Jane wants to type at a rate of 200 words per minute. Thus, the correct expression will be equal to 200 when $x = 12$. Only (D) does this: $100 + \frac{25}{3}(12) = 200$

16) **➡ C**

Concept(s) Tested: Data Analysis

In 2010:

Not poor = Total population − Number of poor

$= 305.7 − (15.7 + 22.6 + 3.7 + 3.5) = 260.2\ million$

17) **➡ B**

Concept(s) Tested: Data Analysis, Measures of Center and Spread

In 1995:

% of poor 65 and over:

$$= \frac{Number\ of\ poor\ 65\ and\ over}{Total\ number\ of\ poor} \times 100\%$$

$$= \frac{3.3}{14.4 + 16.5 + 2.2 + 3.3} \times 100\% = 9\%$$

18) **➡ B**

Concept(s) Tested: Problem Solving, Algebra

Since we know how much Ximena spends on gas relative to x we can find x's value:

$$240 = 4x + \frac{4}{5}x \rightarrow 240 = \frac{24}{5}x \rightarrow$$

$$(5)240 = (5)\frac{24}{5}x \rightarrow 1200 = 24x \rightarrow x = 50$$

Thus, her total spending is

2(50) + 10 + 240 (fuel) + 3(50) + 4(50) + 4(50) + 20(50) = 1,900

The difference in income and spending is her "pocket money": 2,127 − 1,900 = 227

19) **➡ C**

Concept(s) Tested: Problem Solving, Ratios and Percentages

The total number of wins needed to qualify is:

Total wins needed = (0.6)(30 games) = 18 wins

The season is two–thirds over. The number of games that have been played is:

$$Games\ played = \left(\frac{2}{3}\right)(30) = 20\ games$$

With 10 games remaining, the player must win:

$$\frac{8\ wins}{10\ games} \times 100\% = 80\%$$

20) ➡ B

Concept(s) Tested: Algebra
Write the first equation in terms of x:

$y - x = 3$
$y = x + 3$

Substitute this equation into the quadratic:

$x^2 - 7(3 + x) + 31 = 0$
$x^2 - 21 - 7x + 31 = 0$
$x^2 - 7x + 10 = 0$
$(x - 5)(x - 2) = 0 \rightarrow x = 5, 2$
When $x = 5$, $y = 3 + 5 = 8$, and when $x = 2$, $y = 5$

21) ➡ A

Concept(s) Tested: Graphs and Functions
Write the inequalities in slope-intercept form and sketch them on a coordinate plane:

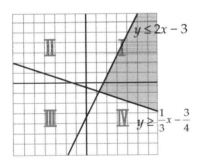

22) ➡ C

Concept(s) Tested: Data Analysis
In January, Peter has $200 in his account. In May, he has $400, a positive change of $200.

23) ➡ C

Concept(s) Tested: Problem Solving, Inequalities
The number of rides Connor can ride can be modeled as a linear inequality, with constant 4.50 (the price of admission), slope 0.79 (the price per ride), and y the maximum amount that can be spent:

$4.50 + 0.79r \le y$
$4.50 + 0.79r \le 16$

To find the maximum value for r, solve the inequality:

$4.50 + 0.79r \le 16$
$0.79r \le 11.5$
$r \le 14.6$

The maximum number of rides is 14.

24) ➡ C

Concept(s) Tested: Problem Solving, Graphs and Functions
The y-intercept is the value of the function when $x = 0$:

$y = (5000)(0.98)^0 = 5000$

This is the amount in the account before any time has passed.

25) ➡ A

Concept(s) Tested: Problem Solving, Algebra
Pat can inspect $\frac{1}{5}$ of a case in one hour, and James can inspect $\frac{1}{3}$ of a case in one hour. After Pat works alone for one hour, there is $\frac{4}{5}$ of the case remaining. If x is the number of hours it takes Pat and James, working together, to inspect the remaining portion of the case:

$$x\left(\frac{1}{5} + \frac{1}{3}\right) = \frac{4}{5}$$

$$x\left(\frac{8}{15}\right) = \frac{4}{5}$$

$$x = \frac{3}{2}\ \text{or 1.5 hours}$$

26) ➡ C

Concept(s) Tested: Problem Solving, Graphs and Functions
Convert the quadratic equation to vertex form:

$y = -4x^2 + 16x + 6$
$y = -4x^2 + 16x - 16 + 6 + 16$
$y = -4(x^2 - 4x + 4) + 22$
$y = -4(x - 2)^2 + 22$

The vertex is (2, 22). The maximum value for y is 22.

27) ➡ **D**

Concept(s) Tested: Geometry

Area of $\triangle ABC = \frac{1}{2} \times base \times height$

$\frac{1}{2}(AC)(BD) = \frac{1}{2}(AB)(CE)$

$(AC)(7) = (8)(9)$

$AC = \frac{72}{7} = 10\frac{2}{7}$

28) ➡ **A**

Concept(s) Tested: Problem Solving, Ratios and Percentages

For the first company:

Price $= 100(0.95)^t$,

where t is the number of 6–month periods in 5 years.

For 5 years, $t = 10$:

Price after 5 years $= 100(0.95)^{10} = 100(.5987) = 59.87$

For the second company:

Price $= 100(0.89)^t$,

Where t is the number of years.

For $t = 5$:

Price $= 100(0.89)^5 = 100(.5584) = 55.84$

The difference is:

Price difference $= 59.87 - 55.84 = 4.03$

29) ➡ **D**

Concept(s) Tested: Problem Solving, Geometry

Let x be the length of the sides of the original square sheet. The volume of the box is the product of the length, height, and width:

Volume $= 4(x - 8)(x - 8)$

$576 = 4(x - 8)^2$

$144 = (x - 8)^2 \rightarrow x - 8 = \pm 12 \rightarrow x = 20, -4$

The length of the sides is 20 centimeters.

Area $= (20cm)(20cm) = 400 \text{ cm}^2$

30) ➡ **D**

Concept(s) Tested: Problem solving, Geometry

We must determine the price of each pizza size in $inches^2/dollar$. Do so by calculating the surface area (SA) of each size using the formula

for the surface area of a circle (πr^2) and dividing this value by the price:

Small SA: $\pi(6)^2 = 36\pi$

Medium SA: $\pi(8)^2 = 64\pi$

Large SA: $\pi(9)^2 = 81\pi$

To find the ratio of $inches^2/dollar$ for each size:

Small: $\frac{36\pi}{10} = 3.6\pi$ $inches^2/dollar$

Medium: $\frac{64\pi}{14} = 4.57\pi$ $inches^2/dollar$

Large: $\frac{81\pi}{18} = 4.5\pi$ $inches^2/dollar$

Thus, the best $inches^2/dollar$ ratio is 4.57π, and choice (D) is correct.

31) ➡ **290**

Concept(s) Tested: Graphs and Functions

$f(x) = x^2 + 1$

$f(4) = 4^2 + 1 = 17$

$f(f(4)) = f(17) = 17^2 + 1 = 290$

32) ➡ **7**

Concept(s) Tested: Problem solving, Algebra

Express the word problem using numbers and variables, then solve for x:

$\frac{2}{3}(8 + x) = 10 \longrightarrow 8 + x = 10\left(\frac{3}{2}\right) \longrightarrow$

$8 + x = \frac{30}{2} \rightarrow 8 + x = 15 \rightarrow x = 7$

33) ➡ **384**

Concept(s) Tested: Graphs and Functions

The slope of line l is $\frac{2}{3}$ and the y-intercept is 0 because the line passes through the origin. The equation for line l is:

$y = \frac{2}{3}x$

Line l intersects the line $y = \frac{1}{2}x - 4$ when:

$\frac{2}{3}x = \frac{1}{2}x - 4$

$\frac{1}{6}x = -4$

$x = -24$

$$y = \frac{2}{3}(-24) = -16$$

Therefore, $xy = 384$

34) ➡ 1

Concept(s) Tested: Graphs and Functions

To find the value of k, solve the function for $f(2)$:

$$f(2) = \pi(2)^2 - 4\pi(2) + 5\pi$$

$$f(2) = 4\pi - 8\pi + 5\pi$$

$$f(2) = \pi = k$$

Thus, $\dfrac{113(\pi)}{355} \approx 1$

35) ➡ 18

Concept(s) Tested: Problem Solving, Ratios and Percentages

Let $P(A)$ be the probability that it snows tomorrow:

$$P(A) = 0.23$$

Let $P(B)$ be the probability that it snows the day after tomorrow. Then the probability that it will not snow the day after tomorrow is:
$$P(not\ B) = 1 - P(B) = 1 - 0.2 = 0.8$$

Therefore,

$P(A) \cdot P(not\ B) = (0.23)(0.8) = 0.184$, or approx. 18 percent.

36) ➡ 240

Concept(s) Tested: Problem Solving, Ratios and Percentages

Let x be the pre–sale price:

$$[(0.75)x]1.05 = 189$$

$$x = \frac{189}{(0.75)(1.05)}$$

$$x = 240$$

37) ➡ 71

Concept(s) Tested: Problem Solving, Algebra

Let x be the number of pairs of boots and y be the number of pairs of shoes:

$$x + y = 500$$
$$10x + 3y = 2000$$

Substitute the first equation into the second:

$$10x + 3(500 - x) = 2000$$
$$7x = 500$$
$$x = 71.4$$

To determine precisely how many pairs of boots can be made, 71 or 72, test these numbers in the original equations:

$x = 71,\ y = 429$

$10x + 3y = 10(71) + 3(429) = 1997$

If $x = 72,\ y = 428$

$10x + 3y = 10(72) + 3(428) = 2004$

The number of pairs of boots is 71.

38) ➡ 60

Concept(s) Tested: Problem Solving, Algebra

First determine the price of each batch by determining the number of pairs that can be created and multiplying this value by the price per pair:

Boot batch cost: $\dfrac{2,000}{10} = 200 \to 200(300) = \$60,000$

Shoe batch cost:
$\dfrac{2,000}{3} = 666.\overline{6} \to 666$ <u>complete</u> pairs$(90) = 59,940$

Find the difference in prices: $60,000 - 59,940 = \$60$

References

- "A 'Smoking Gun' for Dinosaur Extinction." *NASA's Jet Propulsion Laboratory*, California Institute of Technology, March 3, 2003. http://www.jpl.nasa.gov/news/news.php?feature=8

- Angelp, "3d Vector Business Background," 2015. http://www.vectorbg.net/3d-business-square-background/

- Bagsall, Monte, "A smashing success," *DEIXIS Magazine*. Copyright 2014 by the Krell Institute. https://deixismagazine.org/2014/12/a-smashing-success/

- Bates, Mary, "Monkey Faces Give Clues to Species and Individual Identity," *Wired*. Copyright 2015 by Conde Nast. http://www.wired.com/2015/02/monkey-faces-give-clues-species-individual-identity/

- Boyce, John, MD; Pittet, Didier, MD, "Guideline for Hand Hygiene in Health-Care Settings," MMWR, Vol. 51, No. RP-16, October 25, 2002. http://f.i-md.com/medinfo/material/8cd/4ea7c69144ae30018c1c68cd/4ea7c69244ae30018c1c68d1.pdf

- Chong, Iam (trans. Kristen Chan), "China's Independent Journalists Face High Risks—And are in High Demand." Global Voice, May 26, 2016. https://advox.globalvoices.org/2016/05/26/chinas-independent-journalists-face-high-risks-and-are-in-high-demand/

- Clinton, Bill, "Remarks to the People of Ghana." *Authenticated U.S. Government Information*, March 23, 1998. http://www.gpo.gov/fdsys/pkg/WCPD-1998-03-30/pdf/WCPD-1998-03-30-Pg483.pdf

- Congressional Budget Office, *The Distribution of Household Income and Federal Taxes, 2010*. December 2013, Pub. No. 4613. http://www.cbo.gov/sites/default/files/cbofiles/attachments/44604-AverageTaxRates.pdf

- Cooper, Caren, "Coop's Scoop: Speak for the Trees on next #CitSciChat." *CitizenSci*, April 27, 2015. http://blogs.plos.org/citizensci/2015/04/27/coops-scoop-speak-for-trees-citscichat/

- Graybeal, Carolyn, "Did you know 'storm spotters' in your community keep you safe during severe weather?" *CitizenSci*, June 29, 2015. http://blogs.plos.org/citizensci/2015/06/29/did-you-know-storm-spotters-in-your-community-help-keep-you-safe-during-inclement-weather/

- Haines, Michael and Whaplesl, Robert. "Fertility and Mortality in the United States." EH.Net Encyclopedia, edited by Robert Whaples. March 19, 2008. http://eh.net/encyclopedia/fertility-and-mortality-in-the-united-states/

- Hudson, Rex, *Brazil: A Country Study*. Library of Congress: Federal Research Division, Washington, D.C., 1998.

- Iddo, "Sequencing the Frog That Can Save Lives." Byte Size Biology, October 1, 2014. http://bytesizebio.net/page/2/

- Lewandowski, Eva, "Declining monarch population means increased need for citizen scientists." *CitizenSci*, February 7, 2015. http://blogs.plos.org/citizensci/2015/02/07/declining-monarch-population-means-increased-need-citizen-scientists/

- Lewis, Ricki, "Dan Brown's Inferno: Good Plot, Bad Science." *DNA Science Blog*, January 9, 2014. https://www.google.com/url?sa=t&rct=j&q=&esrc=s&source=web&cd=1&ved=0CB4QFjAAahUKEwj5m-zDltLIAhUY_mMKHdICDBo&url=http%3A%2F%2Fblogs.plos.org%2Fdnascience%2F2014%2F01%2F09%2Fdan-browns-inferno-good-plot-bad-science%2F&usg=AFQjCNExinljjZngStq9pNZSsKsneKJ-jg&sig2=iNej0vS3u86zuEg4-G7U3g

- Malone, John, "The Importance of Geothermal Energy." The Moderate Voice, 2009. http://themoderatevoice.com/the-importance-of-geothermal-power/

- Medosch, Chloe, "Out on a Limb: Dwindling Trees in Cities." *Everyone*, March 5, 2015. http://blogs.plos.org/every-one/2015/03/05/dwindling-trees-in-cities/

- National Institute of Allergy and Infectious Diseases, "Timeline of Human Flu Pandemics," January 14, 2011. www.niaid.nih.gov/topics/flu/research/pandemic/pages/timelinehumanpandemics.aspx

- Reagan, Ronald W., "Explosion of the Space Shuttle *Challenger* Address to the Nation, January 28, 1986." *NASA History Office*, June 7, 2004. http://history.nasa.gov/reagan12886.html

- "Shuttle Flights as of Januarry 1986." *Space Shuttle Mission STS-51L, Press Kit*, NASA, January 1986. http://www.histroy.nasa.gov/sts51lpresskit.pdf

- Silberman, Steve, "Music to Write By: 10 Top Authors Share Their Secrets for Summoning the Muse." *Neurotribes*, November 15, 2012. http://blogs.plos.org/neurotribes/2012/11/15/music-to-write-by-10-top-authors-share-their-secrets-for-summoning-the-muse/

- Stockton, Nick, "Heat, Pollution, and Skyscrapers Make Cities Have More Thunderstorms," *Wired*. Copyright 2015 by Conde Nast. http://www.wired.com/2015/02/cities-thunderstorms/

- Suresh, Arvind (Editor) & Russell, Sharman Apt (Author), "Nature's Notebook: Through the Eyes of a Citizen Scientist." *Scistarter Blog*, March 30, 2015. http://scistarter.com/blog/2015/03/natures-notebook-citizen-science/#sthash.iIgRD7ON.dpbs

- Terranova274, "A series of paired river terraces." *Wikimedia Commons*, November 7, 2012. https://commons.wikimedia.org/wiki/File:A_series_of_paired_river_terraces.jpg#/media/File:A_series_of_paired_river_terraces.jpg

- Turner, Sarah, "Understanding the Decrease in College Completion Rates and the Increased Time to Baccalaureate Degree." Population Studies Center Research Report 626, University of Michigan, November 2007.

- U.S. Department of Labor, Bureau of Labor Statistics, "Audiologists." *Occupational Outlook Handbook*, January 8, 2014. http://www.bls.gov/ooh/healthcare/audiologists.htm

- U.S. Department of Labor, Bureau of Labor Statistics, "Occupational Employment and Wages, May 2014," *Occupational Employment Statistics*. http://www.bls.gov/ooh/business-and-financial/market-research-analysts.htm#tab-6

- U.S. Department of Labor, Bureau of Labor Statistics, "Survey of Occupational Injuries and Illnesses," 1994. http://www.bls.gov/iif/oshwc/cfar0020.pdf

- U.S. Department of Education, National Center for Education Statistics, Integrated Postsecondary Education Data System (IPEDS), Spring 2012, Graduation Rates component. http://nces.ed.gov/pubs2013/2013037.pdf

- U.S. Energy Information Administration, "Energy Prices." *Annual Energy Outlook 2015*, April 14, 2015. http://www.eia.gov/forecasts/aeo/section_prices.cfm

- USDA Foreign Agricultural Service, "Indonesia: Rising Global Demand Fuels Palm Oil Expansion," Oct. 8, 2010. http://www.pecad.fas.usda.gov/highlights/2010/10/indonesia/

- Vespa, Johnathan, "Marrying Older, But Sooner?" *Random Samplings*, February 10, 2014. http://blogs.census.gov/2014/02/10/marrying-older-but-sooner/

- World Bank, *World Development Indicators*, 2011. http://www.afdb.org/fileadmin/uploads/afdb/Documents/Policy-Documents/FINAL%20Briefing%20Note%205%20Income%20Inequality%20in%20Africa.pdf

Made in the USA
San Bernardino, CA
26 June 2018